The Discovery of Cerebellar-Vestibular Syndromes and Therapies

A Solution to the Riddle

DYSLEXIA

Also by Dr. Levinson

A Solution to the Riddle—Dyslexia, Springer-Verlag (1980)

Smart But Feeling Dumb, Warner Publications (1984, Revised 1994)

Phobia Free, Evans (1986)

Total Concentration, Evans (1990)

The Upside Down Kids, Evans (1991)

Turning Around The Upside Down Kids, Evans (1992)

A Scientific Watergate—Dyslexia, Stonebridge (1994)

Feeling Smarter and Smarter, Stonebridge (2000)

The Discovery of Cerebellar-Vestibular Syndromes and Therapies

A Solution to the Riddle

DYSLEXIA

by Harold N. Levinson, M.D.

with 95 illustrations

Stonebridge Publishing, Ltd.

Harold N. Levinson, M.D.
Director, Medical Dyslexic Treatment Center
600 Northern Boulevard, Suite 118
Great Neck, NY 11021
Web site: http://www.dyslexiaonline.com
E-mail: drlevinson@aol.com

Library of Congress Cataloging in Publication Data

Levinson, Harold N
A Solution to the Riddle—Dyslexia

Bibliography: p.
Includes index.
1. Dyslexia. 2. Cerebellum—Diseases. I. Title
RJ496.A5L48 616.85'53 00-100725

Printed in the United States of America.

THE DISCOVERY OF CEREBELLAR-VESTIBULAR SYNDROMES AND THERAPIES
A Solution to the Riddle—Dyslexia
ISBN 09639303-1-1

Dedicated to
my wife Diggy and
daughters Laura and Joy—three
loving and beautiful women

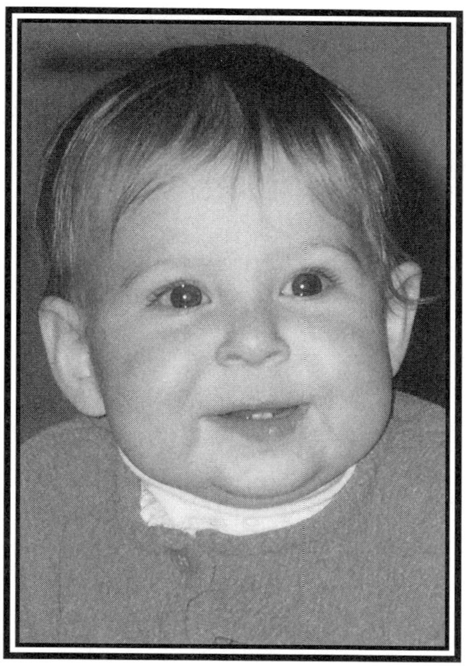

And to Hannah—a new
millennium addition

Contents

Preface

Dyslexia was first described by two English physicians, Kerr and Morgan, in 1896. Interestingly, the *structural cortical* hypothesis initially proposed by Morgan is still held in wide esteem, albeit in slightly modified forms. Despite 80 years of escalating research efforts and mounds of corresponding statistics, there continues to exist a perplexing diagnostic-therapeutic medical void and riddle in which dyslexics can neither be scientifically distinguished from other slow learners nor medically treated; and pathognomonic clinical signs remain as elusive as a suitable neurophysiologic conceptualization.

This book is the outcome of a 15-year-long search for a solution to the riddle characterizing dyslexia. All of my initial attempts at re-exploring the safe old (cortical, psychogenic, etc.) dyslexic paths and ideas led nowhere. Something new was needed. Children and adults were suffering. Educators and parents were bewildered. Answers were needed. The government mandated equal education for the learning disabled. Clinicians were waiting. And traditionalists remained fixated to the theoretical past and blind to the clinical dyslexic reality.

A Solution to the Riddle Dyslexia evolved slowly and "dysmetrically." Scientific confusion and "tripping" were commonplace. Historically accepted convictions were held with perseverative force. Resistance to meaningful change and integration was intense. Interdisciplinary dissention and rivalry were found significantly competing with cooperative efforts. Scientific bias and tunnel vision periodically reigned supreme, often playing havoc with the collection and interpretation of facts. So-called paradoxical and statistically atypical findings were frequently ignored or denied rather than explored and integrated into the clinical-theoretical mainstream. Larger and larger samples were required to provide both a depth and panorama missing from the historical or traditional perspectives of dyslexia and dyslexics.

This book is written in a manner depicting my original investigations, data, reasoning, errors, and resistances toward reaching a meaningful and comprehensive solution. All too often a solution was at hand only to partially dissolve and "blur out" amid periodic flurries of seemingly contradictory information and bursts of "scientific" criticism.

Ironically enough, a solution would never have materialized were it not for the challenge and stimulation provided by unexpected and seemingly unexplainable findings and criticism. In many ways, the analysis of confusing data and/or critical resistance proceeded in a manner similar to the analysis of neurotic symptoms and dreams—from the clinically bewildering defensive perimeter to its latent or subclinical central core. As a result of this analysis, almost all traditional assumptions and convictions as to the nature of dyslexia were surprisingly found to be based on highly selective, biased, and minimal sampling. Interestingly, highly charged and/or confusing content invariably served as a guide to the unknown; and its scientific pursuit led to horizons never before contemplated or explored—eventually leading me to a new, holistic, cosmic perspective of dyslexia.

Although the data and conceptualizations derived from this investigation appear to provide a solution to the dyslexic riddle, I am keenly aware that *all* solutions are incomplete and that multiple solutions may exist. Accordingly, this book is entitled ***A** Solution*—rather than ***The** Solution—to the Riddle Dyslexia.*

I truly hope the reader will utilize the content of this book so as to further expand and modify my current 1980 "dyslexic" horizons and conceptualizations—and thus maintain and even catalyze the forward momentum of the infinite scientific continuum.

Acknowledgments

As any reader must know, ideas alone are insufficient to make things happen. Were it not for the time, energy, and dedicated assistance—ingredients required for success—provided by my wife, Diggy, this research endeavor would have remained incomplete and scrambled. Not only was she an encouraging and steadfast sounding board during periods of scientific confusion and despair, she (1) screened over 1500 kindergarten children for dyslexia in District 26, Queens, New York (Chapter 6); (2) performed over 500 electronystagmographic examinations; (3) obtained the ocular-motor tracking patterns presented in Chapter 9; and (4) typed and retyped the seemingly endless case reports and drafts which eventually culminated in *A Solution to the Riddle Dyslexia*.

Complex and time-consuming statistics were an essential ingredient to this book's final design. Were it not for the time and interest of Godfrey Pyle of the 3M Company and Terry West of Hewlett-Packard, Chapters 6 and 8 would most probably have remained in a state of suspended animation.

Two friends and colleagues deserve special thanks for their professional input and support. Dr. Lawrence Sheff, Director of the Children's Psychiatric Clinic, Long Island Jewish-Hillside Medical Center, Hillside Division, read and reread the initial rough drafts of this manuscript. His open and honest criticism led to this "final" draft. Dr. Robert Cancro, Professor and Chairman, Department of Psychiatry, New York University Medical Center, generously provided me with the time and encouragement needed to complete this seemingly endless research task.

The physicians participating in the "blind" neurologic and electronystagmographic (ENG) vestibular studies deserve special mention. Their combined efforts and data served as a crucial cornerstone for the developing cerebellar-vestibular formulations noted in Chapter 3.

Without the crucial jolts and incentives provided by critics, researchers and their efforts often remain significantly biased and stagnant. As a result of this awareness, Chapter 13 was written and dedicated to the critics and criticism required to holistically conceptualize the complex multidimensional disorder under investigation.

Dr. Jan Frank served as an encouraging positive critic. His help was in sharp contrast to the aims of the negative critics who unwittingly attempted to preserve the traditional dyslexic void and riddle—at all costs. Paradoxically, my negative critics collectively served as a crucial stimulus to succeed. And their negative criticism served to highlight the bias or resistance forces requiring analysis and resolution.

Among the many volunteers participating in this fifteen-year-long research project, one stands out: Milton Surasky, a retired electronics manufacturer, maintained the equipment needed to complete the research constituting this book and aided in founding the DDD (Dysmetric Dyslexic and Dyspraxic) Research Foundation.

Last, but not least, I must thank my dyslexic children and patients. My daughters, Laura and Joy, enthusiastically served as both control and experimental subjects, rounded up friends and neighbors for similar purposes, and tirelessly found themselves collating mounds of pages, charts, and graphs. My dyslexic patients reported their symptoms with a tenacious vigor sufficient to overcome the scientific resistance that often blocks crucial insights and successful treatment. Were it not for the joint need and synergistic determination of dyslexics to overcome their disorder and its symptomatic fallout, this seemingly interminable research effort would have fallen far short of its intended goal—for all dyslexic participants served as catalytic research incentives, and they all deserve nothing short of success.

Authors Note

The Cerebellum and Dyslexia—A New Scientific Millennium

"Science progresses not by convincing the adherents of old theories that they are wrong but by allowing enough time to pass so that a new generation can arise unencumbered by the old errors."

—Max Planck

A new generation of researchers unencumbered by century-old cerebral cortical and related theories have recently begun to rediscover the crucial primary role of the cerebellar-vestibular circuitry in dyslexia and related learning impairments. Because A *Solution to the Riddle—Dyslexia* was the first and only medical text to highlight this cerebellar-dyslexic relationship as well as the existence of "higher cerebellar functions" affecting all sensory processing, cognition, language, attention, affect, etc., this work was initially considered "controversial" by traditionalists.

Interestingly, since the content within this text was recognized to be as valid today as when initially conceived over a quarter of a century ago, it is now often referred to as "pioneering," "revolutionary," "groundbreaking," etc. In other words, a significant scientific progression appears to have "suddenly" occurred concomitant with the onset of a new scientific generation and millennium. Quite clearly, this quantum leap is in full accordance with Max Planck's remarkable insight, an insight as valid today as when initially conceived almost a century ago. Because of this progression in cerebellar-dyslexia research, many have requested that this out-of-print work be republished in its original form so that it might more readily be available to all clinicians and researchers interested in understanding the detailed investigations and reasoning leading to the cerebellar-vestibular origins and treatment of dyslexia and its related learning, attention deficit and phobic or anxiety-based disorders.

Having made this reprint possible, I truly hope that its clinically-based and independently verified insights will finally lead to a resolution of dyslexia and its devastating symptoms, especially those impairing self-esteem. To facilitate the integration of all pertinent source content, I've made two changes: This comment was included here with a few important references containing vital others; and a new title was added in order to highlight the cerebellar-vestibular role in triggering all the many and varied reading and non-reading symptoms found to characterize what I elected to call the *dyslexic syndrome—a* syndrome also significantly characterized by dyslexics with compensated normal and even superior reading scores.

- Leiner, H.C., Leiner, A., and Dow, R.S. 1986. Does the cerebellum contribute to mental skills? *Behavioral Neuroscience 100:* 443–454.

- Rae, C., Lee, M.A., Dixon, R.M., Blamire, A.M., Thompson, C.H., Styles, P., Talcott, J., Richardson, A.J., Stein, J.F. 1998. Metabolic abnormalities in developmental dyslexia detected by ^{1}H magnetic resonance spectroscopy. *The Lancet* 351: 1849–1852.

- Schmahmann, J.D. and Sherman, J.C. 1998. The cerebellar cognitive affective syndrome. *Brain* 121: 561–579.

- Nicolson, R.I. and Fawcett, AJ. Developmental dyslexia: The role of the cerebellum. Submitted to: *Dyslexia: International Journal of Research and Practice.* April 1999

- Levinson, H.Ns. 1984. *Smart But Feeling Dumb.* New York: Warner, 1984. Revised Edition, 1994.

1 The Riddle Dyslexia and a Solution: An Introductory Sketch

The aim of this chapter is to provide the reader with an introductory sketch of both the dyslexic riddle and its solution.

Upon exploration, the dyslexic riddle was found to be a complex melange of fact, fantasy and fiction. The origin of this "scientific scramble" was traced to a series of historically rooted fallacious assumptions and convictions. To date, there exists only a diagnostic-therapeutic medical void in which dyslexics can be neither confidently distinguished from other slow learners nor medically treated. And a vast range of clinical data remains unaccounted for and ignored by currently unchallenged cortical dyslexic conceptualizations. In retrospect, it often appears as if researchers and clinicians were attempting to force highly selected quanta of data into a series of preconceived theoretical molds, rather than developing a clinically unbiased and flexibly expanding unitary hypothesis to fit the total reality of dyslexia. In many ways, the dyslexic riddle and the continuing scientific effort to bolster and rationalize the validity of its dubious theoretical basis are reminiscent of a dreamer attempting to substantiate the reality and logic of his manifest dream content upon waking.

To solve the riddle, the entire theoretical and clinical dyslexic "dream content" had to be re-explored, re-analyzed and dissected into its basic factual, fantasied and fictitious components. Fact and fantasy were then harmonized and interwoven with the clinical spectrum of dyslexia so that the total symptomatic complex could be explained pathophysiologically and the dyslexic diagnostic-therapeutic void resolved. During the scientific working-through process, fascinating insights were generated when exploring the nature and intensity of the resistance forces that shaped and maintained the unique character of the dyslexic fiction and resulting riddle.

Historically Rooted Assumptions

The Cortical Structural Hypotheses

The existence of reading-disabled children of normal and superior I.Q., who manifest reversals and related scrambling difficulties in reading, writing, and spelling, despite adequate emotional and educational stimulation, was first recognized in 1896 by Kerr and Morgan. Morgan's article, "A Case of Congenital Word-Blindness," described a 14-year-old boy experiencing difficulty in learning the alphabet, reading, writing, and spelling. His name was Percy, but he spelled it *Precy*. He wrote *score* for song, *widout* for without, and *Englis* for English. It was stated that Percy's mathematical ability was intact. Hinshelwood (1917) descriptively expanded the dyslexic data base and re-emphasized the existence of familial or hereditary influences. Like Morgan, he attributed congenital word-blindness to a structural dysfunction or agenesis of the left angular parietal gyrus.

Hermann (1958, 1959) was also convinced that congenital word-blindness was of a dominant parietal and genetic origin. He recognized a striking parallel between the right/left confusion, agraphia, and acalculia in Gerstmann's parietal syndrome, and the right/left, graphomotor, and mathematical difficulties characterizing dyslexics.* And on the basis of this symptomatic resemblance, he concluded that word-blindness was a congenital form of Gerstmann's syndrome.

In discussing the directional dysfunction underlying the symptoms of Gerstmann's syndrome and constitutional word-blindness, Hermann (1959, pp. 136–137) states:

> The many points of similarity between the symptoms of Gerstmann's syndrome and of constitutional dyslexia make it highly probable that congenital word-blindness is dependent on the same disturbance of directional function which is responsible for the symptoms of Gerstmann's syndrome.
>
> We know from patients with Gerstmann's syndrome that the function "direction" is disturbed when a circumscribed area in the dominant hemisphere's parietal lobe is damaged. Whether other parts of the brain exercise a regulatory influence on the directional factor cannot be answered at present, but may reasonably be supposed. However, this question is of minor importance for our theme, since we need only keep to a purely descriptive study of the phenomenon of direction and its meaning for symbol functions.
>
> When the behavior of patients with Gerstmann's syndrome is disturbed by impairment of directional function, it is "direction" as an abstraction which is principally involved. The patient can orientate himself perfectly well in those real surroundings to which he is accustomed.
>
> It is particularly, therefore, the concepts of direction which are impaired in Gerstmann's syndrome, whereas actual orientation in space, and especially in the patient's customary surroundings, is either considerably less impaired or

* Gerstmann's parietal syndrome consists of agraphia, acalculia, right/left confusion and finger agnosia (Gerstmann, 1940).

unaffected. A similar state of affairs obtains also in other higher mental and somato-psychic functions. The abstract attitude is lost before the more concrete attitude, the latter being in relation to particular tasks or situations.

Hermann conceptually solidified the "parietal identity" between the two disorders, despite the fact that alexia is not part of Gerstmann's syndrome, conceptual acalculia is most frequently absent in dyslexia, and finger agnosia, a cardinal sign of Gerstmann's syndrome (Gerstmann, 1914), is invariably absent in congenital dyslexia. Furthermore, although Hermann credited Critchley with having described the first recorded case of congenital Gerstmann's syndrome and utilized this case to substantiate his thesis, Critchley regretted having published this study and doubted the existence of Gerstmann's syndrome, much less a congenital form (Critchley, 1969, pp. 84–85):

> Both dyslexia and Gerstmann's syndrome have been ascribed by some to a common factor of directional dysfunction . . . However important, this point can scarcely be fundamental, for a Gerstmann syndrome is certainly not an integral part of dyslexia, even though right–left confusion is commoner in dyslexics than in normal readers, but perhaps only to a slight degree . . . The propriety of thinking in terms of a "constitutional" or "congenital" variety [of Gerstmann's syndrome] is even more suspect. I express this opinion advisedly having been responsible in 1942 for the reporting of what has often been regarded as the first recorded case of congenital Gerstmann's syndrome . . . If then I am unconvinced as to the bona fides of Gerstmann's syndrome, I am even more dubious of the doctrine of a developmental variety.
>
> The acquired dyslexic shares with the developmental dyslexic a certain lack of facility in the full appreciation of verbal symbols; but there the likeness rests, and the analogy should not be pressed further.
>
> Moreover, an acquired alexic may sometimes retain his ability to write. More often, however, he finds it hard to express his ideas on paper, and to draw upon what was previously a very rich vocabulary, without betraying hesitancies, repetitions, omissions and corrections. The graphic efforts of a child with developmental dyslexia are fundamentally different, and resemblances between the two kinds of dysgraphia will not stand up to scrutiny. To speak of a "congenital dysgraphia" in the context of a developmental dyslexia, is not appropriate.
>
> It is still necessary to emphasize these points despite the fact that they were clearly stated as long ago as 1903 at the Societe de Neurologie de Paris . . . Mme. Dejerine stressed that it was important not to confuse the pathological loss of a function with cases of absence of that function.

Although Hermann attributed the directional dysfunction in both Gerstmann's syndrome and congenital dyslexia to a *conceptual* directional impairment, and although Critchley challenged this assertion on the basis that a directional dysfunction is "not an integral part of dyslexia," it appeared to the author that a directional dysfunction *is* indeed an integral part of dyslexia, but that this right/left dysfunction in dyslexia is due to a *nonconceptual, nonparietal* compass-determined memory instability, which is most often compensated for with time, age, and conceptual ingenuity.

Is it possible that Hermann "slipped" scientifically and so failed to clearly distinguish the separate neurophysiologic origins (conceptual vs. compass) of the directional dysfunction in Gerstmann's parietal syndrome and dyslexia—despite his awareness that "other parts of the brain exercise a regulatory influence on the directional factor"? And is it equally possible that Critchley overlooked the crucial role of the directional dysfunction in dyslexia as a result of his failure to appreciate the compensatory ease with which most dyslexics utilize conceptually related clues in order to mask their inability to "reflexly" recall the site rather than the concept of right and left?

In a manner perhaps depicting the ebb and flow of the shifting cortical scientific tides, Kinsbourne and Warrington (1962, 1963a, b, 1964a, b) appeared to re-echo Hermann's Gerstmann-dyslexic conceptualizations, while side-stepping Critchley's criticism, and concluded (1) that both the acquired and congenital forms of Gerstmann's Syndrome were indeed viable clinical entities, and (2) that the conjunction of finger agnosia, right/left disorientation, dysgraphia and dyscalculia characterizing Gerstmann's parietal tetrad was more than coincidental.

Utilizing a nonverbal series of ingeniously conceived "finger order sense" tests to investigate the presence and quality of finger agnosia, they demonstrated decreased "finger order sense" scores in both the acquired and developmental Gerstmann (dyslexic) disorders, and fallaciously assumed that decreased "finger order sense" and finger agnosia were clinically equivalent neurophysiologic parameters. In addition, Kinsbourne and Warrington (1962, p. 56) reasoned (1) that underlying finger agnosia there existed "a specific difficulty in relating the fingers to each other in correct spatial sequence," (2) that "the fingers were treated by the patients in some respects as if they were an undifferentiated mass," (3) that a similar but generalized disturbance of spatial-temporal sequencing was responsible for the total Gerstmann tetrad as well as the occasionally noted and associated ordering difficulties in spelling.

Kinsbourne lucidly summarized his views of the developmental and acquired Gerstmann syndromes as follows (1968, p. 777):

> A developmental syndrome of cognitive deficit is described in which there is selective delay in the ability to recognize, recall and utilize information as regards the relative position of certain items in spatial or temporal sequence. Analogies are drawn between this syndrome and the acquired Gerstmann syndrome found in some adults with parietal lesions in the dominant hemisphere. Such children may present with a selective difficulty in learning to read and write. Their spelling is characterized by order errors and their script by malorientation of individual letters. They show delayed acquisition of "finger order

> sense," simple tests for which are described, as well as of ability to discriminate between right and left. They often also have arithmetic difficulty, and on Wechsler testing show a "performance" deficit, the subtests of Block Design, Object Assembly and Arithmetic being maximally affected.
>
> The developmental syndrome is not necessarily indicative of localized or lateralized cerebral damage. It may represent a developmental lag, which is ultimately made good, but often not before considerable reading backwardness becomes complicated by secondary emotional resistances. At present the management remain empirical.

Although a clear analogy was drawn between the two syndromes and both were considered to be of cerebral origin, a significant difference was noted. The acquired Gerstmann syndrome was neurologically localized to a specific defect within the dominant parietal lobe, whereas the developmental Gerstmann (or dyslexic) syndrome was characterized by the absence of localizing neurologic signs of a similar cerebral defect. As a result of this difference, Kinsbourne (1968, p. 776) was forced to acknowledge that, "The developmental syndrome is not necessarily indicative of localized or lateralized cerebral damage. It may represent a developmental lag."

Interestingly enough, Kinsbourne and Warrington, like Hermann, failed to distinguish the separate (cortical versus subcortical) proprioceptive and compass neurophysiologic origins of the directional dysfunction characterizing the uniquely distinct quality of the acquired and developmental (dyslexic) Gerstmann tetrads. As a result of this oversight, they mistakenly equated decreased "finger order sense" with finger agnosia, thereby overlooking a unitary alternative hypothesis which explained all of the similarities and differences between the two syndromes, and which ultimately led to a solution to the dyslexic riddle.

It is hoped that even this brief historical sketch will serve to demonstrate that simultaneous with the clinical recognition of congenital word-blindness as a medical disorder, there developed the natural pathophysiologic assumption—and conviction—among investigators that the congenital word-blind disorder was of a similar dominant cortical origin as acquired alexia (and/or agraphia) in adult aphasics.

The reasoning utilized to establish a pathophysiologic analogy and identity between the congenital and acquired reading disorders was really quite simple and straightforward. Investigators merely assumed that the very same left-angular and supramarginal gyrus lesion found on autopsy by Broadbent (1872) to be responsible for the acquired loss of reading ability in alexic adults was congenitally present and responsible for preventing children from developing and acquiring normal reading functioning. And since the terms word-blindness and dyslexia were utilized, respectively, by Kussmaul (1877) and Berlin (1887) for the adult alexic disorder, it seemed only natural to apply these very same terms to the congenital reading disorder as well.

The logic underlying the structural cortical assumptions in dyslexia was beyond reproach and appeared as basic as the gravitational analogy indicating that what goes up equals what comes down. However, detailed clinical analytic and comparative studies conducted by the author over many years revealed that significant qualitative and prognostic differences exist between the congenital and acquired (alexic) adult reading disorders. These differences were, surprisingly, found to be due to distinctly separate pathophysiologic mechanisms. As a result, the author was forced to recognize that what goes up need not equal what comes down and that the disorder and mechanisms responsible for the loss of existing function need not equal those responsible for the failure of function to develop normally.

In retrospect, it became apparent that the structural cortical theories of dyslexia required careful re-evaluation. Thus, for example, upon re-analyzing the congenital parietal Gerstmann theories of Hermann, Kinsbourne and Warrington, it appeared that highly selected quanta of clinical data were being utilized—and even forced—to prove their respective cortical dyslexic positions while co-existing refuting data was either selectively overlooked or denied.

The Diagnostic Void in Dyslexia

The unfortunate, but natural and inevitable, cortical assumption and conviction as to the neurophysiologic origin of congenital dyslexia had so blinkered and fixated dyslexic research efforts in a "cortical search" and circular logic that 80 years after Kerr and Morgan initially drew scientific attention to this syndrome there existed, in Hermann's words (1959, p. 17), "not . . . one single symptom nor one straightforward objective finding on which to base this diagnosis." Although historically dyslexia was assumed to be of a structural cortical origin, clinical evidence of such a defect was completely absent. As a result, the cortical structural hypotheses were eventually abandoned by many researchers.

This diagnostic void in dyslexia has been clearly recognized by such outstanding authorities as Critchley and Money:

> To identify the cases of specific developmental dyslexia among the multitude of poor readers is no easy task . . . for there is no single clinical feature which can be accepted as pathognomonic. [Critchley, 1969, pp. 17–18]

> The obvious criterion of reading retardation is that a child is not able to score at the reading achievement level proper to its age and years of instruction. It is a simple matter to identify reading retardation, but far from simple to make the differential diagnosis of specific dyslexia.
>
> The fact of the matter is that no one has yet devised a foolproof way of diagnosing specific dyslexia. There is seldom argument about extreme cases, with their extreme handicap and their tell-tale errors. The problem arises in less severe cases. Rabinovitch said that in his clinic they have often found themselves

making double-barreled diagnoses like "secondary retardation with a touch of primary disability."

The diagnostic problem is even more acute when, among prereaders and beginning readers, one would like to differentiate a prognosis of specific dyslexia from one of "late blooming" or of generalized learning block. To a significant degree the problem hinges around the fact that no one has as yet uncovered any telltale sign or group of signs that are exclusive to the syndrome of specific dyslexia and are not found in other conditions of reading retardation. [Money, 1962, pp. 15–16]

A Typical Descriptive Definition of Dyslexia

In the absence of specific diagnostic neurophysiologic criteria, only descriptive definitions of dyslexia were possible. Hermann's definition and conceptualization of dyslexia is typical of those presented by most researchers and does not significantly differ from that of Kerr and Morgan's.

I shall first endeavor to define congenital word-blindness in the medical sense. The term is to be understood to signify a defective capacity for acquiring, at the normal time, a proficiency in reading and writing corresponding to average performance; the deficiency is dependent on constitutional factors (heredity), is often accompanied by difficulties with other symbols (numbers, musical notation, etc.), it exists in the absence of intellectual defects or of defects of the sense organs which might retard the normal accomplishment of these skills, and in the absence of past or present appreciable inhibitory influences in the internal and external environment. . . . The definition has to be a descriptive one since one does not have one single symptom nor one straightforward objective finding on which to base the diagnosis. On this point, there is no difference from the kind of delimitation one is obliged to adopt with other psychic disorders, where a descriptive definition has to be used and is fully adequate both for practical diagnosis and for detailed scientific study. [Hermann, 1959, pp. 17–18]

A Rationalization and Denial of the Dyslexic Void

Upon analysis, Hermann's argument and underlying motivation justifying the complete adequacy of a descriptive definition of dyslexia for "practical diagnosis and for detailed scientific study," became highly suspect and transparent. The quotation above served to highlight clearly the existence of unconsciously motivated "bias mechanisms" attempting to deny the significance of the diagnostic dyslexic cortical void, while simultaneously rationalizing the validity and adequacy of descriptive definitions for a disorder considered to be of cortical rather than psychic origin.*

* Perhaps motivated by similar "bias mechanisms," Money (1962, p. 17) states: "From the point of view of case management the diagnostic obstacles are not as great as they may seem. Whatever the etiology of reading retardation, the known principles and stages of therapy are the same." Is Money really correct? Or do his

Psychogenic Reflections and Conceptualizations

Perhaps a personal clinical example will be helpful in examining the complex overdetermined nature of dyslexic symptomatology. The author began his career in dyslexia by chance 15 years ago following completion of a psychoanalytically geared psychiatric residency. At that time, educators and clinicians alike within the New York City tutorial reading services considered learning (and/or dyslexic) symptoms to be of psychogenic origin. Needless to say, the author had no quarrel with this familiar and comfortable point of view.

Upon psychoanalytic exploration, the vast majority of learning disabled children were found to experience severely distressing feelings of inferiority, stupidity, and clumsiness. They invariably found school and academic activities frustrating and traumatizing. As a result, they developed and manifested corresponding phobias, inhibitions, mood variations, and acting-out behavior, e.g., temper outbursts, restless hyperactive-like symptoms, etc. In addition, psychosomatic symptoms such as insomnia, enuresis, nail-biting, thumb-sucking, headaches, ocular pain, and abdominal complaints prior to school were not infrequently correlated to academic frustrations and stress. Denial mechanisms were commonplace. Thus, learning disabled and/or dyslexic children often confabulated rose-colored stories of academic and personal success. And frequently they manifested happy-go-lucky or "normal" emotional facades sufficient to mislead many investigators into comfortably defining this disorder as existing "in the absence of past or present appreciable inhibitory influences in the internal and external environment."

Had both dyslexic patients and their physicians jointly denied the subclinical depth and range of the coexisting emotional variables? Although dyslexic symptoms may well be of a primary somatic or cerebral cortical origin, how is a clinician to meaningfully assess and rule out co-existing "appreciable" degrees of emotional traumatization and symptomatic determinants if neurophysiologic diagnostic and related measuring parameters are entirely lacking as somatic points of reference and contrast? And how is a clinician to distinguish dyslexic from nondyslexic learning symptomatology? Were the emotional and learning symptoms in dyslexia of primary psychogenic origin, or were the emotional symptoms secondary reactions to an idiopathic primary CNS or somatic dysfunction?

Inasmuch as (1) the emotional, behavioral and academic symptoms among

---

remarks also represent unwitting attempts at rationalizing away the medical significance of the diagnostic-therapeutic void in dyslexia? For after all, is not the scientific aim of medical treatment geared towards specifically reversing and preventing the pathology created by specific etiologies? And is it possible for "the known principles and stages of therapy" of the reading disabled to be independent of specific pathogenesis?

dyslexics frequently improve in association with psychotherapy, (2) the dyslexic scrambling and reversal mechanisms resemble the psychogenically determined primary process reversal, omission, condensation, and displacement mechanisms characterizing slips, jokes, and dreams, as well as neurotic and psychotic symptoms (Freud, 1900, 1901, 1905, 1916–17, 1925–26, 1932–36), and (3) diagnostic neurophysiologic signs are absent in dyslexia, it seemed only reasonable to conclude that the reading and learning symptoms characterizing dyslexics were of primary psychogenic origin. Thus, for example, among the many psychodynamic mechanisms assumed responsible for reading and related academic difficulties, Pearson and English (1937, pp. 162–163) describe the following psychogenic factors:

> 1. Some unpleasant and painful experience may have occurred during the early efforts of the child to learn to read and, as in cases of arithmetical disability cited above, the child becomes conditioned against reading.
>
> 2. Reading may be the one subject stressed by a hated and severe parent. The child, unable to express his antagonism to the parent openly, does so indirectly through refusal to learn to read.
>
> 3. Reading is the acquiring of knowledge through looking. If a child has been severely inhibited in his peeping activities, all acquisition of knowledge through looking may come under the ban of the child's superego. The problem then is not the inability of the child to learn to read, but his fear to use his vision to acquire knowledge. The best treatment for these cases is that which will reduce the severity of the child's superego, i.e., analytic treatment for his neurosis, of which the reading disability is only a symptom.
>
> 4. As in the cases of stammering, the words and letters themselves may come to represent curious anal-sadistic phantasies. In a case reported by Blanchard the child's distortion of words and reversals of words and letters represented a magical spell by which he poured forth his hate and his fear of various people. He was so consumed by these emotions that he had the compulsion to distort everything he read or wrote, and consequently could not learn to read properly. Such cases in which the reading difficulty is symptomatic of a definite neurosis require analytic treatment.

In 1954, Pearson added fear of sibling rivalry, dread of castration, and reality disturbances to the forever expanding and sometimes repetitive list of psychogenic causes of reading disabilities, and stated (1954, pp. 70–71), "Some reading disabilities may be due to strephosymbolia or to the other causes I have already mentioned, but certainly these causes do not explain the severe cases. Blanchard's studies seem to indicate that they are cases of difficulties in digesting and assimilating learning material."

However, upon analysis of a large reading-disabled or dyslexic sample, the various psychodynamic conflicts and triggers contained within the vast psychoanalytic literature were found to statistically permeate only a small minority of cases. In retrospect, primary psychogenic mechanisms and determinants were found insufficient to explain the specific structure and symptoms characterizing the vast majority of dyslexics.

Furthermore, a review of Blanchard's case and corresponding psychodynamics (quoted by Pearson) led the author to postulate an alternative set of pathogenetic formulations: Might Blanchard's case be suffering from a primary somatically determined symptomatic complex consisting of stammering and associated speech distortions as well as letter and word reversals manifesting during reading and writing? And is it possible that these somatically determined symptoms resulted in frustration, anger, and anxiety, as well as in secondary defensive attempts to rationalize away and deny the underlying organicity or somatic compliance? Had Blanchard and many of her psychoanalytic colleagues similarly denied the organic basis of *both* the academic and emotional symptoms in dyslexia and reading disorders? Might Blanchard have mistakenly confused somatic cause with psychogenic effect in her psychodynamic formulations? And might the "magic spell" described by her patient represent a dyslexic child's defensive or confabulatory attempt to disavow himself of both his somatic disorder as well as the fear and responsibility associated with escalating degrees of uncontrollable anger and frustration?

In any event, the psychodynamic explanations as to the origin of dyslexic symptomatology left much to be desired; and the sampling from which these explanations were derived was minimal, and thus subject to significant personal bias. Something was missing, and it was reasoned that it was somatic if it was not psychogenic.

Lloyd Thompson (1966), in a magnificent summary of the psychoanalytic (and organic) literature pertaining to reading disabilities and dyslexia, appeared to share the author's point of view.* He (1) highlighted and thus emphasized Freud's (1910) view that constitutional factors or "somatic compliance" underlie the tendency to fall ill to psychogenic and neurotic disorders, (2) indicated the denied somatic basis underlying two cases described by Prentice and Sperry (1965) as having "primary neurotic learning inhibitions" and manifesting "spelling errors" as well as "accident-proneness, clumsiness and hyperactivity which are characteristics frequently found in dyslexia," and (3) gently footnoted his criticism of Pearson's failure "to take into account innate or organic factors that bear upon the learning process" (Thompson, 1966, p. 71):

> However, with an "about face" in the same book, Pearson became concerned about the trend in psychiatric reporting and cautioned: "It is necessary to reemphasize it [the organic] because at the present time when there is so much emphasis on the importance of intra-psychic processes in all phases of medicine and education, psychiatrists tend to become over-enthusiastic about dynamic

* For those readers specifically interested in the psychoanalytic literature reviewed by the author and summarized by Thompson, refer to: Freud (1910), Jones (1923), Strachey (1930), Klein (1931), Blanchard (1935, 1936, 1946), Mahler (1942), Sylvester and Kunst (1943), Liss (1935, 1937, 1940, 1941, 1949, 1955), Klein (1949), Rosen (1955), Jarvis (1958), Silverman et al. (1959), Rubenstein (1959), Sperry et al. (1958), Prentice and Sperry (1965).

intra-psychic processes to the complete neglect of physiological and organic processes, for which they seem to have a psychic blind-spot.

Upon recognizing the "somatic denial" characterizing the psychoanalytic formulations of learning disorders and dyslexia, the author was forced to backtrack conceptually and assume that the emotional and behavioral symptoms characterizing dyslexics were secondary manifestations of an underlying primary somatic dysfunction rather than the reverse. This "scientific reversal" would then be consistent with, and could explain, the frequent presence of emotional symptoms in dyslexia, the favorable dyslexic response to psychotherapy, and the inability of psychogenic formulations to explain both the quality and spectrum of symptoms defining the majority of dyslexics. According to this assumed primary somatic point of view, psychotherapy had merely relieved the secondary pressures, anxieties, and phobias contaminating and overlapping the primary idiopathic dyslexic disorder and symptomatology, thereby facilitating symptomatic compensation, spurting, or "late blooming." And inasmuch as "spurting" occurred both with and without psychotherapy, it seemed reasonable to further assume that spurting and psychotherapy may often be unrelated and merely coincidental phenomena.

However, although the author could find no hard and fast primary psychogenic mechanisms significantly responsible for the quality and pattern of dyslexic symptoms and was accordingly forced to assume the existence of a primary somatic dysfunction, he could not *completely* disprove a primary psychogenic dyslexic etiology or a crucial psychogenic-somatic lock and key co-determination. Emotional symptoms and psychogenic mechanisms were certainly highly correlated to dyslexia and no doubt influenced and shaped the final symptomatic outcome. And a possibility most certainly existed that other, more experienced clinicians might be capable of elucidating primary psychogenic determinants overlooked by the author and other researchers of a similar bent. One thing was certain: although definitions of dyslexia were theoretically capable of eliminating emotional and educational etiologic variables, dyslexics and clinicians were not as fortunate. In the absence of hard and fast neurophysiologic parameters, the evaluation and differential diagnosis of dyslexia remained highly speculative and confusing. And as a result of the existing differential diagnostic dyslexic void, the disorder and its conceptualization became "fair game" for any and all clinical specialties and adventurists.

The Cortical Physiologic Hypotheses

In view of the fact that psychogenic determinants were found totally inadequate to explain the symptomatic spectrum of dyslexia, and since the absence of cortical signs in dyslexia appeared to negate the historically accepted structural cortical hypotheses, the author turned to the cortical physiologic theories of Orton and Critchley with the hope of finding a theoretically consistent and diagnostically practical solution. At first glance, these physiologic cortical hypotheses were found both logically and emotionally attractive, and appeared to provide an answer to a most puzzling question: *How can dyslexia be of cortical origin without cortical signs?*

In an effort to reconcile the heretofore irresistible cortical parietal theories of dyslexia with the complete and paradoxical absence of corresponding cortical signs, investigators such as Orton and Critchley were forced to water down the prior structural cortical theories and replace them with neurophysiologic hypotheses more consistent with the clinical reality of dyslexia. They reasoned that a structural cortical dysfunction or agenesis was incompatible with the absence of cortical signs, whereas a cortical physiologic dysfunction was not.

Orton, for example, re-named the dyslexic language disorder resulting in twisted reading, writing, spelling, and math symbols "strephosymbolia" (Orton, 1937), and correlated this syndrome to both speech disturbances and an increased incidence of left- and mixed-handedness. Inasmuch as speech and language functions, as well as the expression of right-handedness, were known to be physiologically localized to functioning within the dominant left cortical hemisphere, Orton assumed that an incomplete or delayed establishment of left cortical dominance was neurophysiologically responsible for the dyslexic speech and handedness correlations, as well as the twisted symbol disturbances characterizing this disorder. Interestingly enough, Orton did not modify his dominance theory of dyslexia following recognition that strephosymbolia was, in fact, unrelated to left- or mixed-handedness.

Although Orton's theory appeared to be a clinical step forward, he neither could reliably prove the derivation and existence of incomplete dominance nor could he experimentally prove its causation of dyslexia. In fact, there was no way to disprove an alternative hypothesis suggesting (1) that incomplete dominance is a result rather than a cause of the dyslexic disorder, and (2) that the speech disturbances characterizing dyslexia were similarly independent of dominance mechanisms and were instead related to the idiopathic somatic basis of dyslexia.

Critchley (1969), in a well-written review of the dyslexic literature and dyslexia, stated (p. 103) that "Orton's theory of visual rivalry from inadequate unilateral occipital suppression is on the face of it too speculative. This idea does not explain why dimensions should be confused in a lateral direction only. Nor does it give any reason why verbal symbol-arrangement alone is at fault, while surrounding objects, scenes and pictures appear in normal orientation." Since Critchley found no hard and fast localizing (cortical) signs in dyslexics despite "scrupulous" neurologic examinations, and because the few "miniscule" signs clinically noted tended to diminish or disappear as a function of age, he reasoned that the dyslexic disorder was due to a specific "cerebral immaturity" or maturational lag of constitutional or genetic origin:

> Cases of "specific" or developmental dyslexia are not always entirely "pure" in the sense of a disability existing in complete isolation. . . . The occasional "impurity" of the syndrome is shown by the elucidation at times, on appropriate testing, of various subtle, tenuous, or miniscule deficits, or "soft" neurological signs—to employ an unfortunate term. . . . Many of these little signs are related to an incomplete maturation of the nervous system, and they are more likely to be found among the younger age-groups, being rarer in dyslexics who have attained adolescence. [Critchley, 1969, p. 73]
>
> In recapitulating the diverse neurological disorders which may be uncovered after close and particular scrutiny, it must be stressed that these findings are by no means integral. Many a dyslexic—perhaps even most of them—shows no such disabilities despite highly alerted and scrupulous testing-procedures. Perhaps these subtle neurological signs should be regarded as epi-phenomena—significant when they occur, but not essential in any consideration as to pathogenesis or aetiology. When such manifestations are found, there seems to be an inverse correlation with the age of the patient. In other words, the younger the subject the more likely it is that neurological signs will be found, while with older dyslexics the greater the likelihood of a negative clinical examination. When neurological disabilities are marked, or when they persist into late childhood, underlying brain damage is probable. The dyslexia would then be of the "symptomatic" or "secondary" kind. [Critchley, 1969, p. 85]

Although Critchley's *specific* cerebral lag theory was consistent with the absence of localizing cerebral neurologic signs, he did not and perhaps could not attempt to explain pathophysiologically the *specific* nature, structure, and pattern of symptoms and signs encompassed by the dyslexic syndrome. Furthermore, he failed to thoroughly examine and explore the full range and significance of dyslexic neurologic signs or "epi-phenomena," as well as the possibility that there existed a clinically hidden CNS dysfunction in dyslexia which was merely compensated for and rendered increasingly subclinical with age.

Instead of recognizing and pursuing the significance of the neurologic signs found, Critchley assumed dyslexia to be a neurologically "pure" disorder, and erroneously considered the positive findings "epi-phenomena" rather than basic and inherent evidence of a more universal dyslexic disturbance. Might Critchley's neurophysiologic oversight or "slip" have been motivated by an unconscious need to preserve the primary role of the cerebral cortex in the pathogenesis of dyslexic symptomatology? Could Critchley's theoretical "cart" have biased and shaped his clinical "horse"?

Inasmuch as both the basis and genetic origin of Critchley's cerebral lag theory of dyslexia were as untestable as Orton's cerebral dominance theory, there was no way to disprove an alternative hypothesis suggesting that "cerebral immaturity," when and if present, may be secondary to a neurophysiologically more specific, noncortical dysfunction, and that the so-called neurologic "epi-phenomena" were overlooked pathognomonic clues to the underlying dyslexic dysfunction. Interestingly enough, this alternative hypothesis would then be consistent with, and could explain, both Orton's and Critchley's theoretical formulations and the absence of cortical signs in dyslexia.

In retrospect, it appears that although Orton and Critchley were clinically forced to abandon the structural cortical theories, they could not altogether abandon the traditionally accepted primary cerebral cortical role in dyslexia. As a result, they substituted vague, nonspecific, and experimentally untestable cortical physiologic hypotheses which offered little or no hope toward further explaining the nature and origin of dyslexic symptoms and dyslexia. Their clinically up-dated theories still remained completely incapable of providing definitive methods for accurate diagnosis, prediction, and incidence determination, let alone a scientific methodology of assessing the assumption that dyslexia was of a constitutional or genetic origin.

In view of the continuing diagnostic-dyslexic void, all reported dyslexic incidence statistics were viewed by the author as highly speculative, and all genetic assumptions about dyslexia based on these speculative incidence statistics were considered subject to significant degrees of error. The only convincing data suggesting a possible genetic etiology for dyslexia was the repeated clinical observation indicating that male dyslexics predominate over female dyslexics by ratios greater than 3:1 and 4:1. However, Vernon (1957) even questioned the sex-linked genetic significance of these ratios by suggesting that males are psychologically more vulnerable to failure than females, and so clinically appear in greater numbers.

Despite extensive research efforts, there continues to exist a perplexing scientific void with regard to dyslexia—best symbolized by the more than 35 synonyms for dyslexia collected by Critchley (1969) in his review of the literature. Untested and unproven theories and conceptualizations abound in number and range from one clinical extreme to another. Some educators and experts have even refuted the existence of dyslexia altogether, and claim this "apparent" disorder is merely the slow end of the learning spectrum. In retrospect, it appears that investigators have attempted to rename the disorder when failing to comprehend and explain it. As a result, there developed a "synonym compulsion," which merely added scientific insult to injury and which has immeasurably fragmented and scrambled any meaningful attempt at reaching a scientifically integrated perspective on dyslexia.

To date, dyslexia has been postulated to be of aphasic, minimal brain damage (MBD), psychogenic, ocular, pedagogic, and even of "phantom" or imaginary origin—depending upon the researcher's specific point of view and/or the sample size and test data utilized for study and analysis. There exists no theory capable of explaining the total clinical range of dyslexia and each hypothesis appears to explain only a "bird's eye view" of the symptomatic spectrum.

For reasons to be explored analytically, investigators have categorically failed either to recognize or to state the limitations of their respective formulations. All too often, large quanta of scientific time and energy have been wasted on intra- and interspecialty rivalry, thereby nullifying or confusing the benefit derived from meaningful multidisciplinary approaches. Although scientific conflict is by no means limited to dyslexic research, the specific quality, intensity, and motivation underlying the critical forces characterizing the dyslexic research effort appeared suspect and so were studied with an analytic eye geared towards recognizing and comprehending the meaning and nature of the bias mechanisms assumed present.

As a result of this study, several questions were triggered: Could the time and energy drain provoked by scientific conflict have an adaptive purpose and direction? Might not scientific haggling indicate that scientists are still actively resisting, and so delaying, the recognition and acceptance of insights required to solve the studied riddle? Might not the multiple theories and synonyms of dyslexia, as well as the ongoing conflicts, signify that, as yet, no one theory reigns supreme and that all existing theories leave much to be desired? And might not the scientific rivalry suggest the existence of denied and displaced emotions of uncertainty, anxiety, and frustrations? Is it possible that all the theories of dyslexia to date have an underlying common denominator and source? Is it equally possible that each of the theories represents but one of many clinical segments constituting the dyslexic panorama and horizon? And might the traditionally proposed but fragmented tunnel-vision perspectives of the dyslexic source be due to unwittingly biased, selective, and minimal sampling?

Upon contemplating a solution to both the existing dyslexic riddle and the resistance forces shaping and sustaining it, the author assumed (1) that in the final analysis all investigators and theories of dyslexia will turn out to be partially right and wrong, and (2) that any meaningful holistic theory of dyslexia will be fully capable of encompassing all the clinical data and corresponding subtheories, and will simply and specifically explain the scientific "dyslexic" scramble as well as the atypical and paradoxical data. In retrospect, one was forced to recognize that so-called conflicting scientific data is seldom, if ever, "paradoxical" or atypical. Upon analysis, these terms were found to highlight illusions created by incomplete or faulty conceptualization and experimentation. All too often, the fault is unwittingly displaced from the scientific conceptualization and investigator to the data and subject matter.

As a result of this realization, so-called atypical, paradoxical, or conflicting data thereafter served to warn the author that conceptual and/or experimental errors were unwittingly involved. The analysis and resolution of each clinical paradox and statistical exception catapulted the evolving research effort a significant step forward.

In an attempt to comprehend and explain the complex and exponentially expanding dyslexic data base, the author was repeatedly forced to abandon or modify one theory after another. For example, the primary psychogenic formulations of dyslexia were reluctantly dropped following recognition of their severe limitations. In despair, the author latched on to and explored the cortical structural and physiologic hypotheses, only to find them similarly incomplete. Despite many years of intensive and extensive clinical research, the nature of dyslexia continued to remain an elusive and tantalizing mystery.

Gilbert Schiffman, past chairman of the President's Panel on the Right to Read, succinctly highlighted the mystery and riddle underlying dyslexia in his written discussion, "Dyslexia As an Educational Phenomenon: Its Recognition and Treatment" (1962, p. 60):

> In summary, I would like to say that I do not believe that any one discipline—whether medical or educational—or any one technique will by itself solve this serious problem. No one discipline will be able to answer these questions: What is the etiology of these disabilities? How can we make an early diagnosis? What are the best pedagogical procedures in remediating these specific language disabilities?

Pre-Solution Questions and Speculations

In a re-determined effort to explain the cortical diagnostic paradox and dyslexic riddle, the author took a deep breath, stepped way, way back, and silently free associated: How was it possible for the dyslexic riddle to have remained completely intact despite 80 years of extensive research efforts and mounds of corresponding scientific papers and books? Have experts been researching for the missing dyslexic needle in the wrong CNS haystack? Is it possible that a solution to this riddle is really quite simple and readily at hand, but that its recognition and grasp have been masked by potently active bias factors and forces? And if, indeed, bias forces exist and continue to scramble the research effort and maintain the riddle intact, what is the source and nature of these scrambling forces?

The dyslexic research effort and riddle may readily be compared to the pre-Freudian attempts at comprehending dreams, slips, and mental symptoms. As long as clinicians limited themselves solely to investigating conscious mental processes and were "blind" to the significance and power of unconscious mental forces, and as long as these hidden forces selectively determined what was scientifically "seen" and what was denied, mental symptoms and phenomena (dreams, slips, etc.) remained a scientific enigma. Although mental theories abounded, they remained as incapable of solving the neurotic and psychotic mental riddle as are the neurophysiologic theories to date in resolving the dyslexic riddle.

Is it possible that neurophysiologically trained clinicians are as psychologically fixated to the cerebral cortex as were the pre-Freudian psychiatrists to conscious mental events and processes? And might similar unconscious bias and resistance forces be responsible for selecting what is seen and searched for, as well as what is ignored and denied?

If, indeed, cortical signs are completely absent in dyslexia, might dyslexia be of a noncortical or primary subcortical neurophysiologic origin? And may a primary subcortical dysfunction result in reactive secondary emotional, cortical and related CNS symptomatic and compensatory expressions? Might researchers have mistakenly "slipped" and reversed primary dyslexic cause with secondary effect in their formulations? Is it possible that pathognomonic noncortical dyslexic signs exist, but that their presence and significance have been repeatedly overlooked or denied by a determined search for only cortical signs and cortical etiologies? And upon objective analysis, might Orton's dyslexic–speech correlations and Critchley's so-called soft and minimal neurologic "epi-phenomena" be recognized as hard and fast localizing pathognomonic signs of the aforementioned noncortical or subcortical dysfunction? Might we not hypothesize the existence of unconsciously rooted cortical fixation and subcortical denial mechanisms that are responsible for shaping and maintaining the current scientific dyslexic scramble?

Might Kinsbourne and Warrington have overlooked the crucial proprioceptive and compass functions of the cerebellar-vestibular (c-v) circuits in determining finger placement, orientation, and direction (or sequence) sense? Are not finger-to-finger (as well as finger-to-nose) placement and sequencing disturbances localizing signs of a c-v dysfunction? Might we not then assume that the presence of a c-v dysfunction is basic to an impaired "finger order sense"?

If, indeed, "finger order sense" is significantly decreased in Gerstmann's acquired syndrome, might we not assume that this decrease is due to the secondary disruption or release of reciprocally dependent and c-v determined proprioceptive placement and directional compass mechanisms by a *primary* dominant parietal defect with associated cerebral localizing signs, i.e., constructional apraxia?

If "finger order sense" is significantly decreased in the developmental (dyslexic) Gerstmann syndrome as well, might we not in a similar fashion assume the active presence of a similar c-v dysfunction? If neurological evidence of a cerebral dysfunction is absent in the developmental (dyslexic) Gerstmann syndrome, might we not be justified in reasoning that the dyslexic syndrome is due to a *primary* c-v dysfunction with, perhaps, *secondary* cerebral manifestations and expressions? Might we not be justified in holistically conceptualizing the directional and sequencing dysfunction as a neurophysiologic resultant of reciprocally active, interdependent cerebral and c-v functional vectors and determinants?

Is this c-v conceptualization of directional and placement functioning not in harmony with (1) von Uexkull's (1957) view that the three semicircular canals determine three-dimensional operational space by acting as a kinesthetically guided navigational compass with significant memory capability and (2) Sir John Eccles's (1973) observations indicating that "the computational machinery of the cerebellum is engaged in a continuous on-going correction of movements in much the same way as occurs for a target-finding missile"?

Moreover, are not these c-v conceptualizations in harmony with Sherrington's (1906) view of the cerebellum as "the head ganglion of the proprioceptive system," Jackson's (1931) and Goldstein's (1936) views of integrational levels and holistic CNS functioning, and Denny-Brown's (1965) cerebral research demonstrating the release of positive and negative tropisms, or instinctive grasp and avoidance responses, secondary to primary frontal and parietal lobe lesions, respectively?

May not *frontal ataxia* be pathophysiologically due to the secondary release or triggering of c-v ataxic functioning by a primary frontal lobe lesion?* If indeed ataxia may be determined by either a primary frontal lobe lesion or a primary c-v dysfunction, then might not the symptomatic similarity between the acquired and developmental Gerstmann disorders be due to the analogous existence of a c-v common denominator, despite the fact that the two syndromes have a separate and uniquely distinct primary CNS localization and pathogenesis?

Have not Kinsbourne and Warrington "slipped" in a manner analogous to Hermann and overlooked the cerebral versus c-v primary determinants of the directional dysfunction in the acquired versus developmental Gerstmann's syndromes? And might not the clinical differences between these respective syndromes be accounted for by their cerebral versus c-v primary pathophysiologic roots? Might not the similarity in the directional disturbances underlying the right/left, calculation, and graphic disturbances in both the acquired and developmental Gerstmann disorders be due to the presence of released and/or primary c-v dysfunction?

If, indeed, dyslexia cannot be neurophysiologically isolated and differentiated from "the multitude of poor readers" and "other conditions of reading retardation," might we not be justified in assuming the existence of a common pathophysiologic denominator for most poor readers, and that what is commonly referred to as specific developmental dyslexia by Critchley and others is merely a highly selected and thus theoretically biased clinical

* See Dow and Moruzzi, 1958, pp. 404–6.

subsample? Has the dyslexic reading disorder and prognosis been unwittingly confused with that of the cortically impaired alexic aphasic?*

Is it really true, as some experts maintain, that *all* dyslexics have "severe" or "refractory" reading disorders, and that dyslexic reading scores must be at least two years behind normal peers? Or have only the severe and refractory dyslexic cases been recognized and thus far referred for clinical study and treatment? Have experts conceptualized the dyslexic disorder on the basis of highly selective and unwittingly biased sampling? Is it possible that the dyslexic reading disorder varies from one extreme to another and that clinicians have been unwittingly attempting to differentiate dyslexics with severe reading disorders from dyslexics with mild and compensated reading disorders, as if dealing with distinctly separate neurophysiologic and etiologic entities? Could this scientific "error" have significantly contributed to the reported lack of pathognomonic diagnostic signs in dyslexia, as well as the resulting differential diagnostic dilemma and paradox?

Interestingly enough, these scientific free associations and their experimental pursuit led to a new conceptualization of dyslexia which encompassed the various traditional theories and their respective limitations, "neurotic" contradictions, and errors. Utilizing the analogy of a dreamer waking and attempting to rationalize the validity and totality of his remembered dream content, it seems as if researchers have inadvertently mistaken highly selected dream fragments for the entire manifest dream content, while confusing the secondarily derived, disguised or scrambled dream content with its underlying subclinical or latent primary source. To comprehend the scientific dream called dyslexia, the unconsciously motivated resistance forces, or dream censors, which scramble insight and resist change, had to be recognized, analyzed, and resolved.

Although the author completely failed to elucidate any primary psychogenic determinants of dyslexia, he did accidentally succeed in unscrambling the dyslexic research effort from the underlying bias and resistance forces found shaping and maintaining the dyslexic riddle. As might have been anticipated, the analysis of the neurotic-like riddle proceeded in a manner and direction similar to the analysis of dreams and neurotic symptoms: from the defensive perimeter to its underlying nuclear core.

During the "blind," intuitive, and scientific exploration of dreams, slips, and neurotic symptoms, one often encounters unexpected and seemingly "paradoxical" verbal and emotional responses, which invariably signify the existence of active defensive efforts at resisting further penetration and

* In defining alexia as a "variant of aphasia" in which there exists an "extreme difficulty in the interpretation of verbal or literal symbols," Critchley (1969, p. 3) clearly distinguishes this disorder from specific dyslexia by virtue of its cortical structural origin and symptomatic severity and quality: "*Alexia*—That variant of aphasia where the most conspicuous feature consists in an extreme difficulty in the interpretation of verbal or literal symbols by way of visual channels."

insight. As a result of this technical insight, resistance mechanisms were, ironically, found to highlight the avenues requiring clinical analytic pursuit and dissection. In a similar technical fashion, the author pursued the so-called unexpected, atypical, and parädoxical clinical and critical data triggered when blindly and intuitively exploring the dyslexic riddle until these defensive clues ultimately led to the dyslexic core and to a resolution of the riddle.

A Solution

Utilizing a truly multidisciplinary approach, the author attempted to integrate the works of outstanding scientists into a conceptual framework wide enough to answer Schiffman's questions pertaining to dyslexia. In the process of solving the dyslexic riddle, the author stumbled into areas of neurophysiologic and mental functioning where questions arose in exponential proportions with every scientific twist and turn—eventually leading to a unique scientific theory of mind and mental events.

In a series of investigations spanning 15 years and encompassing a sample of 5,000 dyslexics, the author:

1. recognized that the so-called "soft" and "minimal" balance, coordination, rhythm, and direction signs characterizing dyslexic and MBD individuals were, in fact, specific, hard, and fast localizing signs of a cerebellar-vestibular (c-v) dysfunction;
2. correlated and proved dyslexia and related learning disorders to be due to a primary c-v dysfunction with secondarily related emotional and cortical manifestations and expressions;
3. hypothesized and proved that the visual reading symptoms of dyslexia are due to a c-v-determined ocular fixation, tracking, and processing dysfunction;
4. highlighted the role of the cerebellum in processing the entire sensory input in a manner analogous to its established role in processing the entire motor output—thereby significantly enlarging Sherrington's view of the cerebellum as the "head ganglion of the proprioceptive system," while simultaneously explaining the nonvisual sensory sequencing symptoms characterizing dyslexics;
5. developed a 3D optical scanner and blurring-speed methodology capable of a rapid and accurate diagnosis and prediction of the c-v-induced fixation and tracking dysfunction in dyslexia;
6. determined the incidence of c-v dyslexia to be approximately 15%–20% of a middle-class population;
7. demonstrated the c-v-determined ocular tracking capacity (blurring speeds) among male and female dyslexics, and among right- and left-handed dyslexics to be identical—thereby experimentally suggesting that sex and handedness may be independent dyslexic variables;

8. speculated as to the genetic and constitutional origins of dyslexia as well as the possible etiologic role of infectious, allergic, toxic, and traumatic c-v factors occurring during early childhood;

9. highlighted the vital dynamic role of c-v compensatory mechanisms in dyslexia—leading to the discovery of reading-score and blurring-speed *compensated dyslexics;*

10. recognized (a) that the dyslexic c-v disorder need not be defined in terms of I.Q. and degrees of reading score impairment, and (b) that the inclusion of these etiologically nonspecific, variable, and overdetermined parameters in prior dyslexic definitions was most likely based on highly selective and minimal sampling, as well as upon the fallacious identity of dyslexic and alexic aphasic reading disorders;

11. neurophysiologically redefined dyslexia as a c-v-determined dysmetric sensory-motor and spatial-temporal sequencing and processing disorder in dynamic equilibrium with compensatory forces—resulting in a diverse spectrum of symptoms in varying states of compensation, decompensation, and even overcompensation;

12. derived new insights into the role of the cerebellum as a dynamic sensory-motor filter that modulates foreground/background, conscious/nonconscious, and motion sickness mechanisms;

13. postulated that the dyslexic disorder is analogous to a subclinical form of c-v-induced motion sickness, and demonstrated the therapeutic efficacy of the anti-motion sickness medications in improving dyslexic symptomatology;

14. developed new pedagogic, neurophysiologic, and psychotherapeutic methods of facilitating compensatory processes and minimizing emotional and educational traumatization and scarring;

15. demonstrated the role of the c-v circuits in the etiology of a group of travel, motion, perceptual, and sensory-motor phobias and inhibitions. In addition, obsessive-compulsive, mood, impulse, and behavior disorders, as well as a group of somato-psychic disturbances (e.g., headaches, stomachaches, ocular disturbances, sleep disturbances, enuresis, etc.) previously thought to be psychosomatic in origin, were similarly recognized to be of a c-v somatic origin. As a result of this insight, these symptoms were successfully treated with a combined pharmacotherapeutic and psychotherapeutic approach.

Although answers to Schiffman's questions initially seemed as remote as did the moon and Martian landings many years ago, in retrospect his questions and their answers now appear minor in number and complexity when compared to the questions and hypotheses raised by the dyslexic studies and patients constituting this book.

Dyslexia was initially viewed by the author with a fascinating "childish mystique," and so appeared to be an intriguing, grandiose scientific world unto itself. This clinically naive perspective was analogous to the manner in which phylogenetic and ontogenetic man (i.e., the child) egocentrically viewed himself and his relationship to the earth, sun, moon, and stars. However, this narrow and psychologically distorted view of a complex multi-dimensional medical disorder was found incompatible with the cosmic perspective required to solve the dyslexic riddle.

The unfolding research effort and concomitant "neuropsychoanalytic" analysis have both "shrunk" and expanded the author's initial neurosis-like dyslexic perspective. No longer is dyslexia viewed as an isolated scientific world unto itself: quite the contrary. Dyslexia is now understood to be a dynamically interacting, complex speck in the infinite scientific cosmos. Its exploration has carried the author, by analogy, from Earth to Mars and back. One hopes that this dyslexic, scientific "space shuttle" will continue to probe the inner mental and outer cosmic worlds in much the same manner as America's remarkable space program not only probes the cosmos, but continues to expand immeasurably the dimensions and quality of earth itself by sheer dint of its cosmic perspective.

The task of viewing dyslexia through both ends of a "space telescope" has not been easy, and the author has often gone astray. Scientific "tripping" and confusion was commonplace and permeated the entire research effort. However, each and every "dyslexic" or "dysmetric" trip and its retrospective analysis resulted in additional spatial-temporal insights and dimensions. And the developing dyslexic cosmos was found to be endless, and at least four-dimensional. The "dyslexic space probe" initially set its course for the psyche and cerebral cortex, and found itself in the cerebellar and vestibular circuitry instead. By analogy, one might better compare this dysmetric scientific journey to that of Columbus rather than to the scientifically sophisticated, computer-guided space probes.

The author's research efforts were hindered at every step by inner and outer unconscious scientific resistance forces, which attempted to fixate the traditional primary cortical role in dyslexia, while at the same time denying the crucial pathophysiologic determinants of the c-v circuitry. The evolution of the c-v dyslexic research efforts and conceptualizations required the continuous analysis and working-through of instinctive resistance forces attempting to maintain in place what might be called a cortical dyslexic "scientific neurosis." In retrospect, one can only wonder at the degree of unconscious perceptual and conceptual distortion required to support the existence of fallacious cortical assumptions and avoid facing the objective c-v dyslexic reality before one's eyes.

Were we merely dealing with a scientific neurosis, or did the reality and data distortion constitute, in effect, a scientific psychosis? And what were the psychodynamic factors and forces motivating this dyslexic scientific neurosis and "folie-en-masse"? In an attempt to answer these questions, the author speculated as follows:

1. Man is infinitesimal in relationship to the universe and his postulated anxiety over "cosmic insignificance" is assumed to require a proportionally defensive megalomania or narcissism.

2. Man's defensive megalomania has been forced to accept a series of scientific blows: (a) The earth is round and not flat, and therefore far larger than man can see and far more complex than his cosmic anxiety will allow him to accept. (b) Man and earth are not centers of the universe, and thus man and his projected image in earth were scientifically "shrunk" to mere specks in the infinite scientific cosmos. (c) Man is not a unique, supreme, God-like being, but merely a derivation of animal form, and thus part and parcel of earth's vast animal kingdom—resulting in what might be termed "phylogenetic anxiety." (d) Man and his conscious mental functioning are significantly governed and dominated by unconscious, repressed, animal-like instincts, drives, and motives; and, as a result, he has been forced to accept a most unpleasant fact—that he is not even master in his own house.

3. Man's last megalomanic hiding place, his conscious linguistic cortex, has now been neurodynamically analyzed and "shrunk" to realistic biologic proportions—bringing man's mental and linguistic functions into closer relationship to his animal "cerebellar subcortical heritage," and thereby creating a "phylogenetic identity crisis" and a defensive subcortical or "cerebellar denial."

4. Man has attempted to cope with his cosmic insignificance and "phylogenetic identity crisis" by megalomanic or narcissistic pseudoscientific defenses of "cortical over-valuation," "cortical confabulation," and "cerebellar denial."

Needless to say, psychotherapists expecting initial gratitude from neurotic patients following analysis of their narcissistic defenses and exposure of their painful, unconscious, past memories of insignificance, helplessness, and vulnerability are indeed naive. For similar reasons, the c-v data, hypotheses, and conceptualizations of dyslexia were not readily or gratefully accepted by all interested colleagues. As might be expected, some reacted most unscientifically. However, the analysis of their criticism and its intensity revealed the emotional roots underlying their scientific "cortical facades" while, at the same time, demonstrating the existence of unconscious resistance forces in dyslexic and neurophysiologic research.

In attempting to revive and integrate the achievements of past and present scientific giants so as to benefit from their truly remarkable insights, the author was forced to wonder why so many of these great works had never before been scientifically integrated and utilized to successfully tackle dyslexia, despite the continuing cry for a multidisciplinary approach. Do the "panoramic" insights and contributions of scientific giants threaten man's attempt to deny his cosmic insignificance? Do man's narcissistic defenses trigger reactive attempts aimed at isolating, denying, or prematurely burying "cosmic insights" in a royal disguise and masquerade of acceptance?

Although the author has apparently come a long way in his scientific exploration and analysis of dyslexia, this exploration and analysis must be viewed as open-ended and interminable. At any given time, one's scientific introduction and summary must be considered to be separated by only infinitesimal spatial-temporal quanta. It is hoped that the "microcontent" contained in this book as well as the author's 1980 "momentary" research perspective will provide the reader with the data and insights required to assimilate, integrate, and re-analyze the continuously expanding literature on dyslexia.

2 The Spectrum and Panorama of Dyslexia: The Retrospective Study

The author began his "dyslexic career" by chance in 1965 as a psychiatric consultant to the Special Reading Services of the New York City Board of Education. At that time, the prevailing opinion within the Special Reading Services (SRS) was that reading disabilities were due to psychogenic factors.* This opinion was presented at the 1958 American Orthopsychiatric Symposium on Learning Disabilities by Jerome Silverman, Margarette Fite, and Margaret Mosher—3 members of a typical SRS clinic team consisting of psychiatrist, psychologist, and social worker. In their paper, "Clinical Findings in Reading Disability Children—Special Cases of Intellectual Inhibition," the authors analyzed the data derived from a study of 35 SRS children (29 boys/6 girls) with severe learning problems, and clearly stated that "work with these children has shown repeatedly that the reading disability is only one aspect or symptom of a more basic disturbance in the child's emotional life," and that "physical and developmental factors . . . while they do not appear crucial in the origin of the reading problem, may be contributory." In addition, Silverman, Fite, and Mosher formulated a profile of a typical SRS child and then summarized their psychogenic concepts regarding the etiology of disabilities—which, of course, contrasted sharply with the views of researchers espousing a somatic or developmental pathogenesis.

> This child would be male, nine years old, and in the fourth grade. He would have at least average intelligence—usually above average intelligence—and probably would be doing nearly as poorly in arithmetic as in reading. In the classroom he would appear to suffer from severe anxiety, hyperactivity, depressive

* The Special Reading Services was established by the New York City Board of Education in 1955 and dissolved approximately 10 years later during New York's school decentralization crisis. It's concept was jointly resurrected in a modified form by the author and Mr. Maurice Wollen, Superintendent of Staten Island Schools, and became known as The First Grade Supportive Reading Program (SRP). Data derived from this program are reviewed in Chapter 3.

> trends and fearfulness. He would usually have periods of excessive day-dreaming and distractibility. These symptoms occurred in two-thirds of our children. In his early school history we would probably find an absence of kindergarten experience, a chronological age of below six years on entering the first grade, and various unfortunate early school experiences such as frequent changes of school or teacher, serious illnesses or accidents, excessive absences. . . .
>
> Disabilities then may occur 1) because of the child's conflict in acquiring knowledge—he suffers a general inhibition in learning and does not allow himself to learn generally or to learn by learning reading or by reading; and 2) through conflicts displaced to use of vision for learning arising during the important phases of his psychosexual development. There must be freedom for the active and aggressive purpose of seeing and knowing, and utilizing "giving out" what is seen and known; freedom passively to take in and without conflict, and with gratification to chew or digest the food of knowledge. Indeed, since seeking knowledge can represent aggressive activity, if the child has learned this is dangerous or prohibited for him, he cannot permit himself the aggression or curiosity necessary to search or look actively for knowledge, or even the aggression necessary to enable him actively to master a skill—reading. Moreover, one may learn to read but not be able to derive pleasure of any sort from the reading skill. The ability to learn to read does not necessarily imply the ability to experience pleasure in reading itself, or the ability through reading to accumulate or use knowledge. [Silverman et al., pp. 78–79]

Having just completed a psychiatric residency, and having had only minimal clinical experience, the psychogenic hypotheses of reading disorders were readily accepted and explored. However, with increasing clinical experience, it soon became apparent that psychodynamic factors alone were insufficient to explain the diverse range and structure of symptoms displayed by the majority of SRS children. Since vital psychogenic determinants were missing, it seemed reasonable to assume that neurodynamic, rather than psychodynamic, factors and mechanisms were playing havoc with the reading and learning processes of SRS children.

In an attempt to scientifically enlarge the author's initial psychogenic "tunnel perspective" of reading and learning disorders, the role of neurophysiologic determinants was researched and explored. Accordingly, it appeared that the vast majority of reading-disabled SRS children examined fell within the diagnostic criteria defined by dyslexia: an idiopathic reading disorder traditionally assumed to be due to a cortical dysfunction or maturational lag.

As a result of the highly specific SRS selection and clinical referral criteria, the vast majority of reading-disabled children examined might be readily characterized and defined as dyslexic: (1) To be accepted by the SRS, a child must be two or more years behind his/her peers and of normal or superior I.Q. (2) To be referred for clinical neuropsychiatric evaluation, an SRS child must be failing to respond to one hour of biweekly tutoring. Reading disorders hereafter were assumed due to psychogenic and/or cortical factors, and all referred SRS children were examined neurologically and psychiatrically in an effort to establish specific differential diagnostic criteria.

This chapter contains the data and insights derived from the retrospective study and analysis of the clinical/educational records of 1,000 reading-disabled children neuropsychiatrically examined within the SRS. As a result of this study, a diagnostically significant grouping of dyslexic symptoms and three unexpected etiologic correlations was statistically demonstrated and qualitatively explored.

The dyslexic symptomatic complex was found to consist of reading, writing, spelling, math, memory, directional, speech, and grammatical dysfunctions in varying combinations and intensity. The three etiologic correlations revealed:

1. Reading disorders were negatively correlated with primary psychogenic determinants.
2. Reading disorders were negatively correlated with primary cortical determinants.
3. Reading disorders were positively correlated with so-called "soft" balance, coordination, and rhythmic signs; and the latter signs were recognized to be diagnostic of a cerebellar-vestibular dysfunction, and suggested a cerebellar-vestibular dyslexic pathogenesis.

In order to simplify the presentation of data, this chapter is separated into three parts, and artificially divided into quantitative and qualitative studies. The quantitative study contains detailed qualitative descriptions of the symptoms and mechanisms that were found to define statistically the dyslexic syndrome, as well as the aforementioned dyslexic etiological correlations. The qualitative study contains the clinical dissection and discussion of a single dyslexic case typical of those contained within the sample of 1,000. This case has been presented clinically so that the reader might more readily grasp the method and reasoning utilized to detect and dissect the cerebellar-vestibular (c-v) "needle" from the massive clinical dyslexic "haystack." Interestingly enough, the quantitative study was, in fact, a noncomputerized qualitative data analysis of a large clinical sample, whereas the qualitative case study contained a mass of data requiring both quantitative and qualitative analysis.

Inasmuch as handedness and sex have been historically related to dyslexia, these correlates were determined and utilized as points of reference for follow-up studies. Ten percent of the children were observed to be left-handed and the male/female ratio was noted to be 5:1 (Fig. 2–1).

The Nuclear Symptomatic Complex in Dyslexia

A dual quantitative-qualitative analysis of the clinically determined SRS data demonstrated the existence of a nuclear symptomatic complex of diagnostic significance in dyslexia. This complex consists of reading, writing,

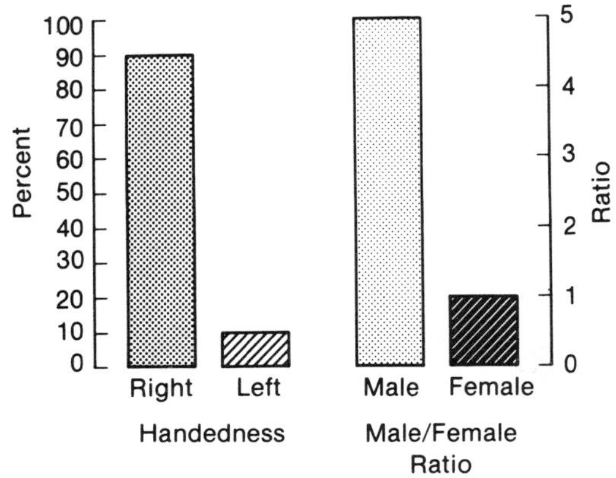

Fig. 2–1. The retrospective study of 1,000 neuropsychiatrically examined reading-disabled or dyslexic children in the Special Reading Services revealed 90% to be right-handed and 10% left-handed. Mixed-handedness was not evaluated. Male dyslexics predominated over female dyslexics by a ratio of 5:1.

spelling, math, memory, directional, speech, and grammatical disturbances. Although the so-called "typical" or "pure" dyslexic might be conceptualized as manifesting all of these symptoms in severe form, most reading-disabled children exhibit varying degrees and combinations of the symptoms defined by the nuclear complex. Each child within this sample demonstrated, and was characterized by, a unique spectrum of dyslexic functions which specifically varied in clinical intensity from severely deficient to compensated and even overcompensated (Fig. 2–2).

The functions within the dyslexic complex were specifically explored and dissected so as to clarify the underlying mechanisms shaping and determining their manifest form. Interestingly enough, each and every function was found to be a complex dynamic vector derivative of multiple, interacting dysfunctioning and compensatory mechanisms. This clinically derived, dynamic conceptualization of dyslexic functions and symptoms helped explain the pseudocontradictory and pseudoparadoxical nature of the extreme variations characterizing dyslexic data and conceptualizations to date. In retrospect, it appeared as if the scientific conflicts due to seemingly contradictory dyslexic findings and diametrically opposed hypotheses resulted from minimal and "biased" sampling, as well as from fixed or static conceptualizations of mental and neurophysiologic functioning. These dyslexic pseudoconflicts were eventually resolved by dramatically enlarging both the width and depth of the currently existing data base and perspective —utilizing a psychoanalytic-like exploratory methodology, a psychodynamic-like or neurodynamic scheme of symptom formation, and large scale sampling.

All the children within this reading-disabled sample were asked an endless series of exploratory questions designed to gather clinical insights: Tell me about your symptoms. Why do you read, write, and spell the way you do? Show me how you make your mistakes. What makes your symptoms

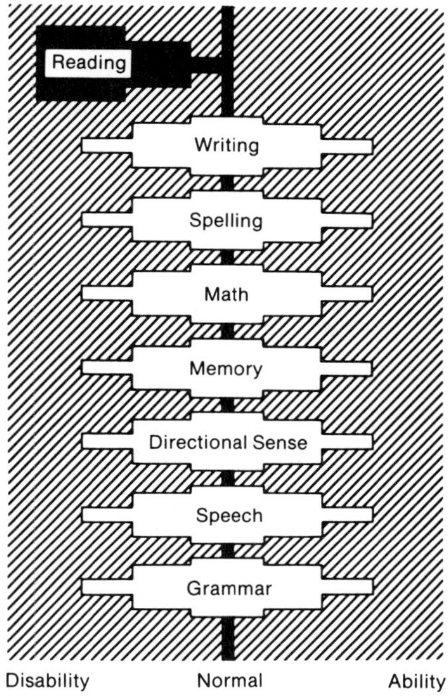

Fig. 2–2. The nuclear symptomatic complex in dyslexia and the functional variations and scatter found upon examining a large dyslexic sample. Severe reading disability may be found associated with any combination and intensity of normal versus abnormal writing, spelling, math, memory, directional, speech, and grammatical functioning.

worse, and what makes them better? Why do you read slowly and use your finger to point? Why does your writing slant? Why do you tilt your head and paper when you write and draw? Why can't you remember the words you study? Why is it harder to remember certain words? Why can't you add or multiply? What's wrong? Do you have trouble understanding the math? Or do you have trouble remembering math tables? Why do you have difficulty remembering right and left? Can you explain the meaning of right and left?

Although the answers to these and countless other questions did not result in the expected psychogenic solution of dyslexia, the data generated did elucidate the complex, fluctuating, and variable nature of the dyslexic disorder under scrutiny. Were it not for the unexpected insights derived from this massive, dual quantitative-qualitative investigation, a solution to the dyslexic riddle would never have materialized.

Inasmuch as descriptive terms such as hyperactivity, distractability, impulsivity, and aggressiveness permeated the clinical records of the sample under study, and since it was difficult to determine whether this descriptive syndrome was a nuclear, or inherent, primary part of the dyslexic symptomatic complex, or merely a secondary reaction to it, a compromise approach was taken. The syndrome was analyzed and described, but not included within the dyslexic complex. It was anticipated that later investigations by the author would clarify its nature and role in dyslexia.

A Qualitative Analysis of the Dyslexic Complex

Reading

The reading disturbances in dyslexia were qualitatively analyzed and found to be of several distinct types. All dyslexic children in the sample manifested a specific visual and/or phonetic perceptual, and related memory, instability for letters and words—and many resorted to defensive guessing, confabulation, and phobic avoidance.

Orientational and directional dysfunction appeared to scramble the normal reading mechanisms and resulted in a host of "typical" dyslexic reading errors. For example, *b* was confused with *d, p* with *q, was* with *saw,* and *on* with *no.* Words, syllables, letters, and parts of letters were frequently skipped over and omitted, Thus, *p* might be seen and read as *o* or *l, t* as *i, dog* as *do,* and *read* as *red.* At times, letters, syllables, and even words, were inappropriately inserted during the reading process and *go* might be read as *going* or *gone,* and *us* as *bus.* Letters and syllables of successive words were periodically fused or condensed, and read as new words. *The cat,* for example, might be seen and read as *that.* Omitted letters, syllables, and words were inadvertently displaced to more distant parts of the same sentence or paragraph, seeming to appear from space. These reading errors were characterized by omission, insertion, displacement, condensation, rotation, reversal, substitution, and guessing tendencies (Fig. 2–3).

Considering that (1) dyslexic reading errors resemble the errors and distortions found in "Freudian slips," (2) dyslexic reading mechanisms resemble the psychodynamically determined primary process mechanisms responsible for neurotic symptoms and the scrambled manifest content characterizing dreams and psychoses, and (3) manifest anxiety, denial, phobic, and inferiority mechanisms were characteristically present, the author initially assumed that the reading errors and mechanisms in dyslexia were of psychogenic origin. This assumption was entertained despite the fact that the dyslexic reading errors and mechanisms were found upon analysis to be devoid of both the psychic determinism and the symbolic content, intent, and meaning usually characteristic of slips, dreams, and neurotic symptoms.

The author found it difficult to detach himself scientifically from familiar and comfortable psychogenic assumptions, despite the recognition that psychodynamic formulations alone were incapable of explaining the dyslexic reality. The analysis and exploration of this emotionally rooted need to fixate and hold on to the familiar, while simultaneously avoiding the anxiety-laden unknown, led to the realization and recognition that similar "neurotic" tendencies had permeated and scrambled the entire research effort in dyslexia to date. To solve the dyslexic riddle, the neurotic scientific fixations to the past and present had to be resolved, new and anxiety-ridden paths had to be explored, and a more objective scientific equilibrium had to be re-established. Upon resolving the fixation to the

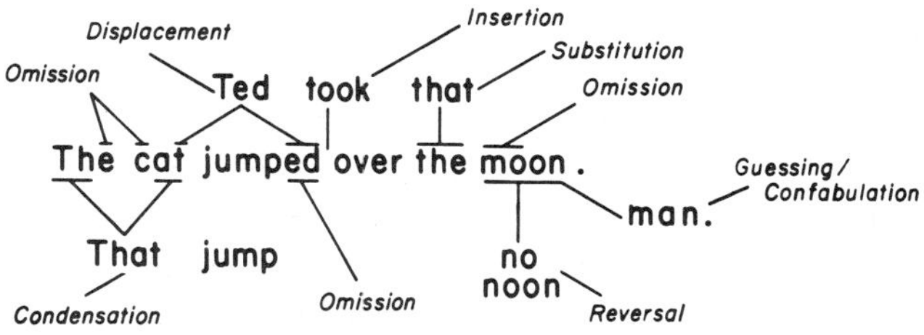

Fig. 2–3. The "typical" dyslexic errors and mechanisms triggered when a reading-disabled sample attempts to read the sentence, The cat jumped over the moon. By means of an error analysis and diagram, the mechanisms underlying the dyslexic reading performance are reconstructed: omissions, insertions, displacements, condensations, rotations/reversals/scrambling, substitutions, guessing/confabulation.

psychogenic dyslexic hypotheses, an exponentially expanding series of additional observations and associated insights materialized.

Occasionally, dyslexics reported active and conscious letter, word, and sentence movement, i.e., oscillopsia, scrambling and reversals, partial and complete blurring, changes in word size, and so on. Not infrequently, this perception of active word movement occurred in association with such symptoms as vertigo, nausea, headaches, ocular tension, and even abdominal pain—resembling the experiences and sensations triggered when reading in a car speeding over bumpy roads. Compensatory squinting, blinking, and head-nodding appeared to minimize these perceptual illusions, whereas fatigue, bright sun, and fluorescent lighting, together with various background "noises" or distractions, were often found triggering or intensifying these disturbances. Periodically, blinking and head movements were required to free the eye from perseveration-like fixation pauses so that the ocular fixation and sequential tracking process underlying reading might continue.

Large, widely spaced black or colored print tended to decrease the clinical or subclinical visual scrambling difficulties, whereas small, newspaper-like grey print intensified these disturbances. Compensatory finger pointing, slow reading, and re-reading were noted to minimize dyslexic reading errors and improve reading comprehension, whereas rapid reading most often resulted in increased visual scrambling and reading errors. Exceptional cases were found capable of grasping the gist of rapidly scanned sentences and paragraphs. However, upon careful scrutiny, these rapid scanners were surprisingly found to have ocular fixation and sequential scanning or scrambling dysfunctions similar to the slow-reading, finger-pointing dyslexics. The rapid scanners had merely learned a compensatory, "intuitive" technique of grasping the meaning of a jumbled or scrambled input. Some rapid scanners were even found to be spontaneous "mirror readers," and several cases were noted to read from right to left and bottom to top. Mirrors and prisms which aligned the reading content with the specific direction of gaze often improved reading speed and comprehension.

In general, a majority of dyslexics demonstrated a remarkable ability for reading and comprehending experimentally presented "mirror content"—an observation suggesting that the presence of dyslexic scrambling mechanisms may trigger the adaptive compensatory development of sequence-independent visual comprehension functions.

In retrospect, the so-called exceptional dyslexic readers were found to be typical dyslexics who merely developed exceptional compensatory reading styles. The insight that divergent, and even contradictory, manifest symptoms may have a similar underlying basis eventually led to a clearer understanding of the crucial role of compensatory and defensive mechanisms in dyslexia. Although clinical and educational focus is invariable directed to the nonreader and the poor reader of normal or superior I.Q. who is failing to progress academically according to expectations, a significant number of "typical" dyslexic children within the SRS were found to respond favorably to tutoring. Their reading scores approached and occasionally surpassed their nondyslexic peers, and as a result they were discharged from the clinical-educational service.

Occasionally, nonreaders and poor readers with "typical" reversal, tracking, and memory disturbances showed a sudden spurt: something seemed to "click," and suddenly they began to progress. For this reason they were viewed pedagogically as "late bloomers," and their dyslexic disorder was considered by some investigators to be merely due to a transient developmental lag rather than a CNS dysfunction. However, reversals, slow reading, and tracking disturbances frequently continued to characterize the "late bloomers" reading performance. These observations suggested the continued active presence of dyslexic scrambling or error mechanisms, which were merely rendered subclinical by overlapping and coexisting specific compensatory forces. The persistence of writing, spelling, math, directional, and other "dyslexic" disturbances in "late bloomers" further indicated that the CNS maturational lag hypothesis of dyslexia fell short of explaining a majority of clinical phenomena and left much to be desired. The "late bloomer" did not really outgrow his dyslexic disorder. He merely compensated for it.*

Despite the fact that visually related symptoms appeared to dominate the clinical stage and foreground in dyslexia, there existed sufficient evidence to suggest that a host of parallel and interdependent auditory, proprioceptive, and motor mechanisms were acting as crucial symptomatic and com-

* The recognition and study of compensatory dyslexics and dyslexia triggered intriguing questions: Why did definitions and conceptualizations of dyslexia ignore the existence of compensated dyslexia? What motivated this highly selected and universally accepted tunnel-vision perspective of dyslexia?

pensatory background determinants. These silent determinants were more specifically highlighted by later studies. For example, the crucial role of proprioceptive sensory and related memory signals in selecting appropriate visual-motor tracking and processing reading reflexes was not fully appreciated until the author attempted to dissect and comprehend the mechanisms underlying a fascinating clinical paradox enabling some dyslexics to recognize and understand larger words more easily than smaller words.

In order to explain this clinical phenomenon, the author reasoned as follows. In the presence of visual memory instability, larger word configurations are characteristically more difficult to process and recognize. To understand the reverse situation, one had to assume the coexistence of nonvisual compensatory reading mechanisms aiding visual recognition. Among the many explanatory possibilities, it seemed most reasonable to assume that the scanning of larger and more complex visual gestalt configurations must result in greater degrees of proprioceptively guided ocular-motor signals and related memory clues which facilitate visual word recognition.

Although this proprioceptive, ocular-motor theory of word recognition was initially developed and utilized to explain a seemingly atypical, paradoxical clinical event, further studies indicated the neurophysiologic universality of this analogy for normal, dyslexic, and perhaps even alexic, visual perception in aphasic adults. For example, alexics may recognize visual written forms only when specifically tracking the letters and words with their eyes—a phenomena called Westphall's maneuver. Furthermore, pedagogic observations indicate that multisensory and rhythmic motor and coordination activities are often helpful in facilitating reading and learning in dyslexia (Ayers, 1972; Delacato, 1959; Gillingham, 1956, 1960 Mourouzis et al., 1970). Needless to say, both independent sets of clinical observations support and further explain the proprioceptive-motor role in normal, abnormal, and compensatory learning.

In a similar fashion, the pursuit of still another dyslexic reading paradox led to an even greater degree of insight. Dyslexics were atypically found capable of spelling words they failed to visually recognize. This initially confusing observation led to the assumption that some dyslexics must *know* or comprehend words better than they can *see* them. To explain this curious phenomenon, the author reasoned as follows: if words are scrambled or blurred because of impaired reflex ocular fixation and scanning mechanisms, the paradoxical occurrence of reading misperception, despite the presence of normal and even superior learning comprehension and spelling memory functions, may readily be understood.

Interestingly enough, the neurodynamic formulations derived from attempts to explain statistically unusual or minority events inadvertently led to a deeper understanding of the scrambling mechanism characterizing the majority of dyslexics. And as a bonus, in conceptualizing the reading recognition process as a summation of separate but interrelated and overlapping ocular-motor and reading comprehension functions, a theoretical basis was provided for specifically explaining Westphall's maneuver, as well as the benefit dyslexic children may occasionally derive from optometric and pedagogic ocular-motor exercises (Pierce, 1977; Halliwell and Solan, 1972; Greenspan, 1975–76).

Writing

The writing performance of dyslexic individuals most often reflected disturbances in graphomotor and spatial coordination. Pencils were awkwardly but tightly held. The writing was slowly and meticulously executed in an apparent attempt to compensate for underlying disorganizing tendencies analagous to those scrambling the dyslexic reading process. The writing most often manifested a "sloppy" appearance, and it often drifted from the intended angle, direction, and spatial position. In addition, associated and complicating difficulties with spelling and grammatical recall appeared to jumble further the dyslexic writing impairment.

Although printing was easier than script for many dyslexics, the reverse was true for others, and some even exhibited "artistic" writing for both—suggesting the existence of specific and distinct writing and compensatory mechanisms for each writing style. During writing and drawing, dyslexic children were frequently noted repositioning their heads, bodies, and arms, while angling the paper as if searching for stable and comfortable perceptual-motor reference points. These positioning maneuvers were also observed during reading, and highlighted the existence of positional reading and writing preferences. For example, some dyslexics preferred reading or writing with their heads angled to one side and close to the page, despite normal visual acuity. Others preferred reading and writing in reclining positions, suggesting the existence of position-dependent sensory-motor reading and writing mechanisms in dyslexia. Some preferred mirror writing, a symptom suggesting a directional determinant to graphomotor functioning. Mirror writing (and spelling) occurred both with and without graphomotor incoordination—indicating the existence of multiple overlapping mechanisms determining the graphomotor output. And oddly enough, mirror writing did not invariably correspond to mirror reading, as was clinically anticipated. The existence of mirror reading without mirror writing, and vice versa, highlighted the circuit-specific nature and expression of the directional dysfunction underlying and permeating dyslexic symptomatology.

Figures 2–4 and 2–5 illustrate the graphomotor performance of dyslexic children. The letters and words are poorly formed, spaced, and directed, and the sentences tend to drift off the horizontal. Grammatical details, such as periods, commas, capitals, are carelessly omitted. Spelling errors are frequent. Letters and syllables may be omitted, reversed, fused, or displaced from one word to another—thus resembling the dyslexic reading errors.

Copying—Script (10 min.)

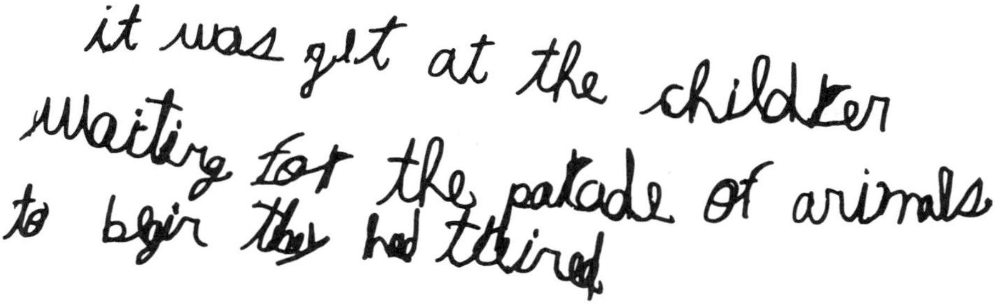

Copying—Printing (more rapid)

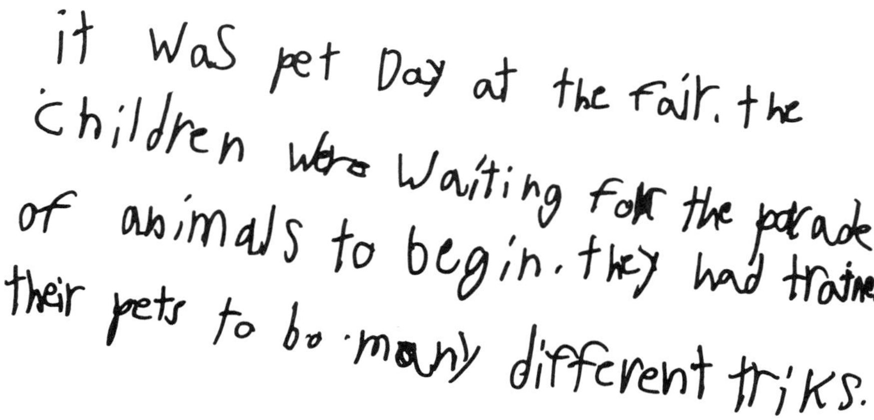

Fig. 2-4. An 8-year-old dyslexic was instructed to copy, "It was pet day at the fair. The children were waiting for the parade of animals to begin. They had trained their pets to do many tricks." Translating the printed form into script was very difficult. It took 10 minutes to translate and copy two sentences. Grammatical detail was lost and letters and words were omitted, reversed, and poorly formed and spaced. Copying the printed form was more rapidly performed. However, capitalization was both omitted and improperly added. Letters were omitted, reversed, and poorly constructed and spaced.

Spelling

Spelling was deficient among the majority of dyslexics, and the quality of the spelling errors was found to be similar to the errors characterizing the reading and writing process. For example, writing was spelled *writting,* story–*storie,* spell–*spellss,* running–*runing,* catch–*cash,* gone–*go* or *goes.*

A qualitative analysis of these spelling errors revealed obvious and typical

Twelve boys were waiting in line at a party to play a game. A picture of a lion hung on the wall before them. They first put large paper bags over their heads so they couldn't see. Each of the boys then tried to pin a ribbon on the lion's tail. They put ribbons on the lion's legs, head, and body. All missed its tail. So none of them won the prize.

Fig. 2–5. An 11-year-old dyslexic was instructed to read and then copy several printed sentences into script. The writing drifts significantly from the horizontal. Letters are poorly formed and spaced, as well as inappropriately omitted, inserted, and condensed. Occasionally, letters from successive words are fused or condensed. Grammatical details such as crossing t's are intermittently and carelessly omitted.

disturbances in visual and/or phonetic sequential word recall. In addition, the spelling errors were found to be significantly determined and shaped by the motor channel utilized for testing. For example, it was not unusual to find children for whom written spelling was complicated by graphomotor incoordination and scrambling tendencies. As a result, their written spelling was found worse than their oral spelling. However, other fascinating variations were also noted. Children manifesting graphomotor scrambling and

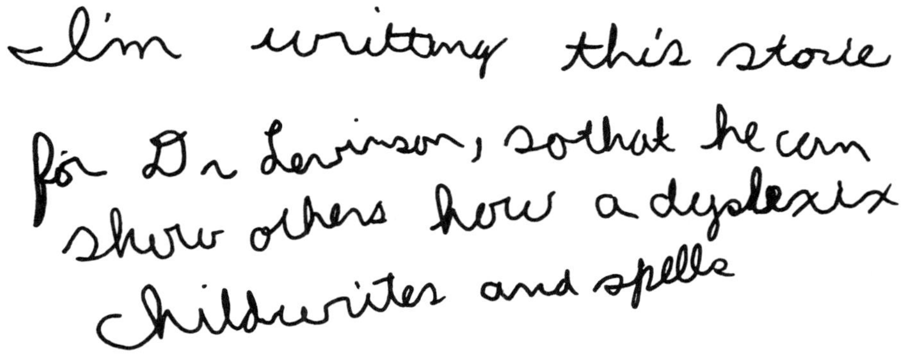

Fig. 2–6. Graphomotor spelling errors of a bright 10-year-old dyslexic girl. A neurodynamic analysis of the spelling errors suggests a dysfunction in the visual-motor memory of letter sequences and the use of compensatory phonetic recall. Letters and letter pairs are perseverated, and at times inappropriately fused or condensed. Moreover, the spelling disorder is complicated by graphomotor incoordination, drifting, and the omission of grammatical details. Interestingly enough, this girl's oral spelling was found to be superior to her graphomotor spelling, suggesting that the motor channel utilized to test spelling may significantly alter the performance.

compensated memory functioning not infrequently exhibited poor written spelling and normal, or even superior, oral spelling. The reverse situation was true as well: children manifesting impaired auditory sequencing and speech dysfunctioning were typically found to be deficient in oral spelling. And the oral spelling deficiency was occasionally found to be more severe than the corresponding written spelling performance—provided graphomotor functioning was relatively intact. In the presence of compensated visual memory functioning, additional spelling variations were noted, i.e., dyslexics with normal and even superior spelling ability.

A comparison of the spelling samples in Figs. 2–6 and 2–7 demonstrates the variations in intensity characterizing each function within the nuclear symptomatic complex in dyslexia.

Mathematics

Mathematical functioning varied significantly among dyslexic children, and was found dependent upon the specific pattern of interaction between underlying dysfunctioning and compensatory mechanisms. Most dyslexics experienced no difficulty with mathematical conceptualization, and so conceptual acalculia was statistically absent in this dyslexic sample. However, many dyslexics demonstrated an impaired or uncertain "computer memory" for addition, subtraction, and especially multiplication recall. As a result, they were often found resorting to compensatory finger, speech, and eidetic

One morning a boy made a boat.
"Where can I play with it?" he asked.
Father said, "Come with me in the car.
We will take your boat with us."
Soon the boy called, "Please stop.
I see water. May I play here?"
"Yes," said Father. "Have a good time."

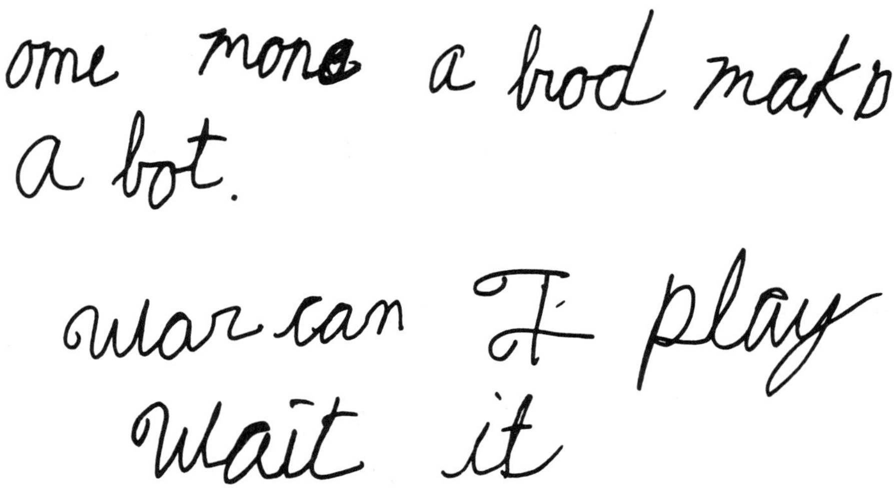

Fig. 2–7. Spelling performance of an 8½-year-old dyslexic girl asked to write a few sentences she just read. Her visual-motor memory for sequential letters is severely deficient. Letters and syllables are omitted or substituted for one another, and guessing or confabulation is determined by randomization plus phonetic cues.

image counting. Since compensatory finger and speech counting utilized touch, proprioceptive, auditory, and even motor signals, whereas eidetic image counting utilized visual and ocular-motor proprioceptive, and even rhythmic, signals for stabilizing memory functioning, it seemed highly reasonable to assume that the so-called conceptual mathematical difficulties in dyslexia were often caused by nonconceptual sensory-motor sequencing and related memory difficulties. Furthermore, the fact that dyslexics spontaneously and successfully utilized sensory-motor and rhythmic functions to compensate for reading and mathematical recall suggested the thesis that primary sensory-motor mechanisms are crucial for normal learning, and that the disruption of these mechanisms may result in learning disabilities.

Graphomotor incoordination and associated reversals, scrambling, and column malalignment invariably complicated mathematical memory functioning and resulted in a host of "careless" errors (Fig. 2–8). To minimize these motor, spatial, and scrambling errors, some dyslexics preferred mental calculations to written calculations, and thus avoided coexisting graphomotor scrambling mechanisms. Occasionally the reverse was noted. Some dyslexics were incapable of mentally retaining or visualizing numbers for calculations. As a result, they were forced to write down the numbers so that they might be *seen* and thus conceptually utilized. Interestingly enough, math performance was often found to improve dramatically if graph paper was utilized to minimize column malalignment and scrambling, and if the mathematical "foreground" is relatively free of neighboring detail, clutter, or "background noise."

These observations clearly demonstrate the manner and degree to which mathematical functioning is dependent upon nonconceptual and heretofore unrecognized perceptual-motor and related memory functions.

Directional Sense

Specific disturbances in right/left directional sense and memory were encountered frequently enough in this dyslexic sample to warrant a distinct category. The neurodynamic analysis of the right/left errors suggested the presence of a specific impairment in remembering or knowing where right and left were as spatial directions, while ruling out the existence of a primary linguistic or conceptual disturbance.

Dyslexic children knew that right and left were directions. They just didn't know or remember where these directions were. When tested, dyslexic children who could not recall the location of right and left would often guess. Once they guessed, all future directional responses during the immediate testing were consistent. This clinical observation clearly suggested that the concept of right and left as directions was intact, and that only its spatial localization or long-term right/left memory function was impaired.

With time, training and maturation, most dyslexic children eventually learn not only their own right and left, but the examiner's as well. Needless to say, if the concept of right and left were primarily linguistically (or gnostically) impaired, one would expect a randomization to the right/left guessing patterns rather than the consistency which was invariably found. In addition, many dyslexic children who experienced initial difficulty recalling right and left spontaneously devised and utilized compensatory memory clues to enable or facilitate recall, further suggesting the existence of a memory—rather than conceptual—dysfunction. For example, a dyslexic child with a scar on his right hand would visually utilize the scar to recall his right/left reference points, unless the speed with which the questions were asked did not allow him adequate reasoning or compensatory time. Not infrequently, dyslexic children utilized proprioceptive

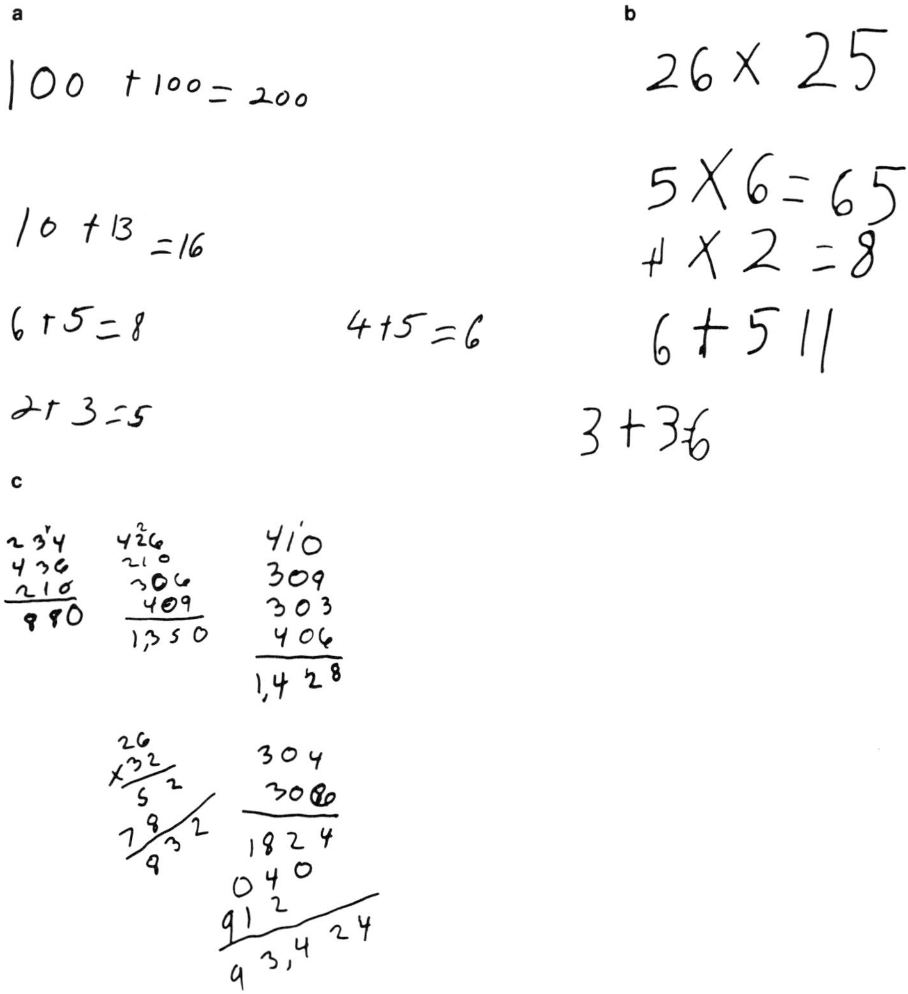

Fig. 2–8. The mathematical errors in dyslexia may be of several distinct overlapping types.

(*a*) "Simple" addition calculations such as 100 + 100 and 2 + 3 are *remembered*, whereas more difficult calculations are *forgotten* and the answers guessed at or confabulated.

(*b*) A similar memory instability for multiplication. When asked to write and multiply 2 × 6 and 2 × 5, the 9-year-old mentally condensed the numbers, writing 26 × 25. When asked to write and calculate 5 × 6, he guessed at an answer, and the guess was merely a condensation of the two numbers written. He did understand and remember 4 × 2 = 8, but reversed the 4. As noted, he recalled addition, but forgot to put in the equal sign when adding 6 + 5, and belatedly added it to the equation 3 + 3 = 6.

(*c*) The multiplication ability of a 10-year-old dyslexic. The numbers are occasionally poorly formed and the column alignment drifts to the right. Needless to say, graphomotor and spatial incoordination may result in careless errors, despite superior conceptual and memory ability.

and other compensatory sensory-motor and related directional memory clues —e.g., the right hand is the one currently experienced as stronger, or the one remembered as having sustained a painful past injury, or the one visualized as holding a pencil or throwing a ball.

Occasionally, dyslexics were considered to be negativistic on the basis of their hesitant, ambivalent, and anxiety-laden avoidance of handshaking and/or eye contact. Only in retrospect were these "anti-social" avoidance symptoms recognized to be due to primary somatic, rather than primary psychogenic, disturbances. Thus, upon neurodynamic exploration, hand contact was avoided because of right/left uncertainty and the anticipated embarrassment of using the wrong hand. In a similar fashion, upon analysis, eye contact was avoided in order to minimize (1) ocular perseveration, (2) directionally confused and dysmetric ocular scanning mechanisms, and (3) the catastrophic discomfort triggered when "forced" to fixate moving facial features during communication.

For some dyslexics, simultaneous listening and looking were more than they could "take" physiologically, and as a result they tended to sacrifice direction-dependent looking or eye contact in order to preserve the direction and sequence of auditory verbalizations and comprehension. In retrospect, it appeared as if dyslexics could not simultaneously coordinate and integrate directional and/or sequential visual, auditory, proprioceptive, and motor processing.

Chance remarks spontaneously made by several dyslexic children triggered the scientific pursuit and insight that eventually added an entirely new dimension in understanding the directional dysfunction and its significance in dyslexia: "Swimming under water with my eyes closed gets me completely confused and scared and I don't know where I am . . . The same thing happens when I dive. That's why I won't go diving anymore. When I open my eyes underwater I'm fine." Another patient stated: "Once when I was scuba diving, I meant to swim up and I was actually going down. I realized I was going the wrong way only because the pressure began to hurt by ears. I never went scuba diving again." For some, even the water's temperature and depth seemed to be important directional symptomatic variables.

Disorientation (and/or vertigo) was also clinically observed in some dyslexic children during eyes-closed Romberg testing. Upon opening their eyes, the disorientation and vertigo disappeared. These observations suggested that visual suppression tends to trigger vestibular reactivity, whereas visual fixation tends to inhibit vestibular reactivity.

Sleep disturbances and phobias were not uncommonly found related to disorientation phenomena. Occasionally a dyslexic child refused to sleep in the dark; others insisted on watching television until falling asleep. Analysis of these sleep difficulties revealed the existence of "sleep disorientation and vertigo" and its avoidance by insomnia. Watching television enabled children to "doze off" with their eyes open, thus avoiding the vertigo, disorientation, and catastrophic anxiety triggered by visual suppression and associated sleep mechanisms.

Upon recognizing the primary somatic role of disorienting and vertiginous experiences in triggering secondary catastrophic anxiety, avoidance, and phobic mechanisms, the author was forced to abandon the traditionally accepted assumption that mental symptoms such as insomnia and phobias invariably have a primary mental derivation. These observations clearly indicated that mental phenomena may have a hidden or denied somatic origin, regardless of the coexistence of independent neurotic factors and the absence of neurologic signs. As a result of this realization, the reported fantasies, fears, and anxiety dreams of getting lost suddenly took on a new primary somatic significance and determinism.

Could dream fantasies of getting lost, being abandoned, flying, falling, spinning, etc., be the expression of disorienting and vertiginous sleep sensations and signals?* Further psychodynamic and neurodynamic clinical explorations revealed that tunnels and elevators often triggered the same disorienting reactions as scuba diving, and that acceleration and deceleration motion signals intensified these disorienting and anxiety experiences. In addition, an occasional child reported flying disorientation and even prolonged jet lag, whereas others reported motion sickness and motion-avoidance or phobic phenomenon. Looking out of a plane or car window appeared to reduce or eliminate these motion-related symptoms—once again highlighting the significance of ocular fixation in minimizing motion-related symptomatic phenomena. On the other hand, specific and/or complex "crowded" (colored and/or uncolored) background visual patterns ("noise") tended to provoke disorientation and anxiety responses similar to those elicited by ocular and visual suppression.

Although each of the disorienting triggers was found to be statistically "atypical," there intuitively seemed to exist a typical background pattern, or unity, to these apparently dissimilar triggering stimuli. In attempting to comprehend the common thread unifying the "disorienting data," the following themes and generalizations were recognized. Visual fixation and orientation mechanisms tended to minimize and/or inhibit disorientation, vertiginous, and anxiety sensations, whereas visual suppression and/or reduced orientation and input data (scuba diving, sleep, eyes closed, etc.) appeared to trigger or exaggerate these disorienting sensations. Paradoxi-

* Electronystagmography (ENG) studies later revealed the triggering of spontaneous nystagmus in patients only upon closing their eyes, and its disappearance upon opening their eyes. This observation, together with the recognition of position-dependent nystagmus and vertigo in a significant percentage of dyslexic children, suggested the conceptualization of subclinical nystagmus and vertigo tendencies and raised the question, Was there a relationship between spontaneous and positional nystagmus with eyes closed, sleep disorientation and/or vertigo and the tracking nystagmus of dream content or REMs?

cally, both visual overloading ("noise," "crowds," and specific visual colors and patterns) and visual deprivation appeared to trigger or release the very same sensations.

In retrospect, these seemingly contradictory and paradoxical observations suggested that both visual suppression and visual overloading minimized or scrambled the significance of visual orientation mechanisms, triggering disorienting and vertiginous responses in susceptible dyslexic individuals. The triggering of disorientation, vertigo, or imbalance phenomena during Romberg testing with eyes closed and rotation-stimulation studies suggested that these symptoms were due to an underlying vestibular dysfunction. The assumed presence of a vestibular dysfunction could then further explain why the opposing experiences of excessive motion and immobility (sensory-motor deprivation) may result in similar disorienting experiences and anxiety reactions, depending on whether the vestibular dysfunction was hyper- or hypoactive and reactive. Furthermore, it seemed reasonable to assume that hypoactive vestibular functioning might adaptively result in stimulation-seeking motion activity, whereas hyperactive vestibular functioning would result in attempts to avoid and minimize symptom-triggering types of motion stimulation activity.

Vestibular hypo- and hyperreactivity are traditionally and oversimplistically diagnosed on the basis of response to caloric stimulation. However, this and later studies demonstrated vestibular reactivity to be highly gestalt- or stimulus-specific, and even direction-specific. As a result, hypoactive caloric responses may coexist with normal rotation responses and hyperactive visually triggered responses. In addition, vestibular reactions to the various specific motion triggers were found to vary significantly. Car sickness may exist in the absence of plane and seasickness. Escalator or elevator motion sickness and anxiety reactions may exist in the absence of car, plane, and seasickness. Not infrequently, the direction of the motion stimuli appears crucial in determining vestibular response. Thus *up* and *down* as well as *clockwise* and *counterclockwise* motion stimuli may result in significantly differing vestibular responses. Furthermore, vestibular conditioning for a specific motion or a specific stimulus direction may not apply or be transferred to the same motion in a different direction, or to another type of motion input or configuration. Only upon recognizing the complex circuit-related sensory and direction-specific nature of vestibular functioning and compensation, were the diverse and often confusing clinical findings in dyslexia eventually understood.

If, indeed, a vestibular dysfunction were responsible for the directional dysfunction characterizing dyslexics, the "triggering unity" of water, tunnels, and elevators might readily be conceptualized. If the vestibular-cerebellar circuitry is hypothesized to be a sensory-dependent compass, media that decrease the reception of vital sensory data and signals could result in disorientation, especially in the absence of visual compensatory mechanisms. And if the vestibular compass is as dependent on the reception of electromagnetic and gravitational signals as are the guided-missile compass systems, then electromagnetic, gravitational, and microwave shielding environments, as well as inherent disorganization of compass sensory receptivity, would result in disorientation and anxiety responses. As a result of this conceptualization, water, tunnels, and elevators might be viewed as *shielding environments.* These shielding environments alone, or in combination with excessive motion and related sensory (visual) overloading, could explain the various triggers found responsible for the observed "disorienting data" (Fig. 2–9).

However, the fact that only right/left disorientation is statistically present in dyslexia must still be explained. *Up/down* and *front/back* disorientation is seldom noted. To explain these directional variations, the author reasoned as follows. If the gravitational force field is recognized to be asymmetric, and if its primary vector is vertical when compared to the relatively mild right/left and front/back force vectors, then mild receptive compass disturbances most likely would be imperceptive to only the minimal right/left and front/back gravitational vector signals. In addition, front/back orientation is largely determined and strongly reinforced by innumerable nongravitational visual, proprioceptive, and touch signals—rendering front/back memory and conceptualization developmentally "easy." On the other hand, visual compensation and reinforcement for right/left memory uncertainty and instability is obviously of only minimal help when compared to its significance for front/back, and even up/down memory. Right/left orientation is assumed to be primarily dependent on gravitational asymmetry and the accruing "abstract" memory for right and left. Since right/left memory is dependent upon such delayed compensatory memory functions as the writing and throwing hand, the stronger or weaker hand, etc., it seems understandable why only right/left disorientation statistically manifests in dyslexia, and why it is least likely to respond to early developmental or compensatory mechanisms.

Although right/left uncertainty is a frequent symptom in dyslexia, it is only one of innumerable subclinical directional compass disturbances and manifestations. A retrospective analysis of the dyslexic signs, symptoms, and functions indicate that directional disturbances permeate and influence almost all sensory, motor, speech, memory, and thought functions, and that the appearance and pattern of directional "slips" is often significantly dependent upon, and determined by, the neurophysiologic equilibrium existing between the inherent strength of specific sensory-motor functional areas and their specific overlapping compensatory mechanisms and forces. The study of factors and forces triggering compass confusion and catastrophic anxiety reactions intuitively led to a similar study of adult phobic and anxiety triggers, and resulted in fascinating insights into the somatic determinants of emotional disorders.

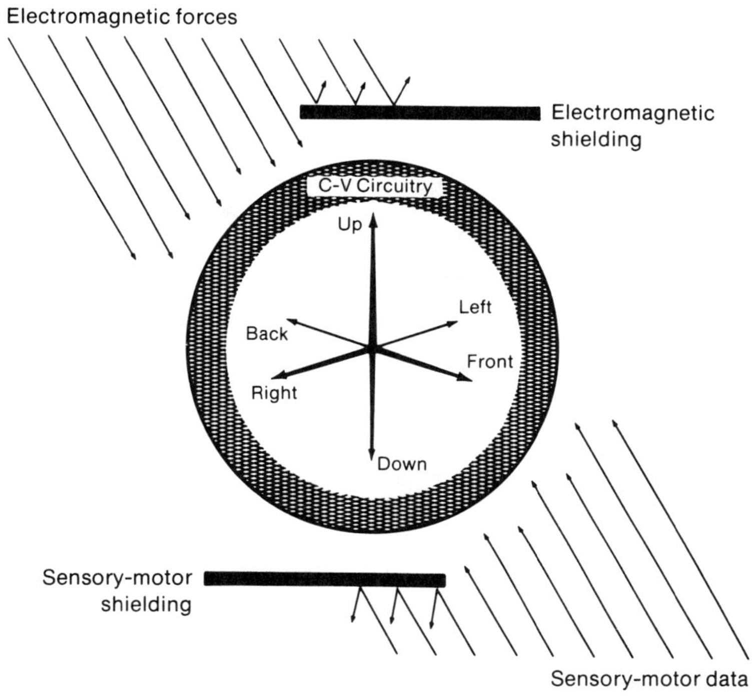

Figure 2–9. The cerebellar-vestibular compass. A qualitative analysis of the directional disturbances characterizing the vast majority of dyslexics led the author to conceptualize the c-v circuits as analogous to a dynamic, complex compass and guided-missile system, which computes and imparts direction to all CNS functions. This compass system was envisioned as inherently dependent upon the appropriate reception and processing of external electromagnetic forces and internal sensory-motor data. Disturbances in either the reception or processing of external or internal compass-dependent data may result in degrees of disorientation and impaired direction-related somata-psychic functioning.

Paradoxically, although specific direction-related cerebral, sensory-motor and "conceptual" functions may be secondarily effected by a primarily impaired c-v compass, compensatory directional functioning appears to be highly dependent upon primary cerebral conceptual and memory cues.

Memory

Both sequential and single types of memory disturbances for sensory, motor, temporal, and directional events appeared to characterize the dyslexic sample examined. Dyslexic children, for example, manifested impaired visual and/or phonetic letter and word recall as well as difficulty in remembering the days of the week, the months of the year, a series of instructions, spelling sequences, multiplication tables, speech and thought sequences, ideas, directions, colors, and so on.

The delay experienced by some dyslexic children in learning to name specific colors was initially considered to be a developmental form of color agnosia—once color blindness was ruled out—and tended to substantiate clinically the classical correlations of alexia and color agnosia (Poetzl, 1928; Hécaen, 1962). Upon clinical dissection, this fascinating pseudo-agnostic or pseudo-aphasic word-finding difficulty was found to be due to either an inability to remember the names of infrequently observed colors or a type of "color blurring" for only specific color configurations.

A significant number of dyslexic children experienced difficulty learning or remembering how to tell time. Upon analysis, this symptom was found to be multidetermined and due to overlapping but separate neurodynamic mechanisms. Some dyslexics would forget instructions rapidly and become confused. Others experienced the numbers as blurred, reversed, or scrambled; still others could not recall either the direction of the watch hand signifying *before* and *after* or which hand represented minutes or hours. As a result of these scrambling, directional, and memory disturbances, dyslexic children were fallaciously considered to have a primary conceptual inability in learning to read time.

Furthermore, the clinical data was characterized by delays in the memory retention and/or learning of such diverse balance, coordination, and rhythmic motor functions as speech, hopping, skipping, running, tying shoe laces, buttoning and zippering clothes, and holding and using pencils, crayons, scissors, knives and forks. Interestingly enough, the symptomatic dissection of this diverse array of clinical disturbances revealed the surprising existence of an underlying subclinical dysfunction in primary proprioceptive placement and related sequential memory affecting a varying spectrum of seemingly unrelated temporal-spatial motor functions.

In attempting to explain the reason why dyslexic children experienced difficulty in selectively recalling only specific letters, words, numbers, names, colors, directions, and motor tasks, the author assumed that both sequential and single sensory-motor memory functions were category- or function-specific and circuit-related, rather than generalized. Thus, memory-related difficulties with one sequence or event by no means implied the existence of similar difficulties with all related sequences and events. Often, difficulty with one memory channel or function triggered either compensatory "savant" functioning in another channel or secondarily impaired the development of related and dependent conceptual functions. As a result, mixed combinations of poor, adequate, and even superior sensory-motor memory functions were invariably found clinically coexisting in any one patient, and resulted in the typical dyslexic scatter-function pattern so often "paradoxically" observed.

Although this clinically derived qualitative description of sequential and single memory disturbances appeared adequate to account for the total range of memory disturbances noted in the dyslexic sample, one cannot assume that all memory disturbances noted are primary. The clinical variation in memory functioning clearly suggests that memory is a complex interdependent and overdetermined variable, which may significantly affect, and be affected by, related sensory-motor and conceptual functioning. Only a continuing research effort will determine the neurophysiologic validity of clinically separating memory function into sequential and single types. In retrospect, one might even speculate that single memory dysfunction may develop into a special compensated form of sequential memory dysfunction.

Speech

Delayed expressive speech development, together with articulation, slurring, and stuttering errors, were recognized in approximately one-third of the referred sample. The articulation and slurring difficulties appeared to be due to spatial-temporal incoordination or scrambling of the speech musculature and its unfolding sequential motor patterns. Inasmuch as stuttering appeared related to a scrambling disturbance in the timing and/or temporal flow of the motor patterns, with resultant difficulties in stopping and starting, and since stuttering errors were not infrequently associated with articulation and slurring errors, it appeared reasonable to view the stuttering disorder as part and parcel of the dyslexic or dysmetric temporal-spatial speech syndrome.

Although primary receptive aphasic speech disturbances were distinctly absent in this dyslexic sample, an occasional dyslexic reported experiencing an unusually long delay between hearing and comprehending a language sequence. As a result, they often found themselves either requesting speakers to repeat themselves as if they had not heard what was said, or forgetting what was said and repeating it later on as if it was their own thought. This interesting difficulty was expressed by a patient as follows: "I find myself saying, 'What?' and by the time I've asked the question I know what was said. . . . And at other times I'll say something only to find out I've just repeated something told to me." This temporal receptive speech impairment appeared to mirror the temporal expressive speech delays noted in slurring, stammering, and stuttering, and seemed also consistent with the temporal-spatial sequencing disturbances generally characterizing the speech dysfunctions in dyslexia.

Auditory imperception or scrambling for specific and sequential phonetic sounds was not infrequently observed. This disturbance appeared to parallel the visual scrambling and blurring phenomena previously described, and often provoked both speech and spelling errors.

Occasionally, dyslexics manifested a "loose" and telescopic quality to their associative speech or thinking styles, and as a result tended to be rapid, wordy, and rambling in their spontaneous descriptions. This interesting speech pattern appeared independent of anxiety factors, and tended to resemble a schizophrenic's "loose associations" and tangential thinking. However, these dyslexic children were not psychotic, and lacked autistic preoccupation and projective thinking mechanisms. They merely seemed to forget momentarily the direction of their thought sequences and/or the thoughts and words themselves. Occasionally, the temporal spacing between words and sentences was shorter than normal and even dysmetric.

Later studies noted nonpsychotic "absent-minded" adult dyslexics to manifest similar loose, wordy, and rambling speech patterns—clearly demonstrating the need to qualitatively and diagnostically distinguish dyslexic speech patterns from schizophrenic patterns (Kasanin, 1964). Upon analysis, this loose, absent-minded dyslexic thinking style prone to slips was found to be due to the very same underlying memory, directional, and temporal-spatial dyscoordination mechanisms characterizing dyslexic reading, writing, and spelling errors.

Not infrequently these so-called absent-minded individuals intend to say or do one thing and wind up saying or doing another, even the opposite of what was originally intended. Forgetting is commonplace. As a result, the dyslexic's speech and action patterns may often exhibit a disoriented and disjointed, even comical, quality, which many clinicians fallaciously consider due to primary psychogenic determinants. However, upon analysis, the dyscoordination or slip between intention and speech or motor response was most often found lacking a primary emotional causation, and appeared qualitatively consistent with the dyslexic symptomatology. In retrospect, these slips invariably provoked secondary emotional attempts at compensation; and the unsuspecting psychiatrist and psychologist will unwittingly mistake secondary defensive reaction with primary causation. For example, some dyslexics become embarrassed, blush, and retreat socially as a result of their slips, while others attempt to joke and rationalize them away.

Paradoxically, some dyslexics were found to demonstrate highly organized, crystal-clear thinking and expressive styles. Upon analysis, many of these individuals were found to have had subtle and compensated speech impediments during their early childhood. In retrospect, their highly condensed speech patterns appeared to be defensive or adaptive attempts at minimizing speech output and thinking errors. Although these dyslexics were often incapable of spontaneous free-associative and reflective speech, they were more than capable of performing these very same functions in silence. For example, when asked to freely think aloud about a question, they could not or would not. But they could, and would, invariably produce the answer after a silent pause—clearly demonstrating their highly developed, silent associative and reflective thinking capacities. Following recognition and resolution of their guarded or defensive speech mechanisms, many learned to think aloud and to express themselves without embarrassment or fear of criticism. Later adult studies not only confirmed these observations but revealed the existence of dyslexics who were capable of free association and reflection only when writing. Their fluent and lucid writing styles appeared to be motivated similarly by dyslexic verbalization difficulties which were compensated for by gifted and/or unhampered writing functions.

Because the ability to free-associate is a cardinal and essential prerequisite for candidates being evaluated for psychoanalytic therapy, and since this ability may be nonverbally present, it behooves psychiatrists and psychoanalysts to explore seriously these clinical considerations in their diagnostic-treatment assessment of psychoanalytic patients.

Grammar

Analysis of dyslexic written and speech samples frequently revealed the presence of grammatical disturbances, although it was often difficult to determine whether these disturbances were of primary, secondary, or even tertiary, origin. For example, periods, commas, capitals, verbs, and adjectives were frequently omitted or inappropriately used in the written samples of dyslexic children, who nevertheless grasped the conceptual meaning and significance of these and other grammatical functions. Some, however, experienced great difficulty comprehending the meaning of written grammatical formulations, although their speech functions were found to be grammatically intact, and even superior. Often the reverse was also found: children manifesting intact and even superior grammatical written functioning appeared to exhibit grammatical disturbances in speech. As a result of these clinical observations, grammatical functioning was considered dependent on, or related to, underlying circuit-specific motor and memory functions. In addition, these clinical observations clearly demonstrated that conceptual functions may be secondarily delayed or impaired by a primary disturbance in nonconceptual sensory-motor and memory mechanisms.

Overactivity, Distractability, and Impulsivity

Terms such as hyperactivity, distractability, impulsivity, restlessness, and aggressive and regressive acting-out, appeared frequently to characterize the developmental and educational records of the reading-disabled children under scrutiny. However, very few of these children manifested this behavioral complex when tutored in the small SRS groups, or when neuropsychologically examined by the author in one-to-one clinical circumstances. Of course, these paradoxical behavioral observations resulted in paradoxical conclusions and confusion. How were hyperactive, distractable, and impulsive children transformed into attentive angels? Were their teachers or peers at fault? Do these children require one-to-one emotional contact? Or do they require less background stimulation and frustration? Are these situation-specific and stimulus-specific "hyperactive" children milder variants of the aimless, continuously active, driven "perpetual-motion machines" characteristic of the "true" hyperactivity-distractability syndrome? Or do significant qualitative and etiologic underlying differences determine these quantitative variations? Pending resolutions of these questions, the stimulus-specific, mildly hyperactive child will be referred to as overactive.

Further analysis of the SRS developmental histories differentiated congenital overactivity from reactive overactivity. Congenitally overactive children frequently improve with age, until once again triggered to overactivity and distractability by the anxieties and frustrations associated with academic failure and the complexities of classroom situations. The reactive group reveals no history of congenital overactivity and first manifests in association with academic anxieties and frustrations. Although continued study of these overactive groups may eventually reveal that congenital overactivity is of somatic origin and reactive overactivity is of psychogenic origin, the author would not be entirely surprised to find these groupings artificial and clinically based on quantitative, rather than qualitative, differences.

Overactivity and distractability may appear and disappear independently of one another. Distractable children were occasionally noted to be motorically calm. And overactive children may demonstrate intense concentration for interesting subject material. These observations suggest that overactivity and distractability may be due to separate, but related and interacting, mechanisms, which may be selectively triggered and compensated. Distractability appeared to be related to a failure in selectively inhibiting background stimulation, whereas overactivity appeared to be related to a failure in selectively inhibiting or neutralizing motor, anxiety, and related events. Of course, overactivity may fragment concentration and vice versa.

To date, the author has clinically correlated the overactivity-distractability syndrome with the dyslexic symptomatic complex. The syndrome appears to be either somatically predisposed or psychogenically triggered by catastrophic anxiety situations, and tends to respond favorably to the sympathomimetic amines. Further studies will attempt to elucidate its situation-specific nature and determine its neurophysiologic relationship to the dyslexic symptomatic complex and "true" hyperactivity.

This syndrome and its management have been remarkably reviewed by Werry (1968). Historically, the hyperactivity-distractability syndrome has been similarly correlated to learning disorders by Laufer and Denhoff (1957), Werry et al. (1966), and Bakwin and Bakwin (1966). Its treatment with sympathomimetic amines dates back to 1937 (Bradley, 1937; Connors and Eisenberg, 1963), and the paradoxical sedative effect of CNS stimulants in hyperactive children remains unclear—although Laufer et al. (1957) suggest that these drugs may increase the CNS disorganization threshold by some action on the inhibitory areas of the reticular activating system (Magoun, 1963, pp. 158–77).

Psychogenic and Neurophysiologic Correlations

Psychogenic Correlations

All reading-disabled SRS cases manifested the nuclear symptomatic complex, albeit in varying combinations, intensities, and degrees of compensation—despite the fact that the dyslexic sample varied significantly in socioeconomic, cultural, educational, racial, I.Q., and psychological backgrounds. It was not uncommon to find reading-disabled or dyslexic children with stable and healthy emotional, educational, and cultural backgrounds who manifested severe degrees of the symptomatic complex. The opposite was true as well. At times, emotionally, educationally, and culturally deprived children were noted to manifest only mild degrees of the dyslexic complex. These observations clearly suggested that the dyslexic complex was independent of primary psychogenic determinants.

There existed no scientifically adequate, primary psychodynamic explanation or hypothesis capable of explaining the specificity, choice, structure, intensity, and variability of the dyslexic symptomatic complex and its underlying mechanisms. Most frequently, the coexisting emotional symptoms were found to be either secondary to, or independent of, the reading (or dyslexic) disorder and its symptomatic manifestations.

As previously stated, the resemblance of dyslexic scrambling mechanisms to the primary process mechanisms underlying dreams, slips, and neurotic and psychotic symptoms initially suggested a psychogenic identity. However, dyslexic errors and mechanisms lacked the psychic determinism, meaning, and symbolic representation responsible for the content of dreams, slips, and psychogenic symptoms—highlighting a crucial pathogenetic distinction. Inasmuch as the dyslexic errors and mechanisms were not psychogenically determined, it became evident that dyslexia was not of psychogenic origin and that dyslexia must have a primary neurophysiologic derivation. And yet the similarity between *primary process* and dyslexic mechanisms begged for an explanation. Were the dyslexic and primary process mechanisms similar but qualitatively different? Or did the neurophysiologic regression during sleep and psychogenically determined symptom formation in some way trigger or release mental processes and forces similar to those released by the neurophysiologic dysfunction assumed to underlie dyslexia?

Neurophysiologic Correlations

A retrospective analysis of the neurophysiologic data clearly revealed:

1. Reading disorders were negatively correlated with cortical signs, despite the fact that cortical signs were specifically investigated and searched for.
2. Reading disorders were positively correlated with various so-called soft or minimal cerebral signs—signs traditionally denoting a nonspecific

and nonlocalizing neurophysiologic significance, and frequently utilized by clinicians to infer the existence of a cortical dysfunction when cortical signs are absent.

3. These so-called soft signs most often reflected balance, coordination, and rhythm disturbances, and were retrospectively found to be hard and fast parameters of c-v dysfunction.

Negative Cortical Correlations

Proven hard and fast cortical signs, such as agnosia, ideational apraxia, aphasia, primary conceptual impairment and concrete thinking, impaired I.Q., abnormal cerebral reflexes (i.e., Babinski reflexes), cerebral paresis, cerebral sensory loss, extinction phenomena, as well as deficiencies in point localization and two-point discrimination, were distinctly and/or statistically lacking from the analyzed data—despite the fact that these cortical signs were specifically searched for during the clinical examinations (Nielson, 1946; Brain, 1965).

Approximately 4% of the cases had a history of seizure phenomena, i.e., febrile convulsions, grand mal, and petit mal epilepsy. In addition, 1% of the children in this study had been examined by neurologists, and occasionally the symptoms comprising the symptomatic complex of dyslexia were considered to be aphasic, agnostic, apraxic, and conceptual in nature and origin (Fig. 2–10). However, upon analysis of the terms' usage, often what was called "apraxia" was, in fact, a c-v dysmetria reflecting a spatial-temporal incoordinational and/or rhythmic impairment, rather than an ideational dysfunction (Denny-Brown, 1958). Word hesitations and reversals, as well as slurring and articulation errors, in association with defensive speech avoidance phenomena were frequently mistaken for aphasic disturbances. The inability to recognize words or remember and name specific colors was fallaciously considered to be evidence of visual agnosia and/or aphasia. Right/left directional uncertainty, and the resulting handedness and speech "slips," were erroneously viewed as disturbances in cerebral dominance. The memory uncertainty underlying dyslexic mathematical functioning was clinically confused with parietal acalculia. And the specific sensory, motor, and eidetic attempts at memory compensation were mistaken for concrete thinking and functioning secondary to a primary conceptual impairment.

The Circular Logic in Dyslexic Research

Inasmuch as the neurophysiologic localization and pathophysiology of dyslexia and its symptomatic manifestations were unknown, and thus considered idiopathic, it seemed confusing to refer to dyslexic symptoms with terms

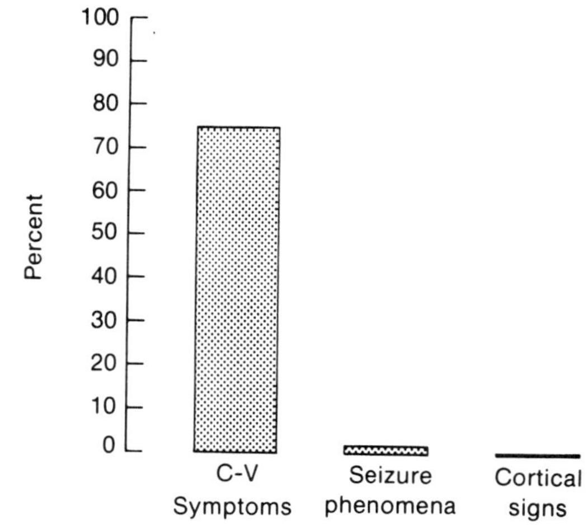

Fig. 2–10. Incidence of cerebellar-vestibular signs and symptoms found upon a retrospective analysis of the case records of 1,000 neuropsychiatrically examined dyslexic children. As noted, 75% of the children evidenced cerebellar-vestibular signs, as compared to a statistically negligent incidence of cortical signs.

specifically denoting exact cerebral localization and implying proven pathophysiologic impairment. This circular reasoning can be outlined as follows:

1. Dyslexia is an idiopathic congenital reading disorder.
2. Dyslexia is assumed to be of cortical origin based on the proven cortical parietal origin of acquired alexia in adult aphasics.
3. The existence of severe and scrambled reading symptoms in otherwise normal children appeared to be convincing evidence that the dyslexic disorder was of a cortical structural or physiologic origin—despite the absence of hard and fast cortical signs.
4. The presence of coexisting speech, motor, memory, conceptual, perceptual, and dominance difficulties merely clinched the cortical neurophysiologic diagnosis of dyslexia and established its identity with acquired adult parietal alexia (and Gerstmann's syndrome). For, after all, are not aphasic, agnostic, conceptual, perceptual, and dominance disturbances pathognomonic indicators of cortical dysfunctioning?

However, are not assumptions confused with conclusions? And are we not reasoning in circles? If, indeed, dyslexia is a disorder of unknown neurophysiologic origin, how can its idiopathic reading and related symptoms be utilized to specifically and definitely establish its neurophysiologic site? Although the absence of hard and fast cortical signs in dyslexia does not mean that the cortex is intact and plays no role, this absence most certainly requires an explanation—as does the need to prove a cortical etiology in dyslexia via confabulated cortical terminology and a circular logic.

Positive Cerebellar-Vestibular Correlations

Approximately 75% of the retrospectively analyzed dyslexic case histories contained past or present developmental evidence of balance, coordination, and rhythmic motor disturbances (Fig. 2–10). For example, dyslexic children frequently manifested a developmental delay and/or difficulty in crawling, sitting, standing, walking, and speech. Running, skipping, hopping, kicking, throwing, and swimming were often troublesome. Difficulties were experienced in tying shoelaces and in buttoning and zippering clothes. Riding a two-wheeler (even a three-wheeler) and participation in sports activities were delayed and/or avoided. Knives and forks, pencils, crayons and scissors were awkwardly held and poorly utilized. Tripping, falling, and other clumsy accidents were characteristic. In addition, these developmental symptoms were significantly correlated with one or more of the following hard and fast c-v neurophysiologic signs: positive Romberg, tandem walking imbalance or ataxia, articulatory speech disorders, dysdiadochokinesis, fine tremor, hypotonia (i.e., pes planus, scoliosis, etc.), head tilting, nystagmus, and a spectrum of dysmetric disturbances during finger-to-nose, finger-to-finger, heel-to-toe, writing, drawing, and ocular scanning testing.*

Bender Gestalt and Goodenough Figure Drawing Errors

The analysis of the Bender Gestalt and Goodenough figure drawing errors in dyslexia revealed, in most cases, a clear-cut and characteristic disturbance in spatial orientation and placement. For example, the Bender Gestalt designs were typically rotated, reversed, or angled from their intended directions. And during the drawing performance, dyslexics were frequently observed tilting and shifting their heads, bodies, copying paper, and even the Bender Gestalt stimulus cards, in what appeared to be compensatory gyroscopic attempts at finding a comfortable drawing position. These positioning movements seemed identical to the previously described dyslexic reading and writing compensatory positional preference maneuvers, and suggested the existence of an underlying dysfunctioning gyroscopic system and compensatory neurophysiologic attempts at re-stabilization.

The rotation errors and associated positioning maneuvers, together with tilting of the Bender Gestalt and Goodenough figure drawings from their intended horizontal and vertical axes, and steering difficulties during angle formations, suggested that the automatic co-pilot or the inner spatial and directional steering "gyroscopic" mechanisms of the vestibular apparatus and c-v circuitory was impaired.

Inasmuch as the so-called soft, nonspecific and nonlocalizing CNS errors and mechanisms determining and shaping the Bender Gestalt and Goodenough figure drawings appeared similar to the errors and mechanisms

* There existed only one case with clinical nystagmus, and two cases manifesting a fine writing tremor. Although the fine tremor was initially thought to be of psychogenic origin, upon reflection it appeared that the fine tremor was of c-v origin, and that psychological and/or anxiety factors merely intensified the tremor so that it become clinically and visibly apparent.

defining the dyslexic symptomatic complex, and since these findings were correlated to negative psychogenic factors, negative cortical signs, and positive c-v signs, it seemed reasonable to assume that the Bender Gestalt and Goodenough errors and mechanisms in dyslexia were also of c-v neurophysiologic origin.

In retrospect, it was recognized that the dysmetric or dyslexic writing and drawing samples contained the projected evidence of clinical and subclinical neurodynamic c-v dysfunctioning and compensatory mechanisms. Thus, graphomotor tilting was assumed to reflect the projected presence of a subclinical c-v imbalance or destabilization, and suggested the existence of a corresponding inner tilt to the c-v compass and "gyroscope" which, in addition, seemed also responsible for the c-v-determined symptoms of vertigo, disorientation, and ataxia. The articulation errors, or disjointed Bender Gestalt and Goodenough errors, were assumed related to or determined by the dysmetric proprioceptive and visual-motor dysfunction characterizing finger-to-nose, heel-to-toe, and finger-to-finger placement. Furthermore, the absence or disappearance of graphomotor errors with age suggested the corresponding development of subclinical compensatory gyroscopic tilting and placement mechanisms. As a result of this reasoning, a neurodynamic dimension was added to the traditional psychodynamic and developmental interpretation of the Bender Gestalt and Goodenough projected content and performance (Bender, 1938, 1951; Goodenough, 1926). It is hoped that this dual neurodynamic/psychodynamic research perspective will enrich both neurophysiologic and psychogenic formulations, and facilitate their differential diagnostic separation.

Bender Gestalt Designs

Figure 2–11 indicates the Bender Gestalt designs children are requested to draw and represents the normal expected pattern for children of SRS age. Figures 2–12, 2–13, and 2–14 illustrate the rotation, drifting, coordination, articulation and angle formation errors characterizing dyslexic Bender Gestalt drawing samples. In retrospect, these errors were recognized to be due to underlying graphomotor disturbances in intended placement and direction, as well as in coordinated spatial motor integration. These errors were triggered by the specific spatial-motor coordination tasks required by the gestalt-specific Bender cards rather than by primary psychogenic determinants. The card A stimulus frequently triggered rotation errors, whereas cards 1 and 2 provoked drifting errors. Articulation errors were released by cards A and 4, and angle formation difficulties were typically provoked by cards A, 7 and 8. Stimulus card 6 triggered disturbances in smooth rhythmic coordination flow, and frequently resulted in zig-zagging.

Although specific visual configurations statistically provoked characteristic patterns of graphomotor dysfunction, large-scale sampling and analysis were required to recognize both typical and atypical responses, as well as their specific underlying neurophysiologic dysfunctioning and compensa-

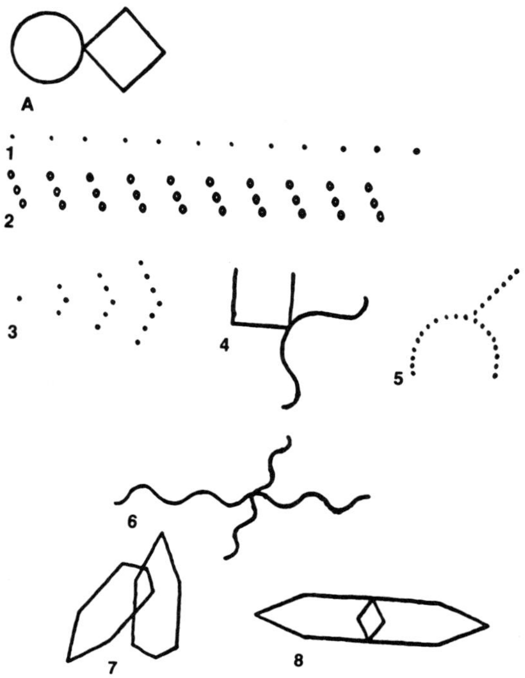

Fig. 2–11. The Bender Gestalt stimulus cards. Children are requested to draw 9 Bender Gestalt stimuli. For children of SRS age, the graphomotor drawing performance should closely approximate the illustrated Bender Gestalt stimulus figures. These figures thus served as the expected norm for the SRS group tested, and variations from this graphomotor norm were qualitatively analyzed for the presence of underlying psychodynamic and/or neurodynamic mechanisms.

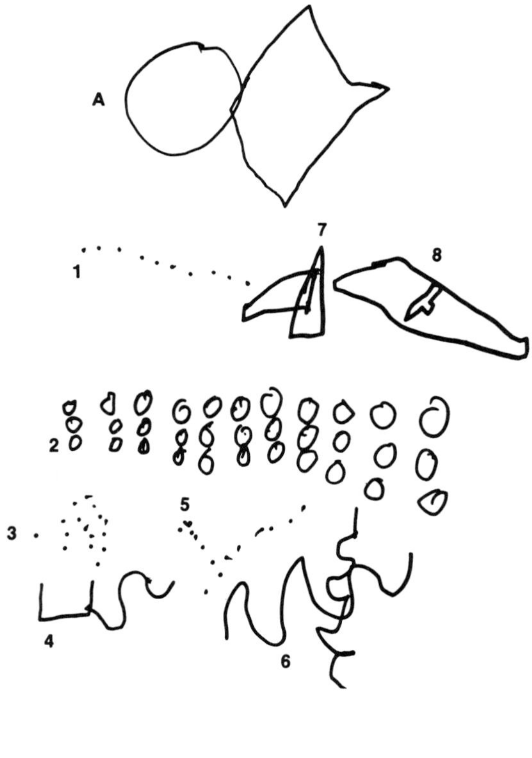

Fig. 2–12. Bender Gestalt performance by a 10½-year-old dyslexic girl. Articulation and angle formation errors were triggered by cards A, 4, 7, and 8. Directional disturbances resulting in drifting, rotation, and angle formation errors were triggered by cards A, 1, 5, 7, and 8. In addition, card 6 triggered zig-zagging rather than a smooth rhythmic flow, and card 2 provoked graphomotor instability in maintaining constant size and space as a function of repetition and time.

Fig. 2–13. Bender Gestalt performance of a 10-year-old dyslexic boy. Articulation and angle-formation errors were triggered by cards A, 4, 7, and 8. Directional or drifting errors were triggered by cards 1 and 2. Card 6 provoked dysmetric zig-zagging rather than a smooth rhythmic flow.

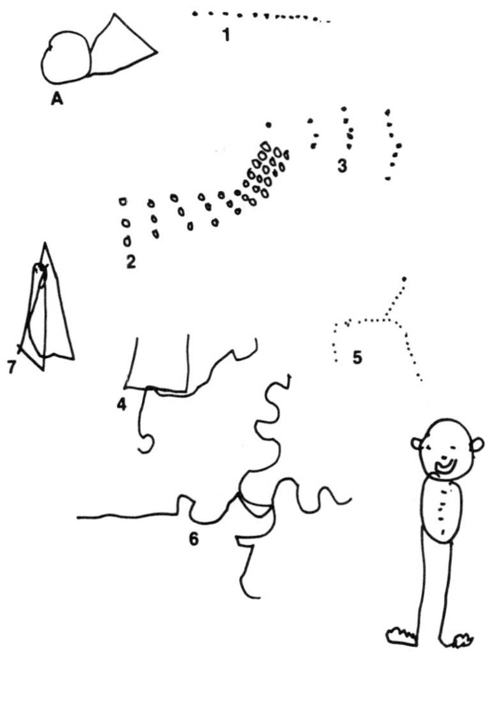

Fig. 2–14. Bender Gestalt and Goodenough figure drawings of a 10½-year-old dyslexic boy. Cards A, 4, and 8 were found to trigger angle-formation errors. Orientational and directional disturbances were provoked by card 2. Card 6 triggered zig-zagging. The figure drawing is simplified, detail is minimized and the arms are omitted in an effort to avoid the catastrophic anxiety triggered by complex graphomotor tasks.

tory mechanisms. Age has been found to be a potent developmental force in shaping both normal and abnormal Bender Gestalt performance. However, until this study, the specific developmental and dysfunctioning neurophysiologic mechanisms responsible for the Bender Gestalt output remained unknown, as did their specific relationship to c-v functioning, dysfunctioning, and compensation.

Goodenough Figure Drawings

Goodenough figure drawings (Fig. 2–15a–d) illustrate the tilting and articulation errors characterizing dyslexic drawings. In addition, their form and size were more frequently found to reflect neurodynamic, rather than primary psychodynamic, mechanisms—although the latter were noted to be secondary and/or independent overdetermined variables. For example, hands and fingers were characteristically either omitted, simplified, or hidden behind the body trunk. Upon a dual neurodynamic-psychodynamic investigation, the reason for this simplification and avoidance was found to be an intent to minimize dysmetric motor functioning while simultaneously avoiding catastrophic, rather than masturbation and castration, anxiety. Although masturbation guilt and anxiety may also be reflected in the Goodenough drawings, whenever present these anxieties were found to be coexisting and overlapping rather than primary determinants. In addition, stick figures and reduced figures were typically found to reflect neurodynamically determined motor simplifications, with perhaps a blend of contaminating secondary feelings of inferiority.

As a result of the insights derived from the c-v mechanisms correlated to normal and dyslexic functioning, it appeared reasonable to view the Goodenough figure performance in terms of neurodynamic projections of the c-v-modulated sensory-motor body scheme. Goodenough errors exceeding developmental norms may hereafter safely be viewed as reflecting the body-image distortions resulting from specific patterns of c-v and related CNS and psychogenic dysfunctioning, as well as from defensive attempts at compensation and/or catastrophic anxiety avoidance.

An Initial Review of the Cerebellar-Vestibular Literature

Once the fallacious cortical assumptions were filtered out of the massive clinical data base in dyslexia, a clear and obvious neurophysiologic relationship was recognized between the clinical c-v neurologic signs in dyslexia and the nuclear symptomatic complex. So obvious was this dyslexic–c-v correlation that, in retrospect, the author was forced to ask, If indeed this relationship was real, why had it been previously overlooked and/or denied? And were other significant signs and symptoms of c-v dysfunction overlooked or denied as well?

Fig. 2–15 a–d. The somatically determined errors provoked when dyslexics are requested to draw a person. As noted, the figures are frequently tilted and details such as hands, fingers, feet and facial features are omitted. (*d*) A stick figure illustrates the simplification of the arms, legs, and trunk, although the facial features are detailed. These Goodenough figure drawing errors were viewed as projections indicative of underlying disturbances in c-v-determined spatial, directional, graphomotor and proprioceptive integration. In addition, some of the simplification or omission errors were assumed to represent compensatory attempts at avoidance of dysmetric performance and the resulting catastrophic anxiety.

Table 2–1. Symptoms of Cerebellar Deficiency

Neurocerebellar Lesions
Muscular hypotonia
Disturbances of posture
Abnormal attitudes: Shoulder, body, and/or head tilt or rotation
Static tremor
Disorder of movement (ataxia)
Dysmetria
Tremor (movement)
Adiodokokineses
The rebound phenomenon
Associated movements
Ocular disturbances
Weakness of conjugate ocular deviation
Skew deviation
Nystagmus
Disorders of articulation and phonation
Disorders of gait
Abnormalities of the reflexes
"Pendular" knee-jerk
Barany's pointing test
Lesions of the Flocculonodular Lobe
Balance and gait disturbances
Vertigo

Data from Brain, 1955, pp. 52–55.

These questions motivated a careful and detailed review of the c-v neurophysiologic literature. Two tables and a textual quotation have been abstracted from neurologic, neurophysiologic and vestibular texts, respectively, and clearly confirm the relationship between dyslexia and c-v signs and symptoms. Table 2–1 was abstracted from the author's medical school text on neurology by Brain (1955), and Table 2–2 from Dow and Moruzzi's highly specialized and brilliant text, *The Physiology and Pathology of the Cerebellum* (1958). A review of the tabulated cerebellar signs clearly demonstrates that the signs, symptoms, and mechanisms permeating the dyslexic sample were indeed of c-v neurophysiologic origin. In addition, the following concisely written text from Dolowitz (1967) clearly describes the balance and spatial orientation functions of the vestibular apparatus. Dolowitz magnificently elucidates the role of this system in maintaining "both equilibrium and spatial orientation and hence the ability of locomotion." Interestingly enough, the crucial computer role of the cerebellum in integrating the "constant stream of impulses from the eye, ear and proprio-

Table 2-2. The Most Common Symptoms of Cerebellar Deficiency, Classified According to the Division of the Cerebellum Thought Primarily Responsible for the Symptom When Diseased or Damaged (Dow and Moruzzi, 1958)

Symptoms, in Order of Frequency	Division of the Cerebellum Responsible for Symptom: Focculo-nodular Lobe	Anterior Lobe of Corpus Cerebelli or Medial Part of Corpus Cerebelli	Posterior Lobe of Corpus Cerebelli or Lateral Parts of Corpus Cerebelli
1. Disturbance in gait	x	x	x
2. Ataxia of isolated movements of upper extremity			x
3. Spontaneous nystagmus	x		x?
4. Adiadochokinesis			x
5. Ataxia of lower extremity			x
6. Abnormal head posture	x		
7. Hypotonia			x
8. Disturbance in station	x	x	x
9. Past-pointing and spontaneous deviation of the limbs			x?
10. Stewart-Holmes phenomenon			x
11. Dysmetria			x
12. Tremor			x
13. Cerebellar speech disturbance			x
14. Pendular knee jerk			x
15. Cerebellar "fits"		x?	
16. Cerebellar catalepsy		x?	
17. Positive supporting reaction		x?	

ceptive senses" so as to "maintain balance and normal terrestrial position" was omitted (p. 86):*

> Balance and spatial orientation are maintained by streams of afferent impulses which are generated by the ocular system, the vestibular system, and the proprioceptors (muscles, joints, viscera, and skin). These impulses are acted upon and interact at conscious and subconscious levels. The proprioceptive impulses of the muscles and tendons and especially of the joints of the neck have an extreme influence on the interaction. Regulatory systems in the brain and spinal

* Is the omission of the "cerebellar" computer role in integrating and regulating the sensory-motor input merely an oversight? Or is this omission a "Freudian slip" motivated by unconscious scientific resistance mechanisms?

> nervous structures act like computers, taking the constant stream of impulses from the eye, ear, and proprioceptive senses, regulating them to constantly alert the body to maintain balance in its normal terrestrial position. Thus these sense organs provide a running commentary on both the external and internal environment of the individual from which the central nervous system collects an integrated pattern which maintains both equilibrium and spatial orientation and hence the ability of locomotion.

Moreover, the author's clinically derived conceptualizations of a sensory-dependent c-v navigational compass affecting both inner mental and outer operational space were found, in retrospect, to be mere echoes of Jakob von Uexkull's "zoologically derived" formulations (1957, pp. 14–17):

> When we move our limbs freely with our eyes shut, we know the exact direction and extent of these motions. Our hands trace paths in a space called our *motor sphere*, or our *effector space*. We measure all these paths by infinitesimal units, which we shall call *directional steps*, since we know the direction of each step perfectly, through kinesthetic sensations or *direction signs*. We distinguish six directions, or three pairs of opposites: right and left, up and down, forward and backward. . . .
>
> It is of the utmost importance to us that paths once traced are retained very easily. This is what makes writing in the dark possible. This faculty is called *kinesthesia*, a word that explains nothing. . . .
>
> Cyon's great contribution is that he traced the three-dimensional character of our space to a sense organ situated in the middle ear, the so-called semicircular canals [Fig. 2–16a], whose position roughly corresponds to the three planes of operational space. This relationship is so clearly proven by numerous experiments that we can make the assertion: all animals possessing the three canals also have a three-dimensional operational space. . . .
>
> [Figure 2–16b] shows the semicircular canals of a fish. It is obvious that they must be of paramount importance to the animal. This is further evidenced by their internal structure, a tubular system in which a liquor moves under nervous control in the three spatial directions. The motion of the liquid faithfully reflects the movements of the whole body. This indicates that the organ has an added significance beyond projecting the three planes into the animal's effector space. It is apparently destined to act as a compass—not as a compass that always points to the North, but as a compass for the fish's own "front door." If all the movements of the whole body are analyzed and marked according to three directions in the canals, then the animal must be back at its starting point whenever it has reduced the nervous markings to zero as it moves about.
>
> There is no doubt that a compass for the front door is a necessary spawning ground. Determination of the front door by visual cues in visual space is insufficient in most cases, since the entrance must be found even if its aspect has changed.

A dysfunction of the vestibular system alone, or in combination with its integrating and regulating computer, the cerebellum, may well account not only for the motor imbalance and spatial incoordination noted in dyslexia, but for the visual, auditory, proprioceptive, and directional dys-

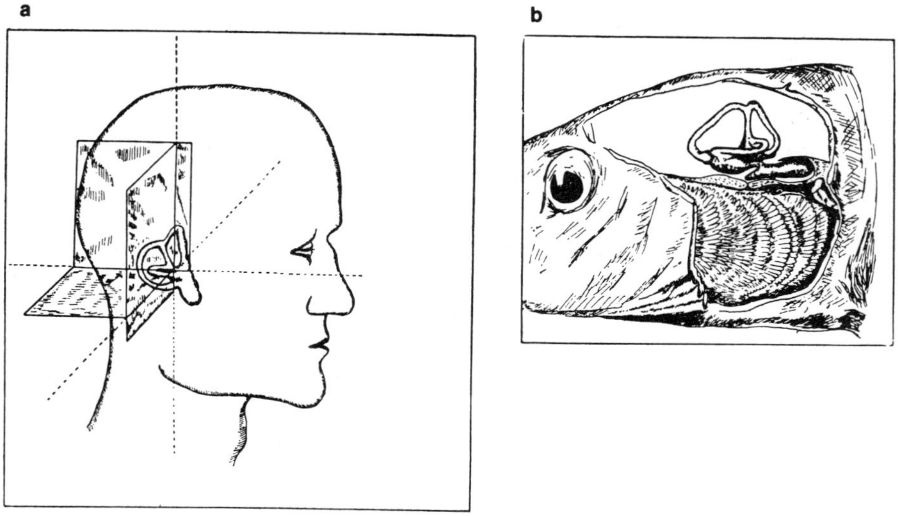

Fig. 2–16. Reproduced with permission from von Uexkull, 1957.

coordination as well. The crucial role of the cerebellum in integrating and regulating the total sensory and motor system will be further discussed in Chapters 4 and 7.

Soft and Minimal Neurophysiologic Signs

The so-called soft and minimal balance, coordination, rhythm and direction-related signs in dyslexia were retrospectively recognized to be of c-v origin, and were viewed as neurophysiologically specific and of localizing significance. The author reasoned as follows: If balance, coordination, and rhythm signs reflect a c-v neurophysiologic origin, they most certainly are not soft or minimal signs of CNS or cerebral dysfunction. They must be, in fact, hard and fast neurophysiologic parameters reflecting c-v function and dysfunction.

In retrospect, the author realized that these unrecognized or denied c-v signs were considered soft and minimal only when utilized as indirect parameters reflecting cortical dysfunction in the absence of cortical signs. The real meaning of soft and minimal was thus recognized to symbolically represent fallacious cortical dyslexic assumptions due to "soft" and "minimal" neurophysiologic insight.

A Resolution of the Circular Logic

In contrast to the traditional dyslexic circular logic, the author reasoned as follows:

1. Dyslexia is assumed to be of primary psychogenic and/or cortical origin.

2. Primary psychogenic determinants and cortical signs were found to be absent in dyslexia.
3. Balance, coordination, rhythm and direction-related "soft" signs were often present in dyslexia.
4. Inasmuch as balance, coordination, and rhythm signs were recognized to reflect c-v dysfunction, these signs were viewed as specific hard and fast clinical parameters.
5. If dyslexia correlates with negative psychogenic determinants, negative cortical signs, and only so-called "soft" positive c-v signs, dyslexia is most probably of c-v, rather than cortical, origin.

This new c-v dyslexic assumption could then explain:

1. The absence of psychogenic determinants and cortical signs in dyslexia.
2. The inability of all previous investigators to find pathognomonic, tell-tale or hard and fast (cortical) signs diagnostic of dyslexia.
3. The lack of any medical progress in developing a pathophysiologic scheme of dyslexia. For example, there is no current neurophysiologic or neuropsychologic way of diagnosing, predicting, treating, preventing, defining, and understanding dyslexia—despite 80 years of intensive and escalating research efforts.

Needless to say, a scientific needle in the wrong haystack cannot be found no matter how diligent the search.

The Retrospective Study (N = 1)

In the absence of a clear understanding of the psychological and physiologic origins of dyslexia and related learning disabilities, victims of these disorders are often subjected to "shotgun" diagnostic batteries of psychiatric, neurologic, psychological, educational, optometric, ophthalmologic, and pediatric tests and examinations. Most often, the children, families, and researchers are overwhelmed and flooded with a volume of reports and a mass of names, numbers, and test scores, which at times appear contradictory and inversely proportional to the medical-educational-diagnostic-therapeutic yield. Retrospectively, one was forced to wonder if this testing compulsion and accompanying data collection were not symptomatic reflections of a defensive attempt at dealing with urgent patient needs as well as scientific anxieties over innumerable uncertainties. Of course, the retrospective analysis of voluminous case reports and data, which was unwittingly biased by selective sampling and interpretation, was not easy. And the attempts to find common threads and denominators within seemingly inconsistent and biased data made looking for a needle in a haystack easy.

In order to illustrate these points, Andy's case is presented here, and will be followed up by a similar case in Chapter 4.

Andy S. is "typical" of the many dyslexic cases retrospectively analyzed, except that he received independent psychological, psycho-educational, and neuropsychiatric evaluations by outstanding clinicians in the dyslexic and learning disability field. The presentation and analysis of Andy's case and clinical findings will serve to illustrate clearly the traditional "cortical dyslexic" point of view previously shared by the author, as well as the retrospectively derived c-v view of dyslexia.

In addition, the author thought it more objective, and thus wiser, to present the reader with the independent, original clinical data of one thoroughly examined and analyzed dyslexic case, rather than to rely entirely on a highly condensed and summarized version of the c-v findings noted in the clinical records of 1,000 dyslexic cases. In order to preserve the flow of ideas and transitions while conserving time and space, the dyslexic data indicative of the c-v "needle" has been abstracted from the clinical "haystack" and analyzed.

The Author's Retrospective Clinical Findings

Andy is a bright 8½-year-old third-grader with severe reading, writing, spelling, and directional difficulties. Since he was failing to respond to biweekly tutoring within the SRS, Andy was referred to the author for neuropsychiatric examination. A retrospective analysis of Andy's neuropsychologic data revealed only positive c-v signs, i.e., positive Romberg, dysdiadochokinesis, tandem dysmetria and imbalance, finger-to-thumb sequencing and placement difficulties, and a partially compensated speech articulation impairment.

During eyes-closed Romberg testing, Andy exhibited difficulty in maintaining his arms and fingers on the same spatial plane. Upon opening his eyes, Andy spontaneously and automatically corrected for this spatial placement disturbance. These fascinating but simple clinical observations strongly suggested that Andy's spatial placement difficulties were due to the existence of an underlying cerebellar-vestibular-determined proprioceptive placement and integration dysfunction, which was compensated for by visual targeting and organizing mechanisms upon opening his eyes. Interestingly enough, Silver (1960) assumed this phenomenon to represent a failure in establishing cerebral dominance.

In addition, when experiencing imbalance during eyes-closed Romberg testing, Andy's arms and fingers began to move. Prechtl (1962) assumed these movements were choreiform in nature and thus to be of extrapyramidal origin. In contrast, the author viewed these very same "choreiform-like" finger movements to be analogous to the nystagmoid and/or swaying movements resulting from a c-v dysequilibrium and attempts at compensating for the imbalance as well as for the ensuing anxieties. The author's assumptions were strengthened when these movements as well as the associated vertiginous sensations disappeared together upon Andy's opening his eyes.

Psychological Evaluation

In 1968, Andy was psychologically evaluated for his difficulties by M. Fite, the Supervisor of Psychologists, Bureau of Special Reading Service. He was found to have a V.I.Q. of 129, P.I.Q. of 115 and a WISC Full Scale of 123. The report states, "He manifested a mature vocabulary, quick comprehension and excellent capacity for organization of thought. . . . Real problems exist when eye-hand coordination is required and there was awkwardness in block manipulation, drawing and handwriting. . . . Lateral dominance was not clearly developed, he did not know right from left, held a pencil awkwardly and his visuo-motor difficulties seemed due to motor problems. . . . He blinked his right eye, rubbed his left eye frequently and complained about the bright light of the telebinocular—raising a question as to whether an obscure eye defect might exist."

Retrospective Considerations

1. Is it possible that Andy had photophobia and blurred vision due to an underlying c-v dysfunction—resulting in defensive blinking and other attempts at retinal shielding when confronted by bright light?
2. Could a c-v-induced dysmetria or incoordination explain Andy's "real problems . . . with eye-hand coordination," as well as his "awkwardness in block manipulation, drawing and handwriting"?
3. Might not a c-v dysfunction result in a gravitation-related compass confusion and secondary directional errors in remembering and utilizing lateralized or direction-dependent functions? Might not this directional disturbance result in a delayed establishment of lateral preference, lateral consistency or "lateral dominance"?
4. If, indeed, Andy's dyslexia was truly part of a language dysfunction, and his severe reading, writing, and spelling difficulties were of primary aphasic, agnostic, and/or conceptual origin, could he have obtained a WISC verbal I.Q. of 129 despite the devastating presence and effects of catastrophic and examination anxiety? Would Andy's speech and thinking functions be described as mature, quick, and excellent if he were suffering from a true aphasic disorder?
5. Might we not expect Andy's verbal I.Q. to be greater than his performance I.Q. if his cortical and language functions were intact and only a c-v motor dyscoordination exists?

Psycho-educational Re-evaluation

Because Andy's dyslexic symptoms persisted, he was re-evaluated by Katrina de Hirsch when 10½-years-old (de Hirsch, 1952, 1957, 1963, 1965, 1966). Selected quotations from her detailed report to the author are presented, analyzed, and discussed here so that the reader might better appreciate the background from which the author's c-v dyslexic insights were derived:

> In spite of excellent intellectual potential this youngster had to repeat a grade and is now badly floundering in school. . . . Andy's father [a physician] is a poor speller and a slow reader and . . . has some directional confusion. Andy's older sister, an excellent student, has a fairly severe spelling disability . . .
>
> The parents recognized that the boy was quite hyperactive and they remember that his coordination was not the best . . . he had difficulty remembering nursery rhymes . . . A speech defect . . . has disappeared after he got some help.
>
> He is explosive and impulsive and his frustration threshhold is quite low. One gets the impression of a highly irritable CNS and one never doubts that Andy is "organic." He still whirls on the Schilder test and there are very marked concomitant movements in the uninvolved hand when he attempts to touch fingers to thumb.
>
> Andy . . . does not know which is his right and which is his left hand and he carries a pencil in his right pocket so as to remember.
>
> He was at first quite unwilling to draw a man . . .
>
> Andy's Bender Gestalt . . . is very poor indeed . . . his considerable visuomotor difficulties are all too apparent. Andy—perhaps to compensate for some basic disorganization—is rather compulsive and insisted on counting all of the dots.
>
> Auditory memory span fluctuates . . . He made several mistakes also on the auditory discrimination test . . . his speech used to be very poor . . . one still hears him mispronounce some words. "Distestablmentarism" is an example.
>
> On the Gray Oral Reading Test . . . (he) scored only grade 2.4 . . . The trouble is that he has such difficulties focusing on the paper—the lines are simply writhing for him—as do individual words. One sees it in his frequent reversals too: "grader" for "garden" . . .
>
> One is struck by the disinhibition, the complete lack of control in the graphomotor level . . . His (writing) broke down when the spelling of the words got the least bit complex. He forms all his letters in an entirely atypical and awkward way introducing a number of quite unnecessary steps.
>
> On the Stanford Spelling Test he scored grade 3.2 . . . much of the time the words he puts down have little resemblance to the correct pattern.
>
> Andy's resistance to work . . . seems related to his effort to ward off a catastrophic reaction . . .
>
> Reading therapy should be directed primarily at the stabilization of configurations. Large, widely spaced very black print, the use of a pointer, the picking out of the internal design of words and a strong color might help.

Retrospective Analysis

Katrina de Hirsch has clearly described the reading, writing, spelling, memory, directional, and speech difficulties constituting and defining Andy's nuclear symptomatic complex. This pattern of symptoms was found to be "typical" of the total dyslexic sample within the retrospective study. She recognized that Andy's "coordination was not the best," he "still whirls on the Shilder test," exhibits "concomitant movements in the uninvolved hand" when attempting finger-to-thumb sequencing, has visual motor, graphomotor, and speech incoordination, is a slow reader, and has "such difficulties focusing on the paper."

The incoordination disturbances noted by de Hirsch were found to be consistent with the positive c-v and negative cortical signs characterizing the entire retrospective study, and suggested the possibility that all of Andy's signs and symptoms might be of primary c-v origin. As Andy was found to have a finger-to-thumb sequencing disturbance of a rhythmic and/or proprioceptive placement nature, it seemed reasonable to assume that his concomitant finger movements in the uninvolved hand reflected his compensatory rhythmic attempt to improve sequencing in the tested hand. Most often, concomitant movements are viewed as soft, nonspecific, and independent indicators of CNS dysfunction, and their possible relationship to compensatory mechanisms remains hidden.

Might Andy's motor sequencing or scrambling disorder predispose him to corresponding and related sensory sequencing and scrambling difficulties? Could his whirling on the Schilder test highlight an inhibitory disturbance in the cerebellar modulation of rotation? And might this assumed inhibitory failure explain his graphomotor and behavioral disinhibition as well? Might his "atypical and awkward writing" difficulty requiring "a number of quite unnecessary steps" neurodynamically represent a c-v-induced dysmetric dyspraxia, as well as a resulting compensatory attempt at simplifying the complex writing coordination task into its basic elements? And is not decomposition of movement a clinical sign of c-v dysfunction?

Might Andy's right/left uncertainty be due to a c-v compass impairment with resulting difficulties in interpreting and remembering gravitation-determined direction signals? Are not his compensatory memory attempts at recalling right and left consistent with his superior I.Q. and negative cortical findings? Does Andy have difficulty understanding the meaning of right and left, or is he merely uncertain as to right/left directional location? And might his c-v difficulty affect such other direction-dependent functions as auditory and proprioceptive sequencing, speech, graphomotor, spelling, and memory? Could his difficulty in focusing, his perceptual scrambling, and his reversals and slow reading reflect a c-v-induced ocular fixation and sequential scanning dyscoordination?

If, indeed, Andy has a primary c-v-induced ocular fixation and scanning dysfunction associated with photophobia, horizontal and/or figure–ground reversals (and scrambling), then Katrina de Hirsch's recommendation that he utilize "large, widely spaced, very black print . . . a pointer . . . strong color" to improve "stabilization of configuration" is understandable. Of course, if Andy's reading impairment were of a primary aphasic, agnostic, and/or conceptual origin, these recommendations would be of little help.

Can Andy's assumed c-v-induced perceptual, directional, and motor dyscoordination explain his probic attempt to avoid work, his visual-motor and graphomotor Bender Gestalt and Goodenough figure drawing difficulties, and his "basic disorganization," catastrophic anxiety, and compensatory compulsive attempts? And what is the significance of Katrina de Hirsch's stating that "Andy's father . . . is a poor speller and slow reader . . . and has directional confusion. [And that] Andy's older sister, an excellent student, has a fairly severe spelling disability"? Is Katrina de Hirsch implying the existence of constitutional or genetic etiologic factors in Andy's dyslexia? If so, is she also assuming that the dyslexic disorder may symptomatically be compensated for and manifest itself in variable forms—thus explaining its presence in Andy's father and sister despite their being excellent students?

Neuropsychiatric Evaluation

Finally, Andy was seen by Drs. Archie Silver and Rosa Hagin (Silver, 1961; Silver and Hagin, 1960, 1964, 1965) when 12 years old. Their report states:

> On my examination I find definite evidence of a structural defect of the central nervous system. This defect primarily affects his fine motor coordination and praxis, the establishment of cerebral dominance, and creates perceptual defects in the visual, auditory and tactile areas. He has, in addition, what appears to be an aphasic component with inability to select words to convey his meaning. This is particularly true when he must write the words.
>
> Emotional factors make our problem more difficult particularly since the anxiety in his household is contagious and Andy's index of anxiety rises with that of his parents. We are aware of his problems of identification with his father, his conflict with his sister, his phobias and his tendency towards depression. At this point, however, I would put the stress on attempts to improve his neurologic maturation.
>
> Dr. Rosa Hagin has also seen Andy. She found that his Jastak Oral Reading Test scored at grade 3.6 and his Jastak Spelling at 2.8. In view of his deficits Dr. Hagin suggested the following retraining methods. First, perceptual stimulation through rhythmic writing, form perception and auditory sequencing. When these are mastered . . . then we would go ahead through teaching of word attack skills through single letter phonics taught by sound-tracing. Following that reading in phonetic materials and writing of stories to insure transfer of phonics into spelling. Points 2, 3, and 4 should come only after the first recommendation is mastered.

Retrospective Considerations

If, as Dr. Silver states, a structural defect of the CNS primarily affects Andy's fine motor coordination and praxis, and if, according to the author and neurophysiologists, fine motor incoordination and dysmetric praxis are hard and fast c-v localizing signs, then might not Andy's "structural defect" and resulting symptomatic display be due to a c-v dysfunction? And if, indeed, Andy's structural defect affects the establishment of lateral dominance—which Dr. Silver equates with, and calls, "cerebral dominance"—and if this structural defect is due to a c-v dysfunction, then might not Andy's delayed lateral (and cerebral) dominance be due to a c-v-related directional disturbance? If, indeed, the author's neurophysiologic reasoning is correct, why were Andy's c-v-determined symptoms "imperceived" or denied? And why was Andy's clinically apparent delay in establishing a consistent dominant hand (lateral dominance) confused or equated with a hypothesized delay in establishing cerebral dominance?

The neurologic report states that Andy "has, in addition, what appears to be an aphasic component with inability to select words to convey his meanings. This is particularly true when he must write the words." Of course, aphasic difficulties are hard and fast localizing signs of cortical dysfunction. However, previous clinical reports indicate that Andy has no aphasic speech component at all: just the opposite. Andy's verbal abilities are superior, his V.I.Q. is 129, and his verbal qualities are described as superior by the SRS supervisor of psychologists: "He manifests a mature vocabulary, quick comprehension and excellent capacity for organization of thought."

If a subtle aphasic speech component were indeed present, would not Katrina de Hirsch have found and described it? She found and described only word mispronunciation. "One still hears him mispronounce some words, 'Distestablimentarism' is an example." Are not these "tongue-twisting" speech disturbances typical and characteristic of a c-v dyspraxic, rather than an aphasic cortical, disorder? Since the author and other clinicians found and described no aphasic component to Andy's speech, one must assume that Dr. Silver is most probably in error. And if Dr. Silver is mistaken, one might ask, What error did he make?

In describing Andy's aphasic component and difficulty in selecting words, Dr. Silver states, "This is particularly true when he must write the words." But how can Andy be expected to write words normally if he cannot spell, is clumsy in holding and using a pencil, has severe spatial-motor incoordination and decomposition of movement, and becomes severely anxious and catastrophically threatened when having to perform these most frustrating tasks? In retrospect, it seems that Andy evidenced no aphasic difficulty in selecting words to convey meaning, either verbally or in writing. He appears to have manifested only dysmetric or dyscoordinated speech, graphomotor and spelling difficulties, and secondary psychogenically determined attempts to phobically avoid both his frustrating motor disturbances and his catastrophic testing anxieties by simplifying his verbal and written expressions to words he can more readily articulate, spell, and write. If we consider the concentration and effort required by Andy to cope with his visual scrambling and targeting difficulties along with his speech, graphomotor, and spelling dyscoordination, then slight hesitancy in expression or formulation must be considered pseudo-aphasic—especially in the light of his V.I.Q. of 129.

One might well ask, Why was a simple speech mispronunciation difficulty in a child with a superior V.I.Q. of 129 confused with a cortically determined complex aphasic disturbance? What motivated this neurophysiologic confusion and "cortical confabulation"?

Conclusion

A retrospective analysis of 1,000 dyslexic cases similar to Andy's revealed a surprising correlation of dyslexia and its symptomatic complex with negative psychogenic, negative cortical, and positive c-v signs. In addition, the neurologic and other clinical reports, including those of the author, frequently evidenced "cortical confabulation," "cerebellar denial," and a resulting circular cortical dyslexic logic. For example, idiopathic dyslexic, c-v, and nonspecific symptoms were frequently assumed to be of cortical origin—despite the absence of cortical signs.

Moreover, the neurologic reports often contained a number of misleading assumptions which were written with the conviction reserved only for proven conclusions. Thus, Andy is stated to have "definite evidence of a structural defect of the CNS [which affects] the establishment of cerebral dominance." However, no *definite* evidence is given to support the assumption of Andy's structural CNS defect. The evidence indicative of Andy's handedness or lateral dominance difficulties by no means proves the existence of delayed cerebral dominance. In retrospect, these two misleading and fallacious assumptions reflect two traditional dyslexic hypotheses, i.e., that dyslexia is due to a parietal structural defect and/or that dyslexia is due to a delayed or incomplete cerebral dominance.

One hopes that the reader will note the manner by which historical and traditional theoretical dyslexic assumptions are unwittingly projected into the "clinical stew" and then utilized to elicit and interpret data proving the validity of those assumptions. Were it not for the psychodynamic-like analysis and resolution of this circular logic, and dyslexic "scientific neurosis," a solution to the dyslexic riddle would never have materialized.

As a result of the retrospective study, the author postulated that dyslexia is of c-v, rather than psychogenic or cortical, origin, and designed a series of investigations in order to validate this hypothesis experimentally.

3 Neurophysiologic and Etiologic Correlations in Dyslexia: The Prospective Study

The unexpected discovery of a c-v "needle" in a massive clinical dyslexic "haystack," and the surprising retrospective correlation of dyslexia with c-v dysfunction led to the design of a prospective study. The aim of this new study was to determine specifically the incidence and distribution of c-v and related neurophysiologic signs and symptoms in a reading-disabled "dyslexic" sample. With this aim in mind, 115 consecutively referred reading-disabled children were neuropsychologically examined, and the clinical data tabulated and analyzed. In addition, independent "blind" neurologic and "blind" caloric vestibular function (ENG) studies were performed on random subsamples, and the results similarly quantified and analyzed (Frank and Levinson, 1973).

Utilizing this dyslexic sample and data base, the historically reported relationships between handedness, sex, and dyslexia were investigated. Furthermore, since dyslexia was retrospectively found to be specifically correlated to c-v dysfunction and related symptomatology, it seemed only natural to explore the pathophysiologic role of otitis media and interna in dyslexia. As a result, the historically reported incidence of ear infections, dizziness, and motion sickness were obtained, and the overall data evaluated.

Sample

One hundred fifteen reading-disabled children from the New York City school system were referred to the author for neuropsychiatric testing in an attempt to explore their apparent "refractory response" to special education procedures. This sample was English speaking, ranged in ages between 6½ and 14, and consisted of two distinct populations: (1) 55 children were second- through sixth-graders who were two or more years behind their peers in reading. They consisted of "typical" SRS referrals similar to those described in Chapter 2; (2) 60 children were first-graders who demonstrated significant difficulty acquiring letter and word recognition skills relative to their peers, and most were found to be non-readers by the end of the first grade. They consisted of Supportive Reading Program (SRP) referrals. All but 6 children were found to have at least average I.Q. on initial WISC testing. However, upon re-testing, only 2 demonstrated below-normal I.Q. scores and were thus considered clinically "mixed cases" (i.e., cases exhibiting combined or mixed mental and reading retardation).

Frequency Distribution of Cerebellar-Vestibular, Cortical, and Nonlocalizing CNS Findings

The neurophysiologic signs and symptoms characterizing the reading-disabled, or dyslexic, sample of 115 were tabulated into c-v, cortical, and nonlocalizing CNS frequency distributions (Fig. 3–1).

Cerebellar-Vestibular Findings

Ninety-seven percent of the sample exhibited evidence of a c-v dysfunction, whereas only a maximum of 6% displayed possible cortical signs or symptoms—clearly highlighting the crucial role of c-v dysfunction in dyslexia (Fig. 3–1e). Fig. 3–1a demonstrates the pattern and frequency of c-v signs found in this sample upon conventional neurologic testing. However, a modification of the neurologic testing procedure was found to result in significantly higher proportions of such c-v findings as positive Romberg, tandem dysmetria, finger-to-thumb sequencing difficulties, and dysdiadochokinesis (Fig. 3–1d).

Subclinical Cerebellar-Vestibular Signs and Dysfunction

In the presence of vestibular-cerebellar dysfunction, Romberg imbalance and finger-to-nose dysmetria are seldom detectable unless the eyes are closed and the role of visual compensatory mechanisms are eliminated. ENG demonstrated similar findings. For example, spontaneous and/or positional nystagmus of vestibular-cerebellar origin are seldom detected unless the eyes are closed and the c-v compensatory role of visual fixation and position is eliminated. In addition, visual fixation or concentration has been clinically found to inhibit or suppress the calorically induced vestibular nystagmus. As a result, during ENG caloric testing, patients are specifically instructed to keep their eyes closed. At the termination of each caloric stimulation procedure, patients are requested to open their eyes. The failure of visual fixation in suppressing the calorically induced nystagmus is suggestive of a cerebellar inhibitory failure, i.e., multiple sclerosis.

The author reasoned that if, indeed, c-v-induced disorientation, vertigo,

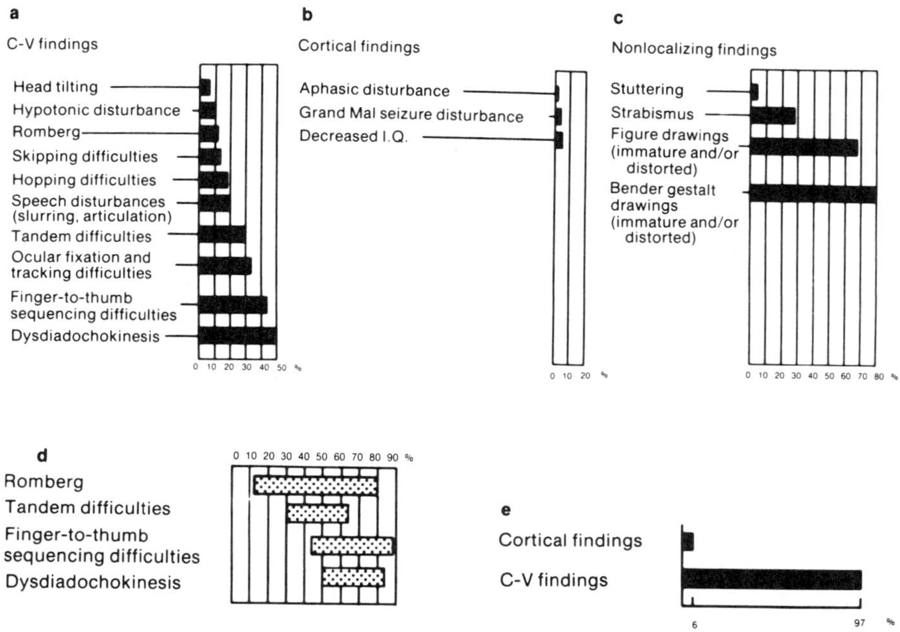

Fig. 3–1. (*a–c*) Frequency distributions of cerebellar-vestibular, cortical, and nonlocalizing signs found in a sample consisting of 115 dyslexics. (*e*) The incidence of c-v versus cortical findings in this dyslexic sample clearly suggests that dyslexia is correlated to positive c-v findings and negative cortical findings. Moreover, inasmuch as the distribution of nonlocalizing findings (*c*) was similarly correlated to positive c-v signs and negative cortical signs, it appeared reasonable to assume distribution (*c*) was either of c-v origin or c-v related. In addition, a new stress procedure for eliciting c-v signs resulted in an increased incidence and pattern of c-v signs depicted by (*d*)—highlighting a methodology for converting subclinical or latent c-v dysfunction to clinically manifest dysfunction.

imbalance, dyscoordination, nystagmus, and dysmetric directional and placement disturbances may be suppressed or compensated for by visual fixation and concentration, then why shouldn't patients be examined for possible c-v dysfunction with their eyes closed. Would this simple eyes-closed procedure not simultaneously minimize c-v-compensatory mechanisms while magnifying subclinical c-v disturbances and render them clinically apparent? As a result of this reasoning, patients were tested for dysdiadochokinesis, tandem placement and balance, and finger-to-thumb sequencing, both with and without their eyes closed.

In addition, eyes-closed Romberg testing was intensified by instructing patients to balance themselves on one foot. Furthermore, right- and left-sided finger-to-thumb sequencing and dysdiadochokinesis were tested for individually in an effort to ascertain c-v "sidedness" data, while simultaneously inhibiting compensatory rhythmic movement of the nontested hand.

Figure 3–1d illustrates the increase in detectable c-v signs upon utilizing this new c-v "stress testing" methodology. This new clinical stress methodology was derived from the combined insights of two additional unpublished clinical neurologic studies consisting of dyslexic samples of 500 and 1200, respectively.

The modified neurologic stress procedure intensified the complexity of the c-v balance, coordination, and rhythm tasks, while simultaneously minimizing visual and other compensatory processes—leading to significantly improved quantitative and qualitative assessments of these c-v neurological parameters.

The data derived from large scale clinical studies clearly demonstrated:

1. that manifest neurologic signs and symptoms are vector resultants of subclinically active dysfunctioning and compensatory processes;
2. that the absence of clinically detectable signs and symptoms by no means proves the absence of subclinical dysfunction, and may indicate that more sensitive diagnostic parameters are required to elicit the underlying dysfunction;
3. that dyslexic compensatory neuropsychologic forces and mechanisms increase as a function of age and are potent factors in shaping the final symptomatic outcome and spectrum; and
4. that compensatory mechanisms must be minimized in order to properly assess the underlying subclinical dysfunction.

A Dynamic Cerebellar-Vestibular Conceptualization of Symptomatology

The dynamic subclinical c-v dysfunctioning and compensatory forces shaping and determining the symptomatic outcome in dyslexia are shown in Fig. 3–2. By means of this dynamic "Freudian" conceptualization of symptom formation in dyslexia, the author was able to explain not only the symptomatic scatter and diversity, but the symptomatic fluctuations characterizing dyslexic individuals and samples. The action of subclinical compensatory forces and mechanisms, for example, could thus explain the existence of normal and even superior functioning within the dyslexic symptomatic complex (i.e., late blooming), as well as the clinical disappearance of dyslexic symptoms and so-called soft signs with age. In addition, fatigue, mood, anxiety, head trauma, infections (i.e., mononucleosis, flu states), allergic and/or seasonal temperature and barometric variations, and hormonal and metabolic changes were found to trigger clinical dyslexic decompensation and symptomatic intensification.

Although dyslexia is often defined and conceptualized as a fixed or static disorder, the clinical observations derived from the retrospective and pro-

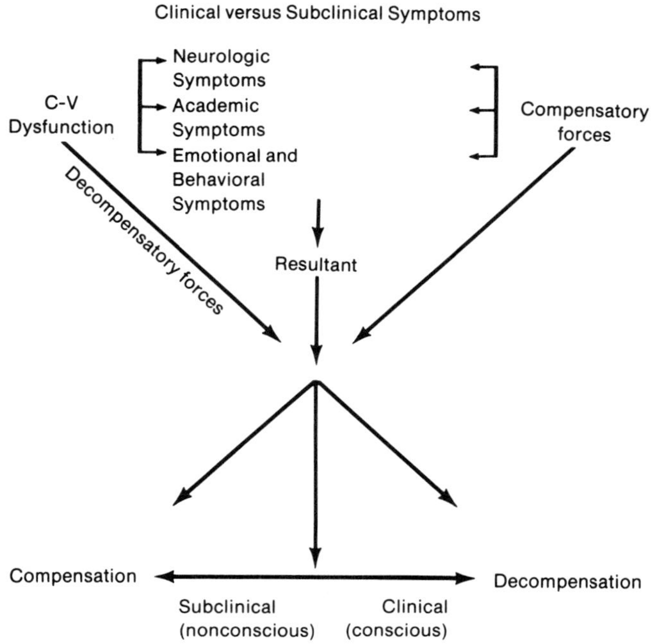

Fig. 3–2. The manner in which c-v-determined neurologic, academic, emotional, and behavioral symptoms are influenced by the presence of coexisting and overlapping compensatory mechanisms. Symptom formation is conceived of as a resultant of dynamically active c-v dysfunctioning versus compensatory forces. The relative intensities of these respective forces will determine whether or not symptoms will become and remain clinical or subclinical.

spective studies have clearly indicated the reverse to be true: dyslexic signs and symptoms were clinically found to be dynamic vector resultants of fluctuating, subclinically interacting dysfunctioning and compensatory forces, and these forces were recognized to be highly dependent upon a complex spectrum of fascinating variables and triggers.

Cortical Findings

The maximum incidence of cortical findings in this reading-disabled or dyslexic sample is approximately 6% (Fig. 3–1e)—clearly demonstrating that dyslexia and clinical cortical dysfunction are statistically unrelated. In addition, Fig. 3–1b depicts the aphasic, seizure, and decreased I.Q. cortical findings in a frequency distribution form.

The analysis and retesting of 6 dyslexic cases with decreased WISC I.Q.s revealed 4 to be normal. Inasmuch as anxiety and a host of dyslexic factors were found to significantly affect WISC functions and result in "pseudodeficient" WISC scores, it became readily apparent that decreased WISC scores alone were insufficient to reliably diagnose truly deficient conceptualization and I.Q.

The two remaining cases with decreased WISC scores demonstrated clinical evidence of cortical and related conceptual dysfunction. Since these cortically impaired cases demonstrated associated patterns of c-v signs and dyslexic symptoms identical to the cortically intact, normal and above-normal I.Q. dyslexics, it seemed only reasonable to assume that dyslexia and decreased I.Q. may coexist and be determined by independent neurophysiologic variables. If, indeed, dyslexia and I.Q. are neurophysiologically unrelated, one might ask why dyslexic conceptualizations frequently require that a child have normal or above normal I.Q. in order to appropriately "qualify" for a true dyslexic diagnosis?

A number of cases showing word-finding hesitations and difficulties were mistakenly considered (compensated) aphasics. In retrospect, these "pseudoaphasic" cases were clearly recognized to have word pronunciation and sequential motor dyscoordination, and/or memory uncertainty disturbances, of c-v, rather than cortical, aphasic origin. These clinical insights eventually led to the holistic conceptualization that the normal speech and language process is a resultant of cortical and subcortical neurophysiologic vectors, and that the speech process may be disrupted by primary cortical and/or subcortical dysfunctioning. This holistic conceptualization of the speech process provides the theoretical basis required to comprehend the presence of language functions in animals and the evolution of this function in cortical man.

A handful of cases were noted to have either a history of grand mal seizures during childhood or abnormal EEGs. As the incidence of cortical seizures in dyslexia was found to be minimal—no higher than in nondyslexic samples—it appeared highly likely that cortical seizures and dyslexia were unrelated as well.

Nonlocalizing Findings

The frequency distribution of such nonlocalizing findings as stuttering, strabismus, and distorted Bender Gestalt and Goodenough figure drawings is illustrated in Fig. 3–1c. Inasmuch as these so-called soft signs were found to be co-existing dyslexic variables, it seemed only reasonable to wonder if they were c-v-related or independent variables.

Although the 5% incidence of stuttering in this sample was not remarkable, the 20% incidence of overall speech disturbances was statistically significant, and clearly suggested a correlation between speech disorders, dyslexia, and c-v dysfunction. If one recognizes slurring, minor enunciation, and sequential speech difficulties to be of c-v origin, then both the quality and incidence of stuttering are consistent with the spatial-temporal nature and incidence of the clinically established pattern of specific c-v-related and determined speech disturbances. In addition, the fact that stuttering often disappeared during singing led to the assumption that stuttering was due to a subclinically operating, dysmetric temporal sequencing dysfunction which may be compensated for by the timing and rhythm provided by singing.

Twenty-eight percent of the dyslexic sample was found, surprisingly, to have strabismus—considered by ophthalmologists to be of peripheral or muscular origin. However, the author suspected (1) that the strabismus, in some of these cases, was of primary central or c-v-mesencephalic origin, and (2) that all cases of peripheral strabismus must be influenced by the asymmetric, centrally determined c-v ocular tonal disturbances. The recognition that peripheral strabismus might complicate, and be complicated by, the dyslexic perceptual disorder, emphasized the need for a careful clinical pathophysiologic dissection of overlapping, overdetermined, and coexisting symptomatology in dyslexia.

Since the balance, coordination, spatial, and directional Bender Gestalt and Goodenough "errors" were both statistically and qualitatively correlated to c-v dysfunction, it appeared highly likely that these "errors" were due to the same c-v mechanisms responsible for the nuclear symptomatic complex in dyslexia.

A Quantitative Analysis of the Nuclear Symptomatic Complex in Dyslexia

The nuclear symptomatic complex was qualitatively delineated and analyzed in the retrospective study. However, in this study an attempt was made to determine the frequency distribution of the symptoms defining the symptomatic complex, as well as their conceptual and performance determinants (Fig. 3–3).

The Dyslexic Reading Symptom

A qualitative analysis and dissection of the dyslexic reading symptomatology led to the recognition of three basic overdetermined disturbances. All children with severe reading disorders manifested visual and/or auditory memory disturbances for letters and/or words. This memory dysfunction was highly correlated with the existence of ocular fixation, tracking, and reversal tendencies, and appeared statistically unrelated to conceptual letter and word disturbances (Fig. 3–3b).

The correlation of dyslexia with only c-v signs clearly suggested that dyslexia was of c-v origin. The qualitative and quantitative analysis of

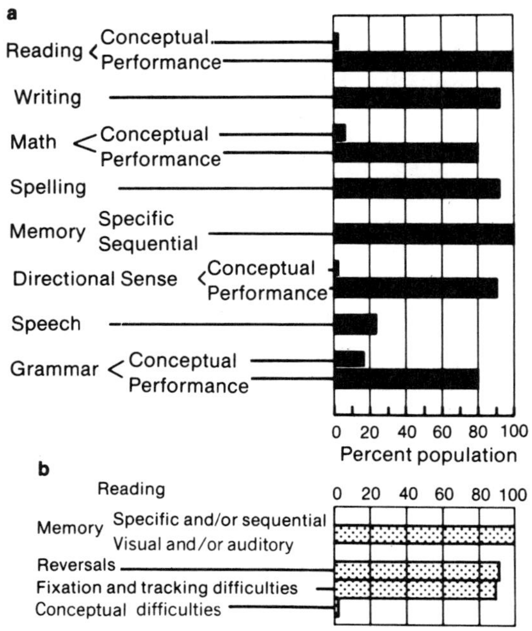

Fig. 3–3. (*a*) The frequency distribution (n = 115) of the conceptual and perceptual vectors of the symptoms defining the symptomatic complex. The performance, rather than the conceptual, vectors were found statistically to be impaired. Moreover, the mechanisms underlying the dyslexic reading symptom were analyzed and (*b*) indicates that the memory uncertainty characterizing this symptom is correlated to the reversal and ocular fixation and tracking performance difficulties, rather than to conceptual impairment.

dyslexic reading mechanisms revealed a clear-cut correlation between dyslexic letter/word memory impairment and ocular fixation, tracking, and reversal tendencies.

Rudolfo Llinas, in a magnificently lucid article, "The Cortex of the Cerebellum" (1975), clearly described the computer role of the cerebellum in modulating: (1) the position of the eyes with respect to the orientation of the head and body, enabling one to clearly fixate points while moving; (2) the rapid eye movements called saccades, which are important in visual tracking; and (3) the refining or revising of motor commands before they reach the eye muscles, so that their movements can be accurately guided and thus controlled.

> In organizing the delicate and precise movements of the eyes the cerebellum is evidently essential; cerebellar dysfunction often disrupts such movements. Two regions of the cerebellum are known to participate in these functions. One is the floccular-nodular area; it regulates the position of the eyes with respect to the orientation of the head and body, enabling one to stare at a fixed point while moving. The other is the cerebellar vermis, which is believed to control the rapid eye movements called saccades, which are important in visual tracking.
>
> In a recent series of experiments at the Air Force School of Aerospace Medicine, James W. Wolfe and I showed that the activation of Purkinje cells by mossy fibers increases about 25 milliseconds before an eye movement begins. . . .

> The implication of this discovery is that cerebellar regulation of movement through the mossy-fiber system is capable of correcting mistakes before they have reached the muscles and have been expressed in actual movement. The cerebellum appears to correct these movements by acting as a brake. . . .
>
> A series of experiments conducted by Anders Lundberg and his colleagues at the University of Göteborg provides a further indication that some cerebellar activity is concerned with the internal state of the central nervous system. They found that one of the main afferent tracts leading to the cerebellum, the ventral spinocerebellar tract, conveys information not about the state of the body or the external environment but about the activity of inhibitory interneurons in the spinal cord. Such an internal monitoring mechanism might be a necessity in a system intended to refine or revise motor commands before they reach the muscles, such as is observed in the cerebellar control of eye movement.

Since ocular fixation and tracking functioning and dysfunctioning are modulated by c-v mechanisms (Barany, 1901–21; Whitteridge, 1968; Bizzi, 1974; Dow and Moruzzi, 1958; Eccles, 1973; Ito, et al., 1973; Llinas, 1974, 1975; Miles, 1975; Pract, 1972), and since only c-v dysfunction was found in and correlated to dyslexia, it appeared reasonable to assume that the reading memory and reversal disturbances in dyslexia are c-v-related as well.

"Blind" Neurologic Findings

In order to confirm the author's c-v neurologic findings in dyslexia, 22 c-v-dysfunctioning dyslexic children were randomly selected and referred to Drs. S. Carter and A. Gold for "blind" neurological examinations.* Dr. Carter examined 6 dyslexic cases, described c-v neurologic signs in 5 cases, and specifically mentioned a "cerebellar deficit" in only 1 case, although he stated that this deficit was of questionable significance. Dr. Gold, on the other hand, examined 16 dyslexic cases, described c-v neurologic signs in all 16 cases, and specifically utilized the term "cerebellar deficit" or "dysfunction" in 14 cases (Fig. 3–4).

Of the "blindly' examined dyslexic cases, 96% manifested evidence of a c-v dysfunction, whereas less than 6% demonstrated historical and/or clinical cortical signs. The data from this blind neurologic study clearly substantiated the author's positive c-v and negative cortical correlations in dyslexia. The (verbatim) c-v signs and symptoms in the blind clinical case reports are abstracted and tabulated according to increasing frequency in Table 3–1 (see also Fig. 3–5).

* Dr. Sidney Carter, Professor of Neurology and Pediatrics, Columbia Presbyterian Hospital, New York, and Dr. Arnold Gold, Associate Professor of Neurology and Pediatrics, Columbia Presbyterian Hospital, New York, participated in this study without any identifying data and without any idea as to the study's research aims. Their neurologic findings and diagnoses are thus typical of their *customary* reports, and were by no means biased by those of the author.

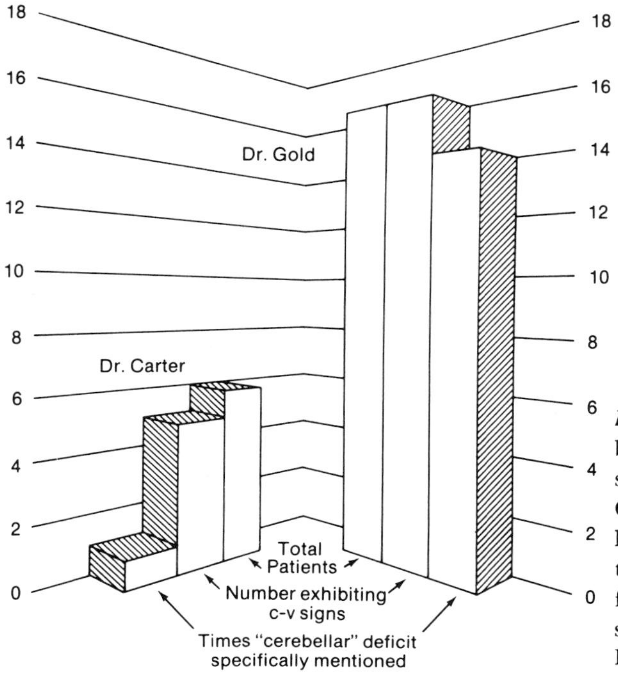

Fig. 3-4. The total number of dyslexic patients sent to Drs. Carter and Gold for "blind" neurologic examinations, and the number of patients found to have c-v signs and stated to have a "cerebellar" deficit.

In view of the fact that only c-v signs and symptoms characterized the blind neurologic study, and since these findings were noted in 96% (21/22) of the dyslexic cases examined, and since the terms "cerebellar deficit" or "dysfunction" was specifically and spontaneously utilized in 70% (15/22) of the case reports, it seemed most surprising, if not remarkable, that (1) the neurophysiologic role of c-v dysfunction in the blindly examined sample was completely overlooked, and (2) the blindly examined c-v-positive dyslexic cases were either nonspecifically diagnosed as minimal brain dysfunction (MBD) or specifically diagnosed as Minimal Cerebral Dysfunction —despite the clinical absence of any and all cerebral signs.

A detailed qualitative analysis of these blindly examined dyslexic cases is included in the appendix so that the reader might review the raw neurologic data substantiating the c-v dyslexic correlations. Several years afer completing this study, deQuiros (1976, 1978) independently correlated vestibular disorders and learning disabilities, thereby adding significant scientific weight to the author's c-v–dyslexic correlations and conceptualizations.

"Blind" Vestibular Function Electronystagmographic Findings

In order to confirm independently and physiologically the presence of c-v dysfunction in dyslexia, 75 dyslexic cases were randomly selected and re-

Table 3–1. Cerebellar-Vestibular Signs Reported in "Blind" Neurologic Examinations (n = 22)

"Blind" Cerebellar-Vestibular Signs and Symptoms	Number of Patients
1. Nystagmus (general)	0
2. Ocular fixation difficulty	1
3. Ocular sensitivity	1
4. Difficulty riding a two-wheel bicycle	1
5. Visual-motor difficulty	1
6. Articulation difficulty	2
7. Decreased muscle tone	2
8. Tandem ataxia	2
9. Mirror movements	2
10. Electronystagmographic abnormality	2
11. Small muscle extraocular incoordination	3
12. Dysdiadochokinesis	3
13. Salivary accumulation	3
14. Hyperextension of muscle and joints	3
15. Speech difficulty (general or non-specific)	4
16. Otolaryngeal incoordination	4
17. Toeing inwards or outwards	4
18. Tandem walking dysmetria	4
19. Difficulty tying shoe laces and/or buttoning clothes	6
20. Slurring of speech	6
21. Pes-planus	6
22. Difficulty hopping	7
23. Difficulty catching, throwing, and kicking	8
24. Visual-spatial or perceptual difficulty	8
25. Rigid and/or awkward holding of pencil	9
26. Finger-nose dysmetria	9
27. Clumsy and/or awkward coordination	11
28. Difficulty with fine or small muscle coordination	11
29. Immaturity and/or distortion of Bender Gestalt drawings	13
30. Graphomotor incoordination, i.e., poor letter formation and spacing	15
31. Impaired succession movements of fingers	17

ferred to seven different medical centers for "blind" electronystagmographic (ENG) caloric vestibular function tests.*

* Dr. James Holman, Clinical Associate Professor of Otorhinolaryngology, Cornell University Medical College, New York, Dr. Noel Cohen, Clinical Associate Professor of Otolaryngology, New York University Medical College, New York, Dr. Kenneth Brookler, Director of the Center for Communications Disorders, Lenox Hill Hospital, New York and others participated in the blind ENG studies without any knowledge of the author's neurologic findings or research aims.

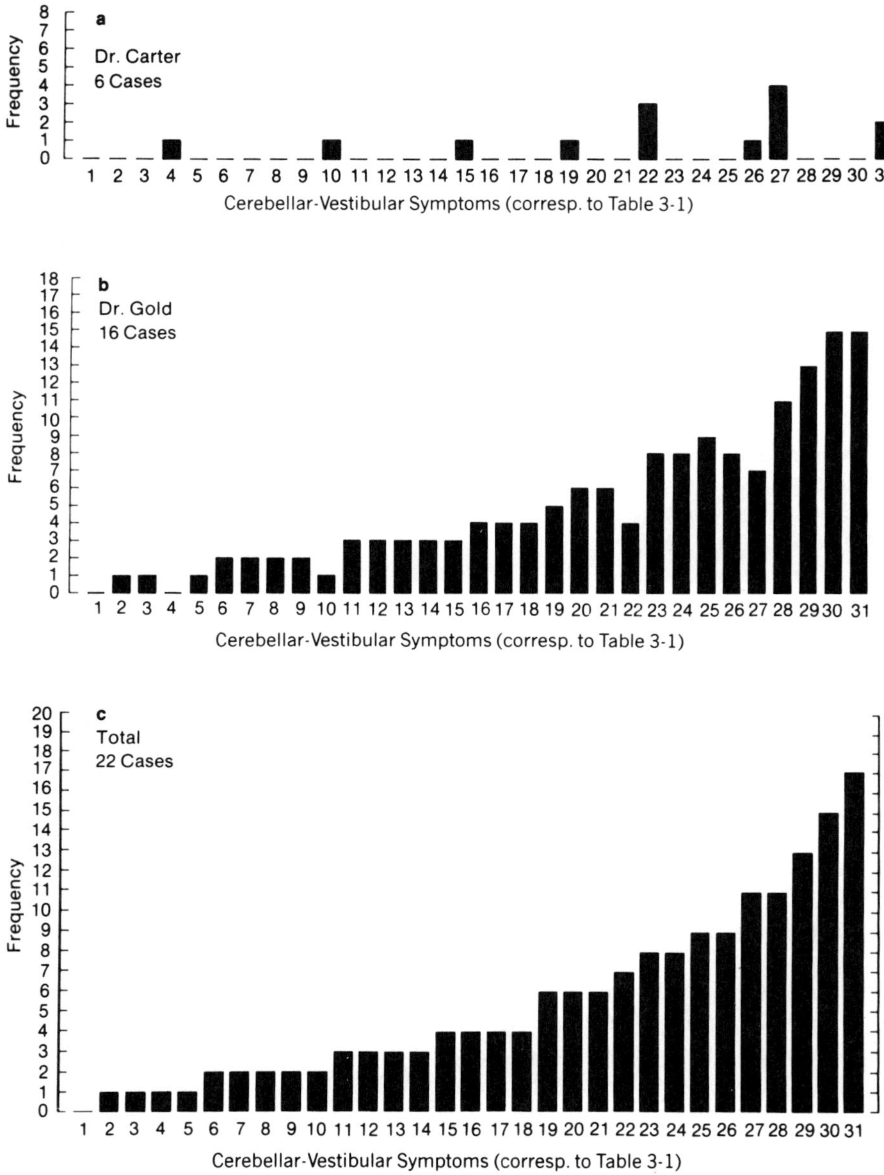

Fig. 3–5. (*a*) Dr. Carter's "blind" c-v findings in a frequency distribution form. (*b*) Dr. Gold's "blind" c-v findings. (*c*) Distribution of their combined c-v neurologic findings.

(Electronystagmography is a technique for objectively detecting, recording, and measuring nystagmus—a rapid involuntary oscillation of the eyeball. Nystagmus may be found in various conditions, but nystagmus of c-v origin can be specifically and qualitatively defined, and thus is useful

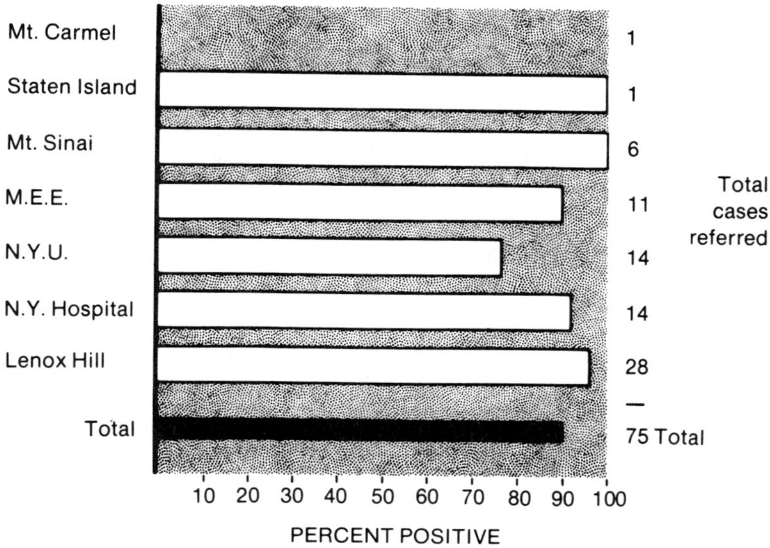

Fig. 3–6. Positive frequency distribution of "blind" ENGs as a function of medical centers where the testing was done, and total percent positive. (M.E.E. = Manhattan Eye and Ear Hospital; N.Y.U. = New York University Medical Center; N.Y. Hospital = New York Hospital/Cornell Medical Center.)

in diagnosing c-v dysfunction. The electronystagmographic monitoring of eye movements is made possible by virtue of the positive corneal potential relative to the retina—the resulting changes in electric potential when the eyes move may be recorded by electrodes placed on the outer margins of the eyes. Electronystagmographic recordings measure nystagmus as a function of vestibular integrity and as a function of vestibular reactivity. In the presence of c-v dysfunction, clinical and subclinical nystagmus is sometimes recordable. If the ears are calorically stimulated with cool and warm water, either individually or simultaneously, electronystagmographic recordable patterns result which provide invaluable information as to the function and dysfunction of the labyrinthine-vestibular-cerebellar circuits [Barany, 1901–21, 1920; Kobrak, 1919–20; Jonglees and Philipszoon, 1964; Brookler and Pulec, 1970; Brookler, 1971], see Appendix D.)

Forty of these cases were audiologically evaluated in order to rule out the presence of coexisting and/or contributing nonvestibular disorders which might effect the ENG. Ninety percent of the 70 completed ENGs revealed some abnormality indicative of a c-v dysfunction, whereas ninety-five percent of the 40 audiologic examinations were reported to be within normal limits (Fig. 3–6). This ENG and audiologic data clearly substantiated the author's clinical c-v findings and conceptualizations, as well as the blind c-v neurologic data.

The blind ENG data more than validated the correlation found between c-v dysfunction and dyslexia. It demonstrated the existence of a c-v-related

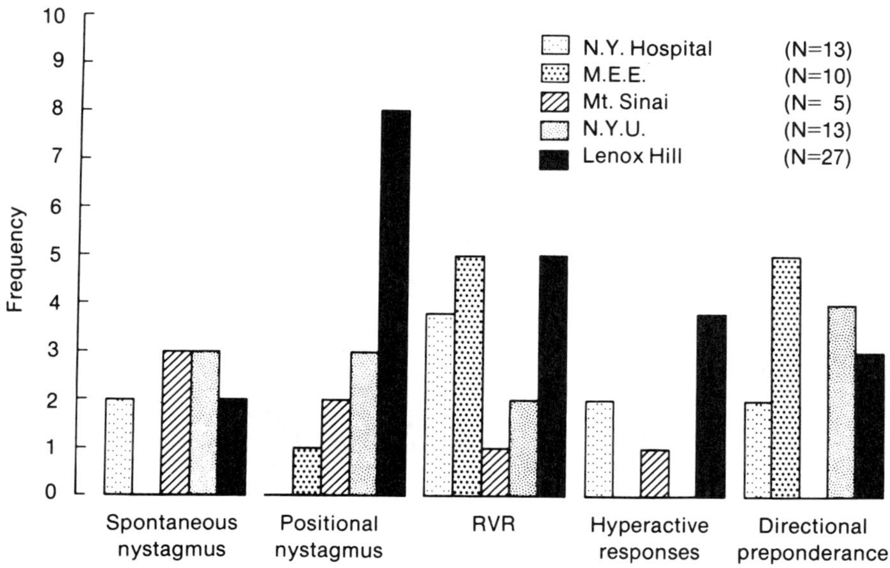

Fig. 3–7. Frequency distribution of spontaneous and positional nystagmus and other ENG pathologic parameters (i.e., vestibular hyper- and hyporeactivity [RVR] and asymmetric vestibular-ocular responses to caloric stimulation [DP]) as a function of hospital center (see Appendix D).

subclinical nystagmus in dynamic equilibrium with compensatory mechanisms, and demonstrated the position-specific and sensory-specific nature of c-v triggers and releases. For example, by means of the ENG technique and recording sensitivity, approximately 20% of the blind ENG sample evidenced positional and/or spontaneous nystagmus, whereas clinical nystagmus was completely absent in the dyslexic sample of 115 (Fig. 3–7).

Inasmuch as ENG-detectable nystagmus was triggered and/or released by (1) only specific patterns of head-neck-body positions, and/or (2) visual suppression (eyes closed), it seemed reasonable to assume that position-dependent and sensory-dependent triggers were capable of provoking c-v decompensation and releasing subclinical nystagmus from compensatory suppression or inhibition. If this reasoning is indeed correct, position-dependent c-v dysfunction and nystagmus could explain the dyslexic reading and writing positional preferences and compensatory maneuvers. In addition, the release of compensated or inhibited nystagmus and c-v dysfunction during visual suppression could explain the vertiginous insomnia, sleep vertigo, c-v related anxiety dreams, and states characterizing a minority of the c-v dysfunctioning dyslexics.

In an attempt to comprehend what appeared to be significant ENG variations among the various hospital centers (Fig. 3–7), the author conducted a clinical ENG caloric, rotational, and optokinetic study of 500 dyslexic children and adults. As a result of this study, the ENG parameters were further explored and expanded, and the ENG diagnostic technique significantly enhanced.* In addition, a series of unexpected and fascinating subjectively reported sensations and experiences were observed and recorded, ultimately leading to the suspicion that dyslexia was merely the sensory-motor scramble resulting from a c-v induced subclinical form of motion sickness.

During caloric and rotational ENG Studies, dyslexics frequently reported sensory-motor, "psychosomatic," anxiety, and phobic symptoms resembling those highlighted by the retrospective study. For example, individuals experienced blurred and scrambled vision, reversals, light, color and acoustic sensitivity, oscillopsia, micro- and macropsia, etc. Balance and coordination "illusions" were commonplace (e.g., spinning, tilting, falling, body-image sensations and distortions), as were such psychosomatic symptoms as nausea, wretching, headaches (generalized and/or localized orbital and migraine types), orbital and abdominal pain, and other symptoms. Fears of fainting, losing control, and even dying, were occasionally reported, and often appeared in association with experiences of disorientation. Sensations of anxiety, panic, and vertigo were commonly confused with one another.

The analysis of this confusion, or Freudian slip, suggested the existence of a common underlying somatic path or source. For example, adult dyslexics frequently and spontaneously compared their caloric stimulation experiences with similar sensations and anxieties noted in cars, elevators, escalators, trains, buses, tunnels, bridges, and so on.

Optokinetic ENG visual tracking and processing studies indicated that "visual overloading" and/or specific visual gestalt stationary patterns may trigger spontaneous nystagmus and a spectrum of emotional symptoms similar to those induced by caloric and rotational vestibular stimulation—perhaps explaining the paradox whereby some dyslexics experience greater difficulty copying visual designs than reproducing these very same designs from memory.

It was recognized that specific and/or generalized visual "overloading" triggers induced the very same motion sickness and/or catastrophic anxiety responses as did visual suppression—clearly highlighting the specificity and sensitivity of the c-v circuits to both visual "crowds" and visual deprivation or suppression.

The c-v "regressive triggers" were found to be not only sensory-specific, but direction-specific as well. For example, motion and visual targeting stimuli in one direction were found to induce or release c-v-related responses that significantly differed from those triggered by the very same stimuli with an opposing directional vector.

* The content of this study will be published as a monograph entitled *Electronystagmography in Dyslexia.*

In general, one can state that the pattern of c-v triggers and responses was unique to each dyslexic individual, and that any and all permutations and combinations could, and should, be anticipated. Since the ENG studies experimentally induced the very same "sensory-motor scramble" and dyscoordination found to characterize the dyslexic syndrome, it seemed reasonable to assume that dyslexia was a c-v form of motion sickness. This overly simplistic model of dyslexia was eventually enlarged and expanded so that the total range and pattern of symptoms defined by the symptomatic complex could be specifically and readily explained to, and understood by, dyslexic children.

Etiologic Considerations and Correlations

Inasmuch as dyslexia is traditionally thought to be of genetic, constitutional, and/or developmental origin, and historically has been correlated to the male sex and incomplete cortical or lateral dominance, an attempt was made to explore and substantiate the validity of these assumptions and variables. In addition, the dyslexic–c-v neurophysiologic correlations provided by the retrospective and prospective studies, and the hypothesis that dyslexia might be conceptualized as a perceptual motor scramble secondary to a subclinical form of motion sickness, suggested the possibility that early childhood otitis media and labyrinthitis may create or complicate the dyslexic disorder. As a result of these considerations, the incidence of otitis media, motion sickness, and vertigo in a dyslexic sample was determined and explored.

Incidence and Correlations of Dyslexia and Handedness

An entire first-grade population (n = 3273) was screened for potential reading disabilities by the Supportive Reading Program (SRP) during the fall of 1971. As a result of this screening, 21% (700) "high-risk" children were selected and pedagogically "immunized" with prophylactic or supportive biweekly reading instruction with the intention of preventing the inevitable emotional scarring and complications observed when clinical and educational intervention is delayed until reading-disabled children are two or more years behind their peers.

Due to this early screening and intervention program, three reading groups resulted: (1) normal readers, (2) "high-risk" children requiring and responding to tutoring, and (3) "high-risk" children failing to respond to tutoring. The latter group of "refractory readers" met the criteria required by most dyslexic conceptualizations and definitions and were referred to the author for neuropsychiatric evaluations.

Incidence of Refractory Readers

Seventy-five of the 700 SRP children failed to respond to reading instruction and were virtually nonreaders by the end of first grade. Of the 75 "refractory readers," 60 were neuropsychiatrically examined and 96% (58/60) were found to have evidence of a c-v dysfunction. The author assumed that 96% (or 72) of the 75 "refractory readers" were c-v-dysfunctioning dyslexics, and thus calculated the minimum first-grade incidence of dyslexia to be 2% (72/3273).*

Both the 21% "high-risk" incidence of poor readers within the total first grade population (700/3273) and the minimum 2% incidence of refractory readers (or dyslexics) were consistent with the statistics presented by most authorities discussing reading disorders and dyslexia. For example, according to "Reading Disabilities in Your Child," a 1970 position paper of the American Association of Ophthalmology:

> The term "dyslexia" is loosely used to describe the condition of a child who is reading two or more grades below his grade level. Approximately one-fifth of all children in the United States have some form of learning disability, including reading disability.
>
> The few children with normal intelligence who have difficulty understanding printed words (dyslexia) should not be confused with the larger group of children who learn slowly for various reasons.
>
> About 2%–5% of all children have some degree of dyslexia in spite of normal intelligence and absence of obvious causes. Their condition is called primary dyslexia or developmental dyslexia. The underlying basis of primary dyslexia is usually present at birth, although the disturbance is not recognized until several years later when the child is required to learn to read. Primary dyslexia affects boys more often than girls.

Left-handedness and Dyslexia

Ever since Orton (1937) correlated left-handedness, speech, and dyslexic symptomatology with incomplete or mixed cerebral dominance, the role of handedness and dominance in dyslexia has received, and continues to receive, wide attention—despite the fact that Orton eventually modified his original left-handed–dyslexic correlations in a rather significant manner. For example, in discussing a paper by John G. Lynn, Orton (1942) stated:

> One probably makes a mistake in attempting to associate too closely conditions like reading disability with handedness pattern. The great majority of my patients with specific reading disability are right handed. Many of them are also right eyed and right footed; in other words many of them have distinctly unilateral motor patterns, but this does not preclude the possibility of

* At the time of this study, the author had not yet discovered the concept of reading-score compensation and was therefore guided by the traditional belief that dyslexics had to have severe reading score deficiencies and were therefore "refractory readers."

> a confusion of dominance in the parts of the cortex which have to do with the reading process, and one sees the same symptoms as in those who do have confusion in the motor patterns.

If, indeed, the majority of Orton's dyslexic patients evidence distinctly unilateral motor patterns, and if dyslexics with and without confused unilateral motor patterns have the same symptoms, then might we not assume that dyslexic symptoms and confused motor patterns are most probably unrelated?

Critchley (1969) reviewed the contradictory and even confusing handedness, dominance, and dyslexic research correlations as follows:

> That many dyslexic children were not strongly right-handed subjects was realized early in the history of "congenital word blindness." With the passage of time increasing importance became attached to this aspect of the problem, and it seemed more and more evident that dyslexic children often lacked a firm and determinate left cerebral dominance. [p. 65]

> The view currently held by most neurologists is that both ambilaterality and dyslexia are the expressions of a common factor, namely immaturity of cerebral development. . . .
>
> Why only a proportion of ill-lateralized children should be dyslexic is not easy to understand. Some psychologists have in the past been reluctant to accept any conception of sinistrality, or of mixed or inadequate dominance, in the context of dyslexia. [p. 70]

> Undoubtedly, however, some dyslexics are unequivocal dextrals with no family history of left-handedness or ambidexterity. In the absence of any closer correlation it is therefore tempting to invoke a hypothesis which would seek to attribute dyslexia to an underlying delayed, or incomplete lateralization of certain cerebral functions. Zangwill (1962) wondered whether there might be two sorts of developmental dyslexia, namely a type occurring in poorly lateralized individuals, as opposed to a type presenting in individuals who are lateralized fully. He had been struck by the frequent associations of retarded speech development, defects of spatial perception, motor clumsiness and other indications of defective maturation in cases of dyslexia presenting an ill-lateralized or else left-handed children. Moreover, Zangwill was impressed by the comparative "purity" of the dyslexia when it presents itself in unequivocally right-handed children, and he suggested that a specific genetic factor might plausibly be assumed in this particular group. [p. 71]

Although Critchley considered Orton's explanation of dyslexic symptoms on the basis of incomplete dominance to be overly simplistic, he nevertheless leaned in favor of evoking "a hypothesis which would seek to attribute dyslexia and its symptomatic severity to an underlying delayed or incomplete lateralization of certain cerebral functions."

Brain (1962) studied handedness and dominance in relationship to aphasia. In accordance with his research, he estimated (1) that 5%–10% of

Englishmen and Americans were left-handed, (2) that left-handedness is twice as common in males as in females, (3) that handedness is due to a hereditary predisposition, and (4) that the establishment of speech centers in the left cerebral hemisphere is to some extent independent of handedness:

> The preference for the right hand is usually the result of hereditary predisposition, and there is evidence that right-handedness is inherited as a Mendelian dominant and left-handedness as a recessive . . . Either hemisphere can function alone for language if the other is severely damaged early in life; in children, aphasia occurs more frequently as the result of right-sided lesions than in adults, and moreover is more transitory. Hence, at birth, it would seem that the two cerebral hemispheres possess an equal potentiality for the localization of the speech functions, but there is a natural tendency, presumably inherited, for the large majority of individuals in the course of learning to speak to establish their speech centres in the left cerebral hemisphere, to some extent independently of whether they are right-handed or left-handed.

If the establishment of both speech and handedness functions are genetically predisposed, and if the speech and handedness functions are to some extent independent of one another, then might we not once again assume that cerebral dominance, dyslexia, and handedness are unrelated?

With this background of conflicting handedness-dominance-dyslexia evidence in mind, the author attempted to test the aforementioned assumptions by determining the incidence of left-handedness in a total first-grade population, as well as among normal, slow, and refractory readers within this population. It was assumed that if indeed left-handedness and dyslexia were truly unrelated, then the incidence of left-handedness among the various normal and impaired reading groups would be the same. In addition, the intensity of speech and dyslexic symptoms was assessed among right- and left-handed refractory readers in order to test Zangwill's (1960, 1962) dyslexic-dominance hypothesis.

Incidence of Left-handedness

The incidence of left-handedness was determined by teacher observation in 3000 first graders. This incidence was distributed in the three reading groups as follows:

Population	Number	Percentage
1. Total population	3000	12%
Normal reading population	2290	12%
2. SRP population	700	18%
3. *c-v* (+) *population:*	112	11%
First-grade refractory c-v (+) readers	58	11%
Older c-v (+) dyslexics	54	11%

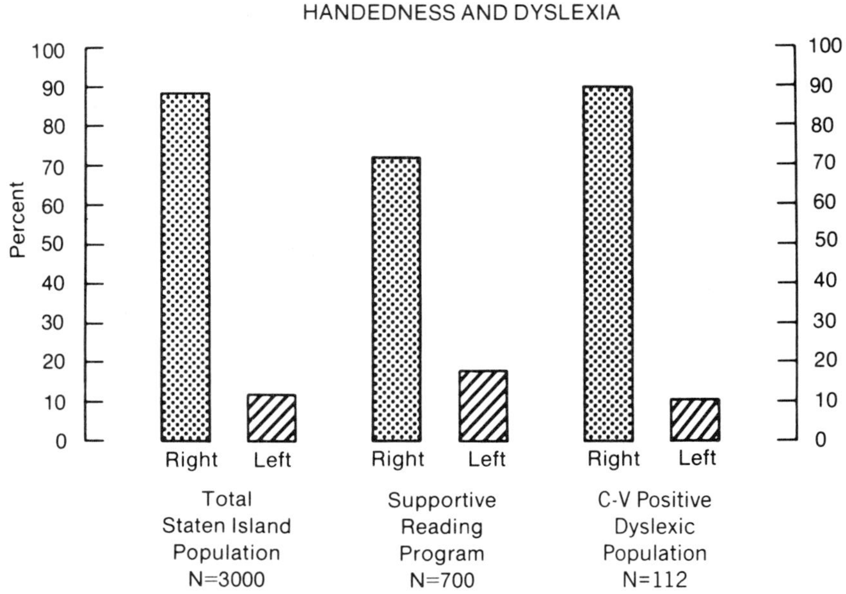

Fig. 3–8. Incidence of right- and left-handedness in the total Staten Island population, the "high-risk" readers within the Supportive Reading Program, and the cerebellar-vestibular dyslexic populations. The distribution of handedness in normal, "high-risk," and refractory or dyslexic reading groups is statistically similar and suggests that handedness and reading category are unrelated.

Fig. 3–8 illustrates this handedness data. Analysis of the data clearly reveals that the incidence of left-handedness is independent of reading levels and groups. Moreover, the 11% left-handed incidence among refractory readers (or dyslexics) is remarkably consistent with the 10% dyslexic left-handedness incidence as determined in the retrospective study—further suggesting that handedness and dyslexia are unrelated. The incidence and distribution of ambilaterality, however, was not determined in this sample, and so its significance and role in normal and dyslexic populations must be considered unknown.

Genetic Determinants of Left-handedness

In an initial attempt to determine the genetic origin of left-handedness among dyslexics, the families of the left-handed c-v-dysfunctioning dyslexics were examined for handedness. It was assumed that if left-handedness in dyslexia was primarily determined by genetics rather than by non-genetic (dominance) factors, then there should exist a significant history of left-handedness among family members.

Analysis of this data (Fig. 3–9) suggests that left-handedness is most probably a genetically determined variant among dyslexics. However, this data

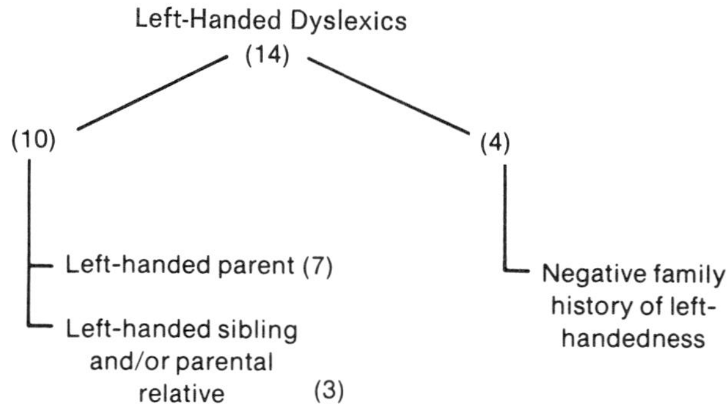

Fig. 3–9. Possible genetic determinants of left-handedness as derived from the historical exploration of the family members of 14 left-handed dyslexics found within the prospective study. Ten of the 14 left-handed dyslexics had a left-handed parent, sibling and/or parental relative, whereas no family history of left-handedness was found in only 4 of the left-handed dyslexics.

by no means eliminates non-genetic handedness determinants in dyslexia. It merely suggests that the latter determinants, if and when present, must play only a minor or complicating role. This data did not test the possible genetic origin of mixed-handedness and/or dominance mechanisms in normal reading versus dyslexic groups.

In an effort to test Zangwill's (1960, 1962) dominance-dyslexic hypothesis, the nuclear symptomatic complex of dyslexia was both qualitatively and quantitatively explored among left-, right-, and mixed-handed dyslexics. Both the quality and intensity of speech and related dyslexic symptoms were found to be independent of handedness—tending to contradict Zangwill's contention that incomplete dominance and severe dyslexic symptomatology were correlated. Furthermore, although the 10% incidence of left-handedness was found to be consistent with Brain's handedness data, there appeared to be no statistically significant male/female incidence difference among left-handed individuals in this and follow-up studies.

Male/Female Ratios in Dyslexia

Dyslexia has been invariably correlated to male/female ratios significantly greater than 1—suggesting that dyslexia is related to a male sex-linked genetic determinant. Critchley (1969) reviewed the pertinent literature to date and states (p. 90):

> It has almost always been observed that developmental dyslexia affects males more often than females. Jastak alone could find no sex difference in his series (1934). The estimate varies from one author to another . . .

We can assume that about 4 males to 1 female may be accepted as a reasonable figure.

Again, Vernon is out of accord on the question of sex-incidence. She believed that the claimed preponderance of boys was because boys who are non-readers create more trouble at school than girls; or at least they bring their disability more forcibly to the teacher's notice, while girls suffer in silence. This again smacks of special pleading. Perhaps, too, according to Vernon, parents take a more serious view of inability to read in a boy than in a girl. However, the explanation which Vernon deemed most likely was that boys with reading disability had super-added emotional disorders, often aggressive in type. Boys are referred to clinics because these latter disorders have brought them to the notice of teachers and parents rather than the disability itself.

Observations such as these, and particularly the last, would not tally with the experience of neurological consultants to whom children with dyslexia are brought by worried parents expressly on account of their paradoxical inability to learn to read. Among such children boys unquestionably outnumber girls.

In an effort to elucidate further the role of sex and genetics in dyslexia, a series of male/female ratios were obtained as a function of reading-score categories and as a function of diagnostic age (i.e., age at which a diagnosis is initially made). Because dyslexia has been viewed traditionally as a genetic, constitutional, and/or developmental disorder, it was assumed that the true dyslexic incidence remained relatively constant from first through sixth grades, and that dyslexic male/female ratios would be independent of diagnostic age and significantly greater than 1 for only refractory or dyslexic reading categories.

If, however, the male/female ratios among dyslexics were found to vary significantly with such factors as diagnostic age, or if nondyslexic male/female ratios were found to be significantly greater than 1, then the sex-linked dyslexic correlations and hypothesis would have to be seriously considered.

The male/female ratio among normal readers in the first-grade Staten Island population (2290) was 1:1 following the removal of approximately 700 "high-risk" children within the SRP. The male/female ratio among the approximately 700 "high-risk" delayed readers responding favorable to SRP instruction was 1.6:1. This data indicates that "high-risk" delayed readers have a significantly greater male/female ratio than normal readers (Fig. 3–10a). The male/female ratio among the first-grade c-v-dysfunctioning "refractory readers" (N = 58) within the SRP was 2.5:1; the male/female ratio among a similar but older sample (N = 54) of second- through sixth-grade c-v-dysfunctioning refractory readers was 4:1 (Fig. 3–10b); and the male/female ratio among the c-v-dysfunctioning third- through sixth-grade refractory readers in the retrospective study was 5:1 (Fig. 3–10c). This data suggests that the male/female ratios in dyslexia increase as a function of symptomatic intensity and diagnostic age.

Because the male/female ratios among poor or refractory readers appears to significantly increase as a function of the age at which initial diagnosis

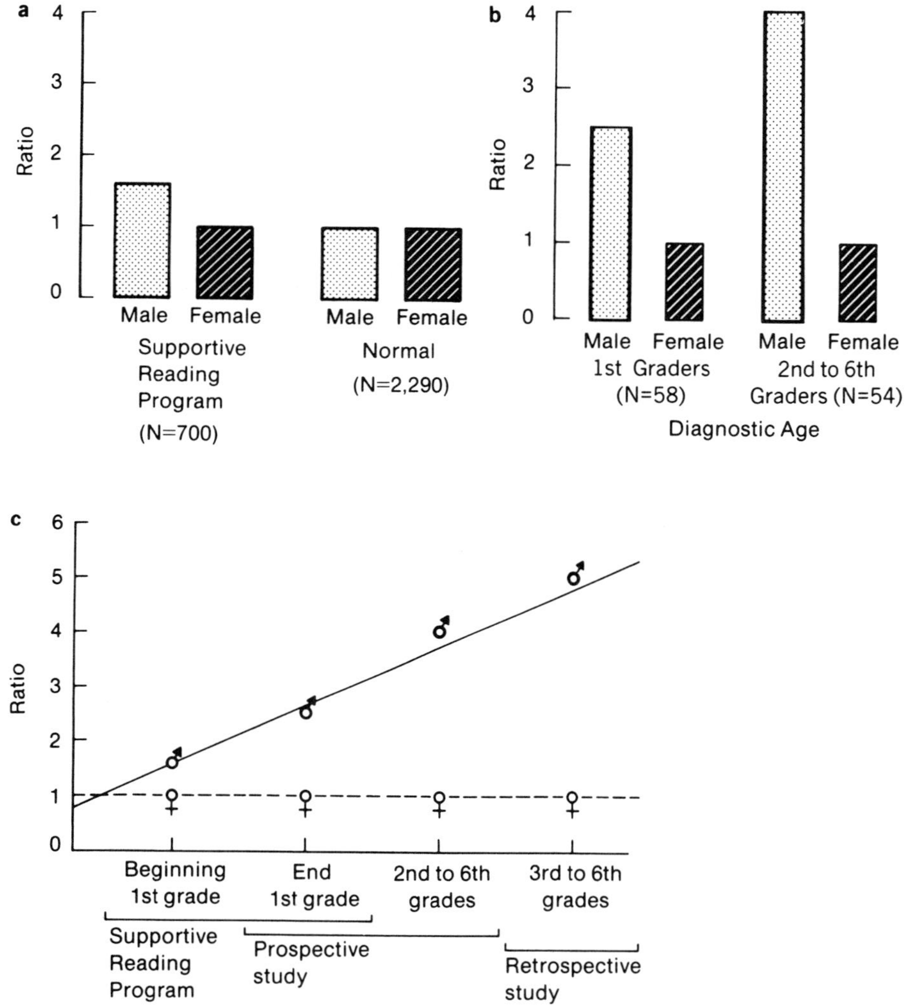

Fig. 3–10. Male/female ratios found among normal readers, "high-risk" Supportive Reading Program delayed readers, and younger and older refractory or dyslexic readers. (*a*) Male/female ratios of normal versus Supportive Reading Program "high-risk" delayed readers. (*b*) Male/female ratios among first-grade versus second- through sixth-grade dyslexics. (*c*) All the male/female ratios with the 5:1 male/female dyslexic ratio found in the retrospective study. The manner in which these ratios increase as a function of diagnostic age and reading severity is clearly demonstrated.

is made, and since all delayed or poor readers show a statistically significant male preference, the data analysis suggests that the clinically reported male/female ratios in dyslexia are most probably referral, rather than true incidence, ratios.

If, indeed, the male/female ratios are greater than 1 for all children with reading difficulties, regardless of diagnosis, and if the male/female ratios increase as a function of symptomatic intensity and diagnostic age, then one must suspect that Vernon (1957) is most probably correct in her assumptions regarding male/female ratios—i.e., that boys with frustrating reading difficulties are more significantly affected emotionally than girls, and as a result clinically appear, and are referred, in greater proportions. According to the data cited above, it seems reasonable to further assume that the degree to which boys are emotionally traumatized is directly proportional to the severity and/or chronicity of the underlying reading disability—thus accounting for the higher male/female ratios found among the older "refractory readers."

Ear Infections, Motion Sickness, and Vertigo in Dyslexia

The incidence and specific localization of c-v dysfunction underlying "dysmetric dyslexia" suggested the etiologic possibility that "harmless" ear infections during early childhood may result in, or intensify, dysfunctioning within the labyrinthine-vestibular-cerebellar circuitry. Inasmuch as the blind ENG study demonstrated positive vestibular dysfunction and negative audiologic findings, the author further assumed that otitis media may result in, or intensify, pre-existing c-v dysfunction despite its healing and clinical disappearance (Frank and Levinson, 1973, 1975–76; Levinson, 1974).

Statistical Data

Of the total dyslexic sample, 50% reported a history of ear infections, 40% reported motion sickness, and 35% reported experiences of positional and/or spontaneous vertigo. This data is summarized in Fig. 3–11. Unfortunately, because nondyslexic control studies were pending and unavailable for statistical comparison, the significance of this data must be deferred.

In an effort to determine statistically whether or not there existed a cause and effect relationship between reported ear infections, on the one hand, and motion sickness and vertigo, on the other, the dyslexic sample was subdivided into those individuals who reported ear infections and those who did not. The corresponding frequencies of motion sickness and vertigo were determined for each subsample. The incidence of motion sickness and vertigo in both groups was approximately the same (Fig. 3–12).

One can either assume that ear infections and vestibular dysfunction are unrelated or that the historical denial of ear infections by no means excludes their past presence. The author assumed the latter alternative, and speculated that ear infections during early childhood must frequently exist subclinically, and may play an etiologically overdetermined and significant role in vestibular dysfunction, "CNS lags," and dyslexia.

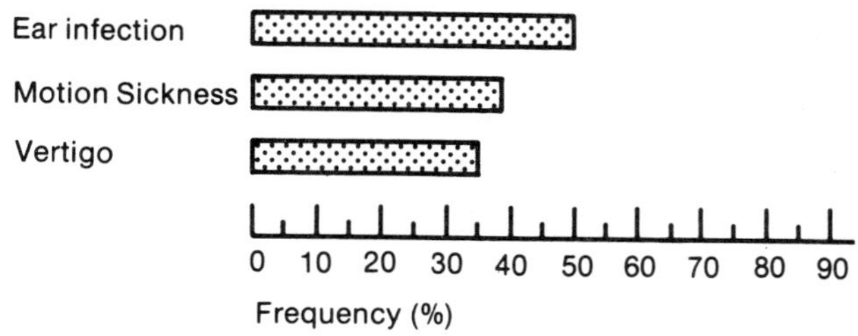

Fig. 3–11. Frequency distribution of ear infections, motion sickness, and vertigo in a dyslexic sample (N = 115).

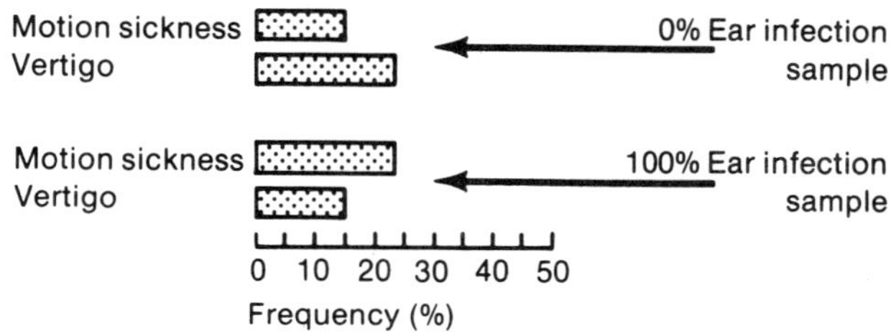

Fig. 3–12. Frequency distribution of motion sickness and vertigo among dyslexics reporting ear infections and those reporting no ear infections. The frequency of motion sickness and vertigo appears to be independent of the reported presence or absence of ear infections.

Genetic, Constitutional, and Developmental Considerations

Genetics

A statistical analysis of the data on dyslexia initially appeared to support the traditional thesis of genetic dyslexia. One-third of the dyslexic sample had at least one family member with a history of reading difficulties. A few dyslexic cases even existed in which all, or nearly all, immediate family members (e.g., 5/5, 5/6, 6/7) had similar symptoms. Although identical-twin dyslexic cases were rare, their presence provided significant "genetic impact" to the data. In addition, the male/female dyslexic ratios of 5:1, 4:1, etc., initially suggested a sex-linked genetic determinant and added a crescendo to the genetic dyslexic data and hypotheses.

However, upon careful reflection, both the hereditary data and resulting assumptions were found to be overly simplistic, naive, and subject to a series of heretofore unrecognized or denied considerations:

1. Because dyslexia is a disorder of unknown origin and uncertain detection, all reported incidence statistics must be subject to significant degrees of uncertainty and error. As a result, all derived genetic infer-

ences must be unwittingly subject to even greater degrees of error. For example, if the commonly reported dyslexic incidence of 2%–5% is correct, then the "family incidence" data cited above must be viewed as genetically significant. If, however, the c-v-dysfunctioning dyslexic incidence is 20%–30%, then the same data may be accounted for by randomization rather than only genetic determinants.

2. Although the historical presence of reading symptoms among family members of dyslexics may be suggestive of c-v dyslexia, historical evidence alone is by no means conclusive of such a diagnosis. For example, nondyslexic reading disorders exist in unknown proportions and can only be differentiated from c-v dyslexia by careful neuropsychologic evaluation. In addition, parents were occasionally found who acknowledged a history of reading problems in order to suggest a genetic, rather than a psychological, determinant, and thus minimize their own sense of responsibility and guilt. At other times, parents were found unwittingly identifying with their children's learning and dyslexic symptoms in order to minimize the impact of hearing such emotionally traumatizing diagnoses as MBD or minimal cerebral dysfunction. As a result of these and other emotional determinants interfering with the reliability and accuracy of the historical content, the historical data was frequently found to be subject to psychogenically determined memory slips and errors.

3. The historical absence of reading symptoms by no means eliminated the presence of c-v dyslexia. Reading-score-compensated c-v dyslexics and/or "late bloomers" were recognized to exist in undetermined numbers, and adult dyslexics were frequently found to deny their learning disorder as a result of intense feelings of embarrassment, stupidity, and inferiority.

4. The genetic significance of the clinically reported and determined male/female ratios of 5:1, 4:1, etc., was sharply reduced when the sex ratios were recognized to be highly selected referral, rather than true incidence ratios.

5. Although the emotional genetic impact of a pair of dyslexic twins is significant, its real genetic meaning is dependent upon unavailable incidence data.

Recognition of the aforementioned "loopholes" in the traditional genetic research efforts in dyslexia by no means implies that genetic factors are unimportant or insignificant. Genetic dyslexia appears to exist—but its incidence and determination requires more comprehensive and sophisticated study.

Constitutional Considerations

Analysis of the data indicated that only 7% of cases had a history suggestive of pathogenetic pregnancy, delivery, and/or prematurity-related constitutional determinants. According to this data, one must either assume that constitutional factors play only a minor role in dyslexia or that the traditional historical indicators of pathogenetic constitutional dyslexic determinants leave much to be desired.

The latter assumption is supported by an unpublished neurologic study of 100 "mild" post-conclusion and/or whip lash injuries sustained during "minor" auto accidents. Of the cases examined by the author, 83% reported such c-v symptoms as spontaneous and/or positional vertigo, blurred vision, memory uncertainty, imbalance and dyscoordination phenomena, tonal disturbances, difficulties in reading concentration and memory, speech hesitations, slurring, stuttering, and word-finding difficulties. In addition, c-v abnormal and ENG abnormal signs were present in almost all cases. As a result of this study, the author reasoned as follows: If indeed "minor"-appearing traumatic precipitants result in a significant incidence of c-v dysfunction, one might readily assume that the c-v circuits are especially sensitive to a significant spectrum of variables relating to toxic, anoxic, traumatic, nutritional, and delivery factors, and that these variables require infinitely more intensive study.

Developmental Versus Structural CNS Considerations

Dyslexia was initially considered to be due to a cortical structural defect. However, the absence of cortical signs in dyslexia led investigators to abandon the structural cortical theory and to assume the existence of a cortical neurophysiologic lag. Although the primary cortical lag theories of dyslexia were consistent with the absence of cortical neurologic signs, they were found inconsistent and incompatible with the discovery that dyslexia was highly correlated to c-v signs and symptoms.

The correlation of dyslexia with c-v signs led to the conviction that dyslexia and its neurophysiologic fallout was of a primary c-v origin. However, was the c-v dyslexic dysfunction of a structural or developmental lag nature? Or were some forms of c-v dyslexia structural in nature, while other forms were developmentally determined? And if there existed c-v developmental dyslexic forms, what factors and forces shaped these developmental delays and/or arrests?

Follow-up or longitudinal neurophysiologic studies of dyslexic children into adulthood, as well as reconstructive studies of adult dyslexics' symptomatology back to their childhood roots, clearly demonstrated the persistence of c-v dyslexic signs despite c-v neurophysiologic and symptomatic compensation. The c-v and dyslexic symptomatic complex did not disappear with age: it was merely compensated for. Although the longitudinal and reconstructive studies highlighted the existence of a c-v dyslexic compensation, rather than a c-v dyslexic resolution, as a function of age, the author found it difficult, if not impossible, to differentiate convincingly between the presence of an incomplete c-v development or lag and a c-v structural dysfunction in the majority of dyslexics.

If, indeed, the c-v circuits required to track and process written and other language symbols are "recent" phylogenetic acquisitions, arising in functional relationship to, and facilitaitng, cortical gnosis and conceptualization, then genetic and nongenetic developmental c-v lags may represent man's ontogenetic recapitulation of his pre-reading state in phylogeny at a time when the cerebellar cortex was one-third its present mass. In other words, delayed and/or incomplete c-v maturation may be postulated to reflect the "dysmetric" evolution of man's language-specific c-v tracking and processing circuits over millions of years. This *ontogenetic* c-v developmental lag hypothesis of dyslexia was indirectly supported by studies suggesting that "the cerebellum has enlarged between threefold and fourfold in [*only*] the past million years of human evolution":

> Excellence in motor coordination is obviously an adaptive advantage, and evidently it is enough of an advantage to sustain the development of a specialized brain center committed primarily to that purpose. The success of the motor coordination center is suggested by the calculations of Sherwood L. Washburn and R. S. Harding of the University of California at Berkeley. They report that the cerebellum has enlarged between threefold and fourfold in the past million years of human evolution. [Llinas, 1975, p. 71]

The author recognized that the c-v tracking, orienting, and processing circuits were clinically stimulus-specific and dependent inbuilt release mechanisms (IRMs) (Lorenz, 1957). Rene Spitz (1945, 1946a, b, 1957, 1965) demonstrated (1) that the ocular tracking and associated "similar response" of infants are maturation and time-dependent IRM's triggered by Gestalt-specific facial and motion configurations, and (2) that psychosomatic and somato-psychic developmental mechanisms unfold in critical relationship to vital, reciprocal mother-infant "dialogue" contact and emotional releasers and triggers. The author was then tempted to speculate that some types of c-v maturational delays may be influenced or caused by the psychotoxic and somato-toxic effects of severe emotional and/or sensory-motor stimulus deprivation occurring during critical stages in an infant's *ontogenetic* CNS development.

The Smiling Response Highlights Critical Developmental Stages

Between the third and sixth month of life, a normal infant will smile when confronted by any face in motion. The key sign or gestalt-stimulus triggering this response was found to be the forehead-eyes-nose sector in motion; even a mask was found to provoke smiling—provided it contained the key visual gestalt elements in motion. Before the third month of life an infant's smiling is a random process, whereas after the sixth month an infant will no longer smile at an *unfamiliar* face or gestalt-specific stimulus which had previously triggered the smiling response.

"Emergence of the smiling response marks a new era in the child's way of life; a new way of being has begun." (Spitz, 1965, p. 119) It is an *indicator* that the convergence and integration of multiple developmental currents within the psychic apparatus has been successfully organized and will henceforth operate as a discrete unit within the psychic system. "These turning points, these organizers of the psyche, are of extraordinary importance for the orderly and unimpeded progression of infantile development . . . However, when the consolidation of the organizer miscarries, development is arrested." (Spitz 1965, p. 119)*

Hospitalism: Total Emotional Deprivation

Spitz (1945, 1946a, b, 1965) clearly described not only the arrest in psychic development, but the tragic irreversible CNS psychosomatic and immunity changes (severe motor, speech, and I.Q. retardation, spasmus mutans, athetoid-like bizarre finger movements, infection liability) eventually leading to a "spectacularly increased rate of mortality" when three-month-old infants are emotionally deprived of mothering or "dialogue" input for more than five months.

In accordance with these observations, c-v or dysmetric dyslexia may be theoretically classified according to primary and secondary types: *Primary dysmetric dyslexia* results from a primary c-v dysfunction due to genetic, developmental, anoxic, toxic, traumatic, infectious, etc., determinants. *Secondary dysmetric dyslexia* results when normal and vital c-v IRMs and circuits fail to unfold properly secondary to severe emotional and/or sensory-motor stimulus deprivation.

Of course, primary and secondary dyslexic types may coexist with each other as well as with varying combinations of CNS and emotional dysfunction—resulting in a biopsychological overdetermined symptomatic spread requiring careful etiologic dissection and treatment.

The Syndrome of Minimal Cerebral Dysfunction

Because the blindly examined dyslexic cases were most often diagnosed as evidencing minimal brain damage (MBD) or minimal cerebral dysfunction (MCD) on the basis of specific cerebellar signs, it seemed wise to review the concept of the "syndrome of minimal cerebral dysfunction" as defined by Carter and Gold (1972). According to this article, the diagnosis of MCD is used to describe children with normal or near normal intellect who demonstrate abnormal behavioral patterns, specific learning disabilities (dyslexia), or both. In addition, speech disorders and poor coordination are said to be the most common presenting complaints.

> Language difficulties are common. Some children remain nonverbal, but more commonly there is delay in the development of speech patterns. Once established, there are problems in the formation of phrases and sentences and a prominent tendency to preserve more immature modes of expression. Speech

* Spitz (1965, pp. 117–118) postulated that psychic organizers act during an infant's "ontogeny" in a manner analogous to the embryonic organizer described by Needham (1931) "as a pacemaker for a particular developmental axis; it is a center radiating its influence."

may be characterized by a paucity, misuse, and poor articulation of words. Flow of expressive language may be either slow, hesitant, or explosive.

Coordination is frequently impaired, and the children are often clumsy and awkward. Poor fine muscle coordination is initially demonstrated by difficulties with buttoning, zippering, or tying shoelaces. Subsequent manifestations are noted in the manipulation of scissors, coloring within a figure, drawing a straight line, and eventually poor handwriting. More gross incoordination is evident in the delay in learning to hop, skip, ride a bicycle, and catch a ball.

Neurologic examination characteristically reveals a paucity of gross abnormalities. However, minimal subtle signs are usually present. Gait may be lumbering and awkward. After 7 years of age, there may be impaired tandem walking and difficulty in hopping and skipping. Examination of the motor system reveals impairment of rapid alternating movements, choreiform activity of extended fingers, and occasional tightness of various muscle groups, including hamstrings, posterior tibials, and pronators. Not uncommonly, there is a right-left confusion and a failure to establish handedness. The deep tendon reflexes may be asymmetric, but the plantar responses are usually physiologic. Eye muscle imbalance of the convergent or divergent types is commonly observed; it tends to diminish with age. Poor speech patterns are often associated with drooling and inability to perform rapid lateral tongue movements. [Carter and Gold, 1972, pp. 879–880]

As the reader will note by referring to these quotations or the article itself, cerebral cortical signs are distinctly absent in this neurologic syndrome. The symptoms and signs defining this syndrome include specific learning problems and specific reading disability or dyslexia, deviant and/or hyperkinetic behavior, and a host of specific dyscoordination, imbalance, and dysrhythmic phenomena, as well as asymmetric tonal disturbances (eye muscle imbalance, asymmetric DTRs, occasional tightness of various muscle groups) traditionally characterizing and defining c-v dysfunction. If only balance, coordination, rhythm and tonal neurologic disturbances characterize the MCD syndrome and/or dyslexia, then are Carter and Gold (1972) correct in stating, (1) "there is no isolated finding that is diagnostic of this clinical syndrome," and (2) "the term Minimal Cerebral Dysfunction appears to be satisfactory, in that it implies impaired cerebral dysfunction without implicating specific areas of the brain"?

Have not the c-v signs characterizing the MCD syndrome and/or dyslexia been denied? Are not cerebral signs characteristically absent in this syndrome? Does not the term cerebral dysfunction imply that a specific area of the brain is impaired? Does it not appear as if dyslexia and the MCD syndrome may be overlapping variations of a unitary panoramic disorder with a common primary c-v denominator and source?

In discussing MCD, Clemmens (1967, p. 32) states:

When cerebral dysfunction exists and the clinical neurological examination is normal, the term "minimal brain damage" or "minimal cerebral dysfunction" is used in designation. The conduct disturbances associated with minimal brain damage are termed "organic behavior disorders." The language problems and learning disabilities that are related to neurological impairment are classified as neuropsychiatric learning disorders. . . .

Characteristic of this impairment is absence of specific neurologic signs, although minor degrees of motor incoordination, non-specific awkwardness, mixed laterality, time and spatial disorientation, or adiadochokinesis (inability to perform rapid alternating movements) can usually be detected. Delayed speech development, mechanical speech imperfections, echolalia (meaningless repetition of others' words), strabismus, visuo-motor impairment, and abnormal electroencephalograms are found in greater numbers than in control subjects.

Upon the retrospective analysis of Clemmens' discussion:

1. There appears to be an unstated equation of brain and cerebral dysfunction, and hence the use of such interchangeable terms as minimal brain damage or minimal cerebral dysfunction. Might this apparent "brain-cerebral" diagnostic identity be viewed as a "linguistic slip" indicating man's scientific preoccupation with his cerebral cortex?

2. There appears to be a *conviction* that cerebral dysfunction exists and that this dysfunction is responsible for "organic behavior disorders" and "neuropsychiatric learning disorders"—despite the stated and seemingly defined absence of specific neurologic (cortical) signs. As an example of this apparent conviction, Clemmens begins his paragraph, "When cerebral dysfunction exists . . ." However, is not the existence of cerebral dysfunction in MBD or MCD an assumption rather than a conclusion, especially as specific cortical signs are invariably absent?

Should not the paragraph have begun with *if* rather than *when*? Even if a cerebral dysfunction were demonstrated to cause some behavioral, speech, and learning disorders, can one reliably assume that a cerebral dysfunction is responsible for *all* organic behavioral, speech, and learning disorders? Did not Critchley (1969), for example, distinguish the reading disorder due to developmental dyslexia from that due to acquired cortical alexia or alexic aphasia? And did he not further distinguish the writing and mathematical disturbances in developmental dyslexia from those due to a parietal Gerstmann's syndrome? Are not the mechanical speech disorders characterizing MCD neurophysiologically distinct from true cortical aphasic disorders?

3. There appeared to be a denial of the specific nature and localizing significance of such c-v signs as "motor incoordination, nonspecific awkwardness, time and spatial disorientation, adiadochokinesis . . . mechanical speech imperfections, strabismus [and even] visuo-motor impairment . . ."* In accordance with this apparent c-v denial, Clemmens (1967) stated,

* Refer to the cases called Martin and Stan P. in Appendix C—found by Dr. A. Gold on "blind" neurologic examination to have visual-motor difficulties and diagnosed by him as having cerebellar dysfunction and benign paraxysmol vertigo respectively.

"Characteristic of this impairment is absence of specific neurological signs although minor degrees (of the aforementioned signs) are found in greater numbers than in control subjects."*

4. There appears to be a conviction that only a primary "injury to or maldevelopment of the cerebrum may interfere with such higher brain functions" (Clemmens, 1967, p. 32) as perception, cognition, judgement, concentration, impulse control, visual and auditory memory, perceptual-motor function, and symbol organization. However, although these higher functions may well be disrupted as a direct result of a primary cortical disorder (Luria, 1966), may we not assume that noncortical or subcortical dysfunctioning may secondarily disrupt an intact cerebral cortex and result in symptomatic cortical expressions, albeit in a more attenuated form? And if primary subcortical dysfunctioning may secondarily result in pseudo-cortical symptomatic mental and behavioral expressions, then is one justified in concluding that the mere presence of cortical-like symptoms is sufficient (or pathognomonic) evidence of a primary cerebral dysfunction, despite the absence of specific cerebral cortical signs?

Because the CNS of infants is remarkably plastic and adaptive to injury and/or dysfunction, might we not assume that an early primary impairment or developmental lag in one part of the CNS (i.e., the c-v system) may result in an adjacent "diaschisis" or "contrecoup-like" adaptive and maladaptive effects in more distant parts of the CNS (i.e., the cerebral cortex)?

> Study of the symptoms in lesions of the cerebellum has shown that it is impossible to come to a real comprehension so long as we regard the symptoms only from the viewpoint of the lesion alone. Real comprehension can only come if we regard the single part as a part of the brain as a whole and the symptoms as performances of the brain deprived of one certain part. Thus, each theory of the function of one part is only possible in the frame of a theory of the brain and, further, of the organism as a whole. Only then, we are able to characterize the particular significance of one single part, that is, as its significance in the performances of the whole organism [Goldstein, 1936, p. 11].

Would this holistic c-v hypothesis not explain the presence of c-v findings in the absence of cortical signs in the MBD majority? Are not these subcortical neurophysiologic assumptions in harmony with Hughlings Jackson's (1931) conceptualization of integrational levels of CNS functioning, Goldstein's (1936) conceptualization of holistic CNS functioning and

* Although echolalia and abnormal EEGs were included by Clemmens in the list of MBD abnormalities, the presence of these signs is most significantly lacking among the vast dyslexic majority. Indeed, the statistical absence of these signs in dyslexia and the occasional presence of these signs in the syndrome referred to as minimal cerebral dysfunction or minimal brain damage may serve to indicate that the latter syndrome contains mixed patterns and groupings of neurophysiologic and psychological disturbances.

the vital role played by both physical and emotional (dialogue) stimuli in triggering, releasing, and/or organizing interdependent functional-structural CNS development, especially at critical developmental stages (Anna Freud, 1946; Lorenz, 1957; Spitz, 1966; Lorenz and Tinbergen, 1957).

If specific cortical signs are absent among neuropsychiatric learning disorders sometimes diagnosed as minimal brain damage, minimal cerebral dysfunction, dyslexia, etc., and if, indeed, the signs reflect the presence of a primary c-v dysfunction, and if a primary c-v dysfunction in young children may result in the nonrelease, scrambling, or delayed development of secondary cortical-dependent or related functions, then the cortical concepts of MBD, MCD, and dyslexia may be determined significantly by fallacious and "biased" cortical neurophysiologic assumptions, rather than by the clinical neurophysiologic reality.

If the neurophysiologic background significance of c-v signs and dysfunction in MBD conceptualizations has been scientifically denied while the resulting manifest secondary cortical expressions have been scientifically "fixated" and confused with the c-v-determined symptomatic source, then a solution has been found for the MBD conceptual paradox in which:

1. The brain has been identified with the cerebral cortex.
2. The term "minimal" has been used for a disorder many might consider severe.
3. A neurophysiologic disorder is assumed to be present despite a normal neurologic examination.
4. A cortical dysfunction is said to be present despite the absence of cortical signs.
5. Neurologic signs are said to be absent despite the stated presence of neurologic signs.

Summary

Of 115 reading-disabled or dyslexic children, 97% revealed evidence of c-v dysfunction. Ninety-six percent of 22 blind neurologic examinations and 90% of 70 completed blind ENGs indicated evidence of a similar c-v dysfunction—clearly substantiating the author's correlation of dyslexia and c-v dysfunction. In addition, the dyslexic sample was further investigated in order to obtain possible correlations and insight into the dyslexic role of handedness, sex, otitis media, and genetic, constitutional, and developmental factors. Handedness and sex were found to be unrelated to dyslexia. Otitis media remained a suspicious unknown.

Genetic, constitutional, and developmental data and considerations were analyzed, raising as many questions as answers. However, in summary one might safely state that dyslexia results from a dysfunction and/or lag within the c-v-related tracking, orienting, and processing circuits. Furthermore, this dysfunction or lag may be of primary genetic, developmental, infectious, toxic, traumatic, or other origin, and/or secondary to severe emotional and sensory-motor deprivations sustained during critical and early developmental stages.

Since dyslexia and its symptomatic complex was correlated to only abnormal c-v signs, the author attempted to explain pathophysiologically the dyslexic disorder on the basis of a primary c-v dysfunction. The c-v pathophysiologic hypothesis of the dyslexic reading disorder will be presented in Chapter 4.

4 A Cerebellar-Vestibular Hypothesis of the Dyslexic Reading Disorder

In view of the fact that dyslexia was found highly correlated only to c-v dysfunction, it seemed natural to explain the dyslexic reading disorder on the basis of a c-v pathophysiology. However, this explanatory task was no simple matter, and its pursuit appeared to result in a neurophysiologic paradox. For example, if, indeed, c-v dysfunctioning is characterized by a dysmetric balance and coordinational motor output, and if the dyslexic reading disorder is characterized by a "dysmetric" visual perceptual input, then how can one neurophysiologically establish that the dyslexic reading performance is of c-v origin? In other words, how can a c-v-determined motor dysmetria result in a visual perceptual dysmetria?

To resolve this output–input dilemma, the author was forced to assume (1) that there exists a c-v-determined ocular-motor dysmetria or nystagmus in dyslexia, and furthermore (2) that this nystagmus secondarily scrambles the visual input. These assumptions were made despite the fact that clinical nystagmus was statistically absent in the dyslexic samples examined. However, no other explanatory theoretical alternative was visible. At this point, the author could empathize with the cortical structural and physiologic theoreticians attempting to explain dyslexia on the basis of a cortical dysfunction despite the absence cortical signs.

In order to reconcile the theoretical need for the presence of nystagmus in dyslexia and its paradoxical clinical and statistical absence in dyslexic samples, the author assumed the existence of a subclinical nystagmus in dyslexia. This assumption was supported by the determination of spontaneous and positional subclinical nystagmus in dyslexic samples during ENG testing.

Interestingly enough, following the formulation of these theoretically "high-flying" assumptions and speculations, God or chance sent a 6½-year-old dyslexic girl named Joan for neuropsychiatric examination. Since Joan manifested direction- and position-dependent *clinical* nystagmus in association with c-v dysfunction and dyslexia, and because the neurodynamic analysis of her clinical findings appeared to verify qualitatively the author's c-v dyslexic reading hypothesis, Joan's case study is presented here: illustrating the manner in which a clinical exception highlighted the hidden c-v dyslexic rule. The appearance of Joan's case led the author to wonder, Does God help those who help themselves, or do we find only that which we consciously or unconsciously search for?

The Role of the Cerebellar-Vestibular Circuits in Ocular Fixation, Tracking, and Processing

The author had assumed (1) that the dyslexic reading disorder was due to a primary c-v-related ocular-motor dyscoordination or nystagmus, which secondarily scrambled the temporal-spatial sequence of the visual input at the retinal site, and (2) that an intact cerebral cortex had difficulty interpreting the gnostic and conceptual significance of the sensory scramble it received. It was further assumed that the degree of the dyslexic reading impairment was primarily dependent upon the degree of c-v-determined temporal-spatial scrambling versus the adaptive capacity of compensatory deciphering and unscrambling mechanisms.

Utilizing this hypothesis, the author was able to explain how a c-v-determined motor dysfunction might result in secondarily related visual receptive or scrambling phenomena. Furthermore, one could also envision how the secondarily or tertiarily related dyslexic difficulty in cortically and gnostically interpreting the visual scramble was, and is, mistakenly considered by many neurologists and researchers to be of a primary cortical structural and/or physiologic origin (Frank and Levinson, 1973).

In an attempt to reconcile and integrate this dyslexic reading scheme with specific and proven c-v neurophysiologic data, the c-v literature was further researched. This research revealed the role of the cerebellum in coordinating the static and kinetic labyrinthine reflex motor system of the eyes, head, neck, and body, so that spatial dimensions and events can be clearly and harmoniously fixated, tracked, and spatio-temporally or sequentially perceived.

> Vestibular reflexes elicited by a position of the head in relation to the dimension of space (Magnus's "Reflexe der Lage"), arising in macular receptors, influencing bulbopontine (Magnus's tonic reflexes) and midbrain (Magnus's "Stellreflexe": righting reflexes) structures, are directly supervised by the cerebellum. The evidence for that is overwhelming . . . A third group of static labyrinthine reflexes is represented by the otolithic reflexes acting upon the eyes. They are clearly affected by ablation of the flocculonodular lobe. . . .
>
> The phasic vestibular reflexes elicited by a movement of the head in relation to the dimensions of space (Magnus's "Bewegungs-reflexe") are also directly supervised by the cerebellum. The reflexes elicited by angular acceleration arise

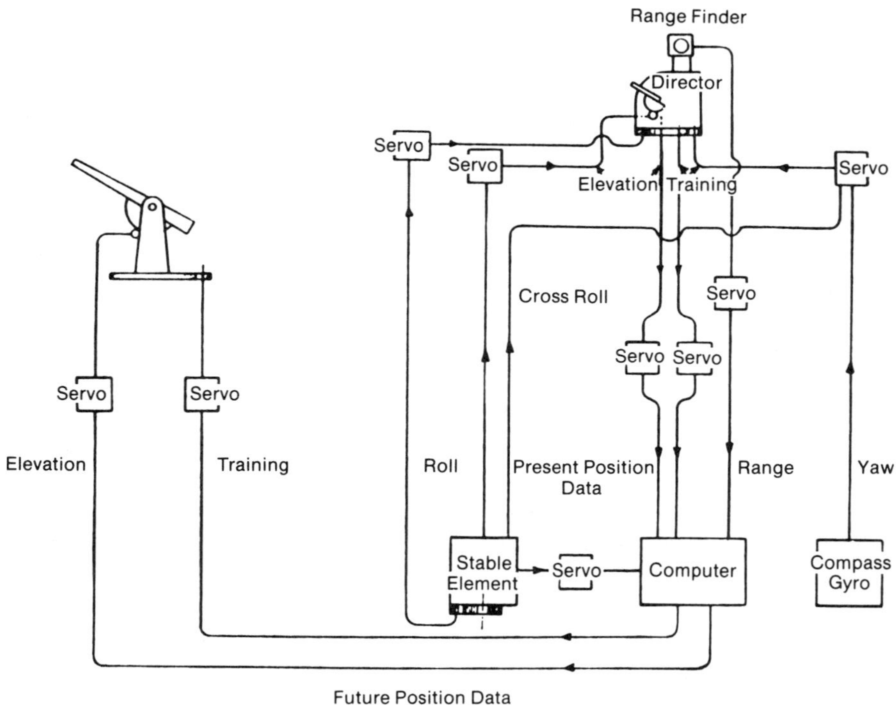

Fig. 4–1. A naval stable platform for a fire control installation. From Gairdner (1947).

> in the ampullary receptors, while those produced by linear acceleration are probably produced by stimulation of the macular receptors. [Dow and Moruzzi, 1958, pp. 273, 287]

The neurophysiologic operation of this dynamic cerebellum-modulated, visual reflex targeting and tracking system may be compared to the analogous need of a naval firing system for a stable platform: in order to provide a moving battleship with an accurate targetting and firing system, the platform on which the firing system is mounted must be stabilized against roll and change of course and pitch by a computer-guided series of servo-mechanisms, or "sensory-motor reflex arcs" (Fig. 4–1).

> No one can track with hand-operated telescopes specks in the sky from a platform rolling erratically and unpredictably . . . In the same way, if the head and eyes are stabilized against movement of the body, it is possible for the fixation reflex to operate to keep the target on the fovea. . . . When the stabilization by the labyrinth breaks down . . . then the visual field will appear to move and visual acuity goes down" [Whitteridge, 1968, p. 1106]

The c-v-modulated servo-mechanisms, or motor gestalt, required to maintain clear visual tracking and processing might also be compared to the analogous action of a computer-guided camera system capable of clearly monitoring the surroundings regardless of relative motion. Just as a disturbance in the camera's computer guidance system might result in a blurred or scrambled image, so also a disruption of the cerebellar computer and/or its labyrinthine servo-mechanisms might be expected to result in a series of ocular fixation, tracking, and processing dysfunctions similar to the dyslexic visual scrambling errors.

According to the qualitative and quantitative clinical data gathered by the retrospective and prospective studies, a majority of dyslexic individuals were found to exhibit ocular fixation, tracking, and/or scrambling (reversal) errors during reading. Moreover, dyslexics often resorted to fleeting head tilting, body shifting, and position-dependent reading preferences in what were recognized as compensatory attempts at restabilizing their inner "platforms" and disrupted "gyroscopic" mechanisms against inner "roll and pitch."

As a result of these c-v perceptual-motor conceptualizations, dyslexic reading errors and associated visual symptoms were viewed as vector resultants and externalized clinical representations of subclinical tracking and processing dysfunction in dynamic equilibrium with compensatory servo-gyroscopic positional shifting mechanisms. The pathophysiology by which the dysfunctioning c-v motor output or platform results in secondary input, or dyslexic reading symptoms, was specifically hypothesized and summarized as follows:

1. The c-v circuits provide a harmonious, well-integrated and stable motor background (platform) for visual perception.
2. This motor background, or motor gestalt, represents the subclinical or subliminal, automatic integrated motor activity of the eye muscles, head, neck, and body, so that ocular fixation and sequential scanning of letters and words can take place in a proper spatial-temporal manner.
3. In the presence of a c-v dysfunction and subclinical nystagmus, ocular fixation and sequential scanning of letters and words are spatially-temporally disordered, and letter and word scrambling results.
4. This primary ocular-motor scrambling, the secondary dysmetric visual perception, and tertiary anxiety lead to deficient memory and comprehension, or dyslexia.

Thus it was postulated that the c-v motor circuits provide the spatial and temporal harmony of the sensory input in a manner analogous to the function of the vertical and horizontal television stabilizers. When these stabilizers go awry, the resulting visual scramble makes interpretation and memory retention difficult and results in c-v or dysmetric dyslexia. As a result of this analogy to television functioning, c-v dyslexia may now be clinically and theoretically distinguished from alexia of cortical origin, in which, by analogy, the television picture is clear but the observer cannot comprehend the meaning and symbolic significance of the visual communication or pattern.

The subclinical nystagmus assumed to be present and responsible for the dyslexic scramble might be compared to the subconscious and subclinical horizontal and vertical sensory drifting which results from inadequately functioning motor stabilizers. Moreover, this television analogy helped account for not only the subclinical nystagmus obtained during ENG, but the compensatory shifting maneuvers manifested and required by dyslexics in order to read, write, and draw more effectively. In retrospect, it appears as if dyslexics were intuitively attempting to compensate for their impaired "TV stabilizers."

The elaboration of this analogy and conceptualization of c-v sensory-motor functioning and dyslexia could then explain neurophysiologically why only certain "sensory channels" and/or gestalt-specific configurations "drift," whereas others remain steady and clear. For example, if, indeed, the c-v circuitry consists of billions of cells and corresponding circuits (Snider, 1958; Llinas, 1974, 1975), and if each circuit complex or "channel" is geared to modulate a specific sensory-motor gestalt (i.e., single and/or sequential configurations), and if compensatory circuits or "channel harmonizers" may be learned or "imprinted" (Eccles et al., 1967), then this hypothetical model of c-v and related functioning is sufficiently broad and dynamic to account for the vast majority of clinically observed sensory-motor phenomena in dyslexics. In addition, Critchley's specific criticism and objection to Orton's dominance speculations can now be better comprehended and theoretically explained:

> This idea does not explain why dimensions should be confused in a lateral direction only. Nor does it give any reason why verbal symbol arrangement alone is at fault, while surrounding objects, scenes and pictures appear in normal orientation. [Critchley, 1969, p. 103]

Furthermore, the TV analogy of c-v functioning was found consistent with the ENG data analysis indicating that the c-v circuits are sensory- and channel-specific, stimulus- and direction-specific IRMs.

If one can envision the dependence of a TV set on antenna functioning and signal receptivity, one can easily explain the c-v response to microwave shielding and sensory deprivation, as well as sensory-motor overloading and dysfunctioning. As a result of these c-v functional analogies, a surprising host and range of fascinating, and heretofore perplexing, clinical dyslexic phenomena can be theoretically accounted for and even explained to children in a manner sufficiently concrete and tangible to be meaningfully understood and emotionally assimilated.

After reading of an experiment performed by von Uexkull, the television analogy of c-v mechanisms was further extended to include "antenna functioning." Von Uexkull (1957) describes an experiment in which a beehive was shifted 2 meters from its original site while most of the bees were out. Upon their return, the bees were observed to gather in the air at the spot where the flight hole—their front door—was previously located.

Not until 5 minutes later did the bees turn and fly toward the hive. If, however, the bees antennae were cut and the experiment repeated, the bees flew directly to the hive at its new location. According to Von Uexkull, these experiments suggest that the bees' antennae must somehow assume the role of an orienting compass for the front door and that antenna-guided orienting mechanisms dominate visual mechanisms—unless the latter are released by the removal of antenna-orientation mechanisms.

Is it possible that although sensory-motor compass receptivity mechanisms in humans have replaced the concretely visible antennae in the bee, compass sensitivity, sensory receptivity, and compensatory orienting mechanisms in man have their functional equivalence in antennae and related signal sensors in our phylogenetic brethren? Might we still possess hidden antennae within our organismic functioning?

Refuting Data and Conceptualizations

Although the author's research and theoretical considerations to date have clearly supported the existence of a c-v-induced primary ocular-motor dysfunction underlying dyslexia and the dyslexic reading disorder, many authorities have either denied such a defect or have attributed its existence to a primary dyslexic reading comprehension impairment.

According to a position paper by the American Association of Ophthalmology (1970), "Faulty patterns of eye movement usually do not cause poor understanding. Rather, they are often the result of having to refix or reexamine the printed page because of poor understanding." Upon reviewing the literature, Critchley (1969, pp. 56, 58) arrived at a similar conviction:

> In aphasic patients who have an alexic difficulty in the comprehension of verbal symbols, the movements of the eyes during the act of attempting to read are necessarily much deranged . . .
>
> As might be expected, unusual ocular movements during attempts at reading occur in the case of developmental dyslexics. Unfortunately the material that has been studied so far is not considerable. At one time it was asserted that abnormal eye movements were the actual cause of backwardness in learning to read. Hildreth (1936), for example, alleged that "reversals of letter-sequence in perceiving certain words are due to faulty eye movements". Witty and Kopel (1936) stated that left eye dominance in some cases results in the eyes moving from right to left during the act of reading, presumably causing difficulty or delay in comprehension. Mosse and Daniels (1959), who described a particular defect in the return sweep from the end of one line to the start of the next ("linear dyslexia"), went on to assert that anomalies in this manoeuvre are responsible for difficulty in comprehension arising in turn from faulty habits of reading which are psychologically determined.
>
> But arguments of this kind are surely topsy-turvy. Faulty eye movements must be regarded as the outcome of a difficulty in reading, and not its cause. An analogy with the disordered reading movements of the eyes shown by aphasic sub-

> jects can be fairly made. A possible exception to this statement may be found in the curious group of cases described by Prechtl and Stemmer (1959, 1962). Out of a series of children with learning difficulties, a distinct neurological syndrome was identified in 50 cases. These children showed clumsiness combined with choreiform movements. In 96% of them the eye muscles were involved, leading to disturbances of conjugate movement and difficulty in fixation and reading. The authors alleged that the chores caused both difficulty in mental concentration and also in fixation during the act of reading. Obviously this report bears little or no relationship to the problem of specific developmental dyslexia.

It is interesting to note that Critchley assumed the eye movement disturbances characterizing alexic aphasia and idiopathic dyslexia to be identical, despite his clear recognition that the alexic reading disorder and the dyslexic reading disorder were due to separate neurophysiologic mechanisms. He attributed dyslexia to a specific cerebral developmental lag, whereas he defined alexia as a variant of aphasia.

Inasmuch as the author correlated dyslexia to a primary c-v dysfunction, and since the c-v dyslexic reading disorder was found to be clinically and theoretically consistent with a c-v-induced ocular fixation and tracking dysfunction (with intact gnosis and conceptualization), it seemed neurophysiologically reasonable to assume that the reading comprehension difficulty in dyslexia was due to faulty eye movements. Since the alexic aphasic reading disorder is characterized by a primary cortical and associated comprehension impairment, it seemed equally reasonable to assume that the faulty eye movements in alexia were due to the underlying comprehension impairment and confusion, as well as the compensatory attempts at searching for meaningful targets in an effort to reduce catastrophic anxiety and deny the underlying aphasic confusional defect.

Furthermore, in view of the fact that the curious group of cases described by Prechtl and Stemmer demonstrate clumsiness and choreiform-like movements as well as ocular fixation and tracking difficulties, and since these learning disabled cases were found by the author to have a primary c-v dysfunction, it once again appears that a "clinical exception" may have highlighted the underlying pathophysiologic ocular-motor rule in dyslexia.

A Clinical Exception Highlights the Cerebellar-Vestibular Rule

According to the c-v reading hypothesis of dyslexia, it was theoretically predictable that dyslexic cases existed and would eventually present with clinically apparent dyscoordination of the cerebellar-vestibular modulated reflex motor background or motor gestalt. Two years after this prediction was made, a pretty, bright, first-grade dyslexic nonreader named Joan walked into my office. She presented with visual scrambling, clinically apparent direction-related positional nystagmus, and associated ocular, head, neck, and body tilting or posturing movements.

Joan's parents had already taken her for psycho-educational, ophthalmologic and optometric evaluations, and handed me the case reports. These "unbiased" clinical reports are presented in abbreviated form in Appendix A so that the reader might more readily capture the "blind" qualitative corroboration of the c-v reading hypothesis of dyslexia without the burden of having to scan the entire clinical "haystack."

Author's Evaluation

Joan was brought for neuropsychiatric consultation because of academic and perceptual difficulties despite a superior I.Q. Her reading, spelling, math, and writing skills were described by her parents as deficient—she was virtually a nonreader and could not spell or write her last name. Letter, word, and number reversals were prominent. Although right/left directional confusion was present, its significance was clinically uncertain as a result of her age.

Joan's medical history revealed the existence of a congenital strabismus, surgically corrected at one year of age, at which time clinical nystagmus became apparent. Between ages 1 and 2, Joan had repeated ear infections and currently is prone to severe motion sickness and episodic vertigo.

Could Joan's ear infections have resulted in, or intensified, her c-v dysfunction and dyslexia? Could her strabismus have complicated her c-v perceptual motor functioning? Could her strabismus have had a c-v component? And might its surgical correction have resulted in a c-v perceptual destabilization as well as compensatory ocular-motor movements (nystagmus) and associated head, neck, and body positioning?

Developmentally, Joan had skipped crawling after initially crawling backwards. She walked by 1, spoke early and clearly, and preferred talking on the telephone to visual games and play. She had difficulty learning to skip, hop, ride a tricycle, tie shoelaces, and button and zipper clothing. "In school she'll memorize her assignments and pretend she's reading, rather than admit she can't do it." Joan is right-handed in a family where half of the members are left-handed. Her father is a professional who most reluctantly admitted to being a slow reader, "I keep skipping over words and losing my place, and have to read slowly and re-read most things. My spelling is horrible and my writing is sloppy. Fortunately, I have always made sure I have excellent secretaries. . . . When I was a child, I also mixed up *b's* and *d's*, and *was* and *saw*." He is also prone to motion sickness and cannot ride in an automobile as a passenger. "When I'm driving, I'm okay. But when I am not driving, I get dizzy and sick, especially if I'm a passenger in the back seat."

Could there be a genetic predisposition to otitis media, vestibular dysfunction, and/or dyslexia?

Joan's writing was poorly formed, spaced, and directed. Her Goodenough figures were simplified to stick forms and she avoided drawing if possible. Her speech was clear and she had an excellent vocabulary and superior expressive ability. During examination, Joan's reading was slow, and characterized by skipping letters and words, reversals, and confusion of similar-appearing words. She acknowledged blurred and episodic double vision as well as reading vertigo, headaches, and ocular pain. When reading and writing, she was observed tilting her head and positioning her body as if searching to obtain a "motor scheme" for visual-motor fixation, tracking, and coordination. Rote arithmetic calculations were uncertain and finger counting was required.

Neurologic examination revealed only c-v signs: positive Romberg, clinical nystagmus accentuated by position and/or visual tracking, head, body, and ocular posturing during reading and writing, difficulty in hopping and skipping, tandem, finger-to-nose and finger-to-thumb dysmetria, and dysdiadochokinesis. Graphomotor and spatial difficulties characterized Joan's writing, Bender-Gestalt designs, and oversimplified drawings. An ENG was not performed. However, her ocular-motor tracking capacity (blurring speed) was significantly reduced.*

Pathophysiologic Evaluation

Joan's case of dyslexia was found to be associated with clinically atypical nystagmus, as well as clinically atypical head, neck, and body tilting or posturing—she appeared to dramatize the manner by which the eyes, head, neck, and body attempt to compensate dynamically for a c-v gyroscopic inability to maintain harmonious ocular balance and adequate visual fixation, tracking, and processing in relationship to the dimensions of space (Dow and Moruzzi, 1958; Whitteridge (1968). Because clinical nystagmus and clinical posturing were statistically atypical in the dyslexic sample, and inasmuch as these symptoms were clinically apparent in Joan's case, clearly demonstrating a gyroscopically impaired motor "platform" for visual fixation and tracking; she tended to validate qualitatively or isomorphically the initially proposed c-v dyslexic reading hypothesis. As a result, Joan's case appeared to be the clinical exception highlighting the c-v dyslexic rule.

A Retrospective Analysis of the "Unbiased" Findings in Joan's Case

A retrospective analysis of the independently determined psycho-educational, ophthalmologic and optometric clinical findings (Appendix A) revealed a clear-cut clinical correlation of Joan's dyslexic symptomatic com-

* See Chapter 5.

plex with a primary c-v dysfunction and related visual scrambling, and secondarily related pseudo-cortical expressions. In addition, her ocular, head, neck, and body tilting and positioning were recognized to be adaptive and reactive manifestations of an underlying, primary c-v destabilization of her motor gestalt for visual fixation, tracking, and processing. The clinically and neurophysiologically derived insights in this case resulted in an enhanced insight into the primary c-v dyslexic pathophysiology and ensuing secondarily and tertiarily related (emotional) clinical manifestations. All too often, the distinction between primary dysfunction and secondary or tertiary, *but topographically distinct,* response is clinically scrambled and confused—and thus the symptomatic and clinical diversity found upon neuropsychologic testing often appears puzzling and paradoxical rather than understandable and natural.

Summary

Inasmuch as dyslexia was found to be significantly correlated to dysmetric c-v balance and coordinational motor output functioning, the author postulated that the dyslexic visual input (reading) disturbances were due to the perceptual scrambling resulting from a primary, c-v-determined nystagmus and dysmetric ocular-motor fixation/sequential scanning dysfunction. The qualitative analysis of a c-v dyslexic girl presenting with statistically atypical clinical nystagmus and associated head, neck, and body positioning movements tended isomorphically to support the author's c-v ocular-motor hypothesis of the dyslexic reading disorder.

Inasmuch as a clear understanding of this clinically atypical case provided invaluable insights into the clinically typical dyslexic rule itself, all future clinical and experimental exceptions were most seriously investigated. It was repeatedly found that a clear understanding of the so-called clinical exceptions almost invariably highlighted the underlying clinical rule.

In order to test the validity of this reading hypothesis, the author designed a 3D optical scanner and a series of investigations in order to measure the c-v-determined ocular fixation/sequential scanning functions in normal and dyslexic individuals. It was anticipated that the ocular fixation and tracking capacity of dyslexics would be significantly deficient when compared to that of normal controls.

Addendum

A Panoramic Hypothesis of the Dyslexic Reading Disorder

The ocular-motor c-v hypothesis was eventually expanded to account for the total spectrum and panorama defined by the nuclear symptomatic complex in dyslexia. For example, although the c-v circuits were known to modulate proprioceptive, motion, directional, and motor signals, the ocular-motor reading hypothesis explained only the c-v role in regulating the visual input. According to this hypothesis, it still remained most difficult to explain the clinical existence of auditory and tactile sequencing and related memory disturbances in dyslexia, as well as the neurodynamic origin of the overactivity-distractability syndrome.

The neurophysiologic examination of several thousand more dyslexic individuals was required in order to convince the author that only primary c-v dysfunction exists in dyslexia, and that all the clinically observed dyslexic symptoms and phenomena were most probably of a primary c-v origin. This enhanced conviction as to the nature of c-v functioning was needed to overcome the resistance barrier imposed by the traditional c-v-functional view, which instructs clinicians that the c-v circuits modulate only the balance and coordinational motor output.

The surmounting of this "tunnel vision" perspective of c-v functioning enabled the author to assume that the c-v circuits must coordinate and harmonize the total sensory input in a manner analogous to its established role in coordinating the total motor output. This enhanced panoramic perspective of sensory-motor c-v function appeared to be in harmony with "common sense" biological logic. For, after all, how were animal species with limited or no cerebral cortical matter able to adaptively coordinate, navigate, and survive if their c-v computers did not rapidly modulate the sensory input with reflex coordinated and adaptive motor responses?

This panoramic sensory-motor hypothesis of c-v functioning was indirectly but convincingly confirmed when antihistamines and/or motion-sickness medications were noted to improve not only c-v motor coordination, but visual, auditory, and tactile sequencing activity as well as directional, memory, behavior, concentration, speech, grammar, and math functions.

As a result of these clinical observations it was postulated that:

1. the c-v circuitry modulates the total sensory input in a manner analogous to its modulation of the motor output;
2. specific and/or sequential memory function is dependent upon the proper integration and/or harmonization of the corresponding sensory input as well as upon c-v-dependent motor circuits and related conceptual feedback input.
3. the c-v circuits receive and modulate the gravitation input, coordinating compass and gyroscopic motor functions so that reality-oriented and goal-directed balance and coordination responses may be facilitated in the service of adaptation and survival. The author was even tempted to speculate that the c-v-determined directional functions were the precursors of intentional and goal-directed action and thinking.

Interestingly enough, these speculations were supported by such outstanding neurophysiologic investigators as Snider and Stowell (1942a, b, 1944), Dow and Anderson (1942), Adrian (1943), and Snider (1943, 1950, 1952, 1958).

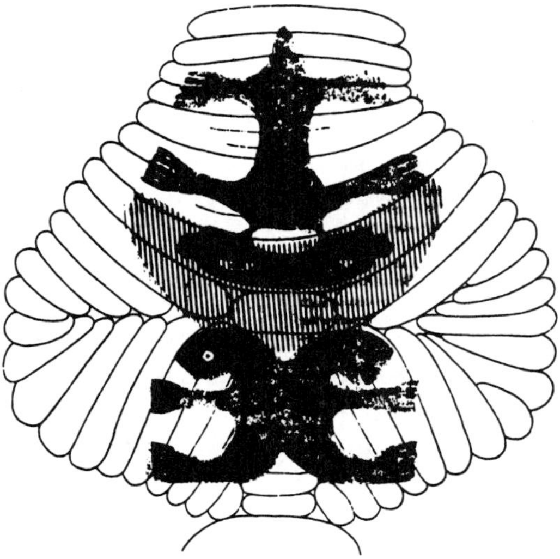

Fig. 4–2. "Homunculi" or projection areas show localization of function in the cerebellum. They show some correspondence to similar projection areas of the cerebrum. Stimuli from the sense organs of touch and from the "proprioceptive endings" that monitor muscle behavior are projected both on the upside-down figure at top and on the partially split figure at bottom. Another projection area, which differs from these in not resembling the body shape, is indicated by the shaded area (*center*). Here auditory and visual stimuli are received. From Snider (1958).

The cerebellar multi-sensory and motor projection areas found by Snider 1958) in the cat are shown in Fig. 4–2—clearly demonstrating the resemblance of this sensory-motor topographic "map" to that neurophysiologically known to exist in the sensory and motor cortical projection areas with which it is interconnected. The reverberating circuits linking the cerebellum to the sensory nerves which connect tactile, visual, proprioceptive, and auditory sense organs to the cerebellum are shown in Fig. 4–3. With this data and summarizing diagram it may readily be seen that a cerebellar (and/or related vestibular) dysfunction may result in a spectrum of tactile, visual, proprioceptive, and auditory sequencing, integrating, and coordinational disturbances. As a result of this panoramic c-v sensory-motor, functional conceptualization, the total dyslexic nuclear symptomatic complex as well as its resulting pseudo-cortical and compensatory functioning became readily understandable.

The Overactivity-Distractability Syndrome

Utilizing a handful of facts, fantasies and analogies, the author attempted to derive hypothetically the somatic basis of both the overactivity-distractability syndrome found characterizing approximately one-fourth to one-third of the dyslexic children and the hyperactivity-distractability syndrome which was only atypically present in referred c-v dyslexics.

The search for a c-v somatic root to the overactivity-distractability syndrome was triggered by the unexpectedly favorable response of these symptoms to anti-motion-sickness medications and antihistamines. Inasmuch as

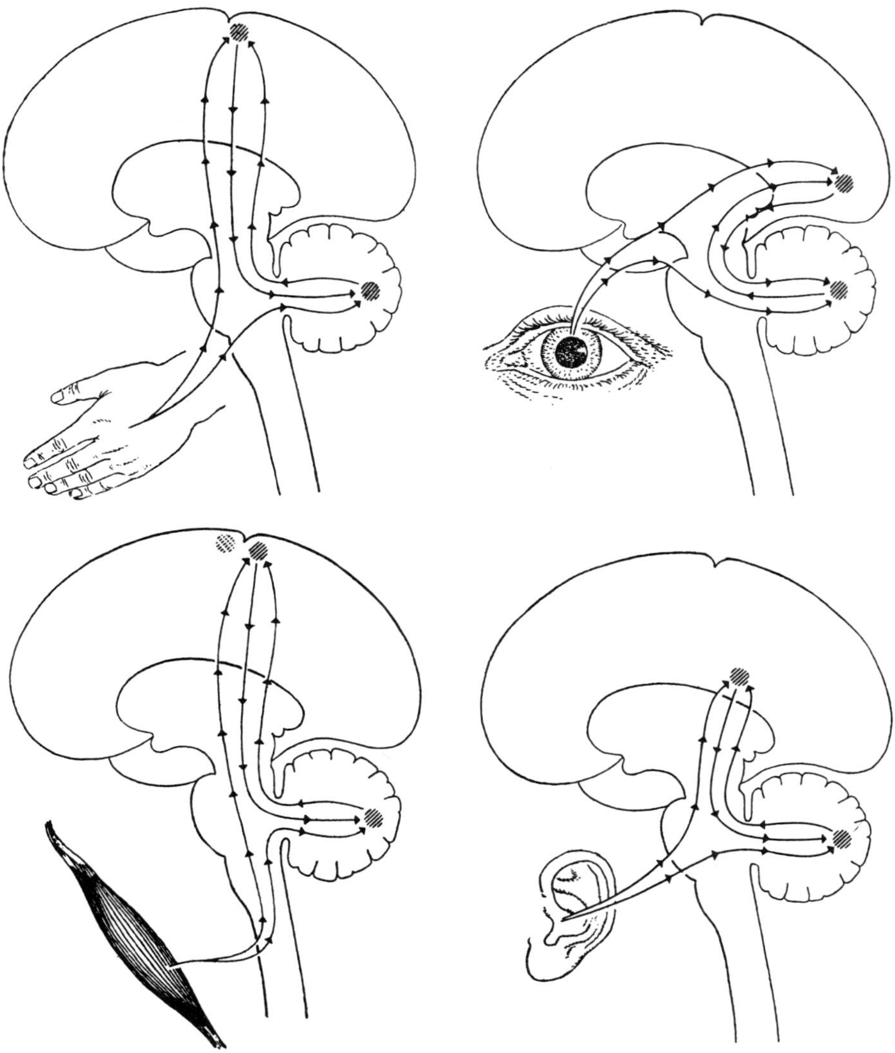

Fig. 4–3. The tactile, visual, proprioceptive, and auditory reverberating circuits linking the various sense organs to the cerebellum. From Snider (1958).

this syndrome improved with the use of medications the author postulated would improve cerebellar inhibitory capacity, it seems reasonable to further assume that overactivity and distractability were due to some selective failure in cerebellar inhibition. Because overactivity and distractability were not invariably clinically fused, it seemed likely that two related cerebellar mechanisms were involved—one resulting in overactivity and the other in distractability.

Since overactivity and hyperactivity appeared to resemble the motor restlessness characterizing extrapyramidal reactions, and because diphenhydramine (Benadryl), an antihistamine, was found to be helpful in neutralizing both phenothiazine-related extrapyramidal overactivity symptoms and c-v-related dyslexic symptoms, it appeared reasonable to assume that a cerebellar inhibitory failure in properly modulating basal ganglia functioning may result in the release of overactivity and anxiety-like impulsivity. In view of the fact that the frontal cerebral cortex is in a feedback relationship with the extrapyramidal system analogous to that of the cerebellum, and inasmuch as the cerebral cortex exerts a major inhibitory and modulating role over basal ganglia functions, it seemed equally plausible to assume that a failure in cerebral–basal ganglia (and cerebellar–basal ganglia) inhibition may result in true hyperkinesis, and furthermore, that methylphenidate hydrochloride (Ritalin) and cortical stimulants facilitate cerebral–basal ganglia inhibition and control.

Neurophysiologically derived inattention or distractability was assumed to be due to a dysfunction within or in relationship to Magoun's (1952, 1963) mesencephalic alerting system (Laufer, 1957). Once again, this alerting system was found to have feedback circuits both to the new brain (cerebral cortex) and to the old brain (cerebellum), leading to the assumptions (1) that a primary cortical and/or c-v dysfunction may result in a secondary failure in mesencephalic alerting and/or impairment in selective background inhibitory mechanisms; and (2) that the CNS stimulants facilitate

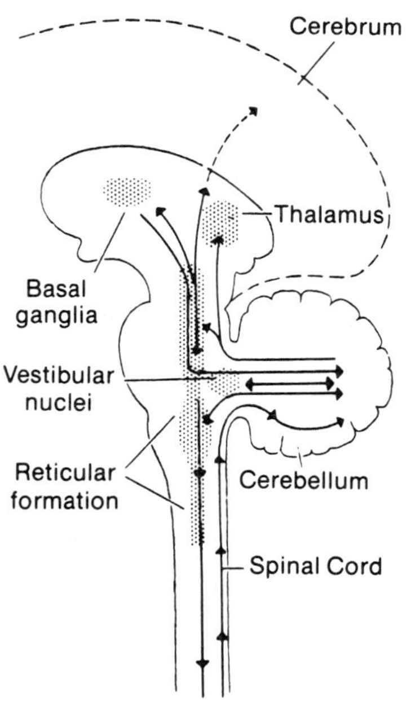

Fig. 4–4. The reverberating circuits linking the cerebellum with the various structures or organs of the brain. From Snider (1958).

both cerebral–mesencephalic and cerebellar–mesencephalic inhibitory capacity.

Because catastrophic and other forms of anxiety were found to trigger, intensify, and/or complicate this syndrome, the role of anxiety in this syndrome required careful etiologic dissection, analysis, and selective treatment. Figure 4–4 illustrates the feedback relationship existing between the cerebellum and related CNS structural and functional systems, and provides the neurophysiologic basis and substrate for these hypotheses and clinical observations.

5 Validation of the Dyslexic Reading Hypothesis: The Staten Island Study

According to the dyslexic reading hypothesis, dyslexic individuals scrambled letters and words because of the presence of a subclinical nystagmus and a related ocular fixation/sequential tracking dysfunction. As a result of this hypothesis, the author postulated that upon optokinetic testing, dyslexics would manifest a statistically significant reduction in tracking capacity when compared to normal controls. The purpose of this study was to measure the c-v-induced ocular fixation and sequential scanning functions in both c-v dyslexic and normal control groups—and thus test the validity of this reading hypothesis.

Theoretical Considerations

The author had assumed the ocular fixation/sequential scanning dysfunction in c-v or dysmetric dyslexia (DD) to be analogous to the tracking difficulty one might normally have experienced while attempting to read a signboard from the window of a rapidly moving train. The "need to see" the signboard will trigger the release of an optokinetic tracking response so that the optical fixation point is maintained and clear vision is preserved. As the train accelerates, a speed is reached at which the physiologic tracking capacity is exceeded, the optical fixation point is lost, and the visual sequence is scrambled or blurred. At this scrambling or blurring point, the author hypothesized, DD has been experimentally and/or physiologically provoked.

The author postulated that if a series of dyslexic and normal individuals seated in an accelerating train were instructed to watch a stationary signpost, the signpost would appear blurred at significantly reduced train speeds for the c-v-impaired dyslexics when compared to normal controls—demonstrating their reduced fixation and tracking capacity. In other words, to maintain stable visual targeting and sequencing of the signpost, the rate of the tracking, optokinetic or "rail-road" nystagmus induced by the accelerating train was reasoned to be proportional to the train's speed. Moreover, it appeared reasonable to further assume that at the blurring-speed endpoint, the maximum induced tracking capacity (MITC) had been exceeded. Inasmuch as blurring speeds were thus assumed to be a quantitatively measurable indicator and parameter of MITC, and since it was postulated that the tracking capacity in dyslexia was reduced, the experimental presence of significantly reduced blurring speeds (MITC) in dyslexic individuals as compared with normal controls would demonstrate the validity of the c-v dyslexic reading hypothesis (Frank and Levinson, 1975–6).

Methodology

Utilizing an analogous experimental and theoretical model, the author designed a 3D optical scanner (Fig. 5–1) capable of simultaneously beaming and recording the speed of independently moving foreground and background visual patterns while the patient sat still. Three measurements were recorded:

Mode I. A foreground consisting of black lettered words and phrases was speeded up against a blank neutral background until blurring was reported by the observer and the "blurring speed" for Mode I was recorded (Fig. 5–2).

Mode II. The same foreground was speeded up against a fixed scenic background and once again the "blurring speed" was recorded (Fig. 5–3).

Mode III. The observer was instructed to fixate the stationary foreground consisting of words, while the scenic background was set in motion. The presence or absence of foreground movement and/or blurring was recorded (Fig. 5–4).

In addition, ocular-motor tracking patterns were obtained during Modes I, II and III in order to help assess blurring and DD neurophysiologically. This data will be presented in Chapter 9.

All blurring-speed testing was performed after visual acuity was ascertained to be 20/20 by means of a Snellen chart and/or school report. The subjects were seated 60 inches away from the screen in an artificially semi-lit room, and told that words were going to be speeded up and move faster and faster until they would become hard to see, foggy, unclear, fuzzy, or blurry: "You don't have to read the words. Just look at them and raise your hand as soon as the words get blurry, or hard to see, or fuzzy, and put your hand down as soon as the letters and words become clear again"*

* In individuals with 20/20 vision, there appeared to exist no significant difference in blurring speeds for right, left, and both eyes. As a result, all future testing utilized coordinated bilateral vision.

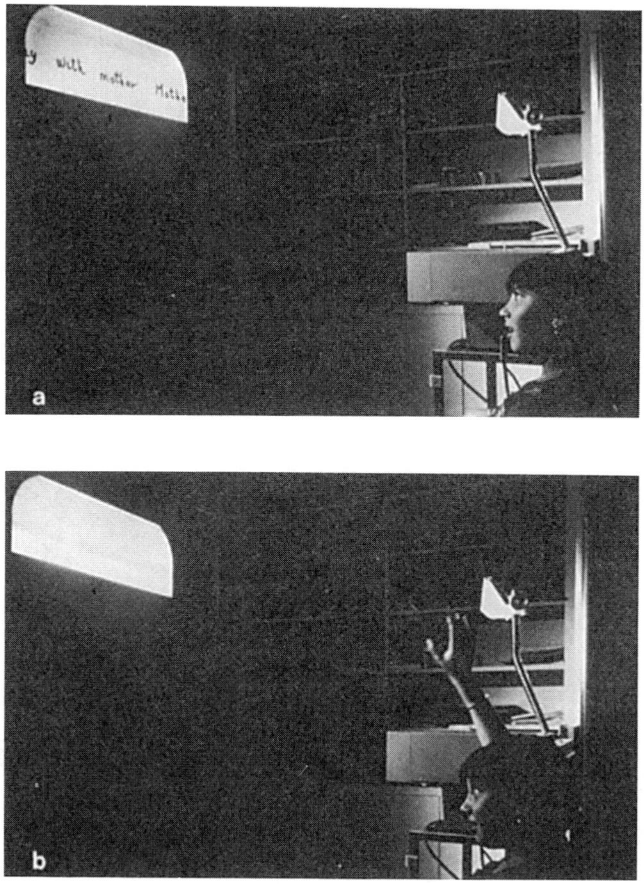

Fig. 5–1. (*a*) A subject watching the moving sequence of words projected by the 3D optical scanner. (*b*) The subject raising her hand upon experiencing the moving word sequence as blurred.

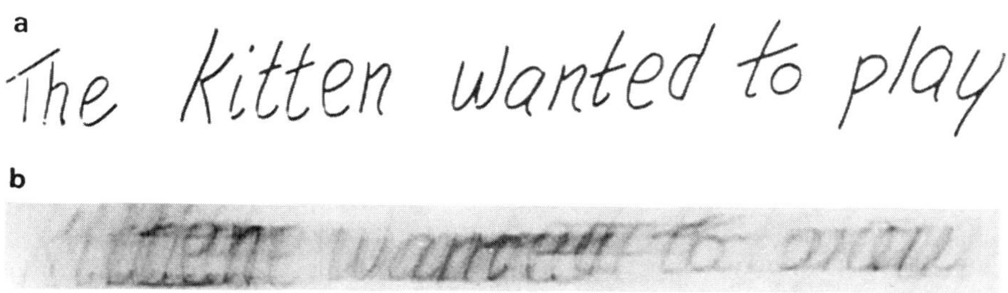

Fig. 5–2. (*a*) A moving sentence foreground and a stationary blank background (Mode I). (*b*) The Mode I blurring-speed endpoint.

a
b

Fig. 5–3. (*a*) A moving sentence foreground identical to Mode I and a stationary colored scenic farm background (Mode II). (*b*) The Mode II blurring-speed endpoint.

(Fig. 5–1). The words and phrases were then speeded up in trial runs from right to left and left to right until the examiner felt convinced that the subject knew what blurring meant.

During these trial runs, the words and sentences were speeded up to above the blurring-speed and then slowed down to the "recognition speed" until there appeared to be a consistent and cooperative response and a positive attitude. The Mode I and II blurring speeds were then recorded

Fig. 5–4. (*a*) A stationary sentence foreground and a moving colored scenic background identical to Mode II (Mode III). (*b*) The Mode III blurring speed endpoint.

for the words and sentences moving from right to left.* For Mode III, the scenic background was set in motion first from left to right and then right to left while the observer was told, "Look at the words and raise your hand

* Right- and left-moving blurring speeds were statistically found to be equal. As a result, blurring speeds were arbitrarily measured from right to left. Inasmuch as *blurring* and *recognition* speeds appeared to be separated by only approximately 0.2 feet per second at the blurring–recognition speed endpoint, and in view of the fact that 0.2 feet per second was found to be diagnostically insignificant, the author assumed that blurring speed = recognition speed.

if they get hard to see or blurry, or if they move." In addition, the size and spacing of the Mode III sentence foreground were sequentially reduced in stages until reaching "footnote" proportions, and each stage was tested for foreground movement and blurring. Foreground movement and/or blurring were reported as Mode III positive. In this study the author did not distinguish Mode III positive foreground movement from Mode III positive foreground blurring.

Sample

Modes I, II, and II blurring-speed data were obtained from a sample of 182 individuals divided into *c-v dyslexic, normal* and *random categories,* and 10 subgroups.

Category Description

The c-v dyslexic population was comprised of c-v abnormal and reading score deficient individuals (Groups 1 and 2) as well as a learning disability first-grade class (Group 3). The *"normal control population"* was comprised of c-v normal and reading-score normal individuals (Groups 9 and 10). The *random sample population* consisted of a c-v and reading-score nonselected sample of nursery school, kindergarten, first-, and second-grade children (Groups 4, 5, 6, 7 and 8).

Group Description

DD Groups. Groups 1 and 2 consisted of 58 children diagnosed as dyslexic on the basis of their poor reading performance and c-v signs and symptoms. Group 1 consisted of 43 dyslexics under age 10 (mean age, 7.8), and Group 2 consisted of 15 dyslexic individuals above age 10 (mean age, 13).* All DD children in Group 1 were English-speaking, with average to above-average I.Q., attending the lower grades in the New York City School System on Staten Island. They were from a low–middle-income mixed racial grouping. The older DD individuals in Group 2 represent a mixture of New York City School children from Staten Island and private practice. Group 3 consisted of a first-grade learning disability class with 18 children whose mean age was 7.4.

Random Sample Groups. Group 4 consisted of a normal private nursery-kindergarten class and Groups 5, 6, 7 and 8 comprised classes tested from one integrated New York City Public School on Staten Island. Group 4 consisted of a nursery-kindergarten class of 21 children whose mean age

* The DD children in this study were separated into Groups 1 and 2 according to age when it became apparent to the author that the dysmetric dyslexics' Mode I word-blurring speeds significantly improved with age and approached normal by 10–12 years of age. This blurring speed age separation was retrospectively recognized to be in error and based on selective sampling.

was 5.3. These children attended a private school and were derived from a middle-income population. Group 5 consisted of a kindergarten class with 24 children whose mean age was 5.8. Group 6 consisted of a first-grade class with 29 children whose mean age was 7.0. Group 7 consisted of a second-grade class in which 9 children were tested and whose mean age was 8.2. Group 8 consisted of a second-grade class with 17 children whose mean age was 8.0.

Control Groups. Groups 9 and 10 consisted of individuals derived from middle-income populations who were neuropsychologically examined and found to have normal or superior reading ability and normal c-v functioning. Group 9 consisted of 15 children whose mean age was 8.7. Group 10 consisted of 26 individuals whose mean age was 40.*

Statistical Methods and Analysis

In an attempt to minimize the confusion which statistics and their presentation often provoke, the author decided to summarize the results of the blurring-speed data analysis before specifically documenting them. In addition, all blurring-speed data found "distracting" were omitted so that the statistical foreground might remain uncluttered and free of "background noise." Hopefully, this dyslexic-like compensatory reading technique will provide the reader with the panoramic overview required to fixate and comprehend better the significance of both the statistical foreground and background.

A Statistical Overview

As a result of this study of blurring speeds:

1. Young dyslexics were found to have a statistically significant reduction in Modes I and II blurring speeds and to be statistically Mode III positive when compared to normal controls—demonstrating an impaired ocular fixation and sequential tracking capacity.
2. Dyslexics were found to demonstrate significantly improved Modes I, II, and III blurring-speed scores as a function of age—suggesting the existence of blurring-speed compensation.

* A word of explanation is in order. The author, in representing the Bureau of Child Guidance, had a purely service function to perform and had no time or authority to clinically examine normal children or adults within the New York City School System. As a result, only the preschool nursery-kindergarten class and the normal controls were privately examined and exact group matching thus was knowingly compromised. Furthermore because of the author's purely service function, it was not possible to administer independent neurologic examinations, ENGs and blurring speeds to all dysmetric dyslexics on the one hand and normal school children on the other.

3. The blurring-speed determinations for the Modes I and II visual gestalts were found to be reproducible to within 0.2 feet per second per patient, and significantly distinct from one another—suggesting that blurring speeds are a function of visual gestalt.

4. The low blurring-speed incidence of dyslexia in the random sample was reasoned to be approximately 10%–15%.

5. Blurring speeds were found to be statistically independent of sex in both normal and dyslexic groups—suggesting that sex is an independent DD variable.

Statistical Analysis and Results

The Mode I and Mode II data for the ten groups tested were analyzed by a one-way analysis of variance, and statistical comparisons were made among the various mean blurring speeds by a Tukey's Test. The resulting statistical means, standard deviations, and relationships for the Mode I and Mode II data are illustrated by Figs. 5–5 and 5–6, respectively. The Mode III data for the ten groups was analyzed by chi square and the results illustrated by Figure 5–7.

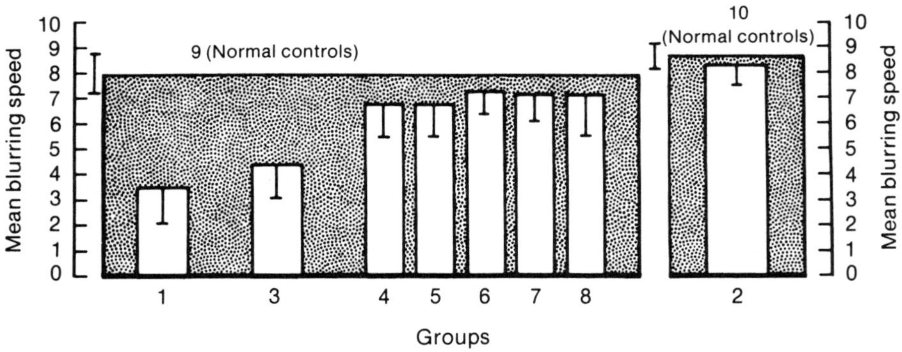

Fig. 5–5. The mean word Mode I blurring speeds and standard deviations for Groups 1–8, and corresponding blurring-speed means and standard deviations of the normal control Groups 9 and 10. The blurring speeds of the younger dyslexics (Group 1) and the learning disability first-grade class (Group 2) are significantly lower than those of the matched controls (Group 9). Interestingly enough, the blurring speed mean of the older dyslexics (Group 2) was not significantly different than that of the background normal controls (Group 10). The mean blurring speeds of random Groups 4–8 are significantly lower than those of the normal controls (Group 9), and the blurring speed difference between the random Groups 4–8 and the control Group 9 represents the presence and incidence of dyslexia in the random sample.

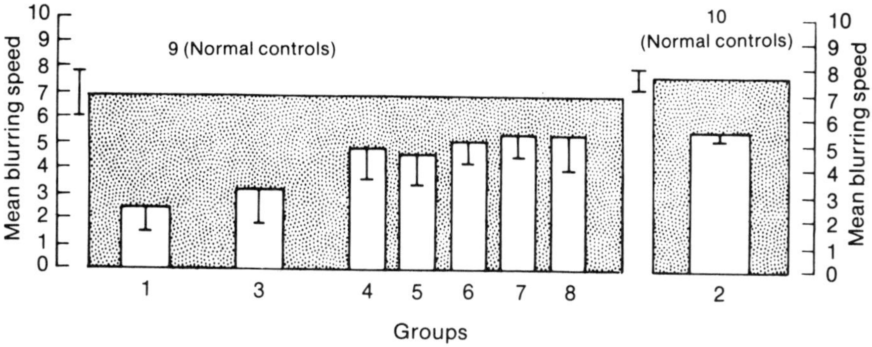

Fig. 5–6. The mean word Mode II blurring speeds and standard deviations for Groups 1–8, with corresponding blurring-speed means and standard deviations of the normal control Groups 9 and 10. The blurring-speed means of Groups 1–8 are significantly lower than those of the matched control Groups 9 and 10. The difference between the mean blurring speeds of random groups 4–8 and the background mean blurring speed of normal control Group 9 reflects the blurring speed incidence of dyslexia within the random groups.

Mode I Statistics (Fig. 5–5)

Young dyslexic children (Group 1) have a statistically significant ($p < 0.001$) lower Mode I mean blurring speed than matched controls (Group 9), substantiating the existence of a tracking dysfunction in dyslexia. The learning-disability first-grade class (Group 3) has a significantly lower Mode I mean blurring speed than random (Groups 4–8), control (Group 9), and older dyslexic (Group 2) samples ($p < 0.001$), suggesting that c-v dyslexics comprise a majority of individuals in this unselected reading-disabled sample. Older dyslexic individuals (Group 2) have a mean Mode I blurring speed which is not significantly lower than matched controls (Group 10), suggesting the conceptualization of Mode I blurring speed compensation as a function of age. The mean Mode I blurring speed for each of Groups 1–10 was found to be significantly ($p < 0.01$) higher than the corresponding mean Mode II blurring speed. In addition, for any given subject and Mode I or II word gestalt, the blurring speed was found to be reproducible to within 0.2–0.5 feet per second at any given trial date. This data tended to further support the evidence suggesting that blurring speed is a function of visual gestalt.

Mode II Statistics (Fig. 5–6)

Young dyslexic children (Group 1) have a significantly lower ($p < 0.0001$) Mode II mean blurring speed than controls (Group 9). The learning-disability first-grade class (Group 3) has a significantly lower ($p < 0.0001$) Mode II mean blurring speed than the control (Group 9) and random sam-

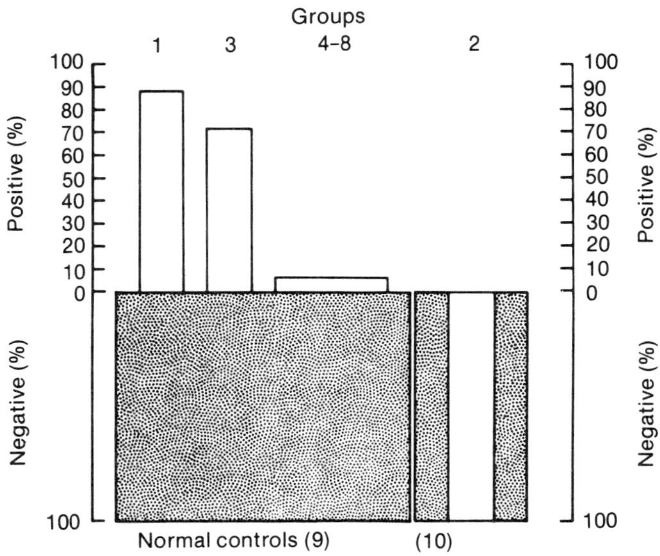

Fig. 5-7. The incidence of Mode III positive in Groups 1-8. The incidence of Mode III positive is highest in the young dyslexic Group 1 and the learning-disability first-grade class (Group 3). The incidence of Mode III positive in random Groups 4-8 reflects the incidence of dyslexia within these categories. Normal control Groups 9 and 10, as well as the older dyslexic Group 2, were 100% Mode III negative.

ple (Groups 4–8). Older dyslexic individuals (Group 2) have a significantly lower ($p < 0.01$) Mode II mean blurring speed than controls (Group 10), suggesting the fascinating possibility that Mode II may be compensated for less than and/or independently of Mode I.

Mode III Statistics (Fig. 5–7)

Young dyslexics in Group 1 are significantly Mode III positive when compared to matched controls in Group 9 ($p < 0.0001$), suggesting the existence of an ocular fixation dysfunction or instability in dyslexia. The learning-disability first-grade class (Group 3) is significantly Mode III positive when compared to control, random, and older dyslexic groups ($p < 0.0001$), lending even further support to the possibility that a significant number of dyslexics might comprise this unselected reading disabled group. Older dyslexic Group 2 individuals were all Mode III negative, clearly suggesting that Mode III positive may be converted to Mode III negative with age (Mode III compensation).

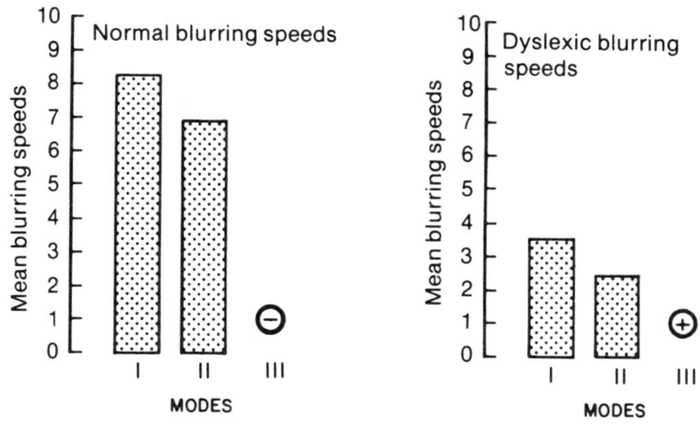

Fig. 5–8. The statistical Modes I, II, and III blurring-speed rule for normal and dyslexic groups in the Staten Island study. The Mode I blurring speed is greater than the corresponding Mode II blurring speed for both normal and dyslexic groups, whereas Mode III is negative for normal groups and is likely to be positive only for younger dyslexics.

The Statistically Derived Blurring-Speed Rule

A statistical analysis of the Modes I, II, and III blurring-speed data clearly revealed a significant correlation of reduced Modes I and II blurring speeds and Mode III positive with young dyslexic groups. The statistically derived blurring-speed rule for normal and dyslexic individuals may be illustrated by Fig. 5–8. In addition, when the dyslexic and control blurring-speed scores were combined, there resulted a clearly bi-modal blurring-speed distribution which seemed "typical."

Exceptions

As one might easily have imagined, the dynamic holistic conceptualization of DD could not be simply measured, and even meaningfully understood, by any one of its parameters alone. Numerous blurring-speed exceptions to the statistical rule appeared in this and later studies and are worthy of mention, especially as their investigation and understanding ultimately led to an immeasurably deeper and greater understanding of DD as well as the statistical blurring-speed rule itself.

DD individuals were found to have various "typical" and "atypical" combinations of Modes I, II, and III: (1) normal Modes I, II, and III; (2) normal Modes I and II, and abnormal Mode III; and (3) normal Mode I, and abnormal Modes II and III. Although these blurring-speed exceptions are

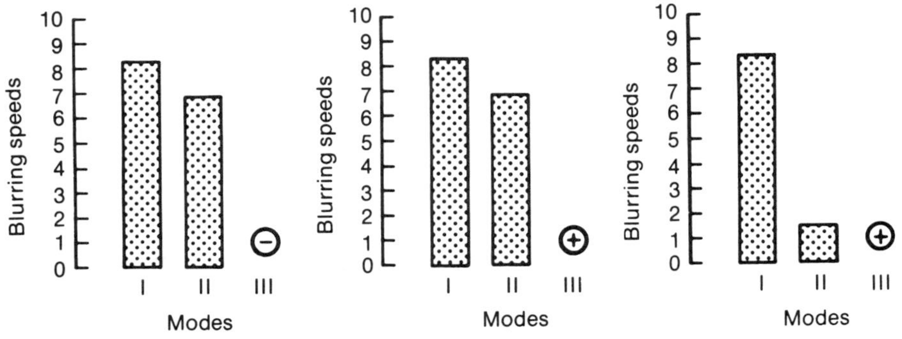

Fig. 5–9. The dyslexic exceptions to the statistical blurring-speed rule in the Staten Island study. Dyslexics may demonstrate normal Mode I, II, and III values, normal Mode I and II with Mode III positive, or normal Mode I with dyslexic Mode II and Mode III positive.

readily illustrated by Fig. 5–9, their underlying determinants remained either highly speculative or completely unknown.

The Incidence of Cerebellar-Vestibular Dysfunction and Dyslexia as Determined by Blurring-Speed Testing

Of 96 children in the random sample (Groups 4–8), 7 were found to have significantly decreased blurring speeds ($p < 0.001$) and c-v signs when examined neurologically. Since some first graders and first-grade holdovers with severe learning difficulties had been placed in the learning-disability first-grade class (Group 3) prior to screening, it was reasoned that the incidence of c-v dysfunction and dysmetric dyslexia as measured by blurring speeds in this population would be higher than 7%—most probably closer to 10%–15%—especially as children with statistically uncertain blurring speeds were not counted. Two of the 7 children with decreased blurring speeds and c-v dysfunction were described as "normal readers" by their teachers. The significance of this initially atypical, unpredictable, and bewildering finding was ignored until scientific necessity demanded its recognition and explanation several years later.

Blurring Speed as a Function of Age

Word Mode I and II blurring speeds increased with age for both normal and dyslexic individuals, whereas Mode III was found to be positive for only young dyslexic individuals, and its incidence dropped sharply with increasing age. In addition, the dyslexic blurring speeds were noted to increase more sharply with age than did the corresponding blurring speeds

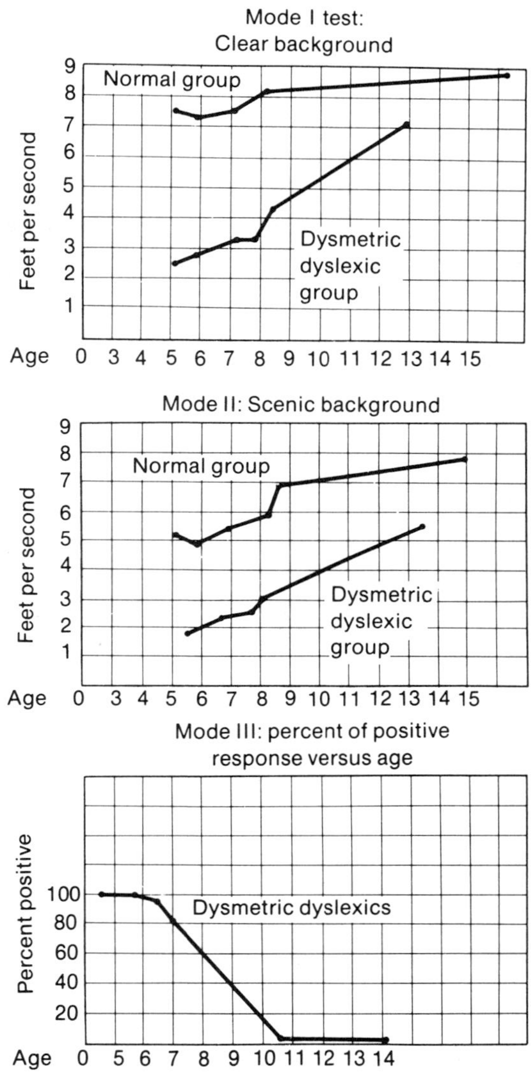

Fig. 5–10. The manner in which both normal and dyslexic Modes I, II, and III blurring speeds are functions of age. As noted, both normal and dyslexic Modes I and II blurring speeds increase with age. According to this data the dyslexic Mode I scores increase with age to a more significant extent than do the corresponding Mode II scores. In addition, Mode III positive changes to Mode III negative rapidly with age—clearly suggesting the concept of blurring-speed compensation.

for normal individuals. This age–blurring-speed relationship is demonstrated for Modes I, II, and III by Figure 5–10, and tended to portray the author's conceptualization of *blurring-speed compensation.*

Male/Female Blurring-Speed Statistics

In an attempt to study the possible role of sex in dyslexia, the male/female Mode I and II blurring-speed means were determined for both dyslexics and normal controls. As illustrated by Fig. 5–11, there exist no significant

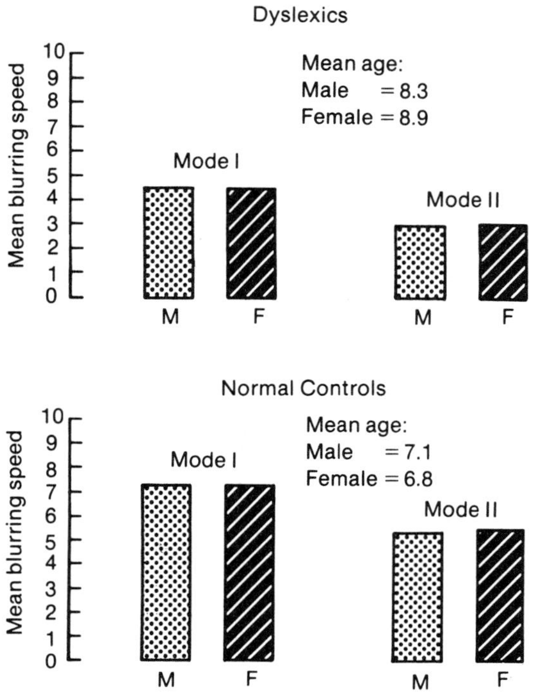

Fig. 5–11. The mean Modes I and II blurring speeds for both dyslexic and normal control categories. No significant difference exists between male and female blurring speeds for dyslexic and normal groups.

male/female differences in blurring speeds among dyslexics and normal controls.

Blurring Speed as a Function of Stimulus Gestalt

Analysis of the blurring-speed data revealed that the Mode I blurring speeds were consistently and significantly higher than the corresponding Mode II blurring speeds ($p < 0.01$). Furthermore, for any one testing and subject, the blurring speeds corresponding to any given Mode I or II visual gestalt were found to be reproducible to within 0.2 feet per second. These findings suggested the existence of stimulus-specific tracking and/or processing circuits. Moreover, since there existed a statistically determined specific and reproducible blurring-speed or tracking circuit for each stimulus configuration, it appeared that the stimulus gestalt triggered and/or selected the c-v circuits tracking it. As a result of these findings, the c-v tracking circuits were assumed to function in a manner analogous to inbuilt release mechanisms (IRMs). In addition, the fact that Mode III positive may at times be converted to Mode III negative by merely changing the foreground visual pattern and/or the direction of the moving background provided additional support for the thesis that the c-v tracking circuits indeed function in a manner analogous to gestalt-specific IRMs.

Recognition Speed

In an attempt to ascertain the reliability of the blurring-speed endpoint, individuals tested were often asked to raise their hands as soon as blurring was experienced and to lower their hands as soon as recognition took place. This endpoint titration process was continued until the difference between blurring and recognition speeds was found to be insignificant and approximated 0.2 feet per second on successive trials. Blurring and recognition speeds were thus viewed as two sides to the same endpoint, and it was postulated that the reliability and application of the blurring-speed methodology could be significantly enhanced and simplified by measuring recognition speeds.

For example, if a series of ten different blurred or unrecognizable visual sequences are slowed down until recognition occurs then: (1) the probability that a subject will be able to guess all ten sequences correctly becomes infinitesimal; (2) confabulatory and/or statistically exceptional responses become readily apparent; (3) the need for the child to understand "blurring" is side-stepped, as are the explanatory-interpretive errors; and (4) the recognition speed can readily be measured in very young children by merely asking them, "Tell me what you see as soon as you see it." As a result of this reasoning, a new experiment utilizing a modified 3D optical scanner was planned, in which recognition speeds would be utilized.

Proof of a Subclinical Nystagmus in Dyslexia

The assumption of a subclinical nystagmus underlying the c-v dyslexic reading errors was originally prompted by the attempt to reconcile seemingly paradoxical clinical data: although the high incidence of visual fixation and tracking errors characterizing the dyslexic reading process appeared pathophysiologically consistent with the scrambling effects of a c-v-induced nystagmus, no neurologic evidence of a clinical nystagmus was statistically detectable in the retrospective, prospective and blind neurologic studies. The author was forced to assume that either the dyslexic reading errors were unrelated to a c-v nystagmus or that these errors were due to a clinically compensated but subclinically active nystagmus. The latter assumption was supported by the evidence derived from Joan's clinical case study, as well as the "blind" ENG data contained in the prospective study.

Joan's case provided clear-cut neurophysiologic correlations between position- and direction-dependent clinical nystagmus and c-v dyslexic symptomatology. As a result of the neurodynamic analysis of Joan's case, the author could more definitively assume that if clinical c-v nystagmus may result in dyslexic reading symptoms, then a c-v-determined subclinical nystagmus might result in similar reading symptomatology.

In addition, the analysis of the "blind" ENG data revealed that of 70 dyslexic children completing blind ENG examinations, 20% were reported to have spontaneous and/or positional forms of a subclinical or ENG-detectable nystagmus. Thus, by means of the increased recording sensitivity of ENG, as well as the special "eyes-closed" and positional techniques for triggering and/or provoking destabilization of the motor gestalt, the incidence of detectable nystagmus in dyslexia was raised from approximately 0% in clinical neurologic studies to 20%. One can assume either that the remaining 80% of the ENG-tested c-v dyslexics have no subclinical nystagmus, or that all c-v dyslexics have a subclinical nystagmus but that present day ENG methodology can detect this nystagmus only 20% of the time.

The author assumed the existence of a subclinical nystagmus in all c-v dyslexics and designed a blurring-speed methodology enabling its detection and measurement. Interestingly enough, although the ENG technique was initially utilized to help standardize the blurring-speed methodology, this methodology was later utilized to re-standardize and modify the conventional ENG technique so that the resulting ENG parameters became more sensitive and reliable indicators of c-v dysfunction. As a result of these ENG modifications, the incidence of ENG-detectable subclinical nystagmus in dyslexia was raised from 20% to over 65%—lending significant support to the thesis that all c-v dyslexics have a subclinical nystagmus. The ENG technique also provided invaluable insight into the dynamic equilibrium existing between clinical and subclinical nystagmus. For example, calorically induced nystagmus is normally suppressed or inhibited upon the subject's opening his eyes (or during concentration), and may once again be released from inhibitory control upon the subject's closing his eyes. These ENG maneuvers clearly demonstrated the existence of dynamic, visually related CNS mechanisms rendering clinical nystagmus subclinical and vice versa.

Furthermore, visual fixation mechanisms were clinically recognized to suppress or minimize motion sickness and such vestibular-related responses as driving "phobias," whereas visual suppression during Romberg testing and sleep occasionally released or triggered vertiginous and/or disorienting reactions, and tended to provoke or intensify "phobic" anxiety responses. Dyslexics were found to be significantly prone to motion sickness, vertigo, and motion phobias only when seated in the back seat of a moving car, whereas these reactions were minimized or eliminated when they were seated up front and able to *see* where they were going. Similar reactions were noted in planes and other moving vehicles as well, and the specific c-v-related response often depended upon whether or not visual fixation and orientation were possible. These fascinating clinical observations further demonstrated the coexistence and dynamic equilibrium existing between subclinical c-v dysfunctioning (e.g., nystagmus) and compensatory mechanisms—contributing significant weight and insight to the developing

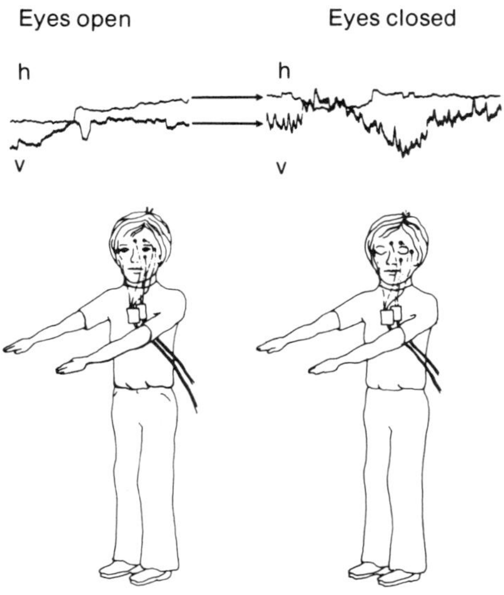

Fig. 5–12. Eyes-open and eyes-closed Romberg positional ENG testing. The clinical insight that eyes-closed Romberg testing produced phobia-related and vestibular symptomatology led to the addition of a Romberg position ENG testing parameter. During eyes-closed Romberg testing, ENG was able to demonstrate the triggering of a vertical positional nystagmus. This evidence not only supported the clinical observations, but added a crucial new ENG testing parameter to the developing ENG methodology.

conceptualization of a c-v-related subclinical nystagmus and dysfunction in dyslexia (Fig. 5–12). However, the blurring-speed methodology and data were needed to statistically validate these conceptualizations. To substantiate and measure the existence of a subclinical nystagmus in dyslexia, several assumptions were made.

If, indeed, there exists a subclinical nystagmus in c-v dyslexia, and if this nystagmus results in clinically apparent fixation, tracking, and processing (reading) errors, then this nystagmus is obviously active and maladaptive and will serve no positive visual tracking function. In other words, the subclinical nystagmus would most probably serve to scramble, and thus reduce, the maximum normal optokinetic tracking capacity, and result in significantly decreased blurring speeds.

By forcing a dyslexic to track visual targets to the maximum physiological limit—the blurring-speed endpoint—an adaptive optokinetic tracking nystagmus will be reflexly triggered and superimposed upon the assumed presence of a maladaptive subclinical nystagmus. The magnitude of the induced tracking nystagmus will be proportional to the speed of the moving target. Inasmuch as clinical or subclinical c-v nystagmus in dyslexia is assumed to serve no adaptive visual tracking function, the normal maximum physiological tracking capacity will be reduced in proportion to the degree or magnitude of the subclinical nystagmus. As a result, it was anticipated that blurring will be experienced and reported by dyslexics at significantly reduced stimulus or blurring speeds; and furthermore, that the magnitude of the subclinical nystagmus will equal the difference between the normal blurring speed and the dyslexic blurring speed.

Perhaps a simple analogy will be helpful in concretizing these formulations. If the normal maximum induced ocular tracking capacity (MITC) and rate is assumed to be 10 oscillations per second, and if this maximum tracking rate corresponds to a visual sequence moving at 10 feet per second, then the MITC or blurring speed may be conveniently expressed in terms of the easily measurable stimulus speed corresponding to blurring, i.e., 10 feet per second. If a c-v-determined and target-independent subclinical (or clinical) nystagmus triggers the eye to vibrate randomly at a rate of 6 oscillations per second, then the residual adaptive or optokinetic tracking capacity will be only (10 − 6 or) 4 oscillations per second, and will correspond to a stimulus or blurring speed of 4 feet per second, assuming tracking compensation has been minimal or technically eliminated.

According to this analogy, the magnitude or degree of the subclinical nystagmus may be conceptualized as proportional or equal to the normal blurring speed ($BS_n = 10$ feet per second) minus the dyslexic blurring speed ($BS_d = 4$ feet per second), or 6 feet per second.

Subclinical Nystagmus Versus Compensatory Tracking

Inasmuch as the blurring-speed methodology demonstrated that dyslexic blurring speeds are significantly below normal controls, the data within this study statistically verified the existence of a decreased optokinetic tracking capacitv or subclinical nystagmus in dyslexia, and added a new dimension to c-v testing and conceptualization. Moreover, since blurring-speed compensation was assumed to be responsible for Modes I and II blurring speeds approaching normal values in older dyslexics, it stood to reason that compensatory tracking mechanisms would have to be technically minimized in order to preserve the efficacy and diagnostic accuracy of the methodology.

Furthermore, since blurring-speed compensation had been demonstrated to be a function of age, it was anticipated that a significant correlation would exist between blurring-speed compensation on the one hand, and dyslexic "late blooming" and/or academic "spurting" on the other. This expectation, however, did not materialize. At times, blurring-speed compensation occurred without late, or even early, blooming and vice versa. This frustrating observation and its retrospective analysis forced the realization that the c-v-determined dyslexic disorder was far too complex to be measured and "tracked" by any one of its diagnostic parameters—for example, blurring speed.

In order to explain blurring-speed compensation without academic compensation and vice versa, as well as the other blurring-speed statistical exceptions, the author was forced to assume that function-specific and/or symptom-specific compensatory mechanisms were operative in c-v dyslexia. For example, if Modes I, II, and III may be independently compensated for, and if mode-specific compensatory functions are not invariably correlated to academic compensation in dyslexia, then the heretofore confusing blurring speed–dyslexic correlations become readily understandable and even expected. One has merely to assume that the dyslexic c-v neurophysiologic and symptomatic fallout is a vector resultant of opposing subclinical dysfunctioning versus specific compensatory forces. This conceptualization of mode-specific and function-specific compensation is then consistent with and could explain the dyslexic blurring-speed curves, which clearly reveal compensation to be greatest for Mode III, whereas Mode I compensation is greater than Mode II. In addition, the function-specific nature of c-v compensatory forces may explain the seemingly paradoxical data indicating that blurring-speed compensation may occur without academic compensation and vice versa.

Blurring-Speed Tracking Equations

The recognition that blurring-speed determinations were vector resultants of opposing and coexisting dysfunctioning versus compensatory tracking mechanisms led to an equation in which these neurophysiologic relationships could be mathematically expressed and illustrated:

$$\begin{aligned} \text{MITC} = \text{BS} = {} & f_i \text{ (normal inherent tracking capacity)} \\ & + \\ & f_2 \text{ (subclinical nystagmus or decreased optokinetic tracking capacity)} \\ & + \\ & f_3 \text{ (compensatory tracking capacity)} \end{aligned}$$

In formulating blurring-speed determinations as a vector summation of normal inherent tracking capacity and subclinical nystagmus versus compensatory tracking capacity, the author was able to encompass the total range of normal and dyslexic blurring speeds—including the statistical exceptions. In addition, according to this clinically derived tracking equation, it became theoretically possible to envision the coexistence of separate but functionally inter-related f_1, f_2, and f_3 tracking circuits.

Several years after formulating this equation, the author "accidentally" discovered the specific compensatory tracking mechanism responsible for a majority of dyslexic blurring-speed exceptions, as well as the Modes I and II compensated blurring speeds in older dyslexics. Elimination of this f_3 mechanism from the blurring speeds of several older Group 2 dyslexics still available for re-testing resulted in a dramatic reduction of blurring-speed values, and highlighted the continued subclinical existence of f_2 in older dyslexics.

If and when f_3 mechanisms can be technically and selectively eliminated from the blurring-speed determinations, so that f_3 approximates 0, then:

1. for c-v normal individuals, $f_2 = 0$ and $BS_n = f_1$
2. for dyslexic individuals, $f_2 < 0$ and $BS_d = f_1 + f_2$

In addition, f_2 can be determined by merely subtracting the dyslexic blurring speeds from matched normal control blurring speeds:

$$f_2 = BS_n - BS_d$$

Because blurring-speed compensation appeared to be significantly greater in dyslexics as compared to normal controls, the ability to selectively eliminate f_3 mechanisms and vectors from the determination of blurring speeds is anticipated to result in a more accurate diagnosis of dyslexia.

Summary

The Staten Island study and its data analysis has revealed a correlation of dyslexia with significantly reduced Modes I and II blurring speeds and Mode III positive. This correlation clearly demonstrated a primary ocular fixation and sequential scanning dysfunction in dyslexia, and thus statistically validated the c-v reading hypothesis in dyslexia. In addition, blurring speeds were found to be both stimulus- and age-dependent as well as independent of sex.

Although the 3D optical scanner and its blurring speed methodology was originally designed to test the c-v reading hypothesis of dyslexia, it was found most useful in diagnosing and predicting c-v dysfunction and dyslexia in young children.

Addendum

An Apparent Statistical Paradox

The gratification derived from the experimental and statistical validation of the c-v dyslexic reading hypothesis was short lived. An interested group of researchers came to New York in order to help develop and improve the 3D optical scanner and blurring-speed methodology. They had little experience with children and dyslexia, but were expert in electronic and statistical design. During their stay in New York, the results of the Staten Island and an additional parallel blurring-speed study were jointly analyzed and verified. In addition, a new 3D optical scanner was designed and a new Mode I, II, and III series of visual gestalt patterns was introduced and correlated to the Modes I, II, and III word gestalt utilized in the Staten Island study.

Upon returning to their home base, this group elected to run a "blind" blurring speed study attempting to duplicate the Staten Island results. The author did not participate in this study's design, implementation, or methodology.

The statistical results of this "blind" blurring-speed study appeared to contradict completely the data and formulations obtained from the Staten

Island and jointly performed parallel blurring-speed studies. The "blind" blurring-speed study sampled an elementary school population and reported:

1. A normal blurring-speed distribution rather than the anticipated completely bimodal distribution obtained in the Staten Island study.
2. A negative correlation of blurring speeds with reading scores and other batteries of psycho-educational test data given to reading-disabled children.
3. A negative correlation of Mode III positive and decreased Mode I and II blurring speeds.

A telephone conversation revealed only that (1) recognition speed endpoints were utilized; and (2) elephant and truck (Modes I, II and III) visual gestalts were utilized for testing. Word gestalts were omitted. How could this be? Did not the group performing this "blind" study duplicate the author's blurring-speed data in New York. What went wrong?

The author's first reaction was to blame the "blind" research team. (They really goofed up! What did they know about children and dyslexia anyway? They must have provoked the children into giving confabulatory responses.) But one comforting thought remained. The honesty, integrity, and dedication of the group was beyond reproach. Even if their findings were in error, their data pointed to inherent but unknown difficulties within the blurring-speed methodology and application; and an attempt was made to understand their data. This task was not easy, especially as the school population and research team were no longer available for a trial rerun.

The unexpected and scientifically devastating results of the "blind" blurring speed study forced the author to re-evaluate the Staten Island data, and attention was refocussed on the statistical exceptions recorded.

The End is Just Another Beginning

The statistical analysis of the Staten Island blurring-speed data validated the c-v dyslexic reading hypothesis, and a parallel pharmacologic study demonstrated the efficacy of motion-sickness medications in dyslexia. Thus the author's initial dyslexic research perspective appeared to be complete. However, the contradictory data introduced by the "blind" blurring-speed study forced a re-evaluation of the blurring-speed technique and the corresponding c-v dyslexic conceptualizations. As a result, the author's dyslexic research effort was off to a new beginning.

In an attempt to resolve the seemingly paradoxical blurring-speed data, the author initiated a series of sequential and parallel investigations. The Queens blurring-speed study (Chapter 6) verified and extended the Staten Island results. A clinical blurring-speed study of 300 c-v-abnormal dyslexic individuals (Chapter 8) not only verified the correlation of dyslexia and decreased blurring speeds, but highlighted the crucial role of compensatory mechanisms in dyslexia. These studies demonstrated two basic dyslexic "facts" to be *fictitious,* and catalyzed the expansion and harmonization of dyslexic theory with both typical and atypical clinical and experimental findings, eventually resulting in a successful classification of the ocular-motor (ENG) tracking patterns in dyslexia (Chapter 9) and a conceptualization of the c-v neurodynamic role of phobias and related mental symptoms (Chapter 12).

Three years after completing the initial unpublished version of this research effort, a "final" version was completed, encompassing new and previously unsuspected hidden dimensions of dyslexia, and resulting in a resolution of the paradoxical blurring-speed data and a panoramic perspective of dyslexia.

6 Blurring-Speed Distribution in a Kindergarten Population: The Queens Study

The Queens blurring-speed study was initiated in an attempt to both substantiate and enlarge the data base derived from the Staten Island study. The entire available kindergarten population (n = 1543) of District 26 in Queens was screened for DD utilizing a new and improved 3D optical scanner and a modified blurring-speed methodology.* The aims were multifold:

1. To determine the statistical Modes I and II blurring-speed distributions as a function of word and elephant visual gestalts—and thus attempt to substantiate the bimodal distribution obtained in the Staten Island study. Inasmuch as an *elephant* (Mode I and II) gestalt was added to a modified Staten Island *word* gestalt, there resulted four blurring speed determinations per patient (word Mode I, word Mode II, elephant Mode I and elephant Mode II).
2. To determine Mode III positive as a function of low blurring speeds and as a function of high or "normal" blurring speeds—and thus attempt to substantiate the prior Staten Island correlation of Mode III positive with low blurring speeds.
3. To determine a statistical low blurring-speed incidence of dyslexia, if possible.
4. To evaluate Modes I, II, and III as a function of sex.
5. To evaluate Modes I, II, and III as a function of handedness.
6. To determine and compare the blurring-speed distributions for additive combinations of the various blurring-speed modalities in an effort to improve the diagnostic accuracy of the methodology: (a) word Mode I and Mode II, (b) elephant Mode I and Mode II, (c) Mode I words and elephants, (d) Mode II words and elephants, (e) total word Modes I and II and elephant Modes I and II.
7. To screen out the low-blurring from the high-blurring (normal)

* The Queens Study was performed under the auspices of Mr. Marvin Weingart, District Superintendent of Schools.

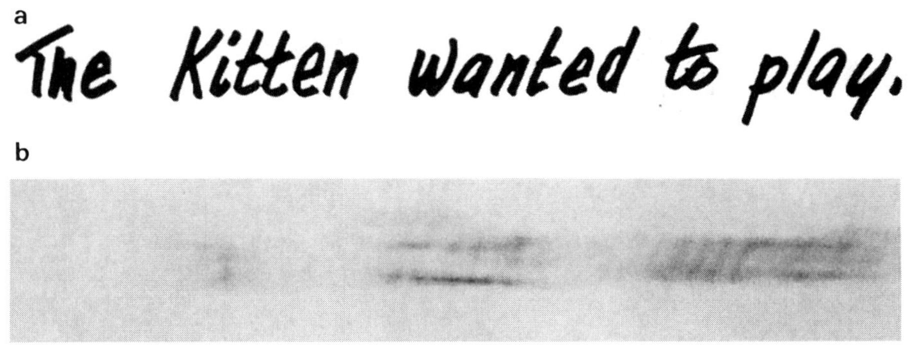

Fig. 6–1. (*a*) The new word Mode I gestalt and (*b*) its blurring-speed endpoint.

children so that more definitive diagnostic evaluation and follow-up studies could be performed on each of the two groups.

Future and follow-up studies will attempt to evaluate blurring speed as a function of (1) age; (2) socio-economic group; (3) ethnic group; (4) emotional background; (5) I.Q. (6) color gestalt; and (7) stimulus distance and angle.

Variations in the Blurring-Speed Methodology—Queens Versus Staten Island Studies

Modes I and II

The Queens blurring-speed study utilized a new 3D optical scanner (II), word gestalt and light intensity. The new word Mode I and II gestalts and their blurring-speed endpoints are illustrated in Figs. 6–1 and 6–2.

As a result of these changes, the Queens word Modes I and II blurring-speed scores were approximately 1–2 feet per second lower than corresponding scores obtained in the Staten Island study. The Queens study also introduced two additional visual gestalts and blurring-speed measurements: elephant Modes I and II. Elephant Mode I consisted of a series of black elephants moving against a blank background (Fig. 6–3a) until reaching a blurring-speed endpoint (Fig. 6–3b). Elephant Mode II contained a moving elephant foreground similar to Mode I and a background consisting of a stationary uniformly colored floral pattern instead of the colored farm scenery utilized in the Staten Island study (Fig. 6–4).

Mode III

The Queens Mode III foreground consisted of only one large, black elephant sequence equal in size, spacing, and saturation to the elephants in

Fig. 6–2. (*a*) The new word Mode II gestalt and (*b*) its blurring-speed endpoint.

Modes I and II. The Mode III background consisted of moving black oblique stripes resembling a picket fence instead of the moving colored scenic background utilized in the Staten Island study (Fig. 6–5).

In the Queens study, the author was primarily interested in determining the correlations of Mode III positive with low versus high blurring-speed populations, so that comparisons could be made with the Staten Island and "blind" Mode III positive correlations. As a result, the elephant Mode III foreground was not graded and tested according to size, spacing, and saturation. By simplifying the Mode III testing in this study, a significantly reduced percentage of Mode III positive is expected as compared with the Staten Island study, but this reduced incidence was not anticipated to effect the Mode III correlation.

Methodology and Procedure

All blurring-speed modes were demonstrated to each kindergarten class as a whole in order to minimize "anticipatory" anxiety. The children were in-

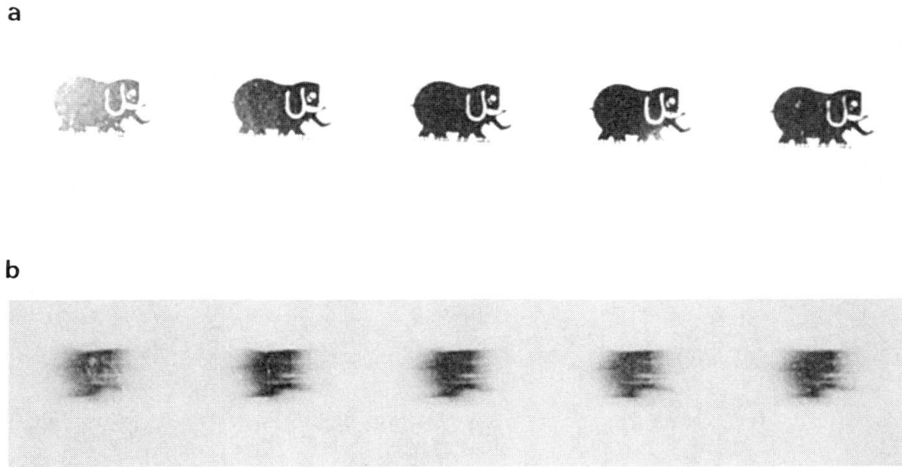

Fig. 6–3. (*a*) The new elephant Mode I gestalt and (*b*) its blurring-speed endpoint.

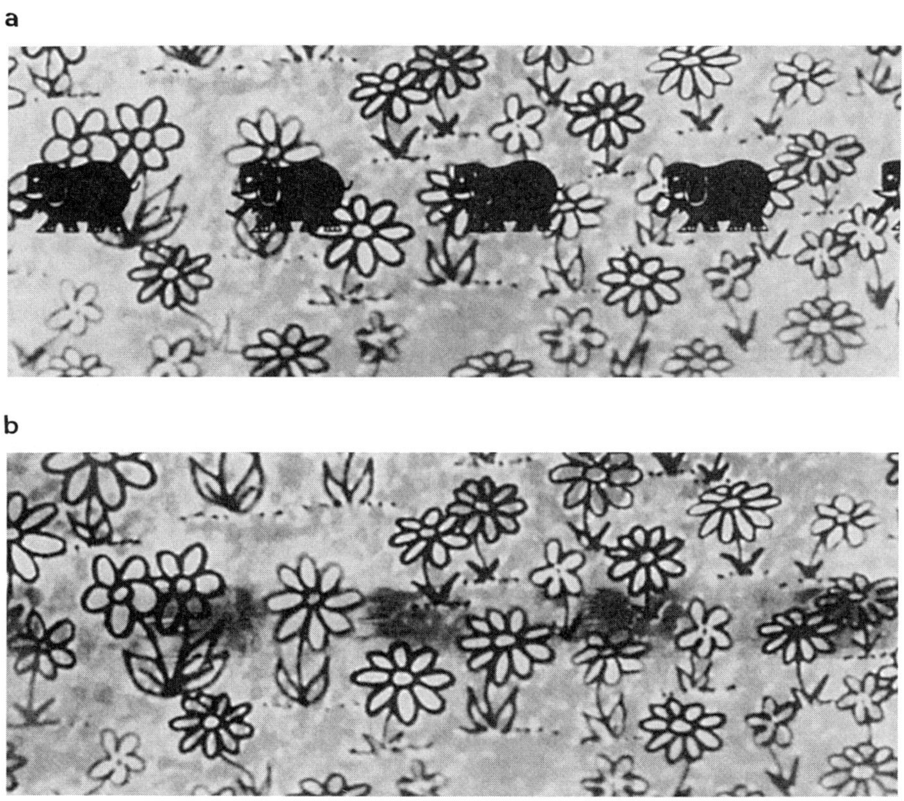

Fig. 6–4. (*a*) The new elephant Mode II gestalt and (*b*) its blurring-speed endpoint.

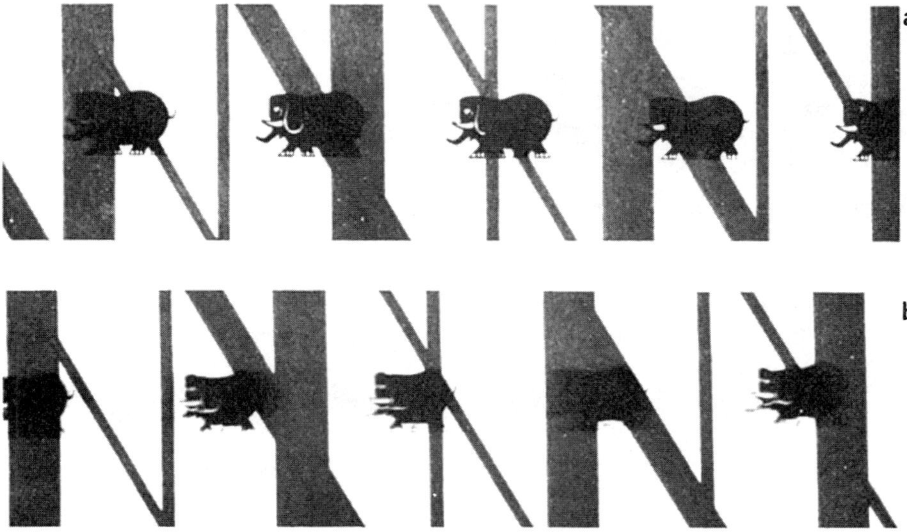

Fig. 6–5. (*a*) The new elephant Mode III gestalt and (*b*) Mode III positive endpoint.

structed to raise their hands as soon as they saw the moving elephants and words become "blurry," "foggy," "fuzzy," "unclear," "hard to see," "smokey," etc. (*blurring speed*) and to put their hands down as soon as the elephants and words became "clear" or "easy to see" again (*recognition speed*).

Children were selected from their class in alphabetical order and the elephant Mode I was utilized to re-demonstrate and re-explain blurry, fuzzy, foggy, unclear, etc. Once again each child was instructed to lower his or her hand as soon as the elephants became clear and easy to see again.

Following clearance and/or correction for 20/20 vision, the blurring-speed measurements were specifically obtained as follows. Elephant Mode I was initially recorded only when two successive repetitions were 0.2–0.5 feet per second apart and the instructions appeared to be reliably understood. Then elephant Mode II, word Mode I, word Mode II, and elephant Mode III were performed and recorded.

Sample

The 1543 kindergarten children tested were derived from primarily middle-income families. Their mean age was approximately 5 years and 9 months. There were 811 males and 732 females. Only 1031 of the entire kindergarten population were reported as either right- or left-handed by their kindergarten teachers; 512 were mistakenly omitted from this handedness classification. Eighty-eight percent (908/1031) were reported to be right-handed and 12% (123/1031) were reported to be left-handed. However, inasmuch as the criteria for deciding handedness was neither formalized nor standardized, and was left entirely to the teacher's observation and interpretation, the reported handedness data must be weighed accordingly.

Statistical Overview

In order to facilitate the presentation and assimilation of the data, the author will provide the reader with an initial statistical overview detailing and illustrating the specific data analysis. The statistical analysis of the data obtained from this sample revealed:

1. Blurring-speed distributions are bimodal regardless of the visual gestalt utilized.
2. Mode III positive is highly correlated to the low-blurring-speed population ($p < 0.0001$).
3. The low-blurring-speed incidence of dyslexia is approximately 15%–20%.
4. Modes I, II, and III are independent of sex and handedness.
5. Blurring speed is a function of visual gestalt.

In addition, predictability limits were obtained for the various blurring speeds and a "reliability index" was added to the evolving methodology so that improbable and/or unreliable data might be statistically detectable. The Queens Study thus verified the Staten Island statistical blurring-speed rule, and ultimately led to a solution to the paradoxical data.

Statistical Data Analysis

Any modal distribution or combination of modal distributions was statistically found to be non-normal, skewed towards lower blurring speeds, and leptokurvic or "spiked." The skewedness appeared to result from a combination of two or more distributions: one centered at a low blurring speed and one centered at a high blurring speed. For illustration and comparison purposes, only the word Mode I and the sum-of-all-modes (word Mode I + word Mode II + elephant Mode I + elephant Mode II) histograms and distributions will be presented and analyzed (Fig. 6–6).

Word Mode I and Sum-of-All-Modes Data

In assuming a bimodal distribution for the word Mode I and sum-of-all-modes blurring speeds, nonlinear least-squares was employed to estimate the incidence of male and female children in each of the low- and high-blurring-speed populations, and to determine their respective means and standard deviations. The statistically derived Mode I and sum-of-all-modes bimodal distributions are illustrated in Fig. 6–7.

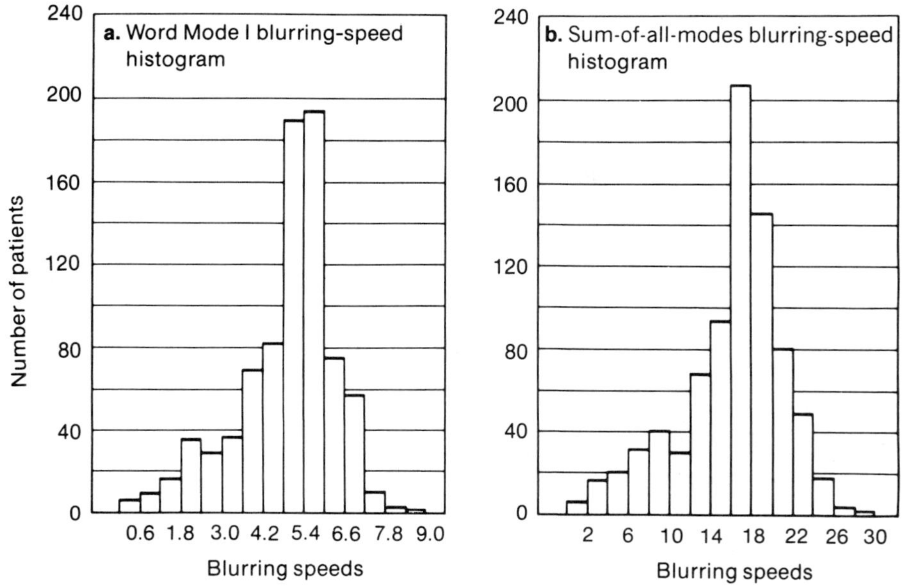

Fig. 6–6. The respective (*a*) word Mode I and (*b*) sum-of-all-modes histograms obtained from the Queens blurring-speed study. The histograms appear skewed towards lower blurring speeds and suggest a bimodal distribution.

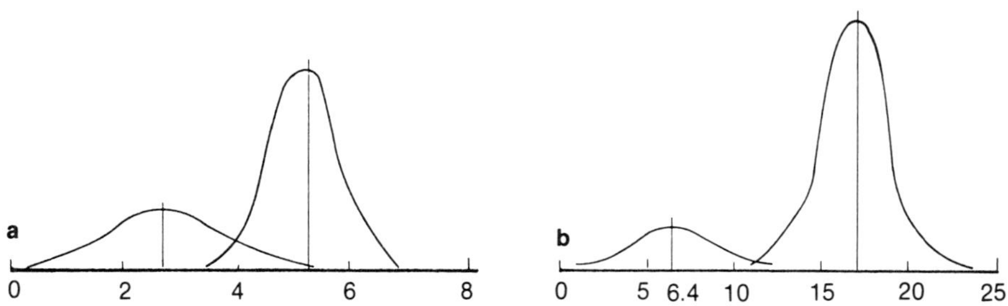

Fig. 6–7. The respective (*a*) word Mode I and (*b*) sum-of-all-modes bimodal distributions statistically obtained by utilizing nonlinear least squares.

Word Mode I Data

The male/female means, standard deviations, and incidence data for the word Mode I blurring-speed distribution are summarized and illustrated by Fig. 6–8. The low-blurring-speed mean (2.7 ft./sec.) is approximately half the high-blurring-speed mean (5.3 ft./sec.), the low-blurring-speed incidence is approximately 20%, and the data reveals no statistically significant male/female differences.

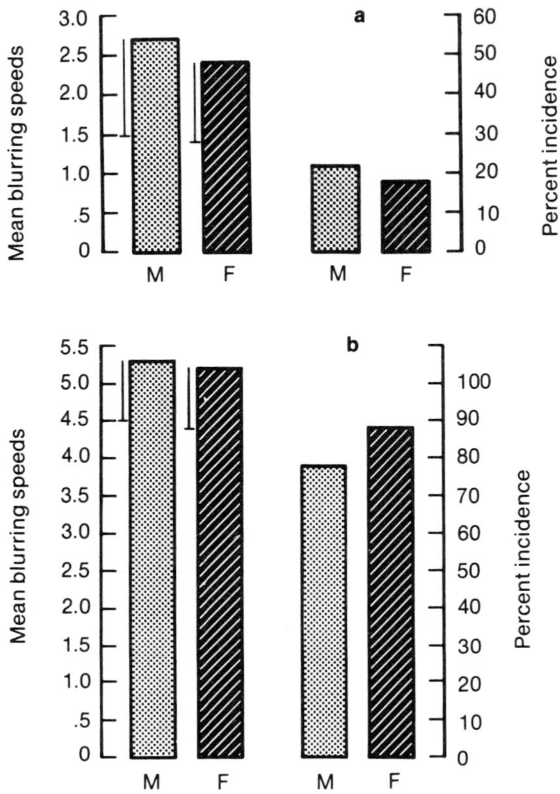

Fig. 6–8. Word Mode I. The male/female means, standard deviations, and incidence data are illustrated for (*a*) low-blurring-speed population and (*b*) high-blurring-speed population.

Sum-of-All-Modes Data

In a statistical attempt to improve the separation of low- and high-blurring-speed populations, a bimodal distribution was obtained utilizing the sum of all four modes (word Mode I and II, elephant Mode I and II) per patient. The male/female means, standard deviations, and incidence data for the sum-of-all-modes blurring-speed distribution are summarized and illustrated by Fig. 6–9. The low-blurring-speed mean (6.4 ft./sec.) is approximately one-third the high-blurring-speed mean (17.1 ft./sec.), the low-blurring-speed incidence is approximately 15%, and the male/female data appears identical.

Mode III Data

Mode III positive incidence data was analyzed as a function of word Mode I distribution, sum-of-all-modes distribution, sex, and handedness. Males and

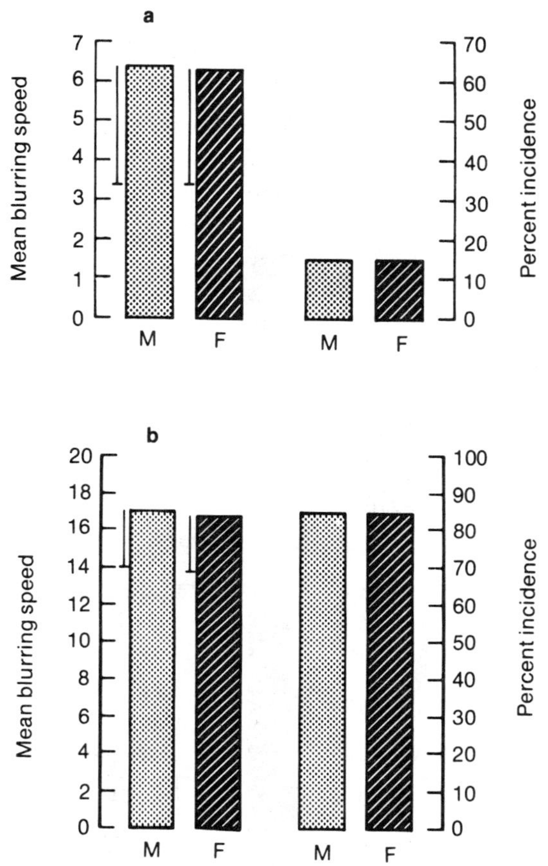

Fig. 6–9. Sum-of-all-modes. The male/female means, standard deviations, and incidence data are illustrated for (*a*) low-blurring-speed population and (*b*) high-blurring-speed population.

females were divided into the low-, overlap-, and high-blurring-speed populations arrived at in the previous analysis, and the percentage of Mode III positive was determined in each of the three groups.

Mode III As a Function of Blurring Speed

The incidence of Mode III positive was found to be significantly higher ($p < 0.0001$) in the low-blurring-speed population (17%) of both the word Mode I and sum-of-all-modes distributions, as compared to their corresponding high-blurring-speed populations (0.5%). These statistical relationships have been summarized in Fig. 6–10. This data clearly substantiated the Staten Island Mode III blurring-speed correlations and contradicted the negative Mode III correlations obtained in the blind blurring-speed study.

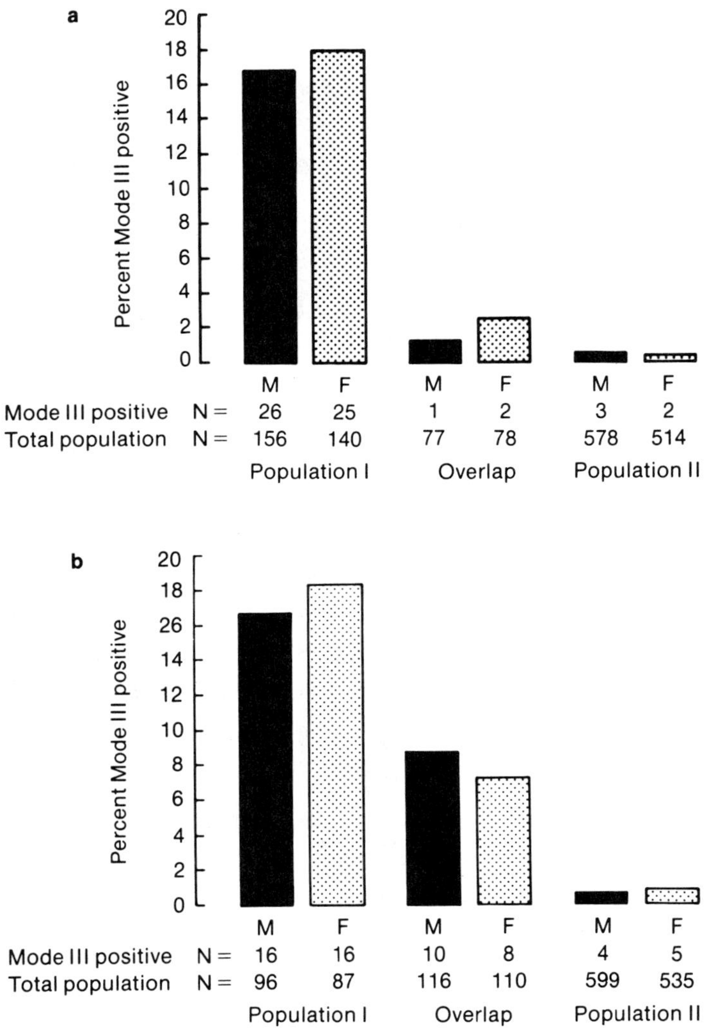

Fig. 6–10. Frequency of Mode III positive as a function of sex. (*a*) Word Mode I distribution. The male/female incidence of Mode III positive is illustrated in the low-blurring-speed, overlap-blurring-speed, and the high-blurring-speed populations. Mode III positive appears independent of sex for word Mode I.

(*b*) Sum-of-all-modes distribution. The male/female incidence of Mode III positive is illustrated in the low-blurring-speed, overlap-blurring-speed, and high-blurring-speed populations. Mode III positive appears independent of sex for the sum-of-all-modes distribution.

Interestingly enough, the incidence of Mode III positive in the Sum-of-all-modes overlap population was found to be significantly higher than the incidence of Mode III positive in the corresponding word Mode I overlap population. This observation and its exploration was crucial in resolving the paradoxical blurring-speed data introduced by the various studies.

Mode III Positive As a Function of Overlap Population

In tabulating and illustrating the relationship between percentage of Mode III positive in low- and high-blurring-speed populations, an unexpected finding materialized: the percentage of Mode III positive was found to be significantly higher in the sum-of-all-modes overlap population (8.6%) as compared to the word Mode I overlap population (1.3%). This fascinating finding has been illustrated for the Mode I and sum-of-all-modes populations by Fig. 6–10. Interestingly enough, this seemingly unimportant and inconspicuous finding provided the first significant clue in resolving the blurring-speed paradox, and will be discussed in greater detail later in this chapter.

Mode III Positive As a Function of Sex

The word Mode I and sum-of-all-modes blurring-speed data were divided into male and female subpopulations, and the percentage of Mode III positive determined in each of the low-, overlap-, and high-blurring-speed analyses. As illustrated in Fig. 6–10, the percentage of Mode III positive is the same for males and females, regardless of category and distribution. In addition, the total percentage of Mode III positive for males (3.7%) was almost identical to the total percentage of Mode III positive for females (3.9%) (Fig. 6–11). Analysis of the Mode III data clearly reveals that Mode III positive is statistically independent of sex.

Mode III Positive As a Function of Handedness

All the children in the Queens study were classified according to recorded or unrecorded handedness, and the percentage of Mode III positive determined in these groups. As demonstrated in Fig. 6–12, the incidence of Mode III positive was statistically similar in all three groups, clearly sug-

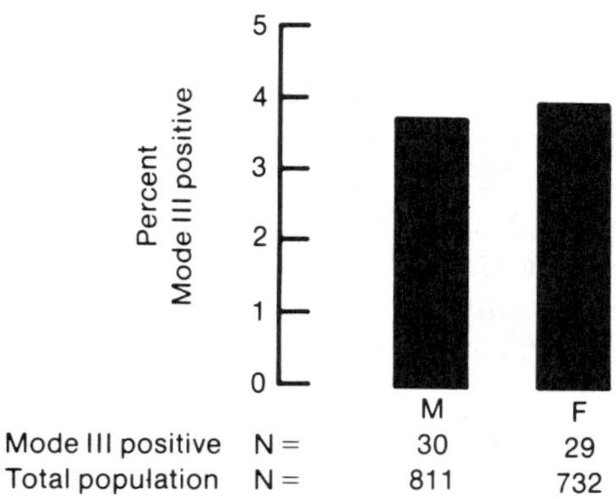

Fig. 6–11. The male/female incidence of Mode III positive in the total Queens blurring-speed distribution. The total incidence of Mode III positive appears independent of sex.

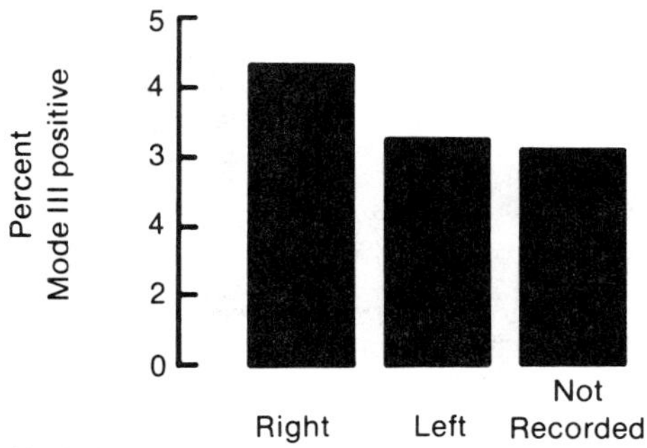

	Right	Left	Not Recorded
Mode III positive	39	4	16
Total population	908	123	512

Fig. 6–12. The incidence of Mode III positive as a function of recorded right-/left-handedness and unrecorded handedness. Mode III positive appears to be statistically independent of handedness.

gesting that it is independent of handedness. This was the first study large enough to obtain statistically significant left-handedness data. Thus far, all the dyslexic handedness data has been consistent, and suggests that dyslexia and handedness are unrelated.

Blurring Speed As a Function of Visual Gestalt

Linear regressions were performed to determine the degree of predictability of the various blurring-speed determinations, given the word Mode I data. For any word Mode I blurring-speed score, all other blurring speeds (word Mode II and elephant Modes I and II) were found to be highly predictable, with correlation coefficients greater than 0.95. The recognition that blurring speeds are a function of visual gestalt and that the various modes are highly correlated (>0.95) resulted in the development of "prediction limits" and "consistency guidelines" so that blurring-speed data can be assessed as to its consistency and/or reliability.

Prediction Limits

Prediction limits of 95% and 99% were determined for the word and elephant modalities. Thus, for any given measure of word Mode I, the inner prediction limits would be expected to contain 95% of all future word Mode II, elephant Mode I, and elephant Mode II observations, while the outer prediction limits would be expected to contain 99% of all future observations. The probability of obtaining a value outside of the 99% prediction limits would most likely be determined by (1) reliability difficulties, and (2) idiosyncratic or specific c-v dysfunctioning and/or compensatory mechanisms.

As a result of the introduction of prediction limits to the blurring-speed methodology, a unique exception among some dyslexics with severe photo-

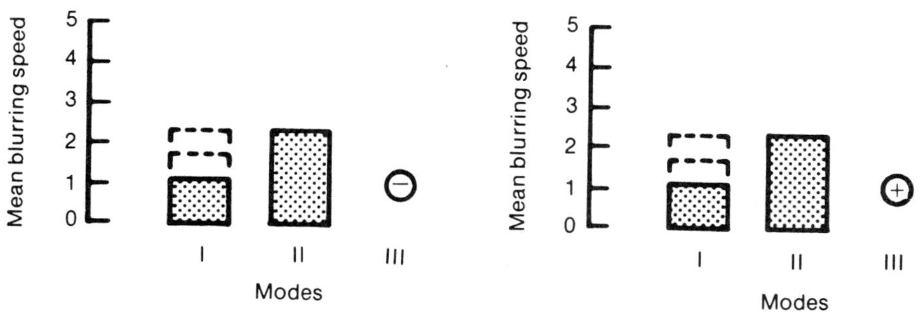

Fig. 6–13. A unique dyslexic blurring-speed exception in which the word Mode I blurring speed is less than or equal to the word Mode II blurring speed. Because Mode I projects greater degrees of light intensity, an occasional light-sensitive photophobic dyslexic individual may "paradoxically" experience greater difficulty tracking Mode I vs. Mode II gestalts. This atypical finding emphasized the manner in which light intensity may decompensate tracking responses and capacity in light-sensitive photophobics, and tended to correlate with phobic responses provoked by specific light wavelengths and intensities (Chapter 12).

phobia was recognized in this study (Fig. 6–13). The increased light intensity of Mode I may fragment the c-v tracking capacity, and thus the Mode I blurring speed may be less than the corresponding Mode II score, whereas the corresponding Mode III response may be positive or negative. Prior to recognizing the specific c-v dysfunction defined by this statistically unusual blurring-speed pattern, this result was considered "unreliable."

Reliability and Unreliability of Blurring-Speed Data

Previous experience with the 3D optical scanner and evolving blurring-speed methodology indicated that children may misunderstand instructions, especially when anxious, and that individuals may attempt to deny their defects and difficulties, and thus confuse or confabulate responses. In addition, subtle changes in the instructions or test situation may unwittingly alter the responses obtained.

In order to minimize unreliable results and detect "improbable" blurring-speed data, a series of statistically determined blurring-speed relationships, or "consistency guidelines," were built into the developing methodology. The Staten Island, Queens, and clinical blurring-speed studies have statistically indicated that, for any given individual:

1. word Mode I is greater than word Mode II;
2. word Mode II is equal to elephant Mode I;

3. elephant Mode I is greater than elephant Mode II;
4. elephant and word Modes III positive correlate highly with significantly reduced Modes I and II blurring speeds, as well as with c-v dysfunction and DD;
5. "accurate" or "true" determinations can be reproduced within 0.2–0.5 feet per second in successive trials;
6. word and elephant Modes I and II blurring speeds must fall within a statistically fixed or predetermined range.

As a result of these experimentally determined formulations, each blurring-speed determination must satisfy criteria 1 through 6 in order to be considered reliable and/or consistent. Following the Queens study, "internal consistency guidelines" 1 through 6 were built into the blurring-speed methodology so that the "reported data" will more closely approximate the "true data." One hopes that the significance of the resulting data and internal consistency guidelines will become more clearly defined and understood as a function of time and experimentation.

Needless to say, "inconsistent" data are clinically and experimentally significant, and point to difficulties with patient, examiner, and test design, as well as unknown and unexplained phenomena, and combinations thereof. It is anticipated that a clear understanding of the data's significance and derivation will eventually result in a stable and reliable blurring-speed methodology.

Comparison of Statistics from the Staten Island and Queens Studies

The low-blurring-speed incidence in the sum-of-all-modes and word Mode I Queens distributions was found to be 15% and 20%, respectively, and appeared remarkably consistent with the 10%–15% low-blurring-speed incidence of the Staten Island Study. Both blurring speed studies demonstrated normal and dyslexic blurring speeds to be independent of sex. And the Queens study was large enough to reveal that blurring speeds are independent of handedness.

The Staten Island blurring-speed study was clearly bimodal without any significant overlap, whereas the Queens study indicated a bimodal distribution with an overlap. The reasons for these bimodal differences remained unknown and were assumed to be due to either the insignificant low-blurring-speed incidence relative to the massive high-blurring-speed incidence in the Queens study or to inherent differences between the two studies. For example, the mean age in the Staten Island study was significantly higher than that in the Queens study, whereas the Queens study had a greater and statistically more significant sample of children.

Could the lower age and larger number of individuals tested in the Queens study have resulted in a more accurate spread of values? Or did the testing of younger individuals and larger numbers introduce greater degrees of error?

A Clue to the Blurring-Speed Paradox: Compensatory Mechanisms

Inasmuch as all blurring speed determinations were encompassed by the sum-of-all-modes distribution, this distribution was hypothesized to be statistically more valid than the others. Three characteristics of the sum-of-all-modes distribution appeared to support this assumption:

1. the male/female low-blurring-speed incidence was identical (15%/15%);
2. this incidence seemed more consistent with the 10%–15% Staten Island low-blurring-speed incidence than did the 20% word Mode I incidence; and
3. the low-blurring-speed mean was one-third that of the high-blurring-speed mean.

However, the sum-of-all-modes overlap population was found to contain a higher percentage of Mode III positive individuals (8.6%) than did the corresponding word Mode I overlap population (1.3%). This interesting finding is clearly demonstrated by Fig. 6–10.

Inasmuch as Mode III positive has thus far not been found in c-v normal individuals, it appeared in retrospect that the sum-of-all-modes distribution might not, in fact, represent a more valid bimodal separation of dyslexics from nondyslexics, as had previously been assumed. Furthermore, the existence of Mode III positive individuals with "normal" Mode I and II blurring speeds highlighted a significant clue in solving the blurring-speed paradox.

Mode III positive has been found to be highly correlated to low Mode I and II blurring speeds ($p < 0.0001$) in both the Staten Island and Queens studies. Is it possible that the combination of Mode III positive and "normal" Modes I and II blurring speeds may be explained by blurring-speed compensation in Modes I and II? The Staten Island study clearly demonstrated that older dyslexics have "normal" Mode I blurring speeds. Might not some younger dyslexics exhibit blurring speed compensation as well? Could compensatory blurring speeds account for the variations found in the shapes of the Staten Island, blind, and Queens blurring-speed distributions? Could subtle changes in administering the test and technique result in higher yields of compensated Modes I and II blurring speeds?

These questions led to the study of, and search for, compensatory blurring-speed mechanisms in dyslexia. Although the aforementioned questions were easily raised, the author could not even speculate as to what these subtle variations in technique might be, and how they might result in higher yields of compensated blurring speeds.

Discovery of a Methodological Oversight

Interestingly enough, the seemingly impossible answer to these questions materialized "by chance," while the author was conducting a parallel *clinical blurring-speed study* (Chapter 8). An adult dyslexic woman tested in a manner identical to that used in the Staten Island and Queens studies spontaneously asked, "Which blurring speed do you want?" What in the world is she talking about?, ran through the author's mind, but instead she was asked, "Tell me about both." Indeed she did. And her reply triggered the insights required to solve both the blurring-speed paradox and the dyslexic riddle: "I have two different blurring speeds. At first I blur out the sequence very rapidly. But then I can [consciously] track *one* elephant or word at a time to a very high speed." The first, *sequential blurring speed,* was recognized to be diagnostic of a c-v tracking dysfunction, whereas the *single-target blurring speed* was recognized to be of a compensatory nature.

As a result of this fascinating but unexpected finding it became readily apparent that dyslexic blurring speeds need not equal dyslexic recognition speeds, and that accelerating tracking speeds need not equal decelerating tracking speeds. If, indeed, there exist two dyslexic blurring-speed endpoints, there must exist two corresponding recognition speed endpoints.

Could the Staten Island study have inadvertently measured diagnostic or sequential blurring speeds for the young dyslexic sample (Group 1) and compensatory single-targeting (and confabulatory) speeds in the older dyslexic (Group 2) sample? A follow-up study of several older Group 2 dyslexic individuals still available for study confirmed this assumption (Fig. 6–14).

Could the blind study have measured primarily *compensatory single-target recognition speeds*? Inasmuch as the blind study measured recognition speeds, it seemed most reasonable to assume that this study inadvertently measured the recognition speed corresponding to compensatory single targeting, and thus yielded seemingly paradoxical and impossible dyslexic blurring speed correlations. Could the Queens study have inadvertently measured more compensatory single-targeting speeds than did the Staten Island study for the corresponding young Group 1 dyslexics? This assumption might then explain the significant Mode III positive incidence found in the Queens overlap population.

In retrospect, there seemed to be little doubt that the elimination of this and other methodological errors in future testing would more accurately separate the c-v dysfunctioning and normal populations. During future blurring-speed testing, individuals would be instructed to look at the whole visual sequence and avoid consciously tracking any one single target. The instructions would be geared more specifically towards obtaining the diagnostically significant blurring-speed endpoint, whereas the role of compensatory tracking mechanisms would hopefully be minimized.

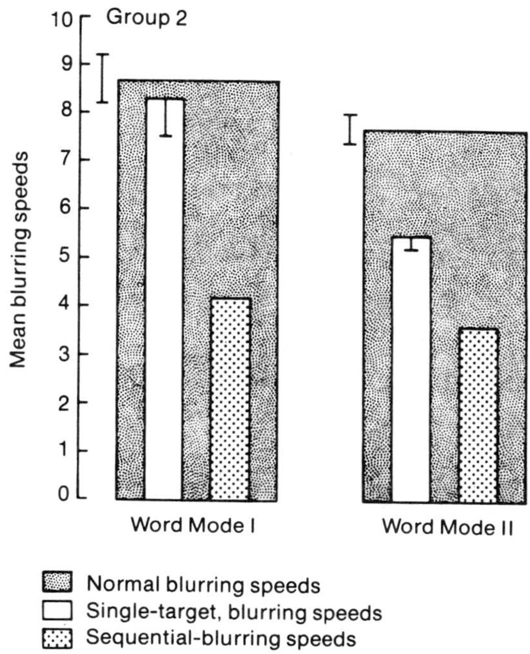

Fig. 6–14. The relationship between older Group 2 dyslexic compensatory (single target) and diagnostic (sequential) blurring speeds vs. normal control blurring speeds (Staten Island blurring-speed study).

Summary

The Queens blurring-speed study was initiated in an attempt to duplicate the Staten Island findings and explain the paradoxical data in the "blind" study. The Queens blurring-speed distribution was found to be bimodal, but not as bimodal as the Staten Island study—highlighting the existence of blurring-speed compensation and unknown methodological complexities. In addition, Mode III positive was found to be highly correlated to low Mode I and II blurring speeds ($p < 0.0001$), refuting the negative Mode III correlation obtained in the "blind" study and corroborating the Mode III findings in the Staten Island study.

The Staten Island study discovered that blurring speed is a function of visual gestalt. This finding was corroborated and expanded in the Queens study. The correlation and predictability of the various Mode I and II word and elephant blurring speeds resulted in a modification of the blurring-speed methodology and led to the establishment of prediction limits and internal consistency guidelines. It is hoped that the technical errors assumed to have occurred in the "blind" blurring-speed study will be minimized and/or readily detected in future "blind" studies. Interestingly, the statistical quantitative techniques of the Staten Island and Queens studies were insufficient to solve and/or comprehend the significance of the exceptions and the dilemma introduced by the "blind" study. A parallel qualitative technique and study was required to discover the presence of sequential versus compensatory single-target blurring and recognition speeds, and thus resolve the blurring-speed paradox. The "accidental" discovery of sequential versus compensatory single-target blurring speeds clearly demonstrated the need for simultaneous and interacting quantitative and qualitative techniques in mental and neurophysiologic research.

As a result of funding cutbacks and other realistic problems, the low- and high-blurring-speed populations of the Queens study could not be clinically examined and distinguished; and the anticipated longitudinal study of blurring speeds as a function of age was not completed. These studies were considered crucial in resolving the significance of the negative correlation of blurring speeds and reading scores obtained in the "blind" study, as well as in elucidating the suspected role of compensatory blurring speeds in determining the shape of the blurring-speed distribution. Because the Queens study found all blurring-speed modalities and combinations to result in similar bimodal distributions, the importance of visual gestalts was minimized and the importance of compensatory blurring speeds and mechanisms highlighted.

In two follow-up studies (and two later chapters), the results and conceptualizations of the Staten Island, Queens, and "blind" studies were extended, and the role of compensatory blurring speeds, reading scores, and neurophysiologic mechanisms were further highlighted.

7 Compensatory Tracking and Reading Scores in Dyslexia

The atypical, paradoxical, and contradictory data introduced by the blind study *forced* the recognition that the blurring-speed methodology was unstable, and that the existing blurring-speed-dyslexic conceptualizations were incomplete and thus dependent upon unknown variables. In an attempt to integrate and harmonize the blind blurring-speed correlations with the Staten Island and Queens findings, the author assumed that all of the data was of equal validity, and that all "paradoxical" data must be due to unique and distinct combinations of overlapping variables and determinants stemming from a common, but hidden, nuclear source.

Once again the author, so to speak, took a long, deep breath, stepped way, way back and free associated: Could the blind study have unwittingly measured compensatory and/or confabulated dyslexic blurring speeds rather than diagnostic and "objective" blurring speeds? Could the use of recognition-speed endpoints rather than blurring-speed endpoints have contributed to these differences?* Could the random and selected reading-score samples in the blind study have been derived from diagnostically unknown, heterogeneous combinations of reading-score-deficient and reading-score-

* The use of recognition speeds may certainly have unwittingly biased or triggered children to confabulate or report "high speeds." Although the author theorized that the use of recognition-speed endpoints in the "blind" study may have resulted in dyslexic compensatory, rather than diagnostic, blurring speeds, a scientifically derived "free association technique" could not envision or even guess at the specific method by which this assumed blurring-speed transformation was effected. Only an experimental approach in which known c-v dyslexic and control populations were tested for blurring and recognition speeds could have validated this assumption. Interestingly, this intended blurring vs. recognition speed study was repeatedly postponed. Could the author have been fearful that his hypothesis was in error and that the methodology and c-v correlations were faulty? Or was the author guided to pattern a research plan by intuitive or unconscious forces he could not comprehend until after this research effort was completed?

compensated dyslexics versus reading-score-deficient and normal non-dyslexic groups? And if, indeed, significantly unknown proportions of compensated and/or confabulated blurring-speeds were statistically correlated to diagnostically unknown reading-score groupings, might the statistical outcome resemble the paradoxical data and correlations obtained in the blind study.

In view of these pre-solution "free associations," the author re-analyzed his dyslexic research for supporting clues. The retrospective analysis of all the studies to date clearly revealed the presence of silently active compensatory and overcompensatory neurophysiologic and neuropsychologic mechanisms tending to neutralize or deny the underlying c-v dysfunctioning and symptomatic fallout.

The c-v symptoms of dyslexic children appeared to diminish with age, and their so-called soft signs became softer and more difficult to diagnose—misleading such investigators as Critchley and Orton into conceptualizing the dyslexic disorder as due to a cortical development lag, rather than to a compensating c-v dysfunction. In addition, the academic performance of dyslexics was found to be favorable provided psychological and educational traumatizations and scarring did not occur. Thus the reading, writing, spelling, and mathematical spatial-temporal dysmetria of many dyslexics so improved by latency and puberty that the author wondered if the so-called late bloomers and developmental dyslexics were not in fact reading-score-compensated dyslexic individuals.

The recognition of reading-score-compensated dyslexics not only explained the heretofore confusing, and statistically atypical, correlation of decreased blurring speeds and normal reading scores found in the Staten Island random sample, but led to the insight that reading scores may significantly vary in dyslexia and that all reading-score-dependent dyslexic definitions and conceptualizations were most probably based on highly selective and biased sampling. In addition, although all reading-score deficient dyslexics were invariably found to have a c-v dysfunction, it did not necessarily follow that all cases with c-v dysfunction had decreased reading scores (Frank and Levinson, 1976).

Could the conceptualization and recognition of reading-score-compensated dyslexics explain the prior diagnostic difficulty in clinically and neurophysiologically distinguishing dyslexics from the multitude of slow learners? Might not the multitude of slow learners comprise a multitude of dyslexics with varying types and intensities of reading and learning difficulties? Would this conceptualization not explain Katrina de Hirsch's intuitive attempts to link Andy's reading-score-deficient dyslexic symptoms with his sister's and father's reading-score-compensated dyslexic symptoms (Chapter 2)?

Since the retrospective study, the author has examined and treated a significant number of medical colleagues, and his experiences have been similar to those shared by Lloyd J. Thompson (1966, p. 117):

Many adults who have had a language handicap in childhood do overcome the disability to a considerable extent, but usually some remnants remain. The writer has observed several colleagues in medicine who had difficulty with spelling and, of course, with writing. Not all of these physicians had a specific disability, but certainly some of them did. One was given to mispronunciation, saying "stench" for stance and calling a refectory table a "refractory" table. Obviously, he could not visualize words and he spelled by ear.

Compensatory Tracking in Dyslexia

Prior to the specific discovery of sequential versus compensatory single-targeting, the author had assumed that compensatory mechanisms played a crucial role in determining and shaping the dyslexic output, and that compensatory tracking mechanisms must, in some way, be responsible for the atypical and paradoxical blurring-speed data.

The existence of compensatory mechanisms was initially suggested by the analysis of the Staten Island blurring-speed data. This data analysis clearly indicated that both normal and DD blurring speeds increased as a function of age, and that the DD word Mode I and Mode II blurring speeds approached normal by 10–12 years of age—despite the continued presence of abnormal c-v clinical and ENG caloric findings. These unexpected but fascinating clinical correlations strongly suggested that DD blurring speeds were not only a function of decreased c-v tracking capacity (i.e., subclinical nystagmus, or f_2), but a function of compensatory scanning capacity (f_3) as well.

As a result of these observations, the subclinical tracking dysfunction (f_2) and the compensatory tracking vectors (f_3) of the blurring speed equation were conceived to be coexisting and overdetermined forces which might significantly alter the constitutionally or genetically determined tracking capacity, or f_1. The blurring speed equation was accordingly formulated as follows:

$$BS = MITC = f_1 + f_2 + f_3$$

The search for specific f_3 compensatory tracking mechanisms determining the Staten Island exceptions and the blind-study data was officially on. As a result of this search, ocular-motor (ENG) tracking patterns were combined with the existing blurring-speed methodology in a special effort to determine additional and more objective parameters for separating DD, non-DD and compensatory tracking patterns. However, the ocular-motor tracking studies were initially of little help, and appeared to add confusing quanta of paradoxical data to the developing blurring-speed "stew"—resulting in significant doubts as to the validity and reliability of the methodology. For example, many dyslexics were found tracking visual targets at speeds far beyond their blurring-speed endpoint, whereas others reported blurring moving targets at low speeds while recognizing them at much higher speeds. Needless to say, the quantity and quality of the paradoxical data had crescendoed and reached a crisis pitch.

Although over 1,000 dyslexic cases were blurring-speed tested with and without corresponding tracking ENG parameters, and although the correlation of dyslexia, c-v dysfunction, and decreased blurring speeds appeared statistically correlated, there remained approximately 15%–20% of "typical" young and older dyslexics manifesting "normal" or compensated Mode I and Mode II blurring speeds. Despite meticulous and painstaking neurologic and neurophysiologic (caloric, rotational, and optokinetic or blurring-speed ENGs) comparison studies of low versus "normal" blurring-speed dyslexics, the specific f_3 compensatory mechanisms theoretically predicted and assumed responsible for the statistically atypical dyslexic blurring-speed variations remained completely elusive. All clinical and theoretical roads led to the presence of f_3 mechanisms—and yet these mechanisms were nowhere to be found. Thus, f_3 remained a theoretical necessity and a clinical mystery.

The f_3 mechanisms and their increase as a function of age, and most probably as a function of ocular-motor facilitation, were theoretically viewed as *ontogenetic* recapitulations of a phylogenetic sequence of events in which man's pre-reading blurring speeds and c-v circuits increased in an adaptive functional relationship to continuously evolving and steadily increasing complex visual tracking and processing needs over an evolutionary time span. The increased compensatory scanning capacity of both normal and DD individuals as a function of age, need and repetition was postulated to have developed by means of a complex, overdetermined resultant of cerebellar learning and increasing cortical-cerebellar feedback control, with increasing myelinization and granulation of the cerebral cortex and its c-v ocular-motor pathways.

In retrospect, it appeared as if ontogenetically developing c-v, cortical, and cortical–c-v feedback circuits were better able to check, neutralize, and inhibit the subclinical nystagmus reasoned to be responsible for the impaired tracking capacity in DD. Furthermore, the development of increased or compensatory tracking capacity in association with cortical-cerebellar myelinization was postulated to represent an ontogenetic recapitulation of the cerebellar-cortical phylogenetic spurt during which man's cortical-cerebellar mass tripled in size over several million years (Eccles, 1967; Llinas, 1975).

Despite years of continuous clinical and theoretical study, as well as large-scale sampling, the missing f_3 mechanism materialized only "by chance," in what ordinarily might have appeared to be a meaningless dyslexic "slip of the tongue." However, the author was both theoretically and clinically "pre-tuned," and so ready and waiting for the dyslexic patient who innocently asked, "Which blurring speed do you want?" Was this chance remark and the realization of its scientific significance due to chance alone? Or would the very same remark have been "imperceived" or denied prior to the considerations and frustrations triggered by the need to comprehend the expanding quanta of paradoxical data? By analogy, it appeared as if the author were acting as an IRM that was ready and waiting to be triggered by a corresponding gestalt-specific key stimulus.

Although the quantitative and statistical exploration of sequential versus single targeting in a large dyslexic/normal control study was deemed crucial, the results to be derived from the clinical blurring-speed study (Chapter 8) were already considered anticlimactic. For a single "innocent" question spontaneously raised by a dyslexic patient, and its qualitative analysis, appeared scientifically sufficient to isomorphically validate the use of blurring speeds in dyslexia and to solve the blurring-speed diagnostic riddle.

As a result of the discovery of sequential versus single targeting blurring speeds, the vast majority of so-called blurring speed exceptions became readily explainable, and so lost the strange and fascinating quality unwittingly attributed to confusing and perplexing data.

To explain the vast majority of blurring-speed exceptions to date, one merely had to assume that all prior testing contained unwitting proportions and modal combinations of sequential and single-target blurring speed, i.e., single-target Modes I and II with Mode III positive or negative, single-target Mode I with sequential-target Mode II and Mode III positive or negative, and so on.

On the basis of this reasoning, a number of older Group 2 dyslexics still available from the Staten Island study were re-tested for sequential and single targeting. As previously noted, their "compensatory blurring speeds" were found to be due to the unwitting measurement of single-targeting rather than sequential blurring speeds (Fig. 6–14). In addition, a follow-up study (Chapter 8) clearly and statistically demonstrated the diagnostic accuracy and consistency of blurring speeds when compensatory single targeting is minimized. When measuring only diagnostic blurring speeds, the incidence of statistically significant low blurring speeds in dyslexic samples was raised from 80% to over 95%. Needless to say, when diagnostic and compensatory blurring speeds were "scientifically scrambled," paradoxical and confusing data reigned supreme.

Utilizing these insights, the author had undertaken the study of acquired c-v adult disorders and factors leading to c-v functional and blurring-speed regression, i.e., multiple sclerosis, post-ECT states, concussion states, toxic states (alcohol and drugs), flu states, mononucleosis, etc. The investigation of these and related disorders via neurologic, rotation and caloric ENG, and blurring-speed studies had led to increased correlations between clinical c-v findings, positive ENG results, and decreased blurring speeds. As a result of these studies, the author developed a broader conceptualization of DD, whereby the resulting symptoms were found to depend upon age of onset, specific sites and types of lesion or dysfunction, and the directional vectors of the dynamic equilibrium existing between c-v regressive and compensatory mechanisms.

It is anticipated that the continued study of adult c-v disorders will yield invaluable information as to both the dysfunctioning and the compensatory natures of c-v and related circuits. In addition, by virtue of the fact that blurring speed was found to measure both compensation and dysfunction or regression, the use of this methodology took on broader and more dynamic dimensions. More specifically, by means of blurring-speed measurements, the author attempted to develop maturation or compensatory curves as a function of time or age, medication, ocular-motor facilitation techniques, and so on.

Symptomatic Fluctuations in Dyslexia

The ability of blurring-speed testing to specifically, accurately and rapidly diagnose c-v dysfunction and dyslexia led to large scale clinical investigations in which dyslexia and its symptomatic complex were studied as a function of time. Young dyslexic children were longitudinally tracked through latency, puberty, adolescence, and even young adulthood; and the symptoms of older dyslexics were both neurodynamically and psychodynamically analyzed and their developmental sequence reconstructed in time to their clinical onset and origin. These longitudinal and reconstructive studies revealed fascinating insights into the compensatory and regressive neuropsychologic triggers and forces determining the manifest clinical symptomatic complex at any fixed time. For any given dyslexic patient, the pattern of symptoms changing with time was found to be truly unique, and dependent upon multiple coexisting and overdetermined variables. Thus, at any given time, specific patterns of symptoms and functions might be compensating while others remain steady or decompensate.

Reading-score-compensated dyslexics were often found referred to psychiatrists and neurologists for the evaluation of such nonreading symptoms as enuresis, headaches, abdominal pain, insomnia, school phobias, height, and motion phobias, obsessive-compulsive neuroses, temper outbursts, acting out and/or delinquent behavior, as well as writing, spelling, math, memory, directional, and balance and coordinational difficulties. Most often, the underlying c-v somatic, dyslexic basis of this symptomatic complex remained completely hidden or subclinical—resulting in unwitting misinterpretations and diagnostic-therapeutic scrambling. The dedicated search for only primary emotional determinants often resulted in fallacious psychoanalytic formulations and such iatrogenic complications as a faulty therapeutic alliance and negative transference/counter transference acting out.

Children presenting for neurologic evaluation because of dyscoordination difficulties were most often diagnosed as having minimal brain damage, minimal cerebral dysfunction, or developmental dyspraxia, and the underlying nuclear pattern of c-v dyslexic symptoms and the secondarily related psychogenic fall-out were significantly overlooked and/or denied.

Reading Scores and Dyslexia

Although every nonreading symptom defined by the nuclear symptomatic complex in dyslexia was found to vary from one extreme to another, and although each of the symptoms within this complex may clinically present as if it were an isolated or unitary symptomatic event, most frequently, mild variations of the associated symptoms within the complex may be clinically detectable upon careful examination, unless compensatory and overcompensatory mechanisms result in "savant-like" symptomatic expressions, i.e., compensatory dyslexic reading and function styles.

Since the author was called upon to examine clinically only reading "refractory" children within the New York City SRS and SRP, and in view of the fact that the reading-refractory children were either nonreaders of normal I.Q. or two or more years behind their matched normal reading peers, and since the traditional conceptualizations of the dyslexic reading-score impairment were identical to the SRS and SRP referral criteria, it seemed most natural to view the dyslexic reading disorder as existing only in severe or "refractory" form, and to believe that dyslexics invariably begin their academic careers as nonreaders. Although Hermann recognized that the reading disorder among dyslexics may be overcome, and Critchley termed these improved readers "convalescent dyslexics," most researchers failed to appreciate either the significance or the extent of the so-called atypical convalescent, late-blooming, or reading-score-compensated dyslexics.

> It was established early that the difficulties in reading are nearly always accompanied by difficulties in writing and spelling. The latter are often more pronounced and persistent than difficulty with reading, which as a rule can be overcome, so that the word-blind person achieves a normal or nearly normal proficiency in reading. [Hermann, 1959, p. 17]

> It is necessary to point out, however, that not every dyslexic child is slow in his reading performance. Particularly does this hold true for the "convalescent" dyslexic, that is one who is beginning to make progress. . . .
>
> In the case of the "cured" dyslexic, defective writing and spelling may continue to appear long into adult life. . . .
>
> As the dyslexic improves with his reading, he and his teachers become increasingly aware of, and concerned with, his conspicuous inability to spell correctly. The time may come, indeed, especially in a teenager or adolescent, when the original delay in the acquisition of reading has been forgotten. . . . The problem now presents itself as an intelligent scholar who is handicapped in his written work by its untidyness and atrocious spelling. [Critchley, 1969, pp. 28, 36, 44]

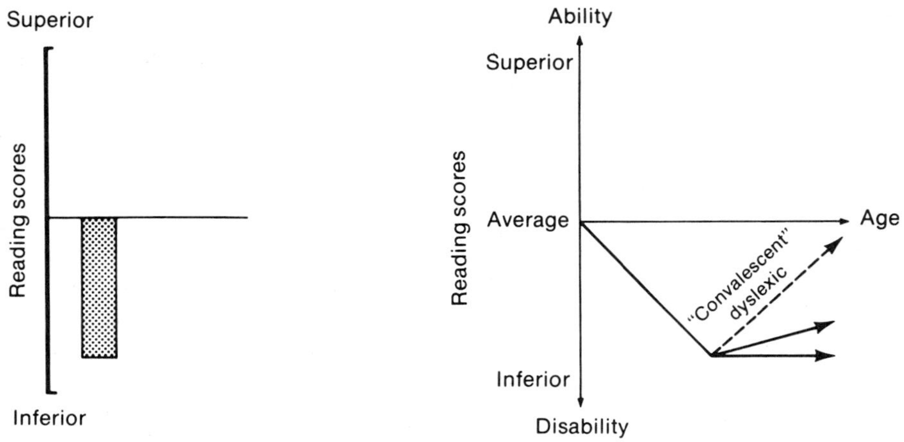

Fig. 7–1. The fixed traditional conceptualization of reading scores and dyslexia, suggesting that these scores are severely depressed and fixed. Inasmuch as this conceptualization of dyslexic reading scores was found to be inaccurate and incompatible with the host of "late-blooming" dyslexic readers and "famous" dyslexics, it appeared in retrospect that the traditional concept of dyslexic reading scores was based on biased sampling resulting from inadequate diagnostic procedures, biased referrals, and the fallacious comparison and assumed identity between alexic reading scores in alexia or acquired aphasia and in idiopathic or developmental dyslexia.

In retrospect, these statistically atypical reading-score-compensated dyslexics were found to be merely highly selected "tips" to the panoramic dyslexic "iceberg." The traditional concept of reading scores and dyslexia is illustrated in Fig. 7–1, whereas the author's newly derived contrasting conceptualizations are illustrated in Fig. 7–2.

As a result of large-scale longitudinal and cross-sectional studies of dyslexic individuals and symptoms, there resulted a mushrooming volume of so-called reading-score exceptions among dyslexics. The author was thus forced to recognize that reading-scores may vary significantly among dyslexics and that the traditional reading-score–dyslexic correlations were most probably based on highly selective and biased sampling. Although the typically described and referred dyslexic is the one who has maximum difficulty acquiring reading and writing skills upon entering school and remains "refractory" to instruction for several years, there exist significant additions and variations to this traditionally accepted prognostic reading scheme. For example, if dyslexics are observed and followed up in an unselected fashion, many improve, compensate, or spurt during latency or puberty, and then stabilize until additional variables (i.e., psychological, maturational, infectious, allergic, hormonal) trigger either further compensation or regression later in life (Fig. 7–2b).

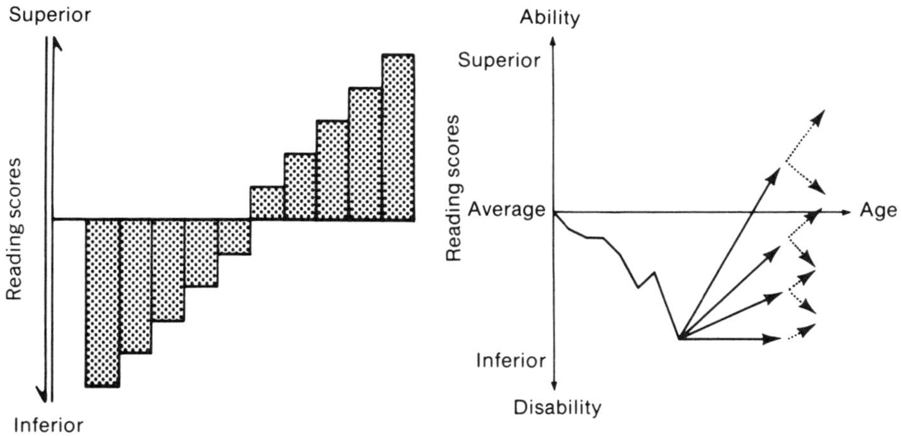

Fig. 7–2. The author's newly derived conceptualizations of reading scores and dyslexia. Reading scores may vary in dyslexia from severely deficient to overcompensated. For any given dyslexic with severe reading score deficiencies, reading scores may vary significantly with age, depending upon a host of variables. This dynamic view of reading score variations in dyslexia is compatible with the total clinical panorama indicating that some dyslexics remain "nonreaders," while others "spurt" or compensate and occasionally become "famous." Moreover, this new view of reading scores and dyslexia is consistent with clinical data suggesting that dyslexic reading performance may regress secondary to toxic, infectious, allergic, endocrinological, and metabolic variables.

Occasionally, young dyslexic children with intact or compensated memory function and/or high I.Q.s are able to perform well when initially starting school. However, they begin to stumble and suffer as the speed, volume, and specific memory requirements of reading, writing, and mathematical tasks increase with increasing grade. All too often, these children are referred for psychological, rather than dyslexic, evaluation and treatment during puberty and adolescence, and are accordingly misdiagnosed as suffering from situational reactions of puberty and adolescence.

These *clinically delayed* dyslexic symptomatic patterns demonstrate a "relative dyslexic decompensation" in later grades and invariably trigger the development of acute emotional symptoms—unless compensatory factors materialize and "save the day." Variations of reading-score function and dyslexia are highlighted by Fig. 7–3.

Not infrequently, c-v-determined mathematical disturbances in reading-score-compensated dyslexics result in acute emotional reactions, and the hidden somatic trigger is most frequently mistaken for a primary psychogenic disturbance. The onset of the emotional episode may occur in later grades, when the specific dyslexic mathematical and/or related memory

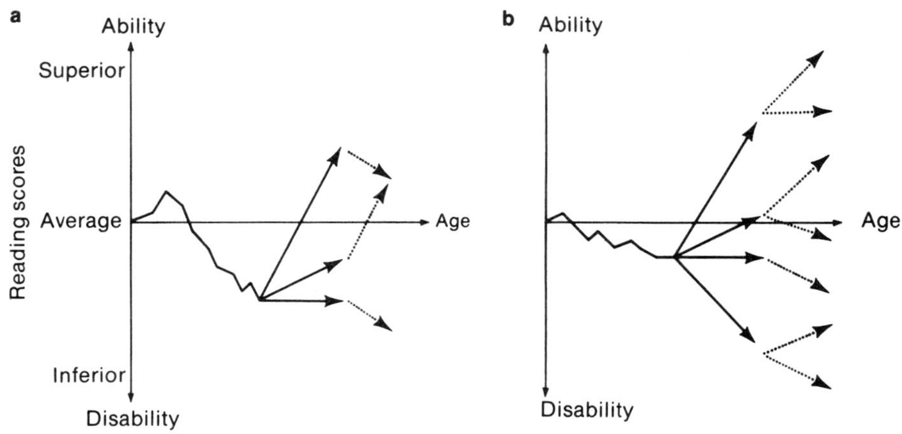

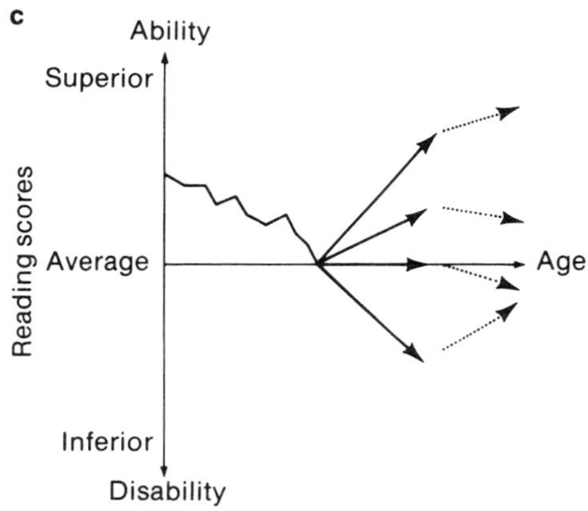

Fig. 7–3. Some additional variations in reading score patterns found among random or unselected dyslexics. Dyslexic reading scores may start out at an average or above-average level, and then decrease with age, grade, and a host of exogenous factors, such as reading volume and speed, until additional intrinsic compensatory or decompensatory mechanisms and vectors once again alter the direction of the resultant reading-score function.

configuration presented for learning triggers catastrophic anxiety responses and defensive attempts to cope with these somatically determined anxieties.

The Fallacy of Reading-Score-Dependent Definitions of Dyslexia

The fallacy of overemphasizing reading scores in the diagnosis of dyslexia may be clearly highlighted by the following two case presentations.

A Mirror-Reading Dyslexic with Superior Reading Scores

Ray is a 30-year-old man referred to the author because of anxiety, depression, temper outbursts, and job-related difficulties. During psychoanalytic and dynamic exploration, he was noted to feel stupid despite an I.Q. greater than 160, and evidenced numerous phobic avoidance phenomena which were initially either denied and/or rationalized. Inasmuch as he spontaneously complained of mathematical and coordinational difficulties, and manifested a compensated speech-hesitation difficulty prone to dyslexic-like "slips of the tongue," he was blurring-speed tested and neurologically evaluated, and found to have a c-v dysfunction. ENG studies were also indicative of a c-v disorder.

A more active and direct historical and exploratory approach was initiated, which revealed the existence of severe vertigo and motion-sickness symptoms that were never spontaneously "free associated" to. Interestingly, he tended to deny all c-v-related symptoms. Moreover, his many travel and motion phobias were elicited only upon direct questioning and confrontation, and were retrospectively recognized to be of a somatic origin.* The resistance mechanisms attempting to deny c-v-related phenomena were found to be extremely potent and required a proportionally intense exploratory approach, once a meaningful therapeutic alliance had been established.

Although a voracious reader, Ray acknowledged great difficulty comprehending certain types of reading material, and evidenced letter and word reversals as well as dyslexic-like mathematical, spelling, writing, and right/left-confused symptomatology. Paradoxically, he was found to be a rapid silent reader despite the fact that his blurring speeds and scanning capacity were significantly impaired. This clinical paradox was resolved upon "accidentally" discovering that he was a mirror reader who scanned reading material from the bottom up and then mentally transposed and translated the memorized page in "correct" fashion. In other words, he developed a compensatory technique of mentally reversing reading content tracked and perceived in an inverted and reversed fashion. Although he would automatically scan a page rapidly, and subconsciously selected only key words for comprehension, he was found unable to read word by word in a normal left/right and top/bottom sequential order without scrambling the words, sentences, and paragraphs. In retrospect, his rapid ability to scan and comprehend reading material was subconsciously modulated and processed, for he could not "see" or recall the key words required for comprehending the total reading gestalt, because his blurring-speeds were found to be one-tenth of normal.

Although his reading scores were found to be above average, he was no doubt dyslexic. A description of his inverted and reversed reading style is presented in his own printed handwriting, for script was impossible for him to perform legibly (Fig. 7–4).

A Case of Pseudo-Dyslexic Psychopathy

John is a 22-year-old college senior referred to the author by his ophthalmologist because of "dyslexia." Upon examination, he revealed a history

* This case will be presented in greater detail in Chapter 12.

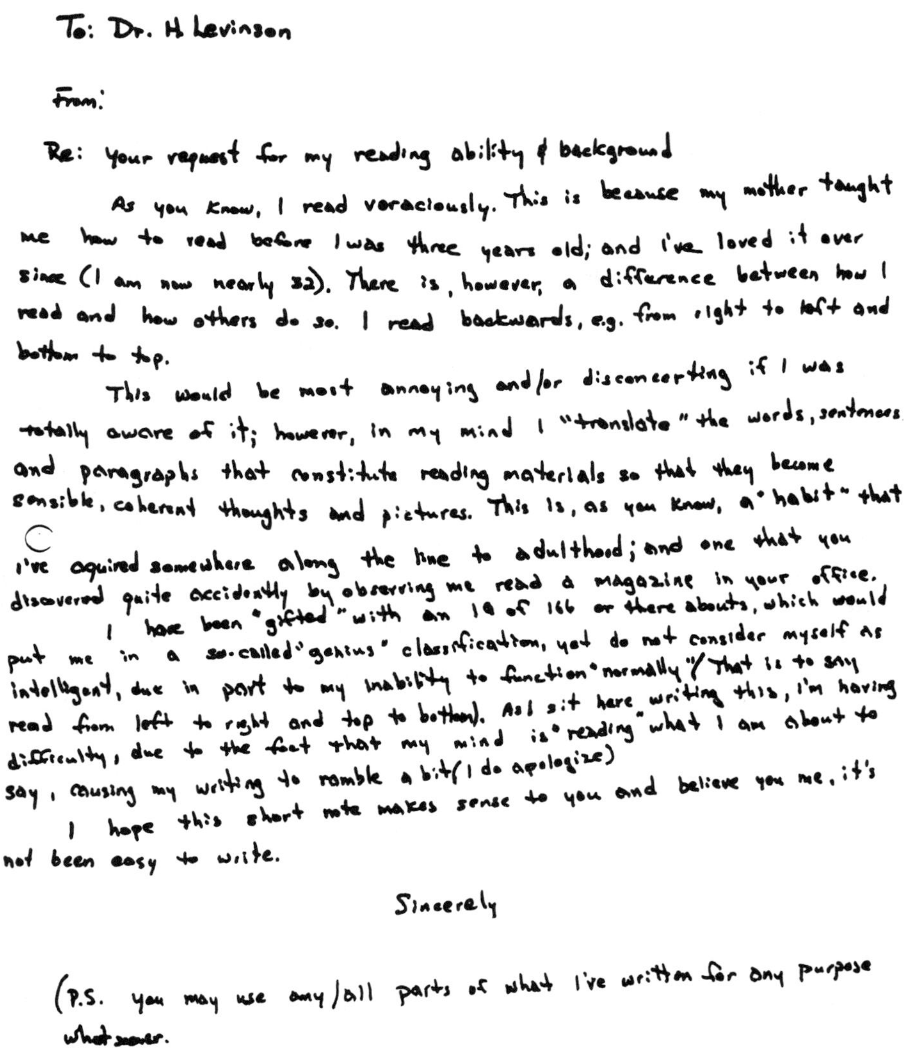
To: Dr. H Levinson

From:

Re: your request for my reading ability & background

As you know, I read voraciously. This is because my mother taught me how to read before I was three years old; and I've loved it ever since (I am now nearly 32). There is, however, a difference between how I read and how others do so. I read backwards, e.g. from right to left and bottom to top.

This would be most annoying and/or disconcerting if I was totally aware of it; however, in my mind I "translate" the words, sentences and paragraphs that constitute reading materials so that they become sensible, coherent thoughts and pictures. This is, as you know, a "habit" that I've aquired somewhere along the line to adulthood; and one that you discovered quite accidently by observing me read a magazine in your office.

I have been "gifted" with an IQ of 166 or there abouts, which would put me in a so-called "genius" classification, yet do not consider myself as intelligent, due in part to my inability to function "normally"/ That is to say read from left to right and top to bottom). As I sit here writing this, I'm having difficulty, due to the fact that my mind is "reading" what I am about to say, causing my writing to ramble a bit (I do apologize)

I hope this short note makes sense to you and believe you me, it's not been easy to write.

Sincerely

(P.S. you may use any/all parts of what I've written for any purpose whatsoever.

Fig. 7–4. This letter illustrates the realizations and observations made by a "gifted" dyslexic who reads in a reversed and inverted manner. The patient initially denied his dyslexic disorder and qualitatively described the manner in which he must compensate for his atypical reading style. This case clearly illustrates the fallacy of inappropriately utilizing reading scores and degrees of reading-score impairment to diagnose dyslexia.

of poor reading, writing, and spelling ability, as well as reading and writing reversals and right/left difficulties. "I needed tutoring until junior high school and was always a few years behind in my reading ability." He demonstrated a slow, hesitant reading cadence, poor spelling ability, and his graphomotor coordination left much to be desired. On Bender Gestalt testing, he rotated some designs and showed angle formation difficulties. His Goodenough figure drawing was "stick" in form, and he still confused right and left.

Neurologic and ENG examinations were found to be within normal limits. His blurring speeds were also well within the normal range. In summary, John presented with "dyslexic" symptoms, significantly decreased reading scores, and absent c-v signs. Was he a dyslexic with compensated or absent c-v signs? Or could he be malingering? Confrontation revealed John to have confabulated his dyslexic-like difficulties in order to qualify for graduate work and school without having adequate grades. Upon re-examination of his reading, writing, spelling, Bender Gestalt and Goodenough designs, he revealed a normal performance.

Significance of the Case Histories

Inasmuch as all current definitions and conceptualizations of dyslexia are dependent upon poor reading-score performance and an absence of telltale neurologic signs, it became immediately clear to the author that any neurologically "normal" individual presenting himself to a neurologist can confabulate a dyslexic history, "deliberately" score poorly on reading, writing, spelling, math, directional, and drawing tests, and thus fallaciously qualify as a true dyslexic.

As a result of these and related clinical observations and considerations, reading, writing, spelling, drawing, I.Q., and related psychological tests were found subject to significant variations, and do not always reflect their intended purpose. They have no built-in reliability index to prevent either malingering or clinical misinterpretation. It is hoped that these case presentations have highlighted the possible error and fallacy of utilizing fluctuating, variable, and neuropsychologically nonspecific quantitative psychological and academic test scores as pathognomonic dyslexic indicators.

Future studies will attempt to elucidate the complex neurodynamic and psychodynamic overdetermined variables shaping the many reading-score variations noted in both dyslexic and nondyslexic groups, and thus establish clear-cut, specific differential diagnostic, prognostic, and therapeutic guidelines, so that clinicians called upon to assess and treat a diverse multitude of reading-disabled individuals will have a fighting scientific chance of success.

Statistically Atypical and Confusing Reading-Score Data

The recognition of reading-score-compensated c-v dyslexics resulted in the immediate harmonization of a large series of seemingly atypical, contradictory, and confusing data with the dyslexic statistical reading-score rule.

For example, two reading-score-normal children in the Staten Island random sample groups were noted to have significantly reduced blurring speeds and c-v dysfunction. The significance of this correlation was just too confusing at that time to be reckoned with, and as a result was just "footnoted" away.

In addition, the initially obtained normal and dyslexic ocular-motor (ENG) tracking patterns corresponding to Modes I, II, and III testing literally defied scientific classification. The data was just too confusing to be meaningfully grouped into distinct normal and DD patterns. At the time of this ocular-motor study, reading-score-normal subjects with normal blurring-speed endpoints were fallaciously considered to be nondyslexic. However, in retrospect, some of the so-called normal subjects were found to be reading-score-compensated dyslexics with single-target compensatory blurring speeds; and their ocular-motor tracking patterns were identical to those of reading-score-deficient dyslexics.

Furthermore, it was initially assumed that if blurring speeds and reading scores were indicators of the c-v dysfunction resulting in dyslexia, reading-score compensation would occur with blurring-speed compensation, and vice versa. However, this expectation did not materialize. Instead, there resulted an endless series of "paradoxical" exceptions. Only in hindsight was it recognized that each of the many indicators or parameters of c-v dysfunction had its own specific compensatory vector counterpart, and that compensation for one symptomatic expression need not and often did not result in either compensatory transfer or generalized compensation.

Interestingly, the realization of function-specific c-v compensatory processes surprisingly led to an explanation for both the success and failure of ocular-motor tracking exercises in dyslexia. The author discovered that tracking exercises improve only the c-v (and cortical) determined fixation and tracking components of the dyslexic reading disorder. Although improved ocular-motor fixation and tracking may clinically result in improved reading scores, tracking facilitation procedures alone did not significantly affect the nontracking c-v "dyslexic circuits," and were thus incapable of reversing either the superimposed secondary emotional symptoms or the CNS lags maintaining the dyslexic status quo.

Might not the existence of reading-score-compensatory variations in dyslexics easily explain the diagnostic dyslexic dilemma whereby reading-score-compensated forms of dyslexia and reading-score-deficient forms of dyslexia were neurophysiologically found to be indistinguishable? If clinicians were indeed unwittingly sampling c-v identical groups and, in addition, were searching only for cortical signs, then it is no wonder why tell-tale and pathognomonic signs were found to be absent in dyslexia.

Last, but not least, the recognition of compensatory blurring speeds and compensatory reading scores in dyslexics, and the possible confusion resulting from their unwitting or "blind" correlations, gave the author sufficient courage to survive and then resolve the devastating blow dealt him by the initial impact of the "blind" blurring-speed study. Were it not for the author's conviction as to the reliability of his own data and its consistency with the total scientific dyslexic reality, the "blind" data would have been isolated and/or denied rather than re-analyzed and eventually integrated into the clinical mainstream. A solution to the dyslexic riddle would have remained a transient and incomplete illusion rather than an incusive scientific reality.

The aforementioned insights catalyzed the recognition that large numbers of reading-score "normal" children referred to the author for psychiatric consultation because of severe speech, behavior, psychosomatic, neurotic, psychotic, anxiety, math, spelling, writing, memory, and inattention disturbances were in fact unsuspected reading-score-compensated c-v dyslexics.

Upon analysis latent or subclinical c-v dysfunction was found to result in a diverse range of primary and secondary "leading" symptoms. Moreover, highly selective sampling and biased clinical referral tended to scramble or mask the underlying unity and interrelationships in this clinical symptomatic spectrum. As a result, each clinical specialty was found to be viewing, and therefore treating, the subclinical c-v disorder by only its highly selected visible symptomatic manifestation. For example, speech therapists were referred, and treated speech disorders; psychiatrists and psychologists were referred, and treated anxiety, neurotic, psychotic, behavioral and psychosomatic disorders; neurologists, ophthalmologists and optometrists were referred, and treated "dyslexics"; otolaryngologists were referred, and treated children with vertigo; and tutors were referred, and treated children with various academic difficulties. Needless to say, overlapping and interdisciplinary referrals were commonplace, and often resulted in a series of isolated views rather than in a truly integrated and multidisciplinary panoramic perspective.

Inasmuch as the perception of "fact" is often noted to be an unstable variable of time and perspective, and because the scientific perception and conceptualizations characterizing dyslexic research were often found to be dependent upon a momentary and highly "scomatized" research glance, it appeared in retrospect that the scientific inability to empathize properly with, and comprehend, dyslexics and their errors must be based on a need to deny one's own dyslexia or the instability inherent in so-called "scientific fact."

The Statistical Rule and Its Exceptions Define Dysmetric Dyslexia

Analysis of the biologic spread of symptoms and compensatory mechanisms in dyslexia resulted in a unique, dynamic conceptualization of this disorder and its diagnostic parameters. Dyslexia was recognized as a c-v-induced scanning and processing disorder in which each symptom was found to have its own qualitative and quantitative determinants. As each symptom may result in specific adaptive compensatory and overcompensatory attempts in which a neurophysiologic and neuropsychologic functional scatter is found, both the dysfunction and its triggered compensatory response must be seen holistically as part and parcel of the dysmetric or c-v dyslexic disorder. Only by viewing compensatory, "gifted," "savant," or overcompensatory functioning as symptomatic expressions of an underlying dysfunctioning c-v stimulus can one explain the existence of DD teachers, scientists, physicians, mathematicians, writers, athletes, artists, and musicians. Inasmuch as each symptom in dyslexia was found to be an overdetermined and dynamically interacting functional complex, one must expect to find significant clinical variations and exceptions to one's expectations. And, indeed, these exceptions were found, analyzed, and integrated into the continuously evolving and forever changing clinical dyslexic reality.

A Reconceptualization of Dysmetric Dyslexia

The clear recognition of specific and independent clinical, symptomatic and blurring-speed compensatory forces in c-v dysfunction and dyslexia resulted in a modification and reconceptualization of the definition of dyslexia—a definition independent of such overdetermined and nonspecific parameters as reading-scores, I.Q., etc. Dyslexia, or DD, was thus redefined as a primary c-v-induced dysmetric sensory-motor and spatial-temporal sequencing and processing disorder in dynamic equilibrium with compensatory forces—resulting in a diverse spectrum of symptoms in varying states of decompensation, compensation, and overcompensation. Thus, the dyslexic reading, writing, spelling, arithmetic, grammatical, graphic, speech, memory, temporal, orientational, and emotional symptoms may appear in any combination and in any degree of compensation and overcompensation. The author's definition and conceptualization of dyslexia, as well as the traditionally accepted point of view, are illustrated in Fig. 7–5. The contrast will highlight the fallacious and incomplete assumptions charactering the traditional descriptive dyslexic concepts, as well as the author's attempt to capture both neurophysiologically and clinically the essence and totality of the dyslexic disorder and panorama.

Dysmetric Dyslexia and Dyspraxia

The fact that some variable form of motor dysmetria, dyscoordination, or developmental dyspraxia tended to characterize the dyslexic population eventually led the author to the concept that dyslexia was, in fact, a sensory-motor organismic dysmetria, and resulted in his adding another *D* (dyspraxia) to the previously defined DD disorder—i.e., dysmetric dyslexia and

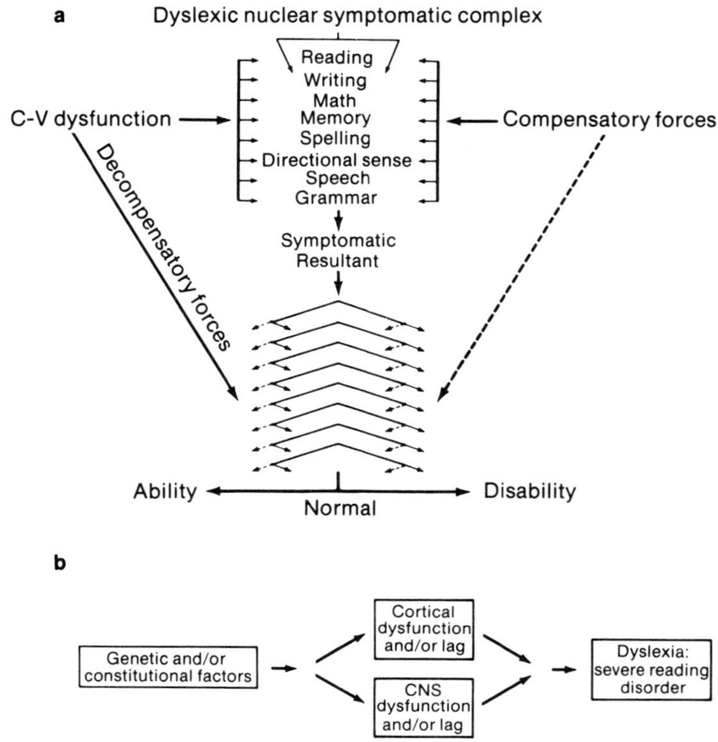

Fig. 7–5. (*a*) The author's clinically derived dynamic concept of dyslexia. This concept depicts the dynamic c-v compensatory and decompensatory vectors determining the symptomatic display at any given fixed point in time. (*b*) The traditional concept of dyslexia. Almost all the assumptions basic to the traditional concept of dyslexia were retrospectively found to be either incomplete or inaccurate.

dyspraxia (DDD).* The term DD was retained for the sake of simplicity and brevity, but hereafter will encompass the total concept signified by DDD.

In accordance with this clinically derived and neurophysiologically con-

* The term "dysmetric dyspraxia" is used as an analogy to the cortical parietal apraxias, and refers to the c-v-determined dysmetric balance, coordination, steering, and spatial orientation disturbances underlying the crawling, walking, sports, speech, writing, and drawing behavior of c-v dysfunctioning children.

The term "dysmetric dyslexia" is used as an analogy to the cortical, parietal, or agnostic alexias, and refers to the dysmetric ocular fixation, sequential scanning, and sensory processing disturbances underlying the reading performance of c-v dysfunctioning children.

The term "dysmetric dyslexia and dyspraxia" (DDD) was conceptualized in order to unify under a common neurophysiologic c-v denominator the broad range of symptoms resulting from a sensory-motor, "organismic" dysmetria.

sistent holistic view of DDD, dyslexic cases may be seen as presenting with varying combinations and intensities of dysmetric dyslexia and dysmetric dyspraxia—depending upon the c-v site, intensity, and distribution of the dysfunction as well as upon function-specific dyslexic and/or dyspraxic compensatory endowments and developments.

Prior to the recognition of reading-score-compensated dyslexia and its c-v origin, the neurophysiologic unity of the dysmetric disorder remained artificially fragmented into distinct developmental dyslexic and developmental dyspraxic disorders. For example, despite Orton's repeated clinical correlation of "developmental apraxia" (abnormal clumsiness) and the syndrome of strephosymbolia, he failed to comprehend the common c-v denominator underlying this correlation. Interestingly, although Critchley clearly described imbalance, dyscoordination, and direction-related walking, talking, and associated motor phenomena among dyslexics, he failed to recognize even a clinical correlation between dyslexia and dyspraxia. Indeed, he considered the dyspraxic symptoms in dyslexia atypical and rare "epiphenomena":

> More banal disorders entailing both motility and spatial notions are seen in those dyslexics who are poor at ball-games; who cannot catch a ball in flight; or who take an unconscionable time to learn to ride a bicycle or a scooter. One must stress firmly however that such dyslexics are in the great minority. . . .
>
> In my series of 125 children presented with reading or spelling problems, 41 had been late in the acquisition of speech. Besides late development of speech, and imperfections in articulation, there may also be demonstrable at times an immaturity of the faculty of *language* as opposed to speech. . . .
>
> However, these disorders of language and of diction are inconsistent, and they are best regarded as being epiphenomena, and rare at that. . . .
>
> Some parents have said that their dyslexic child experiences great awkwardness in expressing himself verbally—stammering and stuttering, and finding himself at a loss for the appropriate words in which to clothe his thought. Other parents have reported differently, stating that their child can emit his ideas well enough in articulate speech, but that he falls down completely when it comes to written work. . . .
>
> Among the motility-disorders which can at times be discerned in dyslexic children is a general *gaucherie* or awkwardness. The gait may be shambling. The child may run in an ungainly fashion, and frequently tumble. Manual dexterity may be so maladroit as to raise the suspicion of a "congenital" type of motor dyspraxia. Because of muscular inco-ordination the dyslexic child may find it hard to bounce a ball, to tie and untie knots, or to fasten and unfasten buttons. These shortcomings were particularly stressed by Rabinovitch (1954) who wrote, "observation of gait, and the performance of motor acts such as dressing, opening and closing doors, and the handling of psychological test-materials, led to the definite impression of a non-specific awkwardness and clumsiness in motor function".
>
> Again I would stress that inordinate clumsiness is anything but an invariable symptom. Indeed it is rare. Of my series of 125 cases, it was noted in 34. When

> present it was more commonly encountered in the very young dyslexics. [Critchley, 1969, pp. 76, 81–83]

William S. Langford (1955), however, came closest to recognizing the neurophysiologic unity between dyslexia and dyspraxia. He described specifically the clumsy syndrome, which he called developmental dyspraxia, noted its presence in normal and poor readers, recognized the development of associated inferiority feelings, deduced that the origin of this disorder is a kinesthetic memory instability for experienced motor patterns, and compared it to the trouble dyslexics have in "getting sequential patterns and words in reading."

> They seem to have trouble in taking their old, more simple patterns and developing new sequences out of them. We see this in the larger and in the small motor muscle activities. Some of these children with severe dyspraxia do not have any associated reading disability or any academic handicap and in a sense they are fortunate because they can compensate with academic success and intellectual achievement. However, many of these children do have concomitant reading difficulties which prevent this compensational achievement in academic lines and theirs is a difficult lot. . . .
>
> There seems to be a difficulty not only in getting the concept of the movements as a whole but also in maintaining the kinaesthetic memory of the pictured movement once they have been through it. This does not seem to be ameliorated as the child grows older and one could think of it as being of the same order as the difficulty of the child who has trouble in getting sequential patterns and letters and words in reading. It is the difficulty in getting a Gestalt impression of things. [Langford, 1955, pp. 4–6]

The resemblance of Langford's views to those of the author's remains truly remarkable—especially as our respective research perspectives were entirely different, and our conceptualizations independently derived. We did, however, have one thing in common: dyslexic children.

Recognition of (1) the crucial function-specific and circuit-specific c-v nature of dyslexic symptoms, and (2) the related dysfunctioning versus compensatory CNS and emotional processes, eventually led to a unified explanation, of the variable forms of the dyslexic reading symptoms, as well as the dyslexic disorder itself.

As a result of these insights, the differential diagnostic and etiologic mystery separating the "dyslexic" reader from the multitude of slow readers was readily solved. The two types of reading disorders were clearly recognized to be merely symptomatic variations springing from a common c-v denominator.

In a similar fashion, a series of "clinically unique" developmental syndromes contained within a Symposium on Developmental Disorders of Motility and Language (1968) were found by the author to have a common c-v source and denominator ["Speech Disorders in Childhood," "Delayed Speech: Developmental Mutism," "Dysfluency and Stuttering," "Cluttering:

Central Language Imbalance," "Auditory Discrimination: Its Role in Language Comprehension, Formation and Use," "Dysacusis," "Right-Left Discrimination," "Cerebral Dominance and Its Disturbances," "Developmental Gerstmann Syndrome," "Syndromes of 'Minimal Cerebral Damage,'" "Developmental Dyscalculia," "Delayed Motor Development," "Developmental Clumsiness," "Dysgraphia and Other Abnormalities of Written Speech," and "Developmental Hyperactivity].

Interestingly enough, Harry Bakwin, Professor of Clinical Pediatrics, New York University School of Medicine, may have intuitively grasped the author's panoramic c-v dyslexic perspective by stating in his foreword to this symposium (Bakwin, 1968, pp. 565–566):

> This volume is limited to a discussion of the developmental disorders of motility and language but many conditions, such as enuresis, motion sickness . . . may properly be included in this category.
>
> The various disorders are closely interrelated . . . Dyslexia, spelling disability, clumsiness and delayed speech are not infrequently seen in the same person. Children with developmental hyperactivity often show visual-motor deficits which probably account, in part, for their learning difficulties.

Although Bakwin intuitively grasped an interrelationship between the various developmental disorders, he remained scientifically fixed to their traditionally established cerebral cortical origin, and thus tended perhaps to separate artificially their pathogenesis on the basis of degrees of compensation, while failing to recognize their unifying c-v basis.

> The developmental disorders of motility and language are manifestations of inborn alterations in cerebral organization. No anatomic lesions are demonstrable, nor are there electroencephlographic changes. It is assumed that the basis is a delay or alteration in the maturation of those areas of the brain which govern motor coordination and language . . .
>
> The developmental behavioral syndromes differ in two ways from that due to cerebral damage: first, in the developmental syndromes there is no history of a damaging injury to the brain; and secondly, no neurological signs are demonstrable . . .
>
> In some children recovery of normal function is complete, and in these the disorder may properly be considered a developmental delay. In others, improvement takes place but is never complete. Here the condition may be regarded as a developmental abnormality. [Bakwin, 1968]

According to the author's developing clinical research effort, very few dyslexics, if any, fully recover or compensate from their "developmental delay." In almost all cases thus far examined, clinical c-v signs and symptoms persist, despite significant and even overcompensated "gifted" symptomatic functioning. Although the persistence of *severe* symptoms into adulthood may suggest the presence of a mixed c-v-cortical disorder, this clinical correlation is by no means universally so. Most often, the compensatory range varies as significantly as the c-v disorder itself, and the manifest vector-resultant at any point in time is determined by the c-v and compensatory equilibrium.

In retrospect, a c-v neurophysiologic common denominator clinically was found to underlie a host of diverse sensory-motor and related mental functioning and dysfunctioning. As stated earlier, various research specialties have been unwittingly viewing highly selected and radiating c-v developmental lines or syndromes as either unique independent parallel disorders, or as disorders radiating from diverse patterns of primarily impaired and/or immature cerebral foci. The clinical-theoretical failure to recognize both the complex sensory-motor functional role of the c-v apparatus and the function-specific, circuit-specific, and time-specific nature of compensatory forces determining dyslexic functional outcome has resulted in a host of theoretically and iatrogenically created clinical entities, as well as a circular logic attributing these entities to a scientifically confabulated primary cerebral source.

A Retrospective Attempt at Explaining the Origin of the Various Theories of Dyslexia

Upon recognizing the complex adaptive range and diversity of the neurodynamic and psychodynamic mechanisms compensating dyslexics for their c-v dysfunction, it occurred to the author that the incidence of undiagnosed, and perhaps even "undiagnosable," dyslexia may be far higher than realized. This thought in turn triggered two further clinical associations. Dyslexics periodically ask, Could everyone have a touch of dyslexia? And neurotic patients repeatedly wondered, Is anyone really normal?

If, indeed, the incidence of c-v dysfunction or dyslexia is very high, if the reading scores among dyslexics range from one extreme to another, and if the concept of "normality" is relative and thus dependent upon only quantitative rather than qualitative variables, then perhaps we have stumbled upon the grain of truth that no doubt underlies the "atypical" research view that dyslexia does not exist and that the so-called dyslexic readers merely represent the slow end of the normal reading distribution. Might we all be touched by degrees and variations of c-v dysfunction and dyslexia? Is dyslexia not then statistically normal?

Encouraged by this analysis of the "nondyslexic" theory of dyslexia, the author attempted to explain similarly the raison d'etre for the other dyslexic theories. Because a denied primary c-v CNS dysfunction secondarily scrambled the cerebrum and psyche, as well as the related ocular, speech and handedness mechanisms, it appeared relatively easy, in retrospect, to comprehend the manner by which the various dyslexic etiologic theories attempted to explain the "manifest epi-phenomena" falling within their rather limited telescopic sights. In order to explain the aforementioned *secondary* scrambling phenomena, there developed a complex host of corresponding etiologic theories espousing the presence of minimal brain damage, minimal cerebral dysfunction, dominant parietal lobe impairment or lag, congenital Gerstmann syndrome, primary psychogenic traumas, primary ocular disturbances, aphasic impairments, cerebral dominance dysfunction or lag, and so on. Needless to say, each of these dyslexic theories explained only a "bird's-eye-view" of the manifest dyslexic panorama. No one theory was capable of explaining and encompassing the other dyslexic theories. And no one theory was capable of explaining and resolving the dyslexic riddle.

Recognition of the twin concepts of compensatory blurring speeds and compensatory reading scores in dyslexia, and the analysis of their variable and complex interactions, led to a resolution and harmonization of the paradoxical blurring-speed and reading-score data with the clinical dyslexic mainstream. In the harmonization and integration process, there developed a panoramic perspective and definition of dyslexia.

8 The Clinical Blurring-Speed Study

The accidental discovery that dyslexics have two blurring speeds led to the realization that the Staten Island, Queens and blind blurring-speed studies were contaminated by unknown mixtures of diagnostic sequential blurring speeds (SBS) versus compensatory single-targeting blurring speeds (STS). In retrospect, it appeared highly likely that the unwitting measurement of STS rather than SBS significantly contributed to the older dyslexic Group II blurring speeds in the Staten Island study, the "overlap" blurring speeds in the Queens Study, the DD recognition speeds in the blind blurring-speed study, and a majority of the so-called paradoxical blurring speeds characterizing the data to date. In a bilateral effort to improve the diagnostic accuracy of the blurring-speed methodology while testing the validity of the Staten Island blurring-speed study, the author initiated a new clinical study aimed at the statistical evaluation of SBS versus STS in DD versus normal controls.

Three hundred proven DD individuals and 25 normal controls were tested for both SBS and STS, and the entire blurring-speed data was then programmed in a manner enabling the computer print-outs to reveal:

1. the total, male/female, and right-/left-handed DD SBS distributions versus normal control blurring speeds;
2. the total, male/female, and right-/left-handed DD STS distributions versus SBS distributions;
3. 95% and 99% confidence or prediction limits for the various diagnostic blurring speeds or SBS;
4. SBS and STS as a function of age;
5. Mode III positive as a function of total DD sample, sex, handedness, age, single-targeting DDs, nonsingle targeting DDs;
6. comparisons of the total clinical DD SBS distributions with the corresponding Staten Island and Queens DD blurring-speed distributions.

Sample

In order to determine the SBS and STS distributions in dyslexia, and to compare these DD blurring-speed distributions to those of normal individuals, the blurring speeds of 300 consecutively diagnosed DD individuals and 25 normal controls were recorded and statistically analyzed. The diagnosis of dyslexia was made on the basis of presenting symptoms, neurologic examination, and ENG testing. The 25 normal controls were DD family members containing a negative history of dyslexic symptoms and an absence of c-v findings upon neurologic examination. The mean age of the DD sample was 17.4; ages ranged from 5 to 50, though 80% of the DD individuals fell within the age range of 7–15. The male/female ratio was 2.4:1 and the right-/left-handed ratio was 9:1. The mean age of the control group was 25.4.

Methodology

Each DD and normal individual was tested for SBS and for the presence or absence of single targeting. When single targeting was present, single-targeting blurring speeds, or STS, were obtained. The compensatory single-targeting mechanisms triggered following the sequential blurring of word and elephant sequences, respectively, are illustrated in Fig. 8–1.

ENG ocular-motor tracking patterns taken during Modes I and II testing reveal sequential tracking to be continuous until the SBS endpoint, following which only single targets are intermittently fixated up to, and even beyond, the normal SBS. The ENG tracking pattern corresponding to the word Mode I SBS and compensatory single-targeting is illustrated in Fig. 8–2.

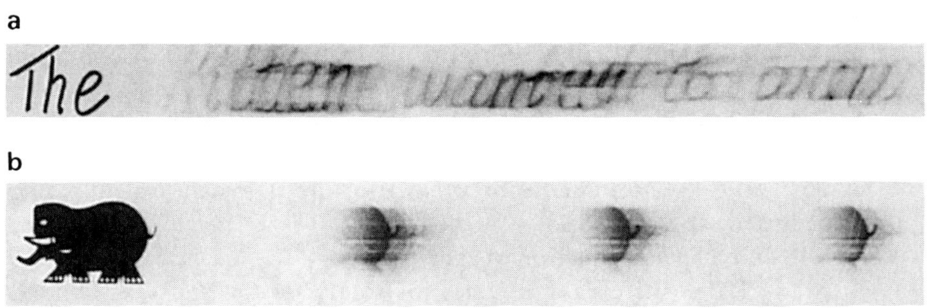

Fig. 8–1. Compensatory single-targeting in dyslexia. Following sequential blurring, compensatory (or learned) single-targeting mechanisms are triggered in order to enhance adaptively the impaired fixation and tracking capacity among dyslexics. The viewer's perception of single-targeted words (*a*) and elephants (*b*), respectively, are shown.

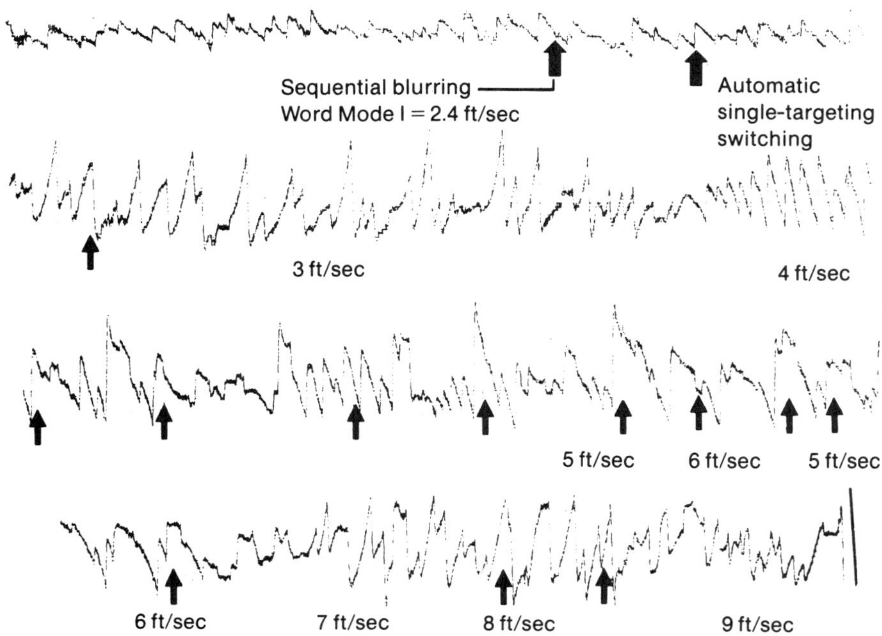

Fig. 8–2. An ENG ocular-motor tracking pattern corresponding to word Mode I testing. The dyslexic individual's sequential blurring speed (SBS) is 2.4 ft./sec. Following sequential blurring, the patient reported intermittent single-target recognition until approximately 8.5 ft./sec. The arrows indicate the single points of word recognition. This ENG pattern corresponding to the onset and duration of single targeting was found to be characterized by large amplitude ocular-motor excursions extending over wide temporal spans. Upon questioning, this wave form corresponded to the dyslexic's conscious intent to fixate and visually hold on to single recognizable targets.

Statistical Overview

In order to facilitate the assimilation and recall of the ensuing statistical sequential analyses, the author has once again chosen to highlight the findings.

1. All DD sequential blurring speed (SBS) means, regardless of visual gestalt or mode, were found to be significantly lower than the corresponding normal control SBS means—clearly indicating that the tracking capacity of dyslexics is deficient relative to normal controls. In addition, DD SBS were found to be independent of sex and handedness.

2. One-third of the DD sample evidenced *single-targeting*, whereas single-targeting was distinctly absent among normal control subjects. As might be anticipated, the STS means were significantly greater than the corre-

sponding and total SBS distribution means. Interestingly, the statistical difference between the diagnostic and compensatory blurring speed means was significantly magnified when the STS means were compared to their own SBS means—suggesting that compensatory tracking speeds may be triggered by the adaptive need resulting from low blurring speeds or severely deficient tracking capacity. STS were found to be statistically independent of sex and handedness.

3. SBS were found to be functions of visual gestalt patterns, and thus 95% and 99% prediction limits were determined.

4. SBS and STS scattergrams appeared visibly independent of age, whereas a regression anaylsis of variance of similar appearing data from another study suggested that both SBS and STS may increase with age.

5. One-third of the DD sample was Mode III positive, whereas all normal controls were Mode III negative. Mode III positive was significantly dependent upon age and independent of sex and handedness. Mode III positive appeared significantly correlated to non-single-targeting dyslexics—suggesting that compensatory Mode III and compensatory single-targeting mechanisms may be interrelated.

6. Statistical comparisons of the clinical, Staten Island and Queens DD blurring-speed distributions suggested the presence of a harmonious relationship between the three independently performed studies.

Statistical Analysis and Results

Normal Blurring-Speed Data

Table 8–1 summarizes the normal Mode I and II blurring-speed data and compares it with the corresponding DD SBS data. Normal control individuals did not evidence Mode III positive or compensatory single-targeting.

Table 8–1. Mean Sequential Blurring Speeds: Total DD Sample vs. Normal Controls

	DD Sample		Normal Controls	
	Mean	Standard Deviation	Mean	Standard Deviation
Word Mode I	3.23	(1.64)	7.46	(0.58)
Word Mode II	2.26	(1.27)	6.23	(0.60)
Elephant Mode I	2.22	(1.23)	6.18	(0.55)
Elephant Mode II	1.54	(1.01)	5.16	(0.53)

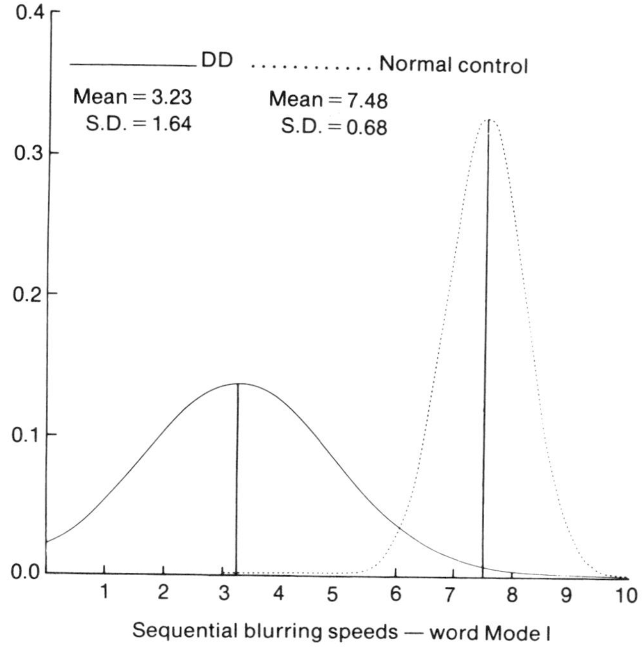

Fig. 8–3. The bimodal distribution resulting from the word Mode I SBS scores. The analysis of the total word Mode I SBS data (300 dysmetric dyslexics and 25 control subjects) resulted in a bimodal blurring-speed distribution. This bimodal distribution was found to be typical of the corresponding word Mode II, elephant Mode I and elephant Mode II blurring-speed distributions.

Dyslexic Blurring-Speed Data

Diagnostic or Sequential Blurring-Speed Distributions

The statistical SBS distribution of the total sample consisting of 300 DD individuals and 25 normal controls was determined for each of the word Modes I and II and elephant Modes I and II blurring-speed modalities. Each of the combined DD and normal SBS distributions was found to be significantly bimodal. The total DD and normal control word Mode I SBS distribution is illustrated in Fig. 8–3. This distribution was found to be typical of the other blurring-speed distributions.

Upon statistical analysis, all the DD Modes I and II SBS means were found to be significantly lower than the corresponding normal control SBS means ($p < 0.001$) (Table 8–1).

The total DD word Mode I SBS distribution was subdivided into male/female and right-/left-handedness distributions. As illustrated by Figs. 8–4

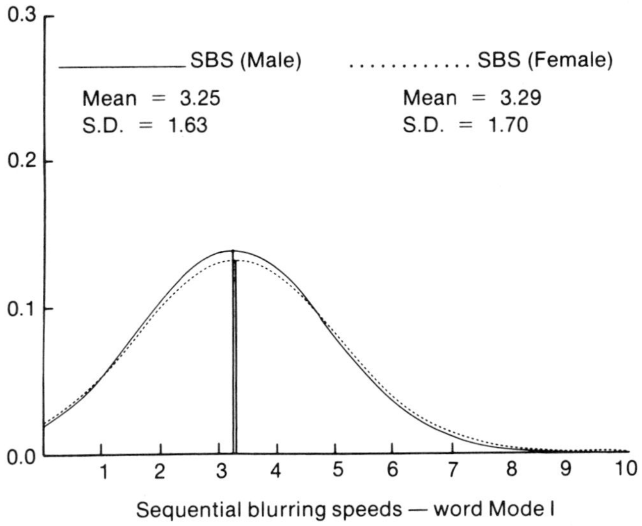

Fig. 8–4. The male and female word Mode I SBS dyslexic distributions. There is no significant difference between the DD male and female SBS distributions.

and 8–5 respectively, dyslexic SBS were statistically and visibly found to be independent of sex and handedness.

Compensatory Single-Targeting Blurring-Speed Distributions

One-third (98/300) of the DD sample evidenced single-targeting. The mean STS (4.52) was found to be significantly higher ($p < 0.01$) than the corresponding total dyslexic SBS mean (3.23). This statistical relationship may be readily seen by comparing the previously illustrated total DD word Mode I SBS distribution in Fig. 8–3 with the STS distribution in Fig. 8–6. In addition, upon statistical analysis the mean word Mode I STS (4.52) was found to be approximately twice the corresponding word Mode I SBS mean (2.59), and the latter value was found to be significantly lower ($p < 0.01$) than the total DD word Mode I SBS mean (3.23) (Fig. 8–6). A similar relationship was found for all the Mode I and II SBS modalities corresponding to their respective STS (Table 8–2).

The total word Mode I STS distribution was subdivided into male/female and right-/left-handedness STS distributions. As illustrated by Fig. 8–7 and 8–8 respectively, compensatory single-targeting was found to be independent of sex and handedness.

95% and 99% Confidence or Prediction Limits

All blurring-speed modalities were found to be highly correlated with each other (>0.87). Thus, given any SBS determination, all other corresponding

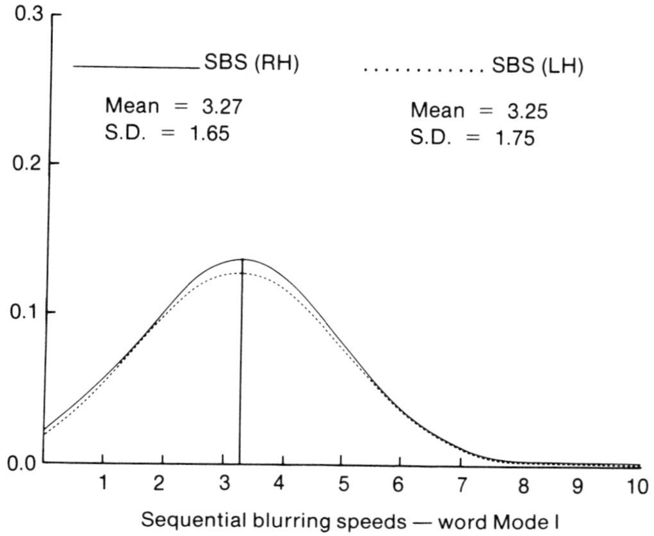

Fig. 8–5. Right- and left-handed word Mode I SBS dyslexic distributions. There is no significant difference between the DD right- and left-handed SBS distributions.

SBS were found to be highly predictable to within 95% and 99% limits (Fig. 8–9). The correlation coefficients as well as the prediction limits for the various SBS modalities are summarized in Table 8–3.

Single-Targeting and Sequential Blurring Speeds As a Function of Age

According to computerized scattergrams, there did not appear to be any visible increase of either SBS or STS with age (Figs. 8–10, 8–11). Unfortunately, these data were not statistically analyzed in time for inclusion

Table 8–2. Mean STS vs. SBS—Dyslexic Single-targeting-positive Sample

	STS		Corresponding SBS	
	Mean	Standard Deviation	Mean	Standard Deviation
Word Mode I	4.52	(1.08)	2.59	(1.52)
Word Mode II	3.37	(0.45)	1.76	(1.15)
Elephant Mode I	3.48	(0.66)	1.69	(1.13)
Elephant Mode II	2.56	(0.26)	1.24	(0.90)

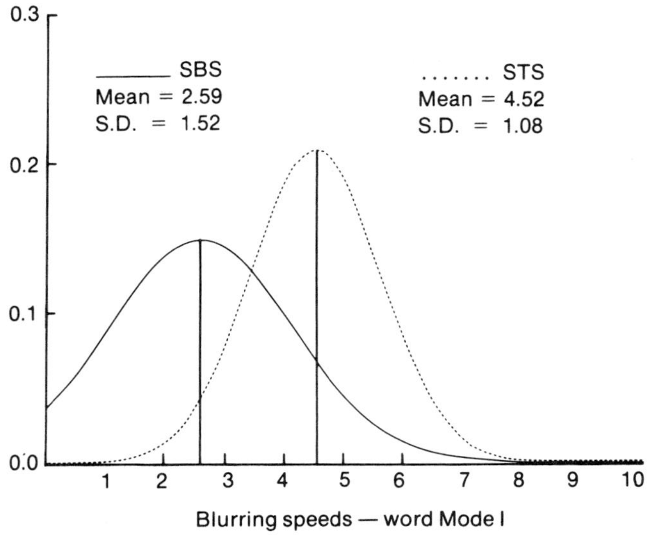

Fig. 8–6. Blurring-speed distributions resulting from a comparison of compensatory STS and their corresponding diagnostic SBS. As a result of this comparison, the SBS corresponding to dyslexics demonstrating single-targeting were found to be significantly lower than the SBS corresponding to dyslexics demonstrating no single-targeting. This statistical observation supported the assumption that compensatory single-targeting might be adaptively triggered by severely impaired tracking capacity.

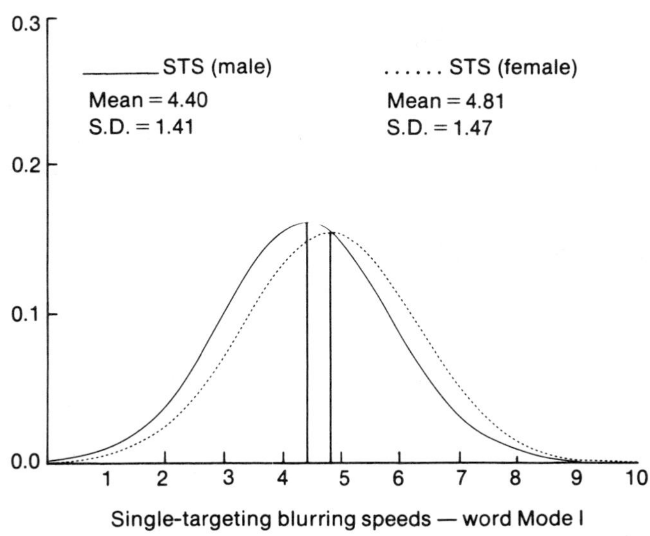

Fig. 8–7. Male and female compensatory STS distributions. Single-targeting appears to be independent of sex.

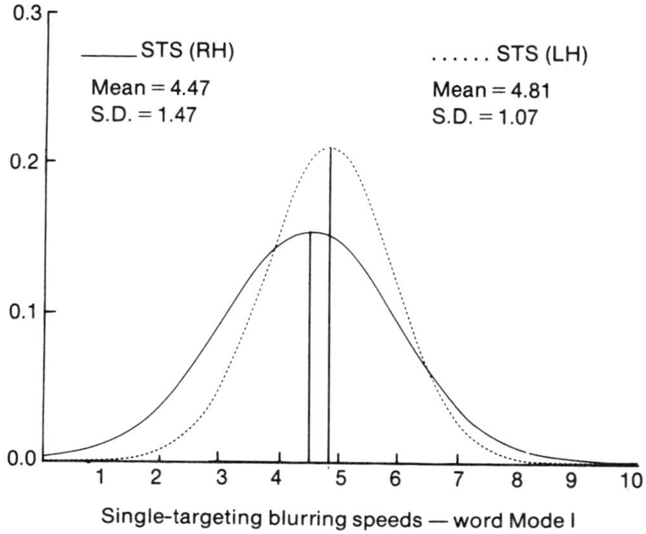

Fig. 8–8. Right- and left-handed compensatory STS distributions. Single-targeting appears to be independent of handedness.

within this chapter. However, similar appearing scattergrams of DD and normal blurring speeds versus age were subjected to a regression approach analysis of variance. The analysis indicated that both normal SBS and DD SBS and STS increased with age—thereby suggesting that the clear-cut Staten Island blurring speed–age correlations were perhaps oversimplified and

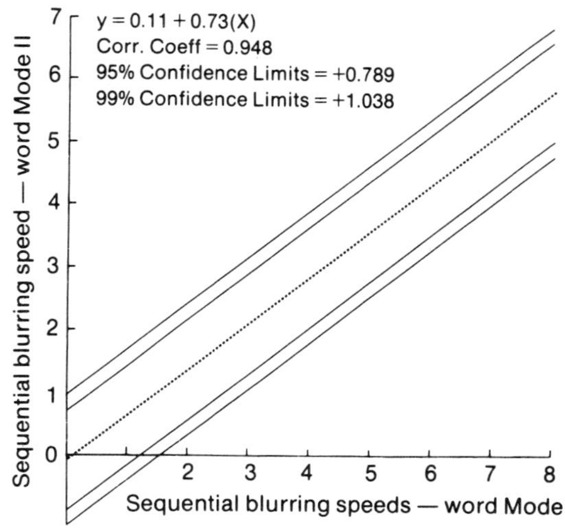

Fig. 8–9. The statistically derived 95% and 99% confidence limits for word Mode I vs. word Mode II. Similar limits were determined for all the sequential-blurring-speed modalities and have facilitated the development of a more reliable and stable blurring-speed methodology.

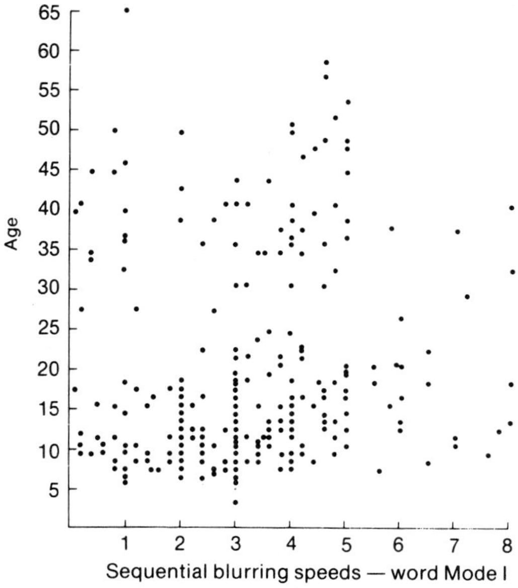

Fig. 8–10. A scattergram illustrating word Mode I SBS as a function of age. Although there appears to be no visible relationship between SBS and age, a regression approach analysis of variance of a similar scattergram did reveal that SBS may statistically increase with age.

exaggerated versions of the true blurring speed–age realistic rule. In retrospect, the naked eye was found insufficient to discern complex and multifactorial biologic patterns. The observation that compensatory single targeting did not dramatically increase with age, as anticipated, led the

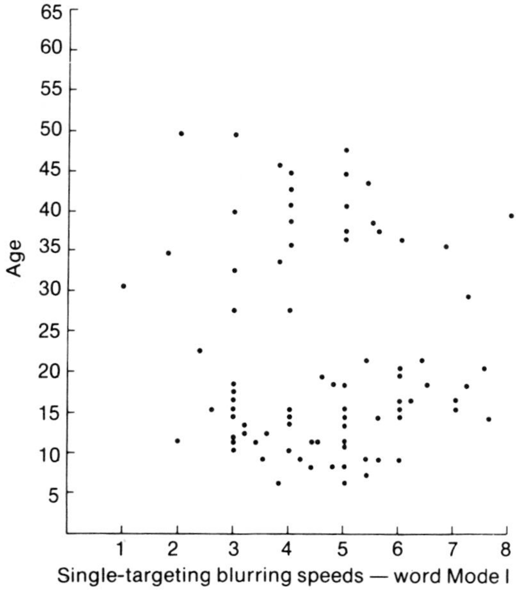

Fig. 8–11. A scattergram illustrating compensatory word Mode I STS as a function of age. Although there appears to be no visible relationship between STS and age, a regression approach analysis of variance of a similar scattergram did reveal that STS may statistically increase with age.

Table 8–3. SBS Equations and Correlation Coefficients

(y)	Equations	(x)	95%	99%	Correlation Coefficient
Word Mode II	$y = -0.11 + 0.73(x)$	Word Mode I	±0.789	±1.038	0.948
Elephant Mode I	$y = 0.09 + 0.66(x)$	Word Mode I	±1.152	±1.152	0.879
Elephant Mode II	$y = -0.14 + 0.52(x)$	Word Mode I	±1.061	±1.397	0.845
Word Mode II	$y = 0.20 + 0.92(x)$	Elephant Mode I	±1.096	±1.443	0.989
Elephant Mode I	$y = 0.52 + 1.10(x)$	Elephant Mode II	±1.036	±1.364	0.904

author to assume neurodynamically: (1) that the development of compensatory single-targeting may be more significantly determined by decreased SBS or tracking deficiency than age, and (2) that compensatory single-targeting may be "forced," induced, or learned at any age, and was thus dependent upon a host of such complex and overdetermined variables as "need," ocular-motor tracking exercises, and so on.

Mode III Positive Findings

Approximately one-third (103/300) of DD individuals were found to be Mode III positive according to the Mode III testing methodology utilized in the Queens study. In addition, Mode III positive was found to be independent of sex and handedness. For example, in a male/female DD sample consisting of 69% males/31% females, the male/female Mode III positive incidence was found to be 70%/30%. In the right-/left-handed DD sample containing 90% right/10% left-handed individuals, the Mode III positive incidence equalled 90%/10%.

The incidence of Mode III positive was found to decrease significantly with age ($p < 0.0001$), and thus clearly confirmed the similar data obtained in the Staten Island study (Fig. 8–12). In addition, by virtue of a slight modification in the Mode III testing procedure there resulted an

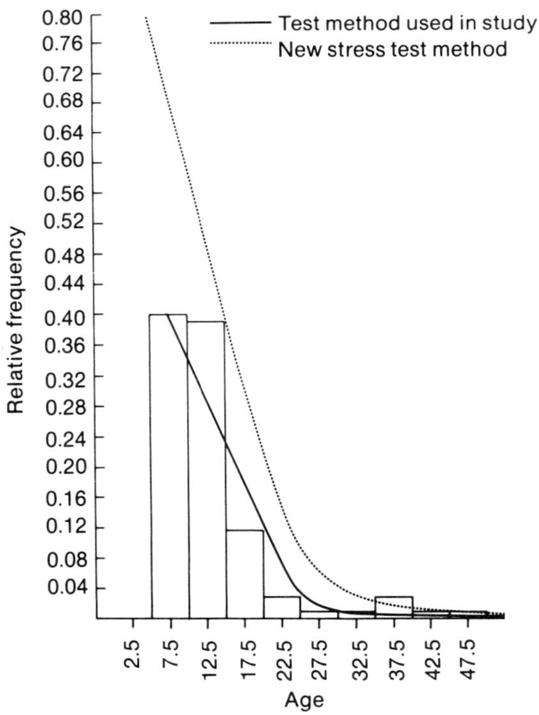

Fig. 8–12. The relationship of Mode III positive and age. The background histogram represents the distribution of dyslexic ages within the clinical blurring-speed study. Mode III positive is rapidly compensated for with age. Moreover, a new Mode III stress test methodology was found to double the Mode III positive yield obtained when testing young dyslexic children.

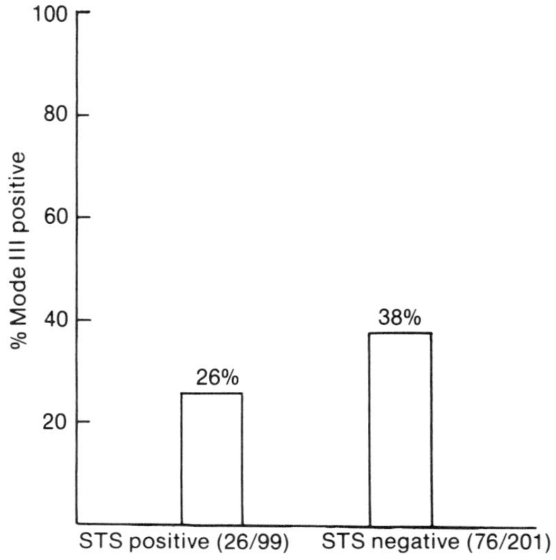

Fig. 8–13. The incidence of Mode III positive findings among single-targeting positive and negative dyslexics. The incidence of Mode III positive was significantly higher ($P < 0.025$) among dyslexics who demonstrate an absence of compensatory single targeting. The positive correlation of Mode III positive and STS negative suggested a failure in common or overlapping compensatory tracking mechanisms to convert Mode III positive to Mode III negative and STS negative to STS positive.

approximate 100% increase in the percentage of Mode III positive yield among dyslexics. For example, if dyslexics are instructed to consciously fixate the moving background, a significant percentage of Mode III negative individuals will be converted to Mode III positive (Fig. 8–12).

Mode III positive was found significantly correlated to DD individuals without compensatory single-targeting ($p < 0.025$). For example, the Mode III positive incidence among STS/non-STS dyslexics equalled 26%/38% (Fig. 8–13). Inasmuch as Mode III negative and STS both indicate the presence of compensatory processes, the correlation between the two was neurodynamically assumed to suggest the existence of overlapping compensatory mechanisms. And because c-v compensation was found to occur despite the residual presence of c-v dysfunction, the author assumed that the cerebral cortex may well play a dominant role in influencing and/or determining c-v and dyslexic compensatory processes.

Comparison of the Staten Island, Queens, and Clinical Blurring-Speed Distributions

Statistical comparison of the Staten Island, Queens, and clinical dyslexic blurring-speed distributions clearly suggested the existence of a harmonious relationship between the three independent studies (Fig. 8–14).

Additional Insights and Atypical Findings

Occasionally, DD patients were found to evidence compensatory single-targeting for only certain visual gestalts and not others—indicating that compensatory single-targeting may be gestalt-specific and circuit-dependent.

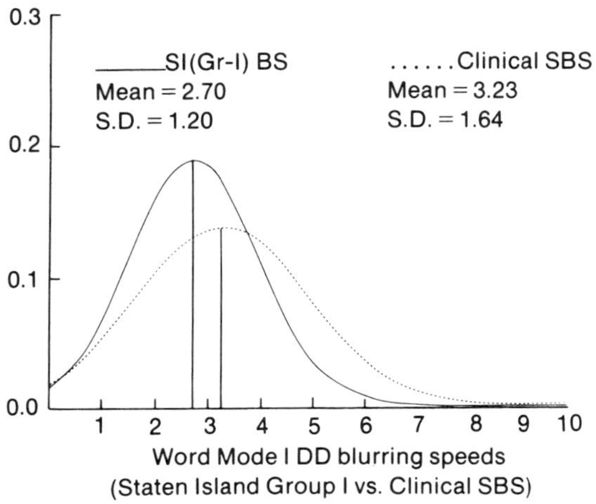

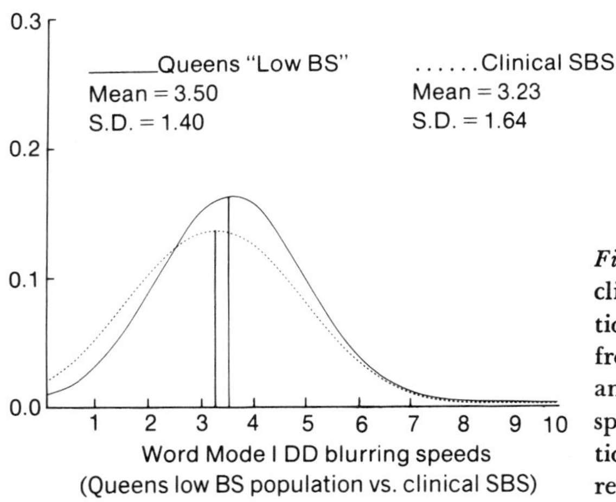

Fig. 8–14. The DD word Mode I clinical blurring-speed distribution compared with that derived from (*a*) the Staten Island study and (*b*) the Queens low-blurring-speed distribution. The distributions from the three studies are remarkably similar.

This initially unexpected observation seemed, in retrospect, consistent with a host of clinical data suggesting (1) that compensatory single-targeting (STS) may be learned or imprinted by forcing DD individuals to track moving targets past their SBS and (2) that c-v compensation is gestalt- and circuit-specific, rather than generalized, and thus that c-v compensatory transfer may be highly restricted and localized. In addition, a small percentage of DD individuals were found to have statistically significant differences in right–left versus left–right blurring speeds.* Directional blurring-speed dif-

* By the time this clinical study was completed, the author had recognized and demonstrated the existence of a series of diagnostically significant blurring-speed endpoints. The description of these endpoints will be thoroughly discussed in Chapter 9.

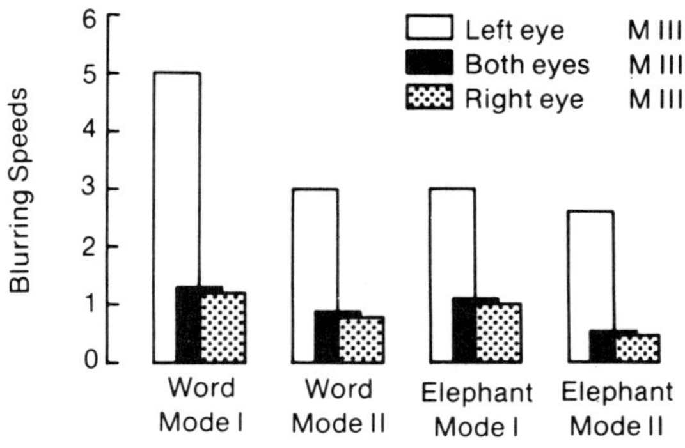

Fig. 8–15. The manner in which blurring speeds may vary as a function of right, left, and both eyes in a dyslexic adult experiencing an acute right-sided unilateral orbital headache. The Modes I and II right-eyed blurring speeds are significantly reduced, as are the blurring speeds corresponding to bilateral visual testing. Interestingly, Mode III was found to be positive when both eyes were tested in the normal binocular fashion, and for right-eyed testing. The Modes I and II left-eyed blurring speeds were borderline low in magnitude and Mode III was negative. During testing, this 30-year-old male was on anti-motion sickness medication (meclizine), thus accounting for his borderline left-eyed blurring speeds. His premedication left-eyed blurring speeds were significantly reduced.

ferences greater than 1–2 feet per second were found to be diagnostically significant of c-v dysfunction. Moreover, the testing of one of these DD individuals indicated that during an episode of unilateral orbital headache, there developed a significant corresponding decrease in blurring speeds in the affected eye. This fascinating exception is illustrated by Fig. 8–15.

Unilateral orbital headaches associated with blurring and vertigo were not uncommonly found characterizing a significant percentage of both young and adult dyslexics, as well as post-concussion syndromes due to "minor" auto accidents and acquired c-v dysfunctioning.* In addition, the early and effective pharmacologic treatment of DD individuals often resulted in an improvement in these orbital headaches, as well as in visual acuity, whereas cessation of the medications at times resulted in a dramatic regression in refraction as a function of time. This observation suggested the possibility that the early diagnosis and treatment of the c-v disorder might prevent otherwise irreversible "somato-somatic" CNS and/or body changes

* This data is contained in an unpublished study in which the author demonstrated that a vast majority of "mild" post-concussion "compensation" and "no-fault" accident cases manifest vertigo, unilateral, and bilateral headaches associated with blurring and c-v dysfunction.

in a manner analogous to the visual impairment resulting from undiagnosed and untreated amblyopia.

A Theoretically Constructed Recognition-Speed Distribution

In an effort to compare the author's clinical blurring-speed study with the results of the blind (recognition speed) study, an attempt was made to convert theoretically the former study into a recognition-speed study. Inasmuch as the blind study did not take into account single-targeting, the artificial conversion of the clinical blurring-speed study to recognition speeds had to deliberately ignore the presence of single-targeting, and thus the highest possible blurring speeds (STS where possible/otherwise SBS) were all fallaciously assumed to be of equal diagnostic significance. To accomplish this conversion, a distribution was obtained in which STS were utilized where possible, and SBS were utilized for the STS negative DD remainder.

The resulting theoretically constructed DD recognition-speed distribution is shifted toward the normal blurring-speed distribution, and the skewed SBS dyslexic distribution is normalized (Fig. 8–16). Moreover, the shaded area in Fig. 8–16, indicating the overlap resulting from the shift, clearly supports the previous speculations suggesting that normal Modes I and II blurring speeds, in association with Mode III positive values, were most likely due to single-target Mode I and II values. However, this shift by no means can account for the results derived from the blind study—suggesting the possibility that the latter study may have inadvertently contained significant degrees of erroneous or confabulatory results. It is hoped that this theoretically constructed recognition-speed distribution will serve as a baseline and point of reference for future recognition-speed studies, which are planned to begin when the 3D optical scanner III has been completed. Because recognition-speed testing may suggest and thus create *higher* blurring-speed values, a comparison of the true recognition-speed curves with the artificially created recognition-speed curve may indicate, and perhaps even measure, the role of "suggestion" in recognition-speed testing.

Summary

The clinical blurring-speed study of 300 proven DD individuals and 25 normal controls confirmed and enlarged the insights derived from the Staten Island and Queens studies. The distribution of blurring speeds was investigated and analyzed. Approximately one-third of DD individuals evidenced compensatory STS, and the mean STS was found to be approximately twice its corresponding SBS mean—suggesting that DD individuals with the lowest SBS are most likely to develop compensatory STS. Although Mode III positive was found to be compensated significantly with age, Modes I and

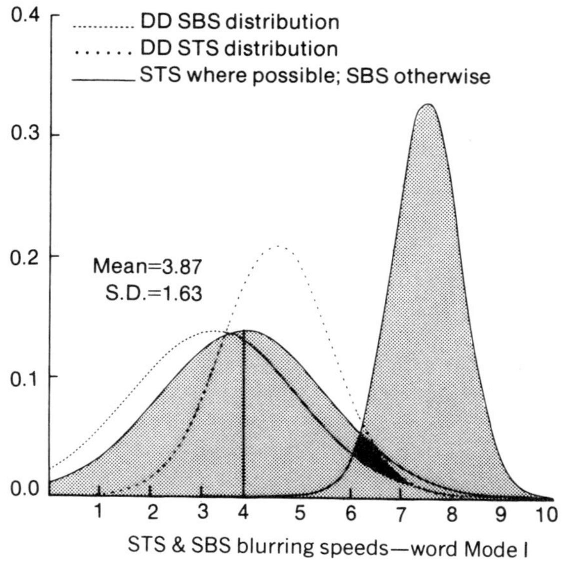

Fig. 8–16. A theoretically constructed recognition-speed distribution. In order to construct this distribution, it was assumed (1) that normal controls did not demonstrate single-targeting and that their recognition speeds would equal their SBS, (2) that the recognition speeds of one-third of the dyslexic population demonstrating compensatory single-targeting would be equal to their STS, and (3) that the recognition speeds of the remaining two-thirds of the non-single-targeting dyslexic population would equal their SBS. As a result of this "artificial" recognition-speed distribution, the DD recognition-speed population (stippled area) manifested as a resultant of two background blurring-speed populations: one-third STS and two-thirds SBS among single-targeting negative dyslexics. The resulting DD recognition-speed population was shifted over to the normal blurring-speed range—creating greater degrees of overlap (shaded area). It was assumed that the Staten Island, blind and Queens blurring-speed studies contained unknown mixtures of dyslexic SBS and STS determinations, to some extent accounting for normal Modes I and II blurring-speed scores among dyslexics with either Mode III positive or negative. As a result of this distribution, it might be easy to envision the effect resulting from increased yields of high "confabulatory" dyslexic blurring speeds or recognition speeds. These confabulatory speeds would significantly magnify the extent of the shaded overlap area.

II SBS and STS appeared significantly more stable with age than did the corresponding Staten Island blurring speed–age correlation. In addition, a few more exceptions were discovered, and a series of diagnostic blurring-speed endpoints were elucidated.

As a result of this study, the vast majority of blurring-speed exceptions to date became explainable, the diagnostic blurring-speed endpoint became a significantally more reliable parameter of c-v dysfunction, and the correlation of compensatory single-targeting and compensatory Mode III suggested the possibility that cortical–cerebellar feedback circuits may play a crucial role in dyslexic and c-v compensatory processes.*

*In a personal correspondence (1977), Sir John Eccles called the author's attention to the research of Gonshor and Jones (1971, 1976a, 1976b), Ito, Nisimaru, and Yamamoto (1973), and Robinson (1976). These papers supported the hypothesis that the cerebellum may serve as a primary vector resulting in ocular-motor tracking compensation.

9 Ocular-Motor Tracking Patterns in Dyslexic and Normal Individuals

Ocular-motor (ENG) tracking patterns were obtained during Modes I, II, and III blurring-speed testing in order to determine the neurophysiologic and "objective" indicators of the blurring/recognition-speed endpoint (Fig. 9–1). It was anticipated that this study might more accurately delineate the diagnostic parameters required to separate DD and non-DD individuals, and thus hopefully provide a solution to the exceptions and the paradox introduced by the blind blurring-speed study.

Initial Attempt at Classification

All initial attempts to classify the DD and non-DD ENG blurring-speed patterns into simple and distinct groups resulted in utter confusion and frustration. The author was forced to postpone completion of the study for two years in the service of preserving his scientific sanity. Many confusing problems arose:

1. DD individuals were found tracking a moving sequence they claimed not to see—a phenomenon eventually understood as "phantom scanning."
2. DD individuals reported blurring at low speeds, and yet at higher speeds claimed they could identify the rapidly moving targets. These seemingly "impossible" observations eventually led to the recognition that dyslexics frequently have two blurring/recognition-speed endpoints. For example, at the SBS endpoint, dyslexics may utilize an STS mechanism, and thus intermittenly fixate single targets up to normal or greater than normal blurring speeds.
3. Reading-score-normal controls occasionally had ocular-motor tracking curves identical to dyslexics. These so-called normal controls were later recognized to be reading-score-compensated dyslexics—a term utilized to encompass both late bloomers and early bloomers.
4. Mode III positive findings occurred with and without the presence of

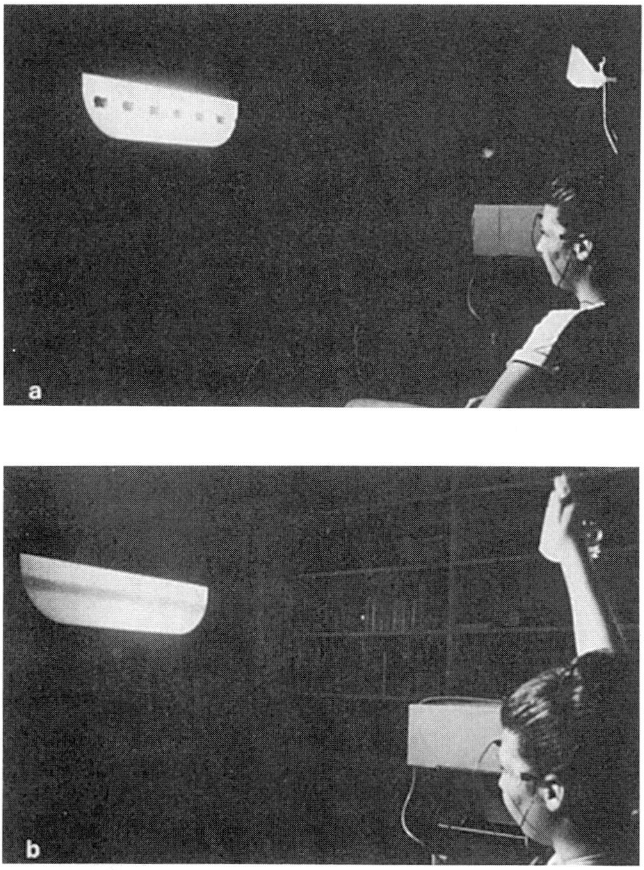

Fig. 9–1. ENG ocular-motor tracking patterns. (*a*) During Modes I, II, and III testing, a child's ocular-motor tracking responses are simultaneously obtained via ENG. (*b*) The child has been instructed to raise her hand at the initiation of blurring.

ENG-detectable nystagmus. At times, Mode III was found to be positive in the presence of normal word and elephant Modes I and II blurring speeds—despite the fact that Mode III positive was statistically correlated to significantly decreased Modes I and II blurring speeds. These "normal" word and elephant Modes I and II blurring speeds corresponding to Mode III positive were retrospectively recognized to be compensatory STS rather than diagnostically significant SBS blurring speeds. The fact that Mode III positive occurred both with and without the presence of ENG-detectable nystagmus was eventually explained by the conceptualization that central c-v processing may be impaired despite compensatory inhibition of the corresponding peripheral nystagmus.

5. Dyslexic individuals exhibited high and low amplitude, slow and rapid velocity, and dysmetric and eumetric tracking curves which changed as a function of time and as a function of ocular-motor tracking exercises—further highlighting the complex interaction of dysfunctioning versus compensatory ocular-motor tracking mechanisms.

6. Ocular-motor tracking curves corresponding to severely deficient blurring speeds did not always correlate with severely deficient reading scores. At times, reading scores would spurt as a function of age, medications, ocular-motor exercises, and so on, while the corresponding blurring speeds and tracking curves remained unchanged—leading to the recognition of function-specific rather than generalized compensatory processes.

7. Mode III positive was noted to be dependent upon the specific foreground/background gestalt or configuration, as well as upon the direction of the moving background. Changes in Mode III from positive to negative often were not reflected in the ENG tracking pattern. This observation was found to support the conceptualization of peripheral versus central tracking and processing mechanisms, as well as peripheral versus central compensatory processes. Thus, compensatory central processing may occur without evidence of peripheral ENG compensation, and vice versa.

In retrospect, this range of diverse and seemingly contradictory findings no longer seems critical and, in fact, should have been expected. Yet consider how a naive investigator might feel when a dyslexic individual blurs at 2 feet per second and continues to track until 9 feet per second. Even worse, how could anyone have explained the manner and method by which a dyslexic might blur at 2 feet per second and identify moving objects at 9 feet per second? And how could Mode III be positive if there exists no detectable ENG evidence of a foreground/background tracking nystagmus? Needless to say, many questions and doubts were triggered regarding the reliability of the blurring-speed methodology and the author's data.

Was it possible that the dyslexic children did not understand directions and reported erroneous data? Even worse, was it possible that the author unwittingly suggested and obtained the blurring speeds and data he expected rather than the "real" blurring speeds?

Initially, all children reporting blurring at low speeds and recognition at high speeds were thought to be confabulating or "playing." Was it possible that many other tested subjects had confabulated as well—without detection? Was all the research time and effort spent in vain?

The initial, oversimplified expectation of a neat ocular-motor tracking and blurring-speed endpoint classification did not materialize. However, the honest but frustrating recognition of ENG tracking exceptions to both the author's expectations and the developing "statistical rule" resulted in a re-determined effort to pursue and comprehend the data. This goal was achieved only after several years of "dysmetric" and painstaking investigations. As a result of these investigations:

1. The traditionally accepted definitions and conceptualizations of dys-

lexia were found to be based on unwittingly selective and biased sampling. Thus, dyslexic individuals were found to have variable and fluctuating reading scores. Dyslexic reading scores were found to vary upon such factors as test, test situations, tester, I.Q., and compensatory mechanisms. Although almost all dyslexics in the initial studies had c-v dysfunction, it did not necessarily follow that all individuals with c-v dysfunction had to have poor reading scores and identical, or "pure," symptoms. Continuing studies eventually led to a redefinition of dyslexia—a definition independent of reading scores.

2. Dyslexics do not track in a manner similar to c-v normal or non-DD individuals. It was surprisingly found that dyslexic individuals often have two significantly different blurring-speed endpoints, i.e., sequential and single-target blurring speeds. This discovery led to a resolution of the blurring-speed paradox. The blind study may inadvertently have measured compensatory STS and encouraged "confabulated" and high speeds, whereas the Staten Island study may have measured primarily diagnostic SBS, and the Queen study may have inadvertently measured greater combinations of the two speeds than did the Staten Island study.

3. The concept of cerebellar inhibition, inhibitory failure, and compensatory tracking resulted in an understanding of: (a) the reflex inhibition of the tracking nystagmus at blurring in normal and compensated dyslexics, and (b) phantom scanning, the failure of the compensatory inhibitory mechanism once blurring occurred and/or the adaptive CNS phantom attempt at searching for recognizable targets.

4. The concept of subclinical nystagmus and subclinical neurophysiologic mechanisms and symptoms resulted in the insight that compensatory inhibition or suppression of the peripheral clinical dysfunction does not imply reversal or elimination of the underlying central c-v disorder. One can thus conceptualize the existence of c-v central and peripheral tracking–processing mechanisms, as well as the existence of corresponding function-specific compensatory mechanisms which can effect one function without the other. One can thus explain blurring without nystagmus and nystagmus without blurring. For example, Mode III positive movement or blurring was found clinically to occur with or without the detectable presence of nystagmus. And Mode III nystagmus may be clinically present with or without blurring. In fact, during compensation, Mode III positive for both directions may change to Mode III negative for one direction before becoming Mode III negative for both directions—clearly indicating the direction-specificity of the compensatory mechanisms.*

The attempt to explain and comprehend what appeared to be contradictory data resulted in neurophysiologic insights sufficient to classify and

* Direction-specific Mode III positive was found to have an interesting parallel in c-v-related phobias. It is not uncommon to find escalator phobics who compensate and can ride up an escalator, but remain fearful of riding down—leading to the recognition of direction-specific c-v phobic mechanisms.

explain the expected as well as the unexpected, the probable as well as the paradoxical and "impossible."

A Second Attempt at Classification

Ocular-motor tracking patterns corresponding to Modes I, II, and III were obtained for normal and DD individuals and the results summarized.

Normal Tracking Patterns

Modes I and II. Moving words, sentences, and elephants induce a tracking nystagmus which attempts to keep the targets in focus. At blurring, there is a sudden "reflex" reduction or inhibition of the rate of the tracking nystagmus, and this rapid decrease in the tracking rate defines blurring neurophysiologically (Fig. 9–2).

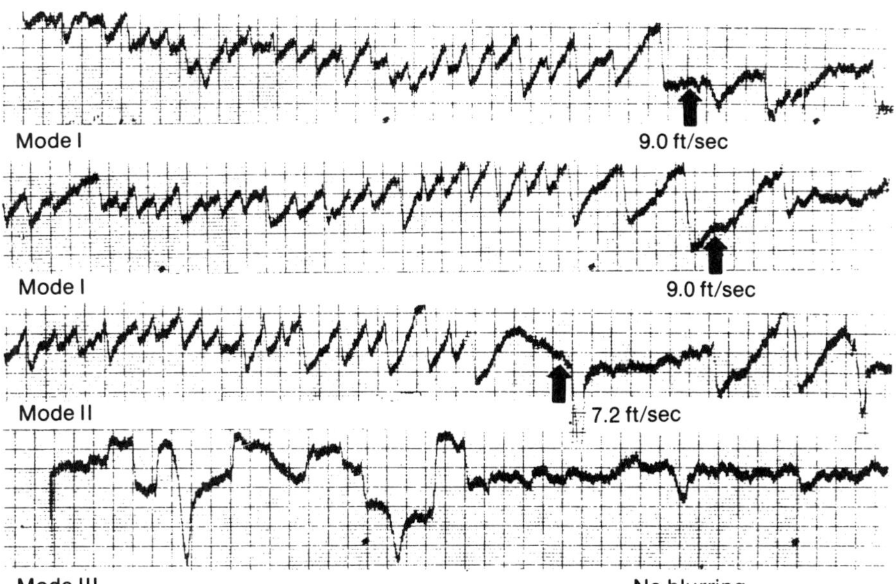

Fig. 9–2. Kenny P. is a c-v normal and reading-score normal 11½-year-old youngster with normal blurring speeds. ENG tracking curves during word Modes I and II blurring-speed testing (3D optical scanner I) reveal a dramatic reduction or cessation of the tracking rate at the blurring endpoint—and this ENG blurring pattern is pathognomonic of c-v normal (and some compensated DDD) individuals. There is no involuntary ocular deflection noted during Mode III testing except for blinking and/or occasional conscious or voluntary background scanning movements. Upon repeated word Mode I testing, the ENG tracking pattern as well as the blurring speed endpoint remain stable and reproducible.

Mode III. During foreground fixation, the moving background does not induce a tracking nystagmus in c-v normal individuals. The tracking pattern is devoid of any significant ocular deflections, and foreground blurring or movement is not experienced (Fig. 9–2).

Dyslexic Tracking Patterns

Modes I and II

Moving words, sentences, and elephants induce a tracking nystagmus which attempts to keep the targets in focus. The tracking amplitude and tracking

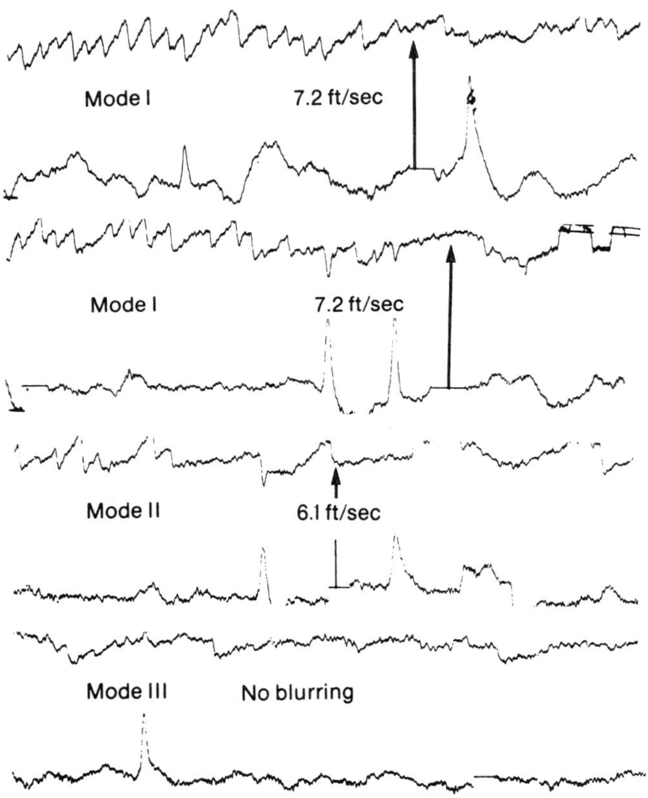

Fig. 9–3. Allison G. is a 12-year-old dyslexic reporting low-borderline word Modes I and II blurring speeds. ENG tracking patterns did not indicate phantom scanning. In fact, cessation of tracking during Mode II testing appeared to occur significantly before blurring was reported and suggested the possibility of a *confabulated* response. This data was taken prior to the recognition of compensatory single-targeting (utilizing 3D optical scanner I). Upon retesting one year later, Allison reported a significantly reduced SBS as well as the presence of single-targeting. Because of inferiority feelings and test anxiety, she was prone to utilizing defensive confabulation.

field is often significantly reduced, the tracking is sometimes dysmetric, and at blurring one of two tracking possibilities results: (1) a "reflex" reduction or inhibition of the rate of the tracking nystagmus similar to normal individuals (Fig. 9–3), or (2) "phantom tracking" or continuous tracking of a blurred sequence at rates substantially higher than the reported blurring speed (Figs. 9–4 and 9–5).

Mode III

Dyslexic tracking patterns for Mode III were of several types:

1. Mode III Positive Patterns With a Corresponding Tracking Nystagmus. While fixating a stationary word or elephant foreground, the moving scenic or striped background induces a foreground/background zig-zag tracking nystagmus, and foreground movement or blurring is experienced and reported (Figs. 9–5 and 9–6). During compensation, foreground movement

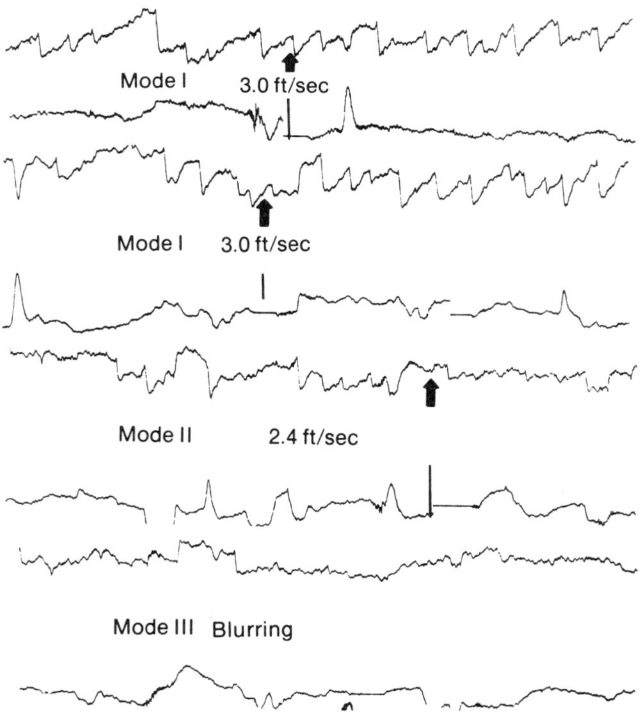

Fig. 9–4. Risa G. is a 6-year-old dyslexic girl reporting a word Mode I blurring speed of 3.0 ft./sec., a word Mode II blurring speed of 2.4 ft./sec., and Mode III foreground blurring. ENG ocular patterns corresponding to Modes I and II were dysmetric, and phantom scanning occurred after the blurring speeds were exceeded. Mode III blurring occurred without evidence of a clear-cut foreground/background nystagmus (3D optical scanner I).

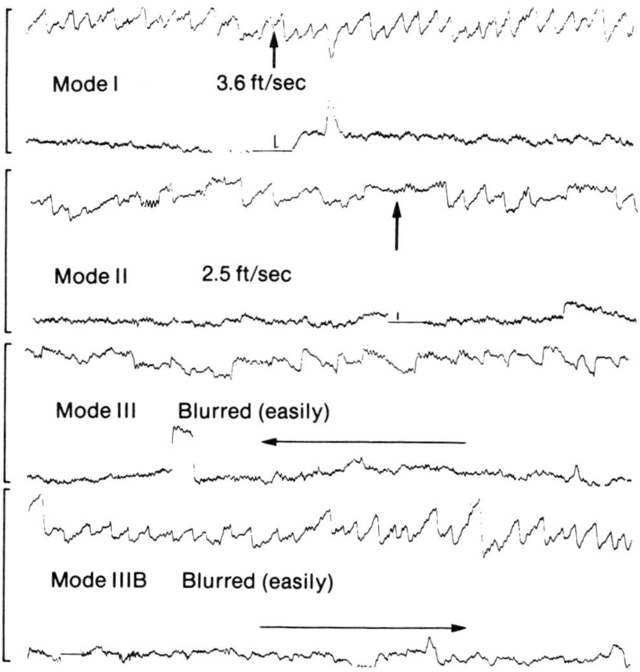

Fig. 9–5. Thomas L. is a 9½-year-old dyslexic boy whose Mode I (3.6 ft./sec.) and Mode II (2.5 ft./sec.) blurring speeds were significantly reduced. He evidenced phantom scanning, i.e., ocular-motor tracking movements in association with blurring or nonrecognition past his blurring-speed endpoint. Foreground blurring occurred during Mode III and was accompanied by a clinically apparent foreground/background-induced tracking nystagmus (3D optical scanner I).

or blurring is at times noted for only one background direction and for only specific foreground/background configurations—clearly demonstrating the direction-specific and gestalt-specific nature of the c-v compensatory processes (Fig. 9–6).

2. *Mode III Positive Without a Corresponding Tracking Nystagmus.* While fixating a stationary word or elephant foreground, the moving background induces no discernible foreground/background tracking nystagmus, but the foreground is experienced as in motion and its apparent speed is described as proportional to the actual speed of the moving background. At increased background speeds, the foreground movement illusion is sometimes experienced as blurred, and thus similar to the aforementioned pattern (Fig. 9–7). During blurring-speed compensation, Mode III positive blurring is at times converted to Mode III positive movement before chang-

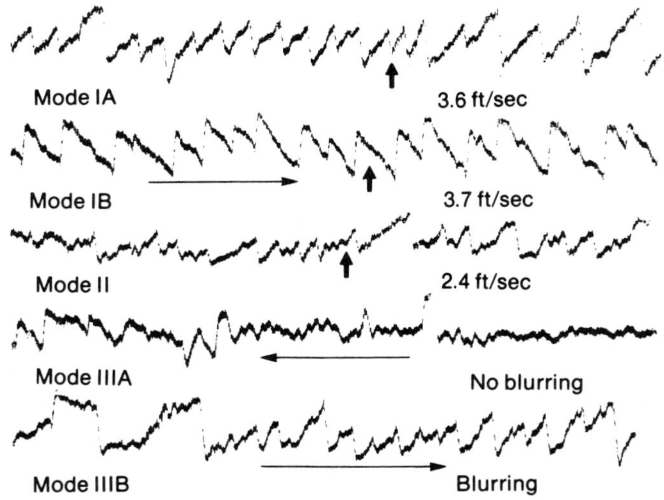

Fig. 9–6. Kathy is a 7-year-old dyslexic girl with deficient word Modes I and II blurring speeds and phantom scanning (3D optical scanner I). When she was 6½, Kathy was Mode III positive for background movement in both right and left directions. After age 7, she was Mode III positive only for backgrounds moving to the right—clearly suggesting that c-v tracking functions and compensation are direction-specific and direction-dependent. At 8½, Kathy was Mode III negative, regardless of the foreground stimulus or background direction. Her brother and father were also dyslexic.

ing to Mode III negative, whereas Mode III positive movement is converted to Mode III negative directly. In addition, by changing the foreground/background visual gestalt, Mode III positive may be converted to Mode III negative and vice versa.

3. Mode III Negative Without a Foreground/Background Tracking Nystagmus. This tracking pattern is identical to the Mode III negative pattern found among c-v normal individuals (Fig. 9–3).

4. *Mode III Negative With a Tracking Nystagmus.* This ENG pattern is similar to individuals reporting foreground blurring and movement, and was found in only one adult who had a fixation nystagmus of apparently cerebellar origin (Fig. 9–8). Interestingly, although fixation and concentration tend statistically to inhibit vestibular nystagmus and associated symptoms, occasionally the reverse occurs. Fixation may actually trigger nystagmus, ocular perseveration, and scrambling in some atypical dyslexics, resulting in "eye contact" and other visual avoidance phenomena. Most often, the c-v somatic roots of the phobic avoidance symptoms remain hidden from clinical view, and thus only psychodynamic interpretations or misinterpretations are offered.

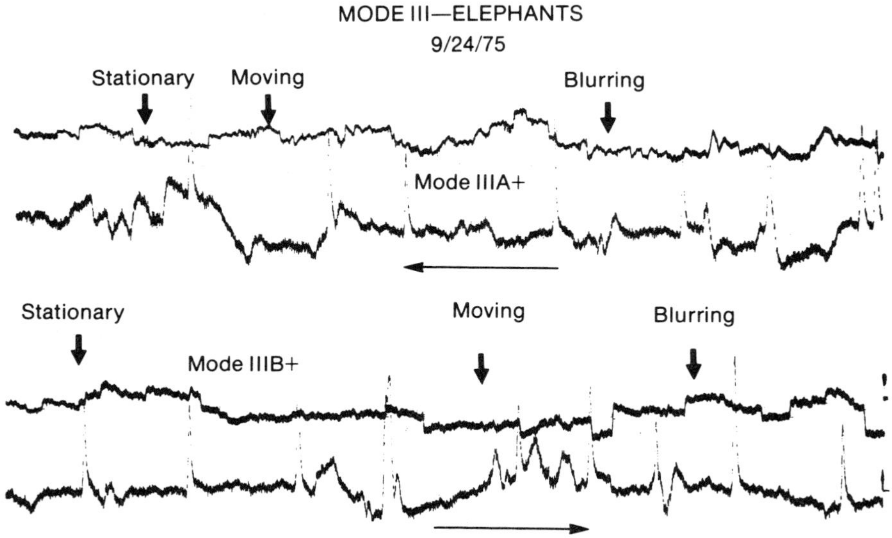

Fig. 9–7. Don is a 7-year-old dyslexic boy with significantly reduced word and elephant Modes I and II. Single targeting was absent. Elephant Mode III was *movement-positive* and *blurring-positive,* despite the absence of (consistent) ENG ocular deflection patterns—suggesting the presence of coexisting peripheral and central c-v tracking and processing mechanisms. For example, a central c-v dysmetria may result in either a corresponding clinical or subclinical peripheral tracking nystagmus—depending upon the presence and intensity of compensatory mechanisms, as well as their specific sites of compensatory action. The author assumed the coexistence of independently acting compensatory mechanisms capable of specifically inhibiting either the foreground movement/blurring experiences, the induced foreground/background nystagmus, or both.

A Third Attempt at Classification

Two discoveries occurring several years apart resulted in a retrospective re-analysis of the total collected ENG tracking curves and blurring speed data, and led to what now appears to be a diagnostically and neurophysiologically successful classification: (1) The recognition of reading-score-compensated dyslexic individuals resulted in the transfer of mistaken normal ENG tracking curves to the DD category—correcting a significant error in the prior classification of tracking data (Figs. 9–9 and 9–10). (2) The recognition that many dyslexic individuals have both diagnostically significant SBS and compensatory STS allowed for the understanding and correction of data which was otherwise confusing, and impossible to comprehend. For example, dyslexic individuals were discovered to blur a moving sequence

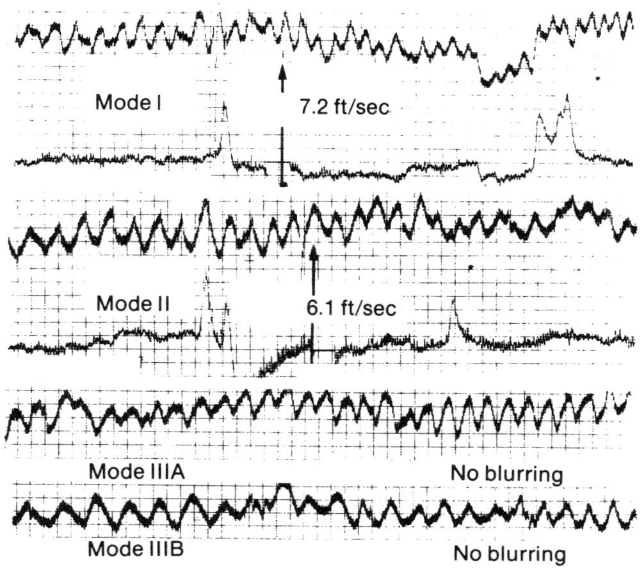

Fig. 9–8. Raymond is a 44-year-old dyslexic male whose ENG tracking patterns corresponding to blurring-speed testing revealed (1) word Mode I blurring speeds at 7.2 ft./sec., with phantom tracking eye movements at higher rates, (2) word Mode II blurring at 6.1 ft./sec., with phantom tracking ENG movements at higher speeds, and (3) a fixation nystagmus during Mode III testing in the absence of foreground movement or blurring (3D optical scanner I).

at sharply reduced tracking speeds. However, a significant number of dyslexic individuals learned to compensate for the sequential tracking difficulty by fixating only single targets, and thus appeared to sacrifice physiologically the whole field for a part.

Because compensatory single-targeting was found to occur significantly only among dyslexic individuals following sequential blurring, and since the SBS in dyslexics were correlated to c-v dysfunction, and since normal individuals statistically presented with only SBS, it appeared most likely that SBS was of diagnostic significance, whereas STS was of compensatory significance and attempted to increase dysmetric fixation and tracking capacity. These crucial insights resulted in a re-examination of the blurring-speed data and tracking curves, enabling the author to make appropriate corrections. As a result of this re-analysis, single-targeting in dyslexia was found to be either absent, poorly developed and lower than the corresponding normal control blurring speed, or "hypertrophied" and greater than the corresponding normal blurring speed.

The recognition of single-target hypertrophy explained the clinical paradox by which DD cases with significantly reduced blurring speeds were

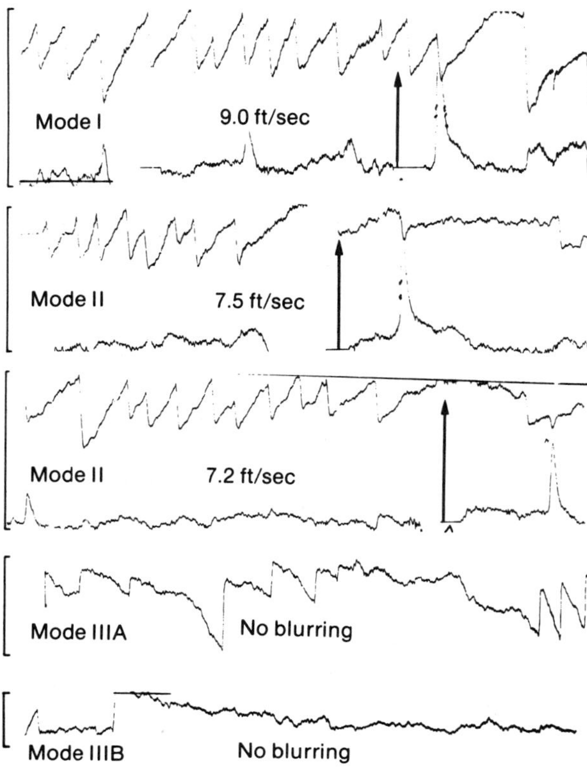

Fig. 9–9. Laura is a 7-year-old dyslexic third-grader who reported normal Mode I (9.0 ft./sec.) and Mode II (7.5 ft./sec.) blurring speeds. Phantom scanning was absent. Mode III was negative (3D optical scanner I). Questioning revealed that Laura experienced sequential blurring at reduced tracking speeds, whereupon she automatically or "reflexly" constricted her visual field to a small fixed locus and selectively tracked the moving targets across a narrow field—perhaps accounting for her large tracking amplitude and reduced rate. Retesting indicated that Laura's SBS was approximately one-half normal and that the reported blurring speeds were, in fact, STS. It is significant that Laura was of superior I.Q. (160). She did not experience any obvious school difficulties or frustration until the third grade—at which point the volume of school work began to expand rapidly and the rate at which she had to read and write multiplied. Her previously denied and compensated DD symptoms suddenly materialized clinically, resulting in frustration, anxiety, and psychosomatic symptoms. Fortunately, she responded most favorably to cyclizine (Marezine) and a modified form of psychotherapy in which the neurodynamics of her DD disorder were explained and her somatopsychically determined anxiety and neurotic-like defenses were worked through and resolved.

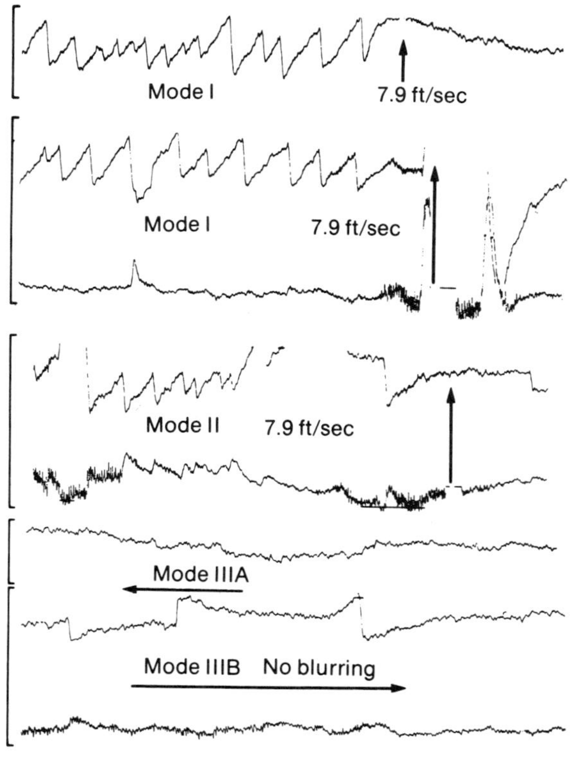

Fig. 9–10. Joy is a 6-year-old bright child with superior reading scores whose blurring speeds were normal. Her ENG tracking pattern indicated ocular deflections which were characterized by high-amplitude excursion and a reduced tracking rate, similar to Laura's. This ENG tracking pattern suggested the possibility that Joy may have single-targeted an object across a scomatized field in a manner similar to Laura (Fig. 9–9). Mode III was negative (3D optical scanner I).

This tracking pattern was obtained prior to the recognition that (1) dyslexic individuals may have compensated and overcompensated reading scores and ability, and (2) dyslexic individuals may utilize compensatory tracking mechanisms; indeed many dyslexics have two blurring-speed endpoints: SBS and compensatory STS. Although Joy's ENG tracking pattern was initially considered normal, retrospective re-interpretation suggests two possibilities: (1) a normal pattern in an individual improperly instructed, i.e. she was not specifically asked to perform sequential targeting and report sequential blurring; or (2) a DD pattern, utilizing compensatory single targeting across a narrow field.

found to be exquisitely sensitive to, and aware of, fine detail. Prior to the recognition of single-targeting hypertrophy, dyslexic cases reporting significantly high blurring speeds were thought to be confabulating. Longitudinal and reconstructive studies of dyslexic individuals with single-target hypertrophy have suggested a corresponding somatically determined personality profile prone to detail and "scomatized" thinking and acting.

Diagnostic Blurring-Speed Endpoints

The author initially thought that all tested individuals perceived the Modes I, II, and III blurring-speed endpoints in a similar fashion, i.e., a dramatic and simultaneous streaking or blurring of the entire sequence into a bar. In retrospect, this naiveté must surely have been due to wishful thinking. Analysis of the ENG blurring-speed data revealed that although c-v normal individuals do have a similar and uniform streaking endpoint, DD individuals have several c-v diagnostic endpoints.

Mode I and II diagnostic endpoints were thus recognized to be of several types:

1. simultaneous sequential blurring or streaking—an endpoint similar to normal individuals;
2. the initiation of single-targeting;
3. intermittent or alternating blurring;
4. image distortion—i.e., the moving sequence appearing to change in size, shape, direction, etc.;
5. subjective sensations of vertigo, nausea, etc.; and
6. stimulus avoidance and/or blinking.

Although the author had already known that the Mode III positive diagnostic endpoint was a complex vector resultant of opposing c-v dysfunctioning versus compensatory quantitative vectors, he "accidentally" discovered that Mode III may be differently experienced by different dyslexic individuals and even by a given dyslexic utilizing differing c-v-related perceptual mechanisms. Mode III positive was thus found to consist of a series of diagnostic foreground endpoints similar to those found for Modes I and II:

1. sequential and simultaneous blurring;
2. single or alternating blurring of only certain elephants and not others;
3. horizontal running movements;
4. vibration of the elephants or oscillopsia;
5. image distortion, i.e., micropsia and/or macropsia, and reversals;
6. subjective sensations of anxiety, vertigo, nausea, blinking, etc. (interestingly, these subjective Mode III sensations were not uncommonly found in c-v-determined and visually triggered phobic individuals);
7. inability to perceive foreground and background simultaneously.

Normal individuals experience no difficulty in simultaneously perceiving both the stationary foreground and the moving background. However, dyslexics fixating the elephant foreground expressed difficulty "seeing" the background—even during only slight background movement. The reverse was accidentally found to be true as well. If dyslexics fixated the moving background, the foreground would either suddenly blur or appear to be in motion. At times, selected elements of the foreground would be "seen" while others disappeared.

As a result of these and a host of related observations, the author realized that dyslexics experienced difficulty in coordinating, integrating, and harmonizing foreground/background dimensions and that the various spatial-temporal dimensions often inappropriately merged—resulting in such typical dyslexic illusions and errors as blurring, movement, reversals, insertions, omissions, and so on.

This expanding insight into the dynamic perceptual forces shaping and determining Mode III positive and negative led the author to the realization that the percentage of Mode III positive might be significantly increased by utilizing techniques geared at minimizing compensatory perceptual processes. In the Staten Island blurring-speed study, compensatory Mode III mechanisms were minimized by reducing the size, spacing, and intensity of the word foreground, and thus the underlying perceptual disturbance was stressed or relatively magnified. Later studies indicated that if Mode III negative dyslexics were specifically requested to consciously fixate the moving background lines, over 50% of the Mode III negative dyslexics would become Mode III posiitve. If Mode III positive dyslexics were similarly instructed, their Mode III positive responses and experiences are significantly intensified. As might have been expected, rare exceptions were found in which background fixation tended to enhance foreground perception—once again highlighting the complexity and variability of the dysfunctioning and compensatory mechanisms shaping dyslexic perception at any point in time and space.

Sequential Scanning Versus Single Targeting

The blurring-speed methodology led to the recognition of two blurring-speed endpoints and two scanning mechanisms in c-v impaired dyslexics. Sequential scanning provides a panoramic continuum to the perceptual field, and at the sequential-scanning blurring speed (SBS), a significant percentage (approximately one-third) of dyslexics continue to track and recognize single targets in an intermittent and discontinuous manner via single targeting. Although the single-target blurring speed (STS) in dyslexics may be less than or greater than the corresponding normal sequential blurring speed, the frequency with which the dyslexic STS equaled the normal blurring speed seemed more than coincidental. In fact, this frequency was responsible for significant degrees of scientific confusion prior to the clear recognition and distinction of sequential and single-target blurring speeds.

Questions and Speculations

Why are the normal sequential blurring-speed endpoints and the DD single-target blurring-speed endpoints so often identical? Is it possible that normal individuals possess cortically determined single-targeting mechanisms and a c-v-modulated peripheral-scanning mechanism which provides a depth and/or continuum to single targeting? If so, c-v dysfunction might impair the peripheral enlargement or sequential panorama of single targeting, and the normally fused mechanisms of sequential and single targeting vision would decompose into their respective component parts: decreased sequential scanning and single targeting.

However, one must then explain why all dyslexics do not possess single targeting. To explain why only one-third of dyslexics have single-targeting mechanisms, the author reasoned as follows: If, indeed, sequential scanning and single targeting are neurophysiologically independent, but functionally related, tracking mechanisms that are normally fused to provide both panoramic and continuous vision with detailed clarity, and if both targeting mechanisms have similar physiologically pre-determined blurring-speed endpoints, then one could explain the frequent correlation whereby the STS is equal to the normal SBS. In addition, if c-v dysfunction may result in either delayed or hypertrophied development of single-target mechanisms, one can further explain the vast majority of STS variations clinically found in dyslexia, i.e., absent, normal, and even hypertrophied single targeting.

The hypotheses regarding independent but related single-targeting and sequential-scanning tracking mechanisms were derived and/or supported by repeated clinical observations in which dyslexic individuals responding favorably to the motion-sickness medications experienced a dramatic enlargement of their tracking field. Cessation of the medication most often resulted in a return to "scomatized" or single-targeting vision. (Visual field defects were absent.) In addition, these medications were found either to provoke selectively the development of single-targeting mechanisms or to result in increased SBS—thereby suggesting that the two targeting mechanisms may indeed be neurophysiologically independent but functionally related. If these medications are assumed to act in a manner analogous to c-v–cortical triggers and stimulants, then one might further assume that single-targeting may indeed be dependent upon c-v stimulation.

Although the chapters are presented in a relatively historical sequence, the derived conceptualizations and insights were by no means smooth and "eumetric." Frequently, confusion and frustration in one study was resolved by data stemming from independent parallel studies. Often, new studies were intuitively or unconsciously designed in order to develop a panoramic and continuous perspective of the unfolding dyslexic disorder.

Phantom Tracking Versus Single Targeting

Dyslexics frequently exhibit phantom scanning and/or targeting following sequential blurring, and their respective ENG tracking patterns have not as yet been clinically distinguished and defined. During phantom scanning, moving sequences are blurred while single-targeted sequences are intermittently recognizable, and the dyslexic subject appears to exert conscious intent and eye-movement control.

Analysis of the phantom-tracking and single-targeting ENG data led to a series of questions and speculations: Is phantom scanning an adaptive attempt to track nonconsciously perceived stimuli to a CNS preset "normal" blurring-speed endpoint? Or does phantom scanning reflect a failure to inhibit tracking once blurring has occurred? Is single targeting a compensatory attempt to see consciously what was previously nonconsciously or phantomly tracked? And is there a relationship between phantom scanning and single targeting, or are they independent tracking mechanisms?

A series of studies designed to provide a computer analysis of the ENG tracking data may cast further light into the possible relationship between phantom scanning and single targeting. These studies may elucidate the manner or mechanisms by which nonconsciously tracked stimuli become conscious, and perhaps explain how phantom tracking is converted into single targeting via adaptive learning processes. Although the author demonstrated that single targeting can be learned, or neurophysiologically imprinted, by encouraging or "forcing" dyslexic individuals to track beyond their SBS, the CNS mechanisms responsible for this "learning process" remain unknown.

Central Versus Peripheral Cerebellar-Vestibular Processing

The conceptualization of central versus peripheral c-v processing was theoretically mandated in order to explain a series of paradoxical blurring speed data: (1) Mode III may be positive with or without the presence of a corresponding ENG-detectable peripheral nystagmus, and (2) nuclear or central dyslexic symptomatology may persist independent of and/or despite blurring-speed and neurologic compensation. However, the "real" meaning and significance of this clinically derived central/peripheral c-v construct was not fully appreciated until the aforementioned data was correlated to, and integrated with, the data derived from both the neurodynamic analysis of innumerable spontaneous dyslexic verbalizations and the clinical dyslexic response to the motion-sickness medications (Chapter 11). The crucial but hidden role of central or centrifugal c-v-determined balance, coordinational, rhythmic, and directional functions in shaping the mental output was not recognized until the retrospective analysis of such spontaneous dyslexic verbalizations as:

I can't balance or juggle two or more thoughts at a time.—My thoughts occasionally become jumbled and scrambled.—I find it difficult to coordinate my thoughts and ideas.—I keep losing my trend of thought.—My thoughts are sometimes hazy.—Occasionally my memory is foggy and events become blurry and difficult to remember.—Sometimes my thinking is sluggish and my thoughts just don't flow smoothly.—I occasionally feel mentally and physically dyscoordinated and "discombobulated."—A thought just blurred out.—I trip and stumble all over my words.—Sometimes I say and I think one thing and do the reverse.—It's impossible for me to concentrate and focus on more than one thing at a time. When I'm interrupted or distracted, I'm lost and I just can't find my place.—Sometimes it's hard for me to concentrate on and remember the whole sequence of what someone has just said. I have to keep making lists for myself so as not to forget things.—Occasionally there is a time lag between what is said and my understanding it. And sometimes I don't hear things said. It is as if it were all a blur.—I find that I can't remember more than three events at a time. For example, if I have to remember six things, I'll have to mentally break them up into two categories of three each and remember each category separately.—I can't seem to coordinate three dimensions. And at times, things appear flat. And at other times, I'll see skyscrapers off balance and tilted to one side.

Interestingly enough, the aforementioned pattern of dyslexic mental events was found to respond most favorably to medications initially designed to improve only c-v reading function.

As a result of these observations, it seemed reasonable to assume that the c-v circuits function inwardly or centripetally in a manner analogous to their external or centrifugal functions, and thus that the c-v circuits are as crucial for harmonizing and modulating inner world or mental events as they are for harmonizing and modulating outer-world sensory-motor events. By analogy, it is as if the c-v vertical and horizontal television stabilizers were monitoring two sets of television pictures: one directed at conscious foreground perception and the other directed at background and nonconscious perception.

These assumptions as to the c-v role in monitoring both inner and outer world phenomena were indirectly but significantly supported by evidence indicating that the REMs of the dreamer scan the inner world's events and space in a manner identical to that of the c-v-modulated optokinetic fixation and tracking movements in scanning outer world events and space (Dement, 1964). Furthermore, if the c-v circuits truly scan and process the inner, unconscious, repressed or latent "dream world," and if cerebellar inhibition provides the background neurophysiologic substrate to what is psychologically recognized as repression, then perhaps the author has stumbled upon another hidden source to the "c-v denial mechanisms" recognized to be permeating and scrambling dyslexic and c-v research efforts.

Practical Therapeutic Applications

A Pedagogic Method of Presenting Reading Material to Young Dyslexics

As a result of the recognition that DD is due to a c-v-related ocular-motor fixation and tracking dysfunction, which secondarily scrambles and/or delays cortical gnostic and conceptual functioning, the author developed a 3D reader in order to facilitate the presentation of reading material to young dyslexics. Reading material is presented to the DD individual in temporal sequence at a fixed locus rather than in the usual right/left, left/right, up/down temporal-spatial sequence. As a result, motor-eye tracking is reduced to a minimum, the fixation point remains relatively constant, and the temporal sequencing speed can be specifically regulated and controlled. The realization that the c-v tracking mechanisms are sensory-specific IRMs resulted in the development of "intensified visual-gestalt triggers," facilitating the ocular-motor tracking and processing response. By intensified visual-gestalt triggers, the author was referring to *larger, darker, colored* and significantly *separated* letters, words, etc., which facilitate symbol tracking and processing mechanisms.

In controlling the fixation locus, the visual-gestalt trigger, and the ocular-motor sequencing speed, one is better able to help DD individuals cope with their temporal-spatial tracking and processing dysfunction until compensatory mechanisms develop.

A Neurophysiologic Method of Improving Ocular Fixation and Tracking

A neurophysiologic method of improving ocular fixation and tracking capacity was accidentally discovered when attempting to standardize and stabilize the blurring-speed methodology. The repeated testing of dyslexics as a function of time occasionally resulted in significantly increased blurring speeds. These increased speeds were initially thought to be due entirely to technical errors until similar increases were noted to occur in conjunction with positive therapeutic responses to the motion-sickness medications. The discovery of diagnostic versus compensatory blurring speeds enabled the author to stabilize significantly the blurring-speed methodology and to clearly distinguish diagnostic and compensatory blurring speeds as a function of ocular-motor tracking exercises and favorable pharmacologic responses. As a result, there evolved a reliable sample of blurring-speed data suggesting that both the motion-sickness medications and specific ocular-tracking exercises may occasionally result in improved SBS and/or STS, and that the compensatory speeds increase more dramatically and frequently than do the corresponding sequential speeds. In addition, further tracking studies suggested that the yield of increased blurring speeds as a function of ocular-motor repetition is higher if dyslexics are "forced" to track moving sequences and objects at or past the blurring-speed endpoint.

The realization that blurring speeds can be neurophysiologically learned or imprinted and that increased tracking capacity may facilitate the reading process, led to the development of a 3D Optical Trainer designed to increase blurring speeds and test their efficacy in improving reading functioning. Although this research effort is still in its infancy, the practical and theoretical yield from its pursuit looks most promising—especially when utilized as part of a holistic therapeutic approach. At the very least, this methodology has provided a neurophysiologic basis and rationale for ocular-motor exercises in c-v dyslexia, as well as a means of measuring tracking changes and possible "compensatory transfer" to other c-v dyslexic functions.

Summary

The attempt to understand and classify the normal and dyslexic tracking curves and corresponding blurring-speed data did not proceed smoothly. In fact, one could easily have labeled this investigation dysmetric. Unexpected and confusing data materialized at every scientific twist and turn and resulted in painful doubts, time-consuming back-tracking, and conceptual reversals. In retrospect, it would have been far easier to have fixated or "single-targeted" the expected data and denied the unexpected, atypical, and seemingly impossible results. However, had the path of least resistance been taken, major discoveries would have been bypassed and the expected data would have remained poorly and incompletely understood. Strangely enough, only the intense frustration and curiosity provoked by the paradoxical blurring-speed and tracking data could have fueled the stubborn determination required to solve the ocular-motor classification problems and provide a theoretical scheme for understanding and/or investigating such phenomena as phantom scanning, single targeting, and central versus peripheral c-v processing mechanisms. In addition, the computerized study of the ENG tracking curves as well as all related dyslexic data may result in more objective neurophysiologic diagnostic and compensatory parameters, as well as a method of predicting symptomatic outcome and therapeutic responses to ocular-motor exercises and medications.

10 Clinically and Theoretically Derived Cerebellar Functions

A series of clinically and theoretically derived speculations regarding cerebellar functions are presented. The data is derived from clinical observations of dyslexics as well as neurophysiologic animal investigations. An attempt has been made to assimilate and integrate the resulting insights (Frank and Levinson, 1976–77) so as to explain:

1. the dynamic sensory-motor foreground/background filter function of the cerebellum;
2. the evolution of the cerebellum;
3. sensory-motor cerebellar learning;
4. the role of the cerebellum in processing the total sensory input;
5. the role of the cerebellum in modulating conscious and nonconscious perception;
6. the role of the cerebellum in motion sickness and motion-sickness mechanisms;
7. the neurophysiologic function of the motion-sickness medications.

It is hoped that the application of these clinically and theoretically derived cerebellar concepts might be a small step in a direction predicted by Eccles et al. (1967, p. 315) at the end of *The Cerebellum as a Neuronal Machine:*

> We are confident that the enlightened discourse between such theorists [communication theorists and cyberneticists] on the one hand and neurobiologists on the other will lead to the development of revolutionary hypotheses of the way in which the cerebellum functions as a neuronal machine; and it can be predicted that these hypotheses will lead to revolutionary developments in experimental investigation.

The Cerebellum as a Dynamic Sensory-Motor Foreground/Background Filter

Mode III Blurring-Speed Observations and Hypotheses

For c-v normal individuals, the Mode III moving background does not induce a foreground/background tracking nystagmus, the fixated• foreground is invariably reported as clear and stationary, and fixation of the moving background does not induce abnormal foreground changes—regardless of stimulus or background direction.

The Mode III testing of DD individuals with significantly reduced Modes I and II blurring speeds often results in a stimulus- and direction-dependent background-induced nystagmus, and foreground movement, reversals, and/or blurring are reported. In other words, the moving scenic background induces or provokes an optokinetic nystagmus, and compensatory attempts to regain foreground fixation and stabilization result in a zigzag foreground/background ENG ocular deflection pattern. This foreground/background nystagmus manifests itself symptomatically and clinically in reversals, scrambling, and blurring.

Fixation of the moving background intensifies or provokes foreground blurring, movement, or scrambling among dyslexics whereas conscious and intentional fixation of the foreground sequence, or single targets within this sequence, minimizes these symptoms. These and related clinical observations clearly illustrate the difficulties experienced by c-v-impaired dyslexics in selectively inhibiting or suppressing background events so as to maintain foreground clarity and prevent foreground/background contamination.

As a result of these clinical observations, it was postulated that the cerebellum plays a vital role in maintaining foreground/background separation by a highly specific and selective process of active background inhibition—thereby acting as a *dynamic sensory-motor foreground/background filter.*

Evolution of the Cerebellum

Sir John Eccles (1970, pp. 3–4) states:

> There is general agreement among neuroscientists that every conscious experience—every perception, thought, and memory—has as its material counterpart some specific spatio-temporal activity in the vast neuronal network of the cerebral cortex and sub-cortical nuclei, that is woven of neuronal activities in space and time in the "enchanted loom" so poetically described by Sherrington (1940).

The cerebellum was postulated by the author to play a silently active role in the function of this mysterious "enchanted loom"—a role not inferior to that of the cerebral cortex. In attempting further to understand cerebellar morphology and function, Eccles et al. (1967, p. 1) trace the evolution of the cerebellum:

> With each further evolutionary development of the brain, this same cerebellar organization seemed to be a necessary adjunct, presumably because it possessed some unique mode of processing information. Hence, these newly evolved components of the brain colonized or developed areas of the cerebellum for this purpose; and most lately of all, the cerebral hemispheres have called forth the great development of the cerebellar lobes. With the evolutionary growth of the brain, the cerebellar hypertrophy has matched the hypertrophy of the cerebrum. This evolutionary story certainly gives rise to the concept that there is some highly significant and unique functional meaning in the neuronal organization of the cerebellum and in the processing of information that is accomplished thereby.

Although Eccles et al. emphasize that "the cerebral hemispheres have called forth the great development of the cerebellar lobes," the author postulates that from a phylogenetic and functional point of view, the reverse was no doubt true as well: the development of the cerebellar lobes or old brain most probably stimulated the development of the cerebral hemispheres and new brain as a response to the organism's need to master increasingly complex environmental stimuli over an evolutionary time span. This cerebellar-cortical "developmental spurt" is postulated to have arisen in relationship to man's attainment of an upright gait and need to master an exponentially expanded sensory-motor horizon. Additionally, if it is assumed that the neurophysiologic and anatomic cerebellar changes in response to "current learning" recapitulate the neurophysiologic and anatomic changes of "evolutionary learning" (evolutionary genetic imprinting) just as ontogeny recapitulates phylogeny, then we can better explain the intimate relationship between stimulus and selected motor response, as well as the reason and way the cerebellar cortex tripled in size in order to cope with, or track and process, man's ever increasing complex environment (i.e., reading and symbolic gestalts).

As a result of this reasoning, one may even speculate that genetically or congenitally determined c-v lags and dysmetric dyslexia represent an ontogenetic indication of an intermediate or pre-reading state in phylogeny.

Sensory-Motor Cerebellar Learning

In describing motor learning in the cerebellum, Eccles et al. (1967, p. 314) state:

> The immense computational machinery of the cerebellum with a neuronal population that may exceed that of the rest of the nervous system gives rise to the concept that the cerebellar cortex is not simply a fixed computing device, but that it contains in its structure the neuronal connexions developed in relationship to learned skills. We have to envisage that the cerebellum plays a major role in the performance of all skilled actions and hence that it can learn from

> experience so that its performance to any given input is conditioned by this "remembered experience." As yet, of course, we have no knowledge of the structural and functional changes that form the basis of this learned response. However, one can speculate that the spine synapses on the dendrites in the molecular layer are especially concerned in this and that usage gives growth of the spines and particularly the formation of the secondary spines that Hamori and Szentagothai (1964) described on Purkinje dendrites. One can, therefore, imagine that in the learning of movements and skills there is a microgrowth of such structures giving increased synaptic function and that as a consequence the cerebellum is able to compute in an especially adapted way for each particular learned movement and thus can provide appropriate corrective information that keeps the movement on target.

If it is hypothesized that sensory learning occurs in the cerebellum in a manner analogous to motor learning, then one can explain the pseudo-agnostic, pseudo-apraxic, pseudo-aphasic, and pseudo-cerebral "higher cerebellar functions" found to be impaired in cases exhibiting DD.*

A search of the literature has revealed a series of animal experiments which indicate that the cerebellum receives and reacts to visual, tactile, acoustic, olfactory, and proprioceptive stimuli. Almost simultaneously, Snider and Stowell (1942, 1944), Dow and Anderson (1942), Adrian (1943), and Snider (1943) reported that the cerebellum (which Sherrington [1906] had called "the head ganglion of the proprioceptive system") is involved in receiving and processing exteroceptive impulses.

In a magnificent article entitled "The Cerebellum," Snider (1958, pp. 84–90) clearly demonstrated the cerebellum's role in modulating sensory input:

> In the back of our skulls, perched upon the brain stem under the overarching mantle of the great hemispheres of the cerebrum, is a baseball-sized, bean-shaped lump of gray and white brain tissue. This is the cerebellum, the "lesser brain". In contrast to the cerebrum, where men have sought and found the centers of so many vital mental activities, the cerebellum remains a region of subtle and tantalizing mystery, its function hidden from investigators . . . Its elusive signals have begun to tell us that, while the cerebellum itself directs no body functions, it operates as monitor and coordinator of the brain's other centers and as mediator between them and the body. . . . As in the cerebrum, the various functions of the cerebellum are localized in distinctly defined areas of its cortex. Detection and plotting of the electrical activity of the cortex has made it possible to map these areas. The control of the body's equilibrium, for example, is localized in the extreme front and rear surfaces of the cerebellum. The proprioceptive areas appear as actual maps of the body on the cortex: two distorted "homunculi", one face-on and the other in double profile back-to-back. . . .

* The concept of "higher cerebellar functions" has been both clinically and theoretically derived, and is used as an analogy to the higher cortical functions so eloquently elucidated by Luria (1966).

> For a long time it was thought that the plotting of these areas had completed the map of the cerebellar cortex in line with the notion that the cerebellum was restricted to the management of the body's equilibrium and muscular activity. However, at the Johns Hopkins University in 1942 Averill Stowell and I undertook an investigation which has established that the cerebellum is equally involved in the coordination of the sensations of touch, hearing and sight. . . .
>
> Our investigation showed also that the tactile, visual and auditory centers of the cerebellum are linked to the corresponding centers in the cerebral cortex by the same sort of feedback loop that connects the proprioceptive areas. . . .
>
> Our studies developed further feedback pathways to the thalamus, the basal ganglia and the reticular formation of the lower brain stem . . . This array of feedback loops should stimulate the cerebral servomechanism of any student of cybernetics. In sum, the cerebellar circuitry is an accessory control system imposed upon the basic ascending (sensory) and descending (motor) circuits of the nervous system . . . One is tempted to see the cerebellum as the great "modulator" of nervous function . . . In the meantime we may have to contend with the possibility that the cerebellum is involved in still more diverse aspects of the nervous system. It becomes increasingly evident that if "integration" is a major function of this organ, trips into the realm of mental disease may cross its boundaries more frequently than the guards in sanitariums suspect.

Furthermore, in their paper delineating the tactile, auditory, and visual exteroceptive role of the cerebellum, Snider and Stowell (1944, p. 351) state:

> One of the most universally accepted teachings of clinical neurology is that the cerebellum is not concerned with any kind of sensation, for true sensory defects have not been found among the disorders which are produced by cerebellar lesions in man. Certainly there is no clinical evidence to indicate that any cerebellar deficit is accompanied by disturbances in touch, auditory or visual perception. Yet we cannot resist wondering whether loss of the cerebellar representations of these three exteroceptive systems does not produce objective and subjective effects which are so subtle that they have escaped present methods of study.

Discussion

The clinically elucidated dyslexic signs and symptoms reported in this book clearly indicate that indeed there are significant disturbances in sequential visual, tactile, auditory, proprioceptive, and directional sensory functioning as a result of c-v dysfunction. However, these sensory disturbances have been fallaciously attributed to cerebral cortical dysfunction or such vague concepts as "minimal brain dysfunction," "minimal cerebral dysfunction," "cerebral immaturity," and "CNS immaturity."

The "finger-order-sense" tests of Kinsbourne and Warrington surely must have elucidated the presence of c-v-determined proprioceptive and directional disturbances in developmental dyslexia (developmental Gerstmann's syndrome), in a manner similar to the author's demonstration of an analogous and equivalent finger-to-finger sequencing or past-pointing defect in these very same children. Furthermore, just as the 3D optical scanner demonstrated a c-v-determined sequential proprioceptive and directional disturbance underlying the dysmetric ocular-motor tracking performance of dyslexics, similar auditory and tactile sequencing disturbances were demonstrated by the 3D auditory scanner and 3D tactile scanner—two additional instruments developed by the author to provide the multisensory parameters required to measure holistically the panoramic c-v sensory-motor dysfunction underlying DD.*

If, indeed, the cerebellum may be considered the "head ganglion of the proprioceptive system" (Sherrington, 1906), and if it is neurophysiologically capable of harmonizing the total sensory input as it is known to modulate the total motor output, then the author may reasonably conceive of the cerebellum as the *head ganglion of the total sensory-motor system.* This panoramic view of cerebellar function could more specifically and accurately explain the total dyslexic nuclear symptomatic complex. On the basis of extensive clinical DD and animal research data, the author postulated:

1. that the cerebellum plays as vital a role in regulating, selecting, ordering, coordinating, integrating, and harmonizing the total sensory input as it is known to play in modulating and harmonizing the motor output—one might even conceptualize this complex series of dynamic sensory-motor functions as constituting body scheme or body image;
2. that the cerebellum is especially well suited to perform these complex functions by virtue of its selective inhibitory, disinhibitory, facilitating, and "learning" functions;
3. that the cerebellum modulates speed perception, spatial orientation, and adaptive motor responses in one's relationship to both inner space (body scheme) and outer space;
4. that the cerebellum modulates a series of higher sensory-motor functions previously assumed to be entirely of primary cerebral cortical origin;
5. that these higher cerebellar sensory-motor functions were triggered by man's development of an upright gait and need to cope with a concomitant exponentially expanded horizon; and that the ontogenetic sequence of walking and talking in children represents a recapitulation of man's c-v, higher cerebellar, and cerebral cortical developmental sequence;

* The early recognition of the panoramic role of the c-v circuits in modulating the total sensory input and motor output led the author to initially postulate that labyrinthitis (otitis interna) and/or otitis media may result in or intensify the dyslexic disorder (Frank and Levinson, 1973; Levinson, 1974). The idea that otitis media may be a significant factor in learning and speech disorders was followed up by Zinkus, Gottlieb and Schapiro (1978). These authors, however, did not appreciate the crucial effect that otitis media had on vestibular-cerebellar-cortical functioning and dyslexia; as a result, they "fixated" only the resulting auditory sequencing and speech difficulties rather than the sensory-motor panoramic dysmetria which may result from a c-v dysfunction.

6. that failure of the c-v circuits to receive properly, modulate, harmonize, and transmit the input to the cortical receiving areas in an interpretable or "proper" form and/or frequency results in secondary pseudocortical dysfunctions; and

7. that Eccles's concept of "synaptic regression" implies also its mirror function of "synaptic facilitation" and that both these concepts are Freudian neurophysiologic echoes, which are clearly described in his brilliant but neglected "Project for a Scientific Psychology" (1895)—crucial for a dynamic neurophysiologic understanding of cerebellar-cortical learning.

Speculations on the Role of the Cerebellum in Modulating Conscious and Nonconscious Perception

Prior to this research effort, conscious and nonconscious mental and perceptual events could not be explained neurophysiologically. Analysis of the blurring-speed and tracking data, however, has led to a new hypothesis of the cerebellar role in modulating conscious and nonconscious events, and the function of bilateral cerebral hemispheres or "two brains"—perhaps enlarging Young's (1962) interesting speculations as to "Why do we have two brains?"

Utilizing the 3D optical scanner and blurring/recognition-speed methodology, blurring or nonrecognition was found to be a *cerebral cortical indicator* of maximum cerebellar tracking capacity. In other words, the dominant cerebral cortex is "blind," and thus cannot "see" and consciously "perceive" a rapid input exceeding its *conscious interpretive threshhold.* However, reading-score-compensated dyslexic individuals with significantly reduced blurring speeds were noted to utilize occasionally a special form of speed reading. These rapid-scanning dyslexics were found capable of absorbing and comprehending both fixated, conscious content and "blurred," "unseen," "background" or "nonconscious" content.

As a result of these observations, the author was forced to assume that DD individuals were able to derive the meaning of a paragraph, chapter, or book by a process of peripheral or background nonconscious perception. How else could one explain overcompensated reading ability on the one hand and decreased blurring speeds on the other? As a gifted dyslexic writer put it, "I've always been amazed by how much I know and how little I read. Reading was always so very difficult and frustrating for me; and yet as a child I scored in the 98th percentile for reading comprehension. I just don't know how I did it." She was amazed to learn that her blurring speeds were one-quarter normal and that she saw "absolutely nothing" when words were moving across a screen at one-half the average word-blurring speed of a 5½-year-old child.

If, indeed, nonconscious perceptions" occur and can be recovered by questioning and associations (as well as comprehension and reading tests), and if conscious or "nonblurred" cerebral perception depends upon the speed of sensory impulses received by the cortex, then the CNS mechanisms determining conscious and nonconscious perception may be conceptualized as follows:

1. Conscious and nonconscious perception depends on the sensory transmission speeds impinging on, or received by, the cerebral cortex.

2. The cerebellum, through its processes of selective inhibition, disinhibition, and facilitation, modulates the input transmission speeds received by the cerebral cortex.

3. Through the processes of selective disinhibition and facilitation, the cerebellum may either fail to slow down the ascending sensory input, or even speed it up, so that the sensory input speeds reaching the perceptual cortex exceed its "interpretive threshold," and blurring or "nonrecognition" is perceived and reported.

4. The cerebellum, by regulating transmission speeds, dynamically influences conscious and nonconscious cerebral perception, as well as foreground/background perception.

5. By virtue of controlling transmission speeds, the cerebellum is especially well suited to serve as a dynamic sensory-motor filter capable of separating the sensory-motor input and output into foreground and background.

6. The cerebral hemispheres have developed as an extension of, and in relationship to, cerebellar function. Instead of viewing the cerebral hemispheres as dominant and nondominant for gnostic perception, both cerebral hemispheres may be considered dominant. One cerebral hemisphere is dominant for foreground perception and the other hemisphere is dominant for background perception. Might this hypothesis not serve to clarify Young's question, "Why do we have two brains?" Holistically speaking, both cerebral hemispheres are in dynamic equilibrium with each other, and the organism as a whole.

7. The cerebellum selects, modulates, and coordinates right and left "brains," and may play a significant role in determining and/or influencing cortical dominance, and even handedness.

8. If, indeed, the right and left "brains" are extensions and reflections of cerebellar function and sensory-motor "processing need," and if Snider and Stowell's findings (1958) of sensory mirrored "homunculi" projection areas in the cerebellum are correct, then one might speculate that: (a) there exist primitive right and left cerebellar "brains" for integrating and/or modulating the sensory-motor input, analogous to the right and left cerebral "brain"; and (b) the basic body-image sense is a reflection of the cerebellum's hypothesized role as the head ganglion of the total sensory-motor system.

9. These speculations imply that a form of "cerebellar dominance" may exist which, in turn, guides and shapes cortical dominance.

Should these hypotheses prove valid, a theoretical gap artificially separating psychoanalysis and neurophysiology will have been bridged; and one hopes that further crossings will eventually contribute a windfall scientific harvest to both fields.

A New Theory of Motion-Sickness Mechanisms

Clinical research with dyslexic individuals has demonstrated that the cerebellum plays as vital a role in modulating the total sensory input as it does in harmonizing the motor output. In addition, blurring-speed data suggests that the cerebellum, via inhibitory-facilitory modulation and control, plays a vital role in regulating and sequencing sensory (and motor) speed transmission prior to its reception by the cerebral cortex for interpretation, perception, and conceptualization. Specifically, it was hypothesized that for normal "cortical interpretation" to take place, the cerebellum must slow down the sensory transmission speed and maintain its sequence so that it falls within the "speed/order" threshold required for proper cortical interpretation. In dyslexia, the cerebellum's inhibitory and sequential ordering capacity is significantly reduced, resulting in sensory dysmetria, i.e., blurring, scrambling and nonrecognition.

One might justifiably ask at this point, What does all this reasoning have to do with motion sickness and motion-sickness medications? The author will answer this question by posing two more: (1) Could the cerebellum modulate motion stimuli as it does visual, acoustic, tactile, and proprioceptive stimuli? (2) If, indeed, motion stimuli are inhibited and regulated by the cerebellum, as are the other sensory input stimuli, might "motion sickness" be justifiably viewed as an "endpoint" representing "cerebellar overloading"?

By analogy, "blurring" and "motion sickness" might be conceptualized as respective cortical and autonomic indicators or signals that the cerebellum's sensory inhibitory and sequential ordering capacity has been exceeded. "Motion sickness" might then be viewed as a homeostatic Inbuilt Release Mechanism which is genetically and environmentally imprinted with survical information, and triggered when the motion input exceeds an adaptive rate. In accordance with this conceptualization, the motion sickness response acts as an anxiety-like warning signal to the organism that something is wrong. One may further speculate that this unpleasant response serves to force the CNS to change its physiologically dangerous state by flight and/or energy discharging reflexes, i.e., wretching, vomiting, etc. Clinically, the motion-sickness IRM and the anxiety IRM appear interrelated, and one often triggers the other.

This c-v (overloading and adaptive) theory of "motion sickness" could then explain many puzzling and previously unanswered questions raised by Bickerman (1972–73):

1. If motion sickness requires vestibular stimulation, how can "motion sickness" occur without motion, and thus without any apparent stimulation of the motion receptors of the vestibular apparatus?
2. How can "motion sickness" be "conditioned," and thus triggered by smell or some other conditioned stimulus? (Once again, "motion sickness" can be triggered by a "learned" or conditioned nonmotion and nonvestibular stimulus.)
3. How and where does "habituation" to rotation and specific motion take place?
4. How can psychogenic factors associated with fear and anxiety lead to the symptoms of motion sickness without motion or vestibular stimulation?
5. Why do the amphetamines and stimulants have as beneficial an effect on motion sickness as any of the other antiemetic drugs, and yet apparently have no direct effect on the vestibular system?

In view of these unanswered questions, Wood and Graybiel (1970) are justified in stating, "The central nervous system mechanisms involved with motion sickness are incompletely understood, hence the actions of drugs in preventing motion sickness are also not understood." Bickerman (1972–73) is equally justified in stating, "The precise pharmacologic activity and site of action of the anti-motion sickness drugs remain uncertain." In introducing the topic he states (p. 459), "Motion sickness has been a recognized clinical entity for over 2,000 years; it is mentioned by Hippocrates. Glaser has referred to it as a 'unique affliction which, in common with childbirth, can cause complete temporary incapacitation without any pathological basis and entirely by reflex mechanisms, though unlike childbirth, it serves no obvious purpose at all.' "

Motion Sickness as a Cerebellar Inbuilt Release Mechanism

When overloaded, the cerebellum is no longer efficiently able to slow down, maintain the order of, and coordinate sensory-motor impulses or stimuli. Under the stress of, and as a reaction to, the specific overloading of motion stimuli, the autonomic nervous system is triggered, on the one hand, and selectively released from cerebellar modulating control, on the other, and reacts with nausea and vomiting. This reaction may be viewed as similar to the warning and discharge function of anxiety—in the service of adaptation and homeostasis.

Just as cerebellar dexterity and coordination varies from individual to individual, so does the cerebellum's ability to modulate selective and specific sensory stimuli—accounting for the significant variation in susceptibility to motion sickness. If Eccles's formulation of motor "learning in the cerebellum" applies equally well for "sensory learning," then the cerebellum is capable of sensory "habituation," conditioning, or "learning"—

thus explaining the decreased motion-sickness response to repeated motion. The concept of "cerebellar conditioning" enables one to understand how conditioned visual, auditory, olfactory, or anxiety stimuli can trigger the cerebellum to react with "motion sickness" in the absence of motion input or vestibular stimulation.

If, indeed, the cerebellum modulates adaptive and homeostatic sensory-motor reflexes, and if the cerebellum is capable of sensory-motor learning, then one may reasonably postulate that the cerebellum modulates both the inborn and the learned warning and anxiety mechanisms required for survival. It seems reasonable to assume further that the cerebellar overloading resulting from anxiety and fear may trigger the release of motion-sickness responses either as an "overflow" phenomenon or as an effort to discharge excessive stimulation and thus maintain homeostatis. Moreover, once the cerebellum is so triggered, it may continue to react to anxiety stimuli via conditioning or learning.

If this reasoning is sound, one might postulate that any disease state of the cerebellum, toxic or otherwise, may selectively trigger the spontaneous release of genetically imprinted or learned motion-sickness mechanisms within its neuronal sphere.

The Hypothesized Function of Anti-Motion Sickness Medications

The amphetamines are known to stimulate the cerebral cortex. Frank and Levinson (1973) postulated that the CNS stimulants charge the reticular activating system, which in turn alerts the cerebellar cortex. It is now possible to hypothesize that via reticular-cerebellar and cortical-cerebellar feedback loops, the amphetamines or stimulants lead to "cerebellar activation," and thus strengthen its ability to modulate, coordinate, and integrate sequential sensory and motor stimuli in a harmonious fashion.

The various other anti-motion-sickness or anti-nauseant medications must directly or indirectly accomplish a similar type of increased cerebellar control, regardless of their varying sites of action or pharmacologic activity. Some drugs may even act via the diencephalon—which Hess (1957) demonstrated is interrelated with the ocular-motor system.

If, indeed, increased cerebellar control leads to its increased capacity to modulate, coordinate, order, slow down, and harmonize its sensory-motor input and output, then the anti-nauseants or anti-motion-sickness medications may be conceived of as "cerebellar (or c-v) harmonizing agents," and are thus postulated to be effective for dysmetric dyslexia and dyspraxia.

11 Anti-Motion Sickness Medications in Dyslexia

The experimental attempt to treat dyslexic individuals with anti-motion sickness medications was based on the following reasoning: (1) If, indeed, the sensory-motor dysmetria underlying dyslexia is of a primary c-v origin; and (2) if the cerebellum modulates the motion input in a manner analogous to its demonstrated role in modulating the visual, acoustic, proprioceptive and tactile input; and (3) if the anti-motion sickness medications improve the functional capacity of the cerebellum (and vestibular circuits) to process and modulate motion input and autonomic motion-sickness reflexes; then perhaps these very same "motion" medications may similarly improve the cerebellum's capacity to modulate and harmonize the non-motion sensory-motor organismic dysmetria characterizing and underlying dyslexia. Furthermore, if these hypotheses are correct, any and all pharmacologically induced therapeutic responses in dyslexia may be viewed as neurophysiologic indicators suggesting that subclinically impaired c-v functional patterns were being compensated for by chemically improved c-v modulating and sensory-motor processing capacity. In addition, the chemically triggered and clinically observed conversion of "dyslexic" to improved or "normal" functioning may be utilized to highlight, and thus explore, the specific c-v neurodynamic role in dyslexic functioning, and to test the c-v potency of specific chemical agents.

One hopes that the insights resulting from this dual therapeutic-investigatory methodology will lead to a predictable pharmacologic scheme for scientifically treating, and possibly even preventing, patterns of dyslexic functioning. In order to test the validity of these assumptions and develop a pharmacologic methodology for the treatment of DD, two large independent samples of proven c-v dyslexics were treated with a series of anti-motion sickness and related medications, and the clinical response patterns were qualitatively and quantitatively analyzed.

Sample and Methodology

The first pilot study contained 250 DD and 30 mixed-DD individuals of varying ages (Frank and Levinson, 1977). The diagnosis of DD was made on the basis of combined neurologic, psychological, blurring-speed, and ENG evidence of c-v dysfunction. Mixed-DD cases had evidence of c-v dysfunction with impaired conceptual ability and decreased I.Q.—and thus were considered to have mixed patterns of c-v and cortical disturbances.

Each individual was treated with one or more of a series of such anti-motion sickness drugs as cyclizine (Marezine), meclizine (Antivert), dimenhydrinate (Dramimine), diphenhydramine (Benadryl), methylphenidate (Ritalin), etc., for a period of approximately two to three months, and the reported clinical (historical) responses and/or parental observations were recorded.* The dosages were individualized by trial and error, and designed to avoid fatigue and side effects. Dyslexic individuals and their parents were instructed to report any and all changes noted during the experimental clinical trials. All participants were advised to expect nothing therapeutically, since the use of medications for the reversal of dyslexic dysfunction was entirely new and highly speculative.

The second study consisted of a series of 200 DD individuals who were similarly treated—except that the insights derived from the first pilot study were applied to the second. As a result, a wider spectrum of medications was utilized, and the ability to determine a positive therapeutic response was more easily and rapidly determined.

Methodologic Considerations

Because these pilot pharmacologic studies were entirely exploratory, and thus significantly "blind," an open-ended clinical-qualitative or historical approach was deemed an essential first step. The author's clinical psychopharmacologic and psychotherapeutic background no doubt facilitated his ability to evaluate the significance of spontaneously reported historical (or subjectively experienced) content, and thus significantly influenced the choice of experimental design. As a result of these and related considerations, it seemed far wiser for the author to scan, and possibly even sketch, the panoramic clinical response pattern to the anti-motion sickness medications before limiting himself in advance to the "blind" but detailed measurements of only a few pre-selected, singly appearing variables suspended in a completely uncharted scientific cosmos.

In accordance with this methodologic philosophy, a "loose" clinical ex-

* For a complete list of the anti-motion sickness medications tested in this study, the reader should refer to Wood & Graybiel (1970). In addition, a wide range of antihistamines were similarly tested for possible efficacy in dyslexia.

perimental design resulted, in which dyslexic individuals were medicated and their favorable therapeutic responses both neurodynamically and statistically analyzed.

Quantitative and Qualitative Results

Utilizing only clinically observed and/or subjectively experienced symptomatic improvement as an indicator of a positive response, the analysis of the total clinical data revealed that well over one-third of both the 250 DD and 30 mixed-DD cases in the first pilot study responded favorably to at least one of the medications utilized. Inasmuch as the first pilot study contained innumerable variables and significant degrees of uncertainty, responses were considered clinically favorable only when they were dramatic in degree and/or extent. In view of the fact that the insights derived from the first study reduced the variables and degrees of uncertainty in the second pilot study, the ability both to trigger pharmacologically and to measure favorable responses improved. Accordingly, 77% (154/200) of the second DD sample evidenced some measure of mild to dramatic improvement in "dyslexic" functioning.

Typical Therapeutic Responses

In accordance with the author's clinical-therapeutic experimental design, all observed and/or subjectively experienced responses to the various medications were carefully documented for each subject. The total collected data was then retrospectively analyzed, resulting in a clinical map which highlighted both the DD response pattern to the anti-motion sickness medications and the corresponding but hidden complex role of the c-v and related circuits in the dyslexic cosmos.

Inasmuch as this composite clinical map and corresponding questionnaire was a development of the first two pilot studies, a majority of the participants were neither uniformly nor thoroughly questioned. Thus, the determination of the frequency distribution of favorable therapeutic responses as a function of both chemical agent and total sample was postponed for a third follow-up study.* In an effort to provide the reader with clinical examples of what the author considered favorable therapeutic responses, a series of typical DD, mixed-DD and adult DD responses are

* This third pharmacological study consisted of the same 300 DD individuals utilized in the single-targeting study (Chapter 8), and 88% of the participants were found to demonstrate some clinical measure or degree of favorable therapeutic response. In this study the author had demonstrated for the first time the efficacy of the so-called anti-depressants in DD.

presented. As the reader will note, the observational historical data has been provided either by parents or the subjective experiences of the patients themselves.

Dyslexic Responses

1. "Jan [8½ years old] had significant spatial disorientation difficulty. . . . If there were 2 or more sentences on the same page she'd lose her place and we had to teach her to track with a pencil. Since starting the medications we find that she no longer uses this pencil and can read longer and longer paragraphs without losing her place, and has stopped reversing *on* and *no*, *what* and *that*. She'll spontaneously pick up a book and attempt to read it without getting discouraged, whereas before she'd only choose books with one picture and two sentences on a page. . . . She also spontaneously started tying her shoe laces. It seems she can coordinate different movements better. . . . She even ventured up a tree and drove her bike down a hill—things she'd never do before. . . . Her handwriting has improved and she no longer reverses the spelling and is writing notes to everyone. . . . Even her drawings have more detail to them and she can better recall what she has seen so as to be able to draw it."

2. "Although Sheila [11½ years old] was reading on grade level, I did not feel her school work reflected what I thought her capabilities to be and I could not understand why she struggled through her school work. Specialists either told me it was maturation or that she was daydreaming too much, an underachiever, not trying, etc. She was down on herself and felt stupid—despite having a 140 I.Q. . . .

"Since she was placed on Antivert, she's become a new child. She reads with ease and you can't stop her from reading. She no longer reverses words. Her spelling, writing, and punctuation have improved. Even some of her sports activities have significantly improved.

"As you suggested, I took her off the medication during the spring recess, and most of her symptoms returned. When I put her back on the medication, everything got better again."

"Before taking the medication, I'd continually lose my place when reading and I'd have to go back over the same page a million times. My writing was big, erratic, and the letters were either too close or too far apart; they'd get bigger and shorter and I'd find it hard to keep on the line. I'd even leave out commas, periods and word endings. I'd get very frustrated and felt very stupid and would get down on myself. Since taking the medication, I see and sound the words out better and everything is just easier to understand. When I read, I don't lose my place, and I find most of the books I read more enjoyable, because I can easily understand it all. I don't mix up or reverse words anymore. When I had difficulty, I'd print, and now I can write cursively and don't use short cuts. For example, before I'd be lazy and write 2 instead of two. . . . Now I get 90s, 95s and 100s instead of 40s, 60s and 70s."

3. "When my son Paul [15 years old] started to take the Marezine we had no idea what would happen as far as the effect on his learning difficulty, dyslexia. After he had been on two pills a day (one in the morning and one at noon) he commented to me that his concentration in school was fantastic. He no longer heard the distracting sounds around him and he said, 'It's as if I'm hypnotized and have to listen and pay attention to what the teacher is saying.'

"I then started to notice an amazing change in his handwriting—it was almost as if another person was doing the writing. The letters were well formed and he no longer left out words or misspelled simple words, which he knew well and had always misspelled in the past.

"Arithmetic was always his worst subject. His marks improved dramatically, as did all his subjects. From complete failures in his subjects he started to get 75s to 100s. His coordination is also better on the Marezine; whereas he had a tendency to trip and drop things before, with the medicine he has control of his reflexes to a great extent. If for some reason he neglects to take the Marezine, I can notice it immediately when I look over his school work for the day—the handwriting once more is scribbled and words that are basic he misspells."

4. "While driving, Stan [17½ years old] noticed he was reading the signs on the parkway faster and clearer. . . . This could be because of greater familiarity.

"When closing his eyes, both feet together, hands and fingers outstretched and upwards, the necessity to continually readjust his balance was greatly reduced . . . almost to the point of being calm. . . . When he went off the medication the swaying under these conditions became quite marked.

"His writing and printing became clearer and appeared on a straighter line. When he went off Dramamine and Ritalin the regression was marked."

5. "Since Tom [16 years old] began taking Marezine and Ritalin on or about August 1, 1974, we noticed the following:

1. About September 1st Tom tried walking a straight line on his heels and touching the end of his nose with his finger tip when his eyes were closed—two tests he had been unable to do when tested in July. He reported with great glee that he was able to do both tests.
2. About the same time he said that he was really feeling great and didn't feel fuzzy or 'spaced out' anymore.
3. Since returning to school in mid-September he has had unusually high grades in his daily work, all As and Bs, except for one C and one F

in a test on which he had misinterpreted the question. He had an 88 on the next test.

4. He says he still hates to study, but that he knows he can do it if he tries. He say that math is 'kind of fun'—a distinctly new adjective for his school work."

6. "John's [7½ years old] handwriting has improved considerably and his interest in math has suddenly mushroomed. He appears to be calculating mentally without using his fingers or pencils and paper for checking and double-checking. He now shows very little right/left confusion. Also, in his piano lessons, he has improved a great deal. He is able to sight read without confusion or losing his place, and only occasionally reverses words. He shows a new and dramatic interest in sports, especially football and baseball. His greatest interest, however, is for schoolwork. He really loves to go to school now.

"However, confusion, difficulty in school, and a general disintegration of personality seems to occur around mid-February and March. I have basically the same problem and find it difficult to concentrate, to complete tasks. I am very disorganized, cannot read well and jump from one thing to another and one word to another, except when on Marezine."

7. "Edward [7 years old] was very agitated and excitable on Marezine and even became confused. According to his reading teacher, he seemed to have an easier time reading when he had taken Dramamine than when he had not. When taking Antivert, however, he showed the most dramatic improvement of all. His concentration, hyperactivity, and reading ability improved greatly. And he recently even developed a great talent for sports. Ed now plays football as a wide receiver and really can catch the long ones. In baseball he can bat well and does a good job in the field. It seems as if everything was suddenly coming together as far as his coordination goes. And he is now for the first time enjoyed by his peers both in sports and socially.

"He had been hitting doubles and homeruns while on the Antivert. And as you requested, I stopped the Antivert for the summer. One day he came home from camp in a foul mood and claimed his team-mates were angry with him. He kept striking out and making field errors. Against your advice, I put him back on the Antivert. Sure enough, he came home very happy that day. I asked him how he did in camp that day and he said, 'Great. I got 3 base hits and my fielding was good.'

"I never told him why I placed him on the medication. I just wanted to see for myself what would happen. Each time I take him off the Antivert the same thing happens. It's really hard to believe. I put him back on it and he performs altogether differently. . . . We have a 15-year-old baby-sitter who, as you now know, happens to be dyslexic. I explained to her why we were taking Ed to the doctor. And sure enough one day she told me that she had gone to see you, started taking ½ tablet of Dramamine three times a day, and she was amazed by her response. Her reading, writing, and gymnastics all improved dramatically. Even her teachers noted a significant change. And they knew nothing about her taking anything."

8. Laura [16 years old]: "Upon taking Marezine I initially became tired but this effect wore off. And then I was suddenly aware of being able to utilize my peripheral vision more effectively. . . . Suddenly my reading speed increased at a rate beyond that which I could comprehend.

"Dimetapp had less of an effect and Antivert seemed to have no effect at all. . . . I also noticed a subtle improvement in my word recall and use. And I don't find myself hesitating, tripping over words like I used to and stuttering any more."

Mixed-Dyslexic Responses

Mixed-DD cases were demonstrated to have qualitative and quantitative therapeutic response patterns similar to regular DD subjects. As previously defined, mixed-DD cases contained c-v dysfunction with evidence of more diffuse CNS impairment (i.e., decreased conceptual ability, decreased I.Q., and evidence of cortical dysfunction).

1. "As per your request, I am writing this letter to advise you on Frank's [16½ years old] progress since our last visit, April 10. His initial dosage of Antivert was 6.2 mg., morning and night. His response to the medicine was good. We notice no drowsiness or any other side effects. After taking the medicine four to five days, we began to notice a general improvement in the areas of his speech and his ability to control his hands, i.e., writing and coloring. . . .

"His schoolwork in the area of writing, is now legible for the first time. He has been able to write complete sentences all on one line, and most of the letters are the same size. His coloring is better, but there is still room for improvement.

"One interesting note. Since medication, we have noticed that Frank no longer puts his pajama bottoms on backwards."

2. "Marty [18 years old] now writes a little more smoothly. He does not reverse his numbers. He is more at ease with us at home. Calm. He can spell a few more words: Manhattan, Bronx Park, license, etc. These are words he could not spell before. He claims he can read better now. Marty can now look at a word and see it as it is. It is no longer bunched up or scrambled. Before taking the Marezine, Ritalin and antihistamines, when he would copy words from a book he would run all the words together and leave no space between the words. Now when he writes, the letters and

words are written separately, as are the sentences. And his punctuation has also improved."

3. "William [6½ years old] has been on Marezine since November 28, 1974. He takes 1 Marezine and ½ Ritalin in the morning; 1 Marezine and 1 Ritalin at lunchtime; 1 Marezine and ½ Ritalin at dinnertime. His writing and overall concentration has improved slightly. I have noticed that he is not rocking as much as he did before taking Marezine and when he reads, he no longer loses his place like he did before.

"These changes have all taken place since he started taking the Marezine. His reading and writing are better. He stays on the lines better. Before he was all over the paper. The Ritalin seemed to calm him down and the Marezine seems to have improved everything else."

Adult Dyslexic Responses

Adult dyslexics were found to respond almost as favorably to the anti-motion sickness medications as did children. The response patterns of two typical adult cases are presented. Both cases were diagnosed "by accident." They brought their children for dyslexic work-up and treatment and were similarly diagnosed and treated.

Evaluation and treatment of numerous adult DD cases clearly revealed that they characteristically (1) deny all c-v-related symptoms unless specifically and skillfully questioned; (2) develop their first manifest or acknowledged vertigo episode during adulthood—a history of previous c-v dysfunction and DD most frequently escapes clinical view; (3) develop various c-v-related travel, motion, coordination, and academic inhibitions or phobias; (4) strive to compensate for their underlying c-v deficiencies, and at times develop overcompensatory and/or counterphobic phenomena.

Two Adult Dyslexic Clinical-Therapeutic Examples

Mrs. B.'s [35 years old] written report of her own reactions to the anti-motion sickness medications is presented abridged, but unedited with regard to grammar and spelling. Her spelling and grammatical errors were found to be in sharp contrast to her superior conversational vocabulary and grammar.

"I have been on Marizine 50 mg. ½ tablet 3 times a day. This dosage proved to be too strong so I reduced it to ½ tablet 2 times daily, which also made me sleepy and listless. Now I am on ½ tablet once a day and I can function normally. My periods of vertigo or dizzyness and light headedness have seemed to have disappeared. I have more of a desire to want to attempt to read and can do so without difficulty for a period of 15 to 20 minutes at a time, which was not possible before. My coordination seems somewhat improved, which gives me the impetus to try things, that I might not have otherwise tried before. I feel more relaxed which I attribute to the fact that I can go through my chores with more ease and dexterity. My severe headaches thank God have disappeared which also relieves the tensions. Once in a while I do experience a little light headedness but instead of remaining as it once did and become an acute problem for the day, it seems to disappear almost immediately. . . . My handwriting seems the same, it is legible but not the greatest. As far as sports activities are concerned, I haven't participated in any as of yet (since I began the medication) but it is tennis time and I would love to see if there is a difference in my game. . . . I find that my attention span is about the same, but what I do notice is that sometimes I can't focus on a person while talking to him or her. I find that my eyes are wandering, and I must try to focus again. My grasp of words seems to have improved, that is while I'm talking, I can find the right words to make myself understood. There are however periods when I can't express myself as I would like to, but they seem to be farer apart now. . . .

"I seem to be able to filter information more quickly and follow instructions (written) more precisely. I still feel comfortable in a structured environment as opposed to a more liberal one. I guess because of the control and knowing what to expect next. I also can only concentrate on one thing at a time, otherwise I get tense and confused. My memory seems keen enough and I rely upon it for almost everything I do. I have not noticed any correlation between my menstruation and the Dyslexia, except during ovulation the light headedness seems to come through a little more. The improvements that I have noticed as you can tell have been in various areas, attitudes for obvious reasons, and in physical things. I find myself constantly looking for a better way of saying things and drawing a critique on my daily living to see the changes if any. In my case maturation has nothing to do with improvement as I might tend to think for my daughter."

Mrs. I. [43 years old] brought her son for psychiatric treatment. He manifested clinically as an acting-out adolescent who had succeeded in provoking a number of schools into expelling him. However, clinical examination surprisingly revealed him to be a "compensated hyperactive" and dyslexic with a "short fuse." He had been under psychological treatment for several years. At that time, the working diagnosis had been that of an acting-out character disorder, and the treatment plan accordingly advised severe restriction and discipline, with disastrous results. History-taking suggested that Mrs. I. might have DD. Neurologic, ENG and blurring-speed testing confirmed this impression. As a matter of fact, Mrs. I. was the patient who first asked the author which blurring speed he wanted, and thus was responsible for the discovery of sequential versus single-target blurring speeds.

Upon neurologic examination, Mrs. I. was found to have typical c-v dyslexic signs despite normal reading-score functioning. She acknowledged vertiginous episodes initiating in adulthood, although pre-existing evidence of c-v dysfunction was traceable to her childhood. In addition, she reported fears of heights as well as fears of driving on parkways, over bridges, into tunnels, around twisting roads and along mountainous terrain, and an inability to use both side and rear-view mirrors because of orientation difficulties. She described herself as clumsy and accident-prone, and experienced a general lack of coordination and an inability to perceive spatial relationships. For example, she found herself unable to judge the distances, locations, and speeds of other cars in traffic, and thus avoided highways and fast driving conditions. In addition, she reluctantly admitted disorientation and panic when driving too far from home by herself—for fear of becoming lost. Of interest is the fact that Mrs. I. experienced repetitive dreams of falling, car accidents, and getting lost. Fears of being abandoned and lost dated back to her childhood. Furthermore, she frustrated easily, had a quick temper and a "short fuse." She was placed on Antivert and reported her reactions to taking one-half tablet twice a day:

"I am much, much more comfortable driving my car, and am now willing to venture out further and further from home, feeling somehow I will be able to get back. I am using both rear-view and side-view mirrors a great deal now. I find myself turning on the car radio for music while I am driving, once a real no-no. I am not so easily frustrated, and my friends have told me—without my asking—that they 'noticed' that I am much more relaxed now. Of course, I also seem to be able to control my temper more.

"I read without headaches now, *totally*.

"When I used to play bridge, and it was my turn to play out the hand (I won the bid), my heart used to pound terribly from anxiety as I tried to keep track of the 52 cards. I can't even imagine why I love the game so, it makes me so anxious. Yet, lately, my heart does not pound at all; I am not at all anxious, and I don't know why. Maybe I am keeping track of the cards better? My kitchen seems cleaner when I cook—my coordination seems better. At least, there are no eggshells in the scrambled eggs.

"And I'm not so afraid of driving on expressways and will stray some distance from my house. I just don't get as disoriented and as panicky as before. . . . Although I've always loved shopping, the elevators, escalators and crowds in department stores used to drive me crazy and I'd feel faint—like I was going to pass out. I'd get that same feeling when I'd be crossing the street or in a subway. Well, things are better now. I'm not so anxious anymore. When I think back, it seems like I used to get disoriented and confused. I guess you might call it dizzy. . . . That's why I'd always like someone with me—just in case I passed out. Now that I feel better, I can travel alone. And looking down from heights and windows just doesn't create the same panic as before. I'd actually feel like I was going to fall out—even when the windows were closed. It was real bad on an open terrace or train platform. . . . It seems I was always afraid of losing my balance, losing control and fainting and then being terribly embarrassed. . . . I refused to discuss all these feelings because they make me feel crazy or stupid. Now these feelings are still with me—but so much milder. . . . And I know you're probably going to tell me that all are related to my dyslexia and the medications were helpful. And probably they are—but I feel compelled to tell you they're not. And I still can't believe my difficulties are physical. . . . But even these thoughts are stupid—because why would I get these dizzy spells and why do I trip over my own words when I talk and why do I keep making so many typing errors when I'm off the medication. And why does the medication help so much if it were all just in my mind?

"And you know, I don't feel so stupid all the time like I used to. It's like I have more confidence. Even my reading is better and I've always loved reading. But I can remember details more easily.

"And crowded movies used to drive me crazy and I'd have to sit near the exit. And during the movie I'd lose track of events—especially if my husband would talk to me. And then I'd really get anxious and want to run out. After the movie was over and my husband would discuss things with me—I'd feel really bad. I found it hard to remember details or the names of characters, and I'd mix up one sequence with another—just like I did when I was cooking. I'd always leave something out of a recipe and was always spilling or dropping things. . . . All this really makes you feel like you're really retarded."

In summary, both cases highlighted a number of vital points:

1. They were both typical underachievers in families of well-educated individuals and were never previously diagnosed "dyslexic" because their reading-score deficiencies were partially compensated.

2. Their first "remembered" episodes of vertigo occurred during adulthood, although the presence of chronic c-v dysfunction and DD remained unrecognized and dated back to childhood. To date, the clinical data clearly indicates that many DD children will be predisposed to vertigo and c-v-related mental symptoms as adults, and that many adults with vertigo had unrecognized and undiagnosed c-v dysfunction and DD as children.

3. As a result of embarrassment, feelings of inferiority, and stupidity, many sensory-motor dysmetric symptoms, as well as related fears of height, motion, elevators, tunnels, and so on, were never spontaneously verbalized nor connected with their denied and/or unrecognized dyslexia.

4. They were able to clinically describe their disorders and response to medications succinctly, and the majority of favorable responses were found to be dependent upon only specific pharmacologic agents. Thus Mrs. B. responded favorably to Marezine and poorly to Antivert, whereas her daughter, Sheila, and Mrs. I responded in reverse fashion. The specificity of response to the various anti-motion sickness medications was found typical

for all DD individuals, and suggested that even slight pharmacologic structural differences result in significant and diverse symptomatic responses. In addition, favorable responses for any given medication are significantly dose-dependent and time-dependent—much more so than could have been theoretically anticipated.

5. DD-related phobias, inhibitions, and related mental symptomatology were found to improve with a corresponding improvement in c-v sensory-motor functioning, and resulted in a new psychodynamic and neurodynamic conceptualization and treatment for a group of "psychic" disorders."

As a result of limited DD sampling, superficial DD and psychodynamic explorations, and the tunnel vision and scrambling effects of denial mechanisms found permeating and characterizing both dyslexics and researchers, there developed a rather common view by clinicians and educators alike that dyslexia was just a reading or learning disability. The subclinical but devastating emotional fallout resulting from the underlying dysmetric functioning was often overlooked.

A Letter Highlighting the Emotional Fall-out of Dyslexia

It is hoped that the content of a letter from Mrs. B. will convey the fact that the emotional scarring and dislocations resulting from dyslexia are far worse than the more obvious reading and learning difficulties, and that dyslexia, as well as its secondary and tertiary symptomatic fallout, are worthy of early intervention, treatment, and prevention.

"As a person with Dyslexia I too have also sold myself short in many areas, that's putting it mildly. My feelings of ineptness have carried over to all phases of my life, and in order to compensate for them I have either over reacted or just reacted instead of acted towards different situations in my life. . . . I had always felt like I was on the outside looking in, never really a participant. Constantly searching for love and approval, I felt safest if I were to be married and have someone else protect me from the world. I didn't feel that I could make it on my own and therefore never really strived for a college education, using money as the excuse. After listening to others with the same problem and worse I am ashamed that I didn't even try. I still might some day. How is that for a positive thought about one's self. I have watched my movements and thoughts so closely I can tell you as I'm sure you know that this Dyslexia touches all parts of your life. My husband is quite a sports enthusiast and always wanted me to participate with him in either tennis, bicycling, target shooting and I always shyed away not knowing why, well now I do and between the new knowledge that I have and the aid of medication I hope to be by his side a lot more. In our arguments I would frustrate so easily for I couldn't find the words to make my self understood. In fact we went to Marriage Encounter which you might know deals with writing down your feelings in a letter; well his were always so clear that you could almost taste them, but mine would be so disorientated that I was better off not bothering. So I did as I always do, I withdraw from the situation. . . . I could go on for hours spilling my guts and still have more to say. I could never read a recipe and follow through on the directions. I could never read the instructions on one of my children's games to explain it to them, yet if I played the game once I would be able to pick it up right away. My feelings towards my daughter are that of understanding mixed with frustration, for her and for myself. She understands me (before medication because I would give such a detailed explanation of things, she couldn't miss. After all one Dyslexic to another, I talk our language. It must be comforting to her to see me function as a person with no problems inspite of the Dyslexia. After all mommy has it and look at her. (Well she is young yet and maybe she doesn't see or know the scars, and yet maybe she does.) I am just so happy that she can label her problems as I couldn't and put them in the proper perspective."

Positive Response Patterns to the Anti-Motion Sickness Medications

Table 11–1 illustrates and summarizes the qualitative analysis and correlations of the total pattern of DD responses to the various anti-motion-sickness medications utilized in studies 1 and 2. The pattern of favorable DD responses appears to be a mirror-image of the c-v disturbances found characterizing the dyslexic nuclear symptomatic complex in the retrospective study (Chapter 2).

Although this initial pharmacologic research effort was not conducted in a formal double-blind manner, the studies did have "double-blind" aspects in that neither patient nor investigator could anticipate the range and depth of the positive cerebellar neurophysiologic and neuropsychologic responses. In addition, so theoretically consistent and uniform were the patterns of positive c-v responses in each patient that the author was forced to suspect that each patient responding favorably to the anti-motion sickness medications isomorphically validated the hypotheses highlighting the role of the cerebellum in modulating (1) the total sensory-motor input and output, (2) the motion-sickness mechanisms, and (3) the motion-sickness medications in both normal and dyslexic individuals. Chance alone could not have explained the unique c-v pattern of positive therapeutic responses in each fortunate DD patient. A "placebo effect" would probably have resulted in only "reading-score improvement," providing reading tests were sensitive enough indicators of the changes in reading functioning. A placebo effect alone could not have determined the unique specific positive response to only one of several medications used, and the dramatic regression in function when the medication was stopped, switched, or changed in dosage, or when active ingredients were rendered pharmacologically inactive and impotent by immune-like resistance mechanisms.

Table 11–1. The Dysmetric Dyslexic and Dyspraxic Response Pattern to the Cerebellar-Vestibular Harmonizing Agents

Reading Activity
- Increased spontaneous reading activity
- Diminished dysmetric tracking and finger pointing
- Improved fixation ability
- Improved foreground/background differentiation (i.e., decreased blurring and increase in degree of letter blackness)
- Decreased or eliminated reading reversals
- Increased reading speed and accuracy
- Increased interest in reading

Writing Activity
- Increased spontaneous writing activity
- Smoother rhythm and increased legibility
- Improved spacing between letters and words
- Increased horizontality in writing
- Increased use of cursive writing (printing usually easier)
- Decreased writing reversals
- Increased use of grammatical details (i.e., periods, commas, etc.)
- Increased writing speed
- Increased word content
- Decreased number of spelling errors

Spelling
- Increased spelling recall and decreased letter reversals (i.e., insertion and omissions)

Arithmetic
- Increased mechanical alignment
- Increased memory for calculations

Directionality, Spatial Organization, and Planning
- Increased right/left differentiation
- Decreased rotations
- Increased detail in drawing
- Improvement in Goodenough figure drawings
- Improved spacing in writing
- Improved relationships to spatial coordination tasks (i.e., ball playing, catching, throwing, batting, etc.)
- Increased ability to tie shoelaces, etc.

Balance and Coordination
- Increased ability to ride a bike, dribble basketball, etc.
- Decreased clumsiness (i.e., tripping, falling, and various past-pointing and prepointing activities)
- Increased feeling of internal steadiness

Foreground/Background Activity (Sensory)
- Increased foreground clarity

Improved background suppression of irrelevant and distracting events (i.e., visual, acoustic, etc.)
Decreased acoustic blurring and scrambling

Speech
Increased spontaneity of speech
Decreased slurring, where present
Increased rate and improved rhythm of speech
Increased verbal content
Decreased stuttering, stammering, and hesitations

Sequence Activity and Memory
Increase in sequence memory (i.e., days of the week, months of the year, spelling, multiplication, etc.)

Time Sense
Increased sense of time and time sequences

Concentration and State of Consciousness
Improved and increased clarity of consciousness, and associated improvement in memory

Mood
Improved and increased stability of mood

Self Image
Decreased feelings of inferiority and stupidity
Decreased defensive attitude
Increased self-assertiveness
Increased positive attitude

Body Image
Improved—as reflected in Goodenough figure drawings and generalized sensory-motor activity
Improved visual, acoustic, tactile, temperature, olfactory, and proprioceptive modulation

Frustration Tolerance
Increased frustration tolerance
Increased concentration and attention span

Anxiety Tolerance
Increased anxiety tolerance

Socialization
Increased and improved socialization—especially with peers

Acceptance of Symptoms
Decreased denial
Increased ability to tackle, understand, and accept symptoms
Increased ability to ask questions spontaneously

DDD Phobias, Inhibitions, Counterphobias, Characterological Development
Improved

In retrospect, a careful patient-by-patient, in-depth neuropsychologic study, utilizing an analytic, psychodynamic and neurodynamic methodologic approach, proved exceedingly helpful in mapping out what might be considered a new, dynamic and holistic c-v neuropsychologic topography. An initial, formal double-blind pharmacologic approach attempting to measure only the anticipated reading-score changes would have resulted in a "scomatized" and confused bird's-eye view of the dynamic, complex, and overdetermined c-v topography. Surely the forest would have been lost for the trees.

In conducting these initial neuropsychologic and pharmacologic clinical investigations with the anti-motion sickness medications, the author assumed (1) that underlying every positive DD response there pre-existed either manifest or subclinical cerebellar and/or vestibular dysfunction; (2) that in highlighting the cerebellar and/or vestibular functional changes in DD, the anti-motion sickness medications served as an invaluable research tool with which to dissect and analyze cerebellar and vestibular latent and related dysfunctions; and (3) that inasmuch as the anti-motion sickness and related medications were found clinically to improve both c-v and related sensory-motor function and modulation, the term "c-v harmonizing agents" might be conceptually appropriate for classifying all drugs improving c-v and dysmetric functioning, regardless of their structure or known pre-existing anti-motion sickness potency.

In summary, and as a result of the analysis and classification of the positive DD responses to the anti-motion sickness medications, the author recognized:

1. A consistent, broad range of improved cerebellar and/or vestibular functions mirroring the dyslexic disturbances defined within the DD nuclear symptomatic complex.
2. The presence of silently active, vital, and heretofore unrecognized "higher" cerebellar and related functions. The repetitive clinical findings of improvement in sequential thinking, state of consciousness, memory, mathematics, grammar, word-recall, and word-use, as well as improvement in other communication, speech, and "pre-gnostic" sensory and thought functions, led to the development of new conceptualizations of higher cerebellar functions—neurophysiologic functions previously attributed entirely to the cerebral cortex.
3. The somatopsychic unity of c-v function and dysfunction. For example, the neuropsychologic c-v basis of a group of travel and motion phobias was recognized for the first time, and a holistic psychoanalytic and pharmacologic approach to the treatment of c-v-related phobias and counterphobias was developed.

Qualitative Variations Among Favorable Dyslexic Responders

In general, the dyslexic patients treated with the anti-motion sickness medications may be classified as:

1. *Medication dependent.* Some dyslexics require continuous pharmacologic treatment in order to maintain favorable responses.
2. *Medication independent.* Following an initial triggering or catalyzing series of dosages, some dyslexics no longer require medication in order to maintain this favorable response.
3. *Negative responders.* Interestingly enough, the size of this group significantly diminished as more and more drugs were utilized for testing, thereby suggesting that potentially all dyslexic individuals may be positive drug responders.
4. *Medication immune.* A small percentage of medication-dependent individuals who initially responded favorably eventually demonstrated what might be termed a developing resistance to drug potency as a function of time. Changing the drug or stopping it for a period of time, and then re-starting it appeared sufficient in some cases to overcome the factors tending to neutralize drug efficacy or potency.

The ability of medications to restore or reset DD functioning to more normal levels, and the corresponding regression of neurologic functioning following drug withdrawal, indicated that for some individuals DD was a chemically reversible or compensatory disorder. The "reversibility" of DD functioning seemed most apparent when an initial trial of medication resulted in a "lasting" improvement in either blurring speed or dyslexic symptoms—suggesting that the medications were at times able to trigger or catalyze the development of self-corrective processes.

Most DD individuals in these studies did not respond favorably to more than one or two "c-v harmonizing agents"—clearly suggesting that positive DD therapeutic response is a function of pharmacologic specificity. Where two or more drugs were found to be effective, they were invariably potent to different degrees and affected different patterns of DD responses. Inasmuch as DD responses were found to be a function of chemical specificity, and because each drug resulted in specific but differing patterns of DD responses in each patient, combinations of the various medications were utilized for each patient to effect deeper and wider favorable responses in DD functioning. In addition, a computerized research effort is now underway attempting to correlate "dyslexic" neurologic symptoms, blurring speeds, tracking patterns, ENG parameters, and favorable patterns of pharmacologic response, so that a prediction can be made as to which medications or combinations of medications are most likely to be effective for any presenting dyslexic individual.

Electronystagmographic and Blurring-Speed Pharmacologic Correlations

Although the historical assessment of DD therapeutic responses to the various anti-motion sickness medications proceeded relatively smoothly and according to theory, the expected ability to objectively record and quantitatively measure these responses via ENG and blurring speeds did not materialize. All too often, ENG parameters did not reflect the pharmacologically triggered dramatic changes in c-v dyslexic functioning. Blurring speeds were often found to vary independently of clinical therapeutic response.

Electronystagmography

The traditionally accepted "objective" ENG parameters did not significantly reflect the positive therapeutic DD responses to the anti-motion-sickness medications. This observation led a critic to state that if the ENG parameters did not reflect a change, there was no change, and that the anti-motion sickness medications, in his opinion, were even worthless in motion sickness—let alone in dyslexia.

The author reasoned differently. If the traditionally accepted ENG parameters did not measure the clinically observed and historically recorded therapeutic DD changes, perhaps the ENG methodology was at fault and additional ENG parameters were required to detect these changes. As a result of this reasoning, the ENG methodology was re-analyzed and re-explored; and the discovery of new diagnostic ENG parameters, and their addition to the traditionally accepted ENG methodology, led to an increased accuracy of this methodology in detecting c-v dysfunction, and simultaneously increased the ability of ENG to measure pharmacologic therapeutic responses.

Blurring Speeds

The variations in blurring speed as a function of therapeutic response were initially too confusing to be understood, and one easily could have concluded that there was no "real" therapeutic response or that the methodology was faulty.

The discovery of compensatory versus diagnostic blurring speeds led to the recognition that the author had at times unwittingly measured and compared premedication compensatory blurring speeds with postmedication diagnostic blurring speeds—thus accounting for the paradoxical data whereby blurring speeds decreased despite increased therapeutic responses. In addition, there existed a series of heretofore unknown diagnostic endpoints, and as a result, the blurring-speed determinations as a function of medication response were retrospectively recognized to contain significant degrees of error. Moreover, premedication blurring speeds were at times defensively confabulated on the high side, whereas postmedication blurring speeds were more objectively reported. One hopes that the elimination of these errors in future studies will result in more accurate correlations and corresponding conceptualizations.

Central Versus Peripheral Processing Mechanisms

The failure of ENG and blurring-speed testing to detect favorable therapeutic responses may be viewed as indirectly supporting the previously postulated existence of central and peripheral c-v processing mechanisms. If, for example, the ENG and blurring-speed parameters are primarily tapping peripheral processing mechanisms, while the anti-motion sickness medications are primarily effecting central processing mechanisms, then the poor ENG/blurring speed therapeutic response correlations are readily comprehensible. In addition, the complex function-specific nature of c-v compensatory mechanisms tends to further complicate the various c-v diagnostic measuring parameters, as well as the resulting statistical attempts at establishing clear-cut correlations in DD. Furthermore, inasmuch as the dyslexic panorama defined by the equilibrium of c-v dysfunction versus compensatory mechanisms was found to have at least four dimensions, it appeared ludicrous and naive to expect any one single test or group of simple parameters to define statistically and to encompass the DD cosmos.

"If the Facts Do Not Fit the Theory, Then the Facts Are Wrong"

The heretofore unrecognized need for additional ENG diagnostic parameters, as well as the unwitting errors in determining diagnostic blurring speeds, resulted in frustrating confusion, as well as difficulty in harmonizing test facts with theoretical expectations. However, by this stage in the dyslexic research effort, the author had the courage to invoke Einstein's famous tongue-in-cheek remark, "If the facts do not fit the theory, then the facts are wrong." Of course, this approach was in sharp contrast to that taken by the author in the retrospective and prospective studies, whereby the psychic and cortical theories of dyslexia were dramatically changed to fit the c-v dyslexic facts. In retrospect, a failure to have flexibly changed theory with fact and vice versa would have resulted in a continuation of the closed system characterizing dyslexic research efforts for approximately eighty years.

> A closed system is a cognitive structure with a distorted, non-Euclidian geometry in curved space, where parallels intersect and straight lines form loops. Its

> canon is based on a central axiom, postulate or dogma, to which the subject is emotionally committed, and from which the rules of processing reality are derived. The amount of distortion involved in the processing is a matter of degrees, and an important criterion of the value of the system. It ranges from the scientist's involuntary inclination to juggle with data as a mild form of self-deception, motivated by his commitment to a theory, to the delusional belief-systems of clinical pananoia. [Koestler, 1968, p. 264]

This research effort has clearly demonstrated that for science to evolve, a flexible balance must be maintained between justifiable conviction and realistic uncertainty. The unseen but clinically apparent dynamic equilibrium existing between fact, fantasy, and fiction must be continuously activated, analyzed and re-analyzed. For most often, scientific facts and fantasies or theories are neither right nor wrong, but merely incomplete; and at any point in scientific time, only highly selected spatial fragments of a factual totality are perceived, and thus incompletely conceptualized.

Interestingly enough, Lorenz (1957, p. 288) reports that similar convictions were voiced by Jakob von Uexkull and Otto Koehler: "Jakob von Uexkull once said: 'Today's truth is tomorrow's error.' And Otto Koehler countered: 'No, today's truth is the special case of tomorrow.' "

Scientific Fact, Fantasy, and Fiction

Is dyslexia a disorder which occurs only in children of average or above average performance or I.Q.? Or is it independent of I.Q.? Most concepts and definitions stress that to be dyslexic one *must* have a normal or superior I.Q. Is this conviction fact, fantasy, or fiction? The recognition that dyslexia and its nuclear symptomatic complex is of c-v origin, that children with diffuse CNS dysfunction and low I.Q. may also have c-v dysfunction and dyslexic symptoms (mixed-DD cases), and that the anti-motion sickness medications improve the c-v-related symptoms in dyslexic and mixed-dyslexic individuals, clearly demonstrated that dyslexia and its symptomatic complex is independent of I.Q.

Inasmuch as many I.Q.-impaired individuals were noted to have associated c-v dysfunction, and inasmuch as anti-motion-sickness medications were found to improve c-v and related cortical functioning regardless of I.Q., it became readily apparent upon resolving the fictitious dyslexic–I.Q. correlation that new hope existed for the conceptually impaired. The reasoning underlying this new therapeutic approach was quite simple. It was anticipated that improved c-v and related cortical functioning would result in a relative increase in "cortical reserve capacity," and that a generalized CNS improvement would occur. Thus far, the data obtained from the experimental treatment of mixed-DD cases has supported this contention.

This reasoning was found equally valid in the treatment of cerebral palsy, where patients exhibited mixed CNS patterns of motor and c-v disturbances.

A Methodologic Explanation

Placebo controls and double-blind research techniques were deliberately not utilized in these pilot pharmacologic studies. So a word of explanation is in order. The author became a dyslexic researcher by necessity rather than by choice. He experienced his primary task and responsibility as a "healing physician." Thus his ambitions and priorities were directed toward the relief of the pain, suffering, and the inevitable emotional scarring resulting from dyslexia. The diagnostic studies to date were viewed merely as attempts to specifically define the disorder so as to develop multidisciplinary therapeutic approaches. Thus, the results of the various diagnostic studies served merely to catalyze, rather than satiate, the author's ambitions, and inevitably led him to the pharmacologic studies described here.

Suffering children and parents flew in from all parts of the world seeking the author's help as a physician, not as a researcher. They had no other medical alternative. Many had already circled the scientific dyslexic globe. They had been everywhere, seen everyone, and were currently spinning and suffering from "emotional vertigo." Needless to say, the author had a captive audience of "experimental hostages." In their despair, the vast majority would no doubt have participated in placebo control studies. All one had to do was tell the dyslexic children and their parents, "Some children will receive 'real' medications and some 'fake' medications. After each two to three month test period, I will change both the real and fake medications again. Neither you nor I will know who is getting what. When the experiment is all over, I'll perhaps know enough to tell which dyslexics 'really' responded to the medication effect and which dyslexics merely responded to its placebo effect. Needless to say, everyone participating in this experiment may eventually help millions of other suffering dyslexics."

However, the author had perhaps empathized or identified too closely with his patients and their parents, and thus could not bring himself in all conscience to subject a large series of suffering dyslexics to placebos for two to three months per drug for three or more drugs—merely for the sake of scientific design, clarity, and/or the avoidance of possible scientific criticism. The possibility of preventing one more traumatic year in the academic and emotional life of a dyslexic child already feeling stupid and clumsy was deemed infinitely more important and significant than research design. Besides, the author felt more comfortable investigating large numbers of variables with his eyes wide open. It seemed to him there would be time enough to conduct more formal "scientific" studies once the variables were reduced and a scientific methodology worked through. The conviction to omit placebo controls was strengthened by several additional considerations:

1. Some patients, including family members, were already responding dramatically to the anti-motion sickness medications, and thus the decision to treat controls with placebos became even more difficult to rationalize.

2. The author had been successfully treating suffering psychiatric patients for many years. Invariably, his therapeutic decisions were based on the ability to assess properly historical and "subjectively experienced" content. If indeed his psychotherapeutic ability was valid, then why should he not feel as confident in objectively evaluating the historical and/or subjective content of the favorable, unfavorable, and changing dyslexic responses to the various chemical agents while utilizing the contrasting differences in place of placebo controls?

3. The confusing statistical and methodologic data of the "blind" blurring-speed study were solved by the ability of the author to assess the meaning and significance of one patient's spontaneous question—clearly indicating that so-called "objective" research and statistical designs can result in unbelievable confusion and time lags, whereas the ability to assess and judge quickly the significance of historical and/or so-called subjective responses may be rapidly illuminating and scientifically "life-saving." In other words, the author was emotionally biased against unnecessary "blind" scientific studies and biased in favor of historical responses and content.

As a result of these, and perhaps other unknown, considerations, the author proceeded scientifically according to the dictates of his subjective "gut" feelings. In the final analysis, he realized that scientific design and guidelines were only as valid and objective as the scientists and researchers applying them. All too often, so-called objective scientists were found to be unwittingly acting-out the whims of their unconscious subjective feelings and convictions—despite their use and display of traditionally accepted scientific principles, and such objectively convincing visual aids as *P* values, correlation coefficients, curves, graphs, etc.

If, indeed, the author's c-v findings in dyslexia proved to be valid, then scientists have been scientifically searching and utilizing accepted "objective" statistical tools, measures, control studies, etc., either in vain or in error. In retrospect, it often appeared as if (pseudo)objective scientific displays were merely "closed systems" in disguise and that both the underlying bias and its manifest scientific facade were being shaped by unconscious subjective determinants. In retrospect, science and scientists were at times recognized to be merely illusions or dream fragments requiring psychoanalytic dissection, interpretation, and treatment.

Imaginary critics may be anticipated as asking, "If double-blind studies were not performed, how can placebo effects be ruled out? Needless to say, the critics are correct. Placebo effects cannot be ruled out. However, the author will, in turn, pose several questions to his imaginary critics, How probable is it for a placebo to improve such a wide-range of heretofore unknown c-v and related functioning in 77% of dyslexic patients? How probable is it for a placebo effect to be so dose- and medication-dependent as to last for years only while patients are actively medicated? If the placebo effect in dyslexia is highly "potent," then why is it so medication-specific? Why haven't these dyslexic patients responded to educational, psychological, and other possible forms of "placebos"? And if, indeed, more "sophisticated" scientific control methodologies are operationally truly more objective and reliable, then how could these techniques have resulted in, and maintained, the scientific fiction characterizing the traditional dyslexic research efforts to date?

Summary

On the basis of DD clinical observations, blurring-speed data, and corresponding ENGs, the author developed a new conceptualization of cerebellar function and dysfunction, motion-sickness medications, and the use of motion-sickness medications in DD. The experimental use of the "c-v harmonizing agents" in the treatment of DD appeared to validate the hypotheses that:

1. motion sickness is a c-v modulated function or dysfunction;
2. anti-motion-sickness medications and many of the anti-neauseants, anti-emetics, and antihistamines are c-v harmonizing agents;
3. the DD therapeutic response to these c-v harmonizing agents can be useful in investigating the function and dysfunction of the c-v circuits, as well as in measuring the c-v potency of chemical agents.

As a result of two pilot investigations, the author was able to develop a pharmacologic methodology for the treatment of DD and mixed-DD disorders. This continuously changing and evolving methodology was found to be successful in alleviating DD symptoms in over one-third of the first simple, 77% of the second sample, and 87% of a third unpublished pharmacologically treated sample of 300 proven c-v dyslexics. Moreover, a computerized research effort is now underway to correlate dyslexic neurologic signs, symptoms, blurring speeds, tracking patterns, ENG parameters, and favorable patterns of pharmacologic responses for each drug, so that statistically reliable predictions can be made as to which drugs and drug combinations are most apt to produce effective results for any given dyslexic individual.

12 The Cerebellar-Vestibular Role in Phobias and Related Mental Events

The discovery of the c-v role in phobias and related mental events was a natural and inevitable scientific outcome resulting from the correlation of data derived from three simultaneous paths of investigation: (1) the cross-sectional and longitudinal follow-up studies of dyslexic children into adulthood; (2) the retrospective and reconstructive analysis of adult dyslexic symptoms back to their childhood origin; and (3) the independent and simultaneous practice of psychiatry and psychoanalytic psychotherapy (Fig. 12–1).

The in-depth exploratory and follow-up study of dyslexic children into adulthood clearly revealed how feelings of inferiority, stupidity, and clumsiness persist despite significant academic and/or motor compensation, overcompensation, and eventual socio-economic success. In addition, the favorable DD therapeutic responses to the anti-motion-sickness medications clearly revealed how phobic, behavioral, mood-related, and inferiority symptoms dramatically improved in association with improved c-v-determined sensory-motor and academic functioning.

The development of the 3D optical scanner made it possible to screen the parents and siblings of dyslexic children for c-v dysfunction and dyslexia. Interestingly, the vast majority of parents diagnosed as dyslexic did not previously acknowledge their own dyslexic symptoms until they were "caught red-handed." Following diagnosis, analysis, and resolution of their denial mechanisms, as well as symptomatic acceptance, there resulted a flood of "dyslexic" associations and questions: Could my avoidance of sports, cooking, and cleaning be due to my dyscoordination? Could my avoidance of heights and my fears of wide-open spaces be due to my sense of imbalance and fears of fainting? Do I avoid reading books because I have difficulty focusing, and have to read and re-read the same paragraph and page over and over again?

Siblings of dyslexic children were similarly screened. Although some of these children were noted to have positive c-v signs, decreased blurring

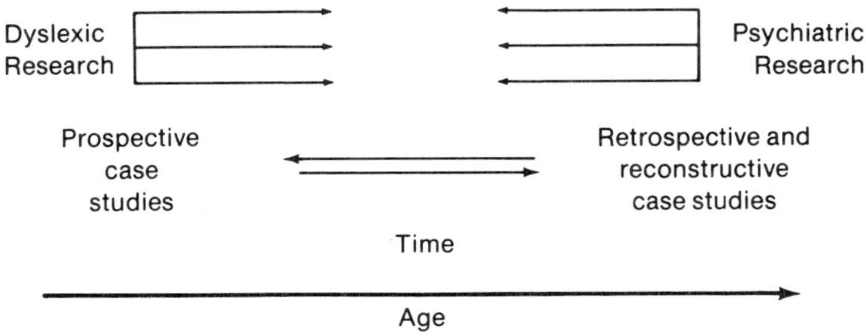

Fig. 12–1. The manner in which the author's "independent" dyslexic and psychiatric research efforts surprisingly resulted in a correlation of dyslexic and psychiatric symptoms with a common c-v denominator and primary pathogenetic source. For example, the follow-up studies of dyslexic children into adulthood revealed that dyslexics were predisposed to feelings of inferiority, mood fluctuation, and phobias. The retrospective analysis of these mental symptoms in adult psychiatric patients revealed that feelings of inferiority, mood variations, and phobias often have a c-v somatic compliance, and that the adult patients had in fact been dyslexic children.

speeds, poor Bender Gestalt and Goodenough designs, and abnormal ENGs in association with emotional symptoms similar to those characterizing the dyslexic complex, their reading scores were occasionally found to be average and, at times, even above average. These cases and findings were initially most confusing and appeared to contradict the author's dyslexic conceptualizations at the time. Only after the recognition of reading-score and blurring-speed compensation in dyslexia were these so-called paradoxical, confusing, and atypical findings reconciled with, and integrated into, a comprehensive theoretical base. Upon historical analysis, these reading-score-normal siblings invariably revealed symptoms relating to the nuclear symptomatic complex of dyslexia and/or to other c-v dysfunctioning (vertigo, motion sickness, etc.).

As a result of the psychiatric, neurologic, and blurring-speed examination of large samples of children referred for emotional symptoms, the author gradually developed an intuitive correlation between specific patterns of emotional symptoms in childhood and c-v dysfunction, dyslexia, and decreased blurring speeds. By the completion of the pharmacologic DD studies, the developing associations between dyslexia and a host of so-called primary psychogenic phobias had crystallized into consciousness—despite intense resistance forces attempting to stem and/or scramble these etiologically significant linkages.

The classical "Freudian" psychoanalytic exploration and treatment of phobias (and related mental phenomena) left as many questions unanswered as did parallel attempts to explain dyslexic symptoms on the basis of either primary psychogenic or cortical determinants. After 15 years of an active general psychiatric practice, it was difficult or impossible for the author to establish a pathopsychology of phobias (and related symptoms) sufficient to satisfactorily explain (1) the form, structure, and choice of the phobic symptom—given the personality profile and circumstances of the patient; (2) the specific symptomatic trigger; (3) the pattern of phobias appearing simultaneously with one another, as well as their progression and resolution; and (4) treatment failure, success, or recurrence.

Inasmuch as the author was simultaneously conducting both an active dyslexic research effort and a psychiatric practice, it seemed only natural for him to wonder:

1. What was the incidence of unsuspected dyslexia in a general psychiatric practice?
2. Did c-v dysfunction and dyslexia correlate with any specific psychiatric disorders and/or symptoms?
3. Could feelings of inferiority in adult psychiatric patients be related and correlated to an unsuspected c-v dysfunction stemming from childhood?
4. Could some or many of the motion, travel, perceptual, coordinational, and spatial-temporal phobias in adults have an unsuspected c-v origin?
5. Could psychiatric patients struggling with either exaggerated sexual and aggressive drives, or the resulting anxiety-motivated defense mechanisms and symptoms, have a c-v-related somatic disturbance in the modulation of instinctual derivatives and/or a resulting dyscoordination or conflict between ego, id, and super-ego?
6. Could adult psychiatric cases presenting with, or developing, vertigo have had latent c-v dysfunction as children?
7. Can nonsymbolic sensory and/or somatic triggers result in a primary c-v neurophysiologic regression and secondarily related mental and emotional regressive functioning?
8. Can the onset, structure, and dynamic fluctuations of a majority of phobias be explained on the basis of a primary c-v dysfunction and secondarily related psychogenic defensive and/or compensatory overdetermining factors?

Methodology and Results

In order to test the author's c-v hypothesis of phobias, quantitative and qualitative studies were performed. One hundred forty-seven consecutive psychiatric patients examined and treated during 1976 and 1977 were tested for c-v dysfunction and DD utilizing blurring speed. Sixteen of the 147 were phobic (2 males/14 females) and all 16 had significantly reduced blur-

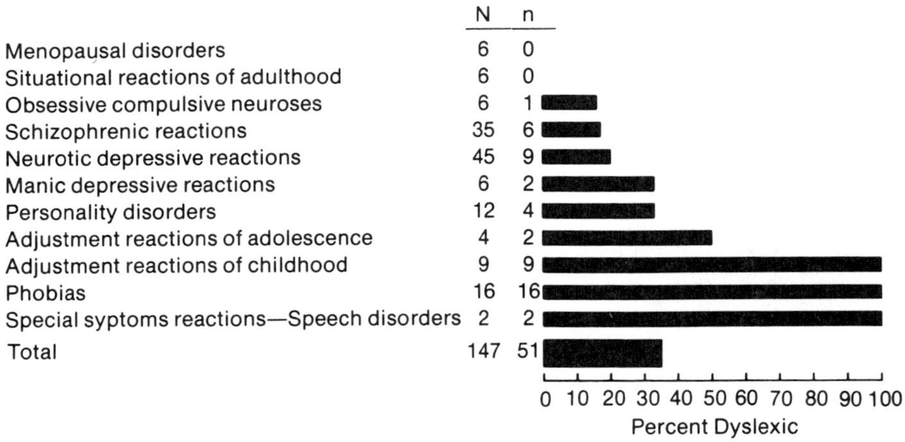

Fig. 12–2. The distribution of dyslexia in a general psychiatric practice. All adults presenting with phobias and all children presenting with special symptoms (speech and behavior disorders, enuresis) and adjustment reactions were found to be dyslexic. N = total patients; n = number dyslexic.

ring speeds as well as a history suggestive of a previous c-v dysfunction and DD ($p < 0.001$). Of the total patient sample tested 35% (51/147) had reduced blurring speeds and DD—approximately twice the blurring-speed incidence of DD found in the Queens study.*

The hidden distribution of DD as a function of presenting or referred emotional symptoms is illustrated by Fig. 12–2, and represents the DD distribution in an unselected adult psychiatric practice. These statistics clearly indicated that:

1. phobic adults were most likely suffering from c-v dysfunction and/or DD;
2. DD children are somatically predisposed to a host of diverse emotional symptoms (i.e., speech disorders, adjustment reactions of childhood and adolescence)
3. DD signs and symptoms permeate and contaminate all psychiatric categories, and thus the DD-related symptoms must be etiologically and pathophysiologically separated and dissected from the non-DD symptoms and diagnostic categories, so that psychoanalytic psychotherapy can be meaningfully and accurately performed.

* This dyslexic incidence was considered minimal in that the diagnostic accuracy of blurring speeds had been improved following this study. Moreover, some acutely psychotic or anxious individuals were thought to have reported either misunderstood or confabulated "high" blurring-speed scores, and checking these patients was difficult.

In addition, all 16 phobic cases were neurodynamically and psychoanalytically explored in order to investigate the dynamic neuropsychologic forces and resulting vector or symptomatic expressions. During this exploratory dissection and analytic process, the personal resistances experienced by the author towards working through a coherent and integrated neuropsychological dynamic structural topography for the DD phobias were found to be no less intense than those experienced during his initial study of the ordinary neuroses as a resident in psychiatry.

Denial of organicity, rationalization, and confabulation were found to be potent defense mechanisms in the c-v-determined phobias, or pathoneuroses, as Ferenczi (1954) termed organic disorders resulting in emotional symptoms. These resistance mechanisms were continuously confronted and reckoned with in the history-gathering, testing, and psychotherapy of the DD patients.

The Traditional Psychoanalytic View of Phobias, Conversion Hysteria, and Anxiety Neuroses

Prior to this dyslexic research effort, the traditional "Freudian" psychodynamic explanation of phobias and conversion hysteria was based entirely on the concepts of conflict, the interaction of unconscious emotional forces, and the displacement of the resulting anxiety and/or emotions onto symbolic objects, situations and/or somatic functions. The significance of coexisting c-v-related symptoms was either clinically denied or considered secondary to psychogenic factors.

This research effort added a fascinating somatic neurodynamic dimension to previous psychodynamic theory, and revealed that:

1. Dyslexic individuals often feel stupid and clumsy as a direct result of a primary CNS-rooted somatic dysfunction or conflict. Psychological attempts to explain these somatically rooted feeling derivatives on the basis of sibling rivalry, family discord, traumatizing teachers, etc., often led nowhere, and merely "iatrogenically" scrambled the patient's free associations and therapeutic alliance with his analyst.

2. Dyslexic individuals are prone to catastrophic anxiety. As a result, they often avoid academic and other sensory-motor areas affected by their temporal-spatial and sensory-motor dysmetria. Indeed, they frequently develop secondary "academic" and "sensory-motor" phobias, inhibitions, and avoidance phenomena, as well as obsessive-compulsive compensatory attempts, in an effort to regain and maintain equilibrium and neurophysiologic control. In time, psychogenic conflicts may crystallize and solidify around this primary, somatically rooted, nuclear catastrophic anxiety core—resulting in an overdetermined somatic-neurotic conflict or pathoneurosis.

3. Dyslexic individuals respond to various nonsymbolic internal and/or

external triggers, which often result in a neurologic c-v functional regression and the automatic generation of catastrophic anxiety. Investigation and analysis of the specific anxiety trigger most often highlighted the underlying neurophysiologic dysfunction triggered.

4. Dyslexic individuals are predisposed to a variety of secondary or tertiary mental and behavioral symptoms, which until this research effort were thought to be entirely of a primary psychogenic origin.

Following recognition of a c-v somatic neurodynamic role in probias, the psychoanalytic literature was reviewed and some fascinating "blind" c-v phobic observations by Fenichel (1945, p. 197, 202–203) are presented:

> Fear of high places later may be replaced by the conversion symptom of getting dizzy spells when looking down from high places. This symptom is physical expression of a mental anticipation of actual falling. . . .
>
> Fears of falling, of heights, car and railway phobias, show at first glance that they are developed in an attempt to fight pleasurable sensations connected with equilibrium stimulation.
>
> This last factor, the struggle against sexual excitation as perceived in the pleasurable sensations of equilibrium, plays a special part in many anxiety hysterias.
>
> Abraham has shown that it is not only exhibitionism and scoptophilia that are warded off in agoraphobia; in cases of fear of going out onto the street, the function of walking itself has acquired a definite sexual meaning, which presupposes an intensified equilibrium eroticism, possibly due to a fixation at the time of learning to walk. . . .
>
> Conflicts around erogenous sensations of equilibrium give rise to equilibrium phobias; but also the development of phobias in general, that is, the establishment of a close connection between sensations of anxiety and of sexual excitement, mobilizes infantile equilibrium eroticism. Often sensations of equilibrium have become the representatives of infantile sexuality in general. . . .
>
> "Something is rotating." Other persons do not remember any pleasure connected with sensations of this kind but do remember anxieties about them, alienations of the body or of certain organs, or fears about space sensations, all of which are the result of the repression of an older pleasure. Anxieties of this kind very often form the core of anxiety hysterias. . . .
>
> Phobias of vehicles, rooted in the warding off of erogeneous sensations of equilibrium and space, have definite relations to the somatic disease of seasickness. The vegetative excitements aroused by equilibrium sensations in a purely physical way have a distinct similarity to sensations of anxiety, and these excitements may have become associatively connected with "too much sexual excitation" in childhood. Neurosis and seasickness, then, may influence each other. Persons with claustrophobia and similar neuroses probably tend more toward the development of seasickness; and an occasional seasickness in a hitherto nonneurotic person may mobilize infantile anxieties and have the effect of a trauma reactivating the memory of a primal scene. There are also conversion hysterias which are an elaboration of vehicle phobias in the sense that vomiting or dizziness, as a physical anticipation of feared equilibrium sensations, may have supplanted the anxiety.

In retrospect, it appeared that although Fenichel clearly described a relationship and correlation of seasickness, vomiting, dizziness, and equilibrium sensation with anxiety, phobias, and conversion hysterias, he completely failed to recognize the crucial importance of primary (and even secondary) c-v neurodynamics and nonsymbolic triggers in their causation and structural determination.

Moreover, a primary failure in the cerebellum's capacity to inhibit, modulate, and/or neutralize anxiety and related emotions may result in the phobics' rapid build-up of anxiety and excitement, requiring projective discharges and displacement onto vehicles and related objects.

Somatic cause and psychodynamic effect were apparently scientifically reversed or scrambled in the unsuspected "pathoneuroses" studied and described by Fenichel. Was this oversight and reversal due to chance alone? Or was it motivated and determined by the very same unconscious c-v denial mechanisms characterizing the dyslexic research effort to date?

Clinical Neurodynamics Versus Single Neuron Potentials

The psychoanalytic-like technique of investigating the DD somatopsychic mental output and neurodynamically "interpreting," or hypothesizing, underlying pathophysiologic and/or compensatory mechanisms, has resulted in a theoretical bridge uniting the "macrocosmic" clinical research of mental events involving billions of neurons, and the "microcosmic" neurophysiologic animal research involving single neurons. For example, the qualitative dissection of DD-related anxiety and phobic driving symptoms indicates that dyslexic individuals prone to motion sickness prefer, or are *compelled,* to sit in the front seat of a moving vehicle if they are not driving, rather than sit in the back seat. Driving or sitting up front where one can *see* tends to minimize or eliminate motion sickness and/or anxiety responses, whereas these very same responses are intensified when seated in the back, where vision is blocked.

On the basis of these observations, it was assumed that ocular fixation and concentration neurodynamically trigger cerebellum-modulated inhibitory mechanisms that diminish vestibular reactivity, vestibular nystagmus, and motion sickness. Thus the vector resultant of c-v dysfunctioning versus compensatory neurodynamic mechanisms was assumed to be responsible for determining whether or not an individual will be a driver or a passenger, and even the latter's specific seating arrangement. Furthermore, some dyslexics experience difficulty integrating simultaneous multisensory inputs with coordinated motor response; as a result, they develop catastrophic anxiety and phobic responses. If, for example, music or auditory stimulation interferes with the reading, working, concentration, or driving performance of dyslexics, they not uncommonly report feelings of being overloaded, flooded, disoriented, dizzy, dyscoordinated, and even off-balance. From a neurodynamic perspective, it would appear as if a cerebellar failure in the selective and reciprocal inhibition of background stimulation by foreground events may lead to foreground/background contamination, stimulus overloading, catastrophic anxiety responses, and c-v regressive functioning (i.e., vertigo, dyscoordination, imbalance, disorientation).

Independent neurophysiologic animal experiments indirectly supported the hypothesized role of the cerebellum in modulating reciprocal sensory-inhibition circuits and motion-sickness responses. Wilson et al. (1975), utilizing single neuron potentials in the cat, demonstrated the role of the cat flocculus in receiving and modulating excitatory inputs from the labyrinth, optic nerve, and neck afferents; and they further demonstrated that the inputs from the three sensory modalities inhibit each other.

Because of the author's success in utilizing "macroscopic" phobic events to infer and explore the existence of underlying "microscopic" neurodynamic mechanisms, this technique was similarly applied to the study of an additional series of mental and behavioral correlates of DD. Thus the internal and external sensory phobic triggers, the resulting neurodynamically determined regressive mechanisms, and the emotional and behavioral concomitants of DD were elucidated. In retrospect, it appears as though a truly interdisciplinary "dialogue" between neurophysiologic animal research and clinical "neuro-psychoanalytic" research has resulted in fascinating theoretical and practical scientific yields.

Neurodynamic Phobic Mechanisms

Dyslexic individuals, via somatic compliance and patterns of "subclinical" c-v dysfunction, were found to have a common nuclear phobic and emotional complex—regardless of significant variations in emotional and personality background profiles. Accordingly, the type, pattern, and variation in c-v-determined phobias and related symptoms may be conceptualized and classified according to the following neurodynamic mechanisms found triggering catastrophic anxiety and secondary related mental symptom formation:

1. c-v overstimulation or flooding;
2. c-v understimulation or deprivation (for example, sensory or electromagnetic deprivation states secondary to microwave shielding result in disorientation and/or failure to function adaptively;
3. c-v failure in specific spatial-temporal and sensory-motor tracking and/or processing;
4. combinations of the above, or "neurodynamic overdetermination."

Upon analysis, the origin of any given fear or pattern of fears and related symptoms was most often found due to multiple overlapping neurodynamic (and psychodynamic) factors. As a result the concept of "neurodynamic overdetermination" was developed in an effort to parallel Freud's "mirror" concept of "psychic overdetermination." And although the neurodynamic phobic mechanisms have been dissected and analyzed in great detail, the resulting data will be presented in a simplified and summarized form.

Cerebellar-Vestibular Overstimulation

A c-v difficulty in processing animate and/or inanimate crowds, patterns, or specific electromagnetic configurations may result in corresponding phobic avoidance responses, regardless of whether the location acts as a sensory source or trigger (i.e., department stores, supermarkets, subways). The "traumatizing" phobic responses to specific light, color, sound, or motion stimuli were most often found to be dependent upon the individual's specific somatic compliance, rather than on the presence of coexisting emotional variables and symbolic mental conflicts.

Cerebellar-Vestibular Deprivation and Microwave Shielding

Closed spaces are recognized to limit neurodynamically the c-v sensory input and thus give rise to electromagnetic shielding—resulting in catastrophic anxiety and such phobic avoidance phenomena as fears of tunnels, elevators, swimming under water, rooms without windows, darkness, sleep, and so on. In addition, if it is assumed that the electromagnetically guided c-v sensory-motor compass is impaired in dyslexia, and if it is also assumed that the need of agoraphobics for "familiar faces and people" may symbolically represent the need for stable electromagnetic reference points, then an interesting somatopsychically determined agoraphobic mechanism may well have been elucidated neurodynamically.

As might have been anticipated, a complex host of neurodynamically determined phobic mechanisms was found to complicate, and thus shape, the agoraphobic's overdetermined expression. For example, fears of vertigo, imbalance, falling, and fainting in wide-open spaces with nothing and no one to hold on to typically characterize the agoraphobic's free-associative responses—but the somatic underpinning to these associations has never before been clearly recognized. In addition, parental and/or marital difficulties, emotional losses, and rejections may complicate or symbolically trigger the agoraphobic disorder by either flooding the c-v circuits or symbolically provoking feelings of being alone, off balance, and having nothing and no one to hang on to emotionally. Unfortunately, only the latter symbolic determinants have thus far been scientifically explored.

Cerebellar-Vestibular Failure in Specific Spatial-Temporal and Sensory-Motor Functions

Difficulty in sensory-motor coordination, balance, and speed perception may result in (1) academic fears; (2) motion fears—i.e., fears of walking, talking, sports, driving, intercourse, and vehicle fears (cars, buses, trains, escalators, elevators, etc.); (3) telephone or communication fears (individuals with specific c-v-related speech and/or auditory sequencing difficulties may frequently manifest speech-related anxiety or phobic symptoms unless compensation occurs); and (4) sensory and/or perceptual phobias (specific sensory forms and/or configurations may trigger clinical or subclinical vertigo, nausea, etc., and a corresponding phobic avoidance of heights, escalators, moving vehicles, moving crowds, etc.).

Symbolic Representations of Somatic Dysfunction

Waiting and anticipation anxieties appear to accompany and permeate the general phobic population, indicating the existence of a generalized neurodynamic mechanism in c-v dysfunction and phobias. Could the waiting, anticipatory, and "trapped" fears symbolize the catastrophic anxiety regarding c-v functional delay and failure in sensory-motor dyscoordination? Might the c-v circuits play a crucial role in modulating such emotions as anxiety, frustration, anger, sex, etc., in a manner analogous to the c-v role in modulating other sensory inputs? Might a c-v failure in neutralizing and/or inhibiting anxiety and other emotions result in rapid build-ups of paralyzing and terrifying emotions?

Might not dysfunctioning c-v mechanisms account for both the severe disinhibited responses to anticipatory anxiety and the "suggestibility" and emotional volatility of hysterics? And is it possible that the characteristic and typical fears of "fainting" and "dying" symbolically represent the fear of c-v somatic failure, and/or the anticipation of such failure, and/or fear of escalating emotions and the loss of emotional control? Might the rather commonly expressed fear of dying or losing control following the ingestion of single and, especially, mixed combinations of medications be a displaced symbolic representation of a c-v somatic failure in processing single, and especially multiple, internal simultaneous stimuli? Is this fear not equivalent to the aforementioned phobias provoked when an individual is confronted by single and/or multiple *external* sensory-motor triggers and tasks? Might the nonadaptive trigger and/or release of motion sickness and related c-v vertigo mechanisms secondary to an impaired or disinhibited CNS system support the thesis that (1) phylogenetically derived IRMs and releasers play a silently active, but inhibited, role in man's mental and behavioral functioning, and (2) decreased inhibitory capacity secondary to CNS dysfunction results in an inappropriate discharge of IRMs and releasers by previously *filtered* internal and external triggers?

Denny-Brown (1952, 1965), for example, has clearly demonstrated the release of positive and negative tropisms (i.e., instinctive grasp and avoidance responses) as a direct result of frontal and parietal lobe lesions. Might not a c-v dysfunction similarly result in the release of primitive needs and drives as well as archaic fears and anxiety responses? Might cannibalistic drives and fears, as well as the anxiety triggered by animals and their shapes, represent the release of archaic, CNS-inhibited mechanisms?

In a magnificent research monograph, *No and Yes,* Rene Spitz (1957) described the manner by which phylogenetically derived feeding reflexes are universally converted to nonverbal *no* and *yes* communication symbols. Is it possible that *universal* phobias may be derived from the disinhibition, dissolution, or release of instinctively derived complex somatic functions similar to those described by Spitz? Inasmuch as universal phobias appeared to be as independent of culture as are the universal *no* and *yes* nonverbal communication symbols, the author reasoned that phylogenetically active primitive reflexes are utilized via "somatic compliance" for emotional expressions and development. For example, fears of swallowing and fears of penetration (i.e., injections, knives, and even intercourse) may be shaped and even determined by phylogenetically derived IRMs serving to ward off the ingestion or penetration of "foreign matter."

Might time-related neurotic phenomena have a somatic source? Dyslexic individuals were occasionally found to be irresistably and/or "deliberately" late for appointments and tasks. They delay initiating events until the last minute, and then are compelled to function in a frenzy. A rather typically heard rationalization for this time-related neurotic behavior was, "I can only function under pressure. Otherwise I'm tired and lethargic." Because psychodynamic formulations were often found insufficient to explain and/or resolve this *need* to rush and function under pressure, the author assumed that neurodynamic mechanisms might be active and determining symptomatic forces. An attempt was made to explore the somatic basis of the aforementioned rationalization.

If, indeed, some dyslexic individuals require anxiety and stress in order to read, work, and concentrate more "normally," then perhaps they are unconsciously driven to perform this neurotic pattern so as to produce CNS stimulants and stimulation endogenously. Might some of these so-called neurotic individuals be somatically predisposed to unconsciously seek out such exogenous forms of stimulation as amphetamines or, perhaps, challenging and dangerous adrenalin-releasing tasks? According to this conceptualization, innate somatic and/or chemical deficiencies may result in an unconsciously rooted psychological and/or behavioral search for exogenous and/or endogenous compensatory mechanisms and pharmacologic agents. Thus, the interaction of somatic need or somatic compliance with co-existing emotional and social influences may result in a spectrum of symptomatic responses, ranging from compulsive lateness to compulsive promptness, addiction to corresponding reaction formations, and so on. Is it possible then that *some* forms of addiction may have a primary somatic source?

Internal and External Triggers

The specific internal and external triggers provoking c-v regression and catastrophic anxiety reactions were pathophysiologically classified as follows:

1. internal and/or external *direct* triggers of c-v regression and catastrophic anxiety;
2. *anticipatory and associative triggers,* associated with and reminiscent of the direct triggers;
3. *symbolic or psychogenic triggers,* which provoke symbolically related specific patterns of underlying neurophysiologic dysfunction. For example, fears of losing dear ones and fears of being abandoned by death or separation may provoke c-v-determined anxiety over loss of somatic stability.

These internal and external triggers have been outlined and summarized in Table 12–1.

Table 12–1. Internal and external triggers that provoke c-v-determined regressive mechanisms and release catastrophic anxiety

Internal Triggers	
Normal	*Abnormal*
Metabolic and/or hormonal variations: pregnancy, post-partum states, menstrual and menopausal states	Metabolic and endocrinologic disturbances: hypoglycemia, etc.
Sensory coordination and integration tasks: visual, auditory, proprioceptive, temperature, smell, taste, tactile, coordination, and integration	Degenerative CNS disorders
Motor coordination tasks: walking, talking, running, swallowing, bending, etc.	Anxiety and mood variations
	Sleep disturbances
External Triggers	
Normal	*Abnormal*
Weather variations: temperature, humidity, barometric conditions, etc.	Allergic phenomena
Altitude changes	Toxic phenomena: alcohol, drugs
Gravitational and/or electromagnetic variations (i.e., microwave shielding environments . . . tunnels, subways, elevators, underwater, etc.)	Infectious disturbances: ear infections, mononeucleosis
Light variations: specific wave lengths, patterns, intensity	Traumatic states: post-concussion and post-ECT states
Motor performances: sports, writing,	Stress situations
Academic performance: reading, writing, spelling, math, memory	

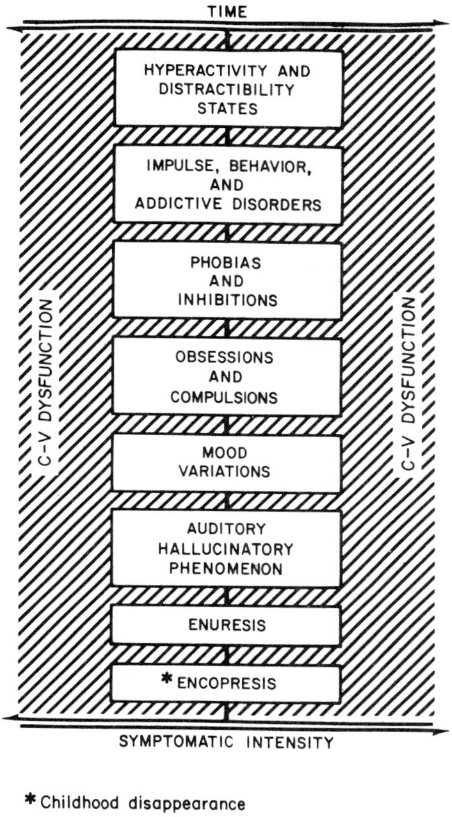

Fig. 12–3. The presenting (foreground) mental, behavioral, and psychosomatic symptoms resulting from a c-v-dysfunctioning background. The time/symptomatic intensity axis serves to highlight the variations of symptomatic intensity as a function of time or age. In addition, any and all symptomatic combinations may occur either simultaneously or sequentially, depending upon a complex host of dysfunctioning and compensatory variables.

Emotional and Behavioral Symptoms of Cerebellar-Vestibular Dysfunction

Inasmuch as c-v dysfunction was observed clinically to result in either primary or secondary decreased CNS capacity to modulate anxiety, anger, mood, attitude, behavior, and perhaps even such instinctual forces as sex and aggression, the author was forced to acknowledge that c-v-impaired individuals were somatically predisposed to neurotic and related mental disturbances (Fig. 12–3). Interestingly, this "somato-psychic" hypothesis of mental symptoms appeared to be supported, if not validated, by the finding that the blurring-speed incidence of DD was twice as high in a psychiatric population compared to a random population.

These observations and data inevitably compelled the author to wonder about the scientific validity and completeness of a host of psychodynamic formulations and treatment approaches. If, indeed, anxiety, anger, behavior, mood, sex, attitude, and so on, are deficiently modulated in c-v dysfunction and DD, is it possible that many psychodynamic formulations of clinically observed mental phenomena have been unwittingly based on "epiphenomena" and/or coexisting independent psychological variables? Furthermore, if the crucial role of nonaffective and nonsymbolic external and internal sensory triggers of subclinical somatic dysfunction has been unwittingly denied or poorly recognized in psychoanalytic and/or psychosomatic research, then one must assume that the current psychodynamic formulations attempting to explain mental phenomena may be as incomplete as were the pre-Freudian attempts to explain similar phenomena on the basis of conscious mental mechanisms. And if the psychoanalytically derived formulations of mental events and symptoms have been unwittingly "biased" by neurodynamic or somatic denial, then has not the application of these biased formulations to both therapeutic and research goals resulted in an iatrogenically induced "conversion blindness," in which only preselected portions of the clinical free-associative field were "seen" and "heard"?

Has accepted fact been found once again to be only fantasy or fiction? Have psychoanalysts and dyslexic researchers been unwittingly propelled into illusionary orbits, fueled by similar "bias" forces and mechanisms? And is it possible that the understanding and resolution of these bias mechanisms will result in a scientifically acceptable cosmic-somatic theory of mental events and mind?

The pursuit of these initially unwelcome, anxiety provoking, and scientifically heretic thoughts and considerations led to a reassessment of the etiologic origins of a diverse diagnostic assortment of complex and overdetermined emotional and behavioral symptoms permeating dyslexic samples. As a result of the reassessment of phobias and a host of related symptoms, as well as their response to the c-v harmonizing agents, it appeared highly likely that at least some individuals experiencing hyperactivity, overactivity, distractability, impulse disorders, phobias, compulsions and obsessions, depressions, stuttering, headaches, insomnia, thumb-sucking, enuresis, tics, and feelings of shyness, stupidity, and clumsiness, were suffering from somato-psychic rather than primary psychogenic and/or psychosomatic disturbances (Fig. 12–3). On the basis of both theoretical and clinical considerations, the author recognized the nuclear symptomatic complex of dyslexia to be wider, deeper, and more variable than initially conceived. In view of these speculations regarding the somatic basis of emotional, behavioral, and mental events, it became apparent that all future patients presenting with either academic or emotional symptoms will hereafter be conceptualized as neuropsychiatric unknowns requiring both neurodynamic and psychodynamic analysis before a final diagnosis and treatment plan is initiated.

In retrospect, although Freud ingeniously recognized and clearly stated the important role of "somatic compliance" in conversion and psychosomatic symptoms, the psychoanalytic investigation of this somatic role has been significantly neglected, and the somatic basis underlying phobias and a host of heretofore considered "pure" primary psychogenic symptoms was altogether denied.

Freud (1910), in a paper entitled "The Psycho-analytic View of Psychogenic Disturbances of Vision," expressed the role of somatic compliance in hysteria as follows:

> We may ask ourselves whether the suppression of sexual component instincts which is brought about by environmental influence is sufficient in itself to call up functional disturbances in organs, or whether special constitutional conditions must be present in order that the organs may be led to an exaggeration of their erotogenic role and consequently provoke repression of the instincts. We should have to see in those conditions the constitutional part of the disposition to fall ill to psychogenic and neurotic disorders. This is the factor to which, as applied to hysteria, I gave the provisional name of "somatic compliance."

Summary of Neurodynamic Hypotheses

Utilizing the previously described neurodynamic technique of investigating the CNS roots and somatic background of mental and behavioral foreground phenomena, the author attempted to integrate and harmonize a diverse array of "psychogenic" events with the c-v disorder they appeared to be functionally correlated with. This neurodynamic exploratory attempt resulted in a series of hypotheses.

Phobias. The psychoanalytic dissection of phobic phenomena led to a series of neurodynamic hypotheses of c-v functioning which, interestingly enough, were corroborated by single neuron animal studies.

Obsessive-compulsive symptoms. The recognition that DD individuals attempted to compensate and even overcompensate for their underlying sensory-motor dysmetria, and resulting catastrophic anxiety and feelings of stupidity, explained the obsessive-compulsive, perfectionistic graphomotor (and related) attempts characterizing a significant proportion of both clinically apparent and clinically "disguised" dyslexics. Moreover, repetitive counting and touching phenomena were frequently identified as attempts to compensate for uncertain dysmetric memory and body-image mechanisms.

In retrospect, it appeared to the author as if some forms of repetitive mental and behavioral phenomena were perseverations resulting from a failure in the normal cerebellar inhibition of nonadaptive memory functioning. Even the ego- and super-ego-determined defensive role of obsessive-compulsive symptoms as reaction formations against *intense* sexual and/or aggressive id derivatives is not incompatible with the concept of a c-v somatic compliance—especially if one assumes that a failure in the cerebellum's capacity to modulate and/or dampen emotions may result in either dysmetric or intense emotional discharges, as well as the corresponding fear of losing control.

Depression and Mood-Related Disturbances

Because depression, cyclothymic variations, irritability, anxiety, and temper outbursts appeared to characterize the DD sample, and varied as a function of hormonal, metabolic, allergic, infectious, and emotional variables, and because these mood-related disturbances often improved in response to treatment with the anti-motion-sickness medications, it appeared reasonable to assume the neurodynamic existence of a dysfunctioning c-v mood-regulating and harmonizing capacity in dyslexia.

Enuresis and Encopresis

Since enuresis and even mild forms of soiling were occasionally found correlated to specific patterns of c-v, rather than psychogenic, disturbances, the author assumed that a failure in the cerebellar modulation of autonomic nervous system reflexes may provide a somatic determinant to these symptoms in a manner analogous to the postulated role of the cerebellum in modulating autonomic responses in motion sickness. Interestingly enough, these "psychosomatic-like" symptoms often improved spontaneously during latency and/or in relationship to the pharmacotherapy of DD, and so appeared to follow a prognostic pattern similar to that of the typically recognized academic dyslexic symptoms with which they were frequently correlated.

It was even possible to explain the "difficulty breathing," tachycardia, and "hypotensive" episodes complicating phobic events by assuming that a c-v regression may result in a dysmetric disinhibition of vital reflex functioning and the secondary generation of complicating catastrophic anxiety responses. Moreover, the emotional trauma "imprinted" by such vital reflex symptoms as difficulty breathing or catching one's breath, rapid and dysmetric heart beats and pulse rates, and feelings of weakness, dizziness, and faintness, may serve as a catalyst or trigger for the onset of a true pathoneurosis.

Auditory Hallucinations

Fifteen nonpsychotic children experiencing auditory hallucinations and two adults still manifesting this intriguing symptom were unexpectedly found to show evidence of a coexisting c-v dysfunction and DD—leading to the assumption that there may exist an underlying c-v-determined somatic compliance. This neurodynamic assumption was initially triggered when a case study was retrospectively recognized, and then proven, to be dyslexic (Levinson, 1966; Frank, 1964).

The patient described by the author in this psychoanalytic study was an orphan named Bonnie [29 years old], who experienced auditory hallucinations, or "voices," despite a lack of evidence supporting a diagnosis of schizophrenia. During psychotherapy, her "voices" were found to represent symbolically those of her fantasized dead mother, with whom she desperately wished to regain and maintain contact. Although the wish-fulfilling nature of Bonnie's hysterical auditory hallucinations and fantasies was obvious and readily explored, the underlying neurodynamic somatic basis would have remained completely denied had this patient not brought her daughter Linda for a dyslexic work-up (Appendix C).

During the neuropsychiatric examination of Linda, Bonnie acknowledged having had similar "dyslexic" symptoms as a child. Suddenly, the heretofore denied c-v somatic basis of Bonnie's previously psychoanalyzed auditory hallucinations, stuttering, feelings of inferiority, phobias of new and high places, fears of the dark, and fears of falling, as well as her academic difficulties in early grades, crystallized into the author's "somatically expanded" consciousness, and accordingly took on an entirely new neurodynamic dimension. In order to explain neurodynamically the c-v basis of auditory hallucinations, the author postulated the existence of cerebellar feedback circuits with the CNS mechanisms and structures modulating sleep and dream states (Morrison and Pompeiano, 1970). Inasmuch as REMs corresponding to dreams were noted by Dement (1964) to be optokinetic tracking movements, and because the c-v circuits were noted to influence concentration, alertness, and states of consciousness, it appeared highly likely that the somatic basis underlying auditory hallucinations and, perhaps, related hypergnostic states (e.g., eidetic imagery) might indeed be c-v determined (Schilder, 1933a b).

Considering that auditory hallucinations and c-v dysfunction were found in non-orphaned individuals with varying emotional profiles and background configurations, it seemed reasonable to assume that Bonnie's auditory hallucinations were *primarily* somatically determined, and thus already present for her unconscious emotional needs and conflicts to utilize for their own symbolic expressions and homeostatically guided energy discharge mechanisms. Since eidetic imagery and other forms of hypergnosis are normal phenomena of childhood which tend to dampen as a function of age, it was further assumed (1) that a failure in the normal cerebellar inhibition or dampening of infantile hypergnosis may result in a continuation of this phenomena into adulthood, and (2) that stress and various psychological and/or compensatory processes may utilize this "open somatic channel." For example, dyslexics may utilize "eidetic image functioning" or "photographic" memory processing in a compensatory manner, thus becoming successful students.

Hyperactivity, Overactivity, and Distractability

The correlation of hyperactivity, overactivity, and distractability with dyslexia (Chapter 3) led to the neurodynamic assumptions that (1) the motor restlessness underlying hyper- and overactive children was related to a dysfunction of the cerebellum–basal ganglia feedback circuits, and (2) the distractability symptoms were related either to the motor restlessness or a dysfunction of the cerebellar–mesencephalic alerting systems. In addition, the recognition that overactive, distractable dyslexics frequently have "short fuses," are impulse-ridden, and are prone to temper outbursts and decreased frustration tolerance led to the further assumption that these somatically determined behavioral phenomena may predispose psychologically traumatized individuals to impulse, behavioral, and addictive disorders in puberty, adolescence, or adulthood.

The Cerebellar-Vestibular Harmonizing Role of the Antidepressants in Dyslexia and Related Mental Phenomena

The combined insights derived from the pharmacologic studies and the neurodynamic mechanisms underlying c-v-related mental phenomena were reciprocally correlated, and catalyzed a new attempt at scientific integration by triggering the following associations.

If, indeed, the CNS stimulants have c-v potency (thus the astronauts were placed on Dexedrine and Scopolomine during their space flights), and if the amphetamines and Ritalin have c-v potency and are thus effective in DD and related overactivity-distractability phenomena, then perhaps such other CNS stimulants as the tricyclic and monoamine oxadise inhibitors have c-v potency as well. Inasmuch as selective tricyclic and/or monoamine oxidase inhibitors (antidepressants) were found to be effective in such diverse mental disorders as depression, enuresis, insomnia, and even phobias, and inasmuch as these mental symptoms were found correlated to c-v dysfunction, and in view of the observations that the antidepressants were periodically found helpful in (adult) dyslexics, it appeared highly likely that the efficacy of the antidepressants in DD and a host of related mental disorders may have highlighted a common underlying c-v neurodynamic denominator.

Future studies will, it is hoped, attempt to distinguish the efficacy of the antidepressants in c-v-related and c-v-unrelated depressions, phobias, enuresis, and "psychosomatic" disturbances, and thus, perhaps, prove the author's c-v–mental correlation while simultaneously adding to the therapeutic efficacy of these medications.

The Foreground Content of a Qualitative Dyslexic Case Study

In an effort to convey to the reader the complex neuropsychological dimensions and quality of the DD phobic disorder under investigation, a case history and interview will be presented. All too often, "dyslexic" case histories are reported in a definitive, oversimplified, and static two-dimensional fashion in which the patient has been reduced to mere psycho-educational quanta of test scores and a predetermined set of hard and soft neurologic parameters.

In retrospect, one can only wonder if these "scomatized" quantitative data presentations do not reflect the existence of a scientific "folie-a-deux" between patients and their examiners. Fortunately, this fascinating scientific interference or resistance phenomena has been psychoanalytically investigated, and is clinically and technically referred to as transference–countertransference resistance. The recognition and resolution of these unconscious feedback resistance mechanisms were found to be as crucial to this research project as they were to the psychoanalytic research and treatment efforts—for behind each analyzed resistance barrier there lurked a wealth of hidden scientific data and insight.

To preserve the foreground flow and continuity of the author's develing c-v–phobia correlations, the crucial data derived from a series of analytic exploratory and treatment interviews of an initially unsuspected dyslexic phobic has been filtered out of its background context, and only a highly condensed summary of his findings will be presented within this chapter's foreground.

Ray was a 30-year-old, white, married male who was referred for psychiatric treatment because of increasing difficulty coping with both personal and business affairs. His temper outbursts were escalating rapidly. Intensifying anxiety and depressive neurotic symptoms were about to cross the border into psychosis. He had been in psychotherapy for several months before a number of suspicious preference and avoidance choices, which could not be explained on the basis of psychogenic determinants, were noted. For example, he worked for an airline, and yet refused to take free air trips. When asked why, he gave various excuses: "I don't like the way they fix the airplanes. . . . I don't like to wait on line. And then you only get bumped at the last minute anyway." Despite both automobile and motorcycle racing experience, he refused to drive in to Manhattan, and continually rationalized this behavior: "It's too crowded there. . . . I hate traffic jams and can't stand waiting." Insightful "free associations" to these phobic avoidance phenomena were not forthcoming, and only denial and rationalization mechanisms were evident.

Ray repeatedly called himself stupid when hesitating or stumbling over words, forgetting a task, or not functioning up to par. The word stupid was apparently a common household term, for his parents had thought nothing of calling either Ray or his brother stupid for anything they could not do well and rapidly. "When my parents would call 'stupid,' we'd ask, 'Which stupid do you want? Big stupid or little stupid'?" His 160 I.Q. and avid reading were insufficient to compensate him for his deep-seated feelings of inferiority.

Three months after his treatment began, I discussed with him some of my research findings in dyslexia and their possible application to air travel. He read the material, claimed to have found it most interesting, and the subject was dropped. Approximately two weeks after handing Ray the DD material, I began to suspect that he might be dyslexic—despite his excellent reading ability and the complete absence of DD-related neurophysiologic clues within his spontaneous productions and free associations. Why was Ray always showing me the books and magazines he was reading? Why did he consider himself stupid despite his 160 I.Q.? Why did he avoid air flights and crowded driving and walking conditions in Manhattan, and yet think nothing of driving cross-country? Why did he feel harassed at work, when in fact he was quite capable of performing his relatively simple tasks? Why did he avoid answering so many of my questions? Why did I give him my DD research papers to read? Why was he impatient with his speech when, in fact, it appeared to be clinically normal—except for an occasional hesitation or slip of the tongue. Why was he compelled to make lists of everything he intended to do? Why was he obsessed with seemingly irrelevant details?

As soon as the suspicion of dyslexia took hold, Ray was actively and directly questioned in detail, and additional history unfolded. He recalled having severe left-sided ear infections when only 6 or 7 years old, and dates his mild left-sided hearing loss back to childhood. "I remember carrying a portable radio real close to my left ear in order to hear it. And I also remember having periodic disequilibrium spells ever since. And my left-sided coordination was always the worst."

"My mother taught me to read when I was around 3 or 4 years old, and I was accordingly placed in gifted classes during the first number of years I attended school. Only later on did I begin to academically stagger and fall by the wayside." This staggering apparently took place in relationship to new and unaccustomed academic demands. For example, he found himself having great difficulty with math; in addition, he found reading technical material most frustrating. It appeared as if sequential memory functioning was deficient and, therefore, he could not keep several mutually dependent facts in his mind at any one period of time. As a result, he frequently experienced secondarily determined conceptual scrambling and confusion. The sequential memory impairment also explained his compulsive need to make lists and concretely obsess over all his daily activities. Single memory events, however, were not difficult for him to remember. Accordingly, he enjoyed history and easily recalled single dates and corresponding names.

He stated that his vision was twice as bad in his left eye as in his right. When reading, he occasionally found the words becoming blurry and scrambled—resulting in his occasionally losing his place and having to re-read sentences and paragraphs. As luck would have it, a chance clinical observation led to the discovery that Ray was an inverted mirror reader; and his own description of this fascinating reading style is presented in Chapter 7.

Further direct historical explorations revealed that Ray had a significant series of phobias. For example, he avoided trains, buses, planes, and even cars in which he was restricted to being a passenger. Tunnels and bridges bothered him severely. He experienced tall buildings as tilting to one side. Crowds made him terribly anxious and frustrated. Upon analysis, he recognized and revealed that crowds, in fact, made him dizzy and disoriented. Claustrophia was intense, and he carefully avoided elevators and confining spaces without windows. Even close and intense emotional relationships precipitated claustrophobic-like responses. Ray's father had been an avid sportsman who avoided reading. Ray avoided sports and tended to be an avid reader. Because Ray's interests were the opposite of his father's, the author initially considered his "interest choices" psychologically determined by oedipal conflicts. However, neurologic studies revealed that both Ray and his father were dyslexic, with distinctly different patterns of c-v dysfunction and compensation. In retrospect, their preference and avoidance behavior were found to be neurodynamically, rather than psychodynamically, determined. If psychological factors were indeed motivating Ray's phobic avoidance of sports, these psychodynamic factors were viewed as playing only a secondary or minor role.

Upon formal neurologic testing, Ray's Romberg was noted to be positive, and he exhibited left-sided past-pointing during finger-to-nose testing. Dysdiadochokinesis was present bilaterally, although it was more severe on the left side. Ocular and tandem dysmetria were clinically evident. Finger-to-thumb sequencing was bilaterally disturbed, but more so on the left. Graphomotor dyscoordination was apparent only for script. Printing was precise and clear. His blurring speeds were approximately one-eighth normal, his Mode III was positive, and his ENG tracking curves were significantly dysmetric. Caloric and rotational ENG stimulation tests were significantly abnormal as well.

Ray was initially medicated with a combination of meclizine (Antivert) and diazepam (Valium). Interestingly enough, Valium tended to catalyze the effect of Antivert while simultaneously minimizing the rapid build-up of anxiety, stress, and anger, and thus tended to prevent the emotional triggering of a neuro-psychological reverberating regression. In addition, both imipramine pamoate (Tofranil) and amitriptyline HCl (Elavil) were found to improve concentration, memory, and c-v functioning. Since Elavil resulted in a delayed fatigue, it was utilized effectively to reduce Ray's severe insomnia.

A retrospective analysis of Ray's multi-faceted symptomatology led to a correlation of his dyslexia with a background of denied, rationalized, and suppressed phobic, obsessive-compulsive, impulse, and speech disorders, feelings of inferiority, clumsiness, and a sundry of so-called psychosomatic disturbances, such as headaches, insomnia, abdominal pain, and even enuresis as a child.

During several years of psychiatric treatment, Ray attempted suicide three times. These attempts initially appeared to be related to marital difficulties and related triggers, sadomasochistic trends, poor impulse control, and severe insomnia, fatigue, and a resulting confusion. Following his first suicide attempt, Ray casually mentioned a relationship between his depressed mood, vertigo, dyscoordination, and the full moon—a relationship recorded, but not taken seriously by the author. His third suicide attempt, however, could not be explained by marital discord or acknowledged primary psychogenic determinants, and appeared to be due to unknown endogenous factors. It consisted of an impulsive ingestion of medication after a night of frustrating sleeplessness. Following this suicide attempt, Ray spontaneously recovered and rapidly felt well again. His depression and suicidal ideation had cleared and disappeared as rapidly and as mysteriously as it had come.

In retrospect, impulsivity, suicidal acting-out, and a rapid dissolution of depression were found characterizing all three of his suicide attempts—despite an intervening persistence of insomnia. Ray's suicidal acting-out was thus psychodynamically unpredictable, leaving the patient and his doctor in quite a desperate dilemma. No doubt motivated by despair, the author noted "by chance" that the patient's third suicide attempt corresponded to the full moon. As a result of this chance observation, the dates of all three suicide attempts were reviewed. Surprisingly enough, all three suicide attempts corresponded to within 24 hours of the full moon's appearance (see also Stone, 1976). Ray described this correlation between mood and lunar cycle in a note reproduced in Fig. 12–4.

A series of clinical observations and associations have been summarized and reported. Are they fact, fiction, or fantasy? No matter. The patient, his mood, and c-v dysfunction will be carefully monitored as a function of the lunar cycle—pending the scientific resolution of the intriguing correlation of c-v function and lunar cycle in this particular patient. Could the assumed grain of truth to this clinically atypical and highly unusual correlation of c-v function and lunar cycle demonstrate a latent universal interaction of man with his cosmic electromagnetic environment? For, after all, are we not all mere functions of lunar time and cosmic space?

Ray's spontaneous correlation of lunar cycle and c-v functioning led the author to wonder if some CNS-impaired individuals were not somatically predisposed, and thus "sensitive," to cosmic electromagnetic influences. The author found himself once again free-associating, theorizing, and attempting to integrate atypical data with the known clinical mainstream. Although the electromagnetic influence on biologic and mental functioning is a field of study still in its infancy, and accordingly has an air of both scientific mystery and "fraud," all "jet laggers" are quite familiar with the disturbances

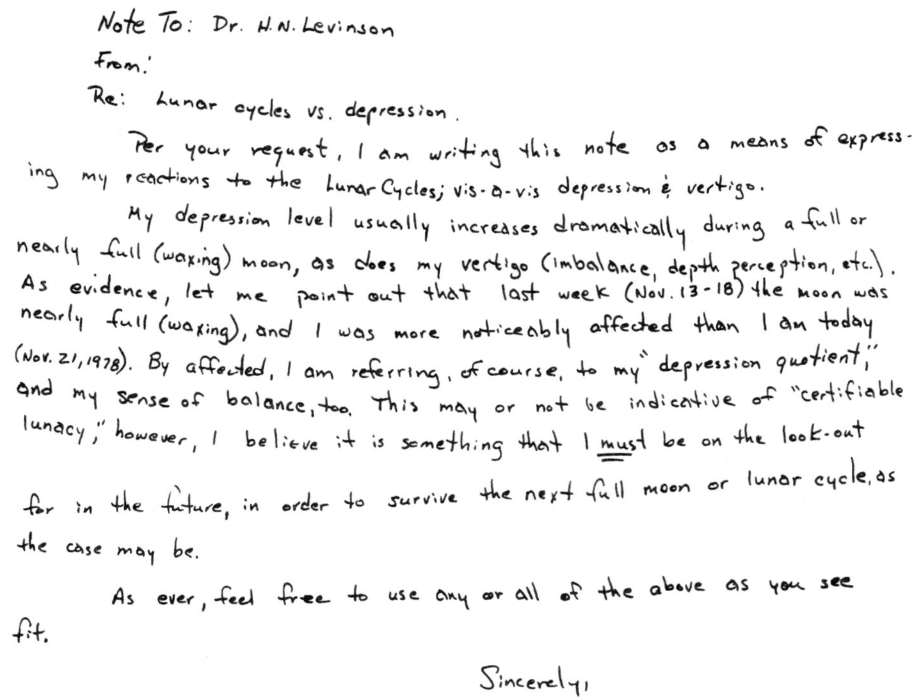
Note To: Dr. H.N. Levinson
From:
Re: Lunar cycles vs. depression.

Per your request, I am writing this note as a means of expressing my reactions to the Lunar Cycles; vis-a-vis depression & vertigo.

My depression level usually increases dramatically during a full or nearly full (waxing) moon, as does my vertigo (imbalance, depth perception, etc.). As evidence, let me point out that last week (Nov. 13-18) the moon was nearly full (waxing), and I was more noticeably affected than I am today (Nov. 21, 1978). By affected, I am referring, of course, to my "depression quotient," and my sense of balance, too. This may or not be indicative of "certifiable lunacy," however, I believe it is something that I must be on the look-out for in the future, in order to survive the next full moon or lunar cycle, as the case may be.

As ever, feel free to use any or all of the above as you see fit.

Sincerely,

Fig. 12–4. A possible relationship between lunar cycles and depression. This letter by a 30-year-old, gifted, mirror-reading dyslexic expresses a spontaneous association and observation suggesting a correlation of insomnia, vertigo, and depression with the full moon. This unexpected correlation eventually led the author to wonder if there was a scientific core to astrology.

that electromagnetic configurations provoke in perceptual-motor function, concentration, mood, vegetative functions, and so on (Aschoff, 1965, 1969; Brown, 1971, 1972; McFarland, 1974; Rockwell, 1975).

In retrospect, the author wondered if our poetic and scientific interest in the sun, moon, and stars did not symbolically represent the manifest content of our latent electromagnetic lock and key unity with the universe. As a result of these "free-associative" thoughts, the author postulated that electromagnetic field theory may play a significantly greater role in biopsychological functioning than our megalomanic defenses against cosmic insignificance will acknowledge. There is a background order to the cosmos which has evolved over billions of years (Sagan and Drake, 1975). Thus cosmic determinism is no more a function of chance than biologic and psychological determinism. No doubt this is what Einstein meant to convey when he commented to Oppenheimer that "God does not play dice with the universe" (Koestler, 1968, p. 200).

Case Summary

By means of an artificial separation of a vast amount of analytically explored DD-related content, an adult phobic case history has been presented so as to delineate the complex qualitative and quantitative somatopsychic and psychosomatic aspects, variations, and ramifications characterizing the heretofore "single-targeted," multidimensional c-v disorder *dyslexia*. The psychoanalytic and neuroanalytic investigation of a large series of adult phobic DD cases clearly revealed a spectrum of c-v somatopsychically related fears, inhibitions, mood, behavior, and personality characteristics, which until now have escaped holistic neurophysiologic and neuropsychological understanding, diagnosis, and treatment. In addition, a host of nonsymbolic, environmentally determined (electromagnetic) triggers of sensory-motor dysfunction (crowds, colors, height, darkness, speed, tunnels, water, temperature, smell, "jet lag," etc.), as well as somatically determined triggers of sensory-motor dysfunction (metabolically determined imbalance, vertigo, body-image fluctuations, etc.) were found to result in catastrophic anxiety reactions and phobic symptom formation.

The belated recognition of a c-v-determined somatopsychic mental, behavioral, and personality profile resulted in a re-evaluation and rediagnosis of a number of so-called primary psychogenically determined disorders in which the somatic basis was actively suppressed, denied, or rationalized, and thus escaped clinical detection (Fig. 12–3). In retrospect, the psychotherapeutic process of these newly recognized pathoneuroses could not be considered complete until their somatopsychic avenues were thoroughly explored and appropriately interpreted. Needless to say, the incomplete or fallacious dynamic formulation of a pathoneurotic symptom's structure and origin can result in traumatic psychoanalytic explorations and "iatrogenic" treatment resistances. For example, just imagine a psychoanalyst "pushing" and/or interpreting "free-associative" content in a predetermined theoretical direction when, in fact, the clues and associations are otherwise directed. In summary, only a dynamic, multidimensional, neuropsychoanalytic approach will insure the DD phobic patient a measure of hope and success.

Electromagnetic, Somatic, and Mental Correlations and Transformations

As a result of the investigation of DD and c-v dysfunction, the author stumbled upon the role of external cosmic and internal metabolic triggers in provoking c-v regressive functioning, catastrophic anxiety, and a host of secondary phobic, conversion, and related mental phenomena. In view of the crucial subclinical cosmic-somatic-mental functional relationship highlighted by the neurodynamic analysis of the c-v phobias, a re-analysis and reassessment of the background determinants of mental functioning was mandated, the pertinent literature was reviewed, and a re-integration attempted.

Electromagnetic Energy and Mental Functioning

The crucial role of nonsymbolic, nonaffective, external electromagnetic and internal chemical (metabolic) triggers in provoking anxiety states, phobias, and related mental symptoms in dyslexia suggested the hypothesis that the c-v filter function was impaired, and that normally inhibited internal and/or external background stimuli were now somatopsychically active, triggering c-v regression, catastrophic anxiety, and a host of defense mechanisms that attempt to regain and/or preserve homeostasis. In addition, the unsuspected or denied interaction of external "cosmic" stimuli with internal somatic structure in determining mental functioning was established. The analysis of this cosmic-somatic-mental interaction resulted in intriguing insights into the relationships between cosmic energy configurations and organismic matter and function.

Organismic Structure as a Function of Cosmic Input

The thesis that organismic structure and function are significantly dependent upon external energy input can be illustrated by a few clinical examples: (1) light deprivation leads to retinal atrophy; (2) sun deprivation leads to vitamin D deficiency; (3) affective and sensory-motor deprivation in newborns leads to psychosomatic disturbances, failure to thrive, illness and even death; and (4) sensory deprivation in adults leads to CNS and mental regression. Of course, the pathologic examples illustrating the crucial relationships between cosmic input and organismic function merely highlight the "tip" of the cosmic-somatic mental "iceberg," and represent only the functional exceptions to the unity defining man's subclinical cosmic-organismic-mental lock-and-key clinical rule.

Observations and Data

Both Sigmund Freud (1939) and Anna Freud (1946) recognized the existence of identification and introjection learning (and defense) mechanisms in children.

Lorenz (1957; also cited by Muir, 1973) described imprinting mechanisms in newborn geese and ducks. These animals can be made to form a filial attachment to one of various stimuli (a man, box, etc.) if exposed to this specific visual configuration during time-specific, critical periods following birth.

Tinbergen (1951; also cited by Muir, 1973) discovered the function of stimulus-specific releasers of stereotyped behavior in birds and fish. The red mark on the adult herring gull's yellow bill, for example, triggers a feeding response in the young. Hawk-like bird models trigger escape reactions in young birds.

Spitz (1946, 1966) described the smiling response in 6–12-week-old children, as well as the specific facial configuration and gestalt models which trigger or release this time-specific response.

Von Frisch (1967, 1974; also cited by Muir, 1973) deciphered the cosmically guided communication mechanisms by which bees recognize and signal the presence and location of nectar.

Eccles et al. (1967) described the structural concomitants of cerebellar motor learning.

Einstein postulated the relationships between space, time, energy, and matter.

An Attempt at Integration

If Eccles et al.'s (1967) description of motor cerebellar learning is equally valid for sensory cerebellar learning, then the *ontogenetic* learning mechanisms of imprinting, introjection, and identification signify the presence of CNS mechanisms by which external patterns of specific electromagnetic configurations are converted to, and/or determine, somatic circuit and structural transformations. These electromagnetically determined "imprinted" circuits may thereafter respond to and/or activate the specific electromagnetic configuration which originally created them. The existence of external electromagnetic releasers which trigger adaptive stereotyped motor and communication responses clearly indicates the existence of somatic CNS structures awaiting vital external stimulus-specific configurations —and thus demonstrates the background existence of an electromagnetic-organismic lock-and-key relationship.

The discovery of releasers and their function in man both demonstrated and solved a fascinating theoretical dilemma. For example, how can one explain the existence of structure which is ready and waiting to be triggered functionally by specific cosmic electromagnetic configurations, without assuming the inheritance of acquired characteristics?

One cannot. Yet lock-and-key sensory-motor functioning is a fact, whereas the inheritance of acquired characteristics is fiction. Is it possible that, over an evolutionary time span, cosmic and environmental forces eventually shaped, and thus "genetically" determined, organismic structure via trial and error and survival of the fittest? If indeed the fittest were best able to process and adaptively react to surrounding environmental forces, then are we not justified in assuming the phylogenetic inheritance of acquired characteristics?

Interestingly enough, these speculations would then be in harmony with the principle that ontogeny recapitulates phylogeny—for ontogeny in a sense represents the imprinting or inheritance of acquired characteristics. Thus, geese that first fixate on a man will follow that man as a parent, as if this imprinted tracking circuit were genetically rather than environmentally or ontogenetically determined or "inherited."

Does not ontogeny recapitulate phylogeny? May phylogeny then be conceptualized as an "ontogenetic recapitulation" of cosmic development—and thus indicate that organismic matter is derived from energy transformations? If these speculations prove valid, then is not matter merely energy transformed? And is not man merely a cosmically determined spatial-temporal configuration or stimulus in the universe?

In summary, the recognition of both the c-v somatic basis of phobias and the significance of electromagnetic triggers has resulted in a new cosmic-somatic perspective of dyslexia, as well as somatopsychic and psychosomatic mental functioning.

Psychosomatic functioning is most often viewed in terms of clinical pathology, whereas the cosmic scope and significance of continuously active, and infinitely occurring mental–somatic centripetal biophysical energy transformations and processes appears to be denied and/or "single-targeted." Man is continuously bombarded by external gravitational, visual, olfactory, acoustic, electromagnetic, and other energy sources; and organismic receptors must eventually reject, neutralize, or convert these energy messages into spatial-temporal imprinted circuits, or matter. Moreover, somatic–mental, or somatopsychic, centrifugally directed signals have been similarly viewed only in terms of pathology, whereas their infinitely larger panoramic perspective appears to have been similarly denied. The programmer of these complex and highly adaptive centripetal and centrifugal forces remains "a ghost in the machine" (Koestler, 1968; Ryle, 1949).

Where is the programmer or Mind hidden which guides the intentionality of these infinitely complex, continuously interacting, centripetal and centrifugal transformations? In Chapter 14, these insights into the c-v somatic basis of mental symptoms, cosmic and somatic triggers, and the unity of cosmic-somatic-mental functioning will be developed into a cosmic field theory of mind.

Summary

The in-depth, cross-sectional, longitudinal study of dyslexic children and their symptoms into adulthood, as well as a reversed parallel retrospective study of dyslexic adults, suggested that phobias and related mental symptoms may have an underlying c-v somatic determination. Quantitative and qualitative studies confirmed this hypothesis. One hundred forty-seven consecutive psychiatric patients were tested for c-v dysfunction utilizing the blurring-speed methodology. Of this random sample of psychiatric patients, 35% were found to have reduced blurring speeds and evidence of c-v dysfunction and dyslexia. Sixteen of the 147 patients were phobic, and all 16 had evidence of reduced blurring speeds and c-v dysfunction ($p < 0.001$). All 16 phobic cases were neurodynamically and psychodynamically explored, and one "typical" qualitative case report was presented. Although not quantifiable, the qualitative case data "speaks for itself."

The results of this research effort clearly demonstrate a neurodynamic relationship between the pattern of temporal-spatial and sensory-motor phobias in adults and the pattern of dysmetric temporal-spatial and sensory-motor functioning in c-v dysfunction and dyslexia.

Interestingly enough, the ratio of male:female phobias in this study was 1:7, suggesting either that women are more prone to phobic symptomatology or that women with phobias are more apt to seek psychiatric treatment.

Recognition of the crucial role of electromagnetics and/or energy input and output in somatic-mental functioning demonstrated the existence of "cosmic denial"—for the psychoanalytic literature is devoid of an acknowledgment of the causal relationship between cosmic triggers and emotional symptoms. The analysis of this resistance force led to an attempt at unifying the seemingly unrelated "Nobel works" of scientific giants, and resulted in speculations tending to integrate energy, matter, and mental functioning. As a result of the analysis of cosmic denial, man and science were found to be merely atypical and exceptional cosmic events which required integration with their cosmic reality and background rule.

13 Criticism and Its Analysis

In drawing this phase of the author's research effort to a close, it appeared as if his foreground presentation and solution might perhaps be a bit too neat, and so may have misled the reader into thinking that this research has gained universal acceptance, and that it has been, and is, beyond critical reproach. The reverse was and is true. Although the DD concepts and insights now appear to be solidly rooted, and growing numbers of successfully treated dyslexic individuals have begun to spread over a wide geographic arc, this research effort, and this book, must be viewed as only a rough scientific first draft, subject to significant retrospective re-working and modification.

During the author's dyslexic "space flight," it often seemed that whatever could go wrong did go wrong. Both internal and external criticism reigned supreme. However, the retrospective analysis of these critical forces had invariably served as an orienting and re-orienting compass and gyroscopic stabilizer—eventually steering and guiding him to a solution to the dyslexic riddle, despite innumerable dysmetric thoughts and trips. Both the quantity and quality of the errors characterizing the dyslexic research effort forced the author to wonder, Were his scientific "errors" and "slips" due to chance alone? Or were they motivated by dynamic unconscious resistance forces similar to those found responsible for transference and countertransference slips and errors?

In retrospect, had things gone smoothly, crucial insights would have remained hidden or denied, and the entire research effort would have been a mere shadow of its present form; for the errors and slips ultimately illuminated the scientific paths requiring exploration, analysis, and a multidisciplinary re-integration.

Almost from the blast-off phase of this research probe, there materialized what might be conceived of as a pattern of resistance forces attempting to maintain the dyslexic status quo by deflecting the author's research effort from its seemingly destined, but unknown, soft landing site. Only in retrospect were these resistance forces recognized as identical to those that initially created the dyslexic riddle. Were it not for the recognition and analysis of these resistance forces, the author's space probe would have been sent spinning wildly into endless space, his space telescope would have fixated only repetitive and traditionally acceptable, but biased, blurred, and cloudy images; and the DD cosmos, as well as its defensive forces, would have remained significantly hidden.

Is it possible that scientists are often unwittingly utilized as mere pawns-in-masquerade by intense and powerful background forces aiming at provoking scientific "scrambling," "vertigo," and "dyslexia"? And is it also possible that all new and meaningful scientific changes or "breakthroughs" are in fact breaking through a cosmic–biologic resistance force or defensive barrier? Do these resistance forces scramble research and researchers in an effort to maintain man's homeostatic balance and equilibrium with both his internal somatic and external cosmic environments?

Is not man's historically rooted need to stem scientific insights and breakthroughs equivalent to his defensive need to suppress id derivatives and breakthroughs?

Does the programmer we call Mind or God actively resist his own discovery?

In the relatively short history of this DD research effort, the author has had to contend with various forms of "well-intended" rationalizations and scientific facades serving intense critical resistance forces. Fortunately, the author's space capsule was only shaken, not shattered or driven from orbit. In the final analysis, the critical thunder of the resistance forces only served to catalyze his scientific curiosity, and re-energize his determination to proceed, come what may.

Unfortunately, the unbiased mass of interested dyslexic individuals, parents, and multidisciplinary colleagues were no doubt initially scared off by the critical roar of, in Audrey McMahon's words (see pp. 295–6), the "erudite big guns with whom no one wished to tangle with publicly." The suffering dyslexic individuals caught in a scientific cross-fire were forced to await the "evolutionary" scientific working-through process. Although scientific and erudite "big guns" never die, they have for the moment faded to only a significant whisper and hum. However, do not be misled by the hum. For, in retrospect, it often appeared as if the resistance force merely changed its facade rather than its intensity and aim. Perhaps its most dangerous disguise of all is premature and/or exaggerated scientific acceptance and adulation—a disguise most often resulting in adulation, satiation, estrangement, and isolation of scientists and their science.

As the reader may well have determined, the primary aim and motivation underlying this interminable research effort and book has been, and still is, the author's commitment to help alleviate the suffering of his patients. One hopes that this book, and this chapter, will serve to catalyze the time-consuming, but necessary, scientific working-through process. By illustrating and analyzing both the author's DD research effort and the critical thunder of the "big guns" directed at its silence and destruction, the evolutionary time span required to determine the final outcome may, perhaps, be dramatically shortened.

In addition, free-thinking and free-minded "scientific" individuals may be encouraged to constructively and scientifically face up to the resistance forces which aim at the transformation of science into a mere dream consisting of puppets and puppeteers dancing to an unknown, unseen, and unheard background traditional tune. By means of a clearer understanding of the determinants of these scientific resistance forces and the resulting scientific inertia, the slow dysmetric momentum of science and scientists may, it is hoped, be catalyzed to acceleration, thereby leading to higher and faster yields of insightful soft landings.

The specific aim of this chapter is to present the reader with both the foreground and background events of an Orton Society meeting whose manifest content was geared towards the scientific review of the author's "blind" and related c-v evidence in dyslexia. Considering that a panel of experts chosen by the Orton Society challenged the author's interpretation of the "blind" c-v data in dyslexia, as well as his c-v dyslexic correlations and conceptualizations, and inasmuch as their criticism served to highlight not only the traditional dyslexic conceptualizations, but the resistance mechanisms shaping and maintaining the current dyslexic manifest dream content and scientific status quo, it seemed scientifically crucial to summarize and analyze the foreground quality and content of the meeting, its critics and criticism.

Background to the Orton Society Meeting of 1975

The need for the Orton Society meeting was triggered by the criticism and disquieting issues raised at a prior scientific meeting. The author and his colleague, Dr. Jan Frank, had initially presented their 1973 research paper entitled "Dysmetric Dyslexia and Dyspraxia—Hypothesis and Study" before The New York Council of Child Psychiatry on November 21, 1974.* Dr. Hart Peterson was scheduled to be the only discussant, but Dr. Archie Silver appeared as a guest discussant.** For differing reasons, both speakers were critical of the c-v dyslexic correlations and reading hypothesis presented by Frank and Levinson.

Dr. Silver quoted a personal study in which he claimed to have found 20%

* Dr. Jan Frank is Professor Emeritus of Psychiatry, Downstate Medical Center, Brooklyn, New York.

** Dr. Archie Silver is Clinical Professor of Psychiatry, New York University Medical College, New York, New York. Dr. Hart Peterson is Director of Pediatric Neurology, New York Hospital, New York, New York.

of children to have clinical nystagmus. In view of Dr. Silver's finding of a 20% incidence of nystagmus distributed evenly among poor and normal readers, and inasmuch as the nystagmus was corroborated by blind neuro-ophthalmologic examination, it appeared to him highly unlikely that the dyslexic reading disorder was due to a c-v-related subclinical nystagmus.

Needless to say, the 20% incidence of *clinical* nystagmus obtained by Dr. Silver in a random population seemed high—especially when compared to the less than 1% incidence of clinical c-v nystagmus obtained by the author, as well as by Drs. Carter and Gold in a highly selected c-v positive dyslexic population (Chapter 3). Is it possible that the diagnosis of clinical nystagmus is subject to significant degrees of error? Might this error be due to a failure in clinically distinguishing c-v nystagmus from such other forms of nystagmus as ocular nystagmus, physiologic nystagmus, etc. (Tolgia, 1975; Gay et al., 1974)? If, indeed, the incidence of true c-v-determined clinical nystagmus is approximately 1% in a c-v abnormal dyslexic population, might Dr. Silver's 20% incidence of nystagmus in a c-v random population reflect the presence of c-v-unrelated nystagmus? Would we not then expect the incidence of c-v-unrelated nystagmus to be distributed evenly in both reading-score normal and deficient groups? Might these considerations not explain both the author's neurologic findings and Dr. Silver's?

Dr. Hart Peterson thought that the concept of a subclinical nystagmus in c-v dysfunction and dyslexia would indeed be most remarkable if it could be experimentally substantiated. However, the statistical data contained within the Staten Island blurring-speed study was not discussed. Because the author had briefly mentioned Dr. Gold's case (Stan P.: see appendix) manifesting and presenting with paroxysmal periodic vertigo and later found to be a c-v dyslexic, Dr. Peterson spontaneously noted a few of his own similar cases in which, according to his recollection, reading difficulties were not significantly outstanding—thereby justifiably suggesting that the c-v dyslexic correlations might indeed be in error.

The concept of reading-score-compensated DD could easily have reconciled and explained both Frank and Levinson's and Dr. Peterson's correlation of periodic vertigo in children with variable reading scores. However, this conceptualization was unknown at the time and was not published until 1976. In fact, Dr. Peterson's constructive criticism served as one of many variables catalyzing the recognition of this concept.

Following recognition of both the existence and significant incidence of reading-score-compensated dyslexics, an alternative but less likely explanation for Dr. Silver's nystagmus data occurred to the author. If, indeed, Dr. Silver correctly diagnosed c-v nystagmus in 20% of a random population of children, and if the distribution of reading-score-deficient versus reading-score-compensated dyslexia is equal, then this hypothesis could be consistent with the 20% incidence of ENG-detectable nystagmus demonstrated in a proven, "blindly" examined sample of c-v-impaired and reading-score-deficient dyslexics (Chapter 3), as well as the equal distribution of nystagmus in reading-score-deficient versus reading-score-normal groups.

In addition, Dr. Peterson did not feel that the blind ENG data and the associated c-v neurologic findings of hypotonia, positive Romberg and dyscoordination reflected localized c-v dysfunction. These views are reflected in edited transcripts of his discussion:

> The cornerstone of this paper [Frank and Levinson, 1973] is an implication regarding the ENG. And the question is: What do these abnormalities mean? I am sorry I am not an electronystagmographer or ENT man. But I do know some ENT men who do not feel that it is valid to attach a [c-v] significance to these abnormalities. . . .
>
> Hypotonia for instance does not need to arise from the cerebellum. It might arise in a variety of areas within the nervous system, including the (cerebral) hemisphere. We mention the Romberg sign. Actually that sign was a sign which was developed to identify patients with Tabes Dorsalis who have posterior column dysfunction. And although certainly patients who have cerebellar dysfunction have more problems balancing when their eyes are closed than when they are open, this is not considered primarily a cerebellar sign. . . . I am not comfortable saying that the [authors'] critical neurological examination identifies cerebellar dysfunction and I am very uncomfortable saying it identifies vestibular dysfunction.
>
> Patients with complete absence of the eighth nerve bilaterally have been studied very, very carefully and were found to have absolutely no clinical abnormality whatsoever except on caloric testing. The only thing is that they are not supposed to go skin diving because they have a little problem with up and down when they are under water.

Having reviewed Robert Barany's magnificent 1916 Nobel lecture entitled "Some New [Caloric Stimulation] Methods for Functional Testing of the Vestibular Apparatus and the Cerebellum" (Appendix D), having been told by all ENT neuro-otologists performing the "blind" ENGs that their reported ENG findings were consistent with a dysfunctioning vestibular system, and having reviewed Dr. Gold's case of benign paroxysmal vertigo and "seen" the manner in which he "specifically" utilized asymmetric caloric stimulation data to diagnose Stan P. (Appendix C) as evidencing a vestibular dysfunction despite the presence of abnormal EEG findings, the author felt justified in maintaining his original ENG-vestibular-dyslexic correlations—despite Dr. Peterson's criticism and objections.

Although Dr. Peterson justifiably raised the possibility that c-v signs may result from either primary cerebral or posterior column disorders, the author's dyslexic data base, the "blind" neurologic dyslexic data base, and the historical dyslexic data base had not found specific hard and fast evidence of cerebral or posterior column dysfunctioning. Inasmuch as the various differential diagnostic non-c-v primary determinants of c-v signs in dyslexia were investigated and ruled out, and inasmuch as only primary c-v determinants were demonstrated and corroborated by "blind" neurologic and ENG examinations, it seemed only reasonable to assume that the c-v signs in dyslexia were of primary c-v origin.

Moreover, the eighth nerve evidence presented by Dr. Peterson in an attempt to refute Frank and Levinson's dyslexic-vestibular correlations paradoxically appeared to support their correlations. If, indeed, individuals with bilateral absence of the eighth nerve "have absolutely no clinical abnormality whatsoever except on caloric stimulation," and except "that they are not supposed to go skin diving because they have a little problem with up and down when they are under water," then might we not assume that both the presence of a caloric stimulation (or ENG) abnormality and an associated impairment in compass- or direction-finding clearly suggests the presence of vestibular signs and dysfunction rather than the "absolute" absence of clinical signs and vestibular dysfunction. Interestingly enough, this assumption was supported by data demonstrating the presence of "genetically" determined dyslexia in several "family trees" manifesting familial eighth nerve degeneration in association with endocrinologic disorders.

In retrospect, it appeared to the author as if Dr. Peterson may have inadvertently denied or refuted the significance of the c-v-dyslexic correlation and data in order to maintain the traditionally accepted views of dyslexia.

For reasons initially unknown, neither discussant contacted the neurotologists performing the blind ENGs, despite the fact that they were affiliated with the same university medical centers. However, both discussants had apparently spoken to Dr. Gold prior to their "critical presentations" and had publicly stated that Dr. Gold refuted Frank and Levinson's interpretation of his blind c-v findings in dyslexia.

Needless to say, this "cerebellar denial" was difficult for the author to comprehend initially. However, the medical editor of *Infectious Diseases* formally verified this denial: "Drs. Sidney Carter and Arnold Gold of Columbia take exception to the inference drawn from their work-ups. . . . In addition, when contacted by *Infectious Diseases,* he [Dr. Carter] stated: 'Both Dr. Gold and I doubt that we interpreted our findings as being consistent with cerebellar deficit.' "*

This "cerebellar denial" should have been anticipated, for it was found to be consistent with the traditionally rooted cortical perspectives of dyslexia, as well as Drs. Carter and Gold's (1972) conceptualization of the syndrome of minimal cerebral dysfunction. As discussed in Chapter 3, neurologic tradition has unwittingly sanctioned the diagnoses of cortically

* This quote was verified by the author. Dr. Carter had written a letter to the editor of *Infectious Diseases* expressing his view that, although he has no record of the cases discussed by Drs. Frank and Levinson, he "doubts" that the findings were consistent with a cerebellar deficit.

determined dyslexia and minimal cerebral dysfunction, despite the fact that the latter diagnoses are characterized by localizing c-v signs and absent cortical signs. If, indeed, researchers and clinicians are unwittingly motivated to "see" cortical dysfunction in the absence of cortical signs and to deny cerebellar (and/or vestibular) dysfunction in the presence of c-v signs, then perhaps there exists a common background resistance force shaping and determining this seemingly "dyslexic," scrambled or paradoxical scientific output. In other words, there appeared to be psychogenically determined and potently active ego-syntonic resistance or defense mechanisms determining and reinforcing the traditional conceptualizations and clinical findings in dyslexia.

Unfortunately there was no time for the author to read Drs. Carter and Gold's blindly examined dyslexic cases to the audience and discussants. In view of the fact that Frank and Levinson's c-v dyslexic clinical, neurologic, and ENG correlations were challenged by the discussants, and inasmuch as their interpretation of the blind c-v findings in dyslexia was challenged by the very same neurologists performing these clinical neurologic examinations, it appeared as if the c-v dyslexic correlations and hypothesis, the 3D optical scanner, and a pharmacologic attempt to treat DD individuals were all placed in scientific jeopardy. The authors' research efforts were thus on trial. And the trial was to take place at a scientific Orton Society meeting.

The Orton Society Meeting

Because of, or despite, the scientific doubts triggered by this meeting, the author and Dr. Frank were invited to present their c-v dyslexic research findings at the New York State Branch of the Orton Society's second annual conference, April 11, 1975. Several months prior to the meeting, Dr. Martha Dencla called and stated (1) that Dr. Gold was invited by the Orton Society to discuss his own and Dr. Carter's "contested" and/or refuted blind cerebellar findings, and that she had accepted the task in his behalf, and (2) that inasmuch as Drs. Carter and Gold did not recall the names and dyslexic cases blindly referred to them by the author, she could not meaningfully discuss the blind neurological data unless she had the case data before her.*

Dr. Dencla was sent a list of the cases with the hope that the apparent scientific confusion over the blind cerebellar findings in dyslexia would once and for all be resolved.

However, our telephone discussion triggered a series of perplexing ques-

* Dr. Martha Dencla is Associate Professor of Neurology, College of Physicians and Surgeons, Columbia-Presbyterian Hospital, New York, New York.

tions: If Drs. Carter and Gold did not recall the names and clinical findings of the dyslexic cases blindly referred to them, why had they not personally requested the data prior to their criticism? Why couldn't Drs. Carter and Gold attend the meeting and discuss the blind neurologic findings? Why was it necessary for a colleague, Dr. Martha Dencla, to act alone in their behalf? How would it have appeared to a scientific audience if both Drs. Levinson and Frank were too busy, and thus unavailable, to present and discuss their own data, and in turn sent a colleague who was completely unfamiliar with the data's determination and its written significance?

Dr. Bernard Cohen called the author at about the same time as Dr. Dencla, and introduced himself as the discussant of the blind ENG findings.* He was sent xeroxed copies of the data. However, another question arose, Why were not the ENT neuro-otologists who participated in the blind ENG study invited to discuss their own findings?

Finally, an agenda of the meeting was received one month prior to the presentation. The author was alloted only 40 minutes to present his retrospective, prospective, blind neurologic, blind ENG studies, the various blurring-speed studies, demonstrate the 3D optical scanner, and describe the rationale for utilizing the anti-motion-sickness medications in dyslexia. Each of the discussants, including Dr. Frank, were given 10 minutes to speak. The time limits seemed impossible for the task. However, the participants were asked to meet jointly one hour prior to the meeting and resolve difficulties before audience presentation. Perhaps this "happy hour" would allow and correct for the time squeeze. Unfortunately, there was no discussion prior to the meeting. Drs. Dencla and Jansky arrived at 8:00 p.m. just as the author was beginning his presentation. Drs. Cohen and Walker did not require any pre-conference clarifications.**

Following the Friday night presentation, I picked up an Orton Society program of scheduled scientific meetings, but unfortunately did not read through it until after the weekend. Much to my surprise, Dr. Gold was scheduled to present Saturday morning on, "Interpretation and Use of Neurological Testing. What Do Hard and Soft Signs Mean in Helping to Diagnose SLD?"

In order to highlight the critical quality of the Orton meeting, the data

* Dr. Bernard Cohen is Assistant Attending Neurologist, Department of Neurology, Mount Sinai Hospital, New York, New York.

** Dr. Jeannette Jansky is Director, Pediatric Language Disorder Clinic, Columbia-Presbyterian Medical Center, New York, New York. Dr. Harry Walker is Director of Research, Rockland County [New York] Children's Psychiatric Center. Dr. Walker was the only one of the four discussants who had *anything* favorable to say. He found the data presented by the authors most interesting and consistent with his own research. However, he justifiably added that the preliminary research findings describing the use of the 3D optical scanner and the anti-motion-sickness medications in dyslexia should be statistically documented.

was subdivided into three segments and presented for the reader's analysis as follows:

1. Descriptions of the Orton meeting by two members of the audience.
2. Criticism: (a) Dr. Dencla's analysis of the "blind" cerebellar neurologic data. (b) Drs. Dencla and Jansky's view of reading scores and dyslexia. (c) Dr. Bernard Cohen's analysis of the "blind" ENG data.
3. Rebuttal and supporting data.

Two Descriptions of the Orton Society Meeting

Only those attending the meeting could really grasp the prevailing charged climate of the discussants and discussion. Qualitative descriptions of the meeting and its scientific climate thus seemed to be in order, both for presentation purposes and analysis.

Audrey McMahon is well known and respected by many in the learning disability field. She was invited by the author to act as a "clinical model" in order to demonstrate to the audience her dyslexic history, c-v signs and symptoms, decreased blurring speeds, abnormal ENG, and her compensatory reading spurt late in her school life. However, so antagonistic and defensive were three of the four discussants that Audrey was spared the embarrassment of participating. Instead, she was asked to describe the meeting so that it might be presented at another time to an audience of interested readers.

> I thought the research session at the N.Y. Orton Society was an unfortunate and confusing event. When new research appears it seems to polarize the public. The traditionalists are threatened, and the public "grasps at anything," rushing in overboard with the result that thoughtful assimilation and consideration of a new concept with mutual respect and intellectual honesty becomes impossible—and the climate antagonistic. The meeting on April 11 turned out to be a premature presentation of "Dysmetric Dyslexia" in which the rationale, hypothesis, procedures, raw data and implications had not been sequentially codified and "translated" into audience oriented lingo and visual aids which weakened the intrinsic impact. In turn the three traditionalists on the panel, some of whom were visibly overemotional, tore into every aspect of the reported study with such ruthless vehemence that the meeting became not a discussion but a confrontation. Few of us in an audience can respect minds which are too closed to concede *any* possible validity in another point of view.
>
> Those people in the audience with whom I spoke who were sincerely interested in getting at the basis of the phenomena evidenced in the study, including the consistency of the tracking scores in different groupings, and in learning more about the validity of the hypothesis, were tongue-tied in the face of the bombardment from the erudite big guns with whom no one wished to tangle publicly, so there were few questions at the close of the session. However, many constructive questions remain valid in my mind:
>
> "Blurring" is a subjective response. Can it be quantified-qualified?

How come *all* the special class children have tracking problems so consistently? Maybe there is something much more fundamental evidenced than only "dyslexia" malfunctions?

How come the chronological age cut off is so consistent at 10? How does this compare with known physiological developmental periods including neuronal and neurohumoral changes? Like myelination as proposed by Dr. Critchley. . . . Where do adults (over 10) fit into the picture? What brain mechanisms do the motion sickness medications mediate? If some but not all patients respond—can you find differentiations? Are the public school studies able to include medication?

Dr. Thomas Rooney, District Principal of the New Hyde Park School District, attended the Friday night presentation (April 11, 1975) by invitation of the author, and attended Dr. Gold's Saturday morning presentation (April 12, 1975) by chance. Dr. Rooney's comments capture the essence of the Orton meetings' manifest and latent content and intent, and thus serve as an independent control to Ms. McMahon's description.

Because the district is embarking on a special training program for teachers about learning disabilities, and since we had become acquainted and I had heard about your invention for the testing of dyslexia, I attended the Orton Society meeting in New York City for the purpose of obtaining background information which would assist me in administering district programs. I was, of course, particularly interested in hearing your presentation on Friday evening. To the best of my knowledge, it was the one new idea, invention or suggestion scheduled for presentation at the conference.

For this reason, if for no other, I was more than amazed at the reception you were given at the conference. I mention "you" purposely because the critics who had so much to say about you did not once mention the invention, testing procedures or analysis of results. Instead, there seemed to me to be a petulant self-righteous revelation by people representing themselves as members of the medical profession about the validity of the qualifications of the cases tested, chiefly by physicians not present at the meeting.

As an administrator of many years experience, I should have been prepared for hearing people slam down a person with a new idea and not discuss the merits of the idea itself. I guess I hoped that in this case, human nature would not prevail and the scientific evaluation of the procedure by disinterested physicians would be presented, which was not done, as you know. Incidentally, the next day I heard the physician who was quoted, or misquoted, the most say that he was not present Friday evening because it was a holy day, but he mentioned that he was not a religious person.

As I review the conference, I find confusion in my thoughts because I went to learn about a malady which has escaped real diagnosis and solution for so many generations and instead heard people who seemed to me, as a disinterested outsider, intent in promoting their previously defined positions.

Since I first heard about your investigation and approach to this problem, I have been interested because it seemed to me, as an administrator, to be logical. My colleagues in this county, with whom I have discussed the procedure, feel the same way. We intend to assist, in every way possible, to bring to fruition the testing of children through the process you suggest. We do this not with preconceived ideas of success, but with the determination that we intend to assist any or all responsible scientists in their quest for a solution to this strange problem which has beset so many children and adults for so long.

Criticism

Dr. Dencla's Analysis of the "Blind" Cerebellar Neurologic Data

Dr. Martha Dencla discussed Drs. Carter and Gold's blind cerebellar findings. The essence of her analysis, as derived from taped and transcribed remarks, was based on the following reasoning:

1. Whenever the concrete word "cerebellar" was not used to summarize the cerebellar findings by Drs. Carter and Gold, she assumed there was no cerebellar dysfunction or deficit—regardless of the presence of cerebellar findings.
2. Whenever Dr. Gold used the phrase, "There were no cerebellar findings other than graphomotor incoordination," she assumed there was no cerebellar dysfunction or deficit—despite the fact that Dr. Gold listed the very same cerebellar findings in his other reports, and then used the summary statement "cerebellar deficit."
3. Whenever Dr. Gold stated there was a mild or moderate cerebellar deficit, she assumed there was no cerebellar deficit, or that the cerebellar deficit and findings were too insignificant to be considered positive.
4. Whenever the reading disorder was not specifically stated by Drs. Carter and Gold to be severe, she assumed the cases were not dyslexic—and thus the presence or absence of cerebellar signs and deficit was considered by her irrelevant—regardless of whether they were termed mild, moderate or severe.

As a result of Dr. Dencla's analysis, one was "forced" to conclude that the author's and Dr. Frank's interpretation of Drs. Carter and Gold's blind cerebellar neurologic findings in dyslexia was in error.

Drs. Dencla and Jansky's Views of Reading Scores and Dyslexia

According to Drs. Dencla and Jansky, to be truly dyslexic a child must have a *severe* reading-score impairment. By severe, they specifically stated that dyslexics must have reading scores that are at least two or more years behind equally matched peers.

Because of their conceptualization and definition of dyslexia, some or many of the reading-disabled cases in the blind neurologic sample were considered to be nondyslexic. To emphasize this point, Dr. Dencla stated that neither Drs. Carter, Gold, Levinson nor Frank really know how to diagnose dyslexia—for we all failed to quantify and document the exact degree of reading-score impairment in the dyslexic sample examined, presented, and discussed.

Dr. Cohen's Analysis of the "Blind" Electronystagmographic Data

Dr. Bernard Cohen reviewed the blind ENG data sent to him. The essence of his taped and transcribed views may be summarized as follows. According to a quoted, published ENG source, approximately 15% of a normal population demonstrates significant vestibular asymmetry and/or ENG abnormalities. This evidence was utilized by Dr. Cohen to sharply reduce the significance and validity of the ENG technique, as well as the reported blind ENG abnormalities and correlations in dyslexia.

Upon direct questioning by the author, Dr. Cohen could not concede the existence of a c-v ocular tracking role underlying the blurring-speed determinations. In stating that "normal" individuals may have abnormal ENG parameters in high percentage and that reduced blurring speeds do not indicate or even suggest c-v dysfunction, Dr. Cohen cast serious doubts on the validity and significance of the ENG technique, the blind ENG data, and the blurring-speed technique and data in dyslexia.

Rebuttal and Analysis

"Blind" Cerebellar Neurologic Evidence in Dyslexia

Drs. Carter and Gold's blind cerebellar findings in dyslexia have been summarized in Chapter 2 and appear in detail in the appendix. Dr. Martha Dencla's analysis of the blind c-v findings has been presented. Her reasoning and comments speak for themselves and require no further comment. In summary, Dr. Dencla did not challenge Drs. Carter and Gold's diagnoses of "minimal cerebral dysfunction" in dyslexia, despite the complete absence of cerebral neurologic signs. Instead, she vehemently denied Dr. Gold's diagnoses of minimal and moderate cerebellar deficit in the presence of obvious and clear-cut cerebellar signs. Her reasoning and arguments thus clearly served to prove the existence of cortical fixation, cortical confabulation, and cerebellar denial mechanisms in dyslexic neurophysiologic research.

Reading Scores and Dyslexia

Both Drs. Dencla and Jansky stated that the diagnosis of dyslexia depends upon the existence of a severe reading-score deficiency. Thus the cases blindly referred to Drs. Carter and Gold with mild, moderate, and/or compensated reading scores were considered to be nondyslexic. Needless to say, this fixed reading-score-dependent definition of dyslexia appeared scientifically arbitrary. Might the views of Drs. Dencla and Jansky be based on highly selective and minimal sampling, as well as on a fallacious comparison and identity between the idiopathic variable dyslexic reading disorder and the severe reading disorder found in cortical alexia? As discussed in Chapter 7, this fixed and traditionally sanctioned reading-score-dependent conceptualization of dyslexia completely ignores or denies the compensatory range of dyslexic individuals, as well as the clinical experience of Knudd Hermann, McDonald Critchley, Lloyd Thompson, and other experts who clearly describe reading-score improvement in dyslexic individuals.

"Blind" Electronystagmographic Evidence in Dyslexia

Dr. Bernard Cohen assumed the existence of vestibular asymmetry and ENG abnormalities in 15% of normal individuals, thus suggesting the presence of "normal ENG pathology." All neuro-otologists blindly participating in this study assumed the opposite point of view, i.e., that the presence of abnormal ENG parameters indicates pathology.

In contrast to Dr. Cohen, the author reasoned as follows. If, indeed, 15% of normal individuals are reported to have abnormal ENG parameters, one must seriously question the "normality" of the control individuals tested. All too often, normality is assumed to exist by the absence of reported clinical symptoms or findings, an assumption which is often invalid. This DD research effort has clearly demonstrated the existence of subclinical c-v signs and symptoms, as well as the existence of symptomatic or organic denial, two phenomena which can easily explain and even create the apparent paradox of "normal pathology," i.e., denied or compensated c-v dyslexic symptoms in association with abnormal c-v neurophysiologic findings, or dyslexic symptoms in the absence of c-v and related neurophysiologic findings.

Unless a clinician is pretuned to the approximately 20% incidence of c-v dyslexia in a random population, as well as the range and diversity of the psychological defense mechanisms utilized by both dyslexics and their parents to deny catastrophically threatening and frightening academic symptoms and such anticipated diagnoses as cerebral dysfunction, brain damage, and mental retardation, the reported "censored" history and the determination of "normality" may well be misconstrued. Crucial c-v and/or dyslexic symptoms are frequently "forgotten" and replaced in a confabulated fashion by "normal" or even "gifted" functioning!

Clinical Insights

As a result of the retrospective analysis of a rather large series of psychologically motivated neurologic errors and slips, the author has found that

1. the presence of c-v signs in association with the reported absence of dyslexic symptoms most often suggests the existence of either denied historical data or compensated dyslexic symptomatology;

2. dyslexic symptoms in the presence of a "normal" neurologic examination suggests the presence of either compensated subclinical c-v findings and/or the clinical denial of existing signs;

3. dyslexic symptoms and c-v signs in the presence of a normal ENG suggests either ENG "compensation" or deficiencies within the ENG technique; and

4. an abnormal ENG in the absence of dyslexic or c-v symptoms suggests the presence of selective compensatory functioning and subclinical c-v dysfunctioning.

Interestingly, although these "errors" were first recognized by the author within his own dyslexic data base and neurologic reports, many of the physicians participating in this research effort were found to have "slipped" in a similar fashion—thereby supporting the author's thesis that psychologically determined errors affect neurologists and neurology as they do psychiatrists and psychiatry, and significantly contribute to the creation of paradoxical clinical and theoretical illusions.

As noted in Chapter 2, Dr. Silver considered Andy to have had a structural cortical defect and evidence of aphasia, apraxia, and incomplete cerebral dominance, despite the fact that no such cerebral evidence was found by the author and other clinicians.

Dr. Carter diagnosed Debbie (Appendix C) as a "normal child," despite her presenting with severe dyslexic symptomatology which intensified with age.

Dr. Frank diagnosed Mark's learning disability and overactivity (Appendix C) to be of psychogenic origin. Mark and his family members were later diagnosed by the author as having significant c-v dysfunction, decreased blurring speeds and abnormal ENGs. In retrospect, it appeared clear that were Mark's symptoms due to a primary psychogenic origin, his dyslexic symptoms would not have significantly improved in a period during which his family circumstances rapidly deteriorated and "went from bad to worse." Had Dr. Frank denied Mark's c-v findings despite his having recognized the c-v denial characterizing the "blind" neurologic study?

Stan P. (6½ years old) was referred to Dr. Gold for headaches and vertigo. On the basis of an abnormal caloric stimulation test and c-v signs almost identical to all "blindly" examined dyslexic cases, Stan was noted to be a superior student, and diagnosed as having benign paroxysmal vertigo or vestibular neuronitis. Six years later Stan was brought to the author by his parents for severe dyslexic symptoms dating back to the beginning of first grade, and most probably existing in kindergarten as well. Could Stan and/or his parents have confabulated a rose-colored performance and thus misled Dr. Gold (Appendix C)?

In a similar fashion Dr. Bernard Cohen examined Holly (Appendix C) in 1976 for vertigo. Although he found no c-v signs and did not perform or recommend caloric or ENG testing, he diagnosed Holly as having benign paroxysmal vertigo, despite the presence of developmental hyperactivity requiring Ritalin. Three year later, Holly was referred to the author for severe emotional, behavioral, spelling, mathematical, writing, directional, and memory difficulties. Although Holly's reading scores were only mildly deficient, she demonstrated severe oscillopsia and associated ocular fixation, tracking, reversal, and directional difficulties during reading. Upon neurologic examination, she evidenced a wide spectrum of severe c-v signs: positive Romberg, dysdiadochokinesis, ocular, tandem, and finger-to-nose dysmetria, finger-to-thumb sequencing disturbances, etc. Caloric and rotational ENGs were significantly abnormal, and her blurring speeds were dramatically reduced. Holly was placed on Antivert for her overactivity, distractability, and dyslexic symptomatic complex, and is currently responding very favorably. As a matter of fact, it was possible to remove the Ritalin required to keep her hyperactivity and distractability in check. Is it possible for Holly to have been neurologically normal in 1976 and to have had severe c-v signs in 1979? Or were her c-v signs and dyslexic symptomatology overlooked in 1976?

John was neurologically examined by Dr. Peterson (Appendix C) when 6½ years old because of organic signs found upon psychological testing for behavior symptomatology. Dr. Peterson's report stated that John "is apparently doing well in school, both academically and behaviorally" and noted "a history of developmental hyperactivity with a normal neurological examination." John was examined by the author at 7 years of age for severe dyslexic symptoms and overactivity requiring special schooling. Cerebellar-vestibular signs were present and blurring speed and ENGs were abnormal. Were John's dyslexic symptoms and c-v signs denied at 6½? And if, indeed, John was neurologically normal, how could one have explained his dyslexic and overactivity symptoms as well as his organic psychological signs?

As a result of the qualitative analysis of a large group of so-called neurologic slips, including those contained in the qualitative analysis of the blind dyslexic data (Appendix B and C), the author assumed (1) that learning disability symptomatology and c-v signs are prone to denial mechanisms, and (2) that these denial mechanisms are a major component of the resistance forces that maintain the dyslexic riddle in force.

Resistance Forces in Neurophysiologic Research in Dyslexia

The manifest critical content of a scientific meeting has been presented and its latent content and intent analyzed. Ironically, the quality and intensity of this meeting's criticism served to propel and catalyze the momentum of the c-v research effort, while dramatically reducing the rate of its public and scientific acceptance. In retrospect, this criticism was found helpful, for crucial questions had remained either unasked and/or unanswered and a holistic assimilation of the c-v research effort and its panoramic perspective was then still to be developed.

In retrospect, both the positive and negative forms of criticism encountered were found to have been crucial determinants in guiding this research effort to a soft landing. The positive criticism highlighted the author's internal resistance and denial mechanisms, whereas the negative criticism highlighted the resistance mechanisms within his critics. The surmounting of each resistance barrier catapulted this research effort a giant step forward. In addition, the qualitative presentation and analysis of the critical content and intent enabled the author to demonstrate to the reader the active role of c-v denial, cortical fixation, and cortical confabulation resistance mechanisms in dyslexic neurophysiologic research.

The recognition that unconscious resistance and bias forces may play a vital role in what we "see" and how we think and reason led the author to initiate the blind ENG and neurologic dyslexic studies at the very beginning of his research effort. The blind studies, however, resulted in a strange paradox: the neuro-otologists performing the blind ENGs were intrigued and fascinated by the correlation of dyslexia with c-v dysfuncton, whereas the neurologists performing the blind neurologic examinations apparently denied their own cerebellar data and/or its significance.

Although the Orton Society meeting was allegedly or manifestly designed to objectively discuss c-v dysfunction in dyslexia, the analysis of the meeting suggested a reversed latent content and intent, thereby proving the existence of cerebellar denial mechanisms in dyslexic research. In summary, Dr. Dencla denied Drs. Carter and Gold's obvious cerebellar findings in dyslexia, while at the same time failing to recognize the fallacy and fiction of their having diagnosed dyslexics as evidencing *minimal cerebral dysfunction* in the absence of cerebral cortical signs. Drs. Dencla and Jansky denied reading-score variations and compensations in dyslexia, and thus highlighted the traditional tendency to equate idiopathic dyslexia with cortical alexia. Dr. Cohen apparently assumed the ENG paradox of "normal c-v pathology," and so denied the validity of the ENG technique, the blind ENG data, and the use of blurring speeds in diagnosing c-v dysfunction and dyslexia—despite his extensive experimental research background in vestibular function (Cohen et al., 1964).

Following the Orton Society meeting, and its analysis, the author was forced to wonder about the origin of these denial and confabulatory resistance mechanisms. Is it possible that the c-v dyslexic research approaches the "unconscious" too closely, and intense unconscious resistance forces are defensively unleashed? After all, were there not surprising similarities found between dyslexic errors and the primary process expressions and mechanisms described by Freud in "The Psychopathology of Everyday Life" (1901), dream content, neurosis, psychosis, etc.? Were not the c-v ocular-motor REM circuits found by Dement (1964) to be tracking the dream content? And might not the primary process dream content and eye movements be linked and governed by common neurophysiologic and neuropsychological cerebellum-modulated mechanisms?

The discovery that numerous phobias, inhibitions, counterphobias, and a spectrum of personality and mental phenomena were somatically predisposed and shaped by c-v dysfunction lent even further support to the hypothesized relationship between the c-v circuits, primary process, and unconscious defensive functioning.

A bright, compensating, dyslexic adolescent asked, "Do dyslexic REMs differ from nondyslexic REMs?" Her question still remains unanswered. Countless other intriguing questions were similarly raised by dyslexic individuals once their denial mechanisms were psychotherapeutically analyzed, worked-through, and a scientific therapeutic alliance established. Both the questions raised and the attempts at their solution have transformed this dyslexic research effort into an open-ended, herculean task. The dyslexic adolescent mentioned above informally analyzed the dysmetric symptoms displayed by her classmates and once again asked, "Is it possible that over 20% of my classmates are dyslexic?" If, indeed, the incidence of c-v dysfunction and/or lag is very high, and if c-v dysfunction is responsible for a host of phobic and related emotional difficulties, and if compensation and overcompensation are significant factors in masking dysmetric and dyslexic symptoms, then the possibility truly exists that dyslexic investigators who deny their patients' clear-cut cerebellar findings may be unwittingly attempting to deny their own c-v dysfunction.

> Valentino Braitenberg of the Max Planck Institute for Biological Cybernetics in Tubingen has calculated that the number of granule cells in the human cerebellar cortex may be 10 times greater than the number of cells previously believed to make up the entire brain. Sanford L. Palay of the Harvard Medical School has commented: "Of the 10^{10} cells in the brain, 10^{11} are in the granular layer of the cerebellar cortex!" [Llinas, 1975, quoting Palay and Chan-Palay, 1974]

In order to further explain the denial of a multilayered organ containing 10^{11} cells in just *one* of its layers, the author reasoned that the force of the "cerebellar denial" must be proportional to the degree and quantity of cerebellar functioning denied. If Braitenberg and Palay are correct in their cerebellar cell calculations and the associated neurophysiologic and neuropsychological functional concomitants, then man's need for "cerebellar denial" must be of astronomical dimensions. Moreover, if the cerebellum is indeed our evolutionary "old brain" and serves as a reservoir for cosmic, phylogenetic, and ontogenetic imprints of the unconscious and repressed past, while simultaneously modulating both inner and outer spatial parameters and determinants, then one might reasonably postulate that "cerebellar denial" is clearly motivated by a summation of all the forces found responsible for man's other great and massive denials.

Summary

Having learned to recognize, track, analyze, and interpret atypical, exaggerated, and paradoxical mental data as a result of the psychoanalytic practice of psychotherapy, and having continuously experienced and analyzed transference (and countertransference) resistance criticism versus "objective criticism" emanating from both neurotic and psychotic patients, the author was fortunately scientifically equipped to recognize, analyze, and constructively interpret the seemingly atypical criticism without losing himself or his research aims in the scientific working-through process and struggle. During this scientific maturation process, the energy motivating the criticism was reactively and consciously converted to curiosity and determination, enabling the author to side-step the magnetic force of the resistance field, and allowing him to reap a significant background harvest. As a result of the insight derived from *criticism and its analysis*, scientists and their scientific content were recognized to be variable functions of their psychic realities and perspectives. Thus, for science and scientists to meaningfully progress, criticism and its analysis must be facilitated rather than denied or suppressed.

14 A Cosmic Field Theory of Mind

In order for science to progress, scientists must be free: free to think and speak, free to daydream and speculate, free to criticize and be criticized, free to be right and wrong, free to be dysmetric, dyslexic, and dyspraxic. This chapter is dedicated to the spirit of scientific freedom. It is the last research chapter in this book, and perhaps the opening chapter in others to follow. Symbolically, it demonstrates the author's belief that knowledge and progress are merely dynamically fluctuating quanta oscillating between any given scientific introduction and summary.

As the author became increasingly aware of the astronomical complexity characterizing the dynamic centripetal (input) and centrifugal (output) forces crucial for conceptualizing such normal mental events as perception, memory, contact, communication, and thinking, as well as such abnormal mental events as phobias, conversion hysteria, inhibitions, and obsessive-compulsive phenomena, it became apparent that the mind's "enchanted loom" was far more complex than its known component parts: structure, circuits, and internal synaptic interaction. For example, although Eccles et al. (1967) beautifully described "the cerebellum as a neuronal machine," they could not find the programmer or Mind in the computer: highlighting the fact that Mind cannot be found in, or localized to, specific brain function and structure. As a result, in "Facing Reality," Eccles (1970) turned to religion and God for answers to Mind's site and method of functioning.

Because Mind could not be localized to structure, and because the author was initially biased against accepting religious explanations for scientific events, he attempted to explain Mind without structural and religious terms. However, in the final analysis the author was forced to renounce his initial religous bias and acknowledge that religious conceptualizations of Mind and mental events come closest to explaining scientifically its site and action—demonstrating that the gulf between scientific and religious conviction and explanation is just one more pseudoscientific illusion.

The author reasoned that for any scientific theory of Mind to be valid, it must be consistent and harmonious with Mind's defining background data. Therefore, in order to attempt a first rough scientific sketch of Mind, it seemed crucial to explore and analyze Mind's existing data base and corresponding "free associations" as if interpreting the manifest content of a dream. By analyzing Mind's manifest "dream content" and the underlying resistance mechanisms shaping its conscious expression, the author hoped to discover Mind's hidden background or latent "dream content," and thus form a theory of Mind.

Mind's Data Base and Its Analysis

Mind exists. Structure exists. Mind is dependent upon and influences structure. Mind cannot be found localized to structure. Mind cannot be explained by structure alone. Could Mind exist apart from, but dependent upon, structure? This hypothesis would certainly be consistent with the clinical and experimental observations and data pertaining to Mind.

Perhaps a quotation from Eccles (1970, pp. 3–4) will prove helpful as a baseline for the analysis of Mind's background roots:

> Every perception, thought and memory . . . has as its material counterpart some specific spatio-temporal activity in the vast neuronal network of the cerebral cortex and sub-cortical nuclei, that is woven of neuronal activities in space and time in the "enchanted loom."

If, indeed, mental events have their counterpart and are woven of neuronal activities in space and time within the "enchanted loom," then may we postulate that neuronal activity may be woven in external synaptic space and time? And if neuronal activities can be woven in external "synaptic" space and time, then would perhaps a simple and heretofore denied solution exist as to the structure, site, and action of Mind? Mind could thus be conceptualized as an external electromagnetic spatial-temporal field configuration and computer, which is derived from and dependent upon structure, and yet exists independent of structure.

Biological and Clinical Observations

Force and field electromagnetic communication theory is not unique to biology, for how else can one explain the sonar and radar guidance mechanisms in the dolphin, salmon and the homing pigeon. How else can we explain how the centripetal and centrifugal forces discovered by Nobel laureate Karl von Frisch (1967, 1974) determine the communication and behavior of bees? Did not the analysis of a bee's unusual behavior enable von Frisch to analyze, dissect, and map out the manner in which a bee

(1) smells the electromagnetic configuration called nectar, and (2) generates a "dance" or electromagnetic signal communicating the presence and site of nectar, via cosmically guided reference points and electromagnetic "servomechanisms" and "feedback circuits."

> Professor von Frisch, now 86, has provided us with detailed knowledge of the extraordinary "language" of bees. By watching marked foragers returning to an observation hive, he concluded that the so-called round dance, in which the homecoming bee moves in a circle, making one or two turns to the left, then reversing to make one or two turns to the right, indicates to the other workers, which soon join in the dance, that a source of nectar has been discovered and will be found in association with the odour adhering to the forager. Another pattern of movement, the waggle dance, in which the forager circles then moves across the diagonal emphatically swinging its abdomen from side to side, transmits a much more complicated message. von Frisch discovered that the pace of the waggle indicates the distance from the nectar source, at ranges of 100–10,000 m. Moreover, the direction of the diagonal indicates the direction of the food source, to an accuracy of 3°. When performed on a vertical surface the dance is even more complex, for the sun is then used as a reference point, and the position of the diagonal relative to the vertical corresponds to the position of the food source relative to the sun. So amazing is the bee's ability to navigate and so remarkable the elaborate coding and decoding of sensory impressions that it involves, that von Frisch's announcement of his early discoveries was greeted with considerable scepticism. The doubts were soon dispelled, but even now, 50 years after his first published work on bees, biologists are still puzzled about how animals find their way and how they use their physiological clocks to correct their bearings for the varying position of the sun. [Muir, 1973]

In retrospect, did not von Frisch discover the forces and fields shaping and determining the bee's "intentional" actions and speech functions? Is it possible that similar force and field mechanisms determine man's function and dysfunction? Are not man's circadian rhythms and clocks "confused" by rapid air flights across large distances with differing time and date meridians? Do we not minimize this "jet lag" by allowing our inner "somatic" rhythms and clocks to adjust to the changing electromagnetic fields operating in each geographic time sphere? Are we not subject to electromagnetic forces and fields? Are we not mere gravitation-dependent specks in the cosmos? And is our movement, direction, and destiny not determined by our position in space?

In a paper entitled "Communication and Empathy," Frank (1961) proposed that empathy in man is a functional, evolutionary derivative of olfaction. Via empathy, one can "smell out" or "tune into" people. In retrospect, it appeared to the author that such communication terms as "beaming in," "zeroing in," "getting a fix," and being "on the same wavelength" must have a "Freudian" symbolic neurodynamic and psychodynamic significance. Might not these terms symbolically indicate man's ability to project and receive electromagnetic signals? And has the latent, background, or unconscious "dream" significance and determination of these various linguistic expressions been denied access to scientific investigation and consciousness by virtue of intense scientific resistance forces motivated by "cosmic denial"?

Interestingly enough, schizophrenic and other psychotic individuals, regressing to the bedrock of their organismic origin, almost invariably develop delusions of being influenced by radio and/or television beams and vice versa (delusions of influencing others). At times, they blank out altogether and their thoughts are interfered with or filtered out of consciousness. How are we to comprehend these latent dream-like symptomatic derivatives?

The neurodynamic analysis of these delusions of influence were assumed, in retrospect, to suggest and represent symbolically the presence of primitive somatic receptive and projected electromagnetic signaling mechanisms in man similar to those described by von Frisch in the bee. Does this assumption not explain the meaning, significance, and universality of delusions of influence, reference, and interference? Would not the existence of electromagnetic signaling and communication mechanisms explain the grain of truth no doubt underlying extrasensory perception and phenomena.

Furthermore, if, indeed, mothers are "tuned into" their newborns by extrasensory mechanisms, have they also been chemically "tuned into" and synchronized with their embryos? Is the reverse true as well? Are embryos and infants tuned into their mothers via chemical and/or electromagnetic reverberating circuits? Have not adopted children been observed clinically and/or psychoanalytically to forever search for their "real" or lost parents (Levinson, 1966)? Do they not then by analogy resemble the homing pigeon or bee instinctively searching for, or tuned into, a specific electromagnetic lock-and-key configuration or gestalt? Is the never-ending search by orphaned children determined only by psychological factors? Or is this search determined by electromagnetic mechanisms as well? May externally induced electromagnetic desynchronization predispose some adopted children to emotional disorders in a manner similar to the method whereby emotional desynchronization may predispose children to neurotic, psychotic, and psychosomatic disturbances? Might we not envision emotional desynchronization, and the resulting illness, as an ontogenetic recapitulation of electromagnetic or phylogenetic desynchronization and illness?

May individuals with genetic, ontogenetic, or acquired traumatic or infectious defects in electromagnetic synchronization or "contact" be predisposed to schizophrenia and the primary nuclear schizophrenic symptom of estrangement—the inability to appropriately "fix" and "cathect," or "lock-in," human foreground objects externally, the inability to normally inhibit the expression of one's own somatic instinctual source, and thus the inability to resist foreground/background emotional and identity contamination, scrambling, and confusion.

As a result of this reasoning, the author assumed that the inability to harmoniously and meaningfully "fix" and cathect object relationships while maintaining normal background emotional separation results in severe catastrophic identity confusion, anxiety, and a host of regressive neuropsychological responses—often to the bedrock of man's mental-somatic existence. Furthermore, the destabilization or desynchronization of emotional "fixation" and emotional "sequential tracking" or cathexis was assumed to result in a series of aphasic-like, typical schizophrenic speech disturbances, as well as compensatory neuropsychological attempts to regain one's bio-emotional equilibrium and mental balance.

In retrospect, it appears as if Freud's use of such terms and concepts as instinctual fixation, object cathexis, object relationships, energy discharges, displacements, projections, introjections, internalizations, condensations, symbolization, omission, and insertion clearly suggested his intuitive understanding of both centripetal and centrifugal energy forces in biomental functioning, development, and dysfunctioning. The author's combined neurodynamic and psychodynamic "pursuit" of the heretofore strange and unusual delusional symptoms of influence, reference, and interference, and his attempt to explain and harmonize this data with the biomental-emotional mainstream of man's existence and derivation from phylogenetic forms, has unexpectedly triggered a series of heretofore denied or repressed insights into (1) the etiology and treatment of nuclear schizophrenia and related psychoses, (2) the nuclear basis of man's communication with both his internal and external environment, (3) the forces maintaining separation of internal and external foreground/background reality, and thus identity, and (4) the source and action of Mind and mental forces.

As a result of a personal communication with Dr. Jan Frank, nuclear schizophrenia was postulated to be a somatopsychically determined disorder primarily of viral and/or genetic origin. Because his analysis of the regressive nuclear schizophrenic's symptomatic trail inevitably led to the presence of traumatic (CNS) fixation points and developmental arrests dating back to the early ontogenetic development of the child, Dr. Frank assumed that a "slow" viral encephalitis occurring *in utero* or during the early part of the first year of life was later triggered to activity during and following puberty by endocrinologic and related somatic and emotional circumstances.

Furthermore, this viral schizophrenia hypothesis appeared consistent with the author's clinical data collected over twenty years, indicating that the recurrent psychotic and "compensatory" schizophrenic episodes most frequently occurred "spontaneously," and were thus independent of current primary exogenous psychogenic and nonpsychogenic triggers—although exogenous triggers did at times precipitate decompensatory bouts. Thus, current emotional conflict and stress, infectious processes, sleep deprivation, airplane flights and "jet lag" were occasionally correlated to acute psychotic episodes. In many ways, the reasoning utilized to deduce clinically the somatic origin of schizophrenia was similar to that utilized to deduce the c-v origin of dyslexia and a host of related somatopsychically determined mental disorders.

A review of the literature by Ornitz (1970), revealed that Schilder (1933a, b), Hoskins (1946) and Bender (1956) discussed the possibility of a vestibular dysfunction in schizophrenia, and that a number of investigators reported abnormal responses to vestibular stimulation in both schizophrenic adults (Pekelsky, 1921; Claude, et al., 1927; Joo and von Meduna, 1935; Lowenbach, 1936; Serel and Vinar, 1937; Angyal and Blackman, 1940; Fitzgerald and Stengel, 1945; and Leach, 1953) and schizophrenic or autistic children (Pollak and Krieger, 1958; Colbert, et al., 1959; and Ritvo et al., 1969). Ornitz (1970, p. 1970) summarized his own data as well as the others':

> Clinical and experimental studies of responses to vestibular stimulation in schizophrenia and childhood autism suggest that central vestibular mechanisms play a fundamental role in the pathogenesis of these conditions. It is suggested that the vestibular system normally regulates the mutual interaction of sensory input and motor output during both REM sleep and waking. The disturbances of perception and motility which occur in schizophrenic adults and autistic children are attributed to vestibular dysfunction during these states of consciousness. This failure of adequate vestibular modulation of perception and motility appears to be maturationally determined.

He did, however, footnote the following comment:

> While the neurophysiologic mechanisms in this paper tend to implicate the vestibular nuclei, particularly the medial and descending vestibular nuclei, the possible influence of cortical or cerebellar or pontine centers on the vestibular nuclei is not to be excluded.

Interestingly enough, the abnormal Bender Gestalt and Goodenough figure drawings of schizophrenics, as well as Holtzman's (1974) abnormal ocular-motor findings in schizophrenia, were also consistent with the presence of a vestibular dysfunction. Although the abovementioned literature demonstrated the presence of vestibular mechanisms in schizophrenia and childhood autism, and investigators were led to postulate that central vestibular mechanisms play a fundamental role in the pathogenesis of these conditions, the author reasoned differently. If, indeed, dyslexia was due to a primary c-v dysfunction, and if the vast majority of dyslexics were neither autistic nor schizophrenic, nor predisposed to such disorders despite their c-v dysfunction, then the vestibular dysfunction characterizing childhood autism and schizophrenia must complicate rather than determine the pathogenic or pathophysiologic basis of their respective disorders.

In other words, childhood autism and schizophrenia were postulated to be of a diffuse CNS origin, and the vestibular findings found characterizing these disorders were merely coincidental or contributory factors.

Might Ornitz's footnote be a clue to the determining pathogenesis and pathophysiology of childhood autism and schizophrenia? According to hypotheses initially proposed by Dr. Jan Frank, and later elaborated upon by the author, the symptoms characterizing nuclear schizophrenia would be dependent upon the pattern of CNS functions impaired, as well as the resulting compensatory neurophysiologic, immunologic and psychological defense mechanisms triggered. Moreover, childhood schizophrenia and/or infantile autism were assumed to be of a distinctly separate pathogenetic origin, despite the presence of similar psychotic and vestibular mechanisms.

These hypotheses are currently under investigation, as is a new screening method enabling the early detection of schizophrenia and a new approach to pharmacologic treatment utilizing transfer factor obtained from recovered schizophrenics. Furthermore, it is anticipated that future investigations will eventually lead to a meaningful pathophysiologic, pathopsychological and pathogenetic classification of the various psychotic and borderline disorders and symptoms affecting both children and adults (i.e., autism, childhood schizophrenia, nuclear schizophrenia, hysterical psychoses, etc.).

Does not normal communication among men consist of patterns of projected and received centrifugal and centripetal electromagnetic signals traversing space without structural interconnections and feedback circuits? Might we not conceptualize this traversed distance as analogous to a giant synapse?

If verbal, symbolic, electromagnetic communication is indeed a phylogenetic elaboration of "empathic" directed electromagnetic communication, and if nonverbal and nonsymbolic forms of electromagnetic communication exist in the animal kingdom as well, then the thesis that (1) ontogenetic or primitive forms of "bee-like" centrifugal and centripetal electromagnetic signaling mechanisms may exist in man, and (2) electromagnetic communication and integration may occur in extracellular space via "giant synapses," appears possible, and even plausible. One may further assume that the frontal lobes and verbal language centers developed in an adaptive functional-morphologic relationship to the limbic system, so as to modulate and dramatically enhance "empathic" directed, electromagnetic signaling and receiving (Frank, 1961). Moreover, it is proposed that the directional and orientational nature of all communication signals must be "guided" by c-v orienting, tracking, and processing functions in relationship to such cosmic reference points as the sun, moon, and stars.

If Mind is conceptualized as a resultant *external* spatial-temporal electromagnetic organismic field derived from all cell units, and if this electromagnetic field is assumed to be in dynamic equilibrium with cosmic forces and capable of "computerized intentionality," then the missing programmer and computer have been found and explained without relying exclusively on structural circuits and religious theory.

One may, thus, speculate that over an almost infinite evolutionary time span, a spatial-temporal electromagnetic computer species developed that could program itself and "think"; and that, furthermore, this "thinking field" with maximum survival value eventually became known as *man*. Upon stretching one's imagination to the limit, man's *organismic mind* may be viewed as an ontogenetic recapitulation of "phylogenetic" and even "cosmic mind." From a psychodynamic point of view, God would then symbolically represent this hypothesized complex, powerful, external, spatial-temporal, invisible electromagnetic field organization influencing and directing man's mental and somatic functioning from within (organismic Mind) and from without (cosmic Mind). This hypothesized electromagnetic computer system called Mind would thus appear to be in harmony with:

1. *Einstein's belief in cosmic determinism.* In stating that God does not play dice with the universe, Einstein clearly expressed his view that there is an inherent cosmic order, and that cosmic determinism cannot be explained by probability and randomization theory alone. Could Einstein's concept of cosmic determinism be termed "cosmic Mind"?

2. *Freud's theory of psychic determinism.* Freud proposed that there is an unconsciously guided inherent purpose, direction, and/or intentional function to such mental events as thoughts, acts, symptoms, dreams, slips of the tongue, memory, etc. No doubt he would have explained man's religious conceptualizations of God, God's Will, and Heaven as unconsciously motivated defensive projections of psychic determinism, as well as personifications of man's mental, super-ego, ego, and id functions and conflicts.

3. *Eccles's theories, as well as those of religious philosophers.* Religious theorists have no doubt (symbolically) termed this invisible and indescribable electromagnetic computer system "God."

In retrospect, it would appear that the difficulties in scientifically explaining the site, structure, and action of Mind were twofold. Via cosmic and subcortical denial mechanisms and forces, it was fallaciously maintained and assumed (1) that Mind existed in structure, and (2) that Mind acted only via structure. However, as long as Mind was conceptually localized and "locked into" somatic structure and internal synapses, and as long as Mind's function was thought to be a resultant derivative only of the total organism, Mind's mosaic site, structure, and action remained impossible to conceptualize scientifically. As long as Mind was assumed to act only via structure, the vast majority of complex mental events remained impossible to understand and explain. It appears, in retrospect, that scientists were linking and/or fusing Mind and its structural origins too closely, and were thus concretely searching for Mind in the wrong clinical-theoretical "haystack."

Interestingly enough, religious conceptualization of God and Heaven have apparently come closest to solving the mind-body problem. If one equates God and His powerful functional descriptions with both Man and Mind, and if one equates God's location in Heaven with external synaptic space, then the external spatial-temporal configuration and function of both Mind and God becomes obvious. If we return to the analogy of the moon probes utilized in the introduction to this research effort, it becomes readily apparent that structure and function may be separated by "light years," and that invisible electromagnetic waves are very effective "sensory-motor" feedback circuits. Thus, although the televised function and action of the moon probe took place on the moon, the Mind guiding this action was on Earth, or perhaps circling somewhere in orbit.

Perhaps these hypotheses regarding cosmic and organismic Mind, as well as the author's reasoning in presenting them, can best be illustrated by a further space analogy. As the reader might recall, many years ago Buck Rogers was a fantasy of spacemen travelling to distant planets. America's moon landing and space probes have transformed this science-fiction daydream into scientific reality. Astronauts, spaceships, and robot structures can be accurately programmed to function and act with direction and intention by minds hundreds of thousands of miles away via electromagnetic "sensory-motor" feedback and integrating forces and field circuits—clearly illustrating the thesis that a functional mind-body unity may exist without the mind being encapsulated and confined to the structure from which it is derived and through which it acts. One hopes that this cosmic field theory of Mind will trigger researchers to apply space-age technology to structural neurophysiologic and psychodynamic theory, and thus once again utilize "science-fiction" as the catalyst with which to transform scientifically acceptable traditional concepts into progress and a new scientific reality.

If this field theory of Mind bears fruit, it will have merely further extended a previous postulate which stated that subclinical neurophysiologic dysfunction may exist despite clinical symptomatic compensation. One might now be forced to reason that Mind may influence and be influenced by peripheral or distant cosmic structures, despite the absence of defined concrete interconnecting neurophysiologic tracts, and furthermore that the cosmos may be conceptualized as a *giant neuronal system.*

The unexpected discovery that phobias (and schizophrenia) and other so-called psychogenic symptoms were of primary neurophysiologic and/or somatic origin, and the recognition that electromagnetic forces and fields may be important in mental and somatic functioning resulted in the following realizations:

1. The presence of mental symptoms does not justify the conviction that these symptoms are of primary psychogenic or mental origin.
2. The absence of clinically detectable neurophysiologic signs does not justify the conviction that there exists no neurophysiologic dysfunction.
3. The presence of "accepted" and/or unchallenged psychodynamics regarding phobias and schizophrenia by no means justifies the conviction that these psychodynamics are completely accurate. In retrospect, it often appeared that psychodynamic formulations were incomplete or unwit-

tingly utilized to explain only the secondary mental reactions to an unrecognized primary somatic dysfunction.

4. The presence of mental and/or motor symptoms in the absence of clearly recognizable and/or "accepted" structural patterns of neurophysiologic dysfunction by no means eliminates a somatopsychic pathogenesis. All too often, neurologists and psychiatrists alike unwittingly diagnosed CNS-impaired individuals as "hysterics" merely because the pattern of their neurologic signs did not live up to traditional expectations. The fact that psychological reactions may "hysterically" exaggerate and distort real CNS injuries, and that significant degrees of neurophysiologic unknowns exist often goes unrecognized and/or denied.

5. Somatic compliance is a crucial determinant in *all* mental phenomena, and thus the latter require both neurodynamic and psychodynamic analysis.

It is hoped that these clinically derived postulates will force psychiatrists and neurologists to rethink and rediagnose so-called primary psychogenic disorders, in which a diagnosis of emotional origin is based solely on apparent neurophysiologic or somatic default and/or the absence of clinically apparent or expected patterns of neurophysiologic findings and circuit impairment.

Furthermore, if Mind is, indeed, a structurally derived and dependent external electromagnetic spatial-temporal configuration with programming capability, is man the only species with Mind? Is Mind an all-or-none phenomenon, or are there species-related functional gradations of Mind? Are there living forms within the cosmos with minds superior to man? If God is a projection of both man and Mind, and if man is not the only species with Mind, then perhaps man's historical worship of animal Gods and multiple Gods supports the aforementioned thesis of multiple Minds or Gods in the cosmos? And if man is only one of many cosmic forms with Mind, man's defensive megalomania will once again have been shrunk to realistic spatial-temporal phylogenetic and cosmic proportions.

Might Man's attempt to limit worship to only one God symbolically represent both the species-specific nature of both Mind and God as well as man's defensive attempt to deny the cosmos and thus minimize his cosmic insignificance and helplessness? If these speculations prove even partially valid, have we not found the basis underlying and motivating cosmic denial, cerebellar-vestibular denial, and cortical confabulation?

Furthermore, if man is viewed as a mere cellular microcosm in the universe, might we not postulate the existence of "cellular determinism" and "cellular Mind"—thus completing the phylogenetic continuum of man and Mind, and at the same time gaining a telescopic or cosmic perspective of man and Mind relative to the universe. Is man not a mere "giant cell" in the universe? And is this "giant cell" not a minor function of cosmic Mind?

There is little doubt that Einstein's dictum about the order of the macrocosm or cosmos is equally valid for the microcosm or atom. Might we not then assume the existence of an atomic Mind?

An Attempt at Scientific and Religious Integration

Following these speculations, the author continued to ponder over the reason (and its scientific significance) why the vast religious majority firmly believed (1) that God created the world, and (2) that God created man in His own image. If God created both the cosmos and man, and if God is cosmic Mind, then might we not assume that cosmic determinism resulted in or created man, and thus that both man and his mental functioning are symbolic projections of God or cosmic Mind, rather than the reverse? Might we not also assume that man's religious convictions and fantasies have been guided and shaped by the primary, somatically rooted origin of both his creation and creator? And is it possible that psychodynamic formulations which identify God as a mere symbolic representation of an individual's father or parents have only scratched the "ontogenetic" mental surface of our cosmic phylogenetic organismic existence? Has cosmic denial misled scientists into confusing and reversing the manifest and latent "dream content" of man's origin and existence in a manner analogous to that whereby the primary cosmic–cerebellar forces and determinants of man's mental and dyslexic functioning were denied and fallaciously attributed to only secondarily related, manifest emotional and cortical variables, respectively?

The author's associations then turned to the contradictions existing between the biblical account of man's origin and the Darwinian account of man's phylogenetic derivation from animal forms. Although both accounts appeared mutually contradictory, and thus "paradoxical," the author intuitively assumed that both the religious and Darwinian theories of man's origin were equally valid, and that a scientific conceptualization was missing which would explain and integrate both theories.

In an attempt to resolve the conflicting theories of man's existence, the author reasoned as follows. If the biblical data as to man's creation are viewed symbolically, their psychodynamic analysis might indicate that God or cosmic Mind is, and has been, "intentionally" directing phylogenetic forms to develop, and thus approach His image, over an evolutionary time span. Just as ontogeny recapitulates phylogeny, phylogeny must be recapitulating, and thus demonstrating its origin from, cosmic development. In retrospect, one was forced to conclude that cosmic Mind has determined phylogenetic and ontogenetic development or evolution. Needless to say, the assumption that cosmic determinism created both inanimate and animate (or organismic) determinism appears objectively sound, and consistent with both religious and scientific theories of the origin of man and matter.

As a result of this reasoning, both the religious and Darwinian views of earth's and man's creation have been harmonized and integrated by means of a holistic and cosmically unbiased psychodynamic formulation, which, in addition, suggests that both religious and nonreligious theories and convictions are of equal scientific validity, and thus worthy of exploration. For "real" science and understanding to progress meaningfully, both religious science and "science science" must be integrated and harmonized with one another, and the sibling-like rivalry and competition between the two must be psychoanalyzed and resolved—for their "neurotically" determined conflict is, and has been, neither truly religious nor truly scientific.

In an effort to comprehend dyslexia and related mental functioning, the author began his research career as a confident agnostic psychiatrist, became an amateur neurologist, and then a humble religious scientist. In retrospect, man could neither have contemplated nor accepted cosmic, organismic, and inanimate Mind in other than the religious concepts of God and Heaven. Inasmuch as religion has supplied man with cosmic insights which science could not, and the reverse as well, it appears obvious that only an integrated religious-scientific "multidisciplinary" approach will enable God's servants to properly treat God's children.

Summary

A theory of Mind has been presented. Is it science or is it science fiction? Or does it really matter?

This dyslexic research effort has clearly demonstrated that science and science fiction are mere conceptual illusions of time and perspective, and that both contain mixtures of fact and fantasy. Science vehemently denies its fiction, whereas science-fiction readily acknowledges its fantasy. In time, research has transformed science into fiction and fiction into science—and thus has established a dynamic relationship between the two.

The role of the scientist is to study and understand fact and fiction, and then attempt their separation, rather than to "prejudge" fact and fiction beforehand. The author initially attempted to explain and understand dyslexia by unwittingly prejudging fact and fiction. This led him nowhere. He then attempted to understand dyslexia as an unknown mixture of fact and fiction. To his surprise, fact became fiction and fiction became fact. Science was thus recognized to be a dysmetric function and illusion of time and space. If, indeed, science is not pure fact and science-fiction is not pure fantasy, then both have "scientific validity," and must be objectively studied and understood.

As a result of these realizations, the author unexpectedly developed, or stumbled over, fascinating new insights into the origin, symptomatic fallout, and treatment of phobias and related mental disorders (i.e., nuclear schizophrenia), and developed a holistic theory of Mind and mental functioning capable of encompassing the panoramic dyslexic-mental complex falling within the analytic range of the author's "orbiting" and dysmetrically guided "space telescope."

Postscript

In an attempt to enrich my rather limited c-v neurophysiologic background, all of Eccles's writings were enthusiastically read. However, after thumbing through the introductory neurophysiologic chapters in *Facing Reality* (1970), I was unexpectedly confronted with Eccles's religious philosophy regarding mind, mental events, and soul. To put it mildly, I was shocked by what I read. My mind began spinning and I developed what clinically might be considered "psychological dyslexia." My reading became dysmetric. I found myself scanning the content rapidly, and merely catching, or almost catching, the gist rather than the sequential details. Sentences, paragraphs, pages, and even chapters were skipped over in an ambivalent attempt to finish rapidly. I felt anxious, upset, disappointed, and '"neurophysiologically betrayed." It was difficult and even impossible to slow down and study what was read. I just wanted to finish and get the book over with. My defenses were up. Blocking was intense. My concentration kept drifting away, and extreme effort was needed to refocus and fixate the content in a sequential fashion. In many ways, the emotions and defenses triggered by the content reminded me of my initial reactions when confronted by a need to read and comprehend Freud's ingeniously written twenty-four volumes.

The resistance forces triggered by *Facing Reality* were working at a fever pitch, and it was initially impossible to ascertain their source and motivation. As a result, I surrendered to their pressure and denied the content. Unfortunately, *Facing Reality* was side-stepped, and its significance remained latent for several more years. Following completion of the dyslexic research efforts, my thoughts were, for reasons unknown, directed towards an attempt at neurophysiologically explaining mind and mental events. Perhaps a new challenge was needed to replace the "old" dyslexic one. Perhaps a solution to the dyslexic riddle provided me with the emotional and neurophysiologic support and background needed to launch a daring new venture. A cosmic field theory of mind was developed.

By this point in research time and space, I had sufficiently "matured" to tackle once again *Facing Reality*. The resistance forces had somehow been worked through and were no longer significantly active. Upon once again tackling *Facing Reality*, it appeared as if my mental formulations were most significantly guided and organized by Eccles's mental tune. Could Eccles's mental tune have unwittingly triggered and organized my clinical-theoretical notes and speculations so that they might be replayed, as if new, via a combined psychoanalytic-psychiatric-neurologic instrumentality?

In order to successfully illustrate Eccles's formulations of mind and mental events, I have decided to present the reader with a few quotations from *Facing Reality* (pp. 64, 83):

> I feel that there is still confusion in the use of such words as mind, mental, mentality, which in some extremely primitive form are even postulated as being a property of inorganic matter! Hence I have refrained from using them, and employ instead either "conscious experience" or "consciousness". . . .
>
> Nor do I believe with the physicalists that my conscious experiences are *nothing but* the operation of the physiological mechanisms of my brain. It may be noted in passing that this extraordinary belief cannot be accommodated to the fact that only a minute amount of cortical activity finds expression in conscious experience. Contrary to this physicalist creed I believe that the prime reality of my experiencing self cannot with propriety be *identified* with some aspects of its experiences and its imaginings—such as brains and neurones and nerve impulses and even complex spatio-temporal patterns of impulses. The evidence presented in this lecture shows that these events in the material world are necessary but not sufficient causes for conscious experiences and for my consciously experiencing self.
>
> If we follow Jennings, as I do, in his arguments and inferences, we come to the religious concept of the soul and its special creation by God. I believe that there is a fundamental mystery in my existence, transcending any biological account of the development of my body (including my brain) with its genetic inheritance and its evolutionary origin, and, that being so, I must believe similarly for each one of you and for every human being. And just as I cannot give a scientific account for my origin—I woke up in life, as it were, to find myself existing as an embodied self with this body and brain—so I cannot believe that this wonderful divine gift of a conscious existence has no further future, no possibility of another existence under some other unimaginable conditions. At least I would maintain that this possibility of a future existence cannot be denied on scientific grounds. . . .
>
> For a final statement of my belief, I would like to quote from an earlier Eddington lecture by Thorpe (1961):
>
> "I see science as a supremely religious activity but clearly incomplete in itself. I see also the absolute necessity for belief in a spiritual world which is interpenetrating with and yet transcending what we see as the material world. . . . Similarly I believe that anyone who denies the validity of the scientific approach within its sphere is denying the great revelation of God to this day and age. To my mind, then, any rational system of belief involves the conviction that the creative and sustaining spirit of God may be everywhere present and active; indeed I believe that all aspects of the universe, all kinds of experience, may be sacramental in the true meaning of the term."

Before concluding this postscript, it appeared to me most worthwhile to present, in addition, the materialist or unitary versus dualistic views of the mind-body problem as brilliantly discussed by Koestler in *The Ghost in the Machine* (pp. 202–204, 219–220):

In his book *The Concept of Mind* (1949) Professor Gilbert Ryle, an Oxford philosopher of strong Behaviourist leanings, attacked the customary distinction made between physical and mental events by calling the latter ("with deliberate abusiveness", as he said) the "ghost in the machine". . . .

By the very act of denying the existence of the ghost in the machine—of mind dependent on, but also responsible for, the actions of the body—we incur the risk of turning it into a very nasty, malevolent ghost.

Before the advent of Behaviourism, it was the psychologists and logicians who insisted that mental events have special characteristics which distinguish them from material events, whereas the physiologists were by and large inclined to take the materialist view that all mental events can be reduced to the operation of the "automatic telephone exchange" in the brain.

During the last fifty years, however, the situation has been almost reversed. While Oxford dons kept snickering about the horse in the locomotive, those men whose life work was devoted to the anatomy, physiology, pathology and surgery of the brain became increasingly converted to the opposite view. It could be summed up in a sigh of resignation: *"Oh, Brain is Brain, and Mind is Mind, and we don't know how the twain meet."* Let me give an illustration of the type of experiment which led them to that conclusion.

Penfield reports: "When the neurosurgeon applies an electrode to the motor area of the patient's cerebral cortex causing the opposite hand to move, and when he asks the patient why he moved the hand, the response is: 'I didn't do it. You made me do it.' . . . It may be said that the patient thinks of himself as having an existence separate from his body.

"Once when I warned such a patient of my intention to stimulate the motor areas of the cortex, and challenged him to keep his hand from moving when the electrode was applied, he seized it with the other hand and struggled to hold it still. Thus, one hand, under the control of the right hemisphere driven by an electrode, and the other hand, which he controlled through the left hemisphere, were caused to struggle against each other. Behind the 'brain action' of one hemisphere was the patient's mind. Behind the action of the other hemisphere was the electrode."

Penfield concluded his memorable paper.* "There are, as you see, many demonstrable mechanisms [in the brain]. They work for the purposes of the mind automatically when called upon. . . . But what agency is it that calls upon these mechanisms, choosing one rather than another? Is it another mechanism or is there in the mind something of different essence? . . . To declare that these two things are one does not make them so. But it does block the progress of research."

Two recent symposia on *Control of the Mind* (1961) and *Brain and Conscious Experience* (1966) were impressive demonstrations of the swing of the pendulum. Sir Charles Sherrington, perhaps the greatest neurologist of the century, was no longer alive, but his approach to the mind-body problem was repeatedly invoked as a kind of *leitmotiv*: "That our being should consist of *two* fundamental elements offers, I suppose, no greater inherent improbability than that

* Delivered at the "Control of the Mind" Symposium at the University of California Medical Centre in San Francisco, 1961.

it should rest on one only. . . . We have to regard the relation of mind to brain as still not merely unsolved, but still devoid of a basis of its very beginning."

Consciousness has been compared to a mirror in which the body contemplates its own activities. It would perhaps be a closer approximation to compare it to the kind of Hall of Mirrors where one mirror reflects one's reflection in another mirror, and so on. We cannot get away from the infinite. It stares us in the face whether we look at atoms or stars, or at the becauses behind the becauses, stretching back through eternity. Flat-earth science has no more use for it than the flat-earth theologians had in the Dark Ages; but a true science of life must let infinity in, and never lose sight of it. In two earlier books I have tried to show that throughout the ages the great innovators in the history of science had always been aware of the transparency of phenomena towards a different order of reality, of the ubiquitous presence of the ghost in the machine—even such a simple machine as a magnetic compass or a Leyden jar. Once a scientist loses this sense of mystery, he can be an excellent technician, but he ceases to be a *savant*. One of the greatest of all times, Louis Pasteur, has summed this up in one of my favourite quotations:

"I see everywhere in the world the inevitable expression of the concept of infinity. . . . The idea of God is nothing more than one form of the idea of infinity. So long as the mystery of the infinite weighs on the human mind, so long will temples be raised to the cult of the infinite, whether it be called Brahmah, Allah, Jehovah or Jesus. . . . The Greeks understood the mysterious power of the hidden side of things. They bequeathed to us one of the most beautiful words in our language—the word 'enthusiasm'—*en theos*—a god within. The grandeur of human actions is measured by the inspiration from which they spring. Happy is he who bears a god within, and who obeys it. The ideals of art, of science, are lighted by reflection from the infinite."

15 A Summary in Cosmic Perspective

The spatial-temporal dimensions of dyslexia and its related cosmic-somatic-mental orbits and defensive "blind spots" have been explored and mapped via multiple qualitative and quantitative scientific "space probes." Interestingly enough, this c-v disorder and its prior psychogenic and cortical etiologic conceptualizations were found to be dysmetric systems "with a distorted, non-Euclidian geometry in curved space, "where parallels intersect and straight lines form loops" (Koestler, 1968).

After fifteen years of exploring dyslexia and its associated scientific resistance forces, fact and fiction as well as theory and conviction were often found to be interchangeable, variable functions of time and perspective. In the attempt to comprehend the complex somatopsychic and psychosomatic intentional functions noted in dyslexia and related mental events, an electromagnetic field theory of Mind was proposed which unexpectedly led to a new understanding and treatment of mental disorders.

Is this cosmic field theory of Mind science or science-fiction? No matter. It must be studied and understood. The observations and thoughts collected during this dyslexic scientific space flight may be poetically summarized in cosmic perspective as follows.

God is cosmic and organismic mind,
Mind is an electromagnetic computer field,
Matter is energy transformed,
Earth is a speck in the cosmos,
Man is a cell in the dust,
Science is an electron in search of its orbit,
Theory is one of many orbits,
Fact is fiction in perspective,
The End is just a new beginning . . .

APPENDIX A

Joan's Case History: Independent Ophthalmologic, Psycho-Educational, and Optometric Evaluations

Selected quotations from previously performed, and thus c-v unbiased, ophthalmologic, psycho-educational, and optometric evaluations are presented so that the interested reader might better appreciate the independently determined data clinically supporting the author's pathophysiologic impression of Joan's dyslexic reading disorder and the dyslexic reading disorder in general.

Psycho-Educational Evaluation

"Reason for Evaluation: Her kindergarten teacher reports that classroom behavior is characteristically distractable, restless, fidgety and inattentive. There are times when Joan seems to be completely lost as to what she is supposed to do. . . .

"She had an eye operation when she was 1-year-old and continues to have astigmatism and a nystagmus. Her parents find her to be a bright, responsive, delightful child at home and question whether her eye problem or a visual problem may significantly account for her difficulties in the classroom. . . . She is very verbal, delightfully curious, and the quality of her thought and expressive language is advanced. . . . Joan has great difficulty in throwing and catching with accuracy. Visual-motor incoordination is very obvious . . . Grapho-motor production seems very labored and generally is quite poor. . . . For example, Joan could not easily make an "X" but persisted in making a "K" and this required very great effort. . . .

"Very early in the testing session, one of the tasks called for the patient looking at the printed test booklet on the table. She immediately asked to have her chair pushed back from the table about one foot so she could see better. Both of her eyes then pulled to the right side and her head tilted to the extreme left. She resorted to this visual side-fixing consistently. Later in the session, Joan complained that her eyes were tired and asked if she could stand up. She moved about three feet away from the table and proceeded to look at the printed material on the table from that distance. . . . When the tasks involved visual discrimination of printed material, the printing of letters, copying of geometric designs, completion of mazes, or assembling of block designs, Joan's behavior changed radically. She became distracted, fidgeted, was often reluctant to try or would want to give up. She tended to be unresponsive to encouragement but would look desperately to the examiner for cues and when they were not forthcoming would make random choices of answers.

"On the Gates MacGinitie Tests, for example, Joan had difficulty in moving smoothly from left to right or from top to bottom of the page; and there were several instances where she adopted a pattern of marking answers in either the first or last columns.

"Joan frequently stated that she couldn't see things well and knew she was going to get them wrong. This sense of helplessness and frustration seemed to trigger behaviors that were alternately immature (whinning and babyish), angry (irascible and distractible), or withdrawing (daydreaming and fantasy). . . .

"Test Results: As measured on the WPPSI, Joan's over-all intellectual abilities are at the upper limit of the Bright Normal Range (Full Scale I.Q. = 118). This summary I.Q. score actually means a wide discrepancy of 29 points between her verbal and nonverbal abilities. Her attained Verbal I.Q. of 101 is indicative of just average ability. In the copying of geometric designs she scored poorly because of rotation, integration, and angulation errors. Joan's inability to perform various visual perceptual tasks was again manifested in the Frostig Test. . . .

"In the first test where Joan was presented with four words—three of which were the same—she had great difficulty in detecting the one word that was different and frequently insisted that all four were the same. Not only did she fail to note differences in words that had very similar configurations (Food—Foot) but she had equal difficulty with some that were dissimilar (cold—held). In contrast, Joan was excellent in auditory discrimination and blending skills."

Ophthalmologic Examination

"Our examination showed that this youngster has a latent nystagmus which allows a vision of 20/25 when both eyes are being used, but drops the vision to less than 20/50 when one eye is covered. When she attempts to look directly ahead, a nystagmus is prominent even with both eyes, but when she uses the lateral gaze, she is much more able to concentrate. A left exotropia can be measured when Joan attempts to fix with her eyes straight ahead, but this disappears when the eyes are rotated to the left or to the right.

"She has a positional and latent nystagmus with the area of minimum activity at either the far right or far left field of gaze. . . .

"I have reassured the family that Joan's congenital defect will not hamper her in her school career and that she will always be able to function independently."

Optometric Examination

"I had the pleasure of examining Joan and her unaided visual acuity was R.E. 20/50, L.E. 20/100 with mixed astigmatic correction.

"Pursuit movements were poor, i.e. a series of short staccato shifts accompanied by an optokinetic (railroad) nystagmus. There also appears to be a rotary component when she begins to fatigue. Saccadic fixation was accompanied by a motor head shift. Joan had considerable difficulty inhibiting her head and when it was held steady, there was severe ocular under-shooting, then correction, with nystagmus of greater amplitude but shorter frequency. The impression of the nystagmus seems to be an 'acuity searching phenomenon' and the head tilt is perhaps her most compensating position that does not produce any diplopia at those times when she does use both eyes at the same time. . . .

"Whenever Joan began to visually concentrate, her eye oscillation rate increased, her head tilted to her left and turned so that her right eye was on her midline. The organization was very poor with no sequence or integration—showing the immature level of visual motor development.

"Supportive and manipulative skills are also below expectation. Bilaterality and directionality on chalkboard activities showed a lot of asymmetry and unequal movements between sides. She could not manipulate the chalk easily, circles were unequal with the left more linear than round and she was totally unable to execute reciprocal movements with her hands. Joan could balance on either foot for ten seconds but could not adequately hop on each foot. Asking to integrate speech with the movement completely frustrated her almost to the level of withdrawal. Labeling of body parts was good, but the awareness and control thereof was a problem. Her constant movement may be contrasted to her nystagmus; perhaps a search for the most efficacious posture and position and while her "motor is running" she can possibly find that position.

"Visual memory demonstrated Joan's response to visual demands. She was able to recognize 'likes' but could not 'see differences.' Her reproductions were of poor size, form and shape with no oblique lines. She verbally recognizes 'I can't make a triangle' and cannot execute the oblique component and cannot differentiate between a square and a rectangle.

Summary and Impressions

"Joan's decreased visual acuity may be a strong contribution to her poor classroom performance. The constant physical movement and her ocular oscillations may be part of her subconscious desire to find the most comfortable, efficient posture in which to perform. However, her inadequate visual judgments; lack of good bilaterality and motor control, poor awareness and reproduction of oblique components, accompanied by more than adequate verbal responses, demonstrate a maturational lag that may be helped by closer teacher/pupil ratio."

APPENDIX B

Verbatim "Blind" Cerebellar Dyslexic Data in 22 Dyslexic Children

In order to confirm the author's c-v neurologic findings in dyslexia, 22 c-v-impaired dyslexic children were randomly selected and referred to Drs. Sidney Carter and Arnold Gold for "blind" neurologic examinations, and the neurologic data quantitatively and qualitatively analyzed.

The specific aim of this appendix is to present the reader with the "raw," "blind" cerebellar dyslexic data base, so that the background from which the author derived his foreground quantitative and qualitative insights may be "seen," and thus independently corroborated.

Inasmuch as the quantitative analysis of the "blind" cerebellar dyslexic findings has already been presented in Chapter 3, the task at hand is "merely" to present abstracted verbatim quotations of the cerebellar (and vestibular) findings characterizing 21 of the 22 "blindly" examined dyslexic cases. Appendix C will include 6 complete and typical "blind" neurologic reports, including Dr. Gold's case of benign paroxysmal vertigo, and the retrospective analysis of these reports. Emphasis (italics) has been added by the author.

Learning-Disability Cases Examined by Dr. Sidney Carter

S.W. is a 9-year-old boy "who demonstrated trouble in hopping on either foot, impaired succession movements in both upper extremities."

G.A. is an 8-year-old boy: "Coordination is somewhat impaired. He is still having difficulty learning to ride a two-wheeler, and he has trouble tying his shoelaces. . . . There was some speech impairment. He had difficulty in hopping on either foot."

S.L. is an 8-year-old boy: "His attention span is short, and he has difficulty in coordination with his small muscles. For example: at age eight, he cannot tie his shoe laces and he has trouble with small puzzles. . . . His clumsiness was evident in his hopping, but the remainder of the examination was not remarkable."

K.E. is an 11-year-old boy: "I had occasion to see Keith . . . because of a history of his having difficulty in school despite what is considered to be a very high

I.Q. . . . I would emphasize a few minor facts in the history: specifically, Keith has always been clumsy but despite that, is good at sports. He had right-left confusion as a smaller child, but this has corrected itself. . . .

"The positive findings were very minimal. There was a very slight unsteadiness on finger-to-nose testing, particularly on the left and he had a very minimal impairment of succession movements—the left more than the right. Quite honestly, I was not particularly impressed by his degree of cerebellar dysfunction. The remainder of his neurological examination was entirely normal. His drawings were well done.

"It was my impression [based on history] that this boy could be classified as having minimal brain dysfunction with his major deficits in the areas of learning, and to a lesser extent, in the area of behavior."

M.E. is a 6-year-old boy: "He was a little late in talking. His attention span was described as being short. He was said to frustrate easily, and his fine motor coordination has always been somewhat impaired. . . .

"On examination . . . he was relatively quiet in the office setting, but was obviously awkward and clumsy. For example: he was unable to hop on either foot. There were, however, no other manifestations of a focal neurologic deficit.

"He seems to fit best into the group of children that have been classified as having the syndrome of minimal brain dysfunction, manifested in his case by behavioral difficulties and clumsiness and awkwardness."

Debbie L. is a six-year-old girl: "I saw little Debbie because of the complaints from the parents indicating that the child was said to have impaired visual perceptual function and to have right-left confusion. . . . At four years of age an optometrist suggested that she might be having visual perceptual difficulties. . . . Some right-left confusion was noted when she was in kindergarten, but this is of no real significance.

"The family and past histories are of significance in that the father is a physician and the mother is an ex-speech therapist. . . . The examination proper was entirely within normal limits. It was my impression that this was a normal child."

Learning-Disability Cases Examined by Dr. Arnold P. Gold

K.G. is a 7-year-old boy: "There was a slight slurring of words which may be due to the delayed eruption of the upper incisor teeth. . . . He held a pencil in a deficient fashion with the index and middle finger over the pencil and very close to the point. This was associated with slight deficiency in graphomotor skills with mildly impaired formation of letters and numbers. His reproductions of the Bender-Gestalt patterns reflected this mild graphomotor difficulty. . . . Station revealed a bilateral pes planus with a tendency to toe outwards. . . . Motor examination showed a mild decrease in muscle tone with slight hyperextensibility of joints involving the intrinsic muscles of the fingers. . . . Cerebellar examination showed normal finger-nose-finger function with reasonably good catching, throwing and kicking. There was, however, a mild impairment of rapid alternating movements such as with alternating pronation and supination. However, small finger muscle coordination such as rapid succession movements involving the intrinsic muscles of the fingers was moderately impaired and associated with mirror movements. . . .

In summary on neurologic examination this seven and a half year old youngster showed evidence of a mild degree of muscular hypotonia with hyperextensibility of joints, and this was associated with a mild to moderate impairment of small hand muscle coordination.

"The family history is of significance in that the father who obtained an equivalency high school diploma had a significant learning disability and when tested, Mr. G., who is of normal intellect, was only able to spell at a third to fourth grade level and his reading was below the fifth grade level with multiple omissions and substitutions. In addition to the learning disability there was a significant speech problem with stuttering which in large part, is related to the frustration that Mr. G. encountered with his academic performance."

D.W. is an 11-year, 11-month-old boy: "He held a pencil in a rigid and awkward fashion in the right hand and his graphomotor coordination was immature for age and letters were poorly printed. Copies of the Bender-Gestalt patterns were likewise deficient with mild distortions and these reproductions were complicated by irregular lines and poor angulations. . . . There was no cerebellar deficit other than that involving graphomotor function. The child encountered no difficulty with throwing, catching, and kicking and on formal cerebellar examination there was no abnormality in finger-nose-finger or the performance of rapid alternating and rapid succession movements."

M.C. is a 6-year-old boy: "Coordination is poor above all for visuomotor and small hand muscle coordination skills. He did not button clothes until 6 years of age. He was unable to tie his shoelaces until recently. . . . Speech patterns were deficient in that the child spoke with a slight to moderate slurring of words and this was associated with salivary accumulation. . . . Prehension was markedly deficient in that he held a pencil in a very awkward fashion with 4 fingers. . . This was associated with deficient graphomotor skills with very poor formation and spacing of letters. . . . The reproductions of the Bender-Gestalt patterns were likewise deficient and in part was related to the poor graphomotor skills but in addition there were distortions and immature reproductions which suggested the presence of an associated perceptual problem with visual spatial difficulties. . . . The gait patterns were characterized by a tendency to toe inwards above all on the right, but was otherwise unremarkable for regular heel, toe and tandem walking. Hopping was slightly deficient. . . . There was a significant cerebellar deficit with finger-nose-finger dysmetria above all on the left and this was associated with poor catching, throwing and kicking. Of greater significance was moderate to marked impairment of rapid alternating rapid succession movements as well as the presence of mirror movements. Cranial nerve examination revealed the previously described speech patterns and this was associated with an immature oropharyngeal coordination with an inability to isolate tongue from mandible on lateral tongue movements.

"The mother had a significant learning disability. Mrs. C. is left-handed and as previously stated has marked right-left confusion. . . . There is one sibling, J., age 8½ years, who is poorly coordinated and has difficulty with spelling, but apparently is an extremely bright boy and has not encountered any significant academic problems.

"In summary, on neurologic examination this 6 year 9 month old child showed evidence of a static encephalopathy of prenatal origin and in view of the prominent history it is highly probable that this is of genetic etiology. This is manifested by a hyperkinetic behavioral syndrome, deficient coordination, poor speech patterns, impaired visual perception and a learning disability as delineated above."

R.V. is an 8-year-old girl: "She was late in both buttoning her clothes and tying her shoelaces. . . . Graphomotor coordination is poor for age and grade placement. A pencil was held rigidly in the left hand and there was slightly deficient formation and spacing of letters. Reproductions of the Bender-Gestalt revealed immature appearing copies that were slightly distorted with irregular lines and poor angulations. . . . Small hand muscle coordination was below that expected for age and there was deficient performance of rapid succession movements, above all on the left.

"In summary, on neurological examination R. . . . showed on examination a mild but definite impairment of cerebellar function which primarily involved small muscle coordination."

A.K. is an 11-year-old boy: "His copies of the Bender-Gestalt were slightly immature with irregular lines and poor angulations. He held a pencil in an awkward and rigid fashion in the right hand and his graphomotor coordination was significantly below that expected for age. He wrote with printed letters that were poorly formed and spaced. . . . Gait patterns were normal with a slight tendency to toe outwards on the left. . . . There was a mild cerebellar deficit which primarily involved fine muscle coordination in the hand with poor succession movements. Cranial nerve examination was unremarkable other than an intermittent and mild convergent strabismus of the left eye. There was excessive salivary accumulation and the child could not dissociate tongue and mandible on lateral tongue movements. . . . There is also impairment of small muscle function involving the oral pharynx and extraocular muscles.

"The family history is of interest in that there are three older siblings; the older two boys had a mild reading and a spelling problem, but presently are doing quite well."

A.H. is a 12-year-old boy: He "spoke with a light slurring of words. . . . His graphomotor coordination was grossly deficient in that there was poor formation of letters and numbers that were poorly written and spaced. The reproductions of the Bender-Gestalt patterns were immature for age with irregular lines but there were no true distortions or rotations. . . . Cerebellar function was normal other than a slight impairment of small finger function with awkwardness in the performance of rapid succession movements. Cranial nerve examination other than the minimal speech deficit was unremarkable. . . . In addition there was a very mild expressive language problem associated with deficient small muscle coordination.

"This disorder is usually secondary to a static encephalopathy of genetic origin and it is highly probable that this is related to the father's disability."

S.T. is a 7-year-old boy: "He spoke with a slight but definite slurring of words and this was associated with salivary accumulation. . . . Copies of the Bender-Gestalt were immature in appearance but at no time was there distortion or rotation. These reproductions had irregular lines and poor angulations. Graphomotor coordination was poor with printed letters that were poorly formed and spaced. . . . There was a cerebellar deficit and this was manifested by slightly awkward gait patterns for regular, heel and toe walking. Hopping was poorly performed and there was evidence of tandem ataxia. In addition to problems with locomotion there was a significant extremity deficit and this was manifested by a minimal finger-nose-finger dysmetria and a moderate to marked impairment of rapid alternating and rapid succession movements. Catching and throwing were poorly performed. It is of interest to note that this youngster's deficit in cerebellar function was most marked in small muscle function.

"It is my impression that this youngster with a hyperkinetic behavioral syndrome shows evidence of organic dysfunction of the central nervous system that primarily involves cerebellar function. *I do not believe that there is evidence of true dyslexia but the child does have a mild learning disability.*"

W.H. is a 9-year-old boy: "The acquisition of developmental milestones revealed a significant delay in motor function and a mild delay in the acquisition of speech patterns. . . . Coordination is stated to be poor for all functions except for walking and buttoning. . . . His speech patterns were poor and this was associated with slurring of words and slight stuttering. . . . Copies of the Bender-Gestalt patterns were immature for age and in addition were slightly rotated to the right with irregular lines and poor angulations. . . . Graphomotor coordination showed that the child held a pencil in an awkward and rigid fashion in the left hand and there was significant deficit in both the formation and spacing of printed letters. . . . Reading was characterized by poor cadence. . . . Station was characterized by a mild pes planus with a slight scoliosis of the thoracic vertebra to the left. His gait patterns were awkward for regular, heel and toe walking. Tandem gait was deficient and hopping was poorly performed, especially on the left foot. . . . There was a significant cerebellar deficit manifested by a moderate impairment of finger-nose-finger function as well as a significant deficit in the performance of rapid alternating and rapid succession movements. He threw only with distal musculature such as observed in females and was very deficient in catching and throwing and kicking. . . . This child with a delay in the acquisition of all developmental milestones showed at the present time deficient motor, cerebellar, and expressive language problems as well as the mild but definite learning disability."

S.D.R. is a 9-year-old boy: "Coordination was stated to be poor for handwriting and catching. He first buttoned his clothes at 5–6 years of age and first tied his shoelaces at 7 years of age. . . . Past history and review of systems revealed that the child has impairment of extra-ocular muscle function for which corrective glasses have been prescribed. There have been many episodes of recurrent pharyngitis and otitis with febrile reactions which rose as high as 105 to 106 degrees. . . . His copies of the Bender-Gestalt were of poor quality. These reproductions were mildly distorted with irregular lines and poor angulation. Graphomotor coordination was deficient with poor formation of both letters and numbers. . . . There was a deficient cerebellar deficit that was manifested by a mild finger-nose-finger dysmetria and a moderate impairment of rapid alternating movement. Catching, throwing and kicking were poorly performed. Cranial nerve examination revealed a prominent alternating convergent strabismus which was most apparent in the right eye. There was a prominent difficulty in the youngster fixing for any prolonged period of time. The eyeglasses tended to correct this problem.

"It is my impression that this youngster with a relative microcephaly shows unequivocal evidence of organic dysfunction of the central nervous system that is often referred to as 'minimal cerebral dysfunction or minimal brain damage.' The evidence to support this impression of neurologic dysfunction is the perceptual problems with visuo-spatial muscle function, above all in the hands, as well as an extraocular muscle imbalance.

"The family history is of interest in that the mother was a slow learner and presently has a marked alternating convergent strabismus. The father likewise had encountered significant problems with academic function.

"Concerning etiologic factors it is possible that this is of genetic etiology and may well be related to the parents who also had significant learning problems."

D.S. is a 7-year-old boy: "His copies of the Bender-Gestalt figures were markedly abnormal with gross distortions, rotations, irregular lines, and poor angulations. These were highly diagnostic of a marked perceptual problem with visuo-spatial difficulties. . . . Graphomotor coordination was likewise deficient with poor formation and spacing of both letters and numbers. The gait was normal for regular, heel and toe walking. There was evidence of slight tandem ataxia. . . . There was a significant cerebellar deficit with poor performance of finger-nose-finger function as well as deficient function in the performance of rapid succession movements, especially that which involved small muscle groups. Catching, throwing and kicking were poorly performed.

"It is my impression that this youngster shows evidence of abnormal neurological function which is commonly referred to as 'minimal cerebral dysfunction.' This is manifested in this youngster by a failure to establish dominance with right-left confusion, the marked perceptual deficit, a mild to moderate cerebellar deficit that was most marked in fine muscle function and finger dexterity. The entire clinical picture is then associated with a marked learning disability that not only involves reading but other spheres of academic function. Etiologic factors appear to be obscure but it is highly possible that there is a genetic basis in view of a paternal uncle who is left-handed and has an associated learning disability."

C.O. is a 7-year-old girl: "The child has frequent falls but on questioning it is more probable that this is secondary to her mild coordination problem with hyperkinesis, rather than any inner ear disease. C. was recently evaluated at Lenox Hill Hospital and apparently vestibular function studies as well as an audiogram was performed and this showed some questionable findings. . . . The child's speech patterns were slightly deficient in that on occasion she showed evidence of poor articulation of words with slurring. . . . Her prehension was slightly deficient in that she held a pencil with the index finger over the pencil and very close to the point. This was associated with poor graphomotor skills and her letters were deficiently formed and poorly spaced. She could produce most numbers but had difficulty with the number 9 which was subsequently written in a mirror reversal. . . . Reproductions of the Bender-Gestalt patterns were grossly deficient with distortions, rotations and immature copies. These were indicative of deficient visual memory as well and impaired visual perception as well as poor visuomotor and visual spatial relationships. . . . Gait was complicated by a slight tendency to toe inwards with mild pes planus. . . . There was a slight deficiency in hopping on the left lower extremity. . . . There was a cerebellar deficit with a slight finger-nose-finger dysmetria associated with poor catching, throwing and kicking and this was associated with a moderate dysdiadokokinesis and poor performance of rapid succession movements. It is of note that despite the impairment of coordination in small finger muscle function, the child had no difficulty in snapping her fingers.

"Mrs. O. . . . shows evidence of a mild learning disability. . . . It is apparent, likewise, when evaluating Mr. O. that he shows evidence of a significant residual learning problem."

N.C. is an 8-year-old boy: "Coordination is stated to be good for walking, running, catching and throwing. In contrast, he has problems with small muscle coordination which involves handwriting, buttoning and shoelace tying. Even at the present time N. is unable to tie his own shoelaces. . . . Prehension consisted of a tripod positioning of the pencil but his graphomotor skills were poor with deficient formation and spacing of both letters and numbers. Reproductions of the Bender-Gestalt patterns were likewise impaired with distortions, irregular lines and poor angulations; in part this was due to the deficient small hand muscle coordination. It is of note that reading is N.'s most proficient subject in that he is reading at grade level and both immediate and intermediate recall was good. Spelling was poor and at the second grade level while number concepts were very poor and limited to finger counting. He was unable to tell time. The child's fund of knowledge and general intellect appeared to be normal for stated chronologic age. Formal neurologic examination revealed bilateral pes planus with the knees in genu recurvatum. . . . His gait was on a slightly widened base but otherwise unremarkable for regular, heel, toe and tandem walking. Hopping was well performed on either foot. Motor examination showed a generalized decrease in muscle tone, and this hypotonia was associated with slight hyperextensibility of joints. . . . There was a mild cerebellar deficit and this primarily involves small finger muscle function such as in the performance of rapid succession movements and this became more impaired when both hands were utilized simultaneously. Cranial nerve examination revealed an alternating divergent strabismus and the child was unable to maintain fixation for any period of time. This was further complicated by photophobia which in part may be due to his present upper respiratory infection.

"In summary . . . N. is an 8 year 5 month old child who showed evidence of a neurologic deficit that was manifested by muscular hypotonia, impaired small hand muscle coordination, an extraocular muscle imbalance, and a learning disability as delineated above. These findings would be consistent with what is commonly referred to as 'minimal cerebral dysfunction or minimal brain damage.' "

M.M. is an 8-year-old girl: "Behaviorally there is evidence of a prominent hyperkinetic behavioral syndrome which is most prominent in the home setting. . . . Past history and review of systems revealed that at 2 years of age the child had a one minute seizure in which she woke up in the morning screaming and this was associated with eye rolling and head shaking. . . . In addition she was clumsy and would frequently fall. . . . At the completion of my evaluation the mother related that the child was seen at New York Hospital for an ENT evaluation which was normal as well as obtaining normal audiogram but apparently the calorics were abnormal. I would be most appreciative if you could supply me further data concerning this vestibular function study. M. was also seen by Dr. Steven K. in neurological evaluation who stated that the child showed no evidence of a neurologic deficit. . . . Physical examination revealed . . . child tended to speak from the right side of her mouth with a tendency to tilt her head to the left. . . . A pencil was held in a rigid fashion with hyperextension of the index finger. Graphomotor coordination was poor in that the child wrote with printed letters that were deficiently formed and spaced. Reproductions of the Bender-Gestalt patterns were moderately deficient with immature reproductions that were distorted and rotated associated with irregular lines and poor angulations; these reproductions were characteristic of a perceptual problem with visuo-spatial difficulties. Auditory memory and auditory perception were likewise deficient. . . . Gait patterns were slightly awkward with a tendency to toe inwards on the left. . . . There was a significant cerebellar deficit that was manifested by a slight left finger-nose-finger dysmetria, a moderate impairment of rapid alternating movements with dysdiadokokinesis and a moderate to marked impairment of small finger muscle coordination with deficient performance of rapid succession movements, above all involving both hands. Catching, throwing and kicking were all poorly performed. Cranial nerve examination revealed a very slight slurring of words and this was associated with a mild impairment of oropharyngeal coordination with an inability to isolate tongue from mandible.

"In summary, on neurologic examination this 8 year, 8 months old child showed evidence of a static encephalography of prenatal or perinatal origin that is commonly referred to as 'minimal cerebral dysfunction or minimal brain damage.' The evidence to support this clinical impression is the impaired auditory and visual perception, the deficient coordination which was most prominent for small finger muscle function, the learning disability as delineated above, and historically a hyperkinetic behavioral syndrome."

P.R. is an 8-year, 11-month-old girl: "At 2½ years of age P. fell from a swing and this resulted in a laceration of the right scalp . . . at 3½ years of age, the child began to present with recurrent eye pain which is often triggered by exposure to bright light or sunlight. . . . Approximately 2 years ago during the course of a routine school physical examination hearing was noted to be deficient on the left side. Subsequent audiological evaluation revealed a nerve deafness on the left. . . . Reproductions of the Bender-Gestalt patterns were mildly deviant from the norm but there were no distortions or rotations. The copies had irregular lines and poor angulations. Graphomotor coordination was poor with deficient formation and spacing of letters and numbers. . . . Gait patterns showed a tendency to toe outwards with mild pes planus. . . . There was a very mild cerebellar deficit with slight-finger-nose-finger dysmetria and a mild small finger muscle coordination such as in the performance of rapid succession movements."

C.S. is a 9-year-old girl: "At 4½ years of age she was seen at the Brooklyn College Speech and Hearing Center where no therapy was suggested and a diagnostic impression of a 'late talker' was made. Coordination is stated to be poor, above all for fine muscle function as manifested by difficulty in tying shoelaces and poor graphomotor coordination. School performance revealed that the youngster is presently in the third grade and is a B student for all subjects other than reading where she has obtained a C grade. . . . Past history and review of systems revealed that the youngster has been seen by an optometrist who states there there is poor eye coordination. . . . Copies of the Bender-Gestalt were significantly below that expected for age and were highly suggestive of a perceptual problem with visuo-spatial difficulties. *Number concepts were adequate for age while spelling and reading were slightly below average. None of these subjects showed gross deficiencies, certainly there was no evidence of a true dyslexic syndrome.* . . . Station was characterized by a lumbar lordosis and the gait was slightly awkward for regular, heel, toe and tandem walking. . . . There was a mild cerebellar deficit with finger-nose-finger dysmetria, above all on the left, poor performance of rapid succession movements and deficient catching, throwing and kicking. Cranial nerve examination was normal other than poor disassociation of tongue and mandible on lateral tongue movements . . . This youngster with a history of a hyperkinetic behavioral syndrome shows a mild to moderate perceptual problem as well as a mild cerebellar deficit. *These findings would be consistent with a diagnosis of minimal cerebral dysfunction or minimal brain damage.*

"The family history is of interest in that Mrs. S. was slow in school and 'had to work to obtain grades.' She is a slow reader and this has continued until the present time. Coordination is poor and she did not participate in physical activities as a child."

M.D. is an 11-year-old boy: "Academically the child has had problems since kindergarten . . . and was nervous and hyperactive. Station was complicated by a slight bilateral pes planus but his gait was otherwise unremarkable for regular, heel, toe and tandem walking. . . . Sensory examination was normal for all modalities including touch, position, vibration and cortical sensation. There was a significant cerebellar deficit with a moderate finger-nose-finger dysmetria above all on the left and this was associated with poor catching as well as a dysdiadochokinesis and above all a prominent impairment of small finger muscle coordination such as with rapid successive movements and this was associated with mirror movements. . . . In summary, on neurologic examination M. shows evidence of a brain damaged syndrome that is characterized by a prominent perceptual problem with visual spatial and visuomotor difficulties, deficient auditory memory, poor cerebellar function, and an associated learning disability."

A Chronological Study of a Case of Benign Paroxysmal Vertigo

S.P. was a 6-year-old youngster when he was first seen by Dr. Arnold Gold.

January 1968: "This six year, ten month old youngster was evaluated with the chief complaint of 'severe headaches.' He was previously diagnosed by Dr. Shapiro and Dr. Bocalli as a vascular migraine secondary to food allergy. . . . The acquisition of developmental milestones revealed that handedness has not been established in that he writes and eats with the right hand and throws and catches with the left. Gait was delayed until 17 months of age. . . . Coordination reveals a child with excellent catching and throwing ability and who does well with fine muscle coordination. At the present time he is an excellent student in the first grade. . . . The family history reveals that the father had 2 vertiginous episodes secondary to a middle ear infection. . . . Approximately two years ago the child began with episodes. . . . All episodes occur at night with the child suddenly gagging, spitting up phlegm and holding his eye (the parents state the right eye; the child the left). There is very little pain but he describes true vertigo with the child spinning around the room and this is associated with a markedly ataxic gait. During the entire episode there is marked photophobia and the child is neither able to lie down or stand but prefers to assume a sitting position. When the episode has terminated there is no residual complaint. . . . Physical examination revealed a bright, verbal youngster who was obviously superior in intellect for his stated chronologic age. . . . Spelling and number concepts were superior. . . . The gait was characterized by the head tilting to the right and the head was maintained stiffly in this position. There was a tendency towards pes planus and genu recurvatum when standing while when walking there was a tendency to toe-in on the left. Motor examination revealed a generalized decrease in muscle tone. . . . There was no evidence of a cerebellar deficit.

"Impression: Episodic vertigo—rule out vestibular dysfunction versus vascular anomalies involving the cerebellum or brain stem."

March 1968: "P. was admitted to the Babies Hospital from January 31st to February 13th, 1968. . . . An electroencephalogram was performed and this was an abnormal record due to well defined bilateral synchronous paroxysmal discharges present both in the alert and drowsy states. . . . An audiogram was performed and this was normal. Vestibular function studies with calorics and rotation tests were normal. These normal studies would rule out a vestibular etiology for the vertiginous spells. . . . Despite the atypical nature of the spells, the possibility of a convulsive disorder must be considered especially in view of the abnormal electroencephalogram. For this reason, the child was placed on Dilantin in the dosage of 100 mg. twice daily.

January 1972: "I had the opportunity to re-evaluate P. on Jan. 14, 1972 . . . the child was last evaluated by me during a hospitalization at the Babies Hospital . . . in Jan., 1968. At that time he was discharged on Dilantin . . . the medication was decreased and ultimately discontinued after a period of six months. P. was essentially asymptomatic until Jan. 10, 1972, when at 4:00 a.m. the child awoke screaming 'help me' or 'I'm dizzy.' This time he was holding his right eye, was unable to open his eyes and complained of headache. The child could not lie down or stand but ultimately could only sit. After a period of three to four hours the symptoms improved and by 12:00 noon P. was asymptomatic. . . . Neurologic examination revealed . . . a slight slurring of words. . . . His reproductions of the Bender-Gestalt patterns were of poor quality and in large part this was due to a slight impairment in graphomotor skills. These reproductions had irregular lines and poor angulations. Academic function was at grade level.*

* This child was referred to the author in 1974 for evaluation of his learning disabilities and upon neuropsychological evaluation was found to have all the signs and symptoms characterizing DDD—including a significant reading disorder. An ENG performed at Lenox Hill Hospital revealed "direction fixed, positional nystagmus, reduced vestibular response—right," during bilateral bithermal caloric stimulation.

"Gait patterns were normal for regular, heel and toe walking but tandem gait was poorly performed. . . . Cranial nerve examination showed a mild bilateral eyelid ptosis. . . . P.'s neurologic evaluation was essentially unchanged from my initial evaluation of the child. At this time, I could not delineate any evidence of head tilt which was previously noted. The episodic 'dizziness' is most unusual for which I did not have an adequate explanation. The possibility of inner ear disease or a vascular etiology must be considered. Despite the abnormal electroencephalogram noted four years ago I would seriously question whether this is a convulsive disorder."

February 1972: "An electroencephalogram was obtained on P. on Jan. 25, 1972. . . . this tracing was only mildly abnormal and was significantly improved when compared to the prior electrical tracing of 1968."

September 1972: "From September 10th until September 13, 1972, P. has presented with daily episodes and as previously noted, these would always awaken him from his sleep. Although they are characterized as being right eye pain, in reality this is a sensation of subjective vertigo which is localized primarily to the right eye, but can also be found on the left side as well, and this is associated with headache. During the episode the child is unable to lie supine or stand and can only walk with his head flexed forward. It is of note that the previously prescribed Dilantin was discontinued over 3 years ago. Antivert, one half of a tablet three times a day was prescribed on September 12th, and as noted no further episodes were experienced after September 13, 1972."

"Gait patterns were normal for regular, heel and toe walking, but there continued to be a mild impairment of tandem gait patterns . . . it is apparent that this is not a migraine headache but the entire clinical picture would be most consistent with either a benign paroxysmal vertigo or intermittent vestibular neuronitis."

November 1972: "Ancillary studies were obtained on P. . . . the electroencephalogram . . . noted . . . this was mildly and nonspecifically abnormal which in itself would not be indicative of a convulsive disorder. I am also enclosing a copy of correspondence from Dr. M.S., as well as the results of the vestibular function studies and audiological evaluation. I do believe that his comments are self-explanatory and certainly the findings would be consistent with benign paroxysmal vertigo. For this reason it is suggested that if spells should occur Antivert should be prescribed on a P.R.N. basis."

October 1972 (Correspondence from Dr. M.S.): "As you will see, the two vestibular labyrinths are symmetrical with cold water but asymmetrical with hot water. This finding is consistent with the diagnosis of benign paroxysmal vertigo. His hearing test remains completely normal."

APPENDIX C

Retrospective Qualitative Analysis of Six Complete "Blind" Neurologic Reports

The positive c-v findings and resulting diagnoses in five dyslexic cases referred to Drs. Carter and Gold are presented, analyzed, and compared to a sixth (and seventh) case presenting with severe dyslexic-like symptoms and absent blind neurologic and ENG findings.

The methodology utilized to analyze the complete blind neurologic data and diagnostic formulations was no different than that utilized by the author to analyze retrospectively his own neuropsychiatric data and conceptualizations. This psychoanalytic-like qualitative research methodology of careful documentation and critical retrospective analysis was found to be as useful in the "dyslexic" research investigations as in the psychoanalytic treatment of neurotic patients—for all too often unconscious "bias" factors and forces play havoc with the collection, perception, and interpretation of data. Only careful and honest scrutiny will facilitate the detection and resolution of the resistance or "bias" forces unconsciously permeating and shaping research efforts and conceptualizations.

Inasmuch as c-v findings were noted and/or specifically stated to be present in 96% of the "blindly" referred dyslexic sample, and inasmuch as a maximum of only 6% of the cases evidenced possible hard and fast signs of cortical dysfunction, it appeared reasonable to qualitatively review the complete "blind" neurologic reports in a manner analogous to that utilized by the author in his retrospective and prospective studies.

Allen

Allen is a 7-year-old exceptionally bright and highly verbal youngster referred to the author for neuropsychiatric evaluation because of reading retardation. His first-grade teacher had described him as "the smartest in his class." When unable to perform adequately, he was noted to become excessively annoyed and prone to temper outbursts.

Allen's dyslexic nuclear symptomatic complex may be summarized as follows: His reading performance was characterized by letter, word and number reversals. He confused *m* and *n*, *n* and *u*, *3* and *E*, *was* and *saw*, *no* and *on*. New words were easily forgotten and he appeared to have the greatest difficulty recognizing small words. Were it not for finger pointing, he would continually lose his place and find himself re-reading the same word and line over and over again. Spelling was severely deficient. For example, he was able to spell his first name but not his last. Graphomotor incoordination and reversals were evident as well. And although math performance was above average in his early grades, it began to deteriorate when he found it difficult to recall the multiplication tables. Restlessness and distractability is apparent only when he becomes frustrated and catastrophically anxious.

Upon neurologic examination by the author, Allen was noted to write with his left hand and to use his right hand for most other tasks. He was right-footed and left-eyed and exhibited significant right/left uncertainty. (His parents were right-handed, but a paternal uncle and maternal grandmother were noted to be left-handed.) On the Schildrer arm extension test, both arms remained on the same level. However, he experienced the right as stronger. Tests of cortical function such as point localization, two point discrimination, stereo, object, and color gnosis, conceptualization, and I.Q. were all well within normal limits. Aphasic and extinction manifestations were absent, as were hyperactive DTRs and Babinski reflexes. The only positive or suspect neurologic findings were mild and situation-specific hyperactivity and distractability, unsteady tandem walking, dysdiadochokinesis, and hypotonia with decreased DTRs in all extremities.

Allen was referred to Dr. Arnold Gold for blind neurologic examination and diagnosed by him as "minimal cerebral dysfunction" (October 1969). Two years later (April 1971) he had a blind ENG performed at New York Hospital which indicated "left canal paresis."

Dr. Gold's Blind Neurologic Report

"Following your kind suggestion I had the opportunity to evaluate Allen in my office at the Neurologic Institute of New York on October 14, 1969. The child was seen for the purpose of evaluating his 'dyslexia.'

"Allen is a 7 year, 3 month old child who is the result of a nine month uncomplicated pregnancy that was terminated by the spontaneous onset of labor of 4 hours duration. The delivery was uncomplicated and the birth weight was 7 lbs. 3 oz. There was no problem in the immediate neonatal period.

"The acquisition of developmental milestones revealed that, if anything, Allen was precocious in his motor development and walked at the early age of 7 months. The parents reported that he never crawled prior to walking. Expressive language function was acquired at a normal age in that the child spoke in words by 14 months and in complete sentences by 2 years of age. Toilet training was completely acquired at 2½ years of age. Coordination was stated to be good or average for walking, running, catching and throwing; and poor for handwriting. He has not yet accomplished buttoning his clothes or tying his shoelaces.

"Academically Allen did well in nursery school, poorly in kindergarten, and at the present time in second grade is again doing well.

"Past medical history and review of systems revealed a fall down a flight of stairs at 2½ years of age with no subsequent ill effects. His left eye was noted to turn in and this has been corrected with glasses. Acute infectious diseases of childhood include measles and scarlet fever. He had pneumonia at 3 years and is allergic to chocolate, wheat, and eggs.

"Behaviorally Allen is not a behavioral problem but shows a mild hyperkinetic behavioral syndrome that is manifested by hyperactivity, poor attention span, impulsiveness, distractibility and the child cries easily and does not play well with his peers.

"Both parents are right-handed. A paternal uncle is left handed and encountered problems in school while the paternal grandfather had amblyopia ex Anopsia with resultant loss of vision in the deviating eye.

"Physical examination revealed a most pleasant, cooperative youngster who had grossly normal verbal intellect. The child wore glasses and had a head circumference of 54 cm. There was no evidence of an intracranial bruit. A brief general physical examination was unremarkable other than a slight tendency towards bilateral epicanthic folds.

"Allen identified all colors as well as shapes which included a circle, square, triangle, and diamond. His copies of the Bender-Gestalt figures were markedly abnormal with gross distortions, rotations, irregular lines, and poor angulations. These were highly diagnostic of a marked perceptual problem with visuo-spatial difficulties. There was a failure to establish dominance in that the child wrote with the left hand and threw and picked with the right-sided extremities. He was left-eyed and there was evidence of right-left confusion.

"Academic performance was significantly below that expected for age in that number concepts consisted of finger counting with a requirement that this be performed in sequence beginning with number one. There was no coin recognition. Spelling was poor and significantly below that expected for age or grade placement. It is of interest that when asked to spell the word look, the youngster stated that it began with the letter 'l' but then wrote it with a letter 'k'. This last feature was suggestive of mirror writing. Reading was poorly performed and at an early first grade level. Graphomotor coordination was likewise deficient with poor formation and spacing of both letters and numbers.

"The gait was normal for regular, heel, and toe walking. There was evidence of slight tandem ataxia. Motor examination showed normal bulk, tone, and strength of all muscle groups. The deep tendon reflexes were physiologic and the Babinski responses normal. Sensory examination was normal for all modalities which include touch, position, vibration, and cortical sensation. There was a significant cerebellar deficit with poor performance of finger-nose-finger function as well as deficient function in the performance of rapid succession movements, especially that which involved small muscle groups. Catching, throwing, and kicking were poorly performed. Cranial nerve examination was unremarkable. I was unable to delineate any evidence of a deviating eye. The funduscopic examination was benign. The visual acuity was 20/20 in both eyes and the visual fields were normal to confrontation.

"It is my impression that this youngster shows evidence of abnormal neurological function which is commonly referred to as 'minimal cerebral dysfunction'. This is manifested in this youngster by a failure to establish dominance with right-left confusion, the marked perceptual deficit, a mild to moderate cerebellar deficit that was most marked in fine muscle function and finger dexterity. The entire clinical picture is then associated with a marked learning disability that not only involves reading but other spheres of academic function. Etiologic factors appear to be obscure but it is highly possible that there is a genetic basis in view of a paternal uncle who is left-handed and has an associated learning disability.

"I do not believe that this youngster could or should continue in his present class placement but it is my opinion that he will require special academic placement in a neurologically impaired class limited to children of normal or near normal intellect without significant behavioral problems."

Retrospective Analysis

Inasmuch as the *only* hard and fast evidence found was "mild to moderate cerebellar deficit," it seemed reasonable for the author to assume that Allen's dyslexic nuclear symptomatic complex was of c-v rather than cortical origin. A consequent attempt was made to explain Allen's clinical findings on the basis of a c-v pathophysiology. Could Allen's failure in establishing *lateral* dominance be due to a genetically determined ambidexterity, and thus be viewed as an independent dyslexic variable? Or is it that his handedness and directional difficulties are due to both his c-v compass dysfunction and inability to harmoniously and correctly select right and left hands for motor tasks? Might his perceptual-motor deficit be due to a c-v-determined sensory-motor dysmetria, with perhaps secondarily related cortical expressions?

Is it possible that the scientific force of the traditional cortical dyslexic theories—including Orton's primary cortical neurophysiologic dominance theory of dyslexia as well as the traditionally accepted minimal cerebral dysfunction syndrome—resulted in a "cortical diagnosis" which ignored the presence of c-v signs and the absence of cortical signs?

Allen is now 17 years old and has been longitudinally followed by the author for the last 10 years. He now reads well, although he still avoids it when possible. He was first tested for blurring speeds in 1974, and his tracking capacity was found to be one-half normal—clearly demonstrating the presence of a c-v-determined ocular fixation and tracking dysfunction underlying his dyslexia. Allen's dyslexic complex responded favorably to Marezine. His reading, for example, became smoother and faster, he no longer stumbled over words, and his reversals all but disappeared. Spelling, mathematical memory (multiplication tables), and his dysmetric writing or graphomotor incoordination improved as well.

Linda (Bonnie's daughter)

Linda is a 9-year-old fourth-grader who was neuropsychologically examined by the author because of severe learning difficulties. Her dyslexic nuclear symptomatic complex manifested as follows. She exhibited letter and word skipping and reversals, slow reading ability and deficient visual and phonetic memory for words. She was a late talker with a mildly slurred and halting or stammering speech, prone to episodic stuttering. In addition, she demonstrated balance and coordination difficulties, graphomotor incoordination, Bender-Gestalt and Goodenough abnormalities, grammatical, spelling, mathematical, and right/left directional uncertainty, as well as difficulty recalling the months of the year in sequence.

Neurologic examination revealed only c-v signs: ocular and tandem dysmetria, dysdiadochokinesis, finger-to-thumb sequencing difficulties and slurred speech. Although described as overactive and distractable both at home and in school, Linda did not present with these symptoms clinically.

She was referred first for psycho-educational evaluation and then for blind ENG and neurologic examinations. Upon psycho-educational evaluation, she was found to have "a variety of developmental deficits in the perceptual-motor, cognitive and language areas." Her ENG was found to be abnormal at Lenox Hill Hospital. Dr. Gold found only cerebellar signs on neurologic examination, diagnosed her as having "minimal cerebral dysfunction or minimal brain damage" and emphatically stated, "Certainly there was no evidence of a true dyslexic syndrome."

Summary of the Psycho-Educational Findings

"*Academic Achievement:* Linda scores 3.1 grade in the Gray Oral Achievement which is not a poor performance. However the manner in which she reads reveals her feelings about the entire experience. For example, this slow moving plodding child becomes impulsive and distractable in the face of this task. She plunges in rapidly, reads a few words and then talks about something in the room and continues in the same fashion throughout. She has very poor word attack skill, reading by contextual clue and looking only at the first letter to make a judgement so that 'would' becomes 'wanted'; 'long'–'large'; 'place'–'palace', etc.

"Linda does more poorly on the test of word recognition, where there is no contextual clue. She scores at 2.3 grade and her difficulty is her inability to see the parts of the word (letters) and their order. Spelling shows the same type of errors and in this she scores 2.0 grade.

"In arithmetic Linda scores at grade level but knows just the addition and subtraction work although she tries the multiplication. Here again she changes her method of approach as soon as there are no words to read,—she slows up and is willing to attend the work at hand.

"Putting words down on paper presents the greatest difficulty.

"*Summary:* Linda has a variety of developmental deficits in the perceptual-motor, cognitive and language areas. Her uneven development makes it much more difficult for her to cope with the demands made at school and at home. She has compensated in many ways for her problem and has tried to divert from the writing-reading problem so that she can do other things. In addition she has developed a passive attitude toward other tasks and becomes anxious and over stimulated when she is required to read or write.

"*Recommendations:* All the above has been discussed with Mr. and Mrs. —. Recommendation was made for a neurological examination."

Dr. Gold's Blind Neurologic Report

"Following your kind suggestion I had the opportunity to evaluate Linda in my office at the Neurological Institute on April 19, 1968. The child was accompanied by her mother who initially was anxious and apprehensive with resultant stuttering but once relaxed, this speech pattern was no longer in evidence. Mrs. — appeared to be a reliable and realistic informant. The child was seen with the chief complaint of a reading problem in the first grade.

"Linda is a 9 year, 2 month old youngster who was the result of a nine month uncomplicated pregnancy that was terminated by induction of labor with a normal delivery and a birth weight of 6 lbs. 8 oz. The immediate neonatal period was unremarkable and the child had a good suck. Subsequently chewing was performed in a normal fashion.

"The acquisition of developmental milestones of this right-handed child revealed that she walked at 12 months but was late in the development of expressive language patterns, with words first in evidence at 2 years and sentences at 3½ years. At 4½ years of age she was seen at the Brooklyn College Speech and Hearing Center where no therapy was suggested and a diagnostic impression of a 'late talker' was made. Coordination is stated to be poor, above all for fine muscle function as manifested by difficulty in tying shoelaces and poor graphomotor coordination. School performance revealed that the youngster is presently in the third grade and is a B student for all subjects other than reading where she has obtained a C grade. The youngster has been previously tutored for all subjects including writing. This tutorial assistance is given twice weekly.

"Behaviorally the child is described as having 'ants in her pants' and this is manifested by a hyperkinetic behavioral syndrome with hyperactivity, short attention span, low frustration threshhold, temper outbursts, impulsivity, and distractability. During this past year there has been a considerable and remarkable improvement in behavioral patterns. Mrs. — states that she is quite permissive with the daughter as apparently her own mother was rigid and strict and the mother's stuttering is related to this poor mother-child relationship.

"Past history and review of systems revealed that the youngster has been seen by an optometrist who states that there is poor eye coordination. There is a nodule on the vocal cord which has resulted in the child's present speech patterns.

"The family history is of interest in that Mrs. — was slow in school and 'had to work to obtain grades.' She is a slow reader and this has continued until the present time. Coordination is poor and she did not participate in physical activities as a child. The father presents with no significant difficulties and there is a 13 year old male sibling who likewise does not present with any problems.

"Physical examination revealed a slightly fidgety youngster who otherwise did not show any other evidence of hyperkinesis. There were multiple bruises over the upper and lower extremities which were related to a bicycle accident. The child spoke rapidly and her speech patterns were hoarse and slurred. She had brown hair and hazel eyes with a head circumference of 51.7 cm. She was right-handed, right-footed, and right-eyed. There was evidence of right-left confusion. General physical examination was unremarkable other than a single left palmar crease.

"She identified colors as well as geometric forms. Copies of the Bender-Gestalt were significantly below that expected for age and were highly suggestive of a perceptual problem with visuo-spatial difficulties. Number concepts were adequate for age while spelling and reading were slightly below average. None of these subjects showed gross deficiencies. Certainly there was no evidence of a true dyslexic syndrome.

"Station was characterized by a lumbar lordosis and the gait was slightly awkward for regular, heel, toe, and tandem walking. Motor examination showed normal bulk, tone, and strength of all muscle groups. The deep tendon reflexes were physiologic and the Babinski responses were normal. Sensory examination was normal for all modalities including touch, position, vibration, and cortical sensation. There was a mild cerebellar deficit with finger-nose-finger dysmetria, above all on the left, poor performance of rapid succession movements and deficient catching, throwing, and kicking. Cranial nerve examination was normal other than poor disassociation of tongue and mandible on lateral tongue movements. The funduscopic examination was benign. The visual acuity was 20/20 in both eyes and the visual fields were normal to confrontation.

"This youngster with a history of a hyperkinetic behavioral syndrome shows a mild to moderate perceptual problem as well as a mild cerebellar deficit. These findings would be consistent with a diagnosis of minimal cerebral dysfunction or minimal brain damage. It is apparent that the child has compensated well for her deficiencies and for this reason I do not believe that a change in school placement is indicated. I would, however, continue with her present tutorial assistance.

"If the hyperkinesis should present as a problem, I would suggest trials with medication and would recommend initially Ritalin in the dosage of 5 mg. two to three times a day. Often this compound or Dexedrine 5 mg. in the morning and a similar dose at noon have a paradoxical response with children who manifest a hyperkinetic behavioral syndrome. Other compounds which could be evaluated include Mellaril 25 mg. two to four times a day or Atarax 50 mg. three to four times daily."

Retrospective Analysis

A retrospective analysis of Linda's case and "blind" neurologic findings clearly revealed a correlation of her academic symptoms exclusively with c-v signs. In addition, for reasons unknown, Dr. Gold's report stated, "Certainly there was no evidence of a true dyslexic syndrome." Needless to say, this rather definitive statement appeared to be most puzzling and required further "analysis" and "associations."

The author reasoned that perhaps Dr. Gold's statement would be more comprehensible if placed in the original context from which it was taken, "Number concepts were adequate for age while spelling and reading were slightly below average. None of these subjects showed gross deficiencies. Certainly there was no evidence of a true dyslexic syndrome." Could it be that Dr. Gold ruled out "true dyslexia" because Linda had only mild difficulties in gross reading, writing, and spelling when he examined her at 9 years of age.

"If the author's analysis is correct, then Dr. Gold is perhaps basing his diagnosis of "true dyslexia" on severe gross deficiencies in reading, writing, and spelling, and not at all on his own neurologic findings or on detailed quantitative psychoeducational test data. In addition, Dr. Gold states, "This youngster with a history of a hyperkinetic behavioral syndrome shows a mild to moderate perceptual problem as well as a mild cerebellar deficit. These findings would be consistent with a diagnosis of minimal cerebral dysfunction or minimal brain dysfunction."

These neurologic "associations" forced the author to wonder how Linda's "blind" neurologic findings are consistent with a cerebral dysfunction? Is it the "mild cerebellar deficit" which is consistent with a diagnosis of minimal cerebral dysfunction? Obviously not, unless one assumes that the presence of cerebellar deficit implies cortical dysfunction. Or is it the "hyperkinetic behavioral syndrome" and/or the "mild to moderate perceptual problem" which is consistent with a diagnosis of "minimal cerebral dysfunction"?

Dr. Gold apparently ruled out specific cortical perceptual problems in his neurologic report: "She identified colors as well as geometric forms. . . . Sensory examination was normal for all modalities including . . . cortical sensation." He did state, however, that "copies of the Bender Gestalt were significantly below that expected for age and were highly suggestive of a perceptual problem with visuospatial difficulties."

Could Dr. Gold have utilized diagnostically nonspecific criteria (i.e., Bender

Gestalt designs) to specifically diagnose and or suggest cortical dysfunction? Although Bender-Gestalt abnormalities may be consistent with a diagnosis of "minimal cerebral dysfunction," Bender-Gestalt abnormalities are also consistent with noncerebral dysfunctions. For example, Dr. Gold's cases of benign paroxysmal vertigo (Stan) and genetic cerebellar dysfunction (Martin) demonstrated abnormal Bender-Gestalt designs. In fact, central to all of Dr. Gold's "blind" neurologic reports are correlations between "cerebellar deficits" and abnormal Bender-Gestalt designs. If the latter have any localizing CNS value at all, one must statistically assume that abnormal Bender-Gestalt designs suggest cerebellar deficit.

Perhaps it is the "hyperkinetic behavioral syndrome" which Dr. Gold considers consistent with a diagnosis of minimal cerebral dysfunction? But why are there then no localizing signs of cerebral dysfunction in cases he describes as hyperactive? Is it possible that c-v-impaired, frustrated and anxious children who have difficulty reading, writing, and spelling become overly active and distractable? This has certainly been the author's experience with many "dyslexic" children. If indeed this is so, then the "hyperkinetic behavioral syndrome" as manifested in this case is also diagnostically nonspecific, and thus cannot be used alone to justify a diagnosis of cerebral dysfunction. For example, one can justifiably say that Linda's "hyperkinetic behavioral syndrome" is consistent with a diagnosis of cortical dysfunction, noncortical dysfunction, c-v dysfunction, emotional dysfunction, etc. This reasoning is not inconsistent with Dr. Gold's, for he diagnosed Martin to have a genetic cerebellar dysfunction despite his hyperactivity.

Martin

Martin is an 8½-year-old third-grader who was neuropsychiatrically examined by the author because of graphomotor incoordination, hyperactive-like symptoms, and a history of having been a "slow, inattentive" reader prone to reversals. His dyslexic nuclear symptomatic complex manifested itself as follows. Throughout first and second grades he was noted to confuse *b* and *d*, *was* and *saw*, and *on* and *no*. In later grades his reading ability significantly improved, and one might easily label him as either an early or late bloomer. His writing was described by his mother as a "jumble" that tended to drift off the horizontal. Periods, commas, and capitals were often omitted, and the spacing between letters, words, and lines was highly irregular. Written spelling was characterized by letter omissions, reversals, and insertions, whereas oral spelling was noted to be somewhat better. Mathematical conceptualization was superior—although written mathematics was subject to significant degrees of "careless" errors" and memory "slips." The multiplication table for 7 remained difficult for him to utilize reliably without double and triple checking. Directional uncertainty persisted and was compensated for by recalling that he had a scar on his right hand. Speech and verbal functions were superior. Overactivity and distractability were not evident during one-to-one examination, although the symptoms manifested at home and at school.

Upon neurologic examination, Martin revealed only c-v signs: tandem dysmetria and dysdiadochokinesis, as well as the subjective experience of spinning vertigo during Romberg testing. His Bender-Gestalt designs and Goodenough figure drawings were characterized by the typical rotation, articulation, and angle formation errors noted in reading-score-deficient dyslexics.

In summary, Martin's dyslexic nuclear complex was characterized by compensated reading scores, significant difficulties with graphomotor functioning (including Bender-Gestalt and Goodenough tests), normal mathematical conceptualization, normal speech, compensated right/left directional sense and memory, and graphomotor-related grammatical, spelling, and mathematical dysfunctioning.

Martin was referred to Dr. Gold for blind neurologic examination with the specific aim of comparing his blind neurologic findings with those of "reading-score-uncompensated" dyslexics. ENG was not performed.

Dr. Gold's Blind Neurologic Report

"Following your kind suggestion I had the opportunity to evaluate Martin in my office on June 16, 1971. The historical data was prepared by his mother who, as well known to you, is presently hospitalized at Long Island Jewish Medical Center. The father, who accompanied the child, provided supplementary historical information.

"Martin is an 8 year, 7 month old child who is the result of a nine month uncomplicated pregnancy that was terminated by the induction of labor and a normal delivery. The birth weight was 7 lbs. There were no problems in the immediate neonatal period.

"The acquisition of developmental milestones revealed motor function was normal and Martin sat alone at 8 months, crawled at 9 months, stood alone unassisted at 11 months and walked unassisted at 12 months of age. He was able to pedal a tricycle by 3½ years and a bicycle by 7 years of age. Expressive language patterns were likewise normally developed and Martin had no problems with either drooling or chewing. Toilet training was established for daytime control by 3 years and for the night time by 6 years of age. Coordination revealed that although Martin's gross motor and visuomotor coordination is stated to be normal the child has significant problems in small hand muscle coordination as evidenced by deficient handwriting, difficulty with buttoning, and problems with tying shoelaces.

"School performance reveals that the child has attended nursery school and kindergarten and presently is in the third grade. He has "constant problems with his handwriting" since starting school.

"Past history and review of systems revealed at 3 years of age the child had an inguinal hernia repair and from 5 to 7 years of age there were three surgical procedures for an extraocular muscle imbalance. The acute infectious diseases of childhood include varicella and rubella. The child had lymphositosis at 7 years of age and is subject to exzema.

"Behaviorally Martin is stated to be hyperactive with a low frustration threshhold, tends to be impatient, has poor eating and sleep patterns. The youngster related during the examination his negative attitudes towards school.

"The family history revealed that the mother, aged 30 years, had cerebral meningitis with no untoward effects. Although it was not related to me initially, Martin described a rather tense relationship between his mother and himself and then stated that she has been hospitalized for the last 11 weeks because 'her mother doesn't love her.' Apparently there has been a similar 'nervous breakdown' prior to the present hospitalization. Mrs. — historically had evidence of an extraocular muscle imbalance and for this reason wore corrective glasses. The father, aged 32 years, stated that he had no problems but following my evaluation of his son in which I stated that there must be a genetic etiology for the small muscle coordination difficulties, Mr. — related that he had the exact clinical picture as Martin when he was of similar chronological age and on testing he too had significant small muscle coordination problems. The discussion with Mr. — ended by his stating 'well it appears that the apple doesn't fall far from the tree.' There is one sibling, Richard, aged 5 years, who does not have any significant problems.

"Physical examination of this 8 year, 7 month old child revealed a youngster who was tense and obviously disturbed by his mother's hospitalization. The child repeatedly expressed negative attitudes towards school and stated that he wanted to be a baseball player.

"This brown-haired, hazel-eyed child had a head circumference that measured 52 cm. and there was no evidence of an intracranial bruit and there was no measurable hypertelorism. Martin was consistently right-handed and right-footed and there was no evidence of right-left confusion. His fund of knowledge was normal, if not superior for his stated chronologic age. Auditory memory was superior for age and the child could consistently produce 8 to 9 digits forward without any difficulty. Reproductions of the Bender-Gestalt patterns were of poor quality and in part this was related to his deficient graphomotor coordination but in addition there appeared to be distortions which would suggest a mild perceptual problem with visuo-spatial difficulties. Graphomotor coordination was significantly deficient with poor formation and spacing of letters. Prehension revealed that the pencil was held in a rigid fashion in the right hand in which there was hyperextension of the distal interphalangeal joints of the index finger. With spelling Martin became so involved in the formation of letters that errors were produced but spelling was only slightly deficient for his present third grade placement. Number concepts were at grade level while reading was superior for age or grade placement and the child read with excellent cadence in a fluent fashion on at least the fourth grade level and there was excellent immediate and intermediate recall.

"Gait patterns were complicated by a mild pes planus but were otherwise unremarkable for regular, heel, and toe walking. There was a slight difficulty with tandem gait. Motor examination showed normal bulk, tone and strength of all muscle groups. The deep tendon reflexes were physiologic and the Babinski responses were normal. Sensory examination was normal for all modalities including touch, position, vibration, and cortical sensation. Cerebellar examination revealed a slight finger-nose-finger dysmetria on the left side while the right was performed in a normal fashion. This was in sharp contrast to a mild to moderate impairment of rapid alternating movements, such as the alternating performance of pronation and supination and there was a significant impairment of rapid succession movements, above all with both hands utilized simultaneously and with fatigue. The cerebellar deficit was most marked on the left side. Cranial nerve examination showed the residual scars from the previous extrocular muscle surgery.

"There was a slight convergent strabismus of the left eye and neither eye could be completely abducted, above all the left. The funduscopic examination was benign. The visual acuity was 20/20 in both eyes and the visual fields were normal to confrontation. Catching, throwing and kicking were all normally performed.

"In summary on neurologic examination this 8 year, 7 month old child showed evidence of a significant cerebellar deficit that primarily involved small muscle coordination and was most apparent in finger function. In addition there was involvement of other small muscle function, notably the extraocular muscles. With a deficit that is so specific to small muscle coordination a genetic etiology is most probable and on questioning and examination Mr. — has a similar problem. In addition there are emotional difficulties related to his mother's illness and recent hospitalization.

"It is mandatory that the school be made aware of Martin's neurologic deficit and that he be stimulated and not frustrated. I have discussed this at great length with Mr. — who will contact the school authorities."

Retrospective Analysis

Martin's case is significant for many reasons. (1) His blind neurologic examination confirmed the presence of cerebellar finding. Upon retrospective analysis, these findings were similar, if not identical, to the majority of dyslexics examined by Dr. Gold and considered to have "minimal cerebral dysfunction." However Martin was diagnosed as having a cerebellar dysfunction "with a deficit that is so specific to small muscle coordination a genetic etiology is most probable and on questioning and examination Mr. R. has a similar problem." (2) Martin appeared to more rapidly compensate for his reading dysmetria than for his dysmetric dyspraxia or graphomotor incoordination—highlighting the need to define the disorder underlying dyslexia as a unitary c-v sensory-motor dysmetria, i.e., dysmetric dyslexia and dyspraxia (DD or DDD) in dynamic equilibrium with compensatory forces.

Inasmuch as Martin's reading ability and reading scores were compensated, and became "normal" despite the presence of residual dysmetric c-v functioning, it soon became apparent that "dyslexia" could not justifiably be defined in terms of a variable, nonspecific and overdetermined symptom such as reading score. As a result of cases similar to Martin, the disorder called "dyslexia" was sharply distinguished from the symptom called "dyslexia" or "poor reading ability," and the definition and conceptualization of DD became independent of reading scores.

Interestingly, Dr. Gold did not elicit Martin's history of slow reading, reading reversals, and tracking difficulties. Would his final diagnosis have been different had he known that Martin was dyslexic and his leading dyslexic symptom was graphomotor incoordination?

(3) As noted in Dr. Gold's history, Mrs. R. had a history of "cerebral meningitis," strabismus, and severe emotional difficulties. Inasmuch as she denied having had similar reading, writing, and drawing difficulties as did her son when initially questioned by the author, and since the author had not yet correlated c-v dysfunction to emotional disorders, she was never examined for c-v dysfunction. In retrospect, this was a significant error—for she expressed feelings of inferiority despite a superior I.Q., had multiple phobias of heights, elevators, escalators, and planes, decompensated psychologically during stress periods, and experienced auditory hallucinations without the schizophrenic thinking and affective disturbances. Could her feelings of inferiority, phobias, auditory hallucinations, and hysterical psychosis have been somatically predisposed by c-v dysfunction? And is it possible that Mrs. R.'s auditory hallucinations were similar to those experienced by Linda's mother—Bonnie F. (Levinson, 1966)? Had Mrs. R. denied her c-v dyslexia and unwittingly led the author astray in what might be considered a countertransference oversight?

In a specific effort to comprehend the reasons why Dr. Gold diagnosed Martin as having a cerebellar dysfunction, and Linda (as well as Allen) as having "minimal cerebral dysfunction," their blind neurologic reports were analyzed and compared.

A careful review of Martin's blind neurologic findings indicated: (1) a history of hyperactivity and inattentiveness; (2) abnormal Bender-Gestalt designs due to graphomotor incoordination and visual-spatial difficulties; (3) a parent with similar graphomotor symptoms; (4) normal number concepts, deficient spelling, and superior reading level (however, omitted was the fact that Martin and Mr. R. both had significant reading reversals and reading difficulties in their early grades and that both remained "slow readers"); (5) significant cerebellar findings; (6) diagnosis: "with a deficit that is so specific to small muscle coordination, a genetic etiology is most probable."

A similar review of Linda's blind neurologic findings revealed: (1) a history of "hyperkinetic behavioral syndrome"; (2) abnormal Bender-Gestalt designs "suggestible of a perceptual problem with visuo-spatial difficulties"; (3) "number concepts were adequate for age while spelling and reading were slightly below average. None of these subjects showed gross deficiencies. Certainly there was no evidence of a true dyslexic syndrome"; (4) a parent with similar academic symptoms; (5) significant cerebellar findings; (6) diagnosis: "This youngster with a history of a hyperkinetic behavioral syndrome shows a mild to moderate perceptual problem as well as a mild cerebellar deficit. These findings would be consistent with a diagnosis of minimal cerebral dysfunction or minimal brain damage." (Inasmuch as Allen's blind neurologic findings and diagnosis were identical to Linda's, the two cases are grouped together and treated as "one" for the sake of convenience and simplification.)

A comparison of both cases indicated that the only difference between the two was the fact that Martin had more thoroughly compensated for his reading disorder than had Linda. Is it possible that this slight quantitative reading-score difference between the two cases was sufficient to have led Dr. Gold to diagnose Martin as having a genetic cerebellar deficit, and Linda as having "minimal cerebral dysfunction"? The answer to this question, interestingly enough, materialized during the qualitative data analysis of Stan P., Dr. Gold's case of benign paroxysmal vertigo.

Stan P.

Stan was 13 years old when brought to the author for the neuropsychiatric evaluation of his severe learning disabilities. Historical summary revealed Stan to be ambidextrous in a family without left-handed individuals. He had to be taught to crawl, stumbling was frequent during early walking, and he was found to be "pigeon-toed." Stan had difficulty learning to tie his shoe laces and button his clothes. His speech was slightly delayed, slurred, and stuttering was occasionally noticed. Toilet training was slow and enuresis was present until 12 years of age.

Stan's dyslexic nuclear symptomatic complex manifested itself as follows. His reading was slow, hesitant, and characterized by letter and word skipping, and poor visual and phonetic word retention. Guessing and confusion of similar appearing words was commonplace. When younger, he confused *b* and *d*, *was* and *saw*, and had been a "mirror writer." Writing, spelling, and math were still deficient. In addition, he experienced great difficulty and delay in learning to tell time and distinguish right from left. At 13, Stan still could not properly recall the months of the year in sequence, and frequently found it difficult to recall specific names and dates.

Neurologic examination revealed only c-v signs: swaying and vertigo during Romberg testing, slurred speech, hypotonia, head tilting, ocular and tandem dysmetria, and severe difficulty with bilateral finger-to-thumb sequencing. Bender-Gestalt designs were mildly deficient, and the Goodenough figure drawing was severely immature. An ENG performed at Lenox Hill Hospital revealed "direction fixed, positional nystagmus" as well as RVR-R (reduced vestibular response—right), during bilateral, bithermal caloric stimulation (Brookler, 1971).

Stan's case is significant in that Dr. Gold had followed him in neurologic consultation from 6 years, 10 months to 11 years of age for unilateral orbital headaches associated with vertigo. During this time span, Dr. Gold failed to recognize and/or elicit Stan's severe dyslexic symptoms, and believed he was an excellent student. On the basis of positive c-v signs, an abnormal caloric stimulation test, graphomotor incoordination, and abnormal Bender-Gestalt designs, Stan was diagnosed by Dr. Gold as having "benign paroxysmal vertigo or intermittent vestibular neuronitis."

What would Stan's diagnosis have been had Dr. Gold "blindly" examined him at 13 for severe academic disturbances? In an effort to answer this question the author thought it wise to analyze Dr. Gold's findings in Stan's case: "The acquisition of developmental milestones revealed that handedness has not been established in that he writes and eats with the right hand and throws and catches with the left. Gait was delayed until 17 months of age . . . At the present time he is an excellent student in the first grade . . . Physical examination revealed a bright, verbal youngster who was obviously superior in intellect for his stated chronological age . . . Spelling and number concepts were superior . . . The gait was characterized by the head tilting to the right and the head was maintained stiffly in this position. There was a tendency towards pes planus and genu recurvatum when standing, while when walking there was a tendency to toe in on the left. Motor examination revealed a generalized decrease in muscle tone. There was no evidence of a cerebellar deficit. Impression . . . Episodic vertigo—rule out vestibular dysfunction versus vascular anomalies involving the cerebellum or brain stem."

Four years later Dr. Gold noted: "Neurological examination revealed . . . a slight slurring of words . . . His reproductions of the Bender Gestalt patterns were of poor quality and in large part this was due to a slight impairment in graphomotor skills. These reproductions had irregular lines and poor angulations. Academic function was at grade level . . . Tandem gait was poorly performed . . . I could not delineate any evidence of a heat tilt which was previously noted . . . The entire clinical picture would be consistent with either a benign paroxysmal vertigo or intermittent vestibular neuronitis."

Retrospective Analysis

Upon analysis of Dr. Gold's meticulous and detailed neurologic findings, Stan was described as exhibiting right-sided unilateral orbital headaches associated with vertigo, photophobia, right-sided head tilting, an incomplete establishment of dominance, delayed acquisition of gait until 17 months of age, pes planus and genu recurvatum, left-sided toeing-in when walking, a generalized decrease in muscle tone, slight slurring of words, a slight impairment in graphomotor skills, deficient Bender-Gestalt patterns characterized by irregular lines and poor angulations, an initially normal caloric stimulation test, an abnormal EEG test, abnormal vestibular functioning on a repeat caloric stimulation test, and a mild and nonspecific abnormality on repeat EEG testing.

Of interest is the fact that on the weight of an initially normal caloric and rotation study, Dr. Gold ruled out a vestibular dysfunction underlying Stan's vertigo, assumed the existence of a convulsive disorder in the light of an abnormal EEG record, and placed Stan on 100 gm of Dilantin twice a day for six months. Because Stan's headaches and vertigo continued, his EEG and caloric stimulation tests were repeated in 1972. In view of the fact that Stan's second EEG showed only a mild and nonspecific abnormality, and his second caloric stimulation test revealed asymmetric vestibular responses to warm water stimulation, Dr. Gold ruled out convulsive and migraine disorders and deemed Stan's clinical picture as "most consistent with either a benign paroxysmal vertigo or intermittent vestibular neuronitis."* In addition, on the basis of neurologic findings similar, if not identical, to all previous dyslexic reports in which a cerebellar deficit was diagnosed, Dr. Gold in this report ruled out a cerebellar deficit.

In an attempt to summarize and harmonize Dr. Gold's neurologic "manifest content," the author reasoned as follows. Inasmuch as incomplete dominance, hyperactivity, distractability, graphomotor incoordination, abnormal visual-motor Bender-Gestalt functioning, spelling difficulties, and cerebellar deficits are found in dyslexic cases variously diagnosed by Dr. Gold as minimal cerebral dysfunction, minimal brain damage, cerebellar deficit, and vestibular dysfunction, it seemed reasonable for the author to assume the existence of a c-v common pathophysiologic denominator underlying dyslexia. Considering that specific hard and fast pathognomonic cortical signs were found statistically absent in this rather large blind neurologic dyslexic sample, it seemed reasonable to further assume that there is no primary cortical defect or dysfunction in dyslexia until proven otherwise.

In retrospect, Dr. Gold's neurologic findings and diagnostic reasoning in dyslexia was found to be identical to those utilized by the author prior to his retrospective study. Interestingly enough, the author's retrospective analysis of Dr. Gold's findings and diagnoses had merely repeated Dr. Jan Frank's retrospective analysis of the author's data. Needless to say, both analyses revealed the crucial but denied role of the c-v circuits in dyslexia, as well as the tendency to attribute dyslexia to a cerebral dysfunction—despite an absence of cerebral signs.

Keith

Keith is an exceptionally bright, 11-year-old, right-handed sixth-grader examined by the author neuropsychiatrically following psychological testing in which behavior difficulties were noted in association with hyperactivity, distractability, and academic disturbances—despite a WISC FSIQ = 132, PIQ = 131, and VIQ = 127.

* Stan P.'s caloric stimulation test was performed by Dr. Malcolm Schvey, Columbia-Presbyterian Hospital, New York, New York. Dr. Schvey stated, "The two vestibular labyrinths are symmetrical with cold water but asymmetrical with hot water. This finding is consistent with the diagnosis of benign paroxysmal vertigo."

His dyslexic nuclear symptomatic complex manifested itself as follows. He experienced difficulty learning to read since first grade, and frequently reversed *b* and *d*, *saw* and *was*, *on* and *no*, etc. Visual and phonetic recall for letters and words were deficient. Often he would confuse similar appearing small words while reading larger words with greater facility and accuracy. Keith's spelling and math performance were deficient, as was his graphomotor coordination. For example, his writing was poorly formed and spaced, and drifted off the horizontal. Sentences often ran together without proper spacing and capitalization. Periods and commas were frequently omitted. Interestingly enough, his Bender-Gestalt and Goodenough figure drawings were exceptionally well executed and appeared consistent with his artistic talent.

Developmental milestones were normal, except for a history of hyperactivity, distractability, impulsivity, and motor incoordination. For example, he experienced difficulty learning to tie his shoe laces, button his clothes, and use a knife and fork, and was described by relatives as "extremely clumsy" and "forever falling and bumping into things." In addition, his speech was characterized by mild slurring and articulation and word-hesitation difficulty. He was found to exhibit sequential memory difficulties as well: "If you tell him to do several things, he'll forget one or two and even do something else. . . . He also forgets his spelling and multiplication tables. At times he'll forget what he just said or what you just said and will either repeat himself or ask me to repeat myself." He still exhibited difficulty recalling the months of the year in sequence and was able to "remember" right and left only by virtue of knowing that his watch was on his left hand.

Keith was orphaned at an early age and his emotional development was found to be exceptionally traumatized. Upon neurologic examination, he evidenced only c-v signs: positive Romberg with right-sided drifting and a subjective sensation of a spinning vertigo, finger-to-nose, finger-to-finger, heel-to-toe, and ocular dysmetria. Interestingly enough, he was not found to be hyperactive or distractable during the one-to-one examination.

In summary, Keith's dyslexic nuclear symptomatic complex was characterized by severe reading, writing, math, spelling, memory, and grammatical disturbances, situation-specific overactivity and distractability, compensated speech and directional functioning, and normal or compensated Bender-Gestalt and Goodenough figure drawings as well as abnormal c-v neurologic findings. Although Keith was subjected to severely traumatizing emotional difficulties throughout his childhood, these psychogenic factors were found to be either secondary and/or independent dyslexic variables.

Keith was referred for "blind" ENG and audiographic evaluations to Dr. Noel Cohen at New York University. Interestingly, his first ENG was normal and the second revealed "a left beating positional nystagmus in the supine and right lateral positions." Upon blind neurologic examination, he was found by Dr. Carter to have minimal cerebellar findings and diagnosed "minimal brain dysfunction." The complete blind ENG and neurologic reports will be presented.

Dr. Cohen's Blind Electronystagmographic Evaluation

December 17, 1971: "This eleven year old boy has been a behavior problem at home and school. He apparently is the product of a normal pregnancy and delivery and has no history of unusual infections, high fever or trauma. His motor development has been normal.

"Examination shows the external ears, canals and drums to be normal. The nose and throat are unremarkable.

"I could find no spontaneous or positional nystagmus. The equilibrium and gait are normal.

"The enclosed audiogram shows the hearing to be equal and normal in both ears.

"Vestibular function tests were performed at University Hospital. The ENG showed neither spontaneous nor positional nystagmus. The responses were equal and normal to bithermal caloric tests.

"In summary, Keith has no demonstrable abnormalities of the ears or vestibular systems."

February 19, 1972: "Re-evaluation of Keith was carried out on 1-31-72. On this examination, the ENG showed a left-beating positional nystagmus in the supine and right lateral positions. The responses to caloric test were again normal.

"The above results seem to agree with your predictions."

Dr. Carter's Blind Neurologic Evaluation

"At your very kind suggestion, I had occasion to see Keith in neurological consultation on April 11, 1972 because of a history of his having difficulty with school work despite what is considered to be a very high I.Q. Keith was brought to my office by his brother-in-law (his legal guardian) Mr. —. This youngster's history is well known to you, and does not bear repetition at this time. I would emphasize a few minor facts in the history: specifically, Keith has always been clumsy but despite that, is good at sports. He had right-left confusion as a smaller child, but this has corrected itself.

"The family and past histories were of significance in that the father died at 53 of cirrhosis of the liver after a long history of alcohol. The mother died in her 40s of Parkinsonism.

"On examination, I noted an alert, pleasant, big cooperative boy. His head measured 53½ cm. The positive findings were very minimal. There was a very slight unsteadiness on finger-to-nose testing, particularly on the left and he had a very minimal impairment of succession movements—the left more than the right. Quite honestly, I was not particularly impressed by his degree of cerebellar dysfunction. The remainder of his neurological examination was entirely normal. His drawings were well done.

It was my impression (based on history) that this boy could be classified as having minimal brain dysfunction with his major deficits in the areas of learning, and to a lesser extent, in the area of behavior.

"I think it makes good sense to have him continue at the C—— School. This is a good outfit that has done well with children of this sort in the past. I suppose he should continue on his Mellaril if it is thought to help him. In general, however, I think the school setting and the emphasis on structured existence will be more important to this boy than medications."

Retrospective Insights

Upon retrospective analysis, Keith's case illustrates that:

1. severe learning difficulties may be accompanied by absent or "minimal" cerebellar signs and normal Bender-Gestalt designs and Goodenough drawings;

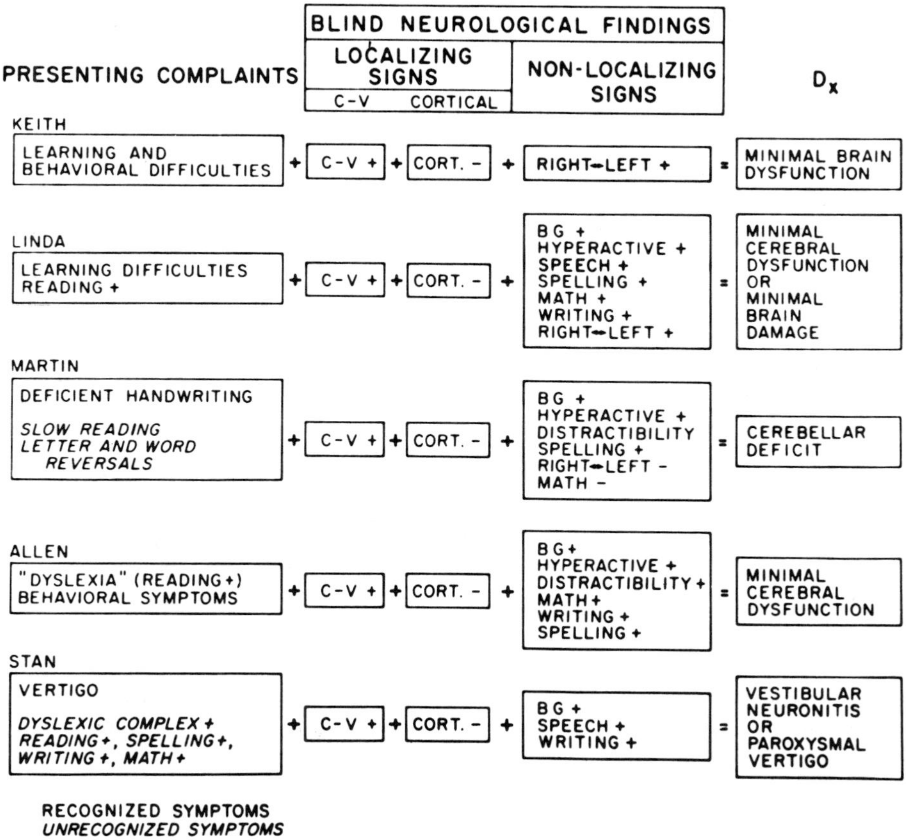

Fig. C–1. Summary of the abstracted "blind" neurologic findings in the first five dyslexic cases. Although positive c-v and negative cortical findings characterize all these "blindly" examined dyslexic cases, the resulting diagnoses vary from minimal brain dysfunction to minimal cerebral dysfunction to cerebellar deficit to vestibular neuronitis or paroxysmal vertigo. As a result of this retrospective data analysis, the author was forced to conclude that the final neurologic diagnosis is often highly dependent upon the presenting symptom and highly independent of the cerebellar findings described.

2. severe underlying emotional difficulties may significantly contribute to hyperactive-like symptoms and drastically complicate the somatic source of the learning difficulties, and yet act as secondary rather than primary etiologic determinants;

3. one negative ENG may be insufficient to rule out c-v dysfunction, and serial ENGs may be as necessary in diagnosing vestibular dysfunction as are serial ECGs and EEGs in the diagnosis of heart and central nervous system dysfunction, respectively;

4. negative ENGs in the presence of positive c-v clinical signs may point to

the presence of compensatory regulatory mechanisms and/or inadequacies in the ENG technique;

5. "minimal cerebellar" signs are scientifically as significant as are "severe cerebellar" signs, and should not be discarded—especially in the complete absence of any other neurologic signs (i.e., negative cortical signs);

6. "minimal cerebellar deficit" or "minimal brain dysfunction" may result in "severe" symptoms and dysfunctioning—clearly demonstrating that "minimal" brain findings are not minimal to the individual manifesting them.

Debbie

Debbie is a 6-year-old brought to the author by her parents for suspected "visual perceptual problems." Upon examination, she was noted to reverse letters, words, and numbers when reading and writing, and still confused right and left. Her Bender-Gestalt designs indicated marked rotations, angle formation, and articulation errors. The neurologic examination was otherwise normal, except for strabismus and possible tandem imbalance and dysmetria.

Inasmuch as Debbie's neurologic findings were "minimal" and of questionable significance, she was referred to Dr. Carter for independent neurologic evaluation and found to be "a normal child." An ENG performed at New York University Medical Center found "no abnormality of auditory or vestibular function."

Dr. Cohen's Blind Electronystagmographic Report

"As you know, the mother of this six year old girl reports that an Army eye doctor stated that Debbie might have a visual perception difficulty in addition to her squint. The mother reports that Debbie scored slightly low in a reading preparedness test in nursery school but appears to be learning to read well. She denies any significant illnesses, hearing loss or difficulty with equilibrium.

"Examination shows no abnormalities of the external ears, drums or canals. The nose and throat are unremarkable. There is a convergent strabismus but no nystagmus.

"The enclosed audiogram shows the hearing to be equal and normal bilaterally.

"Vestibular function tests done at University Hospital showed normal responses to calorics and neither spontaneous nor positional nystagmus. Debbie had difficulty following the optokinetic calibrations signal, but this was probably related to her strabismus. Her eyes were not tested separately.

"In summary, I could find no abnormality of auditory or vestibular function in this six year old girl."

Dr. Carter's Blind Neurologic Evaluation

"At your very kind suggestion, I saw little Debbie on October 28, because of the complaints from the parents indicating that the child was said to have impaired visual perceptual function and to have right-left confusion. This youngster is well known to you, and her history does not bear repetition at this time. I can only note that at four years of age an optometrist suggested that she might be having visual perceptual difficulties. The child has done well in kindergarden and is now in first grade. Some right-left confusion was noted when she was in kindergarden, but this is of no real significance.

"The family and past histories are of significance in that the father is a physician and the mother is an ex-speech therapist.

"The examination proper was entirely within normal limits. Debbie proved to be an alert, petite, bright-acting child who had a mild degree of hirsutism. She is left-handed. Her head measured 51 cm. I could find nothing on my testing which would indicate any impairment of central nervous system function.

"It was my impression that this was a normal child."

Follow-up Evaluation

Debbie was re-evaluated by the author at ages 7 and 8, and her academic or "dyslexic-like" symptoms appeared to intensify with age, grade, and work-load, despite an exceptionally high I.Q. and absent psychogenic determinants. For example, she was still forced to use her finger as a marker during reading in order to minimize tracking disturbances and word scrambling. Both visual and phonetic word memory were still found to be deficient. Spelling and math performance were below grade level. Her Bender-Gestalt designs and neurologic findings remained suspect. Moreover, in order to compensate for her persisting right/left uncertainty, she developed the following technique: "It's hard to remember right and left. But I learned a trick. I squeeze the hand I write with and I know it's my left hand. So the other hand has to be my right hand."

Follow-up psychiatric examination ruled out emotional, cultural, socio-economic, and educational factors as playing a primary etiologic role in Debbie's apparent dyslexic nuclear symptomatic complex."

Debbie remained an enigma for several years. How could she manifest "dyslexic-like" symptoms without any evidence suggesting a primary causation? Is it possible for Debbie's c-v signs to be so minimal and/or so compensated as to have escaped neurologic and ENG detection? In retrospect, and on the basis of significant clinical neurologic experience and ENG expertise, it seemed more than justified to assume that the dyslexic nuclear symptomatic complex may exist in the presence of minimal and/or compensated c-v signs and normal ENGs, and that this complex does not occur in "normal" individuals.

Mark

Before concluding the case presentations, the author thought it wise to provide the reader with an informal case presentation in which Dr. Jan Frank acted as a "control" neurologist for the author. Mark was a bright 7-year-old boy with reading, writing, spelling and speech difficulties as well as "hyperactive-like" behavior. He was initially referred to Dr. Jan Frank for neuropsychiatric evaluation. In the presence of severe family conflict and an absence of neurologic findings, Dr. Frank diagnosed Mark's academic and behavioral symptoms as being of a primary emotional origin.

Six years later, Mark's younger sister was brought to the author for psychiatric consultation, and "by accident" was found to be a reading-score-compensated dyslexic with right/left uncertainty, spelling difficulties, and graphomotor as well as perceptual-motor incoordination similar to that displayed by Martin. Upon further historical exploration, Mark's father, a physician, appeared to have been dyslexic as well. In view of these surprising findings, Mark was neuropsychiatrically re-examined and found to have typical c-v signs: ocular tracking nystagmus, dysdiadochokinesis, tandem dysmetria, and a partially compensated "slurred" speech with difficulty reproducing words such as disestablishmentarian without reversing the phonetic sequence. His ENG was significantly abnormal as were his blurring speeds. Mark's Bender-Gestalt designs revealed significant abnormalities compatible with a c-v-determined graphomotor incoordination. Mark's sister and father were similarly examined and both were found to be dyslexic.

Needless to say, this case highlights an intriguing paradox. For although Dr. Frank corroborated by the author's observation that the so-called soft signs in dyslexia were of c-v origin, he inadvertently overlooked these very same signs during his neuropsychiatric examination of Mark. As a result of c-v denial mechanisms, he mistakenly diagnosed Mark's academic and behavioral difficulties as being of a primary emotional origin. Due to the "accidental" analysis of Mark's case, the author clearly recognized the subjective unconscious forces affecting both the so-called objective neurologic and psychiatric examinations and the decisions as to cause and effect relationships.

The experience gained from the "blind" neurologic examinations and the DD research effort would require or demand that each and every patient referred for either neurologic and/or psychiatric consultation be viewed as a neuropsychiatric unknown, and that all presenting symptoms be analyzed as to (1) primary and direct neurophysiologic expressions, (2) secondary mental expressions of a primary neurologic dysfunction, and (3) mental expressions of primary emotional conflicts independent of (1) and (2).

Summary

The author's "dyslexic career" was meaningfully triggered only after Dr. Jan Frank discovered that the so-called soft signs characterizing the dyslexic data mass presented in Chapter 2 were of c-v, rather than cortical, origin, and after the author's imperception or denial of this c-v dyslexic correlation was "neuropsychologically" resolved and pursued. Once the initial c-v dyslexic insight took hold, it became scientifically obvious, and even simple, to recognize the c-v dysfunction characterizing the vast majority of dyslexics neurologically examined.

So amazing and surprising was this personally experienced scientific phenomenon called c-v denial and cortical confabulation, that its mechanisms and reason-for-being remained an intriguing research stimulus and curiosity throughout the entire course of this dyslexic endeavor. In an effort to comprehend the nature and source of these mechanisms, the author reasoned as follows. If, indeed, the c-v dyslexic correlation and insight was truly correct, and even "easy to see," then why had this correlation and insight remained so completely hidden from clinical view? Had this c-v oversight been caused by chance alone, or had it been motivated by the same active and dynamic defensive forces found characterizing so-called non-scientific slips, errors, and everyday oversights?

Since the author's psychoanalytically geared clinical training and experience had repeatedly demonstrated to him the significance and validity of psychic determinism and its unconsciously motivated source, it seemed only reasonable to assume that if mental events are determined by motives rather than by chance, then psychically motivated mechanisms must be determining and maintaining scientific slips and errors in a manner analogous to the mechanisms motivating dreams, neurotic symptoms, and "Freudian slips" or errors. In line with this reasoning, the author attempted to analyze and discover his own unconsciously motivated mechanisms determining the c-v denial and cortical confabulation initially found permeating his retrospective sample of 1,000 (Chapter 2). In fact, were it not for the analysis and resolution of the defensive "bias" mechanisms creating and maintaining the dyslexic riddle, the retrospective and follow-up studies would have led nowhere.

The analysis of the blind neurologic data in many ways may be viewed as merely a scientific re-enactment and application of the very same reasoning technique utilized by the author to analyze his initially blind dyslexic data in the retrospective study. In fact, the reader might be fully justified in assuming that the validity of the dyslexic insights and conclusions derived from the analysis of the retrospective study is directly proportional to the validity of the conclusions derived from the analysis of the blind neurologic data. In summary, the analysis of the blind neurological data revealed (1) that 21/22, or 96%, of the cases blindly examined had evidence of a c-v dysfunction, (2) that the statistical and neurophysiologic significance of this c-v dysfunction in dyslexia was either denied or not objectively recognized by the neurologic examiners, and (3) that the presence of c-v dysfunction in dyslexia was unwittingly utilized to conclude that dyslexia was of cortical origin—despite the statistical absence of cortical signs.

APPENDIX D

Caloric Vestibular Stimulation and the Electronystagmographic Methodology

The blind ENG data has been quantitatively and qualitatively analyzed, and the summarized results presented in Chapter 3. In this appendix, the reader is provided with (1) Barany's historical discovery of the caloric stimulation test of unilateral vestibular functioning, and (2) a step-by-step description of the current caloric ENG methodology, so that the diagnostic parameters utilized for measuring c-v functioning can be more meaningfully understood, and the blind ENG data more independently and specifically evaluated.

So magnificently clear and lucid is Barany's personal description of his discovery of caloric vestibular stimulation that anything less than a direct quotation from his Nobel Lecture (1916) will do the subject and the reader a great injustice. Later investigators merely utilized electrical methods for measuring the nystagmus induced by caloric vestibular stimulation, added additional diagnostic parameters, and called the process Electronystagmography (ENG).

"The rotary method investigated by Breuer stimulated both sides at once and was, therefore, not satisfactory for clinical use where one-sided testing was nearly always required. The galvanic reaction method discovered by Purkinje and further studied by Hitzig and others did not give results which were suitable for clinical use, and this is still the case today. The caloric reaction method which I discovered was the first to bring light into this obscurity. Only after its discovery was a methodical examination of the function of the semicircular canals made possible. Permit me now to tell you about the history of its discovery.

"As a young otologist I worked in Professor Politzer's clinic in Vienna. Among my patients there were many who required syringing of the ears. A number of them complained afterwards of vertigo. Obviously I examined their eyes and I noticed in doing this that there was nystagmus in a certain direction. I made a note of this. After a time, when I had collected about twenty of these observations, I compared them one with another and was amazed always to find the same note. I then realized that some general principle must be implied, but at the time I did not understand it. Chance came to my aid. One of my patients, whose ears I was syringing, said to me: 'Doctor, I only get giddy when the water is not warm enough. When I do my own ears at home and use warm enough water I never get giddy.' I then called the nurse and asked her to get me warmer water for the syringe. She maintained that it was already warm enough. I replied that if the patient found it too cold we should conform to his wish. The next time she brought me very hot water in the bowl. When I syringed the patient's ear he shouted: 'But, Doctor, this water is much too hot and now I am giddy again.' I quickly observed his eyes and noticed that the nystagmus was in an exactly opposite direction from the previous one when cold water had been used. It came to me then in a flash that obviously the temperature of the water was responsible for the nystagmus. From this I immediately drew certain conclusions. If the temperature of the water was really responsible then water at exactly body temperature should cause neither nystagmus nor vertigo. An experiment confirmed this conclusion. Furthermore, I said to myself, if it is the temperature of the water, nystagmus must be caused in normal cases also and not only in cases of suppurating ears. This I was also able to prove." [From Barany's Nobel Lecture (1916) entitled "Some New Methods for Functional Testing of the Vestibular Apparatus and the Cerebellum."]

Electronystagmography

Electronystagmography (ENG) is an electrical recording technique for the objective detection and measurement of either spontaneous and/or induced clinical and subclinical forms of nystagmus. The ENG monitoring of eye movements is made possible by virtue of the positive corneal potential relative to the retina. As a result of this difference in potential, all corneal or ocular deflection movements are readily detectable by means of electrodes placed on the outer margins of the eyes and a neutral central electrode tuned in to the steady retinal potential.

Dubois-Raymond in 1849 is credited with first describing the corneoretinal potential differences, which later investigators found to be between 300 and 1,000 mV. The source of this potential is considered to be metabolic changes in the receptive layer of the retina and adjacent structures. Spontaneous or induced nystagmus results in an eye deflection (slow component) toward the pick-up electrodes and a corresponding increase in voltage until the rapid return sweep of the nystagmus creates a rapidly falling voltage slope and the cycle continues.

The ENG recorder serves merely to amplify and convert this relatively small corneoretinal potential to a directly proportional recordable signal, i.e., pen deflection.

Nystagmus

Ocular deflections must be differentiated from "true" vestibular nystagmus. Nystagmus of vestibular origin is typically a rapid involuntary oscillation of the eyeball, and characteristically has a slow beat in one direction and a rapid return sweep in the opposite direction; the slope of the voltage amplitude is proportional to the speed of the sweep.

Calibration

Five periorbital electrodes are utilized to record horizontal and vertical nystagmus: two horizontal, two vertical and one ground electrode placed just above the bridge of the nose. Prior to testing for positional and/or induced nystagmus, eye movements are calibrated by adjusting the sensitivity of the electronystagmographic recorder so that a preset 20° horizontal or vertical excursion of the eyes corresponds to a 20 mm amplitude excursion of the recording pen. This calibration of 1° eye movement/1 mm is then utilized to measure and calculate the degrees per second of eye movement deflections during the ENG procedure.

The Lenox Hill Hospital Methodology

Inasmuch as 27 of the 70 completed blind ENGs were referred to Lenox Hill Hospital, and since this center utilized the greatest number of measurable parameters, the author thought it wise to describe in detail the methodology, standardization, and terminology used at this particular institution.

Positional and Spontaneous Nystagmus

Positional and spontaneous nystagmus are tested with the eyes closed in the following positions:

1. Supine 0°—where the patient is lying flat on his back
2. Supine 0° with the patient's head turned as far as possible to the left; and then repeated with the head turned to the right
3. With the patient lying completely on his left side; and then repeated with the patient lying completely on his right side
4. The patient is placed in a supine 30° position for the last recording of positional nystagmus*

Following the above tests, the patient is instructed to open his eyes and ENG recordings are taken for approximately 15 seconds.

Caloric Stimulation

The ears are irrigated first with cool (30° C) and then with warm (44° C) water and six ENG recordings are taken of the patient's bithermal caloric responses. These six ENG recordings correspond to six caloric procedures:

1. 30° C water is infused into the patient's left ear
2. 30° C water is infused into the patient's right ear
3. 30° C water is infused simultaneously into both ears
4. 44° C water is infused into the patient's left ear
5. 44° C water is infused into the patient's right ear
6. 44° C water is infused simultaneously into both ears

A water bath maintains water at 30° and 44° C and is capable of infusing a preset water volume at a fixed rate into each ear independently or into both ears simultaneously. A few minutes are allowed to lapse between caloric tests so that vestibular recovery and re-equilibrium occur. For caloric responses less than 5°/sec, ice water is used to stimulate the ear and an ENG recording is taken.

Interpretation of the Electronystagmographic Data

1. The presence of spontaneous and/or positional nystagmus is considered inconsistent with a normal vestibular system.

* When nystagmus occurs in the supine 30° position, it must be added or subtracted from the nystagmus which occurs during caloric stimulation.

2. The normal nystagmic vestibular response to warm and cool (bilateral) water stimulation falls within a range equal to 5°–25°/second. A nystagmus response of less than 5°/second is considered hypoactive and a nystagmic response greater than 25°/second is considered hyperactive. For nystagmic responses less than 5°/second, ice water stimulation and ENG recording is useful to rule out the presence or absence of a nonresponsive or "dead" labyrinth.

3. "Central dysrhythmia" is defined as an irregular nystagmic response to caloric vestibular stimulation and is indicative of deficient central or cerebellar modulation of the caloric stimulation and ocular motor response.

Cool water irrigation of the test ear induces rapid nystagmic beats to the opposite ear and warm water stimulation provokes a rapid nystagmic response to the same side as the test ear.

In order to obtain additional parameters as to the functional integrity and balance of the c-v system, Jonkees (1964) developed formulae comparing RVR (reduced vestibular response) and DP (directional preponderance):

4. The right ear's overall ENG reactivity to bithermal caloric stimulation with the left ear's ENG reactivity to bithermal stimulation or reduced vestibular response (RVR) or labyrinthine preponderance. If the numbers 1, 2, 3, and 4 are assigned to the traditional caloric irrigation sequence, i.e., 1 = left cool (30° C), 2 = right cool (30° C), 3 = left warm (44° C) and 4 = right warm (44° C), then the difference in excitability between left and right ears to caloric stimulation can be expressed as the percentage of total excitability:

$$\text{RVR} = \frac{(1+3)-(2+4)}{1+2+3+4} \times 100\%$$

When the right labyrinth is less excitable than the left one, a positive value is obtained; a negative value is obtained in the reverse case. An RVR of less than 30% is considered normal.

5. The electronystagmographic responses of bithermal stimulation resulting in rapid beats to the left with those bithermal stimuli producing rapid beats to the right, or directional preponderance (DP). The difference between the right- and the left-beating nystagmus can be expressed as the percentage of the total excitability:

$$\text{DP} = \frac{(1+4)-(2+3)}{1+2+3+4} \times 100\%$$

A directional preponderance to the right results in positive values, and negative values reflect a directional preponderance to the left. A directional preponderance of less than 30% is considered normal.

6. Simultaneous bilateral stimulation—procedure 3 of caloric testing. Five minutes after the onset of the last 30° C caloric stimulus (procedure 2), both ears are simultaneously irrigated for 1 minutes with 250 ml/ear of water at 30° C, and an ENG recording is taken for 30 seconds. Nystagmus is calculated from a 10-second strip containing maximum eye movement deflection.

Following (step 5) infusion of 44° C water into the patient's right ear, the above procedure is repeated utilizing 44° C water (step 6).

Theoretically, a normally functioning vestibular system will not react with nys-

Table D–1. Electronystagmographic Responses to Simultaneous Bilateral Bithermal Stimulation (Brookler, 1971)

Type	Definition	Significance
1	No nystagmus (<2.5°/sec.)	1. Equally normal vestibular responses 2. Equally reduced vestibular responses 3. Equally nonreacting vestibular responses 4. Equally hyperactive vestibular responses
2	Nystagmus in opposite directions (>2.5°/sec.)	RVR
3	Nystagmus in the same direction (>2.5°/sec.)	Pathological DP
4	Nystagmus from only one stimulus (>2.5°/sec.)	Vestibular abnormality

For nystagmus to be significant in the simultaneous bithermal stimulation testing, it must be 2.5°/second or greater.

tagmus (or vertigo) when simultaneously and bilaterally stimulated with 30° C or 44° C water. This added procedure of simultaneous bithermal caloric stimulation was found to be more sensitive than the Fitzgerald-Hallpike individual bithermal caloric stimulation, and is used as an additional caloric test parameter.

The ENG responses to simultaneous bilateral bithermal stimulation were defined by Dr. Brookler as shown in Table D–1.

Comparison of Positive Electronystagmographic Parameters as a Function of Hospital Center

Although 90% of the blind ENGs were abnormal, and thus confirmed the author's c-v–dyslexic correlations, there appeared to be some interhospital methodologic scatter, and resulting differences in their reported abnormal parameters. For example, the analysis of the Lenox Hill Hospital blind ENG dyslexic data revealed a 96% (26/27) positive or abnormal ENG yield. However, were it not for the simultaneous bithermal criteria utilized for measuring abnormal vestibular reactivity, 10 of the 27 cases might have been considered ENG normal, and as a result the percentage positive yield would have been significantly reduced to 63% (17/27).

Interestingly enough, most of the other major hospital centers did not utilize this parameter in their ENG determinations. As a result, the author wondered, If indeed the simultaneous bithermal technique is truly a highly sensitive indicator of c-v dysfunction, then why has not this parameter been utilized by the majority of other hospital centers performing ENGs? Would not their percent positive yield be higher? Or is it that this parameter is still in its experimental stage and requires further validation and research? To further study the interhospital varia-

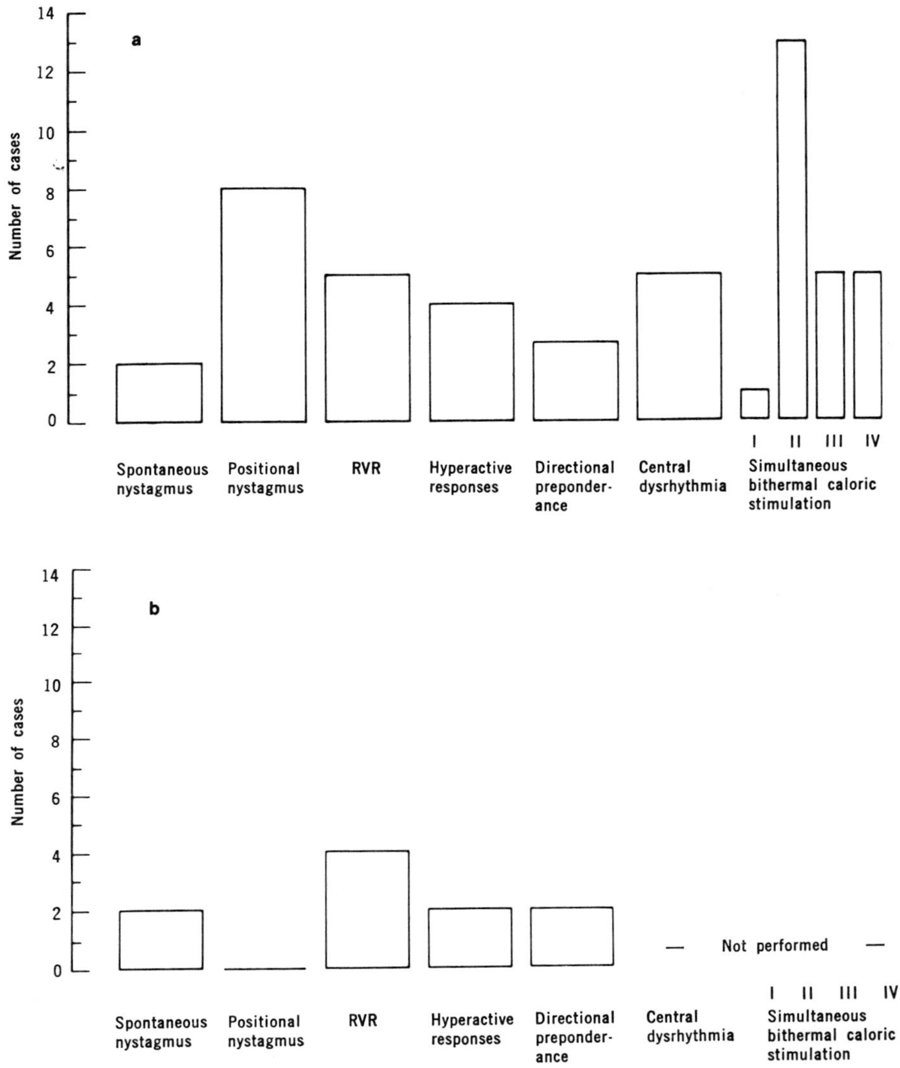

Fig. D–1. Frequency distribution of blind ENG parameters as a function of hospital center: (*a*) Lenox Hill Hospital (27 cases); (*b*) New York Hospital (13 cases); (*c*) Manhattan Eye and Ear Hospital (10 cases); (*d*) Mt. Sinai Hospital (5 cases).

tions as well as the spectrum of currently utilized ENG parameters, the abnormal ENG parameters were analyzed (Fig. D–1) as a function of hospital center, and compared with one another. In addition, the author is currently attempting to (1) re-standardize the ENG methodology utilizing DD and non-DD individuals as controls; (2) correlate positive and negative ENG parameters with positive and negative c-v and/or DD signs and symptoms; and (3) expand the ENG parameters

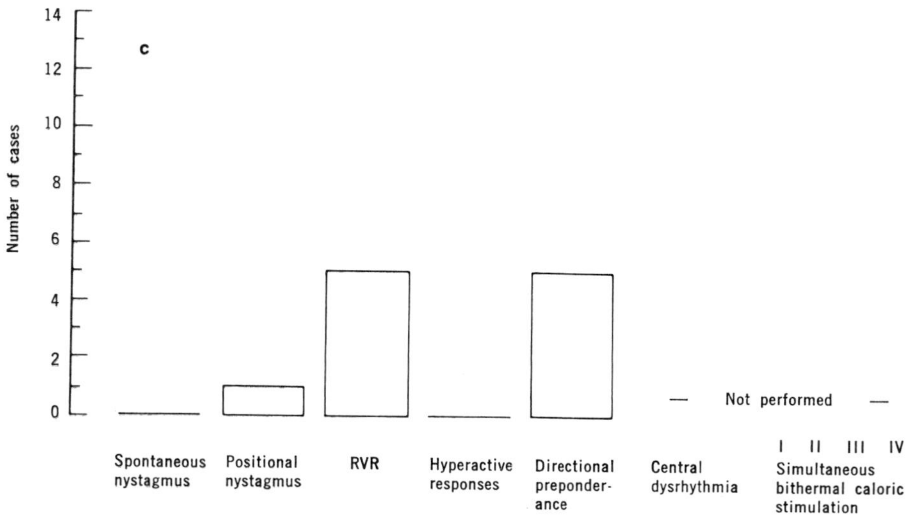

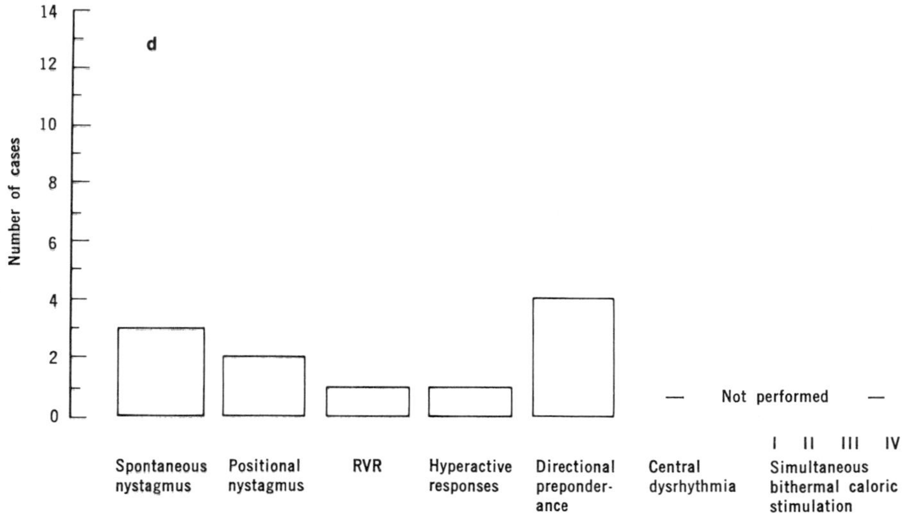

and technique so as to obtain higher yields of more reliable and consistent ENG findings in DD.

Needless to say, prior to this DD research effort, ENG-tested c-v "normal" and abnormal individuals had not been adequately analyzed for c-v dyslexic symptomatology. Thus many so-called normal ENG controls may not have been truly c-v normal. It is hoped that this new ENG study will more clearly define the ENGs of DD children, and provide additional insights into predicting c-v and DD symptoms on the basis of ENG findings.

APPENDIX E

Dyslexia and So-Called Normal Neurologic Examinations

Holly and John were referred to the author for both academic and emotional symptoms, and they were found to have obvious c-v signs and DD. Prior neurologic examinations by Drs. Bernard Cohen and Hart Peterson, respectively, did not reveal either academic symptoms or positive neurologic findings. The presence of historical and neurologic variations and contradictions as a function of examiner was found to be rather commonplace, and the significance of this "scrambling" is specifically discussed in Chapter 13.

Holly

Blind Neurologic Findings

"I examined Holly on October 22, 1976. Her mother's history was that her difficulty began in April, 1976 about six months after her tonsils were removed. She apparently had fluid in the middle ear on the right side which was tapped. She was then well for about a week when she had an episode of dizziness which lasted for about a half hour. During the episode she walked into a wall. This has recurred about 5 times since April, the last episode coming two weeks prior to admission. On several occasions the dizziness has led to vomiting. She apparently was examined by Dr. — who told them of a negative neurological examination and an EEG at Wycoff Hospital which was negative. Skull x-rays were apparently not done.

"She has a past history of hyperactivity which has since receded and had a head injury two years ago but was well in the interim.

"On examination Holly was alert and cooperative. Fields and fundi were normal. Pupils were found regular and equal and reacted well to light. Her eye movements were full and there was no significant nystagmus in any gaze position, or behind Frenzel glasses in any head position. Palate, tongue and voice were normal. Motor power, gait tone and coordination were normal. Reflexes were symmetrical and sensation was intact.

"*Impression:* Episodic vertigo. She has no evidence of CNS involvement now. Skull films were done which were negative. My impression is that this is on a peripheral basis and in my experience it will disappear spontaneously. She certainly seems to fit exactly in the series of Cotte-Rittaud and I thank you for bringing this article to my attention. On history and examination her episodes do not appear to be seizures, nor due to a posterior fossa tumor. I believe she can be followed for development of further symptoms, if they occur."

John

"John, who was the second born child to a healthy 22 year old woman, following a normal pregnancy, was delivered at term and had a 'normal birth weight.' His early development was considered to be normal, however, he was very overactive even before he was ambulatory and the child was described as 'he never walked, he ran.' He was oblivious to dangers, but otherwise healthy. Early developmental landmarks were considered to have been fairly normal with the exception of speech, which was somewhat late in developing. His father recalls that he had not spoken phrases by his second birthday.

"Recently . . . he was evaluated by Dr. — who subsequently had psychological tests carried out by Dr. —. Although the specifics are not available to me, on the WISC and Bender, there apparently were some organic signs with generally normal intelligence. Hence, his referral to my office. Further historical notes are that John can sit and watch television and is apparently doing well in school, both academically and behaviorally. He has only a few friends, but does well with them and did well the preceding 2 years in . . . school. John's gross and fine motor coordination are considered to have been normal, although there continue to be some reversals in letter writing at school. Curiously, John is the only left hander in his family.

"In my office, John was an obviously fidgity boy, who interrupted frequently and was up and out of his chair on several occasions. Nevertheless, he was able to inhibit his hyperactivity when he was engaged or some limits set. His weight was 23.5 kg. and the height 122 cm. Speech revealed a very mild dysarthria. Examination of his gait revealed him to be normal on free walking and running, on toes, on heels and in tandem. He hopped well on either foot. Examination of the cranial nerves revealed a head circumference of 53 cm. The optic fundi were normal. Extraoccular movements were full and conjugate and facial motility was normal. Hearing was intact. There were no adventitious movements of the outstretched arms. Rapid alternating movements were well carried out. Rapid, repetitive finger tapping and sequential finger tapping movements were carried out within the normal limits for a child of 7, bilaterally. Reflexes were symmetrical, without pathological responses. The toes were downgoing bilaterally and sensory function was intact. John missed the first 3 lateralized parts on his own body, but once oriented, was able to identify the next two correctly.

"In summary, John is a 6½ year old boy with a history of developmental hyperactivity, with a normal neurological examination."

The analysis of a series of dyslexic case reports, illustrated by Debbie, Stan P., and Mark in Appendix C, as well as by Hollie and John, has clearly demonstrated that resistance or bias forces have tended to scramble one's recognition of either the panorama of the dyslexic symptomatic complex and/or its underlying c-v pathogenesis. If, indeed, outstanding clinicians are prone to c-v denial and the resulting errors, might their criticism of the author's c-v–dyslexic correlation be similarly influenced by these very same resistance forces? Might we not assume that the diagnostic dyslexic riddle, or the absence of specific pathognomonic neurologic signs in dyslexia, has been significantly determined by c-v denial and perhaps cortical confabulation resistance mechanisms? Has the analysis of both dyslexic case reports and the underlying resistance forces not led to a solution to the riddle dyslexia?

APPENDIX F

Glossary

Acalculia: Inability to comprehend and perform simple arithmetical calculations as a result of a cerebral dysfunction; to be distinguished from dyscalculia of C-V origin.

Agenesis: Absence of tissue; in this text, it refers to the historical theory that word-blindness or dyslexia is due to a structural defect or agenesis of vital cerebral cortical tissue.

Agnosia: The inability to comprehend or recognize the meaning of sensory stimuli and patterns as a result of a lesion or dysfunction of the cerebral cortex.

Agraphia: Inability to express thoughts in writing owing to a lesion of the cerebral cortex; to be distinguished from dysgraphia of C-V origin.

Alexia: Loss of ability to understand the symbolic meaning of written language owing to a cerebral lesion; to be distinguished from dyslexia of C-V origin.

Ambilateral: Affecting both the right and the left sides of the body; ambidextrous, or having the ability to use both right and left extremities equally well.

Amblyopia: Suppression of vision and/or impairment in one eye resulting from strabismus; the brain's attempt to prevent double vision or diplopia; preventable if diagnosed and treated early.

Analogous: Similar in function or form, but not in origin or development; contrast with homologous.

Aphasia: Defective comprehension and/or expression of language owing to agenesis, disease, or injury of the cerebral cortex; to be distinguished from the nonconceptual C-V speech disorders, i.e., stuttering, stammering, slurring, "slips," and even word-finding hesitations due to the same memory instability responsible for dyslexics' difficulty recognizing letters, words, and multiplication tables.

Apraxia: Inability to carry out meaningful, familiar movements in the absence of paralysis or other motor impairment as a result of a cerebral dysfunction; to be distinguished from dyspraxia of C-V origin.

Ataxia: Poor muscular coordination and balance.

Autism: Condition dominated by self-centered, subjective trends of thought or behavior not subject to correction by external stimulation.

Autonomic nervous system: The portion of the nervous system concerned with regulation of the activity of cardiac muscles, smooth muscles, and glands.

Bender-Gestalt drawings: A series of copied designs that often indicates characteristic errors among dyslexics.

Bimodal: A statistical distribution having two peaks—and suggesting two separate and distinct populations.

Blurring speeds: The speed of a moving sequence at which blurring occurs; tested by means of a 3D Optical Scanner; the measure of ocular tracking capacity; *sequential blurring speeds* are diagnostic of C-V functioning, whereas *single targeting* blurring speeds are diagnostic of compensatory factors.

Caloric vestibular responses: Vestibular "inner ear" responses to stimulating the system with warm and cool water; stimulating the fluid within the inner ear results in a recordable eye movement reflex—nystagmus—as well as motion-sickness responses such as motion-sickness symptoms of dizziness, headache, nausea, and abdominal complaints.

Catastrophic anxiety: Anxiety triggered by a dysfunctioning central nervous system; to be contrasted by anxiety triggered by emotional factors, i.e., separation anxiety or castration anxiety.

Cerebellar-vestibular (C-V): Pertaining to the C-V functional system or to this specific localization within the brain.

Cerebral cortex: Thin layer of gray matter on the surface of the cerebral hemispheres; the thinking, speaking brain.

Choreiform movements: Involuntary, jerky movements suggesting a dysfunction within the extrapyramidal system—brain centers responsible for Parkinson's disease; clinically confused with rhythmic or jerky imbalance movements characterizing individuals with C-V dysfunction and dyslexia.

Cognition: Operation of the mind for perceiving, thinking, and remembering.

Confabulation: Conscious or unconscious lying; creating imaginary experiences for self-aggrandisement or to deny memory impairment resulting from organic or psychological disturbances.

Contrecoup: An injury or effect in one area of the skull or brain may result in a transmitted injury or effect to another more distant part of the brain.

Cortical: Pertaining to the cerebral cortex—or to the thinking, speaking portion of the brain.

Counterphobic phenomena: Antiphobic "brave" behavior defensively utilized by individuals to counter their underlying phobic or anxiety-provoking tendencies.

Countertransference: The process whereby emotions and attitudes are unconsciously transferred by a psychoanalyst onto patients; similar to *transference* but having an opposite direction.

C-V mesencephalic origin: Pertaining to the combined C-V and mesencephalic functional systems and/or to the effect of one system on the other; subcortical systems and localization having feedback relationships with the cerebral cortex as well as other subcortical systems.

Cyclothymia: Alternating moods of mild elation and depression; to be contrasted with severe elation and depression found in manic-depressive individuals.

Developmental cerebral lag vs. cerebral injury: A cerebral lag signifies a slow development with associated symptoms without cerebral impairment or injury; a theoretical construct traditionally used to explain the dyslexic syndrome appearing without any clinical evidence supporting a structural cerebral injury or impairment.

Diaschisis: Impaired brain function in areas distant from an injury or a lesion, but functionally connected to it.

Dominant hemisphere: In this text, that cerebral hemisphere that dominates or controls speech and handedness functioning, as well as gnosis or interpretation and conceptualization of the sensory input.

Double-blind drug studies: Studies in which neither patients nor researchers know whether real or fake (placebo) medication is utilized.

Dream content: The remembered, scrambled, or nonsensical manifest content of a dream; to be distinguished from its underlying, unconscious latent determinants which most often remain disguised and hidden from view.

Dysarthria: Imperfect articulation of speech due to central nervous system disturbances affecting muscular control and coordination.

Dyscalculia: Impairment of the ability to perform mathematical calculations; discovered to be related to a C-V-related memory instability in the presence of normal or even superior conceptual ability; to be contrasted with acalculia of cerebral and conceptual origin.

Dysdiadochokinesis: The inability to perform adequately rapid alternating movements; indicative of a C-V dysfunction.

Dysgraphia: Dyscoordinated or "messy" handwriting and drawing; discovered to be caused by directional, spatial, and coordination- and proprioceptive-related memory dysfunctioning characterizing dyslexia of C-V origin; to be contrasted with agraphia of ideational origin, in which the idea or concept for the motor scheme is lost.

Dyslexia: Impaired ability to read as a result of a C-V dysfunction.

Dysmetria: Impaired regulation of distance (spatial and temporal sequencing) and motor response by a dysfunctioning C-V guided missile system.

Dyspraxia: Dyscoordinated motor performance, often related to an impaired C-V guided missile system; to be contrasted with ideational apraxia of cortical origin in which the conceptual motor scheme is lost or severely impaired.

Eidetic: Vivid memory functioning characterized by the exact visualization of events previously seen, i.e., "photographic" memory.

Empirical: Based on experience.

Enuresis: Involuntary discharge of urine, i.e., bedwetting.

Epiphenomena: Coexisting symptoms unrelated to, but affecting, a primary disease or disorder.

Etiology: Origin of a disease.

Eumetria: Proper range, guidance, timing, and coordination of movement; to be contrasted with dysmetria, in which these functions are impaired.

Finger agnosia: An inability to name meaningfully or recognize the fingers of one's own hand as a result of a lesion of the dominant cerebral cortex; part of Gerstmann's syndrome; to be distinguished from a disturbance of "finger order sense"—a C-V-determined proprioceptive dysfunction fallaciously identified with finger agnosia by Kinsbourne and Warrington in their attempt to equate cortically determined Gerstmann's syndrome and C-V-determined dyslexia.

Free-association: The process by which thoughts are allowed to enter one's mind *free* of conscious, logical, or biased restraint; a process utilized by Freud to study hidden, unconscious, primary process thoughts and mechanisms.

Ganglion: A grouping of nerve cells located outside the central nervous system.

Gerstmann's syndrome or tetrad: Finger agnosia, acalculia, agraphia, right/left confusion; a cluster of four symptoms defining a disorder within the dominant cerebral cortex.

Gestalt: A stimulus pattern in which the total configuration contains properties greater than those explained by a summation of the individual elements.

Goodenough figure drawings: The drawings of male or female figures which, upon analysis, often highlight underlying organic and/or emotional determinants.

Graphomotor: The movements required to write and draw.

Gyrus: One of many convolutions characterizing the surface or cortex of the brain.

Hemisphere: Referring to either the right or left hemisphere of the brain, i.e., cortical hemispheres or cerebellar hemispheres.

Homeostasis: The dynamic tendency to maintain or regain normal equilibrium states within the body.

Hypertrophy: A compensatory enlargement of muscles or organs.

Hypoglycemia: Low blood sugar level.

Hypotension: Low blood pressure.

Hypotonia: Diminished muscle tone; frequently caused by a C-V dysfunction; may be partially responsible for pes planus or flat feet, toeing-in or out, scoliosis, etc.

Iatrogenic: An adverse condition caused by a physician's treatment.

Idiopathic: Of unknown origin or causation.

Imperception: Inability to comprehend properly the meaning of an input sequence.

Imprinting: For certain animal species, the object of an instinctive act is often acquired or imprinted. For example, the first animal (or person) seen by some birds after hatching is *imprinted* and thereafter followed as if it were the parent; other birds of the same species, even the real parents, are not recognized as such.

Inbuilt release mechanisms (IRMs): Mechanisms physiologically ready and waiting to be triggered by specific external stimuli during specific time periods, i.e., the smiling response of an infant is triggered by a highly specific visual configuration consisting of the eyes and forehead only during the period from 6 weeks to 3 months of age.

Introjection: An unconscious mental process by which a person incorporates within himself the personality characteristics of another.

Isomorphic: Data having the same form, quality, and common denominator.

Labyrinthitis: Inflammation of the inner ear.

Left-angular and supramarginal gyri: Localized cerebral folds, the dysfunctioning of which leads to acquired conceptual alexia; traditionally assumed to be responsible also for developmental dyslexia, word-blindness, or strephosymbolia.

Macropsia: A perceptual illusion of increased size or shape; frequently of C-V origin.

Minimal brain damage (MBD): A concept fallaciously utilized by many to infer the presence of a cerebral dysfunction in the absence of "hard and fast" cerebral signs, and in the presence of heretofore unrecognized C-V signs.

Megalomania: The defensive need and state of aggrandizing one's own intelligence, power, and abilities, i.e., delusions of grandeur.

Micropsia: A perceptual illusion in which objects appear smaller than they really are; frequently of C-V origin.

Myelinization: The development of the outer myelin sheath surrounding axons of nerve fibers.

Negativistic: Antagonistic or resistive.

Neurodynamic: A concept defined and utilized by the author to encompass the dynamic neurophysiologic mechanisms regulating adaptation, compensation, and homeostasis; a conceptual neurophysiologic analogy to the term psychodynamic.

Neuron: A nerve cell.

Neurophysiologic: Having a neurologic functional determinant.

Nuclear complex: The essential, crucial core elements stemming from, and defining, a disorder, a symptomatic complex, or grouping determined by common nuclear determinants.

Nystagmus: Involuntary rhythmic movements of the eye.

Olfactory: Pertaining to the sense of smell.

Ontogeny: The developing embryonic stages leading to the birth of an individual; recapitulates or mirrors phylogeny—the evolutionary developing stages of the human race.

Optokinetic: Pertaining to eye movements.

Oscillopsia: An optical illusion in which objects or words seem to move, jerk, or wiggle; not infrequently experienced by C-V dyslexics or individuals with C-V dysfunction.

Otitis media: A middle ear infection.

Paradoxical: At variance with the expected norm or rule.

Parietal: In this text pertaining to the parietal lobe of the cerebral cortex.

Parietal lobe: The upper middle portion of the cerebral cortex; the dominant parietal lobe controls and determines the interpretation of the sensory input; the angular gyrus within this dominant lobe determines the interpretation of written symbols; injury to the angular gyrus results in alexia and has been fallaciously assumed to be responsible for dyslexia.

Paroxysm: Spasm or seizure.

Pathognomonic: Signs or symptoms with which a diagnosis can be made with certainty.

Pathophysiologic: Pathology or symptoms having a physiologic rather than a psychogenic or emotional origin.

Perseveration: An irresistible, repetitive fixation to a thought, a sensory stimulus, or motor act, owing to an organic brain dysfunction; to be distinguished from an analogous obsessive-compulsive symptom of psychogenic or emotional origin; possibly providing the somatic compliance underlying some obsessive-compulsive symptoms.

Phonetic: Related to the sounds attached to visual letter and word configuration.

Phylogeny: The evolutionary developmental stages of the human race; recapitulated by ontogeny—the embryonic stages characterizing the developing human.

Post-ECT states: Postelectroconvulsive therapy states.

Praxis: The motor acts determining action.

Primary process: Unconsciously and psychogenically determined thinking mechanisms characterizing dreams, Freudian slips, as well as neurotic and psychotic symptoms; mechanisms characterized by mental forces responsible for clinical symptomatic scrambling; scrambling mechanisms characterized by displacement, condensation, reversals, representation by the opposite, etc.; to be contrasted with conscious, logical, or secondary process thinking mechanisms characterizing normal waking, thinking, and speaking.

Proprioception: The sensory input derived from muscles, tendons, and joints; Lord Sherington referred to the cerebellum as "the head ganglion of the proprioceptive system"; the author extended this concept and referred to the cerebellum as "the head ganglion of the total sensory input"; the sensory input guiding and determining motor responses, our position in space; the summation and integration of this vital input determines body scheme and body image functioning.

Pseudo: A false resemblance.

Psychodynamic: The dynamic mechanisms regulating mental functioning and homeostasis; often utilized to characterize the unconsciously motivated defense mechanisms; utilized by the author to develop an analogous concept—neurodynamic.

Psychogenic: Having an emotional origin.

Rapid eye movements (REMs): Eye movements observed during the dream period of sleeping; eye movements scanning the dream images of our inner dream· world; assumed by the author to be regulated by the C-V system, the system which regulates the eye movements scanning outer world visual events.

Regressive functioning: A deterioration or backward slide in functioning; to be contrasted with *facilitated,* habituated, conditioned, or enhanced functioning.

Right/left dysfunction: An inability to *conceptualize* the meaning of right and left as symbolic meaningful entities suggests a disturbance within the cerebral cortex; an inability to *know* or *remember* "instinctively" where right and left are in directional space suggests a compass-determined disturbance of C-V origin.

Romberg testing: Having individuals stand with their feet together and their arms outstretched—most often with their eyes closed—to test for an imbalance of C-V origin.

Rotation responses: Responses triggered when the inner ear system (and its surrounding fluid) is subjected to rotation; usually consists of eye movement reflexes and motion-sickness reactions.

Savant functioning: "Gifted" but isolated functioning sometimes found among the mentally retarded.

Scientific neurosis: Neurotic-like, illogical, or fallacious scientific slips, errors, and beliefs determined and maintained by unconsciously rooted bias forces; called a "follie-en-masse" when shared by a group or mass of individuals; called a "scientific psychosis" when the erroneous belief is *severely* disoriented and resistive or antagonistic to scientific reality and logic; "tongue-in-cheek" analogies to the ordinary neuroses and psychoses.

Scotoma: Blind spots.

Semicircular canals: Three semicircular-shaped canals within the vestibular system corresponding to the three dimensions of space; they sense and determine compass or direction-related orientation mechanisms and responses.

Slip: As utilized in this text, Freudian-like slips of organic origin must be distinguished from Freudian slips or errors that have an underlying emotional determination or symbolic meaning.

Soft neurological signs: So-called nonlocalizing and/or nonspecific signs suggesting an immaturity or dysfunction within the central nervous system; recognized by the author to be of localizing and specific C-V origin.

Somatic compliance: Somatic or physical determinants (compliance) predicted by Freud to underlie and shape the quality of all neurotic and psychotic symptoms; a determinant frequently ignored or denied by psychoanalytic and psychologically trained researchers or therapists.

Somato-: Denoting a relation to body or physical functioning; in contrast to *psychic* or mental functioning.

Somatopsychic: Highlighting the role of somatic functioning and/or dysfunctioning in determining psychic or mental responses; in contrast to the concept *psychosomatic,* in which psychic influences determine somatic or physical responses.

Spasmus mutans: Nodding spasm.

Spatial: Pertaining to space.

Strabismus: A malalignment of the eyes as the result of either peripheral muscle weakness and/or tonal imbalance—often of a hidden central C-V mesencephalic origin.

Strephosymbolia: Synonym for dyslexia or word-blindness.

Subcortical: Brain structures and systems situated beneath the cerebral cortex, i.e., the C-V system, the mesencephalic system, the diencephalic system or the extrapyramidal system.

Synapse: The space between interconnecting nerve cells through which nervous impulses are transmitted via electrochemical means.

Tachycardia: Excessive or rapid heartbeat.

Tandem walking: Heel-to-toe walking, impaired as a result of C-V dysfunction.

Temporal: Pertaining to time.

Tetrad: A group of four related signs, symptoms, or entities.

Transference: The unconscious transfer of thoughts and emotions stemming from one's past and repressed childhood onto one's therapist or analyst or key figures in one's current environment.

Unilateral occipital suppression: Suppression of one-sided occipital lobe (cortical) functioning.

Vector derivative: An outcome of multiple, often hidden, underlying forces and factors.

Vertigo: Dizziness, usually of C-V origin.

Vestibular: Pertaining to the inner ear system.

Vestibular neuronitis: Inflammation of vestibular neurons.

References

Adrian, E. D. (1943) Afferent areas in the cerebellum connected with the limbs. Brain 66:289–315.

American Association of Ophthalmology (1970) Dyslexia: Your Child's Reading Disability. Washington, D.C., American Association of Ophthalmology.

Angyal, A., and Blackman, N. (1940) Vestibular reactivity in schizophrenia. Arch. Neurol. Psychiat. 44:611–620.

Aschoff, J. (1965) Circadian rhythms in man. Science 148:1427–1432.

Aschoff, J. (1969). The desynchronization and resynchronization of human circadian rhythms. Aerospace Med. 40:844–849.

Ayers, A. J. (1972) Sensory Integration and Learning Disorders. Los Angeles, Western Psychological Services.

Bakwin, H. (1968) Delayed speech: Developmental mutism. Pediatric Clin. North Am. 15(3):627–638.

Bakwin, H., and Bakwin, R. M. (1966) Clinical Management of Behavior Disorders in Children. Philadelphia, W. B. Saunders.

Barany, R. (1916) Some new methods for functional testing of the vestibular apparatus and cerebellum. In Nobel Lectures, Physiology and Medicine, 1901–1921. Amsterdam, Elsevier, 1967, pp. 500–511.

Barany, R. (1920) Zur Klinik und Theoric des Eisenbahnnystagmus. Acta Oto-Laryngol. (Stockh.) 3:260.

Bender, L. (1938) A Visual Motor Gestalt Test and Its Clinical Use. New York, American Orthopsychiatric Association Research Monograph No. 3.

Bender, L. (1947) Childhood schizophrenia. Clinical study of 100 schizophrenic children. Amer. J. Orthopsychiat. 17:40–56.

Bender, L. (1956) Schizophrenia in childhood—Its recognition, description and treatment. Amer. J. Orthopsychiat. 26:499–506.

Benson, D., and Geschwind, N. (1968) Cerebral dominance and its disturbances. Pediatric Clin. North Am. 15(3):759–770.

Benton, A. (1968) Right-left discrimination. Pediatric Clin. North Am. 15(3):747–758.

Bickerman, H. A. (1972–73) Drugs for disturbances in equilibrium. In Modell, W. (ed.) Drugs of Choice. St. Louis, C. V. Mosby.

Bizzi, E. (1974) Coordination of eye–head movements. Scientific American 231:100–106.
Blanchard, P. (1928) Reading disabilities in relation to maladjustment. Mental Hygiene 12:772–793.
Blanchard, P. (1935) Psychogenic factors in some cases of reading disability. Amer. J. Orthopsychiat. 5:361–374.
Blanchard, P. (1936) Reading disabilities in relation to difficulties of personality and emotional development. Mental Hygiene 20:384–413.
Blanchard, P. (1946) Psychoanalytic contributions to the problem of reading disabilities. In Eissler, K., et al. (eds.) The Psychoanalytic Study of the Child, Vol. II. New York, International Universities Press, pp. 163–187.
Brain, R. (1955) Diseases of the Nervous System. London, Oxford University Press.
Brain, R. (1965) Speech Disorders. 2nd edn. London, Butterworth.
Broadbent, W. H. (1872) On the Cerebral Mechanisms of Speech and Thought. Med.-Clin. Trans., London, 55:145–194.
Brookler, K. (1971) Simultaneous bilateral bithermal caloric stimulation in electrostagnomography. Laryngoscope 4:101–109.
Brookler, K., and Pulec, J. (1970) Computer analysis of electrostagnomography records. Trans. Amer. Acad. Ophthalmol. Otolaryngol. May–June 1970, pp. 563–575.
Brown, F. (1971) Some orientational influences of non-visual terrestrial electromagnetic field. Ann. N. Y. Acad. Sci. 188:224–241.
Brown, F. (1972) The "clock's" timing biological rhythms. American Scientist 60:756–766.
Carter, S., and Gold, A. (1972) The syndrome of minimal cerebral dysfunction. In Barnett, M. H. and Einhorn, A. (eds.) Pediatrics. New York, Appleton-Century-Crofts.
Claude, H., Baruk, H., and Aubry, M. (1927) Contribution a l'etude de la Demence Precoce Catatonique: Inexcitabilite Labyrinthique au cours de la Catatonie. Rev. Neurol. 1:976–980.
Clemmens, R. L. (1976) Minimal brain damage in children. In Frierson, E., and Barbe, W. (eds.) Educating Children with Learning Disabilities. New York, Appleton-Century-Crofts.
Cohen, B., Suzuki, J. Shanzer, S., and Bender, M. B. (1964) Semicircular canal control of eye movements. In Bender, M. B. (ed.) The Oculo-motor System. New York, Hoeber.
Colbert, E. G., Koegler, R. R., and Markham, C. H. (1959) Vestibular dysfunction in childhood schizophrenia. Arch. Gen. Psychiat. 1:600–617.
Connors, C. K., and Eisenberg, L. (1963) The effects of methylphenidate on symptomatology and learning in disturbed children. Amer. J. Psychiat. 120:458–464.
Critchley, M. (1942) Phasic disorder of signalling (constitutional and acquired) occurring in naval signal men. J. Mt. Sinai Hosp. N.Y. 9:363–375.
Critchley, M. (1953) The Parietal Lobes. London, Edward Arnold.
Critchley, M. (1968) Developmental dyslexia. Pediatric Clin. North Am. 15(3):669–676.
Critchley, M. (1969) The Dyslexic Child. Springfield, Ill., Charles C. Thomas.
de Hirsch, K. (1952) Specific dyslexia or strephosymbolia. Folia Phoniat., Basel 4:231–248.

de Hirsch, K. (1954) Gestalt psychology as applied to language disturbances. J. Nerv. Ment. Dis., 120:257–261.

de Hirsch, K. (1957) Tests designed to discover potential reading difficulties at the 6-year-old level. Amer. J. Orthopsychiat. 27:566–576.

de Hirsch, K. (1963) Two categories of learning difficulties in adolescents. Amer. J. Orthopsychiat. 33:87–91.

de Hirsch, K. (1965) Early identification of specific language disabilities as seen by a speech pathologist. In Dyslexia in Special Education. Pomfret, Conn., The Orton Society.

de Hirsch, K., Jansky, J. J., and Langford, W. S. (1966) Predicting Reading Failure. New York, Harper and Row.

Delacato, C. H. (1966) The Treatment and Prevention of Reading Problems. Springfield, Ill., Charles C. Thomas.

Dement, W. C. (1964) Eye movements during sleep. In Bender, M. (ed.) The Oculo-Motor System. New York, Hoeber.

Denny-Brown, D. (1952) The biological tropisms of the cerebral cortex. Arquivos de Neuro-psiquiatria 10:399–404.

Denny-Brown, D. (1956) Positive and negative aspects of cerebral cortical functions. North Carolina Med. J. 17:295–303.

Denny-Brown, D. (1958) The Nature of Apraxia. J. Nervous Mental Disease 126: 9–31.

de Quiros, J. B. (1976) Diagnosis of vestibular disorder in the learning disabled. J. Learning Disabilities 9:39–58.

de Quiros, J. B. (1978) Neurophysiological fundamentals of learning disabilities. San Rafael, Calif., Academic Therapy.

Dolowitz, D. A. (1967) Testing vestibular spinal reflexes. In Specter, M. (ed.) Dizziness and Vertigo. New York, Grune & Stratton.

Dow, R. S., and Anderson, R. (1942) Cerebellar action potentials in response to stimulation of proprioceptors and exteroceptors in the rat. J. Neurophysiol. 5:363–371.

Dow, R. S., and Moruzzi, G. (1958) The Physiology and Pathology of the Cerebellum. Minneapolis, University of Minnesota Press.

Eccles, J. C. (1969) The inhibitory pathways of the central nervous system. Springfield, Ill., Charles C. Thomas.

Eccles, J. C. (1970) Facing Reality. New York, Springer-Verlag, 1970.

Eccles, J. C. (1973) The cerebellum as a computer: Patterns in space and time. J. Physiol. 229:1–32.

Eccles, J. C., Ito, M., and Szentagothai, J. (1967) The Cerebellum as a Neuronal Machine. New York, Springer-Verlag.

Fenichel, O. (1945) The Psycho-analytic Theory of Neurosis. New York, Norton.

Ferenczi, S. (1954) Disease or pathoneurosis. In Richman, J. (ed.) Further Contributions to the Theory and Technique of Psychoanalysis. New York, Basic Books.

Field, J., and Magoun, H. (ed.) (1968) Neurophysiology. Vol. 2. Philadelphia, Williams & Wilkins.

Fitzgerald, G., and Stengel, E. (1945) Vestibular reactivity to caloric stimulation in schizophrenics. J. Ment. Sci., 91:93–100.

Frank, J. (1961) Communication and empathy. In Proceedings of the Third World Congress of Psychiatry. Toronto, University of Toronto Press/McGill University Press.

Frank, J. (1964) Nosological considerations in the group of schizophrenias, hysterical psychoses. Read at the Sixth International Congress of Psychotherapy, London, England, on Friday, August 28, 1964.

Frank, J. (1968) Nosological and differential diagnostic considerations in schizophrenias and regressophrenias: Clinical examples. J. Hillside Hospital 17:116–135.

Frank, J., and Levinson, H. (1973) Dysmetric dyslexia and dyspraxia—hypothesis and study. J. Amer. Acad. Child Psychiat. 12:690–701.

Frank, J., and Levinson, H. (1975–76) Dysmetric dyslexia and dyspraxia—synopsis of a continuing research project. Academic Therapy 11:133–143.

Frank, J., and Levinson, H. (1976) Compensatory mechanism in cerebellar-vestibular dysfunctions and dysmetric dyslexia and dyspraxia. Academic Therapy 12:1–24.

Frank, J., and Levinson, H. (1976–77) Seasickness mechanisms and medications in dysmetric dyslexia and dyspraxia. Academic Therapy 12:133–149.

Frank, J., and Levinson, H. (1977) Anti-motion sickness medications in dysmetric dyslexia and dyspraxia. Academic Therapy 12:411–425.

Freud, A. (1946) The Ego and the Mechanisms of Defense. New York, International Universities Press.

Freud, S. (1895/1950) Project for a scientific psychology. In Pre-Psycho-Analytic Publications and Unpublished Drafts. Vol. I, 1886–1899. London, The Hogarth Press.

Freud, S. (1900) The interpretation of dreams. Standard Edition, Vols. IV and V. London, The Hogarth Press.

Freud, S. (1901) The Psychopathology of Everyday Life. Standard Edition, Vol. VI. London, The Hogarth Press.

Freud, S. (1905) Jokes and Their Relation to the Unconscious. Standard Edition, Vol. VIII. London, The Hogarth Press.

Freud, S. (1910) The Psychoanalytic View of Psychogenic Disturbances of Vision. Standard Edition, Vol. XI. London, The Hogarth Press.

Freud, S. (1916–17) Introductory Lectures on Psychoanalysis. Standard Edition, Vol. XV. London, The Hogarth Press.

Freud, S. (1925–26) Inhibitions, Symptoms and Anxiety. Standard Edition, Vol. XX. London, The Hogarth Press.

Freud, S. (1932–36) Introductory Lectures on Psychoanalysis. Standard Edition, Vol. 22, New Introductory Lectures and Other Works. London, The Hogarth Press.

Freud, S. (1939) An Outline of Psychoanalysis. New York, W. W. Norton.

Frierson, E., and Barbe, W. (1967) Educating Children with Learning Disabilities. New York, Appleton-Century-Crofts.

Gairdner, J. O. H. (1947) J. Inst. Elec. Engineers (London) 94(iia):208.

Gay, A., Neuman, N., Keltner, J., and Stroud, M. (1974) Eye Movement Disorders. St. Louis, C. V. Mosby.

Gerstmann, J. (1924) Fingeragnosie: Eine umschriebene Storung der Orientierung am eigenen Korper. Wien. Klin. Wchnschr. 37:1010.

Gerstmann, J. (1940) Syndrome of finger agnosia, disorientation for right and left, agraphia and acalculia. Arch. Neurol. Psychiat. 44:398.

Ghelarducci, B., Ito, M., and Yagi, N. (1975) Impulse discharge from flocculus purkinje cells of alert rabbits during visual stimulation combined with horizontal head rotation. Brain Res. 87:66–72.

Gillingham, A. (1956) The prevention of scholastic failure due to specific language disability. Bull. Orton Soc. 6:26–31.

Gillingham, A., and Stillman, B. W. (1960) Remedial Training for Children with Specific Disability in Reading, Spelling, and Penmanship. Cambridge, Mass., Educators Publishing Service.

Goldstein, K. (1936) The function of the cerebellum from a clinical standpoint. J. Nerv. Ment. Dis. 83:1–12.

Gonshor, A., and Melville Jones, G. (1971) Plasticity in the adult vestibulo-ocular reflex arc. Proc. Canad. Fed. Biol. Soc. 14:11.

Gonshor, A., and Melville Jones, G. (1976a) Short-term adaptive changes in the human vestibulo-ocular reflex arc. J. Physiol., London 256:361–379.

Gonshor, A., and Melville Jones, G. (1976b). Extreme vestibulo-ocular adaptation induced by prolonged optical reversal of vision. J. Physiol., London 256:381–414.

Goodenough, F. L. (1926) Draw-a-Man Test: The Measurement of Intelligence by Drawings. Yonkers, N.Y., World Book.

Greenspan, S. B. (1975–76) Effectiveness of therapy for children's reversal confusion. Academic Therapy 11:169–178.

Halliwell, J. W., and Solan, H. A. (1972) The effects of a supplemental perceptual training program on reading achievement. Exceptional Children April 1972, pp. 613–619.

Hécaen, H. (1962) Clinical symptomatology in right and left hemisphere lesions. In Mountcastle, V. B. (ed.) Interhemisphere Relations and Cerebral Dominance, Baltimore, Johns Hopkins Press.

Hermann, K. (1959) Reading Disability, Copenhagen: Munksgaard.

Hermann, K., and Norrie, E. (1958) Is congenital word-blindness a hereditary type of gerstmann's syndrome? Psychiat. Neurol., Basel, 136:59.

Hess, W. R. (1949) The central control of the activity of internal organs. In Nobel Lectures: Physiology and Medicine. New York, Elsevier, pp. 247–258.

Hess, W. R. (1957) The Functional Organization of the Diencephalon. New York, Grune & Stratton.

Hildreth, G. (1936) Learning the 3 R's. Minneapolis, Minneapolis Educational Publishers.

Hinshelwood, J. (1917) Congenital Word-blindness. London, H. K. Lewis.

Holzman, P. S., Proctor, L. R., Levy, D. L., Yasillo, N. J., Meltzer, H. Y., and Hurt, S. W. (1974) Eye-tracking dysfunctions in schizophrenic patients and their relatives. Arch. Gen. Psychiat. 31:143–151.

Hoskins, R. G. (1946) The Biology of Schizophrenia. New York, W. W. Norton.

Illingworth, R. S. (1968) Delayed motor development. Pediatric Clin. North Am. 15(3):569–580.

Ingram, T. T. S. (1968) Speech disorders in childhood. Pediatric Clin. North Am. 15(3):611–626.

Ito, M., Nisimaru, N., and Yamamoto, M. (1973) Specific neuro-connection for the cerebellar control of the vestibulo-ocular reflexes. Brain Res. 60:238–243.

Jackson, J. H. (1931) Selected Writings of John Hughlings Jackson. J. Taylor (ed.) London, Hodder and Stoughton.

Jarvis, V. (1958) Clinical observations on the visual problem in reading disability.

In Eissler, K., et al. (eds.) The Psychoanalytic Study of the Child, Vol. 13. New York, International Universities Press, pp. 451–470.

Jastak, J. (1934) Interferences in reading. Psychological Bulletin. 34:244–272.

Jennings, H. S. (1930) The Biological Basis of Human Nature. New York: W. W. Norton.

Jones, E. (1923) The child's unconscious. In Papers on Psychoanalysis. London, William Wood.

Jongkees, L., and Philipszoon, A. (1964) Electronystagmography. Stockholm, Oto-Laryngolica Suppl. 189, pp. 00–00.

Joo, B., and von Meduna, L. (1935) Labyrinthreizungsuntersuchungen bei Schizophrenie. Psychiat. Neurol. Wchschr. 37:26–29.

Kasanin, J. S. (1964) Concluding remarks. In Kasanin, J. S. (ed.) Language and Thought in Schizophrenia. New York, Norton.

Kerr, J. (1897) School hygiene, in its mental moral and physical aspects. Howard Medal Prize Essay, J. Roy. Statist. Soc. 60:613–680.

Kinsbourne, M. (1968) Developmental Gerstmann Syndrome. Pediatric Clin. North Am. 15(3):771–778.

Kinsbourne, M., and Warrington, E. K. (1962) A study of finger agnosia. Brain 85:47.

Kinsbourne, M., and Warrington, E. K. (1963a) Developmental factors in reading and writing backwardness. Br. J. Psychol. 54:145.

Kinsbourne, M., and Warrington, E. K. (1963b) The developmental Gerstmann syndrome. Arch. Neurol. 8:490.

Kinsbourne, M., and Warrington, E. K. (1964a) Disorders of spelling. J. Neurol. Neurosurg. Psychiat. 27:224.

Kinsbourne, M., and Warrington, E. K. (1964b) The development of finger differentiation. Quart. J. Exp. Psychol. 15:132.

Klein, E. (1949) Psychoanalytic aspects of school problems. In Eissler, K. et al. (eds.) The Psychoanalytic Study of the Child, Vol. 3–4. New York, International Universities Press, pp. 369–390.

Klein, M. (1931) A contribution to the theory of intellectual inhibition. Internat. J. Psychoanal. 12:206–218.

Klein, M., and Magnus, R. (1920) Ueber die Unabhängigkeit der Labyrinthreflexe von Kleinhirn und über die Lage der Zentren für die Labyrinthreflexe in Hirnstamm. Arch .f. d. ges Physiol. 178:124–178.

Kobrak, F. (1919–20) Zur Frage einer exakten Messbarkeit der Senzibilitat des Vestibularapparates. Arch. Ohren. Nasen. u. Kehlkopf. 105:132–134.

Koestler, A. (1968) The Ghost in the Machine. New York, MacMillan.

Kussmaul, A. (1877) Cited by Lhermitte, J., and de Ayuriaguerra, J. (1942) Psychopathologie de la Vision. Barris, Massan.

Langford, W. S. (1955) Developmental dyspraxia—Abnormal clumsiness. Bull. Orton Soc. 5:3–9.

Langford, W. S. (1966) Predicting Reading Failure. New York, Harper & Row.

Laufer, M. W., and Denhoff, E. (1957) Hyperkinetic behavior syndrome in children. J. Pediat. 50:463–473.

Laufer, M. W., Denhoff, E., and Solomons, G. (1957) Hyperkinetic impulse disorder in children's behavior problems. Psychosom. Med. 19:38–49.

Leach, W. W. (1953) The measurement of nystagmus in normals and schizophrenics. Dissertation Abstr. 13:598–599.

Levinson, H. (1966) Auditory hallucinations in a case of hysteria. Br. J. Psychiat. 112:19–26.

Levinson, H. (1974) Dyslexia: Does this unusual childhood syndrome begin as an ear infection? Infectious Dis. 15:15.

Liss, E. (1935). Libidinal fixations as pedagogic determinants. Amer. J. Orthopsychiat. 5:126–131.

Liss, E. (1937) Emotional and biological factors involved in learning processes. Amer. J. Orthopsychiat. 7:483–489.

Liss, E. (1940) Learning—Its sadistic and masochistic manifestations. Amer. J. Orthopsychiat. 10:123–129.

Liss, E. (1941) Learning difficulties. Amer. J. Orthopsychiat. 11: 520–524.

Liss, E. (1949) Psychiatric implications of the failing student. Amer. J. Orthopsychiat. 19:501–505.

Liss, E. (1955) Motivations in learning. In Eissler, K., et al. (eds.) The Psychoanalytic Study of the Child, Vol. 10. New York, International Universities Press, pp. 100–116.

Llinas, R. (1974) Motor aspects of cerebellar control. The Physiologist 17:17–46.

Llinas, R. (1975) The cortex of the cerebellum. Scientific American 232:56–71.

Lorenz, K. (1957) Companionship in bird life. In Schiller, C. H. (ed.) Instinctive Behavior. New York, International University Press.

Lorenz, K., and Tinbergen, N. (1957) Taxis and instinct. In Schiller, C. H. (ed.) Instinctive Behavior. New York, International University Press.

Lowenbach, H. (1936) Messende Untersuchungen uber die Erregbarkeit des Zentralnervensystems von Geisteskranken, vor Allem von Periodish Katatonen, mit Hilfe Quantitativer Vestibularisreizung. Arch. Psychiat. 105:313–323.

Luria, A. R. (1966) Higher Cortical Functions in Man. New York, Basic Books.

McFarland, R. A. (1974) Influence of changing time zones on air crews and passengers. Aerospace Med. 45:648–658.

Magnus, R. (1914) Welche Teile des Zentralnervensystems müssen das Zustandekommen der tonischen Hals- und Labyrinthreflexe auf die Körpmuskulatur vorhanden sein? Arch. f. d. ges. Physiol., 159:224–249.

Magoun, H. W. (1952) The ascending reticular activating system. A Res. Nerv. & Ment. Dis. (Proc., 1950), 30:480–492.

Magoun, H. W. (1963) The Waking Brain. 2nd edn. Springfield, Ill., Charles C. Thomas, pp. 158–177.

Mahler, M. S. (1942) Pseudoimbecility: A magic cap of invisibility. Psychoanalyt. Quart. 11:149–164.

Manni, E. (1950) Localizzazioni cerebellari corticali nella cavia. II. Effetti di lesioni delle parti vestibolari del cervelletto. Arch. Fisiol. 50:110–123.

Meyers, S., Caldwell, D., and Purcell, G. (1973) Vestibular dysfunction in schizophrenia. Biological Psychiatry 7:255–260.

Miles, F. A., and Fuller, J. H. (1975) Visual tracking and the primate flocculus. Science 189:1000–1002.

Miller M. (1968) Dysacusis. Pediatric Clin. North Am. 15(3):729–746.

Money, J. (1962) Dyslexia: A post-conference view. In Money, J. (ed) Reading

Disability: Progress and Research Needs in Dyslexia. Baltimore, Johns Hopkins Press.
Morgan, W. P. (1896) A case of congenital word-blindness. Br. Med. J. 2:1378.
Morrison, A. R., and Pompeiano, O. (1970) Vestibular influences during sleep. Arch. Ital. Biol. 108:154–180.
Mosse, H. L., and Daniels, C. R. (1959) Linear dyslexia. A new form of reading disorder. Amer. J. Psychother. 13:826–841.
Mourouzis, A., Wemple, D., Wheeler, J., Williams, L., and Zurcher, S. (1970). Body Management Activities. Dayton, Ohio, MWZ Associates.
Muir, E. (1973) The Nobel Laureates. Lancet 2:893.
Needham, J. (1931) Chemical Embryology. London, MacMillan.
Nielsen, J. N. (1946) Agnosia, Apraxia, Aphasia. Their Value in Cerebral Localization. New York, Hoeber.
Ornitz, E. M., and Ritvo, E. R. (1968) Neurophysiologic mechanisms underlying perceptual inconstancy in autistic and schizophrenic children. Arch. Gen. Psychiat. 19:22–27.
Ornitz, E. M. (1969) Disorders of perception common to early infantile autism and schizophrenia. Comp. Psychiat. 10:259–274.
Ornitz, E. M. (1970) Vestibular dysfunction in schizophrenia and childhood autism. Comp. Psychiat. 11:000–000.
Orton, S. P. (1937) Reading, Writing and Speech Problems in Children. New York, W. W. Norton.
Orton, S. P. (1942) Discussion of a paper by Dr. J. G. Lynn. Arch. Neurol. Psychiat. Chicago, 47:1064.
Paine, R. (1968) Syndromes of "minimal cerebral damage." Pediatric Clin. North Am. 15(3):779–801.
Palay, S. L., and Chan-Palay, V. (1974) Cerebellar Cortex: Cytology and Organization. New York, Springer-Verlag, 1974.
Pearson, G. H. J. (1954) Psychoanalysis and the Education of the Child. New York, W. W. Norton.
Pearson, G. H. J., and English, O. S. (1937) Common Neuroses of Children and Adults. New York, W. W. Norton.
Pekelsky, A. (1921) Transitorischer Anystagmus bei Katatonie. Is der Nystagmus Willkurlich unterdrukbar? Rev. Neuropsychopath. 18:97–102.
Pierce, J. R. (1977) Optometric development vision therapy and academic achievement. Review of Optometry. 114:48–63.
Poetzl, O. (1928) Die optisch-agnostischen sturungen. Leipzig, Deuticke.
Pollack, M., and Krieger, H. P. (1958) Oculomotor and postural patterns in schizophrenic children. Arch. Neurol. Psychiat. 79:720–726.
Pracht, W. (1972) Vestibular and cerebellar control of ocular-motor functions. In Dichgansand, J., and Bizzi, E. (eds.) Cerebral Control of Eye Movements and Motion Perception. Basel, Karger.
Prechtl, H. F., and Stemmer, J. C. (1962) The choreiform syndrome in children. Dev. Med. Child Neur. 4:119–127.
Prentice, N. M., and Sperry, B. M. (1965) Therapeutically oriented tutoring of children with primary neurotic learning inhibitions. Amer. J. Orthopsychiat. 35: 521–531.

Reuben, R., and Bakwin, H. (1968) Developmental clumsiness. Pediatric Clin. 15(3): 601–610.

Ritvo, E. R., Ornitz, E. M., Eviatar, A., Markham, C. H., Brown, M. B., and Mason, A. (1969) Decreased post-rotatory nystagmus in early infantile autism. Neurology 19:653–658.

Robinson, D. P. (1976) Adaptive gain control of vestibulo-ocular reflex by the cerebellum. J. Neurophysiol. 39:954–969.

Rockwell, D. (1975) The "jet lag" syndrome. Western J. Med. 122:419.

Rosen, V. H. (1955) Strephosymbolia: An intrasystemic disturbance of the synthetic function of the ego. In Eissler, K., et al. (eds.) The Psychoanalytic Study of the Child, Vol. 10. New York, International Universities Press, pp. 83–98.

Rubenstein, B. O., Falick, M. L., Levitt, M., and Ekstein, R. (1959) Learning impotence: A suggested diagnostic category. Amer. J. Orthopsychiat. 29:315–323.

Ryle, G. (1949) The Concept of Mind. London, Hutchinson's University Library.

Sagan, C., and Drake, S. (1975) The search for extraterrestrial intelligence. Scientific American 232:80–89.

Schiffman, G. (1962) Dyslexia as an educational phenomenon: Its recognition and treatment. In Money, J. (ed.) Reading Disability: Progress and Research Needs in Dyslexia. Baltimore, Johns Hopkins Press.

Schilder, P. (1933a) Experiments on imagination, after-images, and hallucinations. Amer. J. Psychiat. 90:597–611.

Schilder, P. (1933b) The vestibular apparatus in neurosis and psychosis. J. Nerv. Ment. Dis. 78:1–23, 137–164.

Serel, M., and Vinar, J. (1937) Lesions of the vestibular apparatus in schizophrenia. Cas. Lek. Cesk. 76:213–218. Cited by Fitzgerald, G., and Stengel, E.: Vestibular reactivity to caloric stimulation in schizophrenics. J. Ment. Sci. 91:93–100.

Shames, G. (1968) Dysfluency and stuttering. Pediatric Clin. North Am. 15(3):691–704.

Sherrington, C. S. (1906) The Integrative Action of the Nervous System. New York, Charles Schribner's Sons.

Sherrington, C. S. (1940) Man on His Nature. London, Cambridge University Press.

Silver, A. A. (1961) Diagnostic considerations in children with reading disability. Bull. Orton Soc. 11:5–11.

Silver, A. A., and Hagin, R. A. (1960) Specific reading disability: Delineation of the syndrome and relation to cerebral dominance. Compr. Psychiat. 1:126–134.

Silver, A. A., and Hagin, R. A. (1964) Specific reading disability. Amer. J. Orthopsychiat. 34:95–102.

Silver, A. A., and Hagin, R. A. (1965) Developmental language disability simulating mental retardation. J. Amer. Acad. Child Psychiat. 4:485–495.

Silver, A. A., and Hagin, R. (1974) Fascinating journey: Paths to the prediction and prevention of reading disability. Presented at the World Congress on Dyslexia. Rochester, Minnesota, November 8, 1974.

Silverman, J. S., Fite, M., and Mosher, M. (1959) Clinical findings in reading disability children—Special cases of intellectual inhibition. Amer. J. Orthopsychiat. 29:298–314.

Snider, R. S. (1943) A fifth cranial nerve projection to the cerebellum. Federation Proc. 2:46.

Snider, R. S. (1950) Recent contributions to the anatomy and physiology of the cerebellum. Arch. Neurol. Psychiat. 64:196–219.

Snider, R. (1952) Cerebro-cerebellar relationships in the monkey. J. Neurophysiol. 15:27–40.

Snider, R. (1958) The cerebellum. Scientific American 174:84–90.

Snider, R. S., and Stowell, A. (1942a) Evidence of a projection of the optic system to the cerebellum. Anat. Rec. 82:448–449.

Snider, R. S., and Stowell, A. (1942b) Evidence of a representation of tactile sensibility in the cerebellum of the cat. Federation Proc. 1:82.

Snider, R. S., and Stowell, A. (1944) Receiving areas of the tactile, auditory and visual systems in the cerebellum. J. Neurophysiol. 7:331–357.

Spector, M. (1968) Electrostagnomography in the office. Arch. Otolaryngol. 87: 255–265.

Sperry, B. M., et al. (1958) Renunciation and denial in learning difficulties. Amer. J. Orthopsychiat. 28:98–111.

Spitz, R. A. (1945) Hospitalism: An inquiry into the genesis of psychiatric conditions in early childhood. The Psychoanalytic Study of the Child, Vol. 1. New York, International Universities Press.

Spitz, R. A. (1946a) Hospitalism: A follow-up report. The Psychoanalytic Study of the Child, Vol. 2. New York, International Universities Press.

Spitz, R. A. (1946b) Anaclitic depression: An inquiry into the genesis of psychiatric conditions in early childhood, II. The Psychoanalytic Study of the Child, Vol. 2. New York, International Universities Press.

Spitz, R. A. (1957) No and Yes. New York, International Universities Press.

Spitz, R. A. (1966) The First Year of Life. New York, International Universities Press.

Spitz, R. A., and Wolf, K. M. (1946) The smiling response: A contribution to the ontogenesis of social relations. Genet. Psychol. Monogr., 34:57–125.

Stone, M. (1976) Madness and the moon revisited. Psychiatric Annals 6:170–176.

Strachey, J. (1930) Some unconscious factors in reading. Internat. J. Psychoanal. 11:322–332.

Sylvester, E., and Kunst, M. S. (1943) Psychodynamic aspects of the reading problem. Amer. J. Orthopsychiat. 13:69–76.

Thompson, L. (1966) Reading Disability. Springfield, Ill., Charles Thomas.

Thorpe, W. H. (1961) Biology, Psychology and Belief. London, Cambridge University Press.

Tinbergen, N. (1951) The Study of Instincts. London, Oxford University Press.

Tolgia, J. (1975) Clinical evaluation of nystagmus. Hospital Medicine. May 1975, pp. 36–54.

Vernon, M. D. (1957) Backwardness in Reading. A Study of Its Nature and Origin. London, Cambridge University Press.

von Frisch, K. (1967) Honey bees—Do they use direction and distance information provided by their dances? Science 158:1072–1077.

von Frisch, K. (1974) Decoding the language of the bee. Science 185:663–668.

von Uexkull, J. (1957) A stroll through the worlds of animals and men. In Schiller, H. (ed.) Instinctive Behaviour. New York, International Universities Press, 1957.

Warrington, E. K. (1967) The incidence of verbal disability associated with retardation reading. Neuropsychologia 5:175.

Weiss, D. (1968) Cluttering: central language imbalance. Pediatric Clin. North Am. 15(3):705–720.

Wepman, J. S. (1968) Auditory discrimination: Its role in language comprehension, formulation and use. Pediatric Clin. North Am. 15(3):721–728.

Werry, J. S. (1968) Developmental hyperactivity. Pediatric Clin. North Am. 15(3): 581–599.

Werry, J. S., Weiss, G., Douglas, V., and Martin, J. (1966) Studies on the hyperactive child. III. The effect of chlorpromazine upon behavior and learning. J. Amer. Acad. Child Psychiat. 5:292–312.

Whitteridge, D. (1968) Central control of eye movements. In Field, J., and Magoun, H. (eds.) Neurophysiology. Vol. 2. Philadelphia, Williams & Wilkins.

Wilson, V. J. (1975) The labyrinth, the brain and posture. American Scientist, 63: 325–332.

Wilson, V. J., Maeda, M., and Franck, J. I. (1975) Inhibitory interaction between labyrinthine, visual and neck inputs to the cat flocculus. Brain Res. 96:357–360.

Witty, P. A., and Kopel, D. (1936) Sinistral and mixed manual ocular behaviour in reading disability. J. Educ. Psychol. 27:119–134.

Wood, C. D., and Graybiel, A. (1970) A theory of motion sickness based on pharmacological reactions. Clinical Pharmacology and Therapeutics, 11:621–629.

Young, J. S. (1962) Why do we have two brains? In Mountcastle, V. B. (ed.) Interhemispheric Relations and Cerebral Dominance. Baltimore, Johns Hopkins Press, 1962.

Zangwill, O. L. (1960) Cerebral Dominance and Its Relation to Psychological Function. Edinburg, Oliver and Boyd.

Zangwill, O. L. (1962) Dyslexia in relation to cerebral dominance. In Money, J. (ed.) Reading Disability: Progress and Research Needs in Dyslexia. Baltimore, Johns Hopkins University Press.

Zinkus, P., Gottlieb, M. I., Schapiro, M. (1978) Developmental and psycheducational sequelae of chronic otitis media. Amer. J. Dis. Child 132:1100–1104.

Index